Philips'
ILLUSTRATED
ATLAS
of
THE WORLD

Editor

Dr Bernard Stonehouse, Postgraduate School
of Studies in Environmental Science,
University of Bradford

Consultant Editors

T. W. Freeman, Emeritus Professor of Geography,
University of Manchester

R. J. Harrison-Church, Emeritus Professor of
Geography, University of London (LSE)

Professor H. B. Rodgers, School of Geography,
University of Manchester

Professor Clifford T. Smith, Centre for Latin American
Studies, University of Liverpool

Philips'
ILLUSTRATED
ATLAS
of
THE WORLD

GEORGE PHILIP
LONDON·MELBOURNE·MILWAUKEE

Contributors

Robert and Monica Beckinsale (RB, MB); William C. Brice, Reader in Geography, University of Manchester (WB); Dr David Cotton, Postgraduate School of Studies in Environmental Science, University of Bradford (DC); Professor Ian Douglas, School of Geography, University of Manchester (ID); Maureen Douglas, Research Assistant, Department of European Studies and Modern Languages, University of Manchester Institute of Science and Technology (MD); Professor T. H. Elkins, School of European Studies, University of Sussex (THE); David J. Fox, Department of Geography, University of Manchester (DJF); Professor T. W. Freeman (TWF); Professor R. J. Harrison-Church (RJH-C); Professor B. W. Hodder, Department of Geography, School of Oriental and African Studies, University of London (BH); Amna Homoudi, Department of Geography, University of Khartoum (AH); Dr George Kay, Head of the Department of Geography and Sociology, North Staffordshire Polytechnic, formerly Professor of Geography at the University of Rhodesia (GK); Dr Richard I. Lawless, Assistant Director, Centre of Middle Eastern and Islamic Studies, University of Durham (RL); A. T. A. Learmonth, Professor of Geography, the Open University (AL); Stephen F. Mills, David Brice Centre for American Studies, University of Keele (SFM); Dr W. T. W. Morgan, Department of Geography, University of Durham (WM); Alan B. Mountjoy, Department of Geography, University of London (Bedford College) (AM); Dr Judith Pallot, Lecturer in the Geography of the USSR, University of Oxford (JP); John Sargent, Reader in Geography, School of Oriental and African Studies, University of London (JS); F. B. Singleton, Reader in Yugoslav Studies, University of Bradford (FS); Dr Bernard Stonehouse (BS); P. A. Stott, Chairman of the Centre of South East Asian Studies, School of Oriental and African Studies, University of London (PS); Dr Graeme Whittington, Department of Geography, University of St Andrews (GW).

For George Philip

Editor Lydia Greeves
Art Editor Frank Phillips
Designer Brenda Burley
Picture Research Thelma Gilbert
Maps and map index prepared under the direction of B. M. Willett, Alan Poynter and Raymond Smith.

First edition Autumn 1980

British Library Cataloguing in Publication Data

Philips' illustrated atlas of the world.
  1. Atlases, British
  I. Stonehouse, Bernard
  912   G1019

ISBN 0 540 05371 6

Filmset in England by
Tameside Filmsetting Limited,
Ashton-under-Lyne, Lancashire

Printed in Italy

CONTENTS

EUROPE
14–69

ASIA
70–103

OCEANIA
104–115

NORTH AMERICA
116–133

Picture Acknowledgments

Aspect Picture Library: p. 19 (*top left*) J. Alex Langley; p. 25 (*top left*) Brian Seed; p. 33 (*centre*) J. Alex Langley; p. 47 (*bottom*) Helmut Gritscher; p. 52 (*top left and top right*) Bob Davis; p. 54 (*bottom*) A. Clifton; p. 79 (*bottom left*) J. Alex Langley; p. 93 J. Alex Langley; p. 98 (*top left*) Tom Nebbia; p. 101 (*top left*) J. Alex Langley; p. 103 (*centre right*) Bob Davis; p. 109 (*centre left*) John Thornton; p. 129 (*top left*) Phetri; p. 162 Peter Campbell; p. 166 J. Alex Langley; p. 172 (*bottom left*) Bryan Alexander; p. 172 (*top right*) T. Nebbia.
J. Allan Cash: p. 31 (*centre right*); p. 160.
Bruce Coleman Ltd: p. 9 Wedigo Ferchland; p. 11 (1) Mike Price; (2) Chris Bonington; (3) Gerald Cubitt; (5) Clara Calhoun; (6) Klaus D. Francke; (7) D. Vollmar; p. 14 (*top left*) Neyla Freeman; (*centre left*) Bill Brooks; (*bottom left*) Pekka Helo; p. 15 Nicholas de Vore; p. 17 (*top*) Chris Bonington; p. 19 (*top right*) Chris Bonington; p. 25 (*top right*) Chris Bonington; p. 31 (*bottom centre*) Jennifer Fry; p. 52 (*bottom right*) Eric Crichton; p. 57 (*centre left*) David Goulston; (*bottom right*) Fritz Prenzel; p. 64 Prato; p. 67 (*top right*) C. B. Frith; (*bottom left*) Bruce Coleman; (*bottom right*) C. B. Frith; p. 70 (*top left*) Dieter and Mary Plage; (*bottom left*) Dieter and Mary Plage; (*bottom right*) Jonathan T. Wright; p. 71 M. P. Kahl; pp. 72–73 C. B. Frith; p. 74 (*top*) Douglas Botting; (*centre left*) Douglas Botting; (*bottom left*) Jonathan T. Wright; (*centre right*) Douglas Botting; p. 77 (*top*) Jonathan T. Wright; pp. 78–79 Jonathan T. Wright; p. 79 (*top left*) Jonathan T. Wright; p. 82 (*top*) Norman

Owen Tomalin; p. 87 Chris Bonington; p. 89 (*centre left*) Norman Myers; (*centre right*) J. Houzel/la vie; p. 97 (*centre right*) Chris Bonington; (*bottom right*) Norman Myers; p. 104 (*bottom left*) W. E. Ruth; p. 105 Nicholas de Vore; p. 110 (*top right*) V. Serventy; p. 112 (*top centre*) Graham Pizzey; (*centre*) David Goulston; p. 116 (*top*) Bill Brooks; (*bottom left*) Gene Ahrens; (*bottom right*) Nicholas de Vore; p. 129 (*centre*) Norman Owen Tomalin; p. 131 M. P. L. Fogden; p. 134 Peter Ward; p. 135 (*top*) Jen and Des Bartlett; (*bottom*) M. Freeman; p. 139 Bruce Coleman; p. 142 Hans Reinhard; p. 143 (*top*) F. Sautereau; p. 144 M. Freeman; p. 145 Wolfgang Bayer; p. 146 (*bottom right*) Nicholas de Vore; p. 150 (*top right*) Jen and Des Bartlett; p. 151 (*bottom right*) Inigo Everson; p. 154 (*top right*) Lee Lyon; (*centre*) M. Philip Kahl Jr; (*bottom right*) Gerald Cubitt; p. 155 Fritz Vollmar; p. 161 (*bottom*) Peter Ward; p. 164 Christian Zuber; p. 169 Simon Trevor; p. 171 Bruce Coleman; p. 175 (*top right*) Francisco Erize; (*centre right*) Francisco Erize.
Colour Library International Ltd: p. 11 (8); (9); p. 17 (*bottom*); p. 20 (*top left*); p. 22 (*top right*); p. 23 (*top right*), (*top left*); p. 26; p. 29; p. 32 (*top centre*); p. 34; p. 35 (*centre right*); p. 40 (*top left*); p. 43; p. 44; p. 63; p. 81; p. 84 (*top*); p. 90; p. 92 (*top left*); p. 95; p. 100 (*centre left*); p. 103 (*bottom right*); p. 107 (*top right*); p. 108 (*bottom right*); p. 109 (*top centre*), (*centre right*); p. 115 (*bottom*); p. 119; p. 122–123 (*bottom centre*); p. 127; p. 130 (*bottom left*); p. 132 (*top right*); p. 133; pp. 158–159.
Christopher Drew: p. 154 (*bottom left*).

Mary Evans Picture Library: pp. 174–175 (*bottom centre*).
Susan Griggs Agency Ltd: p. 13 (1) Pushkin; (2) Adam Woolfitt; (3) Julian Calder; (4) R. Ian Lloyd; (5) Engelbert; (6) Jehangir Gazda; p. 19 (*bottom right*) Adam Woolfitt; p. 20 (*bottom right*) Adam Woolfitt; p. 23 (*bottom left*) Anthony Howarth; p. 25 (*top centre*) Anthony Howarth; p. 35 (*top left*) Adam Woolfitt; p. 36 (*top left*) Reflejo; p. 40 (*bottom right*) Adam Woolfitt; p. 49 Anthony Howarth; p. 54 (*top*) Tor Eigeland; p. 56 (*bottom right*) Adam Woolfitt; p. 59 Adam Woolfitt; p. 66 (*top*) Cam Culbert; p. 79 (*centre top*) Julian Calder; p. 80 Anthony Howarth; p. 84 (*bottom*) Tor Eigeland; pp. 88–89 (*top centre*) Jehangir Gazdar; p. 92 (*top centre*) Ivan Polunin; (*top right*) Cam Culbert; p. 101 (*top right*) Philip Modica; p. 108 (*centre right*) John Marmaras; p. 147 (*centre left*) Reflejo; p. 167 Adrianne Leman.
Novosti Press Agency: p. 79 (*centre right*) S. Edisherashvili.
Axel Poignant: p. 115 (*centre left*).
Spectrum Picture Library: p. 27.
Mireille Vautier: p. 25 (*bottom left*) Vautier; p. 89 (*bottom centre*) Mireille Vautier; p. 103 (*top left and centre left*) Vautier-Decool; p. 117 Vautier-Decool; p. 120 Vautier-De Nanxe; p. 121 Vautier-De Nanxe; p. 126 (*top left*) Vautier-De Nanxe; p. 130 (*top right*) Vautier-Decool; (*bottom right*) Vautier-De Nanxe; p. 132 (*top left*) Vautier-De Nanxe; p. 137 (*top left*) Vautier-Decool; (*bottom right*) Vautier-Decool; p. 138 Vautier-Decool; p. 140 Vautier-De Nanxe; p. 146 (*centre left*) Vautier-Decool; p. 147 (*top left*) Vautier-De Nanxe; (*bottom left*) Vautier-De Nanxe; p. 149 (*top left*) Vautier-Decool; p. 151

(*centre left*) Vautier-Decool.
Vision International: p. 11 (10) Paolo Koch; p. 47 (*top right*) Paolo Koch; p. 82 (*bottom*) Angelo Hornak; p. 97 (*top centre*) Paolo Koch.
ZEFA Picture Library (UK) Ltd: p. 11 (4) H. Steenmans; p. 18 W. F. Davidson; p. 20 (*top right*) J. Pfaff; (*bottom left*) G. Mabbs; p. 22 (*bottom right*) David Corke; p. 30 Ronald Sheridan; p. 32 (*bottom centre*) W. F. Davidson; p. 33 (*top*) K. Kerth; p. 33 (*bottom*) Starfoto; p. 36 (*top right*) Haro Schumacher; (*bottom right*) Icelandic Photo; p. 39 Jörg Trobitzsch; p. 46 (*top*) W. H. Müller; p. 46 (*bottom*) Rosmarie Pierer; p. 48 Tom; p. 50 M. Fugère; p. 56 (*top left*) Ursula Bagel; (*bottom left*) H. J. Krueger; p. 61 Kurt Goebel; p. 66 (*bottom*) J. Schörken; p. 69 K. Kerth; p. 77 (*bottom*) Dr David Holdsworth; p. 79 (*centre below*) K. Scholz; p. 83 Günter Heil; p. 92 (*bottom centre*) K. Röhrich; p. 96 J. Bitsch; p. 98 (*bottom right*) H. Weyer; p. 100 (*top left*) Kurt Göbel; p. 104 (*top left*) A. Foley; p. 108 (*top left*) G. Sirena; p. 111 (*top right*) F. Park; p. 112 (*bottom centre*) D. Baglin; p. 123 E. Hummel; p. 125 Dr H. Kramarz; p. 126 (*centre*) E. G. Carle; (*bottom centre*) Kurt Goebel; p. 129 (*top right*) Klaus Benser; p. 137 (*bottom left*) Karl Kummels; p. 141 K. Kerth; p. 143 (*bottom right*) H. Strauss; p. 146 (*top right*) Klaus Benser; p. 147 (*bottom right*) G. Ziesler; p. 149 (*top right*) Klaus Benser; p. 150 (*top left*) L. Mau; p. 151 (*top left*) Dieter Grathwohl; p. 157 H. Hoffmann-Burchardi; p. 161 (*top*) Vontin; p. 163 G. Sirena; pp. 170–171 J. Rushmer; p. 172 (*bottom right*) P. Bading.

INTRODUCTION

Philips' Illustrated Atlas of the World is designed for those whose interests go beyond the printed map. Good maps remain a prime source of geographical information – some would say the most important single source. The more they are examined, the more they tell, and an atlas ungenerous of its maps is unworthy of the name. But there is more to the world than maps alone can show, especially to a generation brought up on travel films, TV documentaries and well-illustrated magazines. For them the world is already a colourful, lively place, part-known and well worth further study in broad, cross-disciplinary fields. And for them text and pictures must find a place in a modern atlas, preferably close to the maps, and complementing them with details of topography, climate, history, peoples, wildlife, economic activity, and national problems and aspirations. These are the details that distinguish one land from another, one community from another, and help to present the world as a place of infinite variety and interest.

In planning this atlas, therefore, we have sought text from a team of writers who know their areas well in more than a narrow geographical sense, and have matched their writing with a wide selection of colour photographs, setting both text and illustrations as close as possible to the maps they represent. To keep the text readable and within bounds, only minimal statistical data are included; precise values are tabulated in the section of statistical information on pp. 176–82. Regional climates are summarized in the margins of the maps they refer to. In the climatic tables temperatures are given as monthly and annual means; rainfall appears as monthly means and annual totals. Stations are listed in north-to-south sequence, and all appear on the map alongside; where alternative names are given on the map, the more prominent of the two appears in the table, and both versions are listed in the index.

This atlas owes much to the patience and skill of its in-house editor, Lydia Greeves, and to its designer, Frank Phillips. I thank also the four distinguished geographers who have acted as Consultant Editors.

Bernard Stonehouse

MAP KEY

CONVERSION SCALE

Abbreviations of measures used — ft Feet; mm {Millimetres / Millimeters} cm {Centimetres / Centimeters} m {Metres / Meters} Km {Kilometres / Kilometers} mb Millibars

City and Town symbols in order of size

∴	Sites of Archæological or Historical Importance
———	International Boundaries
— — —	International Boundaries (Undemarcated or Undefined)
·········	Internal Boundaries
⌒	Principal Roads
- - - -	Tracks, Seasonal and other Roads
⌐---⌐	Road Tunnels

∿	Principal Railways
∿	Other Railways
-⌐----⌐-	Railways under construction
⌐---⌐	Railway Tunnels
....	Principal Canals
.——.	Principal Oil Pipelines
———	Principal Air Routes
✧	Principal Airports

--⌐3386⌐--	Principal Shipping Routes (Distances in Nautical Miles)
∿	Perennial Streams
--------	Seasonal Streams
⊂⊃	Seasonal Lakes, Salt Flats
⁖⁖	Swamps, Marshes
⌄	Wells in Desert
▭	Permanent Ice
⋈	Passes
▲ 8848	Height above sea-level
▼ 8050	Depth below sea-level } in metres
1134	Height of lake-level

ft	m
30 000	9000
	8000
24 000	7000
	6000
18 000	5000
	4000
12 000	3000
9000	
6000	2000
3000	1000
Sea-Level 0	500 / 0 Sea-Level / 500
1000	1000
	2000
2000	3000
	4000
3000	5000
	6000
4000	7000
	8000
5000	9000
	10 000
6000	11 000
	12 000
7000 fathoms	m

THE EARTH'S SURFACE

Our earth is one of nine planets encircling the sun – the fifth in order of size, with a mean diameter of 12,734 km (7,960 miles). At its centre lies a dense, iron-rich core, immensely hot and mostly molten. Swirling movements within the core produce the earth's magnetic field. Surrounding the core is a thick, semi-molten mantle, composed of peridotite – a complex oxide of iron, magnesium and silicon that appears at the earth's surface as a dark, crystalline rock. The mantle too is hot, its temperature kept high by radioactivity. Core and mantle together make up all but a tiny fraction of the earth's bulk. Chilled by its constant journey through space, the earth has a solid outer casing, wafer-thin in proportion to its size. This crust of silicate rocks, only 6 km (3.75 miles) thick under the oceans and up to 35 km (22 miles) thick under the continents, is the rugged surface we live on.

From the human viewpoint the earth's surface is mountainous and varied, thrown into immense folds and carved by weathering on an enormous scale. But viewed from outer space the highest ranges of mountains are no more than trivial bumps that disappear against the curved profile of the planet. From the peak of Mount Everest 8,848 m (29,029 ft) up in the Himalaya to the deepest ocean trench 11,033 m (36,198 ft) below sea-level is a total thickness of only 19.9 km (12.5 miles), less than one third of one per cent of the earth's radius. On a model of the globe 2 m (6.5 ft) in diameter the oceans could be represented by a film of water of average depth 1.2 mm (.05 in), and the highest mountain massifs would rise less than the thickness of a match above the general level. It would be difficult to smooth the surface of the model sufficiently to represent truly the tiny ridges and scratches – lesser mountains, hills, canyons and river valleys – that make up much of the earth's relief.

Tensions and Forces in the Crust

Geologists of the early nineteenth century recognized that mountain ranges resulted from stresses, especially tensions, upthrust and lateral pressures, within the earth's crust. Earthquakes and such shattering events as the Krakatoa eruption (a volcanic implosion in the Sunda Strait that destroyed a large island in 1883) indicated the strength of the forces involved. But the true nature of crustal movements, mountain building forces, and indeed the origin of the continents themselves have only recently come to light.

The earth's crust is now seen as a patchwork of shifting plates, that move slowly in relation to each other. The motive power beneath them is probably convection currents within the semi-liquid mantle on which they float. There are six major plates, five of them carrying continental masses, and several minor plates that fill up the interstices. Thin and low-lying, the plates form much of the sea bed between the continental masses. They are composed mainly of basaltic rocks, and are slowly but constantly changing shape.

Where two plates are drawing apart, new material is added to their edges from the mantle beneath; where plates converge, one disappears beneath the other and its edge melts into the circulating mantle. Movements between the plates are slight, mostly from 1 cm (.4 in) to 10 cm (4 in) or more each year. Rates of movement are determined mainly from the rate at which new sea bed has formed between diverging plate boundaries along the mid-oceanic rifts.

Continental Drift

The familiar pattern of continents on modern maps of the world has evolved from completely different patterns of the past. Movements of the continents can be traced back to a period some 250 million years ago when all were clustered together in a single supercontinent, *Pangaea*.

Evolution of the Continents

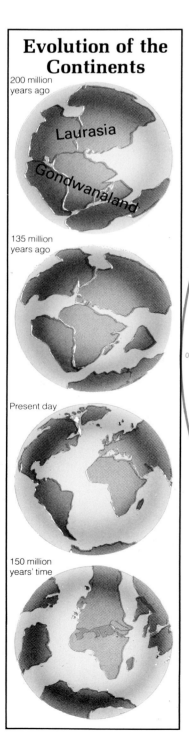

200 million years ago

135 million years ago

Present day

150 million years' time

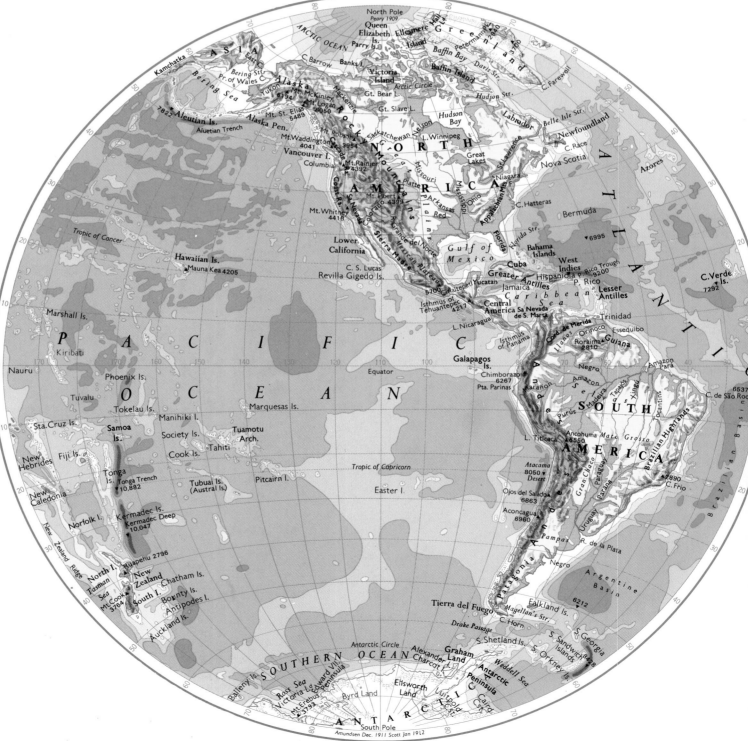

About 200 million years ago this great land-mass split longitudinally to form two lesser supercontinents; *Laurasia* included most of Europe, central and northern Asia, Greenland and North America, while *Gondwanaland* included India and all the southern continents of today.

As Laurasia and Gondwanaland drifted apart, both split latitudinally. Greenland and North America drifted westward from Asia, and the Gondwana complex fragmented into its component parts; last to divide were Australia and Antarctica, which were probably united as recently as 50 million years ago. These breaks occurred along boundaries that correspond with the present edges of the continental shelves, new sea floor welling up from the mantle and spreading between the continental blocks as they drifted apart.

The theory of drifting continents, first examined in the early days of this century, explains many aspects of plant and animal geography, and of past climatic changes, that could not previously be understood, and scientists of many disciplines are still working out its implications. The existence of shifting plates – the vehicles on which the continents are moved – has similarly helped to explain how mountains, volcanoes and other major physical features of the earth have come about, for most of the earth's mountain building occurs at plate boundaries.

The Effects of Plate Movement

Where plates are moving apart, the new material welling up may form a line of volcanoes. At present this is happening mostly on the floors of the oceans; the Mid-Atlantic Ridge, a vast submarine mountain range, marks the line of separation between the westward moving American plate and eastward moving African and Eurasian plates. Most of its mountains are submerged; the Azores Islands, Ascension Island and Tristan da Cunha are taller mountains that rise above the ocean surface. Iceland also is part of the Ridge, its volcanic activity reflecting the continuous movement of the drifting plates that tends to tear it apart. Similar ridges occur on the floor of the Southern Ocean and the eastern Pacific Ocean, where there are similar forces in action between diverging plates. Africa's rift valley is another great tension crack.

Where plates converge upon each other mountains arise in different ways according to circumstances. Junctions away from continental masses often produce curved chains of volcanic islands; the Caroline and Mariana Islands, the Philippines, Ryukyus, Japan, and the Kuril and Aleutian chains are mountainous island arcs formed by the north-westward movement of the Pacific sea floor plate. Where a plate abuts against a continental edge, the continent rides up and buckles; marine sediments previously laid down along its edge are folded and lifted, both by direct lateral pressure and by the injection of liquid rock from below. The Rocky Mountains and their outliers were formed in this way when North America over-rode

Volcanoes mark areas of instability.

the Pacific plate; there is little activity there at present, but similar pressure between South America and the eastward-moving Nazca plate is raising the Andes today.

Where continental blocks collide enormous ranges of mountains appear; this has happened along a broad swathe of southern Europe and Asia, where northward movement of Africa, India and Australia has produced range upon range of spectacular mountains, from the Atlas in the east, through the Alps, Carpathians, Caucasus, Hindu Kush and Himalaya to southern China, Indonesia and New Guinea. (BS)

1 : 100 000 000

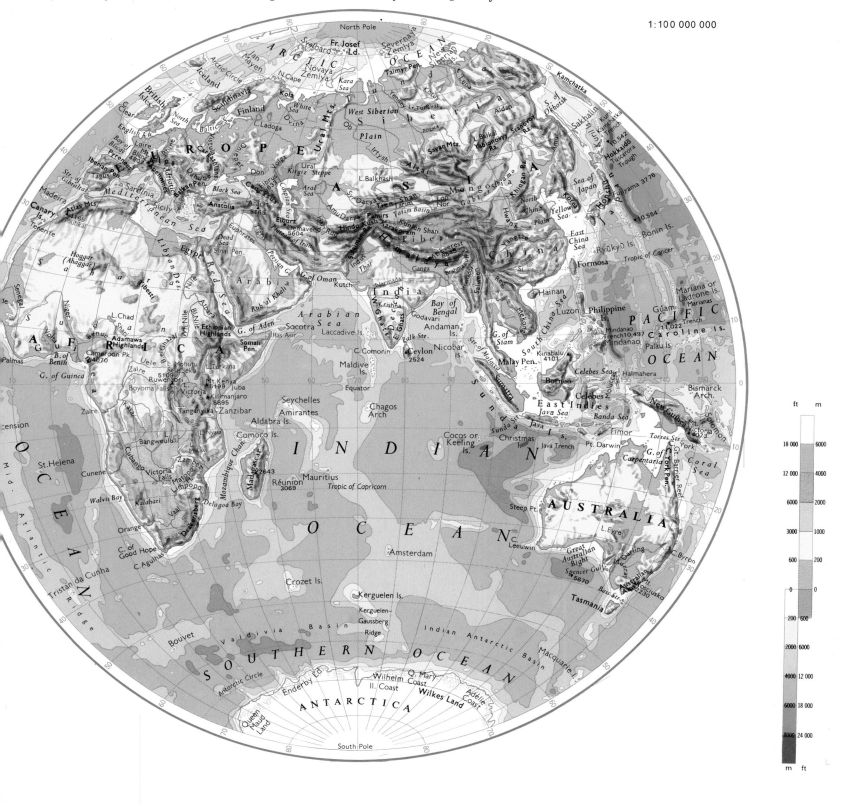

WORLD CLIMATE AND VEGETATION

The climate of an area depends firstly on its latitude; this determines both temperature (whether tropical, temperate or polar) and seasonality (whether winters and summers are similar or different). Secondly climate depends on distribution of atmospheric pressure, for this controls movements of air masses and the day-to-day shifts of wind, cloud and rainfall that make up weather. Proximity of mountains, deserts, oceans, snowfields, lakes and other physical features also strongly affects local climates.

Climate in turn is a controlling factor in determining what kinds of vegetation can grow in an area, either naturally or by human cultivation. Hence the basic similarities of climatic and vegetation maps, both of which have broadly latitudinal bands, with similarly-placed patches of colour. Most systems of climatic classification recognize this correlation, and name climates in terms of the vegetation they support; 'tropical rain forest climate' and 'savanna climate', for example, are useful descriptive terms. Several

systems of climatic classification have been invented; the one most generally used, devised by the German climatologist W. Köppen, is shown in simple form on the map.

Tropical rain forests flourish in a narrow latitudinal band on either side of the Equator, where temperatures are high and rainfall is plentiful throughout the year. They are well developed in the Amazon basin, in central Africa and throughout the East Indies. Seen at their most luxuriant on lowland plains or covering the gentle, lower slopes of mountains, they form a dense canopy of vegetation 15 to 25 m (50 to 80 ft) above ground, with a few taller trees emerging to 35 m (115 ft). There is usually a semi-continuous undercanopy of lesser trees 5 to 15 m high (15 to 50 ft). Epiphytic ferns, orchids, mosses, lichens and climbing plants swathe the trunks and boughs, while between the trees hang lianes and aerial roots.

Green at every level, growing continuously in the hot-house conditions, these forests are immensely productive, with thousands of spec-

ies of plants (often hundreds of kinds of trees alone) per hectare. They produce flowers and fruit throughout the year, providing forage for hosts of insects, tree-frogs, reptiles, birds and mammals. Many of the large animals live in the trees, rather than on the wet ground.

Monsoon (seasonal) forests grow, like tropical rain forests, in hot, rainy climates; however, they are able to survive dry conditions for a few months each year, and are therefore well suited to monsoon climates where dry and wet seasons alternate. They are well developed in South America, north of the Amazon delta and in south-east coastal Brazil, also in Central and West Africa, along the east coasts of India and Sri Lanka, and in Burma, Thailand and Queensland.

Structurally they are similar to tropical rain forests, though seldom so exuberant, and with fewer species. The dry spells encourage a higher proportion of deciduous trees, which shed their leaves and often produce flowers or fruit in the dry season. Trees of one or two species

may become dominant in particular areas. Though intensely green during the rainy season, these forests take on a parched look between the rains. Leaves, dead twigs and other dry debris accumulate underfoot, and fires may sweep through them; fire-prone forests contain a high proportion of trees with thick, flame-resistant bark, which can withstand burning. Both rain forests and monsoon forests are valued for their timber, and include many species (cacao, rubber, kapok, for example) of commercial importance.

Tropical savanna occurs where rainfall is plentiful for part of the year, but insufficient overall to support even seasonal forests. Basically savanna is a mixture of scattered trees and grassland, but it varies considerably with local conditions. Where soils are good and the rains are generous, it can be park-like, with stands of trees and shrubs and a rich variety of luxuriant grasses. On poor soils and in dry conditions the savanna is impoverished, with small scattered trees and thin grass, grading perhaps into semi-desert.

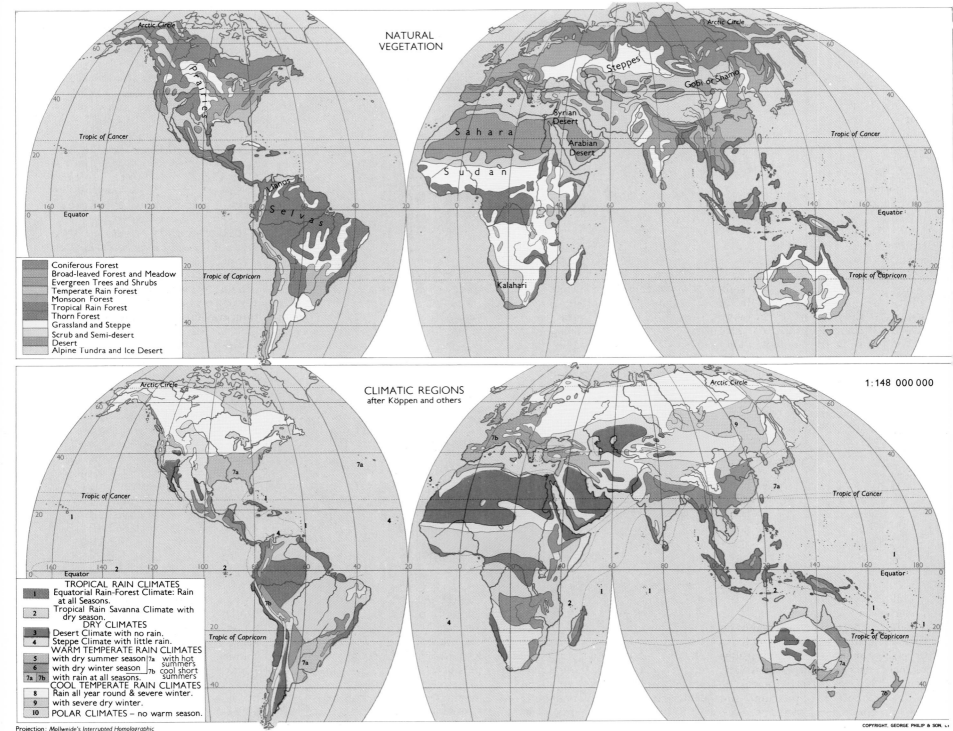

NATURAL VEGETATION

Coniferous Forest
Broad-leaved Forest and Meadow
Evergreen Trees and Shrubs
Temperate Rain Forest
Monsoon Forest
Tropical Rain Forest
Thorn Forest
Grassland and Steppe
Scrub and Semi-desert
Desert
Alpine Tundra and Ice Desert

CLIMATIC REGIONS
after Köppen and others

1:148 000 000

TROPICAL RAIN CLIMATES
1 Equatorial Rain-Forest Climate: Rain at all Seasons.
2 Tropical Rain Savanna Climate with dry season.
DRY CLIMATES
3 Desert Climate with no rain.
4 Steppe Climate with little rain.
WARM TEMPERATE RAIN CLIMATES
5 with dry summer season / 7a with hot summers
6 with dry winter season / 7b cool short summers
7a 7b with rain at all seasons.
COOL TEMPERATE RAIN CLIMATES
8 Rain all year round & severe winter.
9 with severe dry winter.
10 POLAR CLIMATES – no warm season.

Projection: Mollweide's Interrupted Homolographic

1 Rain forest in Indonesia.
2 Monsoon forest in Nepal.
3 A savanna landscape in Africa.
4 The prairies of North America.
5 Semi-desert in flower, USA.
6 Mediterranean scrub in Greece.
7 Alpine forest in Switzerland.
8 Deciduous woodland in England.
9 North American coniferous forest.
10 Tundra vegetation in Canada.

Savanna is widespread across the drier tropics, occurring in South and Central America, on Caribbean islands, in broad swathes between forest and desert in Africa, in Madagascar, India, south-eastern Asia, China and northern Australia. Always seasonal, it alternates between wet and dry conditions, sometimes flooding extensively during the one or two rainy seasons each year, and drying out completely under the hot sun. Highly productive, its grasses, shrubs and herbs are browsed and grazed by herds of mammals, which wander along well-established routes in vast annual migrations. Insects too may be important browsers, and flocks of birds move in at seed-times. Natural and man-made fires help to keep minerals in circulation and promote the seasonal growth.

Semi-arid steppe vegetation occurs in both tropical and temperate regions. Essentially natural grasslands, steppes grow in western North America (the prairies), and southern South America (the pampas); they are widespread in North Africa on both the northern and southern flanks of the Sahara, and occupy much of the southern African tablelands. Western and central Asia include the original steppelands; and similar grasslands extend eastward across Mongolia and northern China, and surround the desert heart of central Australia.

Steppes grow best on good soils where there is adequate rain in spring, at the start of the growing season. Perennial species colonize the deeper soils, sending down long roots to search out the hidden moisture; annual and ephemeral plants flourish on the poorer soils, completing their life cycle while the surface moisture lasts.

In drier regions and areas where the soil is poor, the steppes are green for only a brief season, turning to semi-desert during the long dry months. Xerophytic (dry-tolerant) shrubs replace grass in the least hospitable areas. Steppes were originally cropped by wandering herds of herbivorous mammals (bison, buffalo and wild horses, for example); now they are mostly rangelands for cattle and sheep, or ploughed for cereal-growing.

Deserts occur in tropical and temperate climates, wherever evaporation exceeds or closely matches precipitation. There are many grades of desert, each with its characteristic vegetation. True deserts have little or no reliable precipitation, and may go for several years without rainfall. Their soils are poor, with little or no organic content and no capacity for retaining water; coarse, gravelly soils pack down to form hard pavements, and fine sandy soils blow away, sometimes forming dunes that shift before the winds.

Deserts with these characteristics occur in south-western USA, Mexico, coastal Peru, northern Africa, Arabia, Namibia, in scattered patches across Asia, and in central Australia. Their vegetation is meagre, with coarse grasses and thornbush predominating. Surrounding them are areas of marginal desert where slight rainfall occurs each year, allowing specially adapted plants to survive and flourish.

The amount of rain needed to support this kind of desert and semi-desert vegetation depends on temperature and season; a little rain in winter may be more effective than more during the hot season, when evaporation is high. Cactuses and other succulents can flourish under these conditions, with a relatively rich flora of xerophytic shrubs and grasses, and a rich fauna of insects, reptiles and birds.

Broadleaf evergreen forest and scrub is a tough kind of forest vegetation that grows in Mediterranean lands and other areas where soils are poor, summers are hot and dry, and there is adequate rain in winter. It is characterized by small trees and shrubs, often widely spaced on open ground and forming thickets in hollows where underground moisture collects; the leaves are often dark green and shiny, or grey-green with furry texture – both devices for conserving moisture – and stay on the trees for several years. Grass and herbs cover the ground between sparsely, growing lush and green in spring and early summer, but turning brown and disappearing during the the dry season that follows.

This harsh vegetation, if left to develop, grows to form a dense ground cover – an attractive grey-green forest with trees 15 to 20 m high (50 to 65 ft), and a strong and even luxuriant growth of perennial and annual plants filling the spaces between. In the Mediterranean region much of it has been destroyed by browsing (especially by goats), and by fire and cultivation, leaving only sparse, dried-out remnants in many places where it once flourished. Though broadleafed trees and shrubs predominate, pines and cedars are often characteristic of this attractive vegetation.

Mountain and mild monsoon forest is a high-country version of the evergreen forests that grow in temperate conditions where summers are hot and moist, and winters are cool and relatively dry. Many different forms of this forest appear on mountains throughout the world – in the Andes and Rockies, on the tropical mountains of Central Africa, in the great ranges of Asia and in New Guinea, Australia and New Zealand. Growing on steep slopes, it forms an important protective cover that helps to hold the soil and protect the mountains from erosion.

Though it may grow in the tropics, its mountain habitat provides a relatively cool environment at lower levels; at its upper limits it may be a cool, dank forest with permanent snowfields nearby, though only a few miles from a hot, steamy plain. Mountain forest may be mixed deciduous and evergreen, or exclusively evergreen, with either broadleafed or needleleafed trees predominant. Where it grows at cloud-level it is often a very wet forest, with trunks and branches swathed in mosses and epiphytes, and dense, impenetrable undergrowth. Though not especially attractive to browsing animals, mountain forest is often the haunt of deer, wolves and smaller mammals, and of many birds.

Temperate forests occur in lowlands of middle latitudes, where rainfall is adequate and winters are relatively mild. In the northern hemisphere they are mostly of broadleafed deciduous trees, though cedars, firs and pines may also flourish in these conditions; in the southern hemisphere they are mainly broadleafed evergreens. The great northern forests once covered huge expanses of North America and much of central and western Europe, China and Japan. The southern temperate forests occupied lowland areas of southern Chile, and favoured patches of eastern South America, southern Africa, south-eastern Australia and New Zealand.

During the past five or six centuries great expanses of the northern forests have been cleared, yielding timber for building, fuel and good agricultural land. Temperate deciduous forests are seen at their richest in the south-eastern USA, where the canopy stands at 25 to 35 m (80 to 115 ft), with a dense understorey and a great variety of species. Further north and in western Europe the trees are smaller and less varied, though still highly productive and offering hospitality to many communities of birds and mammals. The maritime temperate forests of the western North American seaboard, with their redwoods, Sitka spruces and Douglas firs, grow the tallest trees on earth.

Coniferous cold forests grow in a broad swathe across the northern hemisphere. On their southern margin they merge into deciduous forest; on the northern edge they stop at the tree-line where the Arctic tundra begins, though there may be a transition zone of open forest (forest-tundra or taiga) between the two. Sometimes called the boreal forest, this band is made up of a very few species of fir, spruce, larch and pine, leavened with more colourful and deciduous birch, alder and poplar.

In composition it closely resembles mountain forests of the temperate regions to the south. Trees that live so far north must be well adapted for cold and drought. Winter temperatures fall far below freezing point and water may be frozen and unavailable to them for at least half the year. Their downward-sloping branches shed the snow which would otherwise build up on them. Their growing season is short – possibly three to four months each year – and they grow slowly on the poor glacial soils which are their normal habitat. The boreal forests support many mammals and birds are plentiful in summer.

Tundra and polar deserts occur in the cold regions of the world beyond the tree line. Tundra is a low, patchy community of mosses, lichens, grasses, herbs and small shrubs, forming a mosaic among the thin, gravelly soils of northern lands. One of the world's most recently developed plant communities, it varies in texture according to locality, soil, drainage, exposure and many other local factors – from a complete ground-cover of well-established plants to a meagre sprinkling of survivors in a hostile world.

Much of the ground is frozen for nine or ten months of the year, thawing out to a depth of a few centimetres or more in spring or summer, but poorly drained and waterlogged. Growth is slow – a dwarf willow or birch several decades old may have stems little thicker than a pencil, and stand only half a metre tall. Productivity is low; the musk-oxen, caribou, hares and rabbits that browse the tundra range widely for their food. Snow cover protects the plants and small tundra animals in winter. Tundra vegetation grows also on Antarctic islands. Polar desert – dry, intensely cold, and almost lifeless – occurs in the high Arctic and Antarctic only. (BS)

THE HUMAN POPULATION

Modern man can trace his descent from ape-like ancestors over a span of about ten million years; before that men and apes are indistinguishable in the fossil record. The timetable of more recent human evolution is far from clear, but relics of the first true men, recognizably akin to our own species, appear in fossil deposits of the East Indies and Africa about one and a half million years old. The bones and artefacts suggest small, scattered communities of nomadic hunters and food gatherers.

They were short people, similar to pygmies of today, living by their wits in forests and on the plains. We know little of their demography or numbers, but their average life span was probably 20 to 25 years, and few would have survived over 30. They would have lived very much at the mercy of their environment, with numbers increasing locally in the good times and cut back fiercely in times of food shortage and crisis. Three to four million is probably a generous estimate for the world population of Stone Age Man up to 100,000 years ago.

Today the human population is estimated, rather more accurately, at about 4.5 billion. It is growing fast, and at a rate that has been accelerating rapidly. Barring some worldwide catastrophe it will almost certainly reach about 6 billion by the end of the century -- an increase of one quarter or more in twenty years. Some estimates are higher; they would have the human population doubling in fifty years or less – well within the life span of today's teenagers.

Early Population Growth

Whichever estimate turns out to be true, this very rapid rate of increase is a relatively new feature in the history of man. The human population probably remained steady at just a few million, with births and deaths closely in balance, well into Neolithic (New Stone Age) times some five to eight thousand years ago. Then, at about the time when people began to settle, to grow and herd food instead of hunting it, and to live in towns, a slow but steady rise in human populations began. Average life expectancy increased and more people survived to old age. There were still the bad times when famine, warfare or disease decimated or even wiped out whole populations. But the spread of settlements and civilization through Asia and Europe probably allowed world population to double every 1,500 to 2,000 years. This gave a total population in medieval times of about 500 million, with a slightly increased life expectancy of 30 to 40 years.

The Population Explosion

Then came a further change – a steady, persistent increase of births over deaths, especially in the societies that were developing both industries and agriculture and expanding into new areas of the world. In these communities food became more plentiful, health and sanitation improved, the means for buying goods and services spread from the privileged few to the masses. As the general quality of life was enhanced, child care improved, and infants – usually the most vulnerable section of any population – began to survive longer. Now the scene was set for an explosive increase in population size. In the short span of two to three hundred years from late renaissance times to the mid-nineteenth century, world population doubled from a half to one billion.

It doubled again to two billion in the next 80 years, as more and more of the world's resources were organized in the service of mankind. Then came a revolution in medical and social care that further enhanced expectation of life, bringing a further doubling to four billion in the 35 years from 1940 to 1975. Now the rate of increase has probably declined, though the momentum of population numbers is still enormous; hence the expectation of a further doubling within the next half century or less.

The Problems of Overpopulation

Population increases on this scale bring problems – especially to the countries in which the bulk of the increases occur. For one reason and another the most recent, and greatest increases in population have occurred mainly in the poorest countries – the ones least able to absorb a large growth in numbers. They tend to have higher birth rates and larger families; in a poor country children – even hungry ones – may be the only assets their parents can acquire in a lifetime, their only mark of success in a hostile, denying world. Medical aid from wealthy neighbours has ensured that more of their babies survive now than ever before; hence the massive increase in numbers in many of the poor countries during recent decades, the high proportion of young people in their populations today, and the inevitability of further massive increases in their populations of tomorrow.

By contrast, in most of the prosperous countries birth rates have declined and the fashionable family size is small; hence their ageing population structures, and proportionally lower contribution to the projected end-of-century world total of humanity. Currently there are five people in the poorest countries to every two people in the rich. Within half a century, if current trends continue, the ratio within the much larger world population will be seven to two or even greater. Millions in the poor countries are starving now, and many see it as inevitable that more will be starving in the world of the future.

The Persistence of Inequalities

The division of the world into rich and poor nations is a relatively

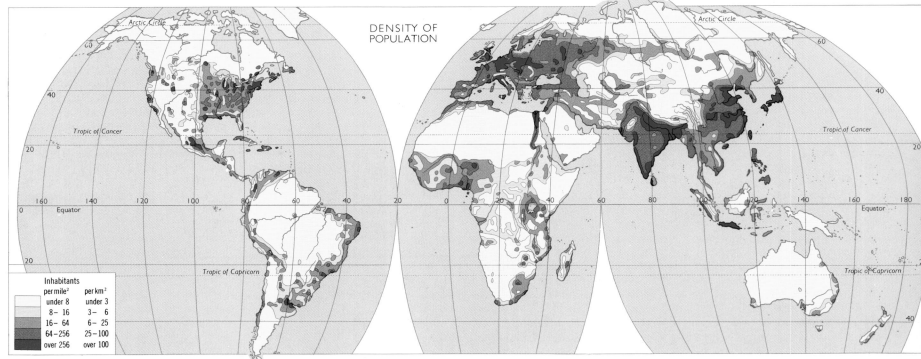

DENSITY OF POPULATION

Inhabitants	
per mile²	per km²
under 8	under 3
8– 16	3– 6
16– 64	6– 25
64–256	25–100
over 256	over 100

1:148 000 000

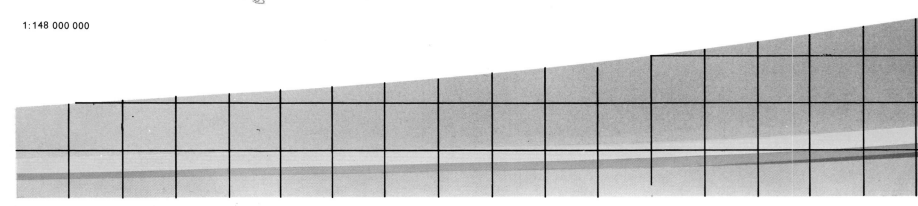

1650   1700   1750   1800

recent happening. Until about three centuries ago practically everyone was poor except for very small, favoured minorities. Over 90 per cent of the world's population lived by farming, using techniques that gave them little more than a subsistence standard of living. When a few communities – the fortunate few that possessed the energy, raw materials, surplus capital and cheap labour at the critical moment – were able to embark on industrialization in the eighteenth and nineteenth centuries, they entered a self-sustaining cycle of events that enabled them to create more and more wealth from their material assets. Wealth spread through these fortunate societies, raising the standards of living of most people within them.

Societies that became rich in this way have in general managed to stay rich, enhancing their living standards from year to year, attracting more and more of the world's goods to their markets, and stabilizing their position of economic superiority. Societies that remained poor – through enslavement or exploitation, through lack of resources or enterprise, or for any other reason – have tended to remain poor and underdeveloped, caught in a poverty trap from which escape becomes more and more difficult.

However, escape is not impossible, as several impoverished societies have shown. China and Japan are countries that, heavily populated and in social and economic chaos only a generation ago, have by widely differing political strategies hauled themselves up from poverty to reasonable levels of hope and prosperity, making use of their large populations to develop both natural resources and skills to the full. (BS)

Human Diversity *Within the human species, Homo sapiens, there are readily discernible differences in characteristics (such as skin colour), and also less obvious but more distinctive group traits, such as blood type. There are nine major human groupings, referred to as geographical races, that relate to major geographical areas: Asian; European; American Indian; African (Negroid); Indic; Polynesian; Melanesian; Micronesian; Australoid. Six are illustrated here.*

1 Asian.

2 American Indian.

3 European.

4 Polynesian.

5 African (Negroid).

6 Indic.

World Population Growth

6,000 m

5,000 m

4,000 m

3,000 m

Oceania

South Asia   2,000 m

Africa

East Asia

South America

1,000 m

North America

Asia pre 1925

USSR

Europe pre 1925   Europe

0

1850   1900   1925   1950   1975   2000

1 Paroportiani Church on Mykonos, Greece. Greece has deep religious traditions richly expressed in the medieval icons, and in the mosaics and frescoes of the fourteenth century.

2 The Jungfrau from Interlaken, Switzerland. Records of ascents of peaks in the Alps date from as early as the fourteenth century.

3 A summer night on the Ontojärvi-See, Finland. Finland has about 60,000 lakes and from the air looks like an intricate blue and green jigsaw puzzle.

4 The Molo waterfront, Venice. A city that is uniquely wedded to the sea, Venice was the centre of a powerful maritime republic from the ninth to the sixteenth century. It is now a major port of northern Italy.

EUROPE

*Purity of race does not exist. Europe is a continent of
energetic mongrels.*

H A L Fisher, *A History of Europe* (1934), Chapter 1

EUROPE

Europe is a small continent, topographically subdivided by shallow shelf seas into a mainland block with a sprawl of surrounding peninsulas and off-lying islands. Its western, northern and southern limits are defined by coastlines and conventions. Of the off-lying islands, Iceland, Svalbard, the Faroes and Britain are included. So are all the larger islands of the Mediterranean Sea, though more on the grounds of their conquest and habitation by Europeans than by their geographical proximity to Europe. The eastern boundary, between Europe and Asia, is hard to define, and conventions for

drawing it differ. Geographers usually set it along the eastern flank of the Ural Mountains, the Emba River, the north shore of the Caspian Sea, the Kuma and Marich Rivers (north of the Caucasus), and the eastern shores of the Azov and Black Seas – thereby including the whole of the western USSR. Politicians often regard the USSR as a separate unit, continental in size, drawing the European border along the boundaries with Norway, Finland, Poland, Czechoslovakia, Hungary and Romania. Bulgaria is European, but all of Turkey is Asian. This convention is followed here.

Europe so defined covers an area of 4.9 million km² (1.9 million sq miles), with a population of 457 million. It extends from well north of the Arctic Circle almost to latitude 34°N, and includes a wide range of topographies and climates – from polders below sea-level to high Alpine peaks, from semi-deserts to polar ice-caps. Its geological structure, and some of the forces that have shaped it, show up clearly on a physical map.

In the far north lies a shield of ancient granites and gneisses occupying northern Scandinavia, Finland and Karelia. This under-

lies and gives shape to the rugged lowlands of this area. The highlands formed later: north and east of the platform lay a marine trough, which was raised, compressed and folded by lateral pressure about 400 million years ago to form the highlands – now well eroded but still impressive – of Norway and north-west Britain.

To the south lay another deep-sea trough, from which a vast accumulation of sediments was raised about 300 million years ago, producing the belt of highlands and well-worn uplands that stretch across Europe from Spain to southern Poland. They include

Projection: Bonne.

the Cantabrian and central mountains of Iberia, the French Massif Central and uplands of Brittany, the Vosges, Ardennes and Westerwald, the Black Forest, the hills of Cornwall, South Wales and southwest Ireland. A third trough, the Tethys Sea, formed still further south and extended in a wide swathe across Europe and Asia. Strong pressure from a northward-drifting Africa slowly closed the sea, to form the present-day Mediterranean, and raised the 'Alpine' mountains that fringe it – the Atlas of North Africa, the Sierra Nevada of Spain, the Pyrenees, the Alps themselves, the Apennines, the Carpathians and Dinaric Alps, and the ranges of the Balkan Peninsula.

More recently still, however, came the Ice Age. The first ice sheets formed across Eurasia and North America from two to three million years ago; during the last million years there have been four major glacial periods in the Alps and three, maybe more, in Scandinavia. The lowland ice melted eight to ten thousand years ago, and the Scandinavian and Alpine glaciers retreated, only Iceland and Svalbard keeping icecaps. The accompanying rise in sealevel finally isolated Britain. (BS)

The Alps are a major barrier but also the most developed of the world's mountains.

An English agricultural landscape.

BRITISH ISLES

Britain stands on the westernmost edge of the continental shelf – two large and several hundred small islands, cool, rainy and windswept. Despite physical closeness to the rest of Europe (32 km or 20 miles at the nearest point – little more than the distance across London) Britain is curiously isolated, with a long history of political independence and social separation from her neighbours. In the past the narrow seas served Britons well, protecting them against casual invasion. Across these seas Britons sailed to explore and exploit the rest of the world. Now insularity is rapidly breaking down, and Britain is closer to federation with Europe than ever before.

The islands are confusingly named. Great Britain, the largest, includes the kingdoms of England and Scotland and the principality of Wales; Ireland was once a kingdom, but is currently divided into the Province of Northern Ireland, under the British Crown, and the politically separate Republic of Ireland. Great Britain, Northern Ireland, and many off-lying island groups from the Scillies to the Shetlands, together make up the United Kingdom of Great Britain and Northern Ireland, commonly known as the UK, Great Britain, or just Britain. Even isolated Rockall, far out in the Atlantic Ocean, is part of Great Britain, but the Isle of Man and the Channel Islands are separate Crown Dependencies with a degree of political autonomy.

The Shaping of the Land

Geologically Britain is the worn-down remnant of a varied, often turbulent past. The oldest and hardest rocks lie mainly in the north and west, with younger, softer sediments in the south and east. The most ancient are the grey sandstone peaks of north-west Scotland and the Hebrides, and the gentler Malvern Hills of south-west England, formed well over 600 million years ago. Helvellyn in the Lake District and the Welsh peaks of Snowdonia are ancient volcanic stumps of similar age. Edinburgh's Castle Rock and its neighbouring peaks are later volcanic remnants, product of an era about 300 million years ago that also gave rise to the limestones, sandstones and grits of the Pennines, the coal measures that supported the Industrial Revolution, and the granites and hard-baked slates of Cornwall. About 180 million years ago warm seas and deserts produced the oolitic limestones of Cotswold cottages, the ironstones, red sandstones and brick-field clays of the Midlands, and the salt deposits that

gave rise to the chemical industries of Cheshire and Durham. Capping these rocks are thick bands of chalk, remnants of a large sea that covered southern Britain and western Europe about 100 million years ago, and now a principal feature of the English lowlands.

For much of the last forty to fifty million years the emerging islands of Britain were tropical or subtropical, facing Europe across a broad sea basin; sands, gravels and clays that accumulated on the sea bed now form the rich and varied soils of the southern counties. The great earth movements of ten to thirty million years ago, that elsewhere raised the Alps, Pyrenees and Himalaya, affected Britain only slightly. In the south they produced the longitudinal folding of the Isle of Wight and the hump-and-sag of the Weald. In the north they released floods of lava that solidified to form the plateau of Antrim, with basalt cliffs at the Giant's Causeway, and the basalt crags of Argyll, Mull and the Inner Hebrides. Throughout this period the climate cooled gradually from tropical to temperate, though as late as two million years ago there were lions and hippopotamus on the plains of lowland Britain, and coral reefs growing in neighbouring seas.

About one million years ago permanent ice formed on high ground, spreading to cover the whole of Britain as far south as the Severn and Thames. The last permanent ice melted nine to ten thousand years ago, leaving a legacy of smooth, bare mountains, wide U-shaped valleys devoid of soil or vegetation, ice-covered lakes and moraine-strewn lowlands. The Dogger Bank, even now only 20 metres (65 ft) deep, formed the corridor that finally linked Britain to the continent, to be submerged as the ice-caps melted and sea level rose. So the British islands took on their familiar shape, with the first Britons already in residence as hunters and gatherers in a chill but slowly-warming environment.

Climate

Despite a subarctic position Britain is favoured climatically. Most other maritime lands between 50° and 60°N – eastern Siberia, Kamchatka, the Aleutian Islands, southern Alaska, Hudson Bay and Labrador – are colder throughout the year, with longer winters, ice-bound coasts and a shorter growing season. Britain's salvation is the North Atlantic Drift or Gulf Stream, a current of surface water that brings subtropical warmth from the southern Atlantic Ocean, spreading it across the continental shelf of Western Europe and warming the prevailing westerly winds.

The coldest parts of Britain, perhaps not surprisingly, are the highlands of Scotland. On top of Ben Nevis (1,343 m, 4,405 ft, the highest peak) mean temperature for the year is about freezing point, and many north-facing gullies contain year-round snow. At sea level mean

summer temperatures range from 11°C (52°F) in the north to 17°C (63°F) in the south, mean winter temperatures from about 5°C (41°F) in eastern and central Britain to 7°C (45°F) in the south-west. Air temperatures seldom exceed 35°C (95°F) or drop below −12°C (10°F); except in the coldest winters snow seldom lies on the lowlands for more than two or three months, usually much less in the south.

The growing season, indicated roughly by the number of months in which mean air temperature exceeds 6°C (42°F), ranges from less than four months in the Scottish highlands to nine months or more on the south-west coast. Most of lowland Britain

Buttermere in the Lake District.

has a growing season of seven to eight months, enough to ensure the prosperity of arable farmers in most years. Britain's reputation for cloudiness is well merited. Mean duration of sunshine throughout the year is about 5 hours daily in the south, only $3\frac{1}{2}$ hours daily in Scotland. At the height of summer only the south-west receives more than $7\frac{1}{2}$ hours of sunshine per day – less than half the hours available. In winter only the south coast, the Severn Estuary, Oxfordshire and a sliver of south-eastern Essex receive more than $1\frac{1}{2}$ hours per day, while many northern areas receive less than half an hour daily. Despite a reputation for rain Britain is a fairly dry country. More than half of the country receives less than 750 mm (30 in) annually, and parts of Essex have less than 500 mm (20 in) per year. The wettest areas are Snowdonia with about 5,000 mm (200 in), Ben Nevis and the north-western highlands with 4,300 mm (172 in), and the Lake District with 3,300 mm (132 in).

British climate is far from static. It was warmer at the time of the Domesday Survey (1086) when vineyards flourished as far north as York, and it cooled throughout the Middle Ages, when Arctic pack ice was reported off Shetland and Eskimos

are said to have visited northern Scotland in their kayaks. Cooling continued into the mid-nineteenth century, followed by a long period of warming up to World War 2. Now Britain's climate may once again be cooling.

Population and Immigration

Despite insularity the British people are of mixed stock. The earliest immigrants – land-hungry farmers from the continent – were often refugees from tribal warfare and unrest. The Belgic tribesmen escaping from Imperial Rome, the Romans themselves (whose troops included Spanish, Macedonian and probably North African mercenaries), the Angles, Saxons, Jutes, Danes and Normans, all in turn brought genetic variety; so did the Huguenots, Sephardic and Ashkenazim Jews, and Dutch, French and German business men who followed them. Latterly the waves of immigrants have included White Russians, Poles, Italians, Ukrainians and Czechs – most, like their predecessors, fugitives from European wars, overcrowding, intolerance and unrest. Often during the nineteenth century Britain took in skilled European immigrants through the front door while steadily losing her own sons and daughters – Scots and Irish peasants in particular – through the back. Most recent arrivals in Britain are immigrants from crowded and impoverished corners of lands once part of the British Empire, notably the West Indies and Pakistan. These and their descendants now make up about 4 per cent of the population of Britain.

Under Roman rule the population of the British island numbered half to three-quarters of a million. By the time of the Domesday Census (1086) it had doubled, and it doubled again by the end of the fourteenth century. The Black Death of the late fifteenth century swept away one in every three or four, but numbers climbed slowly; at the Union of 1707 some six million English and Welsh joined about one million Scots under a single Parliament. By 1801 the first national census revealed 8.9 million in England and Wales, 1.6 million in Scotland; Ireland missed the first two ten-year counts, but probably numbered about 5 million. In 1821 the total British population was 21 million, in 1851 31 million, and in 1921 47 million. Fortunately for all the rate of increase has now declined, and at present Britons number about 59 millions – 55.8 millions in Great Britain and Northern Ireland, and the rest in Eire. Some parts of Britain, notably the south-east and the conurbations, are among the most heavily-populated areas of the world, with higher densities only in the Netherlands and Taiwan. (BS)

Offshore fields produce oil and gas.

The remote and spectacular cliffs of northern County Mayo, Ireland.

A blanket factory in the Cotswolds.

1 : 4 000 000

The DISTRICTS of Northern Ireland have been numbered and can be identified by reference to this table.

1	Londonderry	14	Craigavon
2	Limavady	15	Armagh
3	Coleraine	16	Newry & Mourne
4	Ballymoney	17	Banbridge
5	Moyle	18	Down
6	Larne	19	Lisburn
7	Ballymena	20	Antrim
8	Magherafelt	21	Newtownabbey
9	Cookstown	22	Carrickfergus
10	Strabane	23	North Down
11	Omagh	24	Ards
12	Fermanagh	25	Castlereagh
13	Dungannon	26	Belfast

1 Merseyside
2 Greater Manchester
3 West Yorkshire
4 South Yorkshire
5 West Glamorgan
6 Mid Glamorgan
7 South Glamorgan

Projection: Conical with two standard parallels
West from Greenwich   East from Greenwich
COPYRIGHT. GEORGE PHILIP & SON. LTD.

Climate

Standing in the zone where westerly winds prevail, Britain receives damp, maritime air from the Atlantic Ocean through much of the year, providing a background climate of mild winters and cool summers. Shifting patterns of pressure bring in other air masses to displace the westerlies; those from the continent are hot in summer and bitterly cold in winter, while Arctic air tends to be cool all the year round. Fronts or boundaries between air masses, sweeping almost daily across Britain, provide the familiar, ever-changing patterns of cloud, rain and clear spells that give British weather its variability, and its perennial value as a talking point.

LOCALITY HEIGHT		JAN	JUL	YR
Lerwick	°C	3.1	12.1	7.2
82 m	mm	109	72	1003
Kirkwall	°C	3.7	12.9	7.9
26 m	mm	105	71	950
Edinburgh	°C	3.3	14.8	8.7
134 m	mm	57	83	676
Belfast	°C	3.7	14.7	9.1
67 m	mm	80	94	845
Scarborough	°C	4.1	16.1	9.8
36 m	mm	65	58	647
Birmingham	°C	3.5	16.3	9.6
163 m	mm	74	69	764
Cork	°C	5.5	15.9	10.4
15 m	mm	119	70	1048
London (Kew)	°C	4.3	17.7	10.6
5 m	mm	54	57	593
Cardiff	°C	4.4	16.3	10.3
62 m	mm	108	89	1065
Plymouth	°C	6.1	16.0	10.8
27 m	mm	99	70	950

ENGLAND

Landscape

Visitors to England are often amazed at the variety of the landscape. Physically it has a long history (see pp 18–19). Complex folding, laval outpourings, volcanic upheavals and eruptions, glacial planing, and changes of sea level have all left their marks on the present landscape.

From Northumberland to the Trent the Pennine Range extends southwards as an upland with rolling hills, plateaux and fine valleys, many known as 'dales'. The Range includes two western outliers – the Forest of Rossendale north of Manchester, and the Forest of Bowland in north Lancashire. To either side lie lowlands – those of Lancashire to the west and of Yorkshire and Nottingham to the east. The Eden Valley separates the northern Pennines from Cumbria, which includes the Lake District. This is England's most striking, mountain mass, a circular area of peaks, deep valleys, splendid lakes and crags. The loftiest peak is Scafell, 978 m (3,210 ft). In the southwest Exmoor is a fine sandstone upland, and Dartmoor a predominantly granite area with many prominent tors. Elsewhere are isolated hills, small by world standards but dramatic against the small-scale background of Britain, as shown by the Malvern Hills of Worcester and the Wrekin near Shrewsbury.

The flat landscape of East Anglia, similar to the countryside of Holland.

Much of the English lowland consists of chalk downlands, familiar to continental visitors who enter England through Folkestone or Dover as the famous chalk cliffs. These cliffs are the exposed coastal edge of the North Downs, whose scarped northern slope forms a striking feature in the Croydon area of Greater London. The North Downs continue westward through Surrey to the Hampshire Downs, then south and east as the South Downs, emerging at another of Britain's coastal landmarks – Beachy Head. There is a northward extension of downland through the Berkshire and Marlborough Downs to the Chilterns, then north again into East Anglia to disappear under the edge of the fens at Cambridge. Formerly forested, the downlands were cleared early for pasture and agriculture, and now provide a rich and varied mixture of woodlands, parklands, fields and small settlements. Chalk appears again in the wolds of Lincolnshire and Yorkshire, reaching the sea at Flamborough Head.

Older rocks, predominantly limestones, form the ridge of the Cotswold Hills, and the rolling, hilly farmlands of Leicestershire, the Lincoln Edge (cut by the river Witham at Lincoln), and finally the North York moors. In these older rocks are rich iron deposits, mined in Cleveland to supply ores for the steel towns of the Tees estuary until 1964, and still mined in the Midlands.

England is drained by many fine rivers, of which the greatest are the Thames, the Severn, the fenland Ouse, the Trent, and the great Yorkshire Ouse that receives its tributaries from the many picturesque valleys – the Dales – of the Pennine flank. There are many smaller rivers, and a large number of the old towns that dot England at intervals of 20 km (12 miles) or so were built at their crossing points – generally where dry ground existed above marshes and gave firm sites for building. Chester, for example, was founded on a patch of sandstone beside the Dee; one of the four gates of the Roman town is still called the Watergate. York too was built on firm ground by a river crossing, and so was Manchester. London arose on the site chosen by the Romans for the first convenient crossing place of the Thames, formerly a much broader and shallower river.

Agriculture

England has a rich variety of soils, derived both locally from parent rocks and also from glacial debris or 'drift'. During the twelve thousand and more years since the ice retreated, soils have been enriched, firstly by such natural processes as flooding and the growth of forests, and latterly by the good husbandry of many generations of farmers. Husbandry improved particularly from the eighteenth century onward. The Industrial Revolution was accompanied by an agricultural revolution that resulted in massive increases in crops per hectare and in the quality of livestock.

Through the eighteenth and nineteenth centuries farming became more scientific and more specialized; as the demands from the towns grew, so did the ability of English farmers to meet increasing markets for food. The eastern counties, particularly East Anglia and Holderness (now part of Humberside), became the granaries of England, while the rich, wet grasslands of the west and the midlands turned pastoral – Cheshire cheese is a famous product of this specialization. There were other local products – the hops of Kent and Hereford, the apples of Worcester, and the fine wools that continued to be the main product of the chalk downlands. In south Lancashire potatoes and vegetables became major crops for sale in the markets of the growing northern industrial towns; market gardening and dairying on a small scale developed near every major settlement, taking advantage of the ready market close at hand.

Scenically England still gives the impression of being an agricultural country. Less than 10 per cent of the area is rough moorland, about 5 per cent is forest, and about 10 per cent is urban or suburban, leaving roughly 75 per cent under cultivation of one kind or another. Yet only 3 per cent of the working population is currently employed in agriculture, a figure that has declined drastically in recent years. Loss of rural populations has been an inevitable result of agricultural rationalization and improvements in farming methods. Those who deplore this trend might reflect that, though English farming formerly employed many more labourers, it supported them at little more than subsistence level. However picturesque, the rural villages of nineteenth century England harboured grinding poverty, for which escape to the towns was the only remedy.

Rich Cambridgeshire farmland.

Lincolnshire tulip fields.

The Channel Islands

Guernsey, the second-largest of the Channel Islands, from the south-west.

Lying 16 to 48 km (10 to 30 miles) from the French coast, the Islands cover an area of only 200 km^2 (78 sq miles). The largest is Jersey with 115 km^2 (45 sq miles) and 75,000 inhabitants and the other major island is Guernsey, with 78 km^2 (30 sq miles) and 55,000 people. The other islands are small, such as Alderney with 8 km^2 (3 sq miles) and fewer than 2,000 residents. The Islands have been attached to Britain since the Norman Conquest (1066), but have their own government, with lower taxation than that of Britain. This, combined with a favourable climate and fine coastal scenery, has attracted a considerable number of retired people.

The main produce is agricultural, especially early potatoes, tomatoes and flowers for Britain, and the countryside has a vast number of glasshouses. The soil is now fertile, having been made so by the farmers' skilful use of seaweed and other fertilizers. Jersey and Guernsey cattle are famous breeds, introduced to many countries. Holiday makers visit the islands in large numbers during the summer months, travelling by air or by the various passenger boats, especially from Weymouth. English is the official language but French is spoken widely. (TWF)

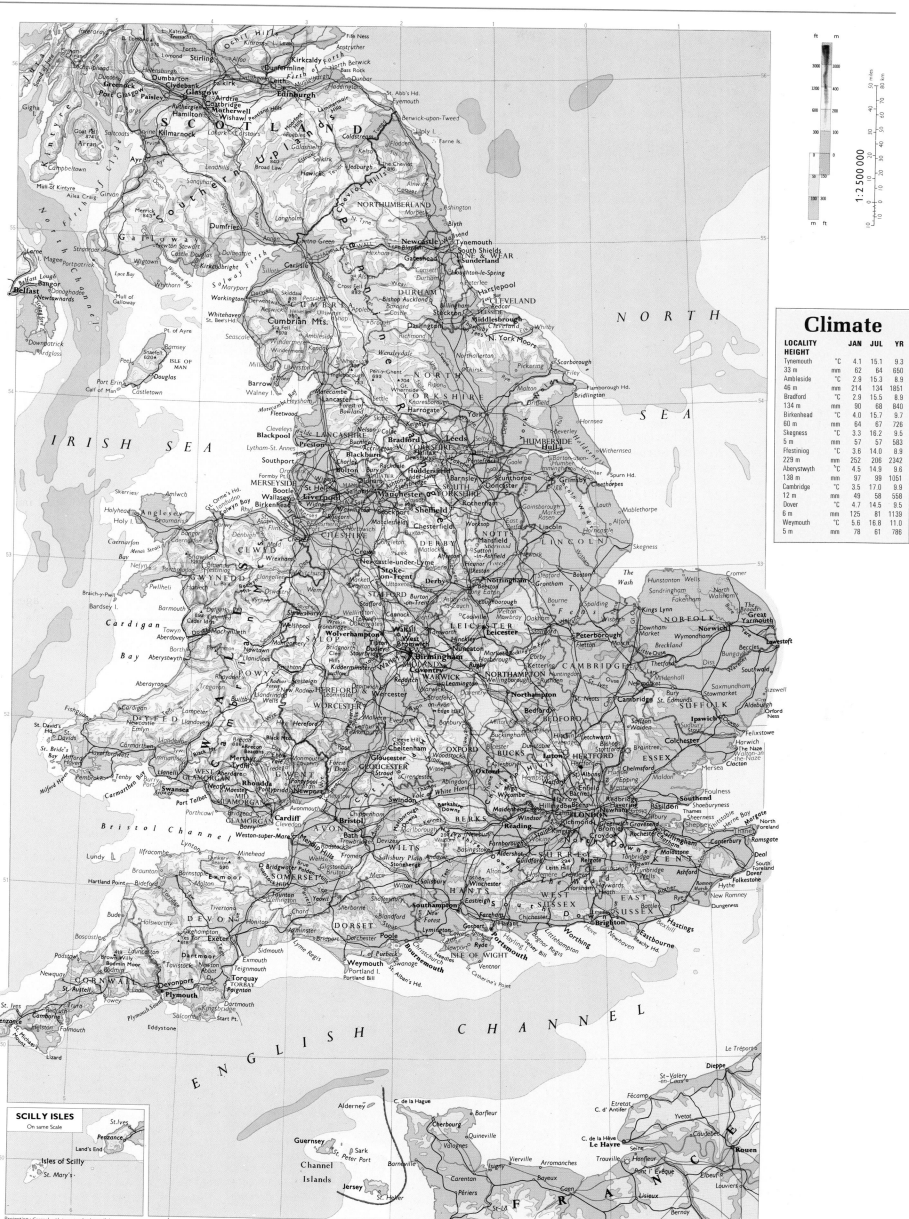

Climate

LOCALITY HEIGHT		JAN	JUL	YR
Tynemouth	°C	4.1	15.1	9.3
33 m	mm	62	64	650
Ambleside	°C	2.9	15.3	8.9
46 m	mm	214	134	1851
Bradford	°C	2.9	15.5	8.9
134 m	mm	90	68	840
Birkenhead	°C	4.0	15.7	9.7
60 m	mm	64	67	726
Skegness	°C	3.3	16.2	9.5
5 m	mm	57	57	583
Ffestiniog	°C	3.6	14.0	8.9
229 m	mm	252	206	2342
Aberystwyth	°C	4.5	14.9	9.6
138 m	mm	97	99	1051
Cambridge	°C	3.5	17.0	9.9
12 m	mm	49	58	558
Dover	°C	4.7	14.5	9.5
6 m	mm	125	81	1139
Weymouth	°C	5.6	16.8	11.0
5 m	mm	78	61	786

1 : 2 500 000

SCILLY ISLES
On same Scale

Projection : Conical with two standard parallels.

West from Greenwich   East from Greenwich   COPYRIGHT. GEORGE PHILIP & SON. LTD.

Industry and Urbanization

England had important reserves of coal, the major fields being on either side of the Pennines (Yorkshire, Lancashire, Northumberland and Durham), in the Midlands (Derbyshire and Nottinghamshire) and in South Wales. These coalfields, and extensive reserves of iron ore, were the basis of the Industrial Revolution of the eighteenth century, and the industrial growth of the nineteenth century, which together resulted in major changes in the English landscape.

Areas which previously had only small populations rose to industrial greatness. Perhaps the most striking example was Teesside where, following the exploitation of the Cleveland iron ores, the town of Middlesbrough grew from a small port (7,000 population in 1851) to a large manufacturing centre. Today Middlesbrough and its neighbouring settlements have almost 400,000 inhabitants. Similarly, small mill villages in Lancashire and Yorkshire grew into large towns while the West Midlands pottery towns and villages coalesced into the urban area of Stoke-on-Trent.

Although the coalfields of the north saw the greatest local expansion of population, London and England's other major ports, such as Liverpool and Bristol, developed too as export markets flourished. These developments were accompanied by significant improvements in communications, including the building of an extensive canal network (with three canals over the Pennines by 1800) and many new roads.

From the 1840s town growth was rapid and by the end of the nineteenth century 80 per cent of the population was urban. While the working class population was mainly housed in slums, the prosperity of the commercial and professional classes was reflected in the Victorian villas that, in varying degrees of splendour, appeared in select areas of the towns.

This phase of expansion continued until World War 1. By the 1930s, however, there were signs that the prosperity of many older and industrial mining areas was threatened and efforts were made to bring new industries to areas of particularly high unemployment, such as the Northumberland and Durham coalfield, West Cumberland, and the South Wales coalfield. In all of these, whole areas had become virtually derelict because their coal was exhausted, or no longer in demand; one such casualty, especially in South Wales, was steam coal for ships, rapidly being replaced by oil. The main areas of industrial growth since World War 1 have been around London and also in the West Midlands. A number of towns, for example Coventry, experienced extremely rapid growth. Conscious planning had the aim of controlling industrial expansion and preventing the indiscriminate growth of some towns, for example Oxford and Cambridge.

Today England is a significant steel producer and most of the steel produced is used in other British industries such as ship-building (Barrow, Merseyside, Tyneside, Teesside) and vehicle manufacture (West Midlands, Merseyside, London area), although, as elsewhere in western Europe, all three industries are currently facing considerable difficulties. Highly-skilled engineering industries are also important and centres include Birmingham, Wolverhampton and Manchester. Textiles are still a major industry, with cotton goods being produced mainly in Lancashire and woollens and worsteds in Yorkshire. Similarly, pottery is still important in the Midlands.

The decline of the coal industry has been offset by the recent development of North Sea oil and gas fields and these are now of major importance to the British economy.

Replanning England

After World War 2 the need for replanning England to take account of the industrial areas was generally accepted. The existence of conurbations where towns had grown into one another was recognized by their listing in the 1951 Census, when they included Greater London, the West Midlands (Birmingham and the Black Country), South-east Lancashire with North-east Cheshire (Greater Manchester), Merseyside and Tyneside. Prolonged discussion followed on the best form of new administrative structure needed in England, and ultimately, in 1974, the new scheme of local government emerged. Many county boundaries were changed but one alteration of particular significance was the definition of some new counties based on the major industrial areas.

In creating the new administrative units of Tyne and Wear, Cleveland, West Yorkshire, South Yorkshire, Greater Manchester and West Midlands, and in redefining Greater London on more generous lines, the planners at last recognized the realities of population distribution in England. However, the highly industrialized areas still cover only a small part of the country. Many towns are developing new industrial areas – the 'industrial estates', housing light industries on their outskirts – and since 1945 government-sponsored 'new towns' have arisen in many parts of the country, in an attempt to stem the further growth of London and the existing conurbations. London has several satellite new towns – Basildon, Harlow, Stevenage and Milton Keynes, for example, most of them founded on small existing settlements. In the north are Washington, Peterlee and Aycliffe, built around old mining villages, with new industries invited in on favourable terms. Powers to develop new towns fortunately go hand-in-hand with powers to protect the remaining countryside against casual despoilment. Agricultural land, particularly at hazard, may be rigorously protected by local

Shipbuilding on the Tyne. This industry is now facing problems.

The UK has pioneered the use of nuclear energy from plants such as this.

planning authorities, and new building kept within bounds.

Preserving the Countryside

In an age when increased prosperity has spread leisure and the means of travel to millions of people, new emphasis has been placed on recreation. One result is the National Parks, another the many scenic areas under the control of the Countryside Commission and other national bodies. In these areas there are special provisions for conserving the beauty of the English countryside, and creating amenities – from car-parks to viewing-points and picnic sites – that help people to enjoy them. Though it is never the intention that National Parks be kept as rural museums, with all development stifled, siting of new buildings, roads and electricity cables is carefully controlled, and national need must be shown before mining and other disruptive activities can be justified.

The Forestry Commission, too, has a mandate to provide amenity sites in its forests, and to landscape new plantings in ways that provide timber, but also maintain the natural beauty of the area concerned. (TWF)

The Borders

The Romans built Hadrian's Wall (AD 122–127) to mark the boundary of their military zone. It runs between Solway Firth and Carlisle to the river Tyne at Wallsend, and its purpose was to deter raiders from Scotland. Now the boundary between England and Scotland, marked by notices on major roads, runs from Solway Firth just south of the village of Gretna Green, and along the main summits of the Cheviot range, of which the highest point is 'The Cheviot', 816 m (2,676 ft). From this fine hill the boundary runs north and reaches the river Tweed, crossing a wide and fertile lowland.

As a whole the Border country consists mainly of the upland country of Northumberland, which is now a National Park, and the similar landscape in Scotland on either side of the Teviot valley. Easy passes run through these uplands but the major routes, used by main line railways and trunk roads, are in the lowlands at either end of the Cheviot range. Many signs of former warfare and unrest may be seen, for whole villages and even some of the private houses were fortified before Scotland and England were united (1707). (TWF)

WALES

United to England in 1535, Wales still preserves a sense of individuality over 400 years later. This separateness rests not on any clear boundary in the countryside, but on history and sentiment. Although only 20 per cent of the population speak Welsh, 75 per cent of the inhabitants do so in the western counties of Gwynedd and Dyfed. The national sentiment is not only expressed through language, but also through literature, the arts (especially music) and political life. Cardiff, the capital, grew rapidly during the nineteenth century with the iron and steel industry and coal mining, but no Welsh town is centrally placed for the whole country. Meetings of the boards representing the colleges of the University of Wales – Cardiff, Swansea, Lampeter, Aberystwyth and Bangor – take place at Shrewsbury, an English border town.

Landscape

With a total area of 20,240 km² (7,800 sq miles), Wales is predominantly mountainous, although two-thirds of the rural area is farmland and one-third moorland. The most famous of the highland areas is Snowdonia, now a National Park covering 2,138 km² (825 sq miles) from Snowdon to Cader Idris. But there are fine upland areas in central Wales, on both sides of the upper Severn valley which cuts through them to the Dovey valley and the coastal lowlands facing Cardigan Bay. South of the Severn, in the counties of Powys and Dyfed, the uplands dominate the landscape and in the Brecon Beacons, south of

The Valleys

Ebbw Vale, South Wales.

The upland of Blaenau Morganwg rises to a height of almost 660 m (2,000 ft) in Craig y Llyn. Before the Industrial Revolution it was a sparsely populated area, with farms on its lower slopes and a few villages on hillsides rather than in the steep-sided valleys. But coal was found in the valleys, varied in type but suitable for use in steamships, domestic fires and industry. Development began from the late eighteenth century, canals served by wagon ways bringing the coal to industrial centres. The main growth came from the mid-nineteenth century: the Rhondda valleys, for example, were not exploited until the 1860s, and many western valleys were developed much later. In some valleys the slopes were so steep that level land was at a premium, used for railways, roads and main streets, and the houses were built above in terraces on the hillsides. Since World War 1, the population of the valleys has been declining, though many new industries have been introduced during the past fifty years to offset the loss of work in mining. Happily, some attempt is now being made to improve the appearance of the valleys. (TWF)

Harlech Castle, built by Edward I c. AD 1283 after his conquest of Wales.

the Usk valley on which the old town of Brecon is situated, they provide another National Park, of 1,303 km² (500 sq miles). Many of the uplands and high lakes are sources of water for Welsh and English towns, including Liverpool, Birmingham, Cardiff and Swansea. Isolated white-washed buildings are a feature of the rural landscape.

Mining and Industry

Some writers on Wales regard the uplands as the country's real heartland, with their sheep pastures and forested valleys, interspersed by farming villages and small towns. But over half the population live in the industrialized area of South Wales, which includes the mining valleys of Gwent, Mid Glamorgan and West Glamorgan, and the towns of Newport, Cardiff and Swansea with their traditional heavy metal industries and newer factories for light industry. All are ports, and Cardiff now has many central buildings for the whole of Wales, including the National Museum and the Welsh Office, though the country's National Library is located at Aberystwyth.

Coal mining developed in association with iron working on the fringes of the upland area of Gwent and Glamorgan, traditionally known as the Blaenau Morganwg. Towns such as Merthyr Tydfil and Ebbw Vale became steel centres, and in time all the valleys where coal was accessible, at first by adits (natural outcrops), and later by mining, attracted settlers. The coal was carried to the ports by railways, and also by canals – for example the Glamorgan canal from Merthyr to Cardiff (opened in 1794), the Monmouthshire canal to Newport (1791), the Tawe valley canal to Swansea (1798). Mining reached its peak by World War 1, and has been declining ever since. Slate quarrying at Llanberis and Bethesda (Gwynedd), which once sent fine Welsh slates all over the world, has also declined.

No other area of Wales is so heavily dominated by mining and industry as Deeside. Flint and the Wrexham areas are also industrialized, with coalfields now in decline and modern light industries taking their place.

The Growth of Tourism

Just as the railways stimulated economic growth in south Wales from the 1840s, so on the north Wales coast they stimulated the growth of holiday and residential towns, notably Rhyl, Colwyn Bay and Llandudno. These attracted English residents, many of them retired people from Lancashire, and the holiday industry boomed. In the motoring age it developed further, so that almost every beach and coastal village had its guest houses, holiday cottages, caravan parks and camping sites. Now tourism has spread to virtually the whole of Wales. In Anglesey, many small places have devoted visitors who favour sailing as well as walking and sea bathing, while this is true also of many ports of the Welsh mainland coast. The south-west, formerly Pembrokeshire but now part of Dyfed, has fine coastal scenery, forming the Pembrokeshire National Park with a coast path 268 km (167 miles) long.

Wales is rich in scenic attraction. The landscape is dominantly agricultural, with mixed farming, notably for dairying, cattle and sheep. Many upland farmers combine agriculture with the tourist trade, providing guest houses or camping centres. Forestry plantations exist in many upland valleys but the main characteristic of the countryside is rural farmland, with country towns placed at distances of 20 km (12 miles) or so from one another. (TWF)

ISLE OF MAN

Covering 590 km² (227 sq miles), the Isle of Man is 50 km (32 miles) long and from 13 to 21 km (8 to 13 miles) wide in its central area. The uplands, pierced by the corridor valley from Douglas to Peel, extend from Ramsey to Port Erin. Mainly agricultural, with some fishing and a few light industries, the island is largely dependent on tourism. The annual Tourist Trophy (motor cycle) races attract many visitors. Douglas, the capital, has over one-third of the island's population. The Calf of Man, an islet to the south-west, is a bird sanctuary administered by the Manx National Trust. Very few people now speak Manx. (TWF)

Hadrian's Wall was 118 km (73½ miles) long. It was evacuated after AD 383.

SCOTLAND

Scotland is a generally cool, hilly and, in the west, wet country occupying about one-third of Great Britain. Physically it can be divided into three parts: the Highlands and Islands, bounded by the edge of the mountains from Stonehaven to the mouth of the Clyde, Central Scotland, sometimes called the central lowland though it is interspersed by a number of hill ranges, and the Southern Uplands, defined in the north by a geological fault extending from Dunbar to Girvan, and in the south by the border with England.

The Highlands and Islands

More than half of Scotland's area is in the Highlands and Islands. These are divided by the Great Glen, from Fort William to Inverness, with its three lochs, Lochy, Oich and Ness (where the monster is prone to appear in the tourist season). The Caledonian canal links these three lochs. Much of the whisky for which Scotland is famous is produced in the Highlands.

The North-West This north-western part of the Highlands has splendid scenery – deep, glaciated valleys dominated by mountains, and only limited areas of farmland, much of it now abandoned.

The financial returns from crofting (small-scale tenant farming) were meagre, and many old croft cottages have become holiday homes. Forests now cover many of the valleys; some of the mountains are deer parks, owned by landlords and let to visitors for seasonal shooting. Railways reach the western coast at Mallaig and Kyle of Lochalsh, from which there are boat services to Skye and the Outer Hebrides, but the future of these lines is uncertain. Roads are in part single track with passing places, although they are gradually being improved. At the various villages there are hotels, guest houses and other accommodation for visitors, and the main commercial occupa-

tions are fishing and home weaving.

The traditional weaving of Harris tweeds in the Hebrides is now industrially organized, with much of the work done in workshops. Skye has splendid climbing in the Cuillin Hills, and the numerous rivers and lakes are favoured by fishermen. Here, as in the rest of the Highlands, efforts to improve local industries have had some success.

The East The highland area east of the Great Glen is a richer country, flanked on the east by the lowlands around Aberdeen, which extend into Buchan and then westward to Moray Firth around Inverness. This is sound farming country, famous for pedigree cattle, and from these low-

Climate

LOCALITY HEIGHT		JAN	JUL	YR
Wick	°C	3.3	12.9	7.9
36 m	mm	85	72	771
Stornoway	°C	4.3	13.3	8.5
3 m	mm	152	93	1297
Nairn	°C	3.1	14.3	8.5
6 m	mm	49	74	612
Benbecula	°C	4.5	13.5	9.0
6 m	mm	142	85	1245
Dundee	°C	2.6	15.1	8.5
45 m	mm	65	89	761
Oban	°C	3.9	13.9	8.9
69 m	mm	146	120	1451
Stirling	°C	2.9	15.4	9.0
46 m	mm	101	87	963
Dunbar	°C	3.5	14.6	8.7
23 m	mm	47	68	568
Dumfries	°C	2.9	15.0	8.8
43 m	mm	106	94	1034
Renfrew	°C	3.1	15.1	8.9
6 m	mm	111	97	1109

left The Island of Skye. Many old crofts are now holiday homes.

below Cumbernauld – a new town for Glasgow's overspill population.

below The countryside near Inverness, north of the Great Glen.

The Clans

A typical glen in the highlands.

Family tradition is much prized in Scotland. The fierce independence of peoples living in isolation, belonging to the same stock and owing allegiance to the same chieftain, for long made Scotland impossible to govern. Surnames often express kinship ('Mac' means 'son of'), or show the location from which a clan originated – possibly a glen, or a few hectares of farmed land. Family cohesion was helped by distinctive patterns of weaving – the tartans – used in the wrap-around kilts, plaids and shawls, originally coloured with natural dyes.

The clan spirit was fiercely tested during the retribution that followed the 1745 rebellion, and tested again during the nineteenth century period of agricultural reorganization, when landlords (often the hereditary chieftains to whom allegiance was owed) dispossessed their tenants to create sheep runs. The massive migration that followed spread Scots to every corner of the world, but clan spirit survived. Visitors from America and countries once part of the British Empire – often direct descendants of the dispossessed – today throng the tweed shops of Edinburgh buying tartans and maps that show where their families originated. Much of the romance surrounding the clans was worked up in the nineteenth century, particularly in the writings of Sir Walter Scott. But family pride – the clan spirit of Scots men and women the world over, is a very real force in the world today. (TWF)

lands tongues of farmland extend into the valleys, the Dee, Don, Spey and others. Aberdeen and Fraserburgh are major fishing centres. Aberdeen has become increasingly prosperous with the oil extraction from the North Sea and so too have many smaller places throughout the Highlands.

Ben Nevis, 1,343 m (4,406 ft), dominating the town of Fort William, is the highest summit in the British Isles (and one of the dullest to climb), and a number of peaks in the Cairngorms, including Ben Macdhui, at 1,311 m (4,300 ft), are of almost equal height. Little known in the past, the Cairngorms have now been developed for winter skiing and summer climbing and fishing. There are still deer forests in the uplands but much of the country is used for sheep farming and tourism. Fort William and a few other centres have modern industry based on local hydro-electricity – aluminium smelting, for example – but Oban is the main holiday centre on the west coast.

In the north, the Orkney islands are connected to Thurso (Scrabster) by boat and also to Aberdeen. Fishing and farming are the main support of the population, with a successful specialization in egg production. The Shetlands have a far harder environment, with craggy hills and limited areas suited to farming, though fishing is prominent, notably at Lerwick. The oil industry has brought great, if temporary, prosperity to some places in these islands.

The Economic Heartland

The Central Lowlands of Scotland include several ranges of rolling uplands – the Sidlaw Hills north of Dundee, the Ochils south of Perth, and the Pentlands extending in a south-westerly direction from the suburbs of Edinburgh. Most of Scotland's population and industrial activity occurs in this central area, and here too are its two largest cities – Glasgow on innumerable small glacial hills (drumlins) in the Clyde Valley, and Edinburgh on splendid volcanic ridges, dominated by Arthur's Seat.

Central Scotland is the economic heartland, and Clydeside the greatest industrial area, of Scotland. Textile industries, engineering and shipbuilding were the basis of the prosperity of Glasgow and its neighbouring towns, which in time grew into one another and held more than a third of Scotland's total population. There is now a wide range of industries in Central Scotland including electronics, printing, brewing and carpet-making.

Edinburgh, with its port of Leith, remained much smaller than Glasgow, with only half its population, but is still the administrative centre, and the seat of the main law courts and the National Museum and Library, as well as of many cultural organizations. A favoured centre for retirement in Scotland, it has an increasing tourist trade, particularly during the Edinburgh Festival in the summer. Much of the central area is rich farmland, especially to the east of Edinburgh where the soils have been upgraded by generations of enterprising farmers concentrating on both stock and crops.

The Southern Uplands

The Southern Uplands, though less spectacular than the Highlands, include many fine hills, rolling moorlands and rich valleys. From the summit of Merrick (843 m, 2,764 ft) in Galloway can be seen the Highlands to the north, the plateau of Northern Ireland to the west, and the Lake District, the Pennines and the Isle of Man to the south. The Tweed with its numerous tributaries and – further west – the Esk, Annan, Nith, Ken and Cree, provide sheltered valleys for farming, and there is splendid agricultural country in Galloway, where dairying has been particularly successful. Cattle rearing with crop production is more general in the drier east, where many farms specialize in beasts for slaughter. The hills are used for sheep rearing. Some of the towns, notably Hawick and Galashiels, are prominent in the textile industry and have a large export trade.

Although tourism is relatively less important than in the Highlands, many people come to see the historic centres, such as Melrose and Dryburgh Abbey. To the west, in Galloway, there has been a policy of afforestation on the poorer soils, and several centres have been opened as small museums and educational sites. The coast attracts tourists and Forest Parks, such as that at Glen Trool close to Merrick, have been well laid out for visitors. In the west the towns are small, though there is heavy traffic to Stranraer, the packet station for the shortest sea crossing to Larne in Ireland. (TWF)

IRELAND

Ireland is the whole island west of Britain: the Republic of Ireland (Eire) is the 26 counties governed from Dublin and Northern Ireland is the six counties that remained part of the United Kingdom from 1921.

Ireland was originally divided into four provinces which gradually emerged as major divisions from Norman times. Three counties of the Republic, Donegal, Cavan and Monaghan, together with the six Northern Ireland counties, formed the old province of Ulster. Connacht, in effect the land beyond the Shannon, includes the five counties of Leitrim, Sligo, Roscommon, Galway and Mayo; Munster comprises Clare, Limerick, Tipperary, Kilkenny, Waterford, Cork and Kerry; while Leinster consists of the heart of the central lowland and the counties of the south-east, Wicklow, Wexford and Carlow, between Dublin and Waterford harbour.

The provinces never had any corporate government, and now have little significance except on the sports field. In the Republic local government is administered through the counties, which developed from Norman times and commonly coincide with diocesan boundaries. In Northern Ireland counties have now been superseded by districts, with boundaries more appropriate for local administration.

Landscape

Physically the main outlines of Ireland are simple. In the western peninsulas of Donegal and Connacht ancient rocks were folded to form mountain chains running northeast to south-west; good examples are the fine Derryveagh range of Co Donegal and the Ox mountains of Co Sligo. The highest peaks, for example Errigal, 752 m (2,466 ft), are generally of quartzite, a metamorphosed sandstone. The same trend is seen also in the long range, including the Wicklow mountains, between Dublin Bay and Waterford Harbour in the south-east and also in the Slieve Bloom of the central lowland. The fine east-west ranges of the south, extending from Waterford to the western peninsulas, and the islands of Kerry and West Cork, were formed at a later period. Much of lowland Ireland is floored by rocks contemporary with the coal-bearing measures in England, and these also form some uplands like those around Sligo. Unfortunately these rocks contain little coal; some is mined on a small scale in the Castlecomer area of Co Kilkenny, and near Lough Allen in the upper Shannon Valley.

The basalt lavas that poured out in the north-east of Ireland, forming the desolate Antrim plateau with its fine scenic cliffs on the famous Coast Road, and the Giant's Causeway, are more recent. Irish soils, however, are largely derived from glacial deposits, and Ireland's famous peat

bogs result from the drainage patterns that emerged as the ice-sheets of the Ice Age decayed.

Agriculture

Agriculture has been the traditional support of the Irish people, though fishing, home crafts and local labouring have been extra sources of livelihood in the poorer western areas. There is a marked contrast between the richest and the poorest agricultural areas. In the eastern central lowland and the south-east, particularly the lowland areas of Wicklow and Wexford, there are splendid large farms, with pastures supporting fine-quality cattle, sheep, and in some areas racehorses. From Wexford, too, rich farmlands extend through the valleys and lowlands westward to the counties of Tipperary and Limerick, and from Waterford to Cork and Killarney. Many of the farms specialize in dairying; milk is taken daily to the creameries, or collected in vans which separate out the cream and return the 'skim' for pig feeding. This is the land of butter and bacon with bacon factories in Cork, Limerick and other towns.

North of the Shannon, in Clare and east Galway, there is intensive sheep and some cattle production; here the glacial deposits are thin and the soils derived from limestones. To the north farming is mixed, with dairying, meat production, and in some cases specialization on crops such as potatoes and barley. Little wheat is grown; oats are better suited to the damp summer climate.

Farming in much of Ireland is prosperous, and aided now by EEC grants. The number of people working on the land declines, but that is due to the introduction of machinery, the union of small farms into larger holdings, and the increased opportu-

Haymaking near Kinsale, Co Cork.

nities of finding employment in the towns, with overseas emigration as an alternative. Rural housing has been greatly improved throughout the whole of Ireland.

Industry

With a current population of some 5 millions (with almost one third in Northern Ireland), Ireland is economically far more prosperous than it was in 1845, when the population numbered $8\frac{1}{2}$ millions. This was the first of the disastrous Famine years. Then, and for years afterwards, there was the hope that Ireland could support a population of as many as 20 millions, with modern industry based on coal, ports such as Galway serving the Atlantic and an intensive agriculture. However, the geologists engaged to look for coal (and other minerals) found that little was available and Galway never supplanted Liverpool or Southampton.

Only in the north-east, especially in Belfast, was there rapid industrial growth from the mid-nineteenth century. Shipbuilding, linen manufacture and other textile industries prospered — shirt making, for example, was prominent in Londonderry. Though these have declined, many new industries have been introduced in Northern Ireland and are still developing despite political strife. In the Republic a policy of industrialization has been vigorously pursued since 1932, with many difficulties and some sceptical comment, but a measure of success.

The Problems of Partition

Given political peace, the prospects for Ireland appear to be bright. The poorer western areas have been aided by government grants and the development of local industries, including the tourist industry. Electricity is universally available. Home industries flourish, especially tweed manufacture. The fishing industry, though never meeting expectations, is increasingly prosperous. The poorer western areas, known from 1891 as the 'congested areas', are not depopulated as in some comparable areas of Scotland, though discarded houses are taken over as holiday cottages, sometimes by people from continental Europe. Many problems have been at least partially solved and the EEC has been a source of help, giving the Republic the feeling of belonging to a wider world than the British Isles.

The present political strife particularly affects Northern Ireland. Politics are dominated by the issue of union or separation, with the split following religious lines. In general, Protestants are Unionists while Roman Catholics have advocated the reunion of Northern Ireland with the Republic. Periodically, political and religious antagonisms have flared into civil disorder, most severely in 1921–2, but again since 1968, accompanied by increased terror.

Whatever the ultimate political solution may be, geographically Ireland is a clear single unit. The country is more varied than is commonly supposed, but with social divisions acquired through historical circumstances rather than from any regional geographical distinctions. However, politically Northern Ireland emerges as a separate entity, having its own social and educational policy, its own laws and social services, its dependence on Westminster for subsidy and security. Union with the Republic seems a remote possibility that recedes as time goes by. (TWF)

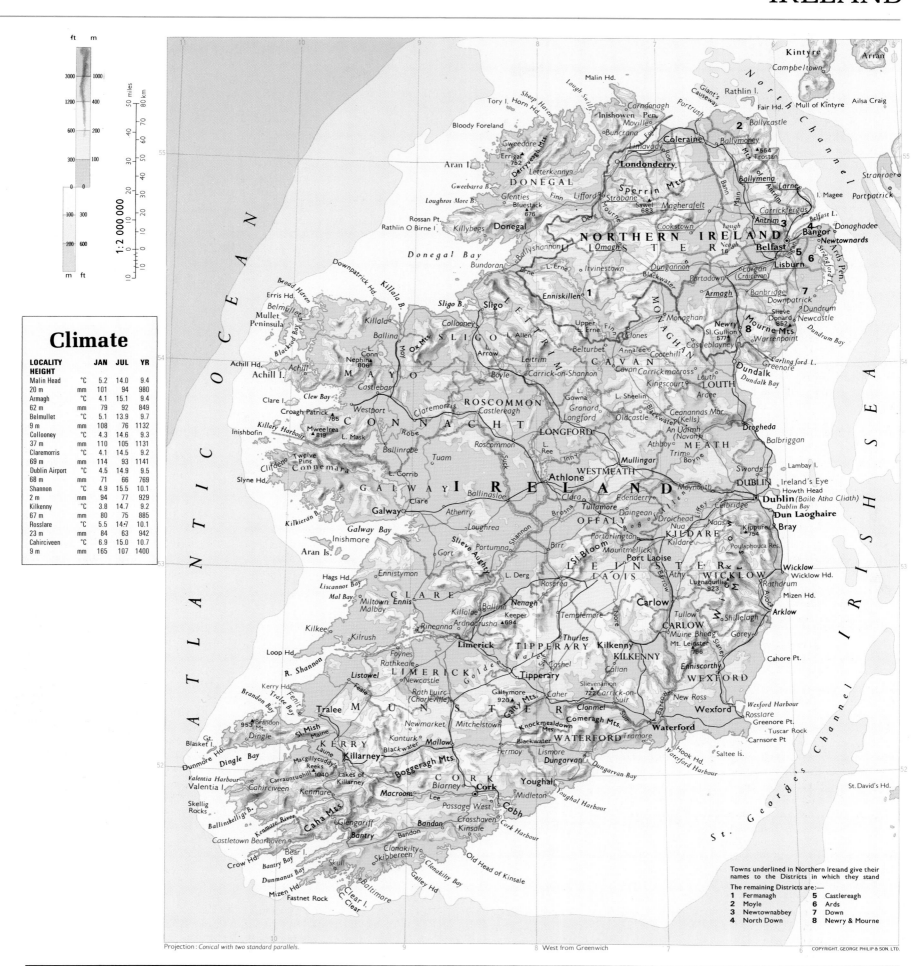

Projection: Conical with two standard parallels.

West from Greenwich

COPYRIGHT. GEORGE PHILIP & SON. LTD.

Climate

LOCALITY HEIGHT		JAN	JUL	YR
Malin Head	°C	5.2	14.0	9.4
20 m	mm	101	94	980
Armagh	°C	4.1	15.1	9.4
62 m	mm	79	92	849
Belmullet	°C	5.1	13.9	9.7
9 m	mm	108	76	1132
Collooney	°C	4.3	14.6	9.3
37 m	mm	110	105	1131
Claremorris	°C	4.1	14.5	9.2
69 m	mm	114	93	1141
Dublin Airport	°C	4.5	14.9	9.5
68 m	mm	71	66	769
Shannon	°C	4.9	15.5	10.1
2 m	mm	94	77	929
Kilkenny	°C	3.8	14.7	9.2
67 m	mm	80	75	885
Rosslare	°C	5.5	14·7	10.1
23 m	mm	84	63	942
Cahirciveen	°C	6.9	15.0	10.7
9 m	mm	165	107	1400

Towns underlined in Northern Ireland give their
names to the Districts in which they stand

The remaining Districts are:—
1 Fermanagh   5 Castlereagh
2 Moyle   6 Ards
3 Newtownabbey   7 Down
4 North Down   8 Newry & Mourne

1:2 000 000

The Plantations

The Normans had never controlled the whole of Ireland; by the late fifteenth century the area of effective English control was only a strip of country in the east, with Dublin as the major port and city. In the sixteenth century, the Tudors attempted to civilize the country by introducing an aristocracy, especially in areas where few if any towns had been established by the Normans. Mary Tudor (1553-8) and her husband Philip of Spain established Queen's and King's county (now Laois and Offaly) in what was then a ravaged part of the central lowland.

Elizabeth I (1558-1603) sent landlords to Ireland, among them Sir Walter Raleigh.

One of the most famous plantations began in 1609 with the London Livery Companies, who organized towns and villages in Derry (renamed Londonderry) and district, and built Derry's cathedral, stately streets and walls, with the aim of creating a Protestant Ascendancy to control the Catholic population. With the new landlords came settlers of British origin, Protestant in religion. Much of the tortured recent history of Ireland originated in the Plantation period. (TWF)

The city of Londonderry.

FRANCE

In area, France is twice as large as the United Kingdom and more than twice the size of West Germany, with a population of about 53 million (compared with the 56 million of the UK or the 61 million of West Germany). France possesses size and space, and though the growth of cities in the years since World War 2

has been spoken of in terms of crisis (*la crise urbaine*), in fact urban expansion is a problem in only a few special areas, notably Paris and its immediate surroundings. In general, France is predominantly rural.

Many French towns show traces of the country's long history. In the south, for example, at Arles and Carcassonne, there are famous Roman remains. Medieval churches are abundant with splendid cathedrals such as Reims, Amiens and Notre Dame, Paris. Traces of the period before the 1789 Revolution include the famous châteaux, many of them built or rebuilt in the eighteenth century, when rich landlords were patrons of the arts.

Frontiers and Administration

Frontiers are a natural concern of continental European countries, but of France's 5,500 km (3,440 miles) almost half consists of sea coast and 1,000 km (620 miles) winds through the mountains of the Pyrenees and the Alps. In general the Pyrenees frontier follows the crest line of the major hills, rather than the watershed between rivers flowing north into France or south into Spain. There are few easy crossings through the Pyrenees, but good coastal routes exist on the west into the Basque country, and on the east from Perpignan to Gerona.

In the south-east of France, Savoie

and the county of Nice were ceded by Italy at the Treaty of Turin in 1860 and in the following year the Prince of Monaco gave Menton and a neighbouring area to France. The cession of Savoie meant that France's territory extended to the summit of Mont Blanc, the highest mountain in western Europe. It also gave France part of the shores of Lake Geneva. Geneva itself is Swiss, but French territory lies within easy walking distance, and special customs arrangements exist so that people from the French countryside may use the city's trading facilities. North of Geneva the frontier runs through the Jura mountains to Basel (Basle) on the Rhine where France, Germany

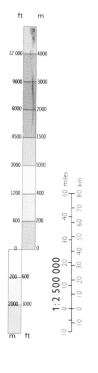

DÉPARTEMENTS IN THE PARIS AREA

1 Ville de Paris 3 Val-de-Marne
2 Seine-St-Denis 4 Hauts-de-Seine

Projection: *Conical with two standard parallels*

West from Greenwich   East from Greenwich

and Switzerland meet. Though Basel itself is in Switzerland, its airport is in France.

North of Basel, for 160 km (100 miles) the boundary between France and West Germany follows the Rhine. Alsace and Lorraine, west of the Rhine, were sought by France and Germany for centuries, and after the Franco-Prussian War in 1870–1 the whole of Alsace and part of Lorraine were returned to Prussia. This frontier remained until the treaty of Versailles, 1919, following World War 1. The frontiers from the Rhine to the North Sea were defined in their present form during the eighteenth century.

Local government in France was reorganized during the French Revolution. In 1790 Turgot defined the départements as areas in which everyone could reach the central town within one day.

Landscape

Highland France Most of France lies less than 300 m (1,000 ft) above sea level, but there are several distinctive upland areas. The most impressive of these are the Alps and the Pyrenees, but they also include the ancient massifs of Brittany and the Central Plateau, as well as the Vosges, and that part of the Ardennes which is within France.

The Alps are formed of complex folded rocks of intricate structure, with relief made even more complicated by the successive glaciations of the Ice Age. Areas of permanent snow exist on Mont Blanc and many other high peaks, and visitors to the upper Arve valley at Chamonix, St Gervais and other holiday centres have easy access to glaciers. The Alps are visited by tourists throughout the year – in winter for skiing, and in summer for walking on the upland pastures (the original 'alps'). In the French Alps, as in the other alpine areas, hydro-electricity has become universal both for general home use and for industries. The Pyrenees are comparable to the Alps, but they lack arterial routes and are crossed by only two international railways.

The Breton massif includes part of Normandy and extends southwards to the neighbourhood of La Rochelle. In general physical character it is a much dissected hilly area. The Central Plateau is more dramatic; it covers one-sixth of France between the Rhône-Saône valley and the basin of Aquitaine, and its highest summits rise to more than 1,800 m (about 6,000 ft); striking examples are the Plomb du Cantal (1,858 m, 6,100 ft) and the Puy de Sancy (1,886 m. 6,200 ft). Volcanic activity of ten to thirty million years ago appears in old volcanic plugs. Earlier rocks include limestones, providing poor

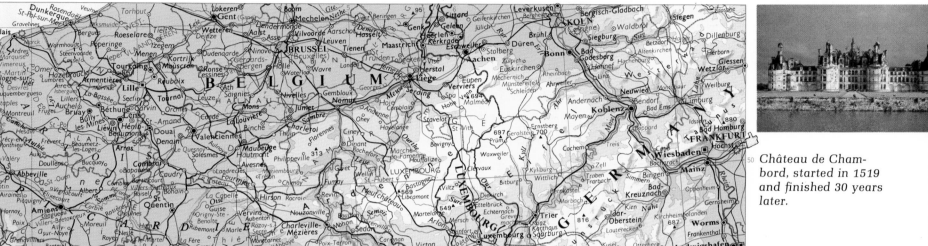

Château de Chambord, started in 1519 and finished 30 years later.

Climate

North-western France, like Britain and the Netherlands, has a temperate maritime climate dominated by warm, damp south-westerly winds. Atlantic air masses alternate frequently with those of polar and continental origins to produce shifting, unpredictable weather. Rain is plentiful throughout the year: winter frosts occur on 60 to 80 days, but snow seldom lies for long except on high ground. The north-east has a more continental climate, with hotter summers and colder winters: frost occurs on more than 80 days in winter, and snow may lie for several weeks, especially in the eastern highlands. The drier continental atmosphere gives clearer skies and sunnier conditions, even in winter.

LOCALITY HEIGHT		JAN	JUL	YR
Boulogne	°C	3.9	16.8	10.4
73 m	mm	57	41	599
Cherbourg	°C	6.4	16.6	11.4
8 m	mm	109	55	931
Paris	°C	3.5	19.5	11.5
75 m	mm	56	59	619
Nancy	°C	0.9	18.1	9.7
212 m	mm	67	60	712
Brest	°C	6.1	15.7	10.9
98 m	mm	133	62	1129
Dijon	°C	1.4	19.5	10.6
220 m	mm	64	58	739
Nantes	°C	4.9	18.5	11.6
41 m	mm	71	47	741
Nevers	°C	2.8	18.4	10.5
176 m	mm	67	60	772
La Rochelle	°C	5.9	19.5	12.7
1 m	mm	71	48	727
Lyon	°C	2.3	20.7	11.5
200 m	mm	52	56	813

EUROPE WEST

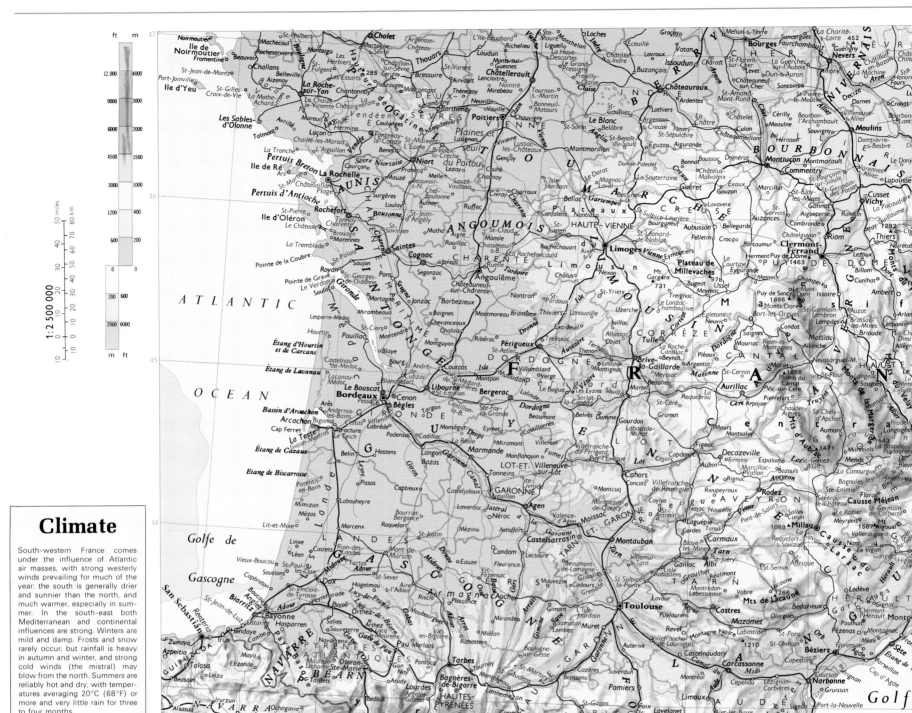

Scale 1 : 2 500 000

Climate

South-western France comes under the influence of Atlantic air masses, with strong westerly winds prevailing for much of the year: the south is generally drier and sunnier than the north, and much warmer, especially in summer. In the south-east both Mediterranean and continental influences are strong. Winters are mild and damp. Frosts and snow rarely occur, but rainfall is heavy in autumn and winter, and strong cold winds (the mistral) may blow from the north. Summers are reliably hot and dry, with temperatures averaging 20°C (68°F) or more and very little rain for three to four months.

LOCALITY HEIGHT		JAN	JUL	YR
Clermont-Ferrand	°C	2.8	19.1	10.9
329 m	mm	25	51	563
Le Puy	°C	0.9	17.9	9.3
714 m	mm	30	55	635
Bordeaux	°C	5.5	19.5	12.5
46 m	mm	90	56	900
Gourdon	°C	4.5	19.9	12.2
205 m	mm	66	52	801
Agen	°C	4.7	20.5	12.6
59 m	mm	60	49	715
Monaco	°C	10.3	23.5	16.4
55 m	mm	61	21	796
Biarritz	°C	7.6	19.7	13.5
69 m	mm	125	90	1475
Marseille	°C	5.7	23.0	14.2
4 m	mm	43	11	546
Perpignan	°C	7.7	23.8	15.5
43 m	mm	39	24	639
Ajaccio	°C	8.1	21.5	14.6
4 m	mm	76	10	672

Projection: Conical with two standard parallels

The lower slopes of Mont Blanc.

soils for agriculture, and coal measures which have been mined for more than a century at St Etienne and Le Creusot.

The Vosges and the Ardennes are areas of poor soil, largely forested.

Lowland France Although France has such striking mountain areas, 60 per cent of the country is in fact less than 250 m (800 ft) above sea level. Fine rivers, including the Rhône, Garonne, Loire and Seine with their many tributaries, drain lowland areas. From the Mediterranean there is an historic route northwards through the Rhône-Saône valley to Lyon and Dijon. North-westwards there is the famous route through the old towns of Carcassonne and Toulouse to Bordeaux on the Gironde estuary, into which the Garonne and the Dordogne flow. This is the basin of Aquitaine, bordered by the Central Massif to the north and the Pyrenees to the south. It is not a uniform lowland – there are several hilly areas while on the coast there is a belt of sand dunes, the Landes, extending for 200 km (125 miles) from Bayonne to the Gironde estuary.

From Aquitaine there is an easy route to the north, followed by the major railway from Bordeaux to Poitiers, Tours, Orleans and Paris. This lowland is generally called the Gate of Poitou, though in place of the word 'gate' the French generally say 'seuil' or 'threshold', which is perhaps more appropriate. Crossing the threshold brings the traveller to the Paris basin, in the heart of which is the great city itself.

The ancient centre of Paris lies on the Île de la Cité, where the Seine was easily crossed. The Paris basin is a vast area floored by sedimentary rocks. Those that are resistant to erosion, including some limestones and chalks, form upland areas. The Loire with its many tributaries in the south-west of the basin, and the Seine with its numerous affluents (notably the Yonne, Aube, Marne,

Notre Dame, Paris, begun in 1163, is the most famous of the Gothic cathedrals of the Middle Ages.

Building the Concorde aircraft at Toulouse.

impenetrable thickets of vegetation. Through most of France this vegetation is known as *maquis*, from the shelter it gives to fugitives: the term *maquis* was given in World War 2 to the resistance forces in hiding. In dry summers the risk of fire is considerable, especially in the south.

Resources and Industry

France is a major producer of iron ore (mostly from Lorraine), and several other minerals are also mined, including bauxite, potash, salt and sulphur. There are coalfields in the north-east, but the output of these does not meet the country's needs. France has reserves of natural gas at Lacq and the

world's first major tidal power station on the Rance estuary in Brittany. In the mountainous areas hydro-electricity is important.

Since World War 2 industrial expansion in France has been marked and has been accompanied by a change in the distribution of population. Before World War 2 France was generally regarded as a country with an even distribution of population between town and countryside, but from the late 1940s there was a spectacular increase in the urban population. In the first post-war planning period, 1947–53, industrial production rose by 70 per cent, agricultural production by 21 per cent and the standard of living by 30 per cent. During the following three years there was further expansion, particularly in the chemical and electrical industries. In the period of the third plan, 1958–61, the success of export industries became notable, particularly in such products as motor cars, aircraft and electrical goods. In this period too natural gas was discovered at Lacq, and such industries as chemicals and aluminium smelting prospered. However, traditional industries, such as textiles and porcelain, are still important.

French life has been, and still is, focussed to a remarkable degree on Paris where traditional luxury industries, such as perfumes, thrive alongside heavy industry. Virtually all the major commercial enterprises of France, for example the multiple shops, have their headquarters in Paris and Paris and district is now estimated to have almost one-fifth of

the total French population. The other important industrial centres are on and around the mining areas and at or near the major ports where imported raw materials are used, for example, Fos, west of Marseille and the steel complex at Dunkerque. The aims of modern planning include the development of regional prosperity, based on such centres as Lyon, Marseille, Toulouse, Nantes, Lille, Nancy and Strasbourg. However, the industrial attraction of the Paris area remains powerful and population growth continues to exceed that of the second largest urban area, Lyon and district.

Generally, as in agriculture, expansion and mergers have transformed the structure of French industry and resulted in the creation of large, economic concerns.

Planning for the Future

Modern economic planning in France has been pursued at a time of great difficulty, which included the loss of the colonial territories in North Africa and South-east Asia, as well as the period of unrest in the 1960s, not only in the universities but throughout the country. Consumer industries have prospered, but some critics say that there is still inadequate provision for social services, including housing. Since World War 2 there has been agitation about the poor standard of housing throughout France, both rural and urban, much of it obsolete and without basic amenities. Rapid urban growth, which still continues, has resulted in overcrowding and even the growth of poor shanty towns to house immigrants, especially those from Spain and North Africa.

Achievement of expansion and prosperity over the whole country has not been easy. In France, as in most other countries, there remains a disparity between the richer and poorer areas. For France this is between the east and the west. Richest of all is the area in closest touch with the great industrial complexes of Germany and the Benelux countries. Though often devastated in European wars, this always emerges in peacetime as one of the most prosperous corners not only of France but of the world.(TWF)

MONACO

Monaco, the smallest state in the world, covers less than 2.5 km² (1 sq mile). It has a remarkable museum of oceanography founded by Prince Albert I, an enlightened ruling prince who served in the French navy. The territory extends over about 3.2 km (2 miles) of coast, and is most famous for the Casino of Monte Carlo, in splendid gardens, surrounded by palatial hotels. The profits from the Casino support public services. Now, as in the past, the attraction of a sheltered site backed by hills, with a high incidence of winter sunshine and an abundance of entertainment, draws thousands of visitors. (TWF)

BELGIUM

Belgium (grouped with the Netherlands as the Low Countries of Europe) is one of the most densely peopled countries in the world, with a population of more than 300 per km² (800 per sq mile). Throughout a stormy history, Belgium's fine cities, including Brussel, Gent and Bruges (Brugge), have maintained their churches and public buildings, though some have been rebuilt after wars. Following the Napoleonic wars, from 1815–30 Belgium and the Netherlands were united as the 'Low Countries', but in 1830, a famous year of ferment in Europe, a National Congress proclaimed independence and in 1831 Prince Leopold of Coburg became King. At The Treaty of London, 1839 (which the Netherlands also signed), Britain, France and Russia guaranteed the independence of Belgium and the famous 'scrap of paper' was upheld when Germany invaded Belgium in August 1914.

The division between Belgium and the Netherlands rests on history and sentiment rather than on any physical features. Belgium is predominantly a Roman Catholic country, while the Netherlands are traditionally Protestant (though about 40 per cent of the population are Roman Catholic). Both were neutral in foreign policy, but in 1940 both were invaded and remained under German occupation until September 1944.

Since the end of World War 2 economic progress has been marked, for the geographical advantages Belgium possesses have given her a position of significance in Europe, especially in the EEC. The unity of the people, however, is less secure. Belgium is a bilingual country, with a division of sentiment between the French-speaking Walloons of the south and the Flemish-speaking people of the north. Flemish is a form of Dutch, and those speaking it are more numerous than French speakers, though more than a million inhabitants of Belgium are able to speak both languages. The areas of French and Flemish speech converge around the capital city of Brussel.

Of the country's universities Louvain (Catholic and Belgium's oldest, dating from 1426) provides courses in both Flemish and French; of the universities founded in the nineteenth century Gent (1816) is Flemish and Liège (1817) French-speaking. At Brussel's Free Univer-

Climate

Belgium and the Netherlands have temperate maritime climates, dominated throughout the year by warm, damp air masses from the Atlantic Ocean. Rapid alternation with polar and continental air masses makes day-to-day weather relatively unpredictable. Summers are cool, with frequent rain; winters are mild, with 40 to 60 days of frost in the lowlands and up to 100 days on the Ardennes plateau. Maritime influences are strongest in the west; summers are hotter and winters colder toward the German border. Luxembourg, further from the sea and generally higher, has a slightly cooler, more continental climate.

LOCALITY HEIGHT		JAN	JUL	YR
Den Helder	°C	2.6	16.9	9.7
4 m	mm	65	64	706
Urk	°C	1.4	17.4	9.5
2 m	mm	63	87	747
Winterswijk	°C	1.3	17.5	9.5
33 m	mm	65	87	755
Vlissingen	°C	3.0	17.3	10.1
1 m	mm	62	71	689
Oostende	°C	2.7	16.3	10.0
10 m	mm	41	62	598
Brussel	°C	1.6	17.4	10.1
100 m	mm	66	95	855
Virton	°C	0.4	16.5	8.9
242 m	mm	75	74	888
Clervaux	°C	-0.1	16.1	7.9
454 m	mm	72	83	885
Echternach	°C	0.9	18.1	9.4
164 m	mm	60	61	731
Luxembourg	°C	0.5	17.9	9.3
330 m	mm	61	60	760

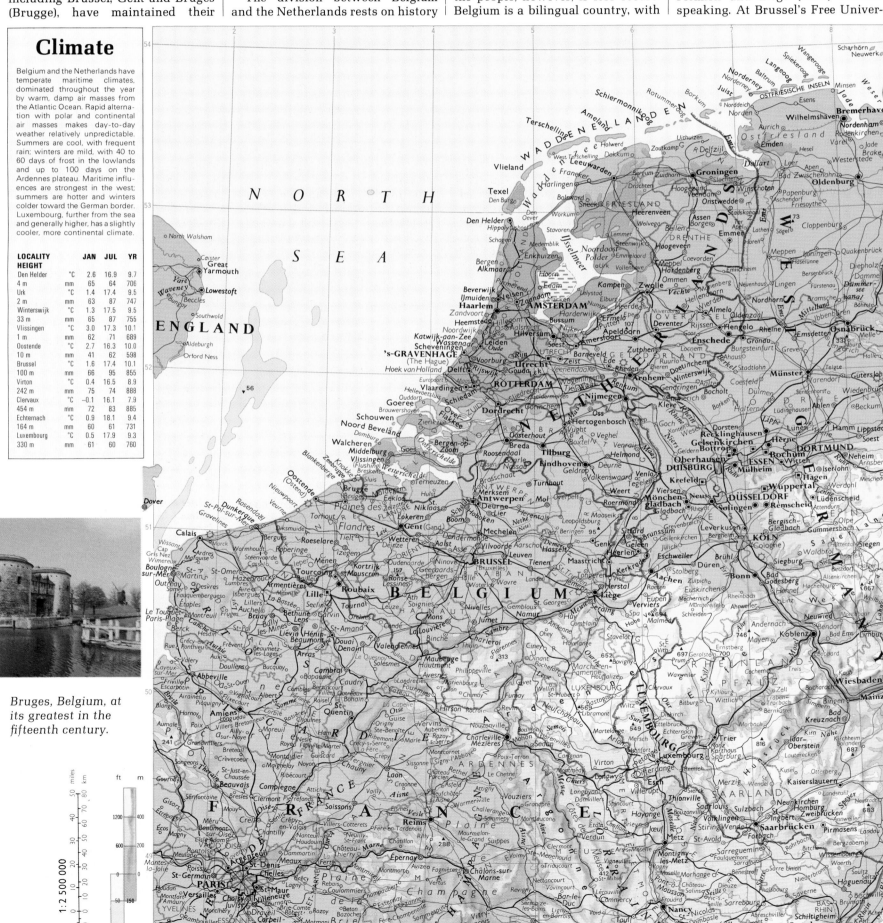

Bruges, Belgium, at its greatest in the fifteenth century.

1:2 500 000

Projection: Conical with two standard parallels   East from Greenwich   COPYRIGHT. GEORGE PHILIP & SON. LTD

Rotterdam, one of the principal ports of Europe.

sity (founded in 1834) the courses are mainly in French but provision is made for Flemish speakers. Gradually the grievances of the Flemish speakers have been removed and in 1974 regional councils were established for Flanders, Wallonia and the Brussel district.

Landscape and Agriculture

Physically Belgium may be divided into the upland of the Ardennes, and the lowland plains, which are drained by the Meuse to the Rhine through the Netherlands, and by the Schelde through Antwerp. The Ardennes, rising in Belgium to about 700 m (2,296 ft) at the highest point, is generally an area of moorland, peat bogs and woodland.

Lowland Belgium has varied soils, including some poor-quality sands in the Campine (Kempenland) area near the Dutch frontier, supporting only heaths and woodland. But in general careful cultivation, sound husbandry and attention to drainage have provided good soils; lowland farming is prosperous, with a strong emphasis on grain crops, potatoes and other vegetables, hops, sugar and fodder beet, with hay. Few hedges exist in the farmed landscape and the holdings are small with intensive cultivation. Traditionally many factory workers of the towns also had a small holding. There is a small area of polders near the coast, in all less than 500 km² (200 sq miles), which is rich agricultural land. Outside the towns density of rural settlement is high.

Industry and Commerce

No minerals other than coal exist in significant quantities and the Belgian emphasis on manufacturing is based on the import of raw materials. The Ardennes includes the country's most productive coalfield (the Campine) in the Sambre-Meuse valley, centred on the cities of Charleroi and Liège. Charleroi is a coal mining and metallurgical city while Liège is the centre of the iron industry. The Campine coalfield is continued into the Netherlands and Germany. Production has declined in recent years as uneconomic mines have been closed. Of major importance is the textile industry, which has existed in the towns of Flanders

from medieval times and in its modern form includes a wide range of products. It is associated particularly with Gent and Bruges (most famed for its medieval architecture). Industry has been diversified and some manufactures, such as glass, are well known in the international market.

Belgium's main port is Antwerp, much modernized since 1956. The main industrial centres are served by ship canals, including one from Gent to Terneuzen 29 km (18 miles) long. Constructed in 1825–7, it can take ships of as much as 61,000 tonnes in capacity. There are canals to Bruges from the North Sea at Zeebrugge, and also to Brussel, both constructed in 1922. Barges of 1,372 tonnes capacity can use the 125 km (79 miles) long Albert Canal, opened in 1939 to Liège, and the Meuse and Sambre rivers are being widened or deepened to take barges of similar capacity. Comparable improvements are being made in the river Scheldt between Antwerp and Gent, and in the Brussel-Charleroi canal. The North Sea ports of Ostend (Oostende) and Zeebrugge cater for overseas trade. Now, as in past centuries, the lowland of Belgium, and particularly the city of Brussel, remains a major focus of commercial and political life in Europe. (TWF)

THE NETHERLANDS

Within an area of 40,844 km² 15,770 sq miles) the Netherlands has a higher density of population than either England or Belgium. To anyone travelling westward from Germany this is at once obvious in the landscape, for the fields are smaller, the villages more tightly concentrated with small neat houses, and the land is cultivated more intensively. In contrast, also, over much of the countryside rivers are at a higher level than the surrounding farmland, with villages sited above the flood-level.

Landscape and Agriculture

Seen from the air, most of the Netherlands is made up of richly cultivated fields, mainly rectangular, with water-filled ditches between them along which farmers travel by boat. Control of water is a major problem, for much of the best farmland lies at or below sea level. Without the protection of dykes and sand dunes along the coast two-fifths of the Netherlands would be flooded. Constant pumping (formerly by windmills and steam pumps, now by automated motor pumps) lifts surplus water from ditches to canals at a higher level, and from canals to the rivers, particularly the Maas, Lek and Waal, which take the Rhine waters to the sea.

The dunes that line much of the coast are carefully guarded against erosion by planting marram grass and, where possible, trees. There are massive dykes to guard the farmland and towns but in 1953 the exceptionally high tides at the end of January broke through coastal dykes and sand dunes, causing widespread devastation.

For over a thousand years the Dutch have wrested land from the sea and the process still continues, with the Zuyder Zee being reduced in size by reclaiming new land for farming, with planned villages and towns. Land use varies. In the west the concentration on bulb farming is marked near Haarlem, in soils of clay mixed with sand. There, too, glasshouse cultivation, combined on many holdings with the growing of flowers and vegetables out-of-doors, is widespread: as one Dutch geographer commented – 'the city is the cradle of horticulture'. Much of the produce is exported, some of it by air to London. Some soils are better suited to pastoral farming, with milk, cheese and butter production. In the areas above sea level, farming is varied, with both cattle and crops, including fruit. Gouda has a famous cheese market and the famous round red-coated Edam cheeses come from northern areas.

Industry and Commerce

Industry and commerce provide support for the greater part of the Dutch population. Mineral resources include china clay, which is abundant, and coal, though mining ceased in 1965. The emphasis of modern industry is on oil, steel, electrical engineering and chemicals. In the area south of Rotterdam a vast new port and industrial area – Europort – has developed. The Dutch are skilled at languages, to which a considerable part of the teaching time is given even in primary schools. This is essential to the country's prosperity, for now as in past centuries the Dutch control a main outlet for the commerce of Europe in the port of Rotterdam, with the Rhine valley and a wider area as its hinterland. The main export markets are in Belgium, Luxembourg and West Germany. Trade with Indonesia recalls the Dutch colonial age. (TWF)

LUXEMBOURG

With a population of about 360,000, Luxembourg covers only 2,586 km² (998 sq miles). The Grand Duchy of Luxembourg formed an economic union with Belgium in 1922. This was extended in 1960 to include the Netherlands under the composite name of Benelux. Luxembourg is a full member of NATO, of the EEC and the United Nations, and is perhaps best known to Europeans as the seat of the Court of the European Communities, of the secretariat of the European Parliament, the European Investment Bank and the European Monetary Co-operation Fund. Rich in iron ore, there is a prosperous iron and steel industry.

The country consists partly of the Ardennes, well wooded and famed for its deer and wild boar, but the more prosperous agricultural areas are in the scarplands of Lorraine. Stock raising, especially of dairy cattle, is important. Crops include grains, potatoes, roots and fruit, and vines in the Moselle valley. The capital city is Luxembourg. (TWF)

Polders

A windmill in Friesland.

Polders are artificial farmlands reclaimed from water. The first were formed about a thousand years ago, when settlers on marshlands found that they could protect their land by building dykes of earth, brushwood (around which mud would accumulate) and stones. The effort was vast, but dry land was created and protected against floods from rivers and high tides. Sluices were made in the dykes to let out surplus water; marshes and peat bogs were gradually drained and the water pumped out to major rivers and canals by windmills. These were replaced in the mid-nineteenth century by steam pumps.

Today some of the most profitable farmland in the Netherlands is polderland, much of it 6 to 7 metres (about 20 ft) below sea level. Within some of the polders the farmland is divided into hundreds of strips separated by water channels and accessible only by boat. Modern polders, including those of the Zuyder Zee, have large fields of great fertility. With modern technology the level of water in each polder can be controlled from central pumping stations. Many older settlements are on dykes, or patches of land known to lie above the highest flood levels. (TWF)

SCANDINAVIA

There are several possible definitions of the term Scandinavia. In the narrow geographical sense it refers to the peninsula shared by Norway and Sweden: in a broader cultural and political sense it includes the five countries of the Nordic Council – Norway, Sweden, Denmark, Finland and Iceland. All except Finland have related languages, and all have a tradition of parliamentary democracy: Finland and Iceland are republics, while the others are constitutional monarchies. There are also strong historical links between them which began in the tenth century when their ancestors, the Norsemen, colonized large parts of northern Europe. All have at different times been governed together, Sweden and Finland separating in 1809, Norway and Sweden in 1905 and Denmark and Iceland in 1944.

Because of their northerly position, and their exposure to Atlantic weather systems, the Scandinavian states have a cool, moist climate not favourable to crops. However, because of the long hours of daylight in the northern summer, some surprisingly good crops are grown north of the Arctic Circle. The Scandinavians were once amongst the poorest peoples of Europe, but during the last century they have become among the richest, making full use of their limited natural resources, and also seizing the opportunities which their maritime position gave them to become major shipping and fishing nations. (FS)

above *Fishing boats and processing plants at Bergen, Norway.*

right *A typically steep-sided Norwegian fjord.*

Unlike her neighbours, Sweden and Finland, which are neutral, Norway is a member of NATO, but refused to join the EEC at a time when Britain and Denmark decided to enter. As a member of the Nordic Council Norway cooperates closely with her Scandinavian neighbours in matters of social welfare and education, and shares with them membership of the European Free Trade Association (EFTA).

The sea has always been a major influence in Norwegian life. A thousand years ago Viking sailors from Norway roamed the northern seas, founding colonies around the coasts of Britain, Iceland, Greenland and even North America. Today fishing, ship-building and the management of merchant shipping lines are of vital importance to the Norwegian economy. Norway's merchant ships, most of which seldom visit the home ports, earn profits which pay for one-third of the country's imports.

Landscape

Norway is a rugged, mountainous country in which communication is difficult. The Norwegian landscape is dominated by rolling plateaux, the *vidda*, generally 300 to 900 m (1,000 to 3,000 ft) high, above which some peaks rise to as much as 1,500 to 2,500 m (5,000 to 8,000 ft) in the area between Oslo, Bergen and Trondheim. In the far north the summits are 1,000 m (3,000 ft) lower. The highest areas retain permanent ice fields, as in the Jotunheim Mountains above Sogne Fjord. The Norwegian mountains have been uplifted during three mountain building episodes during the last 400 million years, and they contain rocks of the earliest geological periods. Intrusions of volcanic material accompanied the uplifting and folding, and there are great masses of granites and gneisses which are the source of Norway's mineral wealth.

There are few large areas of flat land in the country but in the east the *vidda* are broken by deep valleys of rivers flowing to the lowland of south-east Norway, focussed on Oslo. In glacial times the whole country was covered by the great northern ice cap. When it melted about 10,000 years ago it left behind large deposits of glacial moraine, well represented around Oslo in the Raa moraines. Soils of better quality are used for crops and meadows while the less productive sands and gravels remain forested.

NORWAY

The Kingdom of Norway occupies the western half of the Scandinavian peninsula, from North Cape in latitude 71°N to Lindesnes 58°N, a north-south distance of over 1,600 km (1,000 miles). The country covers an area of 324,200 km² (125,200 sq miles), but has a population of only 4 million, most of whom live in the southern part of the country, where the capital, Oslo, is situated. Nowhere in Norway is far from the sea. At the widest point it is only 430 km (270 miles) from west to east, and near the Arctic port of Narvik the Swedish border comes to within 8 km (5 miles) of the Norwegian coast. A third of Norway lies within the Arctic Circle, but the climate is not as severe as might be expected because the Norwegian coast benefits from the moderating effects of the warm waters of the North Atlantic Drift. Even on the Arctic coast, the ports of Hammerfest and Kirkenes remain unfrozen in most winters.

Norway shares a short common frontier in the Arctic with the USSR.

Iceland

The eruption on Heimaey, 1973, a recent example of volcanic activity.

With an area of 103,000 km² (40,000 sq miles) and a population of about 224,000, Iceland is the smallest and most isolated of the Scandinavian countries, far out in the north Atlantic Ocean. Though politically part of Europe, the island arises geologically from the boundary between Europe and America – the Mid-Atlantic Ridge (pp. 8–9). It is indeed a product of the Ridge, formed almost entirely by volcanic out-pourings at a point where the earth's crust is opening at a rate measurable in centimetres per year.

A central zone of recently-active volcanoes and fissures crosses Iceland from Axarfjödur in the north to Vestmannaeyjar in the south, with a side-branch to Reykjanes and an outlying zone of activity around the Snaefellsnes peninsula in the west. During the 1100 years that Iceland has been settled, between 150 and 200 eruptions have occurred in the active zones, some building up substantial volcanic cones. Between AD 1104 and 1970 Mount Hekla, in the south-west, erupted at least 15 times. Its earliest outpourings of ash devastated local farms, some of which have recently been excavated. A huge eruption of 1783 destroyed pasture and livestock on a grand scale, causing a famine that reduced the Icelandic population by a quarter. More recent eruptions include the formation of a new island – Surtsey – off the south-west coast in

1963, and the partial devastation of the town of Vestmannaeyjar-Karpstadur, on neighbouring Heimaey, ten years later. Paradoxically, Iceland is also an island of glaciers and icesheets, with four large ice-caps occupying 11 per cent of the surface, and several smaller glaciers.

Colonized by Viking and British farmers in the ninth century, Iceland became a dependency first of Norway, then of Denmark, though mainly self-governing with a parliament (Althing) dating from AD 930. Recognized as a sovereign state from 1918, the country was united to Denmark through a common sovereign until 1944, when Iceland became a republic. Formerly pastoral, with most of the population scattered in farms and small hamlets, the standard of living depended on the vicissitudes of farming close to the Arctic Circle. Now the economy is based on deep-sea fishing; fish and fish products make up 80 per cent of exports, and living standards currently compare with those of other Scandinavian countries. Geothermal and hydro-electric power provide cheap energy for developing industries, including aluminium smelting and hot-house cultivation; most houses and offices in Reykjavik, the capital, are heated geothermally. The population is concentrated mainly in settlements close to the coast, over half of them in or near Reykjavik. (BS)

Climate

For its subpolar latitude Scandinavia has a relatively mild climate. Summers are cool, with temperatures between 10° and 15°C (50° and 59°F) along the west coast, 5° to 10°C (41° to 50°F) in the mountains and north lands. Sweden and southern Finland have July means of 15° to 20°C (59° to 68°F), in common with much of western Europe. Winters bring strong continental influences, especially to the north and east. Only in a narrow western coastal strip warmed by the Atlantic drift are mean January temperatures above freezing point. This is also the wetter side, with annual precipitations of 60 to 250 cm (24 to 100 in); much of eastern Scandinavia has less than 50 cm (20 in). Iceland, too, has a generally mild climate, with most warmth and moisture in the south-west.

LOCALITY HEIGHT		JAN	JUL	YR
Tromsø	°C	−3.8	12.5	2.9
102 m	mm	96	56	994
Karasjok	°C	−15.5	13.0	−2.3
135 m	mm	17	56	340
Bodø	°C	−2.2	13.3	4.6
33 m	mm	92	63	1063
Akureyri	°C	−1.6	10.9	3.7
7 m	mm	45	32	457
Oulu	°C	−9.8	16.5	2.3
17 m	mm	33	70	514
Reykjavik	°C	−0.3	11.3	5.0
18 m	mm	89	50	779
Vaasa	°C	−7.7	16.1	3.3
6 m	mm	35	62	518
Helsinki	°C	−5.9	17.1	4.8
46 m.	mm	56	68	688
Mariehamn	°C	−3.3	16.3	5.4
4 m	mm	48	45	558
København	°C	0.0	17.7	8.5
9 m	mm	49	71	603

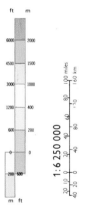

1:6 250 000

Projection: Conical with two standard parallels

37

The Coast and the Islands The configuration of the coast helps to explain the ease with which the Norwegians took to the sea in their early history, and why they have remained a sea-faring nation since. The *vidda* are cut by long, narrow, steep-sided fjords on the west coast, shaped by the great northern ice cap. The largest of these, the Sogne Fjord (203 km, 127 miles long and less than 5 km, 3 miles wide), is the best known but not the most spectacular. Farming is restricted to the limited areas of level or gently-sloping ground beside these sheltered fjords. Cattle and sheep use the slopes above them in the summer but are fed in stalls during the winter. Everywhere fish is caught in the local waters.

Along the coast there are hundreds of islands, the largest group of which, the Lofoten Islands, lie north of the Arctic Circle. These islands, known as the *skerryguard*, protect the inner coast from the battering of the Atlantic breakers, and provide sheltered leads of water which the coastal ferries and fishing boats can navigate in safety.

Norway also owns two groups of islands in the Arctic, Svalbard (Spitzbergen) and Jan Mayen, which were incorporated in the 1920s. Norway shares the mining of coal in Svalbard with the USSR, and there is prospecting for oil and gas. Jan Mayen is used as a base for radio and meteorological stations.

Communications

Until recently communications along the coast were easier by boat than by land. Oslo is linked by rail to the main towns of the south, and a line reaches north to Bodø, latitude $67\frac{1}{2}°$N. Roads are difficult to build and costly to maintain, and are often blocked by snow in winter and spring (snow accumulates to March). There are still several hundred ferries which carry cars across the fjords, but much money has been invested in the building of a north-south trunk road, with bridges across the fjords, to avoid the constant use of ferries. Air transport is of increasing importance and many small airstrips are in use, bringing remote communities into contact with the populated south.

Agriculture

Less than 3 per cent of the land can be cultivated. Two-thirds consists of barren mountains, snow fields, or unproductive wastes, and one-fifth is forested. The barrenness of the soil, the heavy rainfall, winter snows and the short growing season restrict agriculture, especially in the north, though in the long summer days good crops of hay, potatoes, quick-

Climate

LOCALITY HEIGHT		JAN	JUL	YR
Trondheim	°C	-3.8	14.9	5.1
58 m	mm	71	69	870
Kristiansund	°C	1.3	14.1	7.1
39 m	mm	107	89	1151
Røros	°C	-11.7	12.7	0.3
628 m	mm	30	79	481
Lillehammer	°C	-9.1	15.7	3.4
226 m	mm	44	96	691
Geilo	°C	-8.8	11.9	1.3
795 m	mm	43	71	598
Bergen	°C	1.3	15.5	8.1
43 m	mm	143	142	1930
Oslo	°C	-4.9	17.7	6.1
94 m	mm	49	82	730
Stavanger	°C	1.0	15.1	7.8
85 m	mm	93	93	1130
Tonstad	°C	-2.3	15.9	6.4
57 m	mm	161	125	1668
Kristiansand	°C	-1.9	16.5	7.1
23 m	mm	128	104	1401

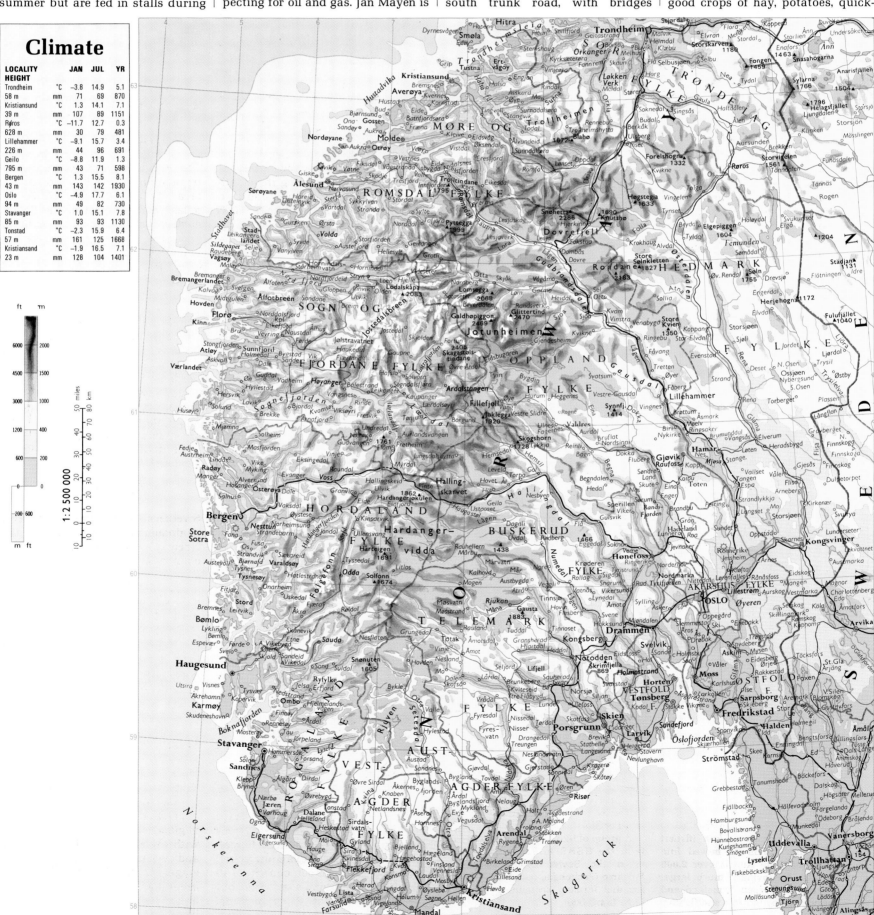

1:2 500 000

Projection: Conical with two standard parallels

East from Greenwich

COPYRIGHT GEORGE PHILIP & SON, LTD.

growing vegetables, even rye and barley are grown.

Mineral Resources and Industry

Iron and lead ores are found in the north, copper in central Norway and titanium in the south. The extent of Norway's mineral resources is not fully known, and prospecting is still revealing new deposits. Oil and natural gas from the sea bed have made a great contribution to the Norwegian economy in recent years. Exploitation of these reserves provides more than enough for the country's needs.

There is no coal in mainland Norway, although some is found in the islands of the Svalbard (Spitzbergen) archipelago in the Arctic Ocean. The lack of coal has been partly compensated for by the development of hydro-electricity, begun in the early twentieth century, when streams flowing down the steep slopes above the fjords were first harnessed. Later, inland sites were developed, and the greatest concentration is in the Rjukan valley, 160 km (100 miles) west of Oslo.

The availability of cheap electricity made possible the rapid growth of the wood-pulp, paper and chemical industries, and later stimulated the metal working industries. Many of the industrial sites are on the shores of remote fjords, where cheap electricity and deep water access for the import of raw materials and for the export of finished products are the determining factors in choosing the location. The aluminium and chemical industries of the south-west coast are typical.

Metal working has developed in the far north since World War 2. After primary treatment iron is exported from Kirkenes to a smelter at Mo-i-Rana, on the coast a few miles south of the Arctic Circle. Coal is imported from Svalbard. The port of Narvik was connected by rail to the Swedish system in 1903, so that Swedish iron ore could be sent from an ice-free port to supply the iron smelters of Germany. This trade is still important.

Rapid industrial development since World War 2 has transformed the Norwegian economy, and has ensured that the Norwegians are amongst the most prosperous people in Europe. The pre-war economy, dependent upon forestry, farming, fishing and seafaring is still important, but the number employed in these industries is dwindling as more and more people move into the new industries and the growing towns. There are still few large towns, and all six of those with more than 50,000 population are on the coast. The largest are Oslo, Bergen and Trondheim. (FS)

The Lapps (Sames)

Norwegian Lapps with their reindeer.

The Lapps are northern hunters, fishermen and herdsmen inhabiting the Arctic areas of northern Scandinavia. The largest group (20,000) live in Norway; Sweden has about 10,000, and Finland 2,500. In addition a small number live on the Kola Peninsula, in neighbouring USSR. Short and dark, Lapps are physically distinct from most other peoples of Scandinavia; their language – Saarme – is akin to Finnish.

There are three main groups – Forest, Mountain and Skolt (fisher) Lapps. They originally moved into Scandinavia from Russia over 2,000 years ago, occupying a much larger area than their present homeland, and living entirely by hunting and fishing.

During the seventeenth century they domesticated the reindeer; many became semi-nomadic reindeer herders, following their animals from winter grazing grounds on the margins of the northern forests to summer pastures on the high Lapland fells. Although many Lapps still keep reindeer, others have adopted settled occupations, merging with the majority population of their country and losing their distinctive culture, language, and ways of life.

A group of Skolt Lapps, transferred from the USSR to Finland in 1944 when the Soviet Union acquired Petsamo (Pechenga), now form a fishing and farming community around Lake Inari. (FS)

FINLAND

Finland, lying between latitudes 60°N and 70°N, is the most northerly state on the mainland of Europe. One third of the total area of 337,000 km^2 (130,000 sq miles) lies within the Arctic Circle, and the northernmost tip reaches to within 32 km (20 miles) of the Arctic Ocean.

The climate of the northern province of Lapland is not as severe as in places in Canada and Siberia which lie in similar latitudes because of the North Atlantic Drift. This keeps the Arctic coasts of Europe free from ice.

Finland enjoys a short but warm summer, with average July temperatures at Helsinki of 17°C (63°F) and 13°C (55°F) in Lapland. Because of the high latitudes, summer days are long and in the Arctic region there is virtually no night during the month of June. Winters are long and cold (Helsinki's January average is −6°C (21°F)) and the days are short. In severe winters the sea freezes for several miles offshore and ice-breakers have to be used to keep the ports open. Snowfall is not heavy, however, and rail and road transport is seldom badly disrupted, even in Lapland.

Landscape

Geologically Finland is made up of a central plateau of ancient crystalline rocks, mainly granites, schists and gneisses, surrounded by lowlands composed of recent glacial deposits. In the 600 million years between the formation of these ancient rocks and the last Ice Age, the surface of the land was worn down to a peneplain. Most of central and southern Finland is below 200 m (650 ft). However, the roots of an old mountain system running north-west to south-east can still be traced across Lapland and along Finland's eastern border with the USSR. Peaks of over 1,000 m (3,000 ft) occur in northern Lapland, near the Swedish and Norwegian borders.

A tenth of the surface is covered by lakes, of which there are estimated to be about 60,000. Concentrated in the central plateau, they are usually long, narrow and shallow, and aligned in a north-west to south-east direction, indicating the line of movement of the ice sheet which scoured out their basins.

Industry and Population

Forests occupy almost 60 per cent of the land surface, the main trees being pine, spruce and birch. Forest-based products, for example, paper, pulp and sawn timber, constitute 40 per cent of Finland's exports, but since World War 2 engineering, ship-building and metal industries have greatly expanded.

Although in area Finland is one of the largest countries in Europe, it is also one of the most sparsely populated, with only 4.7 million inhabitants, giving a density of 14 per km^2 (36 per sq mile).

Between 1150 and 1809 Finland was under Swedish rule, and one of the legacies of this period is a Swedish-speaking minority of 6.5 per cent of the total population. In some localities on the south and east coasts and in the Åland Islands, Swedish speakers are in a majority. Many towns in Finland use both Finnish and Swedish names, for example, Helsinki is Helsingfors and Turku is Åbo in Swedish. (FS)

SWEDEN

The Kingdom of Sweden, with a population of over 8 million and an area of 450,000 km^2 (173,700 sq miles) is the largest of the Scandinavian countries in both population and area. It occupies the eastern half of the Scandinavian peninsula, extending southward to latitude 55°N and having a much smaller Arctic area than either Norway or Finland. The 1,600 km (1,000 miles) long eastern coast, along the shores of the Baltic Sea and the Gulf of Bothnia, extends from the mouth of the Torne river, which forms the border with Finland, to Ystad in the south, opposite the Danish island of Bornholm. Sweden also has a coastline facing west towards the Atlantic, along the shores of the Kattegat – the strait that separates Sweden and Denmark.

Landscape

Sweden's share of the Scandinavian peninsula is less mountainous than Norway's. The northern half of the country forms part of the Baltic or Fenno-Scandian Shield, a stable block of ancient granites and gneisses which extends round the head of the Gulf of Bothnia into Finland. This area contains most of Sweden's rich mineral wealth. The shield land is an area of low plateaux, which rise gradually westward.

South of the plateaux area there is a belt of lowlands between the capital city, Stockholm and the second city, Göteborg (Gothenburg). These lowlands contain several large lakes, the chief of which are Lake Mälar, near Stockholm, and Lakes Vänern and Vättern which lie in the middle of the lowland belt. These are all that remains of a strait which, in glacial times, connected the Baltic with the Kattegat. Changes in land and water level during the later stages of the Ice Age led to the breaking of this connection. Now linked by canals, these lakes form a water route across the country.

South of the Lakes is a low plateau, rising to 380 m (1,250 ft) above Lake Vättern and sloping gently down to the small lowland area of Skåne (Scania).

Sweden's topography has been greatly affected by the Ice Age. The long, narrow lakes which fill the upper valleys of many of the rivers of northern Sweden have been shaped by the action of ice. They are the relics of a much larger lake system which was fed by water from the melting ice sheet and provide excellent natural reservoirs for hydro-electric stations. Some of the most fertile soils in Sweden were formed from material deposited in the bed of such glacial lakes. Elsewhere, glacial moraines and deposits of boulder clay are reminders of the impact of the Ice Age.

Climate

The high mountains which form the spine of the Scandinavian peninsula shut off the modifying influence of the Atlantic weather systems from northern Sweden. This area, therefore, has colder, drier winters than places on the seaward side, but also enjoys warmer and less rainy summers. On the Norrland plateau annual rainfall is less than 508 mm (20 in), July temperatures average 15°C (59°F) and the long summer days of the high northern latitudes make summer time pleasant, although winters are long, dark and cold. The Gulf of Bothnia is affected by ice between November and April, creating problems for shipping.

The southern part of Sweden between the Kattegat and the Baltic is open to Atlantic influences and has milder winters than the northern areas, but summers are also cooler and wetter. Göteborg has average winter temperatures of 0°C (32°F), compared with Stockholm's −3°C (27°F), whilst at Haparanda, at the head of the Gulf of Finland, February, the coldest month, has an average temperature of −12°C (10°F). In summer, however, there is little difference between north and south, most areas having between 15° and 20°C (59° to 68°F).

Forestry and Agriculture

There are extensive coniferous forests throughout northern Sweden. In the south the original cover of mixed deciduous woodland has been cleared for agriculture from the areas of better soil with the typical landscape being farmland interspersed with forest. There are better opportunities for agriculture in Sweden than elsewhere in Scandinavia. Cereal crops, potatoes, sugar beet, and vegetables are grown for human consumption in Skåne and in central Sweden, but by far the greatest area of cultivated land is given over to the production of fodder crops for cattle and sheep. Dairy farming is highly developed, and Sweden is self-sufficient in milk, cheese and butter production.

Industry

Many farmers have left the land since World War 2, attracted by the higher wages and more modern way of life of the towns. Sweden has been able to create a high standard of life based on industry, despite the fact that, apart from the large iron ore deposits, many of the essential fuels and raw materials have to be imported. Most of the iron ore obtained from the mines at Kiruna and Gällivare in Arctic Sweden is exported via Narvik and Lulea to Germany. The development of hydro-electricity has made up for the lack of oil and coal. Sweden is famous for high-quality engineering products such as ball bearings, matchmaking machinery, agricultural machines, motor cars (Saab and Volvo), ships, aeroplanes and armaments (Bofors). In addition to these new industries, the traditional forest-based industries have been modernized. Sweden is the largest exporter of wood pulp in the world, and also produces paper, sawn timber and furniture.

The bulk of the population lives in the area between Stockholm, Göteborg and Malmö, where most industry is also located. (FS)

DENMARK

Denmark is the smallest of the Scandinavian countries in area (43,000 km², 16,600 sq miles), but the second largest in population (over 5 million). It consists of the Jutland (Jylland) peninsula, which is an extension of the North German plain, and a large number of islands, of which 100 are inhabited. The largest and most densely populated of the islands is Zealand (Sjaelland), which lies close to the coast of southern Sweden. Copenhagen (København), the capital city, lies on the narrow strait, The Sound, which leads from the Kattegat to the Baltic.

Control of the entrances to the Baltic – the Great and Little Belts and the Sound – contributed to the power of Denmark in the Middle Ages, when she dominated her neighbours, and expanded her territories to include Norway, Iceland, Greenland and the Faroe Islands. The link with Norway was broken in 1814, and with Iceland in 1944, but Greenland and the Faroes retain connections with Denmark. The granite island of Bornholm, lying 40 km (25 miles) off the southern tip of Sweden, also remains a Danish possession.

Structurally, Denmark is part of a low-lying belt of sedimentary rocks extending from north Germany to southern Sweden, which are geologically much younger than the rest of Scandinavia. The surface is almost entirely covered by glacial deposits, but the underlying strata are exposed as the 122 m (400 ft) high chalk cliffs on the island of Møn. Along the west coast of Jutland, facing the North Sea, are lines of sand dunes with shallow lagoons behind them.

Agriculture

Denmark has few mineral resources and no coal, oil or natural gas. A century ago this was a poor farming and fishing country, but Denmark has now been transformed into one of Europe's wealthiest industrial nations. The first steps in this transformation were taken in the late nineteenth century, with the introduction of cooperative methods of processing and distributing farm produce, and the development of modern methods of dairying and pig and poultry breeding. Denmark became the supplier of bacon, eggs and butter to the industrial nations of western Europe. Most of the natural fodder for the animals is grown in Denmark, with barley as the principal crop.

The Faroes. The population is descended from Norse settlers.

Although less than 10 per cent of the working population are engaged in farming, the scientific methods used and the efficient cooperative marketing system ensure that output remains high. Over one-third of Denmark's exports are of food products, and Britain and Germany are the chief customers.

Industry

From a firm agricultural base Denmark has developed a whole range of industries. Some, like brewing, meat canning, fish processing, pottery, textile and furniture making, use Danish products, while others, like shipbuilding, engineering and metal working, depend on imported raw materials. The famous port of Copenhagen is also the chief industrial centre. (FS)

FAROE ISLANDS

The Faroe Islands, which lie half way between the Shetland Islands and Iceland, have been Danish since 1709. There are 17 inhabited islands, with a total population of 40,000. They are rocky and infertile, with a climate which is characterized by heavy rainfall and strong winds. Fishing is the chief occupation, and Faroese motor vessels are to be found in all the fishing grounds of the North Atlantic. Dried cod is a major export. The capital Thorshavn has fish freezing and drying factories and yards for repairing ships. There is a high degree of local self government, with only foreign relations and defence in Danish hands. (FS)

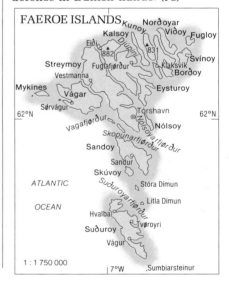

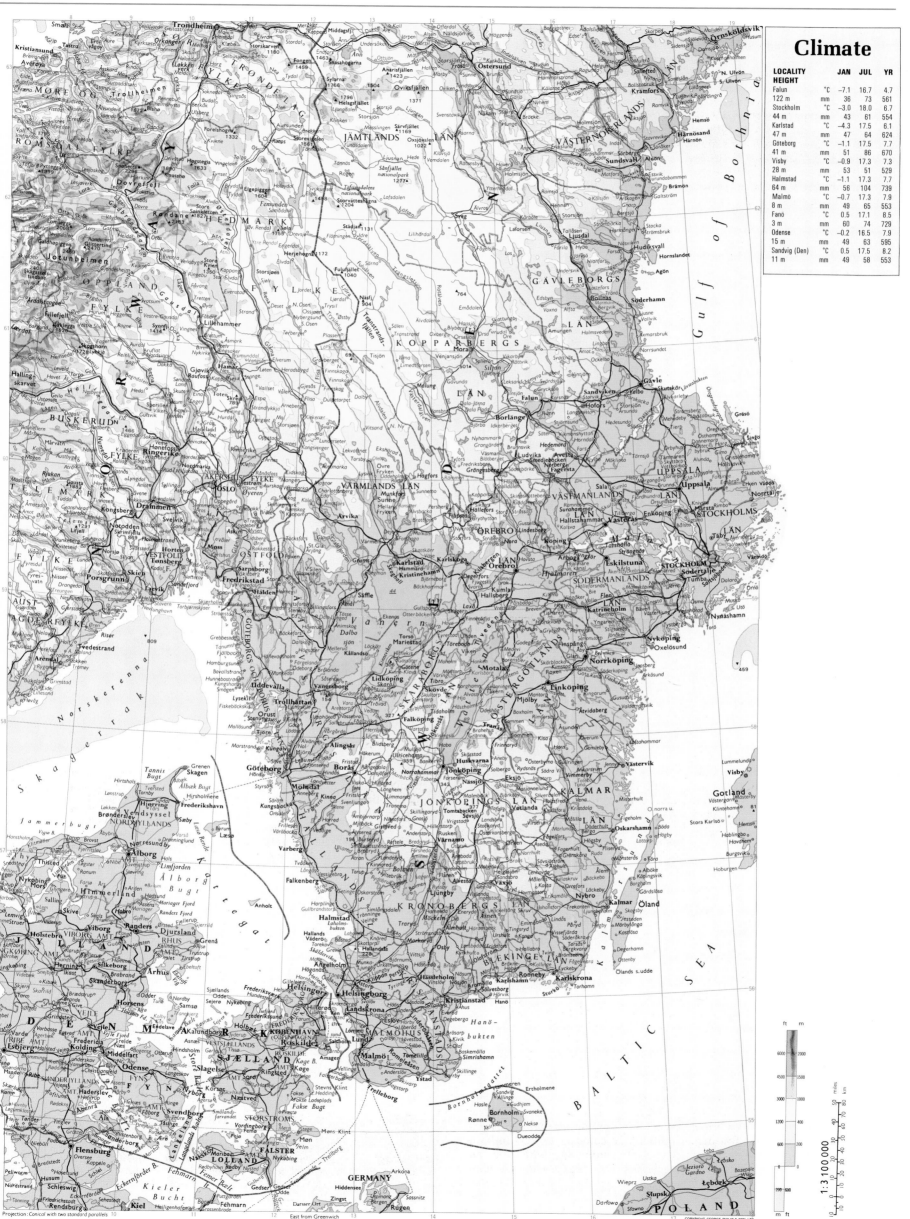

Climate

LOCALITY HEIGHT		JAN	JUL	YR
Falun	°C	-7.1	16.7	4.7
122 m	mm	36	73	561
Stockholm	°C	-3.0	18.0	6.7
44 m	mm	43	61	554
Karlstad	°C	-4.3	17.5	6.1
47 m	mm	47	64	624
Göteborg	°C	-1.1	17.5	7.7
41 m	mm	51	86	670
Visby	°C	-0.9	17.3	7.3
28 m	mm	53	51	529
Halmstad	°C	-1.1	17.3	7.7
64 m	mm	56	104	739
Malmö	°C	-0.7	17.3	7.9
8 m	mm	49	65	553
Fanö	°C	0.5	17.1	8.5
3 m	mm	60	74	729
Odense	°C	-0.2	16.5	7.9
15 m	mm	49	63	595
Sandvig (Den)	°C	0.5	17.5	8.2
11 m	mm	49	58	553

Projection : Conical with two standard parallels

East from Greenwich

COPYRIGHT GEORGE PHILIP & SON LTD.

1 : 3 100 000

CENTRAL EUROPE

Physically, Central Europe is divided into three clear structural belts. In the south, the Alpine fold mountains are at their highest and most complex in Switzerland and Austria, but divide eastwards into the Carpathians and the Dinaric mountains of Yugoslavia, enclosing the basin in which Hungary lies. A second belt, the central uplands, consisting of block mountains, intervening lowlands and some of Europe's greatest coalfields, stretches from the Ardennes across Germany and Czechoslovakia to thin out and disappear in Poland. The third belt, the northern lowland, broadens eastwards, and owes its relief largely to glacial deposits.

Two great rivers dominate the drainage pattern: the powerful 1,320 km (820 mile) Rhine rises in the Alps and crosses the central uplands and northern lowland to reach the North Sea. The east-flowing 2,850 km (1,780 mile) Danube cuts right across the fold mountains at Bratislava and again at the Iron Gates (Portile de Fier) on its way to the Black Sea.

In human terms the major division is a political one. The states situated between the Iron Curtain and the western boundary of the USSR (the superpower which dominates them politically) have a marxist ideology and socialist economies: they are often grouped as 'Eastern Europe' today. Further west, central-European states in the liberal-capitalist tradition are now usually regarded as belonging to 'Western Europe'. (THE)

GERMANY

The unity of the German Empire that was created under Prussian dominance in 1871, centred on the great imperial capital at Berlin, was to last for fewer than 75 years. Even at its greatest extent it left large areas of German-speaking population outside its boundaries, notably in Austria and large parts of Switzerland. Following the fall of Hitler in 1945 a defeated Germany was obliged to transfer to Poland and the USSR 114,500 km² (44,200 sq miles) situated east of the Oder and Neisse rivers, nearly a quarter of the country's pre-war area. The German-speaking inhabitants were expelled as were most German-speaking minorities in the countries of eastern Europe. The remainder of Germany was occupied by the victorious allies.

The dividing line between the zones occupied by the three western

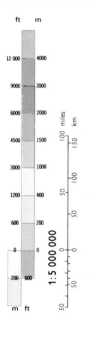

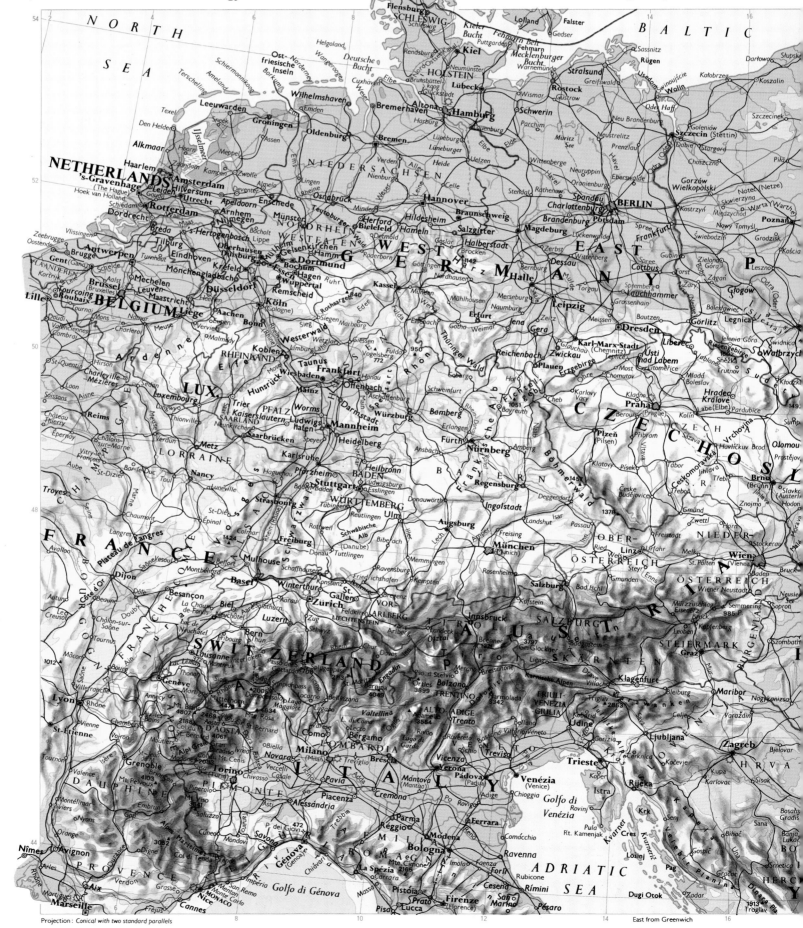

Projection: Conical with two standard parallels

East from Greenwich

allies (USA, United Kingdom, France) and that occupied by the USSR rapidly hardened into a political boundary dividing the country. In 1948 West Germany was proclaimed as the independent 248,000 km² (96,000 sq miles) Federal Republic of Germany, with a capital at Bonn (deemed 'provisional' pending hoped-for German reunification). East Germany became the 108,000 km² (41,700 sq miles) German Democratic Republic. Berlin was similarly divided, the three western sectors of occupation becoming a 480 km² (186 sq miles) enclave embedded in the territory of the GDR, of which the Soviet-occupied East Berlin was deemed to be capital. (THE)

The European Forests

The tree line in Europe – the boundary marking the northern limit of tree growth – runs north of the Arctic Circle. Only the tundra-covered northern area of Lapland and the Kola Peninsula lie beyond it. Practically all of Europe that lay south of the tree line was originally forested. North of the 60th parallel lay dark, sombre evergreen forests, dominated by spruce and pine. Since the last glacial period the evergreen forests have occupied a swathe 1,200 km (750 miles) wide across central Scandinavia and Finland, broken by marshes, moorlands and lakes, and interspersed with stands of willow and birch. Much of it remains today, and is still the haunt of elk, red deer and small populations of wolves, brown bears, and lynx.

To the south of the coniferous forest, Europe was covered with broad-leafed deciduous woodland – an ancient forest of mature oak, ash, birch, beech, sycamore, and a dozen other familiar species. Favoured by the mild damp climate, this rich forest grew in abundance over the lowlands, foothills and warmer uplands of Europe, limited in the south by dry Mediterranean summers, in Hungary and the south-west by the aridity of the plains. Virtually the first industrial resource of European man, the forest suffered a thousand years of exploitation and only remnants survive. (BS)

Autumn woodland in Germany.

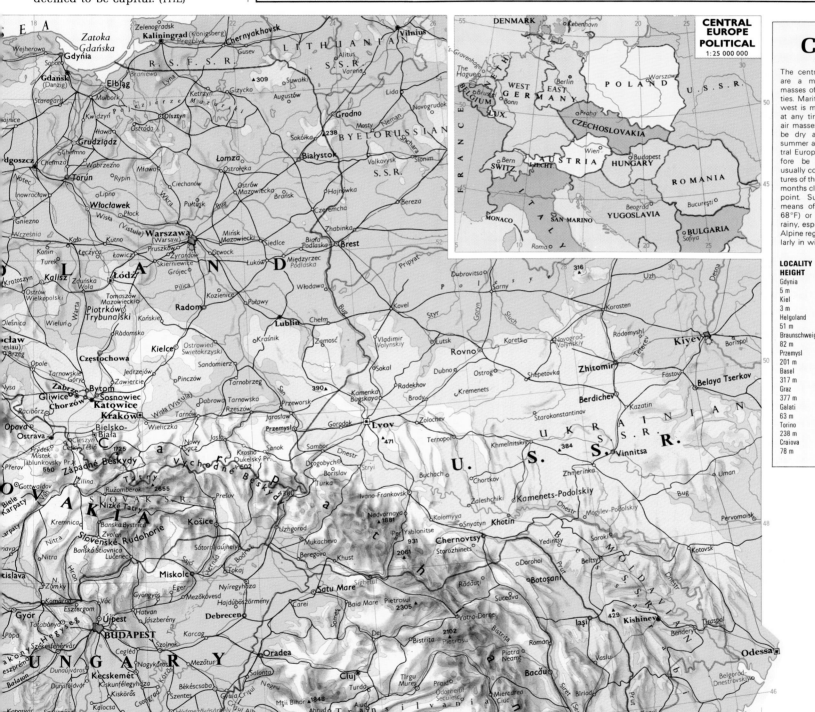

Climate

The central lowlands of Europe are a meeting ground of air masses of widely differing qualities. Maritime air from the south-west is moist and relatively mild at any time of year: continental air masses from the east tend to be dry and extreme – hot in summer and cold in winter. Central European weather can therefore be variable. Winters are usually cold, with mean temperatures of the two or three midwinter months close to or below freezing point. Summers are hot, with means of 15° to 20°C (59° to 68°F) or higher, and tend to be rainy, especially in the south. The Alpine regions are cooler, particularly in winter, and much wetter.

LOCALITY HEIGHT		JAN	JUL	YR
Gdynia	°C	-0.8	17.8	7.9
5 m	mm	33	84	594
Kiel	°C	0.1	17.2	8.5
3 m	mm	63	75	725
Helgoland	°C	1.6	16.5	8.0
51 m	mm	58	79	731
Braunschweig	°C	0.1	18.1	9.2
82 m	mm	43	78	620
Przemysl	°C	-3.3	18.8	8.2
201 m	mm	27	105	656
Basel	°C	0.5	19.5	10.1
317 m	mm	53	86	784
Graz	°C	-2.1	19.5	9.3
377 m	mm	27	127	849
Galati	°C	-2.9	22.9	10.7
63 m	mm	26	44	435
Torino	°C	1.1	24.1	12.9
238 m	mm	23	72	845
Craiova	°C	-2.9	23.3	11.1
78 m	mm	37	47	509

COPYRIGHT. GEORGE PHILIP & SON. LTD.

WEST GERMANY

The Federal Republic of Germany (West Germany) extends from the North Sea and Baltic coasts in the north to the flanks of the central Alps in the south. The country includes only a narrow fringe of Alpine mountains, with the Zugspitze (2,968 m, 9,738 ft) the highest peak. There is, however, a wide section of the associated Alpine foreland bordering Switzerland and Austria, stretching northward from the foothills of the Alps to the Danube. The foreland is largely covered by moraines and outwash plains which, with many lakes, including the Bodensee (538 km², 208 sq miles), are relics of the glacial age, and reminders of the many glaciers that once emerged from the Alpine valleys.

The central uplands of Europe are more amply represented, occupying a broad swathe of West Germany. Four types of terrain are found. Block mountains, for example the Harz, are remnants of pre-Alpine fold mountains shattered and re-shaped by the later earth movements. Uplift was greatest in the south, close to the Alps, producing the Schwarzwald (1,493 m, 4,898 ft) and Vosges and Böhmerwald. Between these great blocks of forested mountains are open basins of sedimentary rocks, their resistant bands picked out by erosion as in the magnificent scarp of the Schwäbische Alb, rising to 869 m (2,851 ft), overlooking the Neckar basin. A third kind of country is provided by down-faulted basins filled with softer deposits of more recent age, notably the Upper Rhine plain between Basel and Mainz. Earth movement and eruptions produced a fourth element, such volcanic mountains as the Vogelsberg (772 m, 2,533 ft), and the hot and mineral springs that gave rise to the famous spas. Here is Germany at the most picturesque, with baronial castles on wooded heights, looking down over vineyards to clustered villages of half-timbered houses, whose occupants still cultivate open-field strips as they did many centuries ago.

The northern lowlands owe their topography mainly to the retreat of the ice sheets. The most recent moraines, marked by forested ridges that may include good boulder-clay soils, are restricted to Schleswig-Holstein. The rest of the lowland is covered with leached older moraine and sandy outwash, so that in many places soils are poor. The glacial period also left behind loess, wind-blown dust deposited along the northern edge of the central uplands and in basins within them, providing some of the country's best soils. The coast is also the product of glaciation and subsequent changes. The low Baltic shore is diversified by long, branching inlets, formed beneath the ice of the glacial period, and now beloved by yachtsmen. The North Sea is fringed by sandy offshore islands, the products of a beach bar now breached by the sea.

Forest and Agriculture

Over a quarter of West Germany is forested, with particular concentration in the Alps, the massifs of the central uplands, and the poorer areas of the northern lowland. It is astonishing that this economically most advanced country has some of Europe's smallest farms, particularly characteristic of southern Germany. Most are used for arable-based mixed farming, with minor livestock enterprises. In the warmer basins tobacco, vegetables and, increasingly, maize are grown. Vineyards and orchards clothe the slopes of the Rhine and its tributaries. Much larger wheat and sugar-beet farms with important livestock enterprises are characteristic of the loess soils on the northern edge of the central uplands. The Bavarian Alpine foreland in the south, and Schleswig-Holstein in the north, are other areas of above-average farm size. The sandy northern lowland, which used to support a poor agriculture based on rye, potatoes and pigs, increasingly specializes in intensive meat and poultry production. Dairy specialization is typical of the milder north-west and the Alpine fringes.

Because of the generally small size of holdings nearly two-thirds of the farmers must seek a supplementary income outside agriculture; this is often a half-way stage to giving up agriculture altogether. Persons employed in agriculture, who were a quarter of the employed population in 1950, now account for well below 10 per cent. With this movement out of agriculture, the average size of holding is steadily but all too slowly rising.

Minerals and Energy

West Germany is the most important coal producer of continental western Europe, but output from the Ruhr, Saar and Aachen fields has dropped since the mid-1950s, owing to competition from oil. Some oil and gas is home-produced, mainly from fields beneath the northern lowland, but most of the oil consumed is delivered by pipeline from Wilhelmshaven, Europort and the Mediterranean to refineries in the Rhineland and on the Danube. Brown coal is excavated from open pits hundreds of metres deep between Cologne and Aachen. This coal is a major source of electricity, although atomic plants built on the coast and principal rivers are expected to be of increasing importance. West Germany's hydro-electric stations are concentrated in the Bavarian Alps. Output could be increased.

The non-ferrous metallic ores of the Harz and other massifs of the central uplands are no longer of great significance, while high-grade imported iron ores have proved more economic than the home ores of the Siegen and Peine-Salzgitter districts. West Germany is a major producer of potash and common salt, mostly from the Werra basin and the northern lowland.

Switzerland

Switzerland has some of the most impressive Alpine scenery in Europe.

The most mountainous country in Europe, Switzerland is also one of the most prosperous. Three-fifths of its territory is in the Alps, of which the two highest peaks are on the Swiss-Italian Border, the Matterhorn (4,478 m, 14,700 ft) and the Monte Rosa (4,634 m, 15,200 ft). The Alps are drained by the upper Rhine tributaries and by the Rhône valley through the lake of Geneva. Numerous lakes add to the scenic attraction of high mountains with permanent snow, and the Alps have become one of the great tourist attractions of the world.

Despite a pastoral image Switzerland is a modern country. Electricity is available everywhere and all the railways are electrified. German is the most widely-used language but French is prevalent in the west and in the Ticino area Italian is spoken. The fourth recognized language, Romansch, is spoken only in the Grisons area.

Agriculture and Industry

One quarter of Switzerland is forested. Agriculture prospers, with both arable and pastoral farming; a wide range of produce is grown, including maize and other cereals, fruits, vegetables, and grapes for a local wine industry. The mountain pastures are still used for summer grazing, though some of the famous migrations of herds and herders up the mountains in summer no longer take place.

Industry is prosperous, especially engineering, both mechanical and electrical, metallurgy, chemicals and textiles. Watch and clock making is perhaps the most famed of all Swiss industries. In addition to agricultural and industrial strength Switzerland also has a world trade in banking and insurance, concentrated particularly in Zürich. Local government is centred on each canton, which has local control over housing and economic development. But Switzerland is a united country – internationally recognized as a permanently neutral power, with an efficient army, active in good causes, and shrewdly trading with all the world. (TWF)

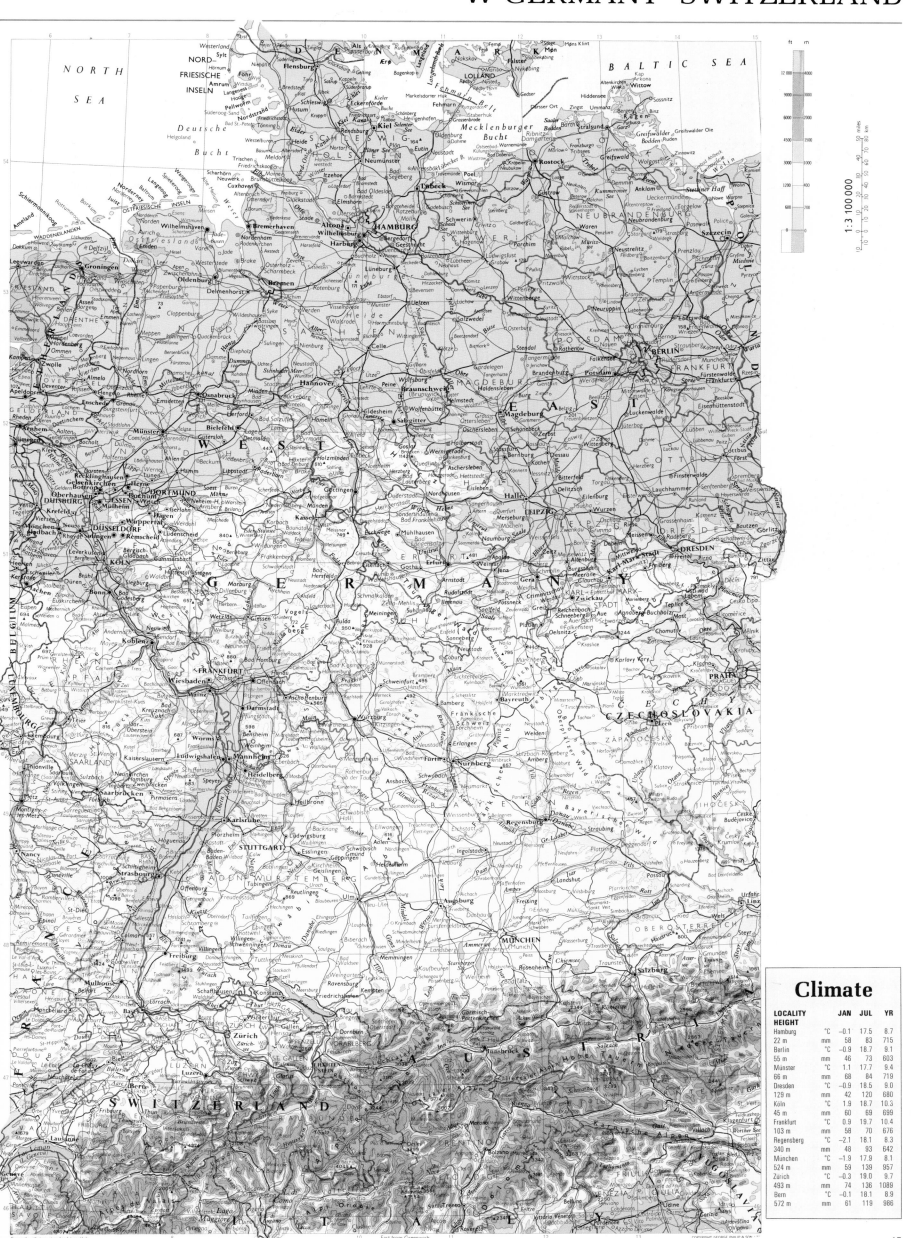

Climate

LOCALITY HEIGHT		JAN	JUL	YR
Hamburg	°C	-0.1	17.5	8.7
22 m	mm	58	83	715
Berlin	°C	-0.9	18.7	9.1
55 m	mm	46	73	603
Münster	°C	1.1	17.7	9.4
66 m	mm	68	84	719
Dresden	°C	-0.9	18.5	9.0
129 m	mm	42	120	680
Köln	°C	1.9	18.7	10.3
45 m	mm	60	69	699
Frankfurt	°C	0.9	19.7	10.4
103 m	mm	58	70	676
Regensberg	°C	-2.1	18.1	8.3
340 m	mm	48	93	642
München	°C	-1.9	17.9	8.1
524 m	mm	59	139	957
Zürich	°C	-0.3	19.0	9.7
493 m	mm	74	136	1089
Bern	°C	-0.1	18.1	8.9
572 m	mm	61	119	986

Neuschwanstein, Ludwig II's castle.

Population and Industry

From Neolithic times the core settlement areas of Germany were the fertile lowlands – areas like the northern edge of the central uplands in Lower Saxony and Westphalia, the upper Rhine plain, the Main and Neckar basins and the Alpine foreland. From these core areas land-hungry medieval peasants advanced to clear large areas of forest in the uplands, and also streamed eastwards to settle in lands beyond the Elbe and Saale. The fragmentation of the Holy Roman Empire into a swarm of competing states had a positive side in the founding and fostering by local rulers, large and small, of a dense system of towns, among them future regional capitals like Hannover, Stuttgart or Munich (München). Contrast with the 'French desert' created by Parisian centralization in France is striking.

When industrial growth came in the nineteenth century heavy industry naturally concentrated in the Ruhr and Saar coalfields, but thanks to the railways other industry could disperse widely to these existing towns. Since 1945 the Ruhr and Saar coalfields have been undergoing a difficult period of conversion, owing to the problems of the now declining coal, steel and heavy engineering industries. By contrast towns away from the coalfields, especially the great regional capitals of southern Germany, have flourished with the development of more modern, and lighter industries

The Wolfsburg Volkswagen works.

(motor vehicles, electrical equipment, electronics), the growth of administrative and office work, and the division among a number of cities of capital functions formerly concentrated in Berlin.

While the inner parts of the greatest cities have tended to lose population, their suburbs and satellites have exploded across the surrounding countrysides, forming vast urban areas of expanding population. In the west and south of the country, an axis of high population growth and high density stretches from the Rhine-Ruhr region (largest of all but checked in expansion by the problems of Ruhr industry) through the Rhine-Main (Frankfurt), Rhine-Neckar (Mannheim-Ludwigshafen) and Stuttgart regions to Munich. In the east and north the densely populated areas are more isolated, centred on the cities of Nürnberg, Hannover,

Bremen and Hamburg.

Since 1950 there has been a tendency for German population to drift towards the more attractive south. Urban population losses have in part been made up by immigrant workers, nearly 2.5 million at their peak in the early 1970s, increasingly joined by their families in a reinforcement of a German native population which at the end of the 1960s entered a period of decline.

Waterways

West Germany has the advantage of the superb Rhine waterway, which from its Alpine sources cuts right across the central uplands to the North Sea. A combination of summer snow melt from the Alps and autumn-spring rainfall in the central uplands gives it a powerful and remarkably even flow. Traffic is at its most intensive between Rotterdam and the Rhine-Ruhr region, where Duisburg is the largest inland harbour of Europe, but standard 1,250 tonne self-propelled barges can reach Basel. Completion of the Rhine-Main-Danube waterway will open a through route to the Black Sea. For north German traffic the Mittelland Canal following the northern edge of the central uplands opens up links to the north German ports and Berlin. Hamburg is Germany's biggest seaport, followed by Bremen with its outport, Bremerhaven. All German ports suffer by being too far from the main centre of European population and economic activity in the Rhinelands; the Belgian and Netherlands ports are closer and at great advantage.

Administration

The system of federal states (*Länder*) created after World War 2 has remained remarkably stable. Marked disparities of size have remained in spite of various reform proposals. Bavaria with 70,547 km² (27,238 sq miles) has the largest area, and North Rhine-Westphalia, with the Rhine-Ruhr region at its heart, has the largest population, over a quarter of the West German total. At the other extreme Bremen has only 706 km² (273 sq miles) and a little over 1 per cent of total population. State capitals like Hamburg or Munich (München), with centuries of power and privilege behind them, have more individuality, vitality and cultural independence than the curious 'provisional' capital created in the small Rhineland university town of Bonn. (THE)

BERLIN

The city is situated in the sandy terrain of the northern lowland of Europe, astride the river Spree. Subjected to four-power occupation in 1945, Berlin was by 1948 politically divided, with the US, British and French sectors isolated as the enclave of West Berlin within the territory of East Germany. Separation was completed in 1961 when West Berlin was sealed off by the

'Berlin wall'. Access to West Berlin from West Germany is limited to three roads, three rail lines, two waterways and three air corridors.

The rapid rebuilding of West Berlin, following wartime devastation, made it 'the shop window of the west'. Institutions such as the University, National Library and museums, situated in the eastern part of the city, were recreated in the west. West Berlin is still an important industrial city but owing to isolation and the loss of its capital functions it needs economic support from West Germany.

In East Berlin there has been a slower but extremely radical reconstruction of the old heart of Berlin, now dominated by a 365 m (1,198 ft) television mast. East Berlin is also an important centre of industry, but has the advantage of not being separated from its natural hinterland in East Germany, of which it is capital. (THE)

EAST GERMANY

The southern part of the German Democratic Republic (East Germany) has a relief pattern of central-uplands type: the Harz, Thüringer Wald and Erzgebirge (Ore Mountains) massifs rise above a varied scarpland terrain, notably the Thüringian Basin, which has the fertile Erfurt lowland at its heart. By contrast the northern lowland owes its relief essentially to relatively recent glaciation. To the south and south-west only eroded remnants of moraine and sandy outwash plains remain, resulting in generally poor soils. Nearer the Baltic the most recent moraines have left behind a confused terrain of hills and lakes, but also areas of good soil developed on glacial till. The movement of water around the edge of the ice sheets carved south-east to north-west stream trenches (*Urstromtäler*). These are now in part occupied by the present rivers, and have also proved convenient for canal construction. Between the central uplands and the northern lowland is a belt of loess, broadening greatly in the lowland of Saxony around Halle and Leipzig, which provides the country's best soils for wheat, malting-barley and sugar beet.

Mineral Resources

East Germany is unique in depending for energy supply on brown coal (lignite), of low calorific value, but economically mined in vast open pits. The older centre of mining was in the lowland of Saxony, between Halle and Leipzig, but the main area of expansion is now in Niederlausitz, south of Cottbus. Brown coal is increasingly reserved for electricity generation, other energy needs and feedstock for the important chemical industry around Halle being met by oil brought by pipeline from the USSR or by tanker through Rostock. The other mineral resource of significance is potash, mined south of the Harz and exported through Wismar.

Industry

As an advanced industrial country of western type the role of East Germany within the communist-block states is to provide technically advanced equipment, receiving in return supplies of raw materials and semi-finished products such as steel. Because of industrial inertia the location of the important machine-building industry has not greatly changed since capitalist times, being heavily concentrated in and around the southern cities of Leipzig, Karl-Marx-Stadt (Chemnitz) and Dresden. Other centres are Magdeburg and East Berlin, which is also the leading producer of electrical equipment.

East Germany inherited a traditional strength in precision and optical industries, mostly located in Thüringia (Zeiss works at Jena), on which has been based important developments in industrial instrumentation and electronics. The government has tried to steer some major new developments into the rural north and east of the country, including shipbuilding at Rostock, oil refining and chemicals at Schwedt, and iron smelting and steel rolling at Eisenhüttenstadt. Just as all manufacturing of significance is nationalized so too nearly all agricultural holdings have been brought into 'agricultural cooperatives', many of over 500 hectares (1,236 acres) and some of over 5,000 hectares (c 12,400 acres). The East German version of the collective farm appears to have proved more efficient than the equivalent in other communist states. In general, the economic outlook is promising.

Communications and Administration

East Germany was left in 1945 with a basically logical if heavily damaged transport system, since the pre-war network had been based on Berlin, which continued as capital of the new republic. The desire to avoid passing through West Berlin meant some adjustment and new construction around the capital. A new ocean port was developed at Rostock, to avoid the use of Hamburg in the Federal Republic. It has the disadvantage that it has no inland waterway access, but south-north rail and motorway links with Rostock have been progressively improved.

In contrast with the system of federal government in West Germany, East Germany has since 1952 been politically divided into fifteen administrative Districts (*Bezirke*) under control of the central government in East Berlin. (THE)

AUSTRIA

The Federal Republic of Austria is composed of nine states, including the capital, Vienna. The present boundaries derive from the Versailles settlement of 1919, which dissolved the Austro-Hungarian Empire.

A mountainous country, more alpine even than Switzerland, Austria has two-thirds of her territory and rather less than a third of the population within the eastern Alps, which extend in a series of longitudinal ridges from the Swiss border in the west almost to Vienna in the east.

The longitudinal valleys between the ridges accommodate much of the Alpine population, but are less effective than might be expected as routes of internal communication. Transverse routes, for example the Linz-Klagenfurt and Vienna-Semmering routes are vital internal links across the eastern Alps to the valleys and basins of Steiermark and Kärnten. The rail and motorway routes over the 1,371 m (4,500 ft) Brenner Pass are more intensively used, but these benefit neighbours rather than Austria. Alpine agriculture, once the mainstay of mountain life, is currently in decline, but skiing and summer tourist industries have brought new prosperity into Alpine areas.

Austria's lowlands include a section of the northern Alpine fóreland, which narrows eastward toward Vienna and contains the Danube basin. This is Austria's most important east-west route, with rail, motorway and river navigation leading through Vienna to Budapest and beyond. Another important lowland is the Burgenland, a rich farming area bordering the eastern Alps and facing south-west toward Hungary.

Industry

Unlike Switzerland, Austria has important heavy industries based in large part on indigenous resources. The mountains are a major source of hydro-electric power. Oil and natural gas occur predominantly in the Vienna Basin and are supplemented by imports from the USSR and from German refineries. Minerals occur in the eastern Alps, notably iron ore in Styria (Steiermark); iron and steel production is located both at Donawitz in the mountains, and also in the Alpine foreland which has become a major centre of metal, chemical engineering and vehicle manufacturing industries. Various manufacturing plants are established also around Vienna.

Vienna stands at a major European crossroads where the Danube is joined by the Moravian Gate route from the northern lowlands of Europe, and by the Alpine route through the Semmering pass. A city of international political and artistic importance, Vienna contains one-fifth of Austria's population (about 7.5 million). Like most European countries Austria experienced low population growth or even slight decline in the 1960s and 1970s. Within the country decline has been greatest in the east, while the west has gained from a higher birthrate, and also from settlement of refugees and the industrialization of the Tirol since World War 2. (THE)

Mieders in the Austrian Tirol, where many folk traditions survive.

Liechtenstein

A multi-national office sign.

Liechtenstein is a tiny (160 km², 62 sq miles), German-speaking state standing at the end of the Eastern Alps, where the Rhine cuts its way northward out of the Alpine chains. A constitutional monarchy, it has surprisingly escaped from being tidied up by incorporation into any of Europe's larger states. Since 1923 Liechtenstein has been in customs and currency union with Switzerland, which also provides overseas representation, but retains full sovereignty in other spheres. The capital, Vaduz, is situated on the *Oberland* plateau above the fields and meadows of the Rhine valley, and is itself overlooked by the royal castle.

Proximity to a major focus of routes linking Austria with Switzerland, and Germany with the Swiss Alps and Italy, brings the country streams of short-term visitors, intrigued by the notion of this miniature state. Behind the town forested outliers of the Rätikon rise to high Alpine valleys, where small-scale tourism is increasing and traditional farming declining. Liechtenstein is best known abroad for her postage stamps, which contribute an important part of the state's income, and as a place of registration for international companies, attracted by extremely low taxation. Since World War 2 there has been quite an impressive growth in specialized manufacturing, the product of a judicious mixture of Swiss engineers, Austrian technicians, Italian workers and international capital. (THE)

EUROPE CENTRAL

HUNGARY

Hungary is a land-locked country of 93,000 km² (35,900 sq miles), occupying the central Danubian lowlands. Until 1918 Hungary was part of the multi-national Austro-Hungarian Empire, but under the peace settlements following World War 1 Hungary lost 70 per cent of her territory to her neighbours Yugo-slavia, Romania and Czechoslo-vakia; 2.6 million Hungarians still live in these countries.

Landscape and Agriculture

There are two large lowland areas, the Great Plain (Nagyalföld) which occupies the eastern half of the country, and the Little Plain (Kisal-föld) in the north-west. Between them a line of hills runs south-west to north-west from Lake Balaton to the Czechoslovak border. Lake Balaton (72 km, 45 miles long) is a favourite holiday resort.

The Hungarian Plains have some of the most fertile agricultural land in Europe, especially in the areas covered by a mantle of loess (a wind-blown deposit dating from the Ice Age), but there are also infertile areas of marsh, sand and dry steppe-land, where crop growing gives way to grazing. In the region to the north-west of the Great Plain, known as Hortobagy, it is possible to see Europe's last remaining cowboys – the gulyas – riding on horseback to round up their cattle. But the expanse of dry steppeland where this way of life is practised is dwindling as irrigation schemes are introduced, and ranching gives way to the growing of rice, tobacco and wheat.

The continental climate, with its spring rains, long, hot summers and cold winters, favours crops such as wheat, maize, sunflowers and vines. Rainfall is around 63 cm (25 in) in the west, but falls to under 50 cm (20 in) in the east.

Industry and Commerce

Hungary has reserves of natural gas, but is poorly endowed with coal and oil; bauxite is one of the few plentiful minerals. Industries have been built up on the basis of imported raw materials, mainly from the USSR. The main industrial centres are in the north, around Budapest and Miskolc, where iron and steel, engineering, and chemicals predominate. Aluminium is manu-factured north of Lake Balaton. (FS)

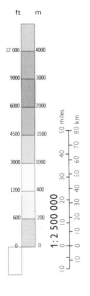

Gulyas, *Hungarian cowboys, on the Hortobagy.*

CZECHOSLO-VAKIA

Czechoslovakia, a land-locked state in Central Europe with an area of 127,870 km² (49,370 sq miles) has a population of about 15 million, of whom some 65 per cent are Czechs, and 30 per cent Slovaks. Of the remaining population, there are over half a million Hungarians, and smaller numbers of Germans, Poles, and Ukrainians. Czechoslovakia came into existence at the end of World War 1, after the collapse of the great Austro-Hungarian Empire. Since 1969 Czechoslovakia has been a federation of two equal nations, the Czechs occupying the western provinces of Bohemia and Moravia, and the Slovaks occupying the eastern half of the country.

Landscape

In the west, Bohemia is a diamond-shaped area, surrounded by ranges of mountains which enclose a basin drained by the river Elbe and its tributaries. In the centre lies Prague, the historic capital city. The mountains are rich in minerals, including iron, lead, zinc and uranium. In western Bohemia there are also reserves of hard coal and lignite.

Moravia is divided from Bohemia by plateau land known as the Moravian Heights. Central Moravia is a lowland. Slovakia consists of a mountain region in the north, part of the Carpathian system which divides Slovakia from Poland, and a southern lowland area.

Agriculture and Industry

Though Czechoslovakia is the most highly industrialized of the East European countries, agriculture remains strong and well developed, with high yields of most crops suited to the continental climate. Food processing industries (brewing, for example) are important in the western provinces. The lowland area of Slovakia is extremely fertile with crops of wheat, barley, oats and sugar beet, and rye and potatoes on the higher ground. Dairying and pig-breeding also play significant roles in the agricultural economy.

Apart from the mineral reserves in Bohemia, there are also good coal reserves at Ostrava, in Moravia, and a number of other mineral deposits. But iron ore is imported to feed the furnaces of the steel industry. (FS)

The historic city of Prague, spread like Rome on seven hills, was founded in the ninth century.

Climate

LOCALITY HEIGHT		JAN	JUL	YR
Praha	°C	-1.7	21.0	9.8
262 m	mm	18	68	411
Opava	°C	-1.5	19.3	8.5
272 m	mm	26	92	587
Kosice	°C	-3.4	19.4	8.7
232 m	mm	30	84	605
Wien	°C	-1.5	19.9	9.7
203 m	mm	39	84	660
Salzburg	°C	-2.0	18.3	8.6
435 m	mm	76	195	1286
Budapest	°C	-1.4	22.1	11.1
139 m	mm	37	56	614
Innsbruck	°C	-2.7	18.8	9.0
582 m	mm	54	134	868
Graz	°C	-2.1	19.5	9.3
377 m	mm	27	127	849
Szeged	°C	-1.4	22.5	11.3
82 m	mm	34	51	556
Pécs	°C	-0.7	21.7	10.9
201 m	mm	40	64	661

![Polish flag]

POLAND

Danzig, acquired after World War 2, is an important outlet for Poland.

The geographical location of Poland has had a strong influence on the country's stormy history. On many occasions powerful neighbours – notably Russia and Germany – have found it easy to invade and occupy Poland. The most recent frontier changes came at the end of World War 2, when Poland gave up territory in the east to the USSR, and in compensation gained parts of East Germany as far as the river Oder.

As a result of these changes Poland lost poor agricultural land in the east, and gained an important industrial region in the west, including the former German cities of Breslau (now called Wroclaw) and the Baltic ports of Stettin (now Szczecin) and Danzig (now Gdansk). Acquisition of a length of Baltic coastline (before World War 2 there was only a narrow access corridor where the Poles developed the port of

Gdynia as a competitor with Danzig) gave Poland a chance to develop maritime interests. Now a major fishing nation, her fleets operate world-wide.

Agriculture and Industry

Before World War 2 Poland was primarily an agricultural country, with 65 per cent of the population dependent upon agriculture, but the post-war industrialization drive has reduced this proportion to about 30 per cent. Poland is still, however, a major supplier of agricultural produce. 65 per cent of the land surface is farmed, about half of this area supporting crops of rye and potatoes.

Poland's industrial development since World War 2 has been striking. Coal, lignite, sulphur, lead, zinc and copper are the main mineral products. Underground salt deposits

Climate

Like other sectors of the European plain, Poland is open to the influence of widely varying air masses, from mild maritime to extreme continental. Winters are long and cold, especially in the east, with two to three months of ice and snow. Nights of sub-zero temperatures often alternate with crisp sunny days. Temperatures climb steeply in spring, and summers are warm with mean temperatures of 15° to 20°C (59° to 68°F) for three or four months and rainfall adequate for cereal crops. Autumn tends to remain pleasantly warm until late October. The Carpathians tend to extremes – warmer than the plains in summer and very much colder in winter.

LOCALITY HEIGHT		JAN	JUL	YR
Suwalki	°C	-5.5	17.1	6.1
165 m	mm	28	96	643
Ostróda	°C	-3.1	17.7	7.3
106 m	mm	33	95	611
Szczecin	°C	-0.7	18.4	8.5
1 m	mm	32	82	546
Białystok	°C	-4.8	17.9	6.9
133 m	mm	28	84	607
Toruń	°C	-2.4	18.5	7.9
46 m	mm	23	99	510
Poznan	°C	-2.0	19.0	8.3
83 m	mm	24	82	514
Warszawa	°C	-2.9	19.3	8.3
110 m	mm	27	96	555
Pulawy	°C	-3.5	19.1	7.9
140 m	mm	24	96	566
Wrocław	°C	-2.7	18.3	8.3
116 m	mm	29	89	584
Krakow	°C	-2.6	19.4	8.6
209 m	mm	28	111	663

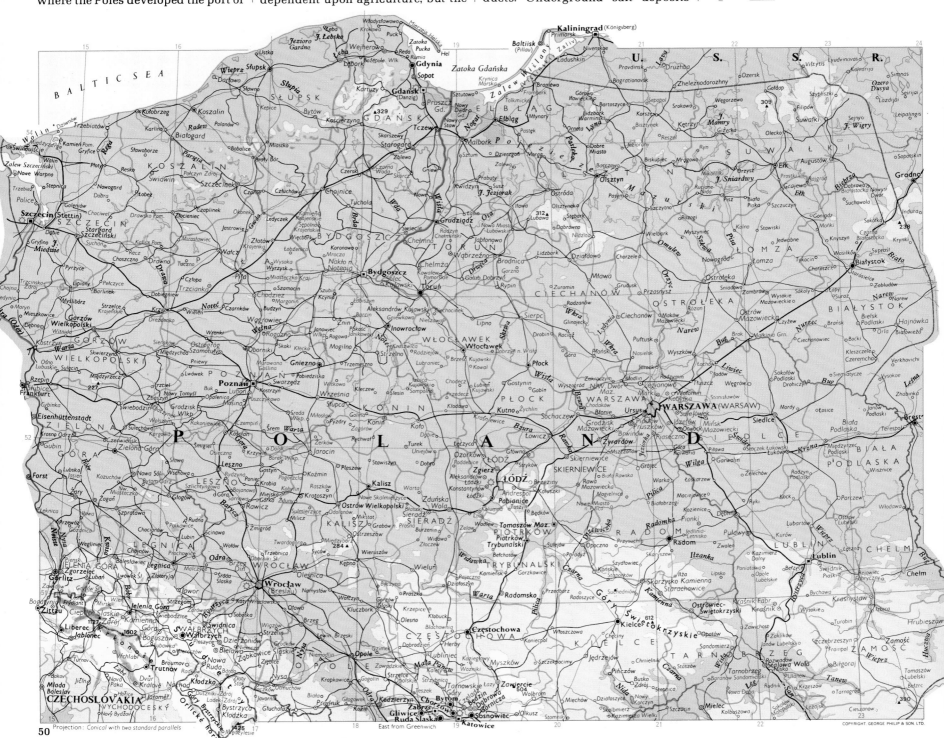

Projection: Conical with two standard parallels

East from Greenwich

COPYRIGHT GEORGE PHILIP & SON LTD

form the basis of important chemical industries. Most of Poland's industrial energy is derived from coal, but oil and natural gas are being developed, and hydro-electric power is being produced in increasing amounts from the Carpathians. Heavy industries include manufacture of steel and cement, and many secondary products.

The historic town of Warsaw, largely destroyed in World War 2, has been faithfully rebuilt. (FS)

ROMANIA

Romania occupies an area of 237,500 km² (91,700 sq miles) between Bulgaria and the USSR, with Yugoslavia and Hungary on the western borders. Romania has a 200 km (125 mile) long coastline on the Black Sea, including the delta of the river Danube. On three sides there are clearly-defined boundaries – the Danube on the south, the coast on the east and the river Prut on the north-east – but on the west the frontier with Hungary crosses the Hungarian plain, cutting across several tributaries of the river Tisza. This area has a mixed population of Romanians and Hungarians, as the western province of Transylvania once belonged to Hungary. Today about 90 per cent of the population is Romanian in a total population of about 22 million. There is also a small German-speaking population. The Romanian language is related to Latin.

Landscape and Agriculture

The landscape of Romania is dominated by a great arc of high fold mountains, the Carpathians, which curve round the plateaux of Transylvania in the heart of the country. Several peaks are over 2,500 m (8,000 ft) high. South and east of the Carpathians are the plains of the lower Danube. The southern arm of the fold mountains is known as the Transylvanian Alps, the legendary home of Count Dracula. Where these meet the Danube, on the border with Yugoslavia, the river has cut a deep gorge – the Iron Gate – whose rapids have now been tamed by the construction of a huge barrage.

There is a great contrast between the fairy-tale landscape of wooded hills in Transylvania and the Carpathians, and the wheat and maize fields of the Danubian lowlands. Romania is still a mainly agricultural country, with an export surplus of cereals, timber, fruits and wine. The climate of the lowland areas reflects continental influences – several months are below freezing point in winter, and summers are hot. In coastal areas annual rainfall is below 450 mm (18 in), rising to over 750 mm (30 in) in the mountains.

Industry

There has been a great drive to develop industries, based originally on the abundant oil and gas resources of areas on the flanks of the Transylvanian Alps. The iron and steel industry, especially the new plant at Galati at the head of the Danubian delta, relies on imported ores from the USSR, but the copper, lead, zinc and aluminium industries use domestic supplies, mainly found in the Bihor Massif in Transylvania.

Bucharest (Bucuresti), the capital, lies between the Danube and the Carpathians. An important industrial centre, manufactures include vehicles, textiles and foodstuffs. (FS)

Climate

Despite remoteness from the Atlantic Ocean, Romania is often engulfed in warm, moist air from the west, especially along the western flanks of the Carpathian arc. The eastern flanks, more open to continental influences, have a harsher climate – colder in winter, hotter in summer, and generally drier. Winters are cold in the lowlands, with one or two months of snow and sub-zero temperatures. In the mountains they are very cold, with temperatures falling to −30°C (−22°F). Summers are correspondingly hot; mean temperatures exceed 20°C (68°F) for two or three months in many localities. Annual rainfall is light (40 to 60 cm, 16 to 24 in) in the lowlands, but exceeds 120 cm (48 in) in the mountains.

LOCALITY HEIGHT		JAN	JUL	YR
Dorohoi	°C	-4.9	20.5	8.4
180 m	mm	26	56	528
Satu Mare	°C	-2.1	21.1	10.4
132 m	mm	43	67	634
Iaşi	°C	-4.1	21.9	9.7
104 m	mm	31	62	509
Tirgu-Sacuesc	°C	-3.7	18.0	7.7
573 m	mm	22	87	524
Sibiu	°C	-4.0	19.9	8.9
407 m	mm	30	82	647
Sulina	°C	-0.3	23.0	11.3
2 m	mm	32	22	357
Caransebes	°C	-0.2	21.3	11.1
230 m	mm	48	74	720
Bucuresti	°C	-3.1	22.8	10.9
92 m	mm	46	53	592
Constanta	°C	-0.3	22.3	11.2
32 m	mm	29	35	379
Calafat	°C	-1.9	23.9	11.9
73 m	mm	45	40	563

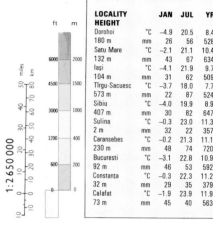

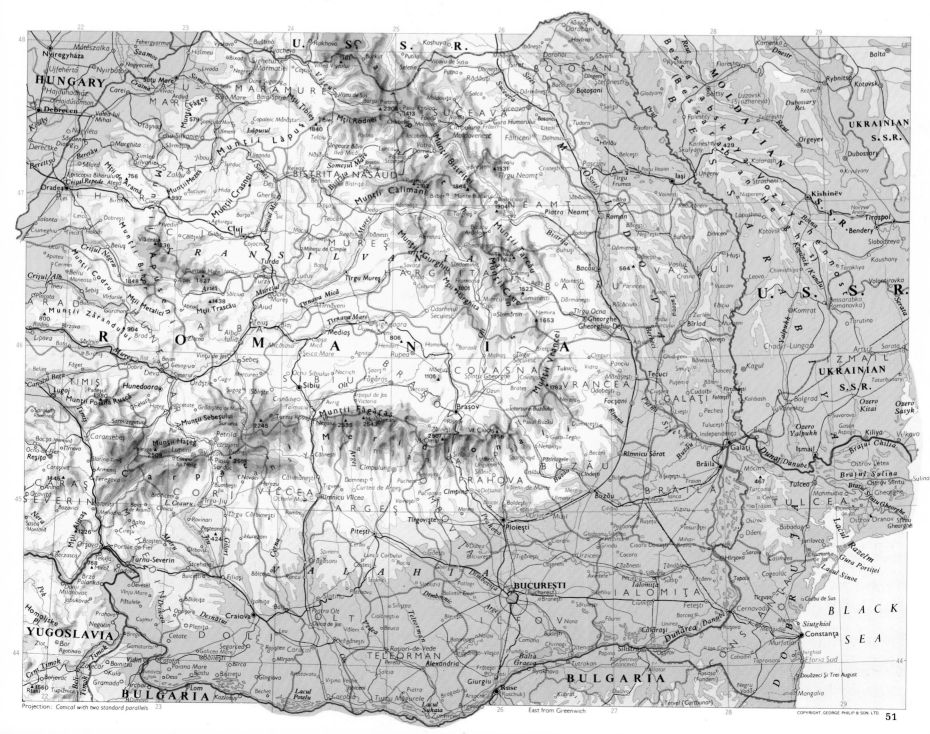

Projection: Conical with two standard parallels

East from Greenwich

IBERIA

The Iberian Peninsula (586,000 km², 226,000 sq miles) is the largest of the three peninsulas jutting southward from Europe into the Mediterranean Sea. Stretching through 10 degrees of latitude it reaches to within 15 km (9.5 miles) of the African coast and extends far enough westward to merit the title of 'the outpost of Europe'. This position is reflected in the fact that early circumnavigations of Africa and the voyages of Columbus to the New World were launched from Iberian shores.

The core of the peninsula is the Meseta plateau, a remnant of an ancient mountain chain with an average height of 600 to 1,000 m (1,900 to 3,280 ft). Huge faulted mountain ranges, such as the Sierras de Gata, de Gredos and de Guadarrama, traverse the plateau obliquely and terminate westward in Portugal as rocky headlands jutting into the Atlantic. Between these upthrust ranges are the wide down-warped basins of Old and New Castile. The plateau is tilted toward the west and its high eastern edge forms a major watershed that overlooks narrow, discontinuous coastal lowlands on the Mediterranean side. The main drainage is through Portugal toward the Atlantic. On its northeastern and southern flanks the Meseta drops abruptly to the Ebro and Guadalquivir (Andalusian) fault troughs; these rise on their outer sides to the lofty mountains of the Pyrenees and the Sierra Nevada respectively.

Politically Iberia includes Spain, the Balearic Islands, Portugal, Andorra, and the Rock of Gibraltar. (RB, MB)

The countryside of Andalusia in the south of Spain.

PORTUGAL

Portugal occupies an oblong coastland (91,641 km², 35,400 sq miles) in the south-west of the Iberian peninsula facing the Atlantic Ocean. Here the Meseta edge has splintered and in part foundered, leaving upstanding mountain ranges particularly in the Serra da Estrêla and its continuation just north of the river Tagus (Tajo) and in the Serra de Monchique.

Agriculture and Fishing

The mild moist airflow from the Atlantic encourages tree growth. Forests reach a height of at least 1,300 m (4,260 ft) in the north and over one-quarter of the country is forested. Pines form the commonest species, especially on the sandy littorals where large plantations provide timber as well as resin and turpentine. Cork oaks abound in the Tagus valley and farther south; Portugal is the world's leading producer of the cork that is derived from their bark. A wide variety of fruits is cultivated, including olives, figs and grapes. Portugal has some of the world's greatest vineyards and is fifth in wine production. Most of the grapes are grown north of the Tagus where the most celebrated speciality is port wine from the Douro valley near the Portuguese-Spanish boundary. The grape juice is transported by boat down the Douro to Vila Nova where it is fortified and stored for export. The lower parts of the Douro and Miño basins produce famous sparkling *vinos verdes* while the vineyards near the Tagus estuary are noted for white table wines and brandy. Algarve with its greater sunshine and aridity specializes more in liqueurs and muscatels.

The Portuguese economy relies heavily on agriculture and fishing, which together employ nearly 40 per cent of the national work force. These industries are mostly undercapitalized and rather primitive, although they provide valuable exports. In the rainy north the pressure of overpopulation causes fragmented and tiny holdings (*minifundia*); in the drier south large holdings (*latifundia*) tend to create monoculture with below-average yields and seasonal unemployment. Recently there has been some investment in irrigation.

The chief general crops are food cereals and vegetables, including a wide variety of beans which form a frequent and favourite item of the Portuguese diet. Maize and rye predominate in the north, and wheat, barley and oats in the south. Of the many farm animals the pig deserves special mention as the forager of the heavy yield of acorns from the cork and evergreen oaks.

The long coastline provides an important supplementary source of livelihood and of foreign tourist currency. The shallow lagoons yield shellfish, especially oysters; the coastal waters supply sardines, anchovy and tunny; the deep-sea fisheries, long frequented by Portuguese sailors, bring hake, mackerel, halibut and, above all, cod.

Industry

Much Portuguese industry is concerned with the products of farm, fishing and forestry but the manufacture of textiles and ceramics is also widespread. Modern engineering associated with a complete iron and steel plant has been established at Seixal near Lisbon (Lisboa). There is some small-scale mining for copper ores and wolfram, one of the problems being a relative shortage of power resources. A small quantity of poor quality coal is mined annually, and is supplemented with foreign imports. Great efforts have been made to develop hydroelectric stations.

Portugal has two conurbations with over 1 million inhabitants. Lisbon, the capital, is the chief centre of the country's financial, commercial and industrial concerns and has a fine sheltered harbour in the large Tagus estuary. Oporto, the main centre for the densely-populated north, has an ocean outport in Leixoes. During recent decades tourism and rapid residential growth have transformed the subtropical coastline of the Algarve, and have led to a substantial increase in its population. (RB, MB)

The cork oak's bark provides cork.

PORTUGAL

BAY OF BISCAY

ATLANTIC OCEAN

SPAIN

MEDITERRANEAN SEA

Strait of Gibraltar

MOROCCO

Projection: Conical with two standard parallels

West from Greenwich

COPYRIGHT. GEORGE PHILIP & SON, LTD.

Climate

Facing the Atlantic Ocean in warm-temperate latitudes, Portugal has a warm maritime climate. Winters are mild and damp, with most of the precipitation between November and March. Summers are very warm, especially in the south where mean July temperatures generally exceed 20°C (68°F). Spain's high relief gives climatic variety. The north, strongly maritime, is mild and damp, with annual rainfall exceeding 100 cm (40 in) at the eastern and western corners. South and east coasts are hotter and drier, with mean January temperatures above 25°C (77°F). The plateau is generally hot and arid in summer, cool and moist in winter, with local climatic variations in the basins and valleys.

LOCALITY HEIGHT		JAN	JUL	YR
Gijón	°C	9.5	19.5	14.1
29 m	mm	114	42	1034
Finisterre	°C	10.1	18.7	14.3
146 m	mm	96	19	843
Valladolid	°C	3.9	21.5	12.1
695 m	mm	37	14	404
Porto	°C	8.9	19.7	14.5
95 m	mm	159	20	1151
Toledo	°C	5.8	26.1	15.0
539 m	mm	35	9	383
Castelo Branco	°C	7.9	24.7	15.7
390 m	mm	123	5	828
Badajoz	°C	8.7	25.9	16.9
203 m	mm	61	3	491
Lisboa	°C	10.9	22.2	16.5
77 m	mm	111	3	708
Sevilla	°C	10.3	28.0	18.8
9 m	mm	66	1	564
Gibraltar	°C	12.5	23.8	17.8
27 m	mm	109	1	863

SPAIN

A global position between coastal north-west Europe and Africa, and between the Mediterranean countries of the Old World and the Americas, made Spain (504,750 km², 195,000 sq miles) a great crossroads. Yet the lofty Pyrenean barrier in the north weakened land contacts with the rest of Europe, while the narrow Strait of Gibraltar in the south encouraged African contacts, lending truth to the cliché that 'Africa begins at the Pyrenees'.

Landscape

The chief feature of Spain is the vast central plateau, the Meseta, which tilts gently towards Portugal. A harsh and often barren area, the plateau is crossed by the Central Sierras, a mountain chain running north-west to south-east. This central divide separates two mountain basins: Old Castile in the north and New Castile in the south.

On the north-eastern and southern edges of the Meseta are large triangular lowlands. That on the north drains to the Ebro and that in the south to the Guadalquivir, the largest river wholly in Spain. Beyond the Ebro trough the land rises to the Pyrenees, which form the Franco-Spanish border, and continue westward in the Cantabrian Mountains. Similarly, the Mediterranean flank of Andalusia rises to a lofty cordillera that culminates in the snowy Sierra Nevada (3,478 m, 11,400 ft). The Mediterranean side of the Meseta has summits of about 2,000 metres (6,560 ft) and drops sharply to narrow discontinuous coastal plains.

Spain has perhaps the widest range of climates of any country in western Europe. The most striking contrast is between the humid north and north-west and the arid rest of the country. Large areas of the country are barren or steppeland, and one-fifth is covered by *matorral*, a mediterranean scrub like the French maquis. A large part of the farmland is used for pastoral purposes but there are rich soils in some of the major river valleys, such as the Ebro and the Guadalquivir, and areas of very productive agriculture, especially where there are *huertas* (irrigated market gardens) and *vegas* (irrigated orchards).

Vegetation

Spain is unique in Europe for the quantity and variety of her plant species, a reflection of varied local environments, a position as a land bridge between Africa and Europe and a long colonial history when many foreign plants were introduced. Generally, moisture-loving plants flourish north of the Central

Sierras and drought-enduring species south of them.

The vegetation falls into three broad categories, forest, matorral and steppe. Forests (10 per cent of the land surface) are today mainly confined to the rainier north and north-west with beech and deciduous oak common. Towards the drier south and east, Mediterranean pines and evergreen oaks take over, and forests resemble open parkland. Widespread clearance for fuel and cultivation and grazing by sheep, goats and cattle have turned large areas into matorral or shrub. This low bush growth, often of aromatic evergreen plants, may be dominated over large tracts by one species: thus *romillares* consist predominantly of rosemary, *tomillares* of thyme, *retamales* of broom. Where soils are thin and drought prevalent, matorral gives place to steppe, mainly of alfalfa and esparto grasses. This clothes considerable areas of La Mancha and the Ebro trough.

Agriculture

Despite the problems of aridity and poor soils, agriculture occupies nearly one-third of the national work force. Irregular river regimes and deeply incised valleys make irrigation difficult and expensive and, on the higher and drier regions, tracts favourable for cultivation are often isolated by expanses of low fertility where only a meagre livelihood can be wrested from the soil. There are, too, problems connected with the size of farms. In semi-arid Spain large estates (*latifundia*) abound with much seasonal employment or share-cropping, while in the rainy north-west and north excessive fragmentation of small farms (*minifundia*) has proved uneconomic.

It is against this picture of difficulties that the great progress made since 1939 by the *Instituto Nacional de Colonización* (INC) must be viewed. The institute, by means of irrigation, cooperative farming schemes, concentration of landholdings, agricultural credit schemes and technical training has re-settled over one-quarter of the land needing reorganization and reclamation. But,

Andorra

Tourism is a major source of income in this tiny medieval principality.

Andorra, a tiny country (450 km², 174 sq miles) perched at the eastern end of the high central Pyrenees, consists mainly of six valleys (the Valls) that drain to the river Valira. The population totals about 30,000, of whom one-third are native born. The rights of the seigneurie or co-principality have been shared since 1278 between the Spanish bishop of Urgel and the French Comte de Foix. The latter's lordship rights passed to the French government, now represented by the prefect of the adjoining département of the Eastern Pyrenees. The Andorrans pay annually in turn a small sum to the Bishop and the Prefect; and each co-prince is represented in their Council by a *viguier*, but in most other respects the co-principality governs itself.

Physically the country consists of deep glaciated valleys lying at altitudes of 1,000 to 2,900 m (3,280 to 9,500 ft). On the north a lofty watershed forms

the frontier with France and is crossed by a road over the Envalira Pass (2,400 m, 7,870 ft); to the south the land falls away down the Valira valley to the Segre valley in Spain, again followed by the same vital highway. In the colder months the Envalira Pass often becomes snowbound and then land communications are with Spain only. The climate is severe in winter and pleasantly cool in summer when, because the valleys lie on a rain-shadow, slopes above 1,400 m (4,600 ft) often suffer from drought and need irrigation.

Andorra has five main sources of income: stock-rearing and agriculture, especially tobacco; tourism; the sale of duty-free goods and of postage stamps; the sale of water and hydro-electricity to Catalonia; and fees from radio transmission services. Probably two million visitors come to see this rare survival of a medieval principality every year. (RB, MB)

generally, crop yields are still low and agricultural techniques backward.

Stock-rearing A large part of the farmland is used solely or partly for pastoral purposes, which are of great economic importance. Spain has about 20 million sheep, mainly of the native merino type which produces a fine fleece. The Mesta, an

old confederation of sheep owners, controls the seasonal migrations on to the summer pastures on the high sierras. Areas too rocky and steep for sheep are given over to goats while cattle, apart from working oxen, are more or less restricted to regions with ample grass and water, for example the north and north-west. Pigs are bred in the cattle districts of the north, and are also kept to forage the acorns in the large tracts of evergreen oaks in the south. Fighting bulls are bred on the marshes (*marismas*) at the mouth of the Guadalquivir. Many working animals are kept.

Arable Crops The typical arable crops are the classical Mediterranean trio of wheat, olive and vine, with maize important in rainier districts and vegetables and citrus fruits where there is irrigation water. Wheat occupies one-third of the cropland and is usually followed in rotation by leguminous pulses or fallow, grazed and so manured by sheep. In dry areas barley, oats and rye, grown for fodder, replace wheat and in the wetter north maize dominates both for grain and feed. Rice is harvested in Murcia, Valencia and the Ebro valley and Spain follows Italy for rice production in Europe.

The Costa Brava, Spain, one of the most popular holiday areas in Europe.

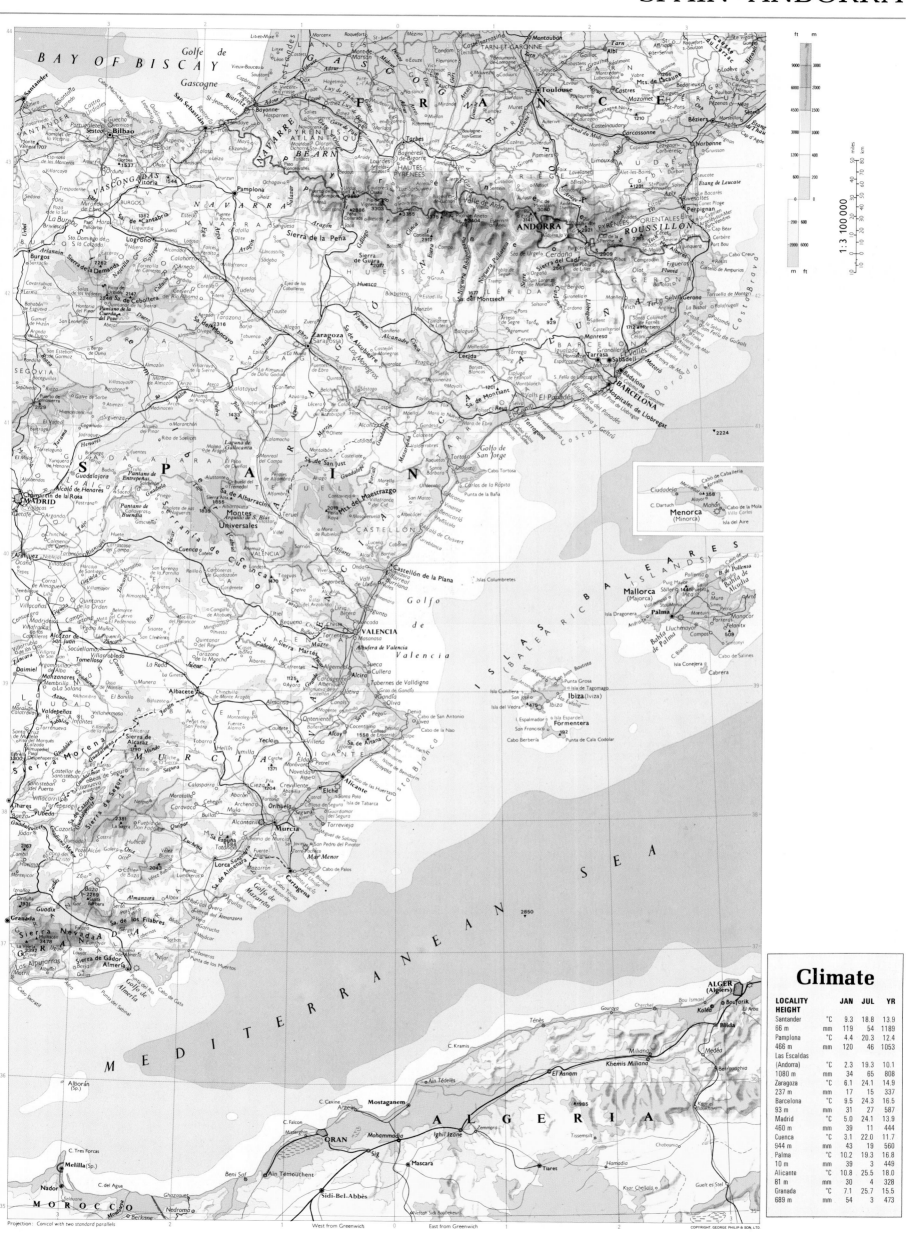

1 : 3 100 000

Climate

LOCALITY HEIGHT		JAN	JUL	YR
Santander	°C	9.3	18.8	13.9
66 m	mm	119	54	1189
Pamplona	°C	4.4	20.3	12.4
466 m	mm	120	46	1053
Las Escaldas (Andorra)	°C	2.3	19.3	10.1
1080 m	mm	34	65	808
Zaragoza	°C	6.1	24.1	14.9
237 m	mm	17	15	337
Barcelona	°C	9.5	24.3	16.5
93 m	mm	31	27	587
Madrid	°C	5.0	24.1	13.9
460 m	mm	39	11	444
Cuenca	°C	3.1	22.0	11.7
944 m	mm	43	19	560
Palma	°C	10.2	19.3	16.8
10 m	mm	39	3	449
Alicante	°C	10.8	25.5	18.0
81 m	mm	30	4	328
Granada	°C	7.1	25.7	15.5
689 m	mm	54	3	473

Projection : Conical with two standard parallels

West from Greenwich   East from Greenwich

COPYRIGHT GEORGE PHILIP & SON, LTD.

Cordoba, the capital of Moslem Spain, was once Europe's largest city.

The port of Seville was a base for Spanish exploration of the New World.

Fruit-growing Fruits occupy a high and honoured place in Spain's agricultural economy. The olive crop, mainly from large estates in Andalusia, makes Spain the world's chief producer of olive oil. Vines cover about one-tenth of the cultivated land and only Italy and France exceed the Spanish output of wine. Sherry (from Jérez) is renowned and there are other fine wines such as the vintages of Rioja. For citrus fruit Spain easily outstrips other European producers, the bulk of the crop being Seville oranges destined largely for Britain for making marmalade. Large quantities of other fruits, especially apricots and peaches, are grown with vegetables as a ground crop in irrigated market gardens and orchards.

Some of the huertas are devoted to industrial crops such as cotton, hemp, flax and sugar beet, while most richer soils in Andalusia are entirely given over to cotton. The poorer steppes yield esparto for paper making.

Maps of modern Spain clearly indicate the tremendous progress made recently in water reservation and river regulation on all the major Spanish rivers. Large new reservoirs have been constructed on the Miño, Duero, Tajo, Guadiana, Guadalquivir and other main rivers as well as numerous dams on the lesser watercourses. The *Instituto Nacional de Colonización* (INC), which directs this work, aims at bringing 70,000 hectares (173,000 acres) a year under irrigation as well as undertaking all kinds of land reclamation, drainage, re-afforestation, settlement schemes and farm cooperative planning.

Mining and Industry

Spain is lamentably short of her own supplies of solid and liquid fuels and in an average year produces only small quantities of poor-quality coal (mainly from Asturias at Oviedo near Gijón) and some lignite from a field south of Barcelona. Small deposits of petroleum found near Burgos and at the mouth of the Ebro have not yet proved economic to develop. Some use is made of nuclear power but the main developments have been in hydro-electricity, especially in Catalonia and the northern coastlands.

In contrast to fossil fuels workable mineral ores are widespread. High-quality iron ores, with substantial reserves, occur in Vizcaya, Santander and Granada. Bilbao, the chief ore-exporting port, has an important integrated iron and steel plant; so have Oviedo, Gijón and several other towns on the north coast, and smaller enterprises are found at Sagunto and Zaragoza. Many localities yield non-ferrous ores in sufficient quantity to broaden the base of Spain's metallurgical industries. The chief workings are for copper at Rio Tinto, lead and silver at Linares and Peñarroya, and mercury at Almadén; in addition, manganese, titanium and sulphur are produced in small quantities and considerable amounts of potassium salts come from Catalonia.

But the major Spanish manufacturing industries are based on agriculture rather than minerals. Textiles, including cotton, wool, silk, jute and linen lead the industrial sector. Barcelona, Catalonia's great industrial, financial and commercial centre, is surrounded by a ring of satellite textile towns, some of which specialize in spinning, as at Manresa and Ribas, and others in weaving, as at Sabadell and Granollers. Cotton fabrics form the chief single product and supply a wide market especially at home and in Latin America. However, Barcelona has a wide variety of light industries, including engineering, and the heavy metallurgical sectors are located mainly at Bilbao and other north coast cities. Madrid has become an important centre for consumer goods, particularly electric appliances.

Food processing industries are concentrated in the north-east, the chief being flour-milling, sugar-refining and oil-pressing. Fish-canning and processing are widespread in the coastal towns and Spain is fortunate in having a long coastline on the Atlantic where the Galicians and Basques are skilled fishermen.

The Growth of Tourism

The relative absence of closely-packed industrial plants and industrial pollution, the historical attractions of the relics of a long history dating from the Greeks and Arabs, and the dry warm sunny climate of the Mediterranean south and east have fostered tourism, the greatest of all Spain's non-agricultural industries. In recent years over 20 million tourists have visited Spain annually and the Costa Brava and Costa del Sol are internationally famous. Equally significant is the great increase in the number of those who come to live permanently or for most of the year in these picturesque coastlands with warm winters and subtropical vegetation.

Communications

The prime communication routes in Spain focus on Madrid, which has radial links to the peripheral cities. First-class highways radiate to the main ports and good motor roads connect all the major towns but minor roads are not macadamised and for so large a country relatively few motor cars are registered. Railways likewise converge on Madrid with minor networks round the regional capitals and main ports. The tracks are not of standard European gauge, about 75 per cent being broad gauge and the remainder narrow. The chief land communications with France run at either end of the Pyrenees and are supplemented by several high-level transmontane rail and road routes. Air travel focusses on Madrid airport and, particularly for tourism, on 40 other civil airports, many of them with busy international services. The large coastal and ocean-going traffic involves 230 Spanish ports, but the bulk of the overseas trade passes through the modernized harbours, in particular Bilbao, Barcelona, Cartagena, Cádiz and Gijón.

Population and Urbanization

The population of Spain is densest on the coastlands and lowlands around the Meseta. Madrid, the capital, in the heart of the tableland, forms a grand exception. Madrid stands on the small Manzanares river, a tributary of the Tagus, and has a long history dating from early Roman times. The Moors first provided it with clean drinking water and Philip II made it the seat of the national government in 1561. A fine metropolis, it has flourished during the decades since the Civil War (1936–9) and now accommodates about one-tenth of the total population of continental Spain. The second Spanish city, Barcelona, is a great commercial and industrial centre and in all ways the core of Catalonia.

The other major cities include Bilbao, the chief urban area of the north coast, long noted for its metallurgy, Cádiz, the naval centre, Seville (Sevilla), the river port and regional capital of Andalusia, Valencia and Murcia, the largest of the Mediterranean huerta cities, Zaragoza, the expanding centre for the

Oranges are a major crop in Spain.

Ebro lowland, noted for food-processing and engineering, and Málaga, the fast-growing nucleus of the Costa del Sol. Toledo, the national capital before Madrid, ranks far below these conurbations in size, but, protected as a national monument, is the finest medieval city that survives almost intact from the golden age of Spain. (RB, MB)

GIBRALTAR

Local rock carvings demonstrate that Gibraltar has been inhabited since Neolithic times. Greeks and Romans also settled here but the first sure date for colonization is AD 711 when Tariq ibn Zaid, a Berber chieftain, occupied it. Although occupied by Spaniards for a short while in the fourteenth century, it remained Moorish until 1462. British naval forces captured it in 1704 and it was formally recognized as a British possession at the Treaty of Utrecht in 1713. In spite of long sieges and assaults it has remained British ever since.

Gibraltar, an outpost of Britain on the southern tip of Spain.

The Rock, as it is popularly known, guards the north-eastern end of the Strait of Gibraltar and lies directly opposite the very similar peninsula of Ceuta, a Spanish enclave in Morocco. It became a naval dockyard and a base for reconnaissance aircraft. The Rock (area 6.5 km², 2.5 sq miles) consists largely of a narrow ridge thrusting south for 7 km (4.4 miles) along the eastern side of Algeciras Bay, rising to 426 m (1,400 ft) at Europa Point. It shelters a spacious anchorage and harbour from east winds with long artificial breakwaters and quays constructed of stone tunnelled from the ridge. On the north there is a low, flat sandy plain used for an airport. Shrubs, partly wild olives, clothe the steeper slopes and provide shelter for the only wild colony of Barbary apes in Europe. Considerable areas of the summit are used as catchments for drinking water, supplemented by diesel-powered seawater distillation.

Population and Industry

Houses cover the slope facing the harbour and spread around two flattish beaches on the south, leaving the precipitous eastern slopes uninhabited except near Catalan Bay. The built-up area (population about 30,000) has an excellent road network but the topography prohibits cultivation and the Gibraltarians rely on the port, the ship-repairing yards, the military and air bases, and on tourism for their livelihood. About 2,400 merchant ships and numerous pleasure craft call at Gibraltar annually and the low import duties, excellent tourist facilities and almost rainless summers make it a popular shopping and holiday centre.

In June 1969, following a long dispute with Spain, and a referendum that showed a wish to remain British, Spain closed the frontier to a large workforce that commuted daily

to work in Gibraltar. Now access to the peninsula is by sea and air only and workers with permits come mainly from non-Spanish territories on a quota system.

Food is brought in fresh daily by ferry from Tangier, with which there are frequent air services. The Gibraltarians are of British, Spanish, Maltese, Portuguese and Genoese descent and are bilingual in Spanish and English. (RB, MB)

BALEARIC ISLANDS

The Islas Baleares group contains five larger islands (Majorca, Minorca, Ibiza, Formentera, Cabrera) and eleven rocky islets, together covering 5,014 km² (1,936 sq miles) and spread over 350 km (218 miles).

Majorca (Mallorca), by far the largest island, has limestone ridges on the north-west and south-east with a plain covered with flat-bedded, very fertile marine sediments between them. Minorca (Menorca), the second-largest island, has limestone plains and small outcrops of crystalline rocks, but nowhere rises above 358 m (1,175 ft).

The typical sunny Mediterranean climate supports an equally typical vegetation. Shrub-growth (*matorral* or *garrigue*) still clothes the highest areas and is grazed by sheep and goats. The rainier upper slopes of the hills have been terraced for olives, carobs and vines while the lower slopes are under market garden crops. The level lowlands are planted with wheat and barley, usually in rotation with beans. Generally, almonds, apricots and carobs are more important here than vines and citrus fruits. The rural economy is essentially peasant with a high degree of self-sufficiency.

Puerto Soller on Majorca, the largest island of the Balearic group.

Population and Industry

Like most Mediterranean islands the Balearics were settled early. Archaeological remains exist from 1,000 BC (Bronze Age) to the Roman period and include boat-shaped burial mounds (*navetas* or *naus*) and conical stone towers (*talayots*) thought to be refuges from piratical raiding parties. Ibiza town and Port Mahon were originally settled from Carthage. During recent times the islands were repeatedly occupied by the British, French and Spanish and remained finally a province of Spain. Port Mahon has fine buildings representing all these changes of ownership. Each different occupation has left its mark; the Balearics in many ways epitomize Mediterranean insular history.

Today the population lives mainly either in agricultural villages some way inland or in small ports around the coast. Power resources and raw materials for manufacture are scarce apart from agricultural products. Textile manufacture (wool and cotton) and food processing are the only widespread factory occupations. Handicrafts flourish in response to a large tourist market and tourism dominates the economy.

Palma, the capital of Majorca and of the province, continues to grow rapidly. It has a fine harbour with regular sailings to Barcelona, Alicante and Valencia for passengers and the export of Balearic surpluses of almonds, grain, textiles and vegetables. It is also a regular port of call for Mediterranean cruise ships and its airport, one of the busiest in Spain, deals with well over one million visitors annually. Manacor, the only other large centre on Majorca, is an agricultural market town near limestone caves and subterranean lakes that attract numerous tourists. Port Mahon is the capital of Minorca, and Ibiza the capital of that small island. (RB, MB)

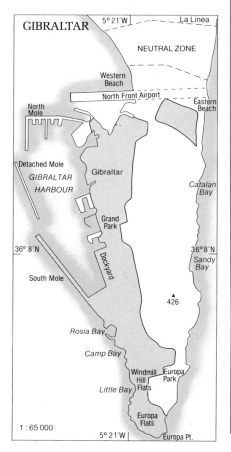

GIBRALTAR

5° 21'W — La Linea

NEUTRAL ZONE

Western Beach

North Front Airport

North Mole

Eastern Beach

Detached Mole — Gibraltar

GIBRALTAR HARBOUR

Catalan Bay

Grand Park

36° 8'N

Dockyard

36° 8'N — Sandy Bay

South Mole

▲ 426

Rosia Bay

Camp Bay

Windmill Hill — Europa Park

Little Bay — Flats

Europa Flats

1 : 65 000

5° 21'W — Europa Pt.

ITALY AND THE BALKANS

The Italian and Balkan peninsulas extend southward into the Mediterranean Sea, together forming the southern periphery of central Europe. In the north of Italy lies the Plain of Lombardy, drained by the river Po and its tributaries: towering above are the ranges of alpine fold mountains – southern outliers of the European Alps – that mark the boundary between Italy and neighbouring France, Switzerland and Austria. A further range of alpine mountains – the Apennines – runs through peninsular Italy and continues into Sicily.

The Balkan Peninsula, between the Adriatic and Black Seas, includes Yugoslavia, Albania, Greece and Bulgaria.

The western Balkans are made up of alpine fold mountains, running north-west to south-east behind the western coasts – the Dinaric Alps of Yugoslavia and the Pindus Mountains (Pindos Oros) of Greece. The Balkan Mountains of Bulgaria represent the southern extension of the great arc of alpine mountains which loop round the lower basin of the Danube. Between them and the Dinaric Alps is a stable, crystalline block, the Rhodopi Massif. (FS)

YUGOSLAVIA

The Socialist Federal Republic of Yugoslavia covers an area of 255,804 km² (98,766 sq miles) but has a population of only 22 million. Few countries of comparable size contain such a diversity of geographical environments and ways of life.

Landscape

There are five natural regions. In the north-west the alpine Republic of Slovenia adjoins Austria and Italy. The mountains continue the main alpine system of central Europe, and include Yugoslavia's highest peak, Triglav (2,863 m, 9,390 ft) in the Julian Alps. The Dinaric region extends behind the coast from Slovenia to Albania; parallel ridges of bare limestone mountains, separated by narrow, marshy valleys, make a formidable barrier between the sea and the northern plains. The

Climate

When western climatic influences are strong in winter over Yugoslavia and the Balkans, they bring rain and snow – often very heavy in the mountains. Bitterly cold air drawn in from the north spreads continental winter conditions with sub-zero temperatures over all but a narrow coastal strip of Yugoslavia, and cold air from the steppes chills north-eastern Greece. Summers by contrast are warm-to-hot and generally dry over the coasts and lowlands; only the higher ground north of the Adriatic has considerable summer rainfall. Mean July temperatures reach 25°C (77°F) and above in most coastal regions, 15° to 25°C (59° to 77°F) in the uplands and mountains.

LOCALITY HEIGHT		JAN	JUL	YR
Zagreb	°C	0.1	22.1	11.7
157 m	mm	55	79	865
Trieste	°C	4.6	23.7	14.3
11 m	mm	68	92	1023
Torino	°C	1.1	24.1	12.9
238 m	mm	23	72	845
Pleven	°C	-1.9	23.3	11.7
109 m	mm	35	82	595
Napoli	°C	8.0	23.6	15.7
110 m	mm	116	19	915
Kerkira	°C	9.9	25.3	17.1
25 m	mm	196	4	1352
Cagliari	°C	10.5	25.5	17.5
7 m	mm	50	1	451
Mitilini	°C	9.9	27.1	17.7
2 m	mm	131	3	739
Messina	°C	11.4	26.0	18.3
54 m	mm	149	20	902
Valletta	°C	12.3	25.5	18.7
70 m	mm	90	0	519

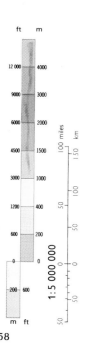

MALTA
1:1 000 000

S.E. EUROPE
POLITICAL
1:25 000 000
Projection: Conical with two standard parallels

Adriatic coast, with its tourist-resort islands and Mediterranean climate, forms a third region. The Balkan mountains are a fourth, lying between Bulgaria and Albania and covering parts of the Republics of Bosnia, Serbia and Macedonia; this is a well-wooded region of ancient, rounded crystalline rocks. The Pannonian lowlands in the north form the fifth region, continuous with the central European plains and drained by the Danube and its tributaries. This is the country's most fertile region, with rich loess and alluvial soils giving good farmland.

Malta

The former British colony of Malta, now an independent, non-aligned republic within the Commonwealth, lies in the centre of the Mediterranean, roughly half way between Gibraltar and Suez. Its strategic importance arises from its position, and from its possession of magnificent natural harbours – notable among them Grand Harbour and Marsamxett; these lie on either side of the rocky peninsula on which the capital, Valletta, stands.

Malta and the neighbouring islands of Comino and Gozo have few natural resources (apart from splendid building stone), and only limited possibilities for agriculture. Yet they constitute

Fort St Elmo, Valletta, between Grand and Marsamxett harbours.

one of the world's most densely populated states, with 310,000 people on their 320 km^2 (124 sq miles) of sun-baked limestone. From the Napo-

leonic period until after World War 2, the Maltese economy depended upon the existence of British military bases. Before the last garrison left in 1979 Malta had already obtained independence, and was developing industries that would replace the income from the military and naval connections. Year-round tourism, taking advantage of the mild Mediterranean winters and the hot, dry summers, brings over 360,000 visitors annually, of whom two-thirds are British. The skill of the dockyard workers is world-famous, and with help from overseas, new facilities, such as the Red China Dock, are being built. (FS)

EUROPE SOUTH-EAST

History and Peoples

Yugoslavia was created after World War 1 from territories which had formerly belonged to the Turkish and Austro-Hungarian Empires. After World War 2, a federation was created under the rule of the Communist Party. Each of the six republics – Bosnia, Hercegovina, Croatia, Macedonia, Montenegro, Serbia and Slovenia – enjoys some degree of internal self-government, and each represents one of the main south Slav ethnic groups. In addition there are two autonomous provinces – Kosovo, which is mainly inhabited by Albanian speakers, and Vojvodina, in which the population includes large minorities of Hungarians, Romanians and other nationalities. The Serbs, Macedonians and Montenegrins have a religious tradition based on the Orthodox Church, while the Croats and Slovenes are Roman Catholic. In Bosnia and Kosovo there are strong Moslem influences. This cultural variety inhibits national unity.

Agriculture and Industry

Yugoslavia's main agricultural area is the northern lowlands. The continental climate, with hot summers, cold winters and early summer rainfall, provides good crops of wheat, maize, sunflower seeds, sugar beet, grapes and tobacco; most of the farms are privately owned. The major cities of Belgrade and Zagreb are in this area, which is by far the most heavily populated. High-quality wines for export are produced in the north, along the Adriatic coast, and in the Balkan region as well. Forest industries provide timber, paper and pulp, and the Balkan mountains are well endowed with coal and non-ferrous metal ores including lead, copper, zinc and silver.

Since World War 2 Yugoslavia has made great progress in industrialization. Before the War about 75 per cent of Yugoslavs lived by peasant agriculture; now only 35 per cent are farmers, and modern methods (involving some collectives and co-operatives) have vastly increased farm output. The main industries are metal-working, chemicals, shipbuilding, manufacture of electrical goods, food processing and wine making. Curiously, the southern areas where the important minerals occur are the least industrially developed. This is partly due to history; the north began to industrialize during the nineteenth century as part of the Austro-Hungarian Empire, while the south remained dormant under Turkish rule. But the mountains, too, have provided formidable transport and communication problems that have helped to keep the south underdeveloped. (FS)

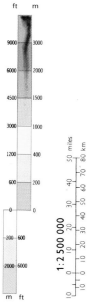

Projection: Conical with two standard parallels

East from Greenwich

Sofia, the capital of Bulgaria.

BULGARIA

The Bulgarians won their independence from the Turkish Empire during the nineteenth century, with the help of Russia. As a Slavonic-speaking people they have strong ties with Russian culture, and in the period since World War 2 they have also developed close political links with the USSR.

About one half of the 8.8 million inhabitants depend on agriculture for their income. The best land occurs in two lowland areas – the Danubian lowlands of the north, where wheat, barley and maize are the chief crops, and the warmer central valley of the river Maritsa, where grain, cotton, rice, tobacco, fruits and vines are grown.

Separating the two lowland areas are the Balkan mountains (known locally as the Stara Planina), which rise to heights of over 2,135 m (7,000 ft). In the south-facing valleys overlooking the Maritsa plains, plums, vines and tobacco are grown. A particular feature of this area is the rose fields of Kazanluk, from which attar of roses is exported world-wide to the cosmetics industry.

South and west of the Maritsa valley are the highly mineraliferous Rhodopi mountains, containing lead, zinc and copper ores. There are also rich mineral veins of both iron and non-ferrous metals in the Stara Planina, north of the capital city, Sofia, and a small coalfield.

Industry is still limited by European standards, but Bulgaria exports large amounts of semi-processed metals, mostly to the USSR and Eastern Europe. Sofia is the chief industrial city, with metal working, and chemical, textile and food-processing industries nearby. (FS)

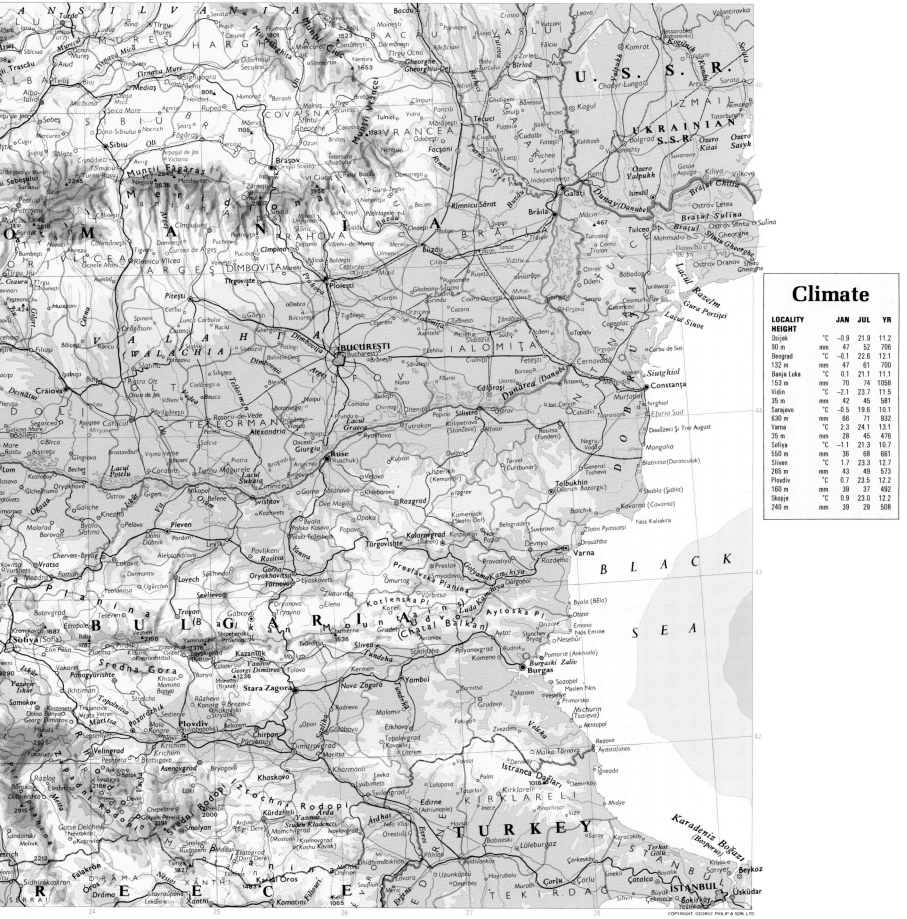

Climate

LOCALITY HEIGHT		JAN	JUL	YR
Osijek	°C	-0.9	21.9	11.2
90 m	mm	47	52	706
Beograd	°C	-0.1	22.6	12.1
132 m	mm	47	61	700
Banja Luka	°C	0.1	21.1	11.1
153 m	mm	70	74	1058
Vidin	°C	-2.1	23.7	11.5
35 m	mm	42	45	581
Sarajevo	°C	-0.5	19.6	10.1
630 m	mm	66	71	932
Varna	°C	2.3	24.1	13.1
35 m	mm	28	45	476
Sofiya	°C	-1.1	21.3	10.7
550 m	mm	36	68	661
Sliven	°C	1.7	23.3	12.7
265 m	mm	43	49	573
Plovdiv	°C	0.7	23.5	12.2
160 m	mm	39	37	492
Skopje	°C	0.9	23.0	12.2
240 m	mm	39	29	508

Climate

The Italian peninsula receives climatic influences from all directions. Winter depressions bring moist air from the Atlantic, causing heavy rain and snowfall, especially in the mountains. January mean temperatures range from 5° to 10°C (41° to 50°F) along the Mediterranean coast, falling to freezing point and below in the Apennines, and especially in the Alps, where cold northern influences are often felt. Only the extreme south of Sicily and Sardinia remain warm in winter. Summers are warm and dry in the north, hot and arid under African influences in the south: July means exceed 15°C (59°F) over all but the highest ground, reaching 25°C (77°F) and above in Southern Italy.

LOCALITY HEIGHT		JAN	JUL	YR
Bolzano	°C	0.1	22.0	12.0
271 m	mm	18	100	781
Ljubljana	°C	-0.8	20.3	10.0
299 m	mm	88	11.3	1383
Milano	°C	2.1	24.3	13.7
121 m	mm	44	64	1017
Venezia	°C	3.0	23.1	13.5
1 m	mm	37	52	770
Rijeka	°C	5.9	23.5	14.3
104 m	mm	132	82	1548
Genova	°C	7.8	15.7	15.7
21 m	mm	79	40	1270
San Remo	°C	10.1	23.7	16.6
9 m	mm	48	20	843
Ancona	°C	5.0	23.6	14.7
105 m	mm	72	34	766
L'Aquila	°C	2.1	21.3	11.9
735 m	mm	86	29	875
Roma	°C	7.8	25.0	16.1
17 m	mm	71	15	744

Projection: Conical with two standard parallels

1:2 500 000

East from Greenwich

ITALY

In 1800, present-day Italy was made up of several political units, including the Papal States, and a substantial part of the north-east was occupied by Austria. The struggle for unification began early in the century, but little progress was made until an alliance between France and Piedmont (then part of the Kingdom of Sardinia) drove Austria from Lombardy in 1859. Tuscany, Parma and Modena joined Piedmont-Lombardy in 1860, and the Papal States, Sicily, Naples (including most of the southern peninsula) and Romagna were brought into the alliance. King Victor Emmanuel II was proclaimed ruler of a united Italy in Turin in the following year. Venetia was acquired from Austria in 1866, and Rome was finally annexed in 1871. Since that time Italy has been a single state — a kingdom until 1946 and then a republic. Both Sicily and Sardinia are included within the state.

Population and Diversity

Since unification the population has doubled, and is now over 56 million. Almost all are Italian speakers; exceptions include small minorities of Austrians and Yugoslavs.

Rapid growth of population, in a poor country attempting to develop its resources, forced millions of Italians to emigrate during the first quarter of the twentieth century. Italy's African Empire enabled some Italians to settle overseas but did not substantially relieve the population pressure. Now there are immigrant Italians to be found on all the inhabited continents. Particularly large numbers settled in the USA, South America, Australia and North Africa. More recently large numbers of Italians have moved for similar reasons into northern Europe.

Almost all Italians are brought up in the official religion of the State, Roman Catholicism, and Catholic religious teaching is compulsory in the schools.

Despite more than a century of common language, religion and cultural traditions, great differences remain in the ways of life of people in different parts of Italy. These can partly be explained in terms of geography. The long, narrow boot-shaped peninsula, with coastal low-

lands on either side of the central Apennines, extends so far south that its toe, and the neighbouring island of Sicily, are in the latitudes of North Africa. Southern Sicily is as far south (36°N) as Tunis and Algiers, while the northern industrial city of Milan (45½°N) is nearer to London than it is to Reggio in Calabria, the extreme south of peninsular Italy. Given their markedly disparate social and historical backgrounds, the long period of isolation that preceded the unification, and widely differing climates, it is hardly surprising that northern and southern Italy retain their independence of character and culture.

The Grand Canal, Venice.

Venice

The city of Venice originally grew up on a group of over a hundred small islands, lying in a lagoon sheltered from the open Adriatic Sea by a sand bar. It now also includes the mainland industrial suburbs of Mestri and Marghera, where two-thirds of the city's population live. 3.2 km (2 mile) causeways carry road and rail links to the mainland, but cars are not allowed in the old city. Boats of all types, from the traditional gondolas to the diesel-powered water buses, use the canals which form the 'streets' of Venice.

Venice was once the capital of an imperial republic which, until overthrown by Napoleon in 1797, controlled much of the trade of the Adriatic and the Eastern Mediterranean. The heart of the city is around St Mark's Square, where stand the cathedral and the Palace of the Doges (Dukes) who ruled the republic.

The unique site and the rich art treasures attract about two million tourists a year, providing a living for the thousands of Venetians who cater for them; tourists, too, help to support such craft industries as glass-blowing, for which the city is famous. (FS)

The Alps and Apennines

Italy's topographical structure is determined mainly by the events of the Alpine period of mountain building, when the main ranges of the Alps and the Apennines were uplifted together. There are traces of earlier periods in the central Alps, between Mont Blanc (4,807 m, 15,770 ft) on the French border and Monte Rosa (4,634 m, 15,200 ft) on the Swiss border, and in the Carnic Alps in the north-east. Here ancient crystalline rocks predominate, although many of the higher peaks are formed from limestone. The Dolomite Alps, famous for their climbing and skiing resorts, have given their name to a particular form of magnesian limestone.

Generally lower than the Alps, the Apennines reach their highest peaks – almost 3,000 m (9,800 ft) – in the Gran Sasso range overlooking the central Adriatic Sea near Pescara. The most frequently occurring rocks are various types of limestone. The slopes are covered by thin soils, and have been subjected to severe erosion, so that in many areas they are suitable only for poor pasture. Between the mountains, however, are long narrow basins, some of which contain lakes. Others have good soils and drainage and provide a basis for arable farming.

Italy is well known for volcanic

Sardinia

Roughly the same size as Sicily, Sardinia has only about one-third the population (about 1.5 million). Sardinia's isolation from the mainstream of Italian life is due partly to its physical position, 480 km (300 miles) from the Italian coast, but the rugged, windswept terrain and lack of resources have also set it apart.

The chief crops on the lowlands are wheat, vines, olives and vegetables, and there are rough pastures for sheep on the scrub-covered hills. Fishing for tuna provides an important source of income for the ports of the west coast. Sardinia is rich in minerals, including lead, zinc, iron ore and lignite. (FS)

Baunei, near Arbatax, east Sardinia.

Climate

LOCALITY HEIGHT		JAN	JUL	YR
Foggia	°C	6.7	20.7	15.9
74 m	mm	55	15	465
Brindisi	°C	9.2	24.9	16.8
28 m	mm	77	14	644
Alghero	°C	9.7	23.1	16.0
40 m	mm	66	2	676
Potenza	°C	3.8	21.6	12.4
823 m	mm	100	18	799
Capo Palinuro	°C	9.7	24.3	16.9
185 m	mm	102	14	773
Cosenza	°C	7.4	24.8	15.7
256 m	mm	164	17	1018
Stromboli	°C	12.1	25.9	18.7
5 m	mm	81	5	532
Palermo	°C	11.9	25.1	18.3
31 m	mm	71	2	512
Catania	°C	10.9	26.5	18.2
45 m	mm	93	3	786
Pantelleria	°C	11.2	24.3	17.5
254 m	mm	48	0	415

Projection: Conical with two standard parallels

East from Greenwich

activity and earthquakes. Three volcanoes are still active – Vesuvius, near Naples, Etna in Sicily and Stromboli on an island in the south Tyrrhenian Sea. Traces of earlier vulcanism are to be found throughout the country. Ancient lava flows cover large areas, and where they have weathered they produce fertile soils. Mineral deposits, such as the iron ores of Elba and the tin ores of the Mt Annata area are often associated with earlier volcanic intrusions. Italy is still subject to earthquakes and volcanic eruptions. During the twentieth century disasters have occurred at Messina (1908), Avezzano (1915), Irpinia (1930) and Friuli (1976).

Lombardy

The great triangular plain of Lombardy, lying between the northern Alps and the Apennines, is drained by the river Po, which flows west to east, rising in the Ligurian Alps near the French frontier, and flowing across a delta into the Gulf of Venice.

The Lombardy Plains are the most productive area of Italy, both agriculturally and industrially. There is no shortage of water, as in the areas further south, although some places are served by irrigation canals. Crops include maize, wheat, potatoes, tomatoes, rice and mulberries. The mulberries are associated with the development of the silk industry. In the Alpine valleys above the Lombardy plain vines are cultivated.

Industry and urban life in Lombardy is long established. Textiles – silk, cotton, flax and wool – metal working and food processing began long before the modern industrial period. Large-scale Italian industry was slower to develop than in Britain and Germany, partly because of the lack of coal, but in Lombardy this is offset by the availability of hydro-electric power from the Alpine rivers, and by the development of a natural gas field in the area of the Po delta. Oil and gas are also imported by pipeline from Austria.

Engineering and metal working are now the most important industries, centred in Milan and Turin.

Central Italy

Central Italy, between the Po valley and the river Tiber, is a transitional zone between the industrially developed north and the poor, agrarian south. It contains Rome, which has survived as a capital city for over 2,000 years.

The area has a glorious history of artistic and literary achievement, but with its limited resources, steep slopes and difficult communications it has been left behind in economic development by the more favoured lowlands of the north.

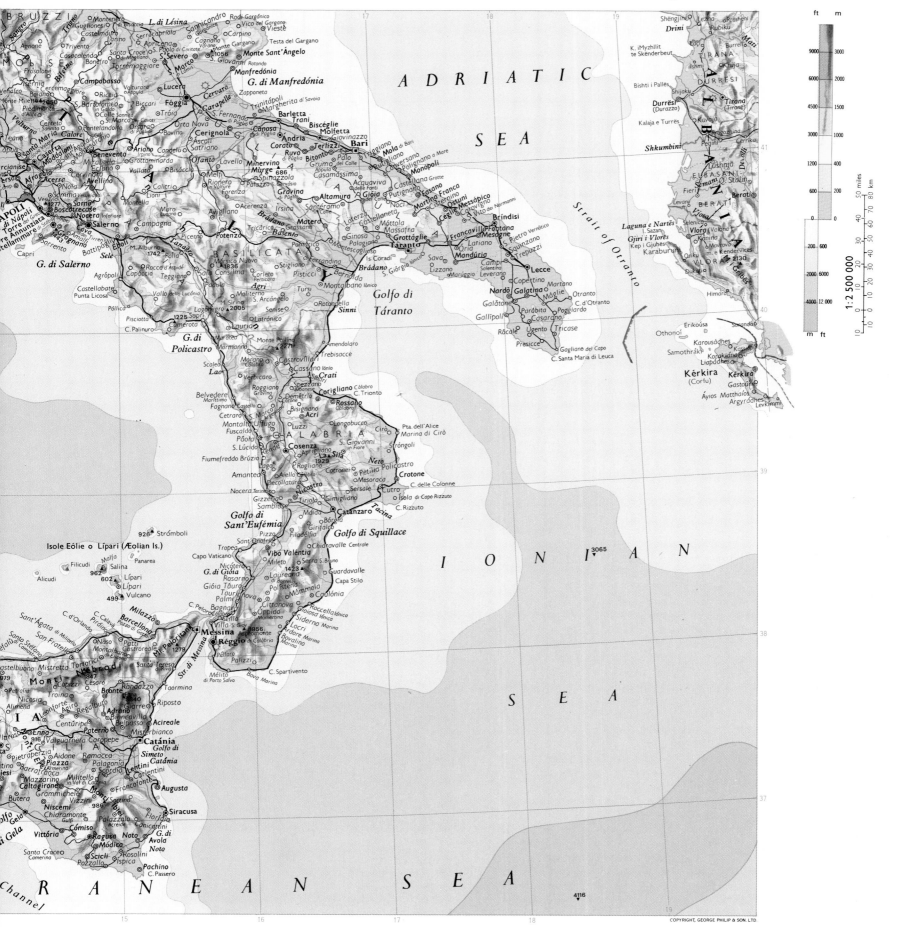

The Mezzogiorno

The south of Italy, known as the Mezzogiorno, is the least developed part of the country. It displays, in less severe form, many of the characteristics of the developing countries of the Third World. Its people depend for their livelihood on Mediterranean crops produced on small peasant farms a few hectares in area. The holdings are too small to lend themselves to modern techniques, although there are some large estates.

The birth rate is much higher than in the north, and there is a serious problem of overpopulation which is partly eased by large scale, often temporary, migration to the cities of the north and to Italy's more developed partners in the EEC, as well as more permanent migration overseas. Migration often exacerbates the problems of the Mezzogiorno, however, as it tends to take away the younger, more active members of society, leaving behind an ageing population. There are also serious urban problems, caused by the rapid growth of cities such as Naples (Napoli), as young people leave the rural areas to live in the slums. As one of Italy's major ports, Naples imports oil, coal, iron ore, chemicals and cotton. These imports provide the raw materials for manufacturing industries. In recent years great efforts have been made by a government sponsored agency, the Cassa di Mezzogiorno, to found new factories in the Naples area, but they have had little effect on the mass poverty and unemployment of the region.

SICILY

Sicily also is an area of great poverty. This triangular-shaped island lies in a strategic position between the two basins of the Mediterranean, and has had a stormy history as each power wishing to dominate the Mediterranean has sought to conquer Sicily. It is a beautiful island, with both natural and man-made attractions to interest the millions of tourists, but it is in a low state of economic development and its people are amongst the poorest in Europe. There is some industrial development around the ports of Palermo, Catania, Messina and Syracuse, based on imported materials or on oil and natural gas found offshore during the 1960s. The only other local industrial materials are potash, sulphur and salt. Despite recent developments, however, a large proportion of the 4.6 million inhabitants live by peasant farming, supplemented by fishing and seasonal work in the tourist industry.

There are few permanent streams on Sicily, as the island experiences an almost total drought in summer. Agricultural possibilities are determined to a large extent by the availability of water. Citrus fruits, vines, olives and medlars are among the chief crops. On coastal lowlands such as those around Catania, Marsala and Palermo, wheat and early vegetables are grown. The rapid growth in the population and the strong family ties which exist amongst Sicilians have led to a situation in which too many people are trying to make a living from tiny parcels of land.

The problems of the Mezzogiorno, including especially those of the Naples area and Sicily, arise partly from geographical limitations and partly from historical circumstances. They are no longer a problem only for Italy, for the stability and prosperity of Italy is a matter of concern for the rest of Europe, and in particular for the countries of the EEC, of which Italy was a founder member. The continuing gulf between north and south has a disturbing effect upon the economic and political health of Italy, a country whose people have contributed so much to the civilization of Europe. (FS)

SAN MARINO

The Republic of San Marino, a tiny independent state, lies 20 km (12 miles) south-west of the Adriatic port of Rimini in northern Italy. Most of the 61 km² (23.5 sq miles) of territory consists of the limestone mass of Monte Titano (725 m, 2,382 ft). Nearly all of the 21,000 inhabitants live in the medieval city, visited by over two million tourists a year. The chief occupations are tourism, limestone quarrying and the making of wine, textiles and ceramics. San Marino has customs treaties with Italy and uses Italian currency, but issues stamps. The state is governed by an elected council and has its own legal system. (FS)

VATICAN CITY STATE

The Vatican State, which lies within the city of Rome, exists to provide an independent base for the Holy See, governing body of the Roman Catholic Church. It is all that remains of the extensive Papal states which, until 1870, occupied most of central Italy. The Vatican consists of 44 hectares (109 acres), including St Peter's Square, with a resident population of about 1,000. The Commission appointed by the Pope to administer the affairs of the Vatican also has control over a radio station, the Pope's summer palace at Castel Gandolfo and several churches in Rome. The Vatican has its own railway station, and issues its own stamps and coins.

The popes have been prominent patrons of the arts and the treasures of the Vatican, including Michelangelo's frescoes in the Sistine chapel, attract tourists from all over the world. Similarly, the Vatican library contains a priceless collection of manuscripts from the pre-Christian and Christian eras. (FS)

Vesuvius

Rising steeply from the Plain of Campania, behind the Bay of Naples, the massive cone of Vesuvius forms one of a family of southern Italian volcanoes, clustered in an area of crustal weakness. Others include the nearby island of Ischia, Stromboli and Vulcano of the Lipari Islands, and Etna in eastern Sicily. Ischia's volcanoes last erupted in the fourteenth century. Stromboli and Vulcano are currently active, emitting lava and gases, and Etna has a long record of eruptions from 475 BC to the present day. Vesuvius, which probably arose from the waters of the Bay some 200,000 years ago, has been intermittently active ever since; over thirty major eruptions have been recorded since Roman times. However, its slopes are forested or farmed, the fertile volcanic soils producing good crops during the quiescent periods between eruptive spells. There are many settlements on its flanks, and laboratories for volcanic and seismic studies.

The most famous eruption of Vesuvius occurred in AD 79, when the flourishing Roman port of Pompeii and nearby town of Stabiae were engulfed in a rain of ashes. Excavations begun in 1748 have revealed streets, shops, houses, frescoes, statues, and many other artifacts of Roman times – even the bread in the bakery. (BS)

Mt Vesuvius: its fertile slopes are covered with vineyards and orchards.

The Forum, Pompeii. Vesuvius had been dormant for centuries before the great eruption of AD 79 that buried Pompeii, Stabiae and Herculaneum. The ruins at Pompeii were first discovered late in the sixteenth century. Most of the site has now been excavated and is a major source of information on daily life in the ancient world.

The Byzantine monastery at Sparti in the Peloponnisos.

GREECE

Mainland Greece consists of a mountainous peninsula which projects 500 km (312 miles) into the Mediterranean from the south-west corner of the Balkans, and an 80 km (50 mile) coastal belt along the northern shore of the Aegean Sea. One-fifth of the total land area of Greece is made up of islands, in the Aegean Sea to the east of the main peninsula, and in the Ionian Sea to the west. The largest island, Crete (8,331 km², 3,200 sq miles), marks the southern limit of the Aegean Sea. Some of the islands of the Dodecanese group in the eastern Aegean lie within 16 km (10 miles) of the coast of Turkey, and northern Corfu in the Ionian Islands is separated from the Albanian coast by a narrow channel less than 3.2 km (2 miles) across.

The main structural features of Greece are the Rhodopi massif (which occupies the area in the north between the Bulgarian and Yugoslav borders and the sea) and the Pindus mountains which extend south-eastward from the Albanian border, to cover most of the peninsula. The island of Crete is also structurally related to the main alpine fold mountain system to which the Pindus mountains belong. Its highest peak, Mt Ida, is 2,456 m (8,000 ft) high. In these ranges limestone rocks predominate. Many of the Aegean Islands, however, are of similar formation to the Rhodopi Massif, and made up of crystalline rocks.

Agriculture

With so much of Greece covered by rugged mountains, only a third of the area is suitable for cultivation, but 40 per cent of a population of over 9 million depend for their living on agriculture. The average size of farm is under four hectares (10 acres). The chief crops are wheat, olives, vines, tobacco, citrus fruits and sugar beet. On the few areas of flat land, mostly around the Aegean coasts in Macedonia and Thrace, larger estates are found. Most villagers keep a few domestic animals, particularly sheep and goats. The mountain pastures are poor, mainly consisting of scrubland, and many areas have been stripped of what tree cover they once had by the activities of goats (which are notoriously destructive of growing trees), and by the need for wood for shipbuilding, house building and charcoal burning.

A Maritime Nation

Greece has been described as a land of mountains and of the sea. Nowhere in Greece is more than 80 km (50 miles) from the sea, and most of the towns are situated on the coast. Greater Athens, which consists of the capital city and its seaport, Piraeus, has 28 per cent of the total population. Thessaloniki (Salonica), the second city, is also a seaport, serving not only northern Greece, but also providing facilities for the trade of southern Yugoslavia. More than a third of the population live in small communities of under 2,000 inhabitants.

Because of the difficulty of wresting a living from their poor but beautiful homeland, the Greeks have throughout their history turned to the sea. In many of the Greek city states of ancient times fishing provided an important supplement to the diet of the people, and this is still true today. In the great days of classical Greece, during the first thousand years before Christ, Greek colonies were established all round the shores of the Mediterranean and Black Seas. For a brief period in the fourth century BC Alexander the Great built a Greek empire which extended from the Danube, through Turkey and the Middle East to the Indus valley of northern India. Even more important to the civilization of the world were the great contributions to philosophy, sculpture, architecture and literature made by the early Greeks.

Mediterranean problems

Occupying a deep, almost land-locked basin, the Mediterranean Sea has a surface area of about 2,500,000 km² (970,000 sq miles). Submarine ridges divide it into eastern and western halves, each subdivided again; much of it is more than 3,000 m (10,000 ft) deep, and the greatest depth, between Minorca and Sardinia, exceeds 5,200 m (17,000 ft). Though it receives fresh water from many rivers, the Mediterranean loses to evaporation far more than it gains. Balance is maintained by an inflow of surface waters through the 12 km (8 mile) wide Strait of Gibraltar. There is a general clockwise circulation of surface waters, but very little tidal movement.

Though more salty than the big oceans, the Mediterranean lacks nutrients and is biologically poor. There are enough small fish (sardines, herrings) to support local industries, but no major fisheries. Blue-fin tuna,

Many beaches are heavily polluted.

large migratory fish, have been taken seasonally for generations, but stocks are now declining, probably due to over-fishing. Monk seals and turtles, once plentiful in many localities, are also seriously depleted by hunting and other pressures from ever-growing human populations. But the Mediterranean's most serious problem is pollution, from the sewage and industrial wastes poured into its enclosed waters. (BS)

Orange groves in the Peloponnisos. Citrus fruits are a principal crop.

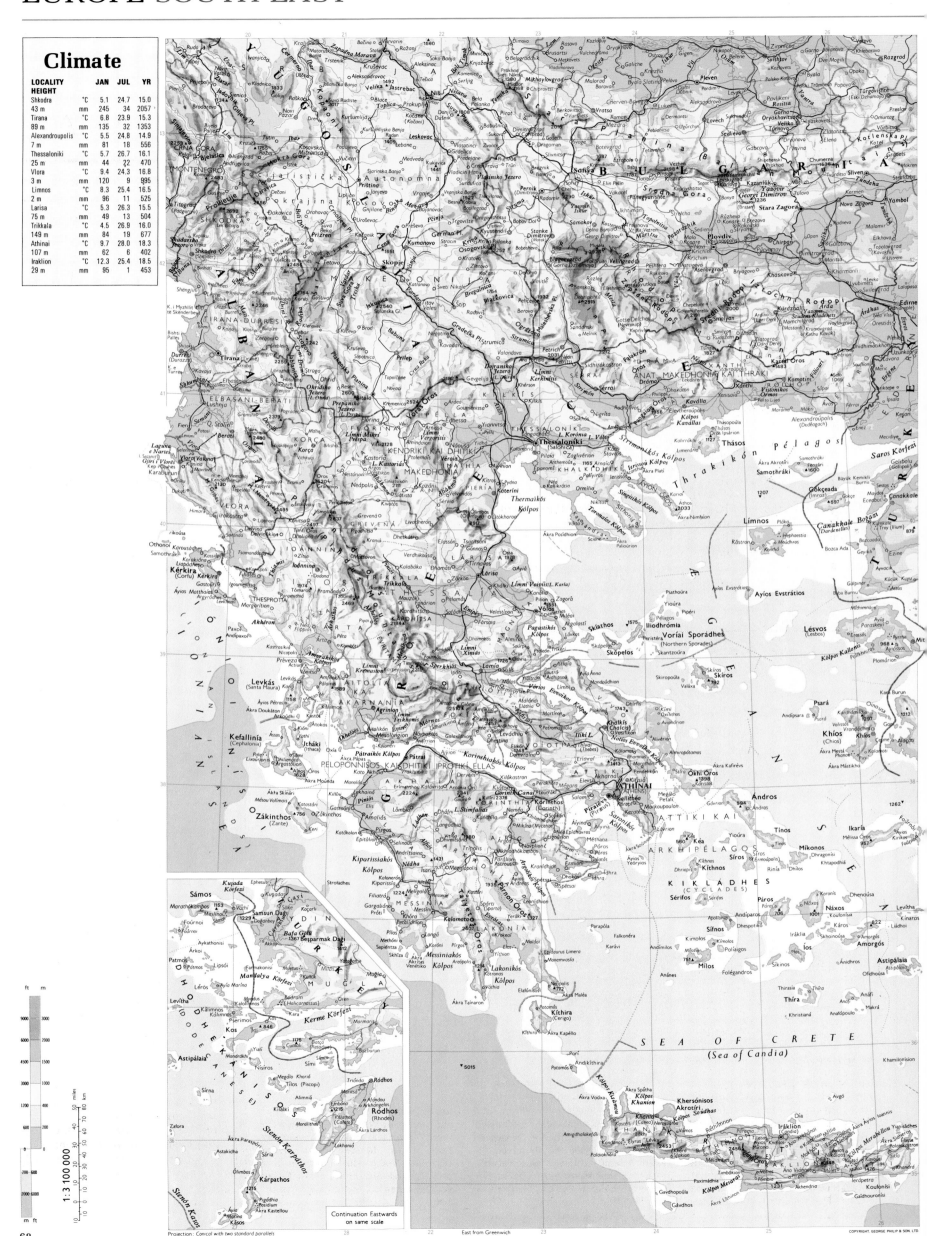

Climate

LOCALITY HEIGHT		JAN	JUL	YR
Shkodra	°C	5.1	24.7	15.0
43 m	mm	245	34	2057
Tirana	°C	6.8	23.9	15.3
89 m	mm	135	32	1353
Alexandroupolis	°C	5.5	24.8	14.9
7 m	mm	81	18	556
Thessaloniki	°C	5.7	26.7	16.1
25 m	mm	44	22	470
Vlora	°C	9.4	24.3	16.8
3 m	mm	120	9	995
Limnos	°C	8.3	25.4	16.5
2 m	mm	96	11	525
Larisa	°C	5.3	26.3	15.5
75 m	mm	49	13	504
Trikkala	°C	4.5	26.9	16.0
149 m	mm	84	19	677
Athinai	°C	9.7	28.0	18.3
107 m	mm	62	6	402
Iraklion	°C	12.3	25.4	18.5
29 m	mm	95	1	453

1:3 100 000

Continuation Eastwards
on same scale

Projection: Conical with two standard parallels

East from Greenwich

COPYRIGHT GEORGE PHILIP & SON LTD

The great epic poems of Greece – the *Iliad* and the *Odyssey*, speak of the exploits of ancient Greek seafarers who travelled around the Mediterranean. Today Greeks are still great seamen and wanderers. Greece is one of the major shipowning nations of the world, though over one-third of Greek-owned ships fly flags of other nations. Large Greek communities are to be found in the USA, Australia, Canada and Latin America; since 1960 many Greek migrants have found work in West Germany, and the admission of Greece to the EEC gives more opportunities for Greeks to find work in western Europe.

Industry

Greece is poorly-endowed with industrial raw materials. There are deposits of iron ore, bauxite, nickel and manganese, but no coal and very small amounts of oil. The possibilities for hydro-electric development are limited because of the irregularity of the streams, many of which dry up entirely during the long summer drought. Thus Greece must import most of her sources of energy – mainly oil and coal. Industrial activity is therefore largely concerned with the processing of agricultural produce – fruit and vegetables, canning, the production of wine and olive oil, cigarette manufacture, textiles and leather-processing. Greece is one of the world's major producers of dried fruits; the word *currant* is derived from the name of the Greek town of Corinth that lies on the narrow isthmus connecting the southern peninsula of the Peloponnisos to the mainland. A 4.8 km (3 mile) long canal, built in 1893, cuts through the isthmus, linking the Gulf of Corinth with the Saronic Gulf.

The tourist industry is of great importance. Overseas visitors are attracted by the warm climate, the beautiful scenery, especially on the islands, and also by the historical sites which survive from the days of classical Greece.

Invasion and Independence

Throughout history Greece has suffered greatly from invasions and conquests. Since the fall of the Byzantine Empire, the source of the Greek Orthodox faith professed by most Greeks, the intruders have included Slavs, Avars, Franks, Venetians, Turks, Italians and Germans. During the nineteenth century, after almost five centuries of Turkish rule, the Greeks began to fight for their independence, but it took a century of struggle before the present frontiers were established. Even now many Greek-speaking peoples live beyond the borders of the country. There are, for example, almost half a million Greek Cypriots, and both Albania and Turkey have Greek minorities. Within Greece there are minorities of Vlachs, who speak a Latin-based language, Pomaks (Bulgarian-speaking Moslems), Macedonians, Slavs, Armenians and Turks, most of whom live in Thrace and Greek Macedonia.

Crete

The island of Crete was the home of the seafaring Minoan civilization, which flourished in the period 3500–1100 BC and has left behind a wealth of archaeological sites and artefacts. Most southerly of the Greek islands, Crete has a milder, more maritime climate than the mainland. The rugged, harbourless south coast, backed by steep limestone mountains, is the more inhospitable side, with winter gales adding to the hazards of navigation. Most of the population live in the lowlands of the north, about a quarter of them in the main centres of Iraklion (the capital) and Khania. Though Greek-speaking, Cretans differ in outlook and culture from the mainlanders; their island suffered long occupation by Venetians and then by Turks, remaining under Turkish rule until 1898, long after mainland Greece had been liberated. About a quarter of the island is under crops; agriculture, tourism and small-scale mining are the main sources of income. (FS)

ALBANIA

Albania, with an area of 29,000 km² (11,200 sq miles), is one of the smaller countries of Europe. It is also one of the most isolated, separated physically and culturally even from the closest neighbours, Greece and Yugoslavia. The Albanian language has no close affinities with other European languages, and the political system, a strict form of Communism, tends to emphasize the country's remoteness.

Albania declared independence in 1912, after five centuries under the rule of the Ottoman Turks. One legacy of this period is the fact that, until the government closed all religious establishments in 1967, over 70 per cent of Albanians were Moslems.

At the end of World War 2, an Albanian People's Republic was formed under Communist leadership, becoming at various times associated politically with Yugoslavia (up to 1948), the USSR (1948–61) and China (1961–77). Since breaking with China, the Albanians have followed a fiercely independent, though still Communist, policy.

Landscape and Climate

Geographical obstacles have reinforced Albania's linguistic and political isolation. The mountainous interior forms a barrier to penetration from the east. The main ranges, which rise to almost 2,000 m (6,000 ft) are continuations of the Dinaric Alps; these run from north-west to south-east, rising steeply from the coastal lowlands. Limestone is the most common type of rock, although in the central area there are igneous masses rich in mineral ores, including copper, iron, nickel and chrome.

There is a great diversity of climate. Along the coast warm Mediterranean conditions make it possible to grow citrus fruits, olives, rice and tobacco. In the mountainous interior cold continental influences bring heavy winter snowfalls.

Industry and Agriculture

Despite great efforts since 1945, helped at different times by the USSR and China, Albania is still one of the least industrialized countries in Europe. This is so although the country has adequate energy resources, including petroleum, brown coal and hydro-electric potential, and a number of useful minerals. Most people still live by farming, however, with maize, wheat, barley, sugar beet and fruits predominant.

Transport is poorly developed, with few good roads. Horses and mules are widely used in rural areas. There are no rail links with other countries. (FS)

The Acropolis

The Acropolis at Athens, built in the fifth century BC.

The Greek word Acropolis means 'high city' and it refers to the groups of buildings dedicated to the gods which were often erected on isolated hills near the ancient Greek cities. The Acropolis of Athens (Athinai) stands on a steep limestone hill 156 m (512 ft) high, dominating the modern city and 1.2 km (three-quarters of a mile) from its centre. The temples (the most famous of which is the Parthenon), are dedicated to the goddess of wisdom, Pallas Athene. The steep sides of the hill were fortified, to act as a defensive citadel in case the city was besieged. From the Acropolis, which lies on the south side of the city, it was possible to see enemy ships approaching the coast of Phaleron Bay and the port of Piraeus a few miles away.

Under Turkish rule the Acropolis, sadly neglected, was used as stables and a powder magazine. Some of the statues decorating the Parthenon were removed to the British Museum by Lord Elgin, becoming the 'Elgin Marbles'. Today the Acropolis is a major tourist attraction, but suffering serious damage from industrial pollution in the Athenian atmosphere. (FS)

1 **1** The Taj Mahal mausoleum, India, built 1632–54 by emperor Shah Jahan.

2 The summit of Everest (8,848 m, 29,020 ft) behind Nuptse ridge, Nepal.

4

2

3 Dancing is one of the many highly-refined traditional arts of Japan.

4 A stilt village in the Tonlé Sap (Great Lake), Cambodia. The lake is one of the richest sources of freshwater fish in the world.

ASIA

The West can teach the East how to get a living,
but the East must eventually be
asked to show the West how to live.

Tehyi Hsieh, *Chinese Epigrams Inside Out and Proverbs* (1948), 588

ASIA

Asia extends from the Mediterranean Sea to the Pacific Ocean and from the tropical islands of the East Indies to the frozen shores of the Arctic. Most of its boundary is shoreline; only the boundary with Europe needs to be defined. This follows the Soviet frontiers with Norway, Finland, Poland, Czechoslovakia, Hungary and Romania, including the whole of Turkey within Asia.

Asia so defined has an area of about 39 million km^2 (15 million sq miles) and a population of 2,700 million, well over half the world's total. Geologically it is made up of two vast sets of rock platforms – the Russian and Siberian in the north, and the Arabian, Indian and Chinese platforms in the south, which for eons have converged upon each other, squeezing between them an enormous extent of sedimentary rocks that were laid down in ancient seas. The platforms provide the great, stable plateaux on the periphery; the sediments have been squeezed and folded into the massive mountain ranges that spread across the continent from Turkey in the west to the Pacific seaboard in the east.

Climatically Asia includes almost every known combination of temperature, precipitation and wind, from the searing heat of Arabia in summer to the biting chill of north-eastern Siberia in winter. Similarly, almost every pattern of vegetation from polar desert and tundra to tropical rain forest can be found within the bounds of this vast continent.

Asia comprises a 'heartland' centred on Siberia, and a series of peripheral areas of widely different character. The heartland includes the tundra wastes of the north, the coniferous forests, and the vast, thinly-populated interior deserts of Mongolia and Tibet. Not entirely desert, some of the heartland was traditionally pastoral and is now responding to new agricultural techniques; the wealth of its minerals is slowly being developed. To the west lie the plains of Russia, homeland of the sixteenth and seventeenth century invaders who, unlike their many predecessors, finally came to settle in the heartland and organize its massive resources. To the south-west lies the 'fertile crescent' of the Tigris and Euphrates valleys (Iraq), possibly the world's first centre of agriculture, and beyond it the Mediterranean coastlands of Turkey, Syria, Lebanon and Israel.

From Iran eastward, right around the shores of the continent and its off-lying islands as far as eastern Siberia, lie the monsoon coastlands that contain and support the main masses of Asia's populations. India, isolated by the northern mountain barrier, has traditionally formed a subcontinent in her own right. China, the second great civilization of Asia, centred on the 'middle Kingdom' of eighteen historic provinces, has expanded steadily over the centuries and is a great influence on neighbouring states, from Vietnam and Malaya in the south to Tibet, Mongolia and Manchuria in the north. Beyond the mainland coasts lie the mountainous but mostly highly fertile islands of the volcanic arcs that skirt the whole eastern edge of the continental shelf. The populations of these islands, already high, are among the fastest growing in the world. Japan, the Philippines and Indonesia between them already muster a population greater than that of the USSR. Only Japan, however, provides a standard of living comparable to those of the West. (TWF)

1:53 000 000

USSR

There are many features of the history and geography of the USSR that serve to distinguish this state from other countries of the world, but size is undoubtedly among the most important. The USSR is the world's largest state and the third most populous. The country covers an area of 22.4 million km² (8.6 million sq miles), equivalent to 15 per cent of the total land surface of the world, and from west to east it spans eleven time zones. The USA is under half the size of the USSR. This territorial immensity has a number of disadvantages; large investments have to be made in the transport system and the long borders are difficult to defend, but set against these are the benefits that derive from the diversity of environments and cultures and the abundance of resources in the country's vast expanses. The great achievement of the Soviet period has been the development of these resources.

Landscape

Diversity certainly characterizes the USSR's landforms, for within the country's borders are to be found rugged peaks and salt flats, glaciers and deserts, marshes and rolling hills as well as broad level plains. In the west the North European Plain, underlain by the ancient peneplained rocks of the Russian platform, occupies the greater part of European USSR. On the eastern side of the plain are the Ural mountains. Popularly seen as the divide between Europe and Asia, the Urals are low and rounded with few peaks rising above 1,600 m (5,248 ft). The eastern slopes of the Urals merge into the West Siberian lowland, one of the great low plains of the earth with extensive low-lying marshes. Still further to the east the Siberian platform, similar in origin to the Russian platform, underlies the Central Siberian Plateau. The relief of this plateau is a good example of a peneplane with its rolling uplands rising 500 to 700 m (1,640 to 2,300 ft) above sea-level and deeply incised river valleys.

The extensive plains of the USSR are surrounded on the south and

The Himalaya include the highest mountains in the world with more than 30 peaks of 7,300 m (24,000 ft).

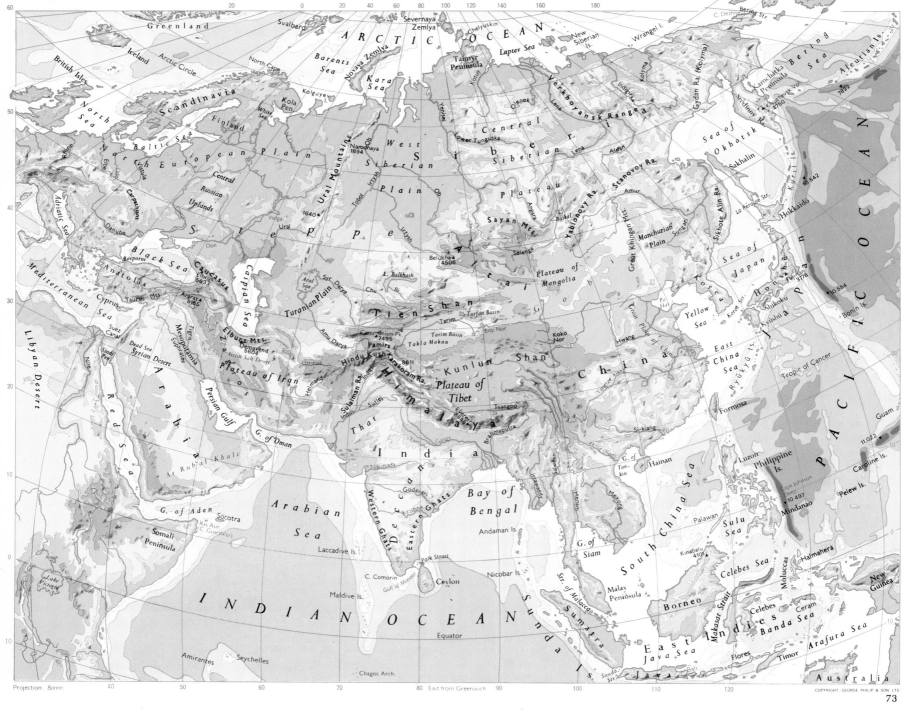

east by mountain ranges of geologically recent origin. The westernmost mountains are the northern part of the Carpathians, acquired by the USSR from eastern Czechoslovakia after World War 2. From the Carpathians other ranges, such as the Caucasus, Pamirs, Tien Shan, Altai and Sayan, describe an arc to end in the East Siberian ranges at the easternmost tip of the Asian land mass. The Kamchatka peninsula is still geologically unstable and volcanic eruptions and earthquakes occur fairly often. The Turanian lowland is another distinctive region. Fringed on the south by the arid peaks of the Central Asian mountains, the Turanian lowland contains extensive rock and sand deserts. These include the Kara Kum, the largest sand desert in Central Asia.

Much of the landscape of the USSR bears the imprint of the last Ice Age in the form of chaotic drainage systems, extensive marshlands, lakes and moraines in the lowland areas and cirques and 'U' shaped valleys in the mountains. Today large areas remain ice-bound. Nearly half the total area of the USSR has permafrost, permanently frozen ground, which may extend hundreds of metres in depth. In the permafrost of East Siberia pre-historic woolly mammoths have been found in near perfect condition.

The rivers that flow across the plains of the USSR are among the longest and most languid in the world. Drainage in European USSR forms a radial pattern with the hub in the Central Russian Uplands west of Moscow. The Volga flows from this area south to the land-locked Caspian sea, the world's largest inland body of water. In Siberia the main rivers flow north to the seas of the Arctic. Shifting channels and irregular flow make these rivers difficult to navigate and they are ice-bound in winter. In the east Lake Baykal (Oz Baykal), the deepest lake in the world, acts as a holding reservoir for the Yenisei river. Central Asia has an inland drainage system with the Syr Darya and Amu Darya flowing north from the Pamir and Tien Shan mountains to the Aral sea.

Natural Regions

Extending latitudinally across the USSR, and corresponding to the major climatic belts, are a series of sharply differentiated natural zones. From north to south these are the tundra, the taiga, the mixed forests, the steppe and the desert. Subtropical landscapes occur around the Black Sea. The dominant natural zones can also be seen as vertical bands in the various mountainous regions.

Tundra occupies at least one tenth of the country and forms a continuous strip north of the Arctic circle from the Norwegian border to Kamchatka. Climatic conditions here restrict plant growth and soil formation so that the region well deserves its name 'bald mountain top', the

meaning of the word tundra in Lapp. Stunted shrubs, mosses, lichens and berry-bearing bushes growing in thin, infertile soils form the vegetation cover of the tundra. They support the herds of reindeer in the region which for centuries have formed the basis of the local tribes' economy.

Taiga Extending south from the boundary with the tundra and occupying nearly half of the country are the coniferous forests that make up the taiga. Different species of tree dominate in different parts of the taiga but throughout the most common are firs, pines and the silver birch. Soils under the forest are *podzols*, a Russian term meaning 'ashy-grey underneath'. These soils are acidic and usually unsuitable for cultivation unless fertilized. A major source of wealth in the taiga has always been its large population of fur-bearing animals such as ermine, sable and beaver. It was the quest for furs that first lured man into this inhospitable environment. Elk, deer, hare, squirrel, lynx and bear, grouse and woodpecker are common.

Mixed Forest In the west and east of the USSR the coniferous forests merge into a zone of mixed forest. This zone is fairly wide in European USSR but it contracts towards the east to form a narrow finger which peters out beyond the Urals. The mixed forest contains both coniferous species and also broadleaves such as oak, beech, ash, hornbeam and maple. Today much of the natural vegetation of the mixed forest zone has been cleared for farming, despite the fact that the soils require heavy application of fertilizers to be productive. From early times the mixed forest has been the focus of settlement for the Russians and it has had to support large numbers of people.

Steppe Sandwiched between the forest to the north and desert to the south is the steppe zone. Hardly any natural vegetation remains in the steppe today as vast expanses have been brought under the plough. The soils of the steppe are *chernozems*, black-earths, and they are among the most fertile in the world. Before conversion into farmland the steppe consisted of extensive grasslands which in the north were interspersed with trees.

Desert In the south the steppe grades into the semi-deserts and deserts extending from the northern end of the Caspian Sea into Central Asia. The desert vegetation is sparse, consisting of various kinds of brush and shrubs, while soils range from unproductive chestnut soils to saline, sun-baked *solonchaks*. Some fertile soils, formed of wind-deposited loess, are to be found in the desert zone, and can be cultivated with irrigation. Elsewhere in the desert and semi-desert agriculture is not viable and pastoral nomadism is the only possible form of land use.

Subtropical USSR The subtropical region of the USSR occupies a restricted area but it is well populated and important for agriculture. In the Crimea reddish soils like those of the

The traditional wooden houses of villages in forested areas.

Coniferous forests occupy about half the area of the USSR.

The Volga is a major artery and site of many industrial plants.

The Kolyma river, east Siberia, frozen in winter.

Mediterranean have formed although brown earths are more common. Olive, juniper, fig, oak, beech and pine are among the dominant species of vegetation. In the subtropical part of the Transcaucasus forests and undergrowth are more luxuriant and monsoonal plants such as bamboo and tung thrive.

Natural Resources

The physical environment of the USSR offers varied opportunities for exploitation. The vast stretches of forest make the USSR the world's largest possessor of soft woods. Although the most extensive stands are found in Siberia, felling has been concentrated in the European part of the country where the wood is of high quality and is readily accessible.

The rivers, lakes and seas have yielded marine and freshwater products from early days. In the eleventh century fishing villages were already established on the northern coast of European Russia for whaling, sealing and fishing. Today fish catches are large on the Pacific coast while, among the freshwater varieties, the

sturgeon continues to be valued for its caviare.

Because of the widespread occurrence of poor soils and harsh climatic conditions, agriculture in the USSR is confined to a relatively small area of the country. Only some 10 per cent can be cultivated and a further 15 per cent can be used for pasture. Most of the arable is in the steppe and forest-steppe and from the time this was first ploughed it has been used for grains, especially wheat. Farming faces problems in this region, however, since it is open to dessicating winds blowing from the deserts to the south-east and there are often unseasonal frosts. There is nowhere in the USSR with conditions like those of the US corn belt.

Other important farming areas are the oases of Central Asia and the Black Sea littoral. In the former, the irrigation of the loess soils has been carried on since ancient times. At present the dominant crop cultivated here is cotton. In the latter, the subtropical conditions allow the cultivation of crops exotic to the rest of the country. The USSR's wines (including champagne), tea and citrus fruits come from this area.

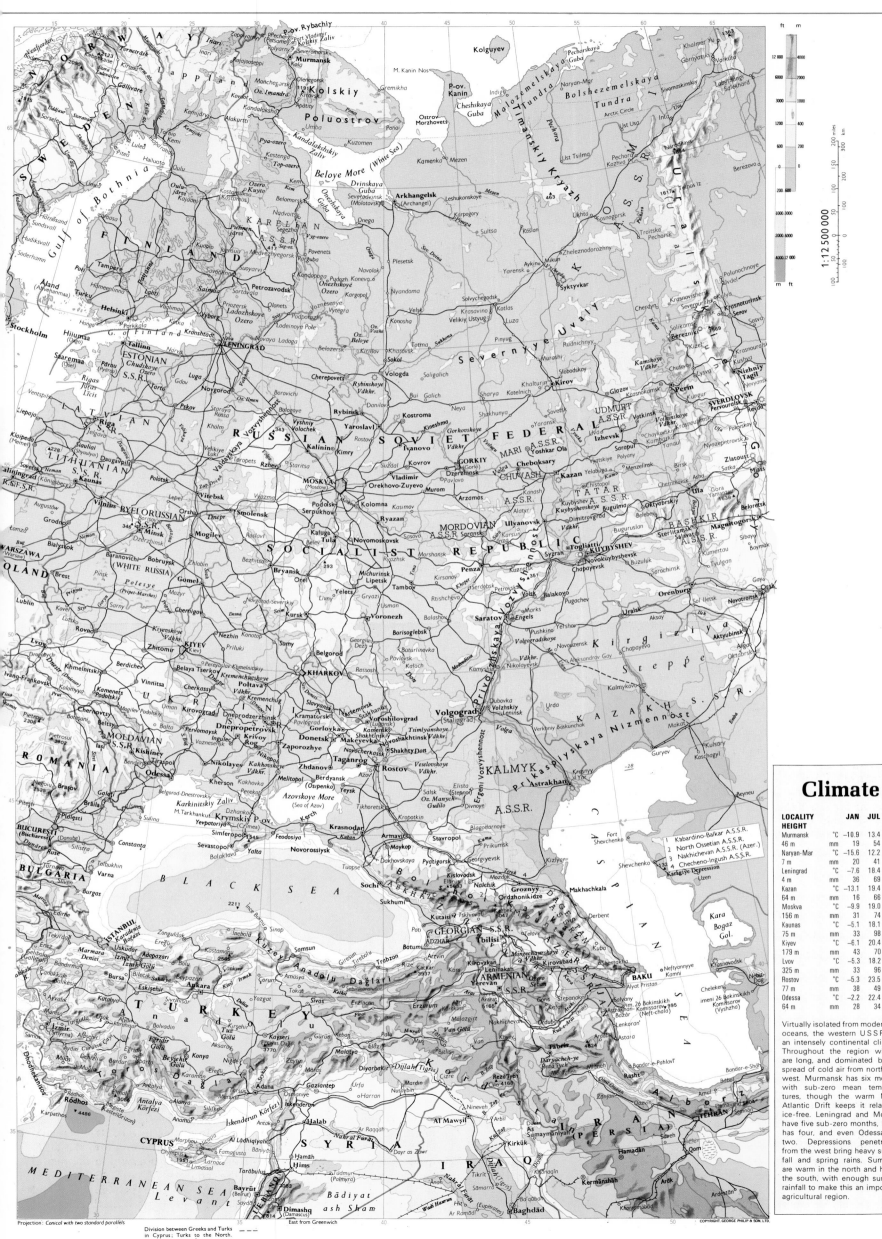

1:12 500 000

Projection: Conical with two standard parallels

Division between Greeks and Turks
in Cyprus; Turks to the North.

East from Greenwich

COPYRIGHT. GEORGE PHILIP & SON, LTD.

Climate

LOCALITY HEIGHT		JAN	JUL	YR
Murmansk	°C	−10.9	13.4	0.2
46 m	mm	19	54	376
Naryan-Mar	°C	−15.6	12.2	−3.2
7 m	mm	20	41	378
Leningrad	°C	−7.6	18.4	4.6
4 m	mm	36	69	559
Kazan	°C	−13.1	19.4	3.1
64 m	mm	16	66	435
Moskva	°C	−9.9	19.0	4.4
156 m	mm	31	74	575
Kaunas	°C	−5.1	18.1	6.0
75 m	mm	33	98	625
Kiyev	°C	−6.1	20.4	7.4
179 m	mm	43	70	615
Lvov	°C	−5.3	18.2	7.0
325 m	mm	33	96	655
Rostov	°C	−5.3	23.5	9.0
77 m	mm	38	49	483
Odessa	°C	−2.2	22.4	9.9
64 m	mm	28	34	389

Virtually isolated from moderating oceans, the western USSR has an intensely continental climate. Throughout the region winters are long, and dominated by the spread of cold air from north and west. Murmansk has six months with sub-zero mean temperatures, though the warm North Atlantic Drift keeps it relatively ice-free. Leningrad and Moskva have five sub-zero months, Kiyev has four, and even Odessa has two. Depressions penetrating from the west bring heavy snowfall and spring rains. Summers are warm in the north and hot in the south, with enough summer rainfall to make this an important agricultural region.

1 Kabardino-Balkar A.S.S.R.
2 North Ossetian A.S.S.R.
3 Nakhichevan A.S.S.R. (Azer.)
4 Checheno-Ingush A.S.S.R.

ASIA

While agricultural resources are limited, mineral and energy resources are abundant and have formed the basis of the USSR's powerful industrial economy. The most notable mineral deposits are found on the Kola peninsula, in East Siberia and the Far East where spectacular discoveries of gold, lead, zinc, copper and diamonds have been made. Iron ore is found in most regions but the most recently opened field is at Kursk south of Moscow.

Energy resources are varied. The coal deposits of the Donbas, Kuzbas, Pechora and Karaganda basins have been most exploited to date. Estimates show the USSR to have sufficient coal to last several hundred years. There are also oil and natural gas deposits which are projected to last for several decades. The main fields are in the Volga-Urals region, West Siberia and Central Asia. Large hydro-power complexes have now been built on many rivers, and there are plans to develop nuclear energy on sites in European USSR in the future.

History

The present size of the USSR is the product of a long period of evolution. In early medieval times the first Slavic state, Kievan Rus, was formed at the junction of the forest and steppe in what is now the Ukraine. As the centuries wore on other states were formed further to the north. All were eventually united under the principality of Muscovy. In the thirteenth century the Slavs suffered a major setback when Mongol hordes from the east penetrated the forests and held sway over the people there, extracting tribute from them.

It was only in the sixteenth century that the Mongol yoke was thrown off as the Slavs under Ivan the Terrible began to advance across the steppe. This signalled the beginning of a period of expansion from the core area of Slavic settlement to the south, east and west. Expansion across Siberia was rapid and the first Russian settlement on the Pacific, Okhotsk, was established in 1649. Progress across the open steppe, the realm of tribal horsemen, was slower but by 1696 Azov, the key to the Black Sea, was secured. A series of struggles in the seventeenth and eighteenth centuries against the Swedes and Poles resulted in the addition of the Gulf of Finland, the Baltic coast and part of Poland to the growing Russian Empire, and in the nineteenth century the Caucasus, Central Asia and new territories in the Far East were added. In this century the USSR has made further gains but also suffered some losses.

Russia has been a centralized state throughout her history. A

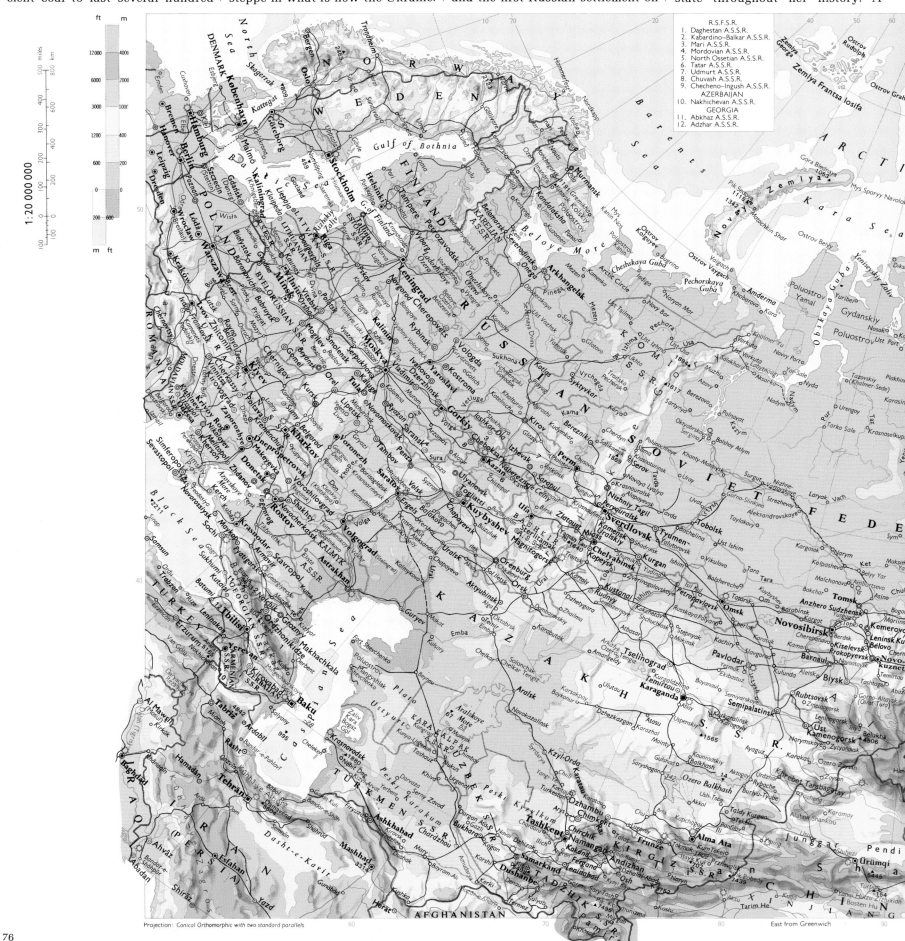

Projection: Conical Orthomorphic with two standard parallels

East from Greenwich

major landmark in the country's history, and indeed in the history of the world, was the 1917 Revolution. In this revolution the Tsarist order was overthrown and a communist government established under Lenin. The years since 1917 have witnessed major changes in the political, social and economic structure of the country. The most dramatic and far reaching of these took place from the 1930s when Stalin instituted central planning of the economy, collectivized agriculture and began a period of rapid industrialization. Since Stalin's death in 1953, Soviet leaders have modified some policies but they have remained true to the general principles of communism.

Peoples

The state that the communists inherited in 1917 was not merely large; it was also made up of peoples of very diverse ethnic and cultural backgrounds. Among the varied peoples the Slavs, consisting of the Russians, Ukrainians and Belorussians, are the most numerous. Other groups include the Turkik and Iranian peoples of Central Asia, the Caucasians, the Baltic peoples, Finno-Ugrians, Mongols and many others. More than one hundred languages are spoken within the present boundaries of the USSR. Under Soviet rule the ethnic diversity of the state is recognized in the existence of federal republics.

The USSR consists of fifteen republics each of which corresponds to a major ethnic group. The Russian republic is by far the largest, occupying three-quarters of the entire country and extending from Leningrad in the west to the Pacific ocean in the east. At the other end of the spectrum in size are tiny republics like Lithuania, Latvia and Estonia in the north-west, and Moldavia in the south-west.

Culturally the most distinctive republics are in the south. Georgia, Armenia and Azerbaijan lying between the Black Sea and the Caspian

Soviet village life has changed little since the Revolution.

An old man at Bukhara market, Uzbekistan. The Uzbeks are a major ethnic group within the USSR.

Climate

LOCALITY HEIGHT		JAN	JUL	YR
Verkhoyansk	°C	−50.3	12.2	−17.2
100 m	mm	5	28	135
Berezovo	°C	−25.0	15.0	−5.3
30 m	mm	15	53	333
Yakutsk	°C	−45.0	17.5	−11.4
163 m	mm	8	41	188
Sverdlovsk	°C	−17.5	16.7	0.0
272 m	mm	13	66	424
Tomsk	°C	−21.1	17.5	−1.7
121 m	mm	28	66	505
Petropavlovsk	°C	−8.3	10.8	1.4
87 m	mm	76	79	912
Irkutsk	°C	−21.1	15.6	−1.9
466 m	mm	13	79	378
Semipalatinsk	°C	−17.5	20.6	8.9
216 m	mm	23	28	295
Vladivostok	°C	−14.2	18.6	4.4
29 m	mm	8	84	599
Krasnovodsk	°C	1.7	28.3	15.6
21 m	mm	13	5	137

Intensely hot in summer and cold in winter, eastern USSR has an even more extreme continental climate than the west, isolated by distance from Atlantic air masses, by mountains from the Indian Ocean, and receiving few influences from the Pacific. Winter isotherms encircle a 'cold pole' centred on Verkhoyansk, where temperatures fall to −60°C (−76°F) and lower. Most of the eastern USSR experiences January means of −15°C (5°F) or below, often with cold winds. July means rise latitudinally from freezing point in the Arctic to 20°C (68°F) and over in the south. Much of Siberia is dry, receiving less than 50 cm (20 in) of precipitation annually. The centre of the USSR is an extensive arid desert.

Boundaries of U.S.S.R.
Boundaries of S.S.R.
Boundaries of A.S.S.R.

ASIA

Sea make up the Transcaucasian republics and Uzbekistan, Kirgizia, Turkmenistan and Tadzhikistan make up the Central Asian republics. The Ukraine and Byelorussia in European USSR, and Kazakhstan occupying a large expanse of steppe and semi-desert east of the Ural mountains, complete the list. Apart from these Union republics, autonomous republics and regions have been set up to recognize smaller ethnic groups. Such, for example, is the Kara Kalpak autonomous republic in Central Asia and the Khanti-Mansi autonomous region in Siberia.

All the ethnic republics and regions of the USSR are firmly bound to Moscow but this does not mean that they have lost their individuality. Cultural contrasts are large even today. In Central Asia, for example, Uzbeks can still be seen wearing their national costumes and haggling in local markets. Although Soviet power has resulted in the abandonment of the Moslem veil, Central Asian women have retained the custom of early marriage and the large family system. The Soviet government has encouraged the development of certain aspects of national cultures and each republic has its own flag, newspapers and official language.

Settlement

Although all parts of the USSR are inhabited, even the most remote, the greatest concentration of people has traditionally been in the European part of the country. It was here that in the centuries before the Revolution the first Russian towns with their fortresses, or *kremlins*, and onion-domed churches were founded. Outside this settled core there were towns and cities which the Russians acquired during their expansion or themselves established on the frontiers. In Central Asia the Russians took over what had once been a flourishing urban civilization, gaining towns such as Samarkand, Khiva and Bukhara with their minarets and palaces.

Since the Revolution changes have taken place in the distribution of population in the USSR so that the former pattern of a small highly populated core and 'empty' periphery has begun to break down. Today the settled area extends into Siberia and, in a narrow band, across to the Pacific ocean. As a result, half the Soviet population is to be found east of the Urals compared with under one-quarter before the Revolution. This redistribution of population has been actively encouraged by the government which has been committed to a policy of developing the east.

Migration to the towns and cities has also been marked since 1917 so that the greater part of the Soviet population is now urban. Some of these urban settlements have been built from scratch during Soviet times and are to be found in the more remote regions of the country. Norilsk, for example, was founded in the 1930s north of the Arctic circle near

to important mineral deposits. The most famous city is the capital Moscow (Moskva). Moscow, like the other cities of the North European Plain, is a mixture of the old and the new. Around the historic buildings at the centre of the city multiple-storey blocks of flats have sprung up separated by wide highways.

While Soviet cities and towns have been the site of vigorous building programmes, villages all over the USSR have changed little since the Revolution. In the forests, people still live in the traditional wooden hut (*izba*), while in the steppe agricultural workers' dwellings are of wattle and daub. Since the Revolution, however, electricity has been introduced and in some villages a range of other services is now provided. But still most villages do not have a modern sanitation system or running water.

Economic Development

A major achievement of the Soviet government has been to transform the USSR from an underdeveloped country into the second most powerful industrial nation of the world. At the time of the Revolution (1917) most industrial development was concentrated in a few centres in the European part of the country: Moscow, St Petersburg (now Leningrad), and the Donbas in the south. Also much was financed by foreign investment and the development of major industrial sectors was unbalanced. On taking power the Communist Party vowed to develop industry rapidly and to introduce it into the backward regions of the country.

As in many other parts of the world, Soviet industrialization was initially based on the iron and steel industry. In Stalin's drive of the 1930s heavy national investment went into expanding production in the already existing industrial areas of European USSR and establishing the industry in the east. During the 1930s new large integrated steel mills were built in the southern Urals and on the Kuzbas coalfield in West Siberia. Later the industry was introduced into the Kazakh republic on the Karaganda coalfield. Most recently a new plant has been established at Kursk in European USSR.

The shift away from coal as a basis for industrial development to alternative energy sources has taken place later in the USSR than in many other countries. Since the 1960s, however, petroleum and natural gas industries have begun to develop rapidly and the same is true of industries based on hydro-electricity. HEP has been especially important in building up industry in East Siberia where massive installations on the river Angara provide the energy for aluminium production.

The introduction of large-scale industry into formerly backward parts of the country has helped to even out levels of development. Regional imbalances in production nevertheless remain large. The pre-revolutionary foci of development

The Grand Cascade in the gardens of the palace of Petrodvorets, built for Peter I in 1721. The palace was designed by Alexandre Le Blond.

have continued to attract a sizeable proportion of available investment and have retained their leading position in Soviet industry. Of the regions developed since the Revolution only West Siberia can be said today to have a well-developed mature industrial structure. Other parts of the country, and especially the non-Russian republics in the south, still have weak industrial economies.

Agriculture While overall industrial production has forged ahead since the Revolution, agriculture has been dubbed the 'achilles heel' of the Soviet economy and in several years since the middle 1960s foreign grain has had to be imported. Since 1965 there has been a notable improvement in yields of all products but even so output and consumption *per capita* can only just keep ahead of increases in population. Some Western commentators ascribe the poor performance of agriculture to concentration on farms too large and too impersonal to be efficient.

Soviet farms are of two types, collective farms (*kolkhozi*) and state farms (*sovkhozi*). The former are, according to the official definition, democratically run producers' co-operatives which, in return for a grant of land, deliver some of their produce to the state. In theory free to run their affairs, they have always

been subject to considerable state interference. State farms are state owned and managed. Until the 1950s state farms were relatively uncommon because they were expensive to run but in the last two decades their number has increased. Today the Soviet sown area is equally divided between collective and state farms. Both types of farm are large, covering on average 6,600 and 18,000 hectares (16,308 and 44,460 acres) respectively in the 1970s. While the greater part of Soviet agricultural output comes from collective and state farms, a large share of market garden produce and some livestock products originate on the so-called personal plots of farm workers. The personal plot is a small but carefully cultivated parcel of land, usually no larger than .5 hectare (1.2 acres) in size, which collective and state farm workers are allowed to work in their spare time. Much of the produce from the plots is consumed at home but some is sold.

Large-scale projects In both agriculture and industry the Soviet government has shown a liking for large-scale projects. Campaigns, as they are called in the USSR, have at times been launched to increase rapidly output of chemicals or machinery, for example. A much-publicized campaign in agriculture was

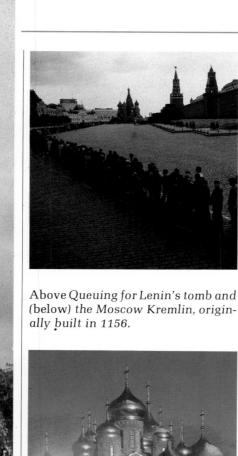

Above *Queuing for Lenin's tomb and* (below) *the Moscow Kremlin, originally built in 1156.*

The fourteenth-century church of St Theodore Stratilata in Novgorod.

The Bolshoi theatre, Moscow, home of the world-famous ballet company.

by inefficiencies in the state distribution system, is obvious in the size of the queues that form whenever scarce products come on sale. Another indication is the existence of a flourishing black-market. In recent years there has been a marked increase in consumer goods production and standards of living have improved considerably. Still, whenever the economy is in difficulties it is the consumer sector that suffers the first cutbacks.

Foreign Trade During Stalin's rule a conscious policy to restrict foreign trade and to be self-sufficient as far as possible was pursued. With the formation of COMECON, the eastern trading block, after World War 2 and the realization that much of Western technology would be useful to her own continued development, the USSR has revised trade policy. Today the USSR trades with all countries of the world, although the Soviet share of total turnover is small. In trading with the West, the USSR exports mainly primary products and imports technology and grain.

Social and Cultural Development

Although the economy has been the main preoccupation of the Soviet government since the Revolution, the social and cultural sides of life have not been neglected. Considerable stress has been laid on education as children are seen as an investment for the future. Popular culture and sports activities have been encouraged and, in planning their towns, the Soviet government has been careful to include a full complement of football grounds, sports centres, cinemas and 'parks of culture'. Most of the larger cities have their own circus. There have also been considerable efforts taken to introduce the mass of the population to the arts. The achievements of nineteenth century music, art and literature, with the work of such men as Pushkin, Dostoevsky, Chekov, Tolstoy, Borodin and Mussorgsky, are known to all Soviet citizens.

After the 1917 Revolution literature was put to the service of the new communist state and writers such as Maxim Gorky and the poet Vladimir Mayakovsky began to produce literature and verse dedicated to the dissemination of revolutionary ideology. The rise of Stalin and the onset of heavy censorship resulted in a general mediocrity in literature after 1930, although Mikhail Sholokov's novels are an exception to this. While official writers have continued to reinforce communist ideology, some dissidents, such as Alexander Solzhenitsyn, have used their writing to protest against the repressive aspects of the Soviet regime.

Art took on an overtly political role after 1917 seeking contact with the workers and peasants of the new state. Censorship in art has resulted in the overwhelming predominance of a few officially sanctioned themes in painting and sculpture: the heroic aspects of World War 2, happy and physically robust work-

launched in the 1950s to bring into cultivation thousands of hectares of hitherto fallow land east of the Ural mountains. As a result of this project, called the Virgin Lands campaign, the sown land of the USSR was doubled in the space of a few years. Following some initial difficulties, and withdrawal from some of the more marginal land, the Virgin Lands are now a principal grain-producing region.

Consumer Goods In the drive for economic development, the Soviet government at first neglected the consumer sector. Growth rates in textiles, food industries and wood-processing, for example, have lagged behind those for iron and steel production. The paucity of consumer goods, which is often compounded

ers and peasants building communism and the role of the Communist Party in all aspects of life.

Architecture too has served the Revolution with architects designing structures supposed to reflect the collectivist basis of the new order. From the 1930s urban design became monumental and grandiose. In Moscow this phase culminated in the building of seven wedding-cake sky-scrapers, one of which houses Moscow University, and in the elaborate design of many of the stations in the metro.

While an overview of the arts in the USSR reveals a rather depressing picture of conformity, there have been notable contributions made in some areas, particularly in the cinema (Eisenstein), theatre and ballet. A main achievement of the Soviet period, however, has been to make 'high culture' accessible to most of the population. (JP)

The Georgians

The Georgians are said to live to a great age. This woman claimed to be 137 in 1973.

At the end of the 1970s there were over three million Georgians in the USSR, the majority living in the picturesque republic of Georgia or Gruzya. The high fold mountains of the Greater and Lesser Caucasus rising above the eastern shores of the Black Sea have for centuries been the home of this fiercely nationalistic people. Georgian history is an unhappy story of successive invasions. Living at the crossroads of the ancient world, the Georgians fell prey to the Macedonian, Persian and Byzantine empires. Later, in the Middle Ages, they were subjugated to the Mongol invaders from the east and in the nineteenth century to the Russians. The Georgian people never succumbed easily: it took the Russians several years to subdue the mountain tribesmen after their nineteenth-century takeover. The greatest flowering of Georgian culture was in the twelfth century during the reign of the celebrated Queen Tamara. Georgian art, literature, painting and sculpture from this era are held in general esteem.

Today Georgians cling to their separate identity. Unlike others in the USSR, they are deeply religious, worshipping in their own church, a Christian orthodox sect. Their language, which is of non-Indo-European origin, continues in daily use. National dance and folk music are the aspects of Georgian culture perhaps best known to outsiders. (JP)

TURKEY

Turkey comprises the broad peninsula of Asia Minor, together with its 'roots' around Lake Van, and in Europe that part of Thrace (Thraki) which lies to the east of the lower Maritsa river. The small but populous district of the Hatay, including Antakya and Iskenderun, was transferred from Syria to Turkey in 1939.

The heart of the country is the high karst plateau of Anatolia, semi-desert around the central salt lake, but mainly sheep country. The Taurus ranges afford summer grazing for the plateau flocks, and also timber. The northern Pontic ranges are better wooded, with fertile plains.

The valleys of the Gediz and Cürüksu, which open westwards from the plateau to the Aegean, export tobacco and figs, while the deltaic plain around Adana grows abundant cotton. The very high and thinly-peopled plateaux and ranges to the east of the Euphrates river produce chrome (near Maras), copper (Ergani) and oil (Batman).

The Republic of Turkey was

Oil is the Middle East's major export and principal source of wealth.

founded after the final break-up of the Ottoman Empire at the end of World War 1. Istanbul, the former imperial capital, which controls the straits between the Black Sea and the Mediterranean, is the country's chief port and commercial city; but

the function of capital has been transferred to the more centrally-placed town of Ankara. Turkey, with a rapidly growing population, now has one of the best railway networks in the Near East, and though lacking in large resources of mineral oil has

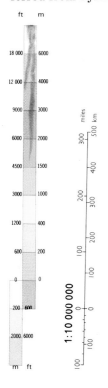

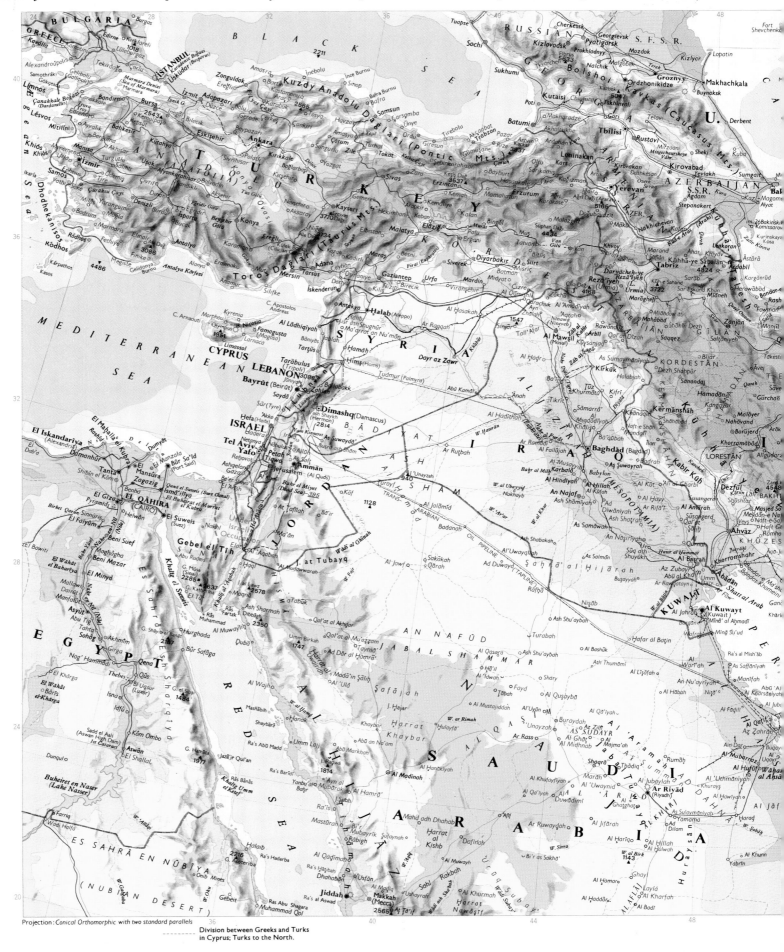

Projection: Conical Orthomorphic with two standard parallels

Division between Greeks and Turks
in Cyprus; Turks to the North.

built up a thriving industrial economy based on imported oil, on coal (from Zonguldak), and above all on hydro-electric power. (WB)

IRAN

The most populous and productive parts of Iran lie at the four extremities – the fisheries, rice-fields and tea-gardens of the Caspian shore in the north, the sugar-plantations and oilfields of Khuzestan in the south, the wheat-fields of Azarbaijan in the west, and the fruit-groves of the oases of Khorasan and Seistan in the east. In between are the deserts of Kavir and Lut, and the border ranges which broaden in the west into the high plateaux of the Zagros, the summer retreats of the tribes of Bakhtiars and Kurds.

The cities of the interior depend on ingenious arrangements of tunnels and channels for tapping underground water, and these have been supplemented by high dams, notably at Dezful. The capital city of Tehran is the crossing-point of the country's two great railways, the Trans-Iranian from the Gulf to the Caspian, and the east-west track from Mashhad to Tabriz, which follows the ancient trade route from China to the Mediterranean. (WB)

CYPRUS

The island of Cyprus is a detached fragment of the mainland mountains to the east. In the south, the broad massif of Troödos, rich in minerals, is a classic example of an ophiolite, or intrusive dome of ancient sub-oceanic rocks. The northern coast is backed by the long limestone range of Kyrenia. The central plain between Morphou and Famagusta is fertile and well-irrigated and grows oranges, flowers and early vegetables. The former forests were cut mainly in classical times to fuel the copper smelteries. Turks settled in the north during the period of Ottoman rule (1571–1878). Greek majority and Turkish minority have lived uneasily together; following an armed Turkish invasion in 1974, the island is currently divided between them. (WB)

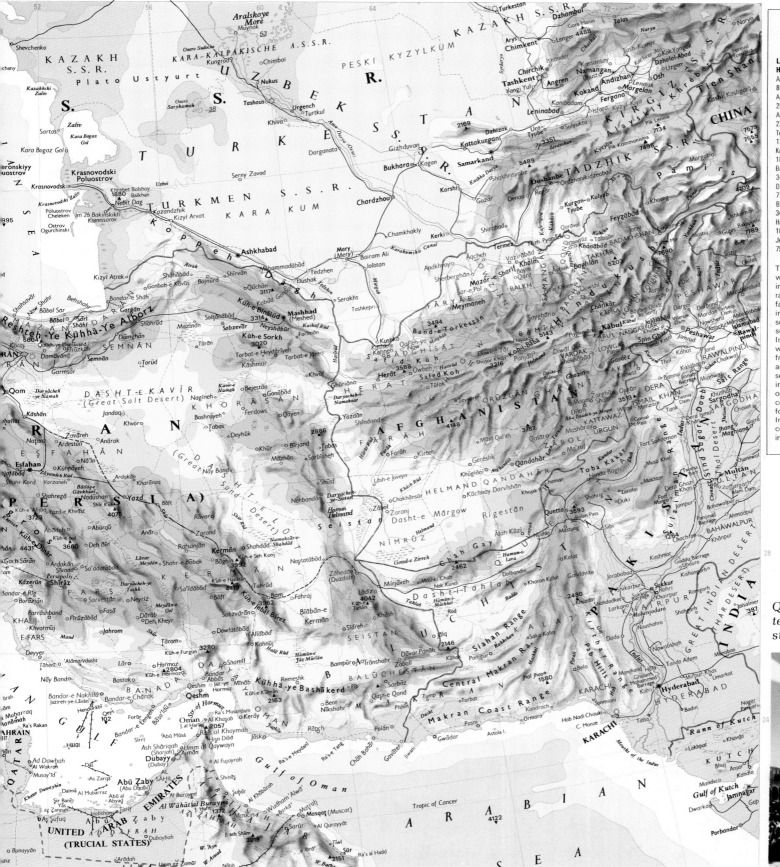

Climate

LOCALITY HEIGHT		JAN	JUL	YR
Ankara	°C	0.0	22.5	11.7
859 m	mm	33	13	345
Adana	°C	8.9	27.8	18.9
25 m	mm	109	5	617
Al Mawsil	°C	6.9	32.5	19.4
222 m	mm	71	Tr	384
Tehran	°C	2.2	29.7	16.7
1217 m	mm	46	3	246
Kabul	°C	-2.8	24.7	12.2
1810 m	mm	30	3	338
Bayrut	°C	13.6	26.7	20.6
34 m	mm	190	Tr	892
Dimashq	°C	6.9	26.7	17.5
718 m	mm	73	Tr	218
Baghdad	°C	9.7	33.9	22.8
34 m	mm	23	Tr	140
Haifa	°C	13.9	27.5	21.7
10 m	mm	175	Tr	663
Jerusalem	°C	8.9	23.9	17.2
755 m	mm	132	0	528

Turkey's long coastline has a warm, almost frost-free climate; in the Mediterranean winters are rainy, in the Black Sea rain may fall all through the year. The interior is drier, with more extreme seasonal temperatures, hot in summer and bitterly cold in winter. Iran and Afghanistan have cool winters, controlled by air masses from central Asia; the mountain areas are very cold, with snow settling and drifting. Summers are intensely hot and rainless, humid on the Gulf and Indian Ocean coasts but drier and more comfortable toward the Caspian Sea. Iraq has hot dry summers and cool winters with rain and snow in the north.

Qom, Iran. Traditional textile industries are still important.

East from Greenwich

IRAQ

Modern Iraq is one of the states created after World War 1 through the partition of the Ottoman province of Syria. The country includes a hilly district in the north-east, and in the west a substantial slice of the Hamad or Syrian Desert; but essentially it consists of the lower valleys and combined deltas of the Tigris and Euphrates. Rainfall is meagre, but the alluvium is fertile and productive when supplied with water. The western desert is nomad country, with good winter grazing, and from here the tribes move in summer with their flocks to the banks of the Euphrates.

The north-east of Iraq includes part of the Zagros mountains, where fruits and grains will grow without the help of irrigation. The Kirkuk oilfield is the country's oldest and largest, and nearby the Lesser Zab river has been impounded behind a high dam. The population here includes many Turks, settled in the times of Ottoman rule, and Kurdish tribes akin to those across the border in Iran.

Upstream of Ramadi and Samarra, the Jazirah or land between the rivers (Mesopotamia) stands too high for irrigation, though the swamp of Tharthar is used to store the excess flow of the Euphrates through a diversionary channel from Samarra. This is dry-farming country or pasture. In the north near the Syrian frontier the block mountain of Sinjar is an oasis of fertility, with an unorthodox Yezidi population (a religious sect).

Downstream of the Jazirah lies Iraq proper, the deltaic plains which, with skill and effort, can be drained and irrigated. The rivers rise rapidly in spring as the snows melt around their sources in Turkey, and are full enough for irrigation throughout the summer. In Abbasid times (750–1258) a long canal ran south from the left bank of the Tigris at Samarra, and five more led from the Euphrates to the Tigris in the vicinity of Baghdad. Further south the rivers passed through a great swamp, which in turn drained to the sea through the Shatt al Arab.

The Mongol invasions of the thirteenth century destroyed this irrigation system, and it was not restored until the present century. Now the spring flood of the Euphrates is stored through the Habbaniyah Escape, which takes off westwards at Ramadi and matches the Tharthar Escape from the Tigris. The canals of central Iraq have been rebuilt, though they do not drain as well as they did earlier, and in consequence a salt crust tends to form and spoil the soil of the cotton plantations. Lower down, a barrage on the Euphrates at Hindiyah and another on the Tigris at Kut control canals which irrigate land reclaimed from the great swamp. Further south still, the banks of the Shatt al Arab are lined with date groves which depend on tidal irrigation.

In addition to the Kirkuk oilfield, which exports by pipeline through Syria and Lebanon, there are reserves of oil near Mosul (Al Mawsil), Khanaqin and Basra (Al Basrah). Baghdad is the capital, Mosul the centre of the northern provinces, and Basra the seaport. A railway joins these three main cities, and from Mosul passes westwards into Syria and Turkey; a branch takes off from Baghdad to Arbil. The main road to Iran leads up the Diyala valley and crosses the Zagros mountains by the pass of Behistun. (WB)

SYRIA

The Republic of Syria, the northern part of the former Ottoman province of the same name, stretches from the Mediterranean to the Tigris, and from the southern edge of the Kurdish plateau in the north to the heart of the Hamad or stony desert in the south. The northern border for most of its length follows the railway from Aleppo to Mosul (part of the old Berlin-Baghdad line). The port of Iskenderun together with the town of Antioch and the valley of the Lower Orontes were transferred to Turkey in 1939. Syria was thus left with only one large harbour, at Latakia (Al Ladhiqiyah), though the country usually enjoys privileged access to the ports of Lebanon.

The Orontes river flows northwards along the great rift valley (see pp. 156–7), through alternating gorges and wide valleys which have been reclaimed through drainage and irrigation. Near Hamah and Hims the ranges of Lebanon and Anti-Lebanon, which flank the valley to west and east, are relatively low, but further south the Anti-Lebanon rises to the Heights of Hermon, whose snows water the gardens of the capital, Damascus (Dimashq), on the eastern or desert side. In the far south, by the frontier with Jordan, the volcanic mass of Mount Hauran supports a group of oases around the town of Suwayda.

Aleppo (Halab) is the second city of Syria, and the capital of the northern districts, set in a well-watered agricultural area. Further east the steppe becomes progressively drier. This was traditionally winter pasture for the nomads who moved in from their summer homes in the mountains of Lebanon, but in recent years, thanks to techniques of dry-farming with machinery, it has become a prosperous farming zone, devoted almost exclusively to cotton and wheat. The water from the Euphrates barrage will extend agriculture in this region. Syria has struck oil at Qarachuk in the 'panhandle' by the Tigris in the far north-east, and a pipeline has been laid from there to the Mediterranean. Another pipeline crosses the desert further south from the Kirkuk fields in Iraq to the sea-terminal at Baniyas. To supplement the railway from Hims to Aleppo and from there

Eastern carpets are world-famous.

along the northern frontier, a line has been laid from Latakia through Aleppo to Al Qamishli. (WB)

JORDAN

After World War 1 the Arab territories of the Ottoman Empire were divided, and one segment became the Kingdom of Trans-Jordan, administered under League of Nations mandate by Britain. On the closure of the mandate in 1946, the kingdom was renamed Jordan, and took over the greater part of Judaea following the partition of Palestine; but recent warfare has resulted in the control of this district – the 'West Bank' – passing to Israel.

Jordan's western frontier thus runs down the centre of the great rift valley (see pp. 156–7) from just south of the Sea of Galilee (Yam Kinneret) to the Gulf of Aqaba, following the Jordan river, the Dead Sea and the Araba trench. The borders with Syria, Iraq and Saudi Arabia were laid out on mainly geometrical lines, including in Jordan a wide area of desert grazing grounds which the tribes need in winter.

The greater part of the country consists of desert and steppe, and the only districts where agriculture is possible are the limited plains and deltas of the rift valley or Ghor, with a strip about 80 km (50 miles) wide of the high plateau just to the east of the edge of the rift. Within this strip of broken land, where the annual rainfall exceeds 20 cm (8 in), the minimum necessary for dry farming, lie the capital Amman, and most of the country's other main towns, Ailun, Irbid and Ma'an. Through it runs the only railway, a metre-gauge track that was part of the former 'pilgrim line'.

To the east, the desert, which includes wide stretches of rough basaltic lavas, becomes progressively drier. The main oasis is by the pools of Qasr Azrak, from where the underground stream of the Wadi Sirhan is followed by a road across Saudi Arabia to the town of Jawf.

Between 1095 and 1291 there were eight major Christian crusades against Moslem powers. Krak des Chevaliers, Syria, was built by the Crusaders.

Petra, Jordan, centre of the Nabataean kingdom from c 312 BC to AD 105.

The western strip of the plateau will grow wheat and barley and tree-crops like olives and vines, but much of it is under pasture. This terrain has been widely damaged by soil erosion, and is being reclaimed through terracing and planting fruit trees.

The Ghor or rift valley will grow cotton and rice, sugar beet and sorghum fodder. However, the land needs water for irrigation and most of this comes from the high storage dam at Wadi Khalid on the Yarmuk river.

Before the partition of Palestine, the economy of Jordan operated closely with that of her western neighbour, and the route to Haifa was the natural avenue for external trade. Now Jordan has two more-distant outlets to the sea, northwards by rail to the Mediterranean at Beirut (Bayrut) through Syria and Lebanon, and southwards by rail and road to Aqaba and the Indian Ocean. Although Jordan has no oil-fields, the country benefits from concessionary supplies from the 'TAP line' (Trans-Arabian Oil Pipeline), which passes through it on the way to the Mediterranean. The main mineral resource is phosphate, which is used for fertilizers. (WB)

LEBANON

The Republic of Lebanon came into existence shortly after World War 1 through the subdivision on ethnic lines of the Ottoman territories in the Levant. This state included most of the Christian communities of the old Ottoman province of Syria, some of which had their origins in the early centuries of Christendom, while others dated back to the Crusades. There is a long tradition of close cultural and commercial contact between Lebanon and France, and many Lebanese have emigrated to Europe or America. The population, dense by the standards of the Near East (over 3 million on 10,000 km², 3,900 sq miles), is about half Moslem and half Christian.

Along the coast are several fine harbours and ports, used since Phoenician times (c 3000–c 1000 BC). The two largest – Beirut (Bayrut) the capital and Tripoli (Tarabulus) – command easy routes by road and rail over the coast ranges. Both the narrow, broken coastal plain and the mountains are well-watered and fertile, producing cotton, tobacco and fruits. Above their cultivated terraces the mountains carry sporadic woods of pine and cedar, much depleted by cutting during the centuries since ancient Egypt and Assyria struggled for their control. East of the coastal range, good cereals can be grown in the Ghor or rift valley. Soil fertility is enhanced through irrigation from the Orontes and Litani rivers (the latter ponded behind a high dam). Further east the Anti-Lebanon ranges, drier and scrub-covered, form the main frontier with Syria.

Lebanon is naturally complementary to Syria and the two countries long maintained a customs union. Damascus (Dimashq), and Amman too, find their easiest sea-outlet in Lebanon, and in Lebanon are the Mediterranean terminals of the great oil pipelines from Iraq (at Tripoli) and from Saudi Arabia (at Sayda). In view of the appeal of the mountain tourist towns, and a high reputation for international banking, Lebanon is aptly called the Switzerland of the Near East. (WB)

ISRAEL

Israel came into existence in 1948 when the British administration withdrew from Palestine and the country was divided. The new state then comprised the coastal plain, the vale of Esdraelon (Jezreel) behind Haifa, the foothills in the south, most of the hill country of Samaria, and half Jerusalem with a corridor to the west. In addition it was the intention of the United Nations that Israel should acquire either Galilee in the north or the Negev in the south, but in the event both these districts were included. The rest of Palestine, mainly Judaea and the rift valley west of the river, was added to Jordan, but subsequently, as a result of recent warfare, its administration as the 'West Bank' was taken over by Israel.

In general, the country is most fertile and best watered in the north, and becomes progressively drier and more desert-like towards the south. The object of the Jordan-Western Negev scheme, the most ambitious of Israel's irrigation enterprises, has been to direct through canals and culverts all the water that can be spared from the Upper Jordan and the streams and drainage channels of the coastal plain southwards to the deserts of the Negev.

In the north, Galilee is rolling hill country with good rainfall and a rich black soil weathered from basalt. Both here and in the hills of Judaea, new pine-woods have been established to fix the soil and hold the water. The Upper Jordan valley is excellent farmland, reclaimed from the swamps of Lake Huleh.

The valley of Jezreel, with a deep alluvial soil washed down from Galilee, is intensively tilled with market gardens. South of the promontory of Carmel, the coastal plain of Sharon is excellent fruit country, but needs irrigation, especially in its southern stretches. Here the drifting dunes have been fixed with grass and tamarisk and reclaimed for pasture.

The Negev Desert

Between Sinai and the rift valley, the great wedge of desert plateau known as the Negev accounts for about half the total territory of Israel. Its bedrock is widely covered with blown sand and loess, which will grow tomatoes and grapes in profusion if supplied with fresh water. Unfortunately the local artesian supplies are too salty for this purpose, but the ancient Nabataean techniques for conserving flood-water have been applied on experimental farms, and piped water brought in from the Yarkon river and further north.

The Negev south of Be'er Sheva' is Israel's pioneer territory, with new towns mining oil, copper and phosphates, factories using the potash and salt of the Dead Sea, and farms experimenting with solar power and artificial dew. Carob trees have been planted for fodder, and dairy farms and plantations of bananas and dates laid out with the aid of the artesian springs of the rift valley or Araba. Elat on the Gulf of Aqaba is a tourist town and Israel's sea outlet to Africa and Further Asia. From here, a pipeline takes imported oil to the refinery at Haifa.

Industry and Communications

To supplement the port facilities of Haifa, Israel has built a new harbour at Kishon, which accommodates the fishing fleet through a ship canal; and a deep-sea port was completed in 1965 at Ashdod to replace the old anchorage at Jaffa (Tel Aviv).

Israel has become the most industrialized country in the Near East. Iron is smelted at Haifa and converted to steel at the foundries of 'Akko. Chemicals are manufactured at Haifa and at Sedom by the Dead Sea. With the aid of a national electricity grid, factories for textiles, ceramics and other products have been widely established in country towns, including the new foundations of Dimona and Mizpeh Ramon in the Negev. Some railways were inherited from the British Administration, but most commercial movement is along the road network. (WB)

AFGHANISTAN

Afghanistan came into existence early in the nineteenth century as a buffer state between Russia and British India, which jointly established and surveyed the boundaries. The great mountain range, the Hindu Kush, can be easily crossed at Kushka, from where the regular road to Pakistan leads by way of Herat and Farah to Qandahar, and then divides toward Kabul and the Khyber Pass or Quetta and the Bolan. Now the Russians have cut a tunnel through the mountains north of Kabul at Salang, and this takes traffic to the USSR by way of the Amu Darya. The deserts of Seistan have recovered some of their former fertility through restoration of the Helmand canals, and the sweet waters of the Hamun support fish, birds and cattle. The hills that border Pakistan are ill-controlled tribal country. Industry depends on hydro-electricity around the capital Kabul, and oil in the northern or Bactrian plains near Mazar-e-Sharif. There are no railways. (WB)

SAUDI ARABIA

During and shortly after World War 1 the Saudis of Najd extended their territory at the expense of the Rashidis and Hashemites, and consolidated their control over the greater part of the Arabian peninsula, including the holy cities of Mecca (Makkah) and Medina (Al Madinah); but the frontiers with neighbours to the south and east remained ill-defined. This mattered little until mineral oil was tapped after World War 2. Since then some disputes have been settled, notably through the division of the Gulf-shore Neutral Zone with Kuwait.

The heart of the state consists of the province of Najd, within which are three main groups of oases. First, the district of Yamama, including the capital city of Riyadh, recovers water from the wells of the Wadi Fatima which cuts through the central scarp of Jabal Tuwayq, the 'pennine' ridge of the country. Second, the oases of Ha'il further north depend on the springs of the sandstones of the Shammar hills. Thirdly, at Buraydah and Unayzah in the district of Qasim the subterranean water of the Wadi ar Rima is tapped through wells and date-groves.

Najd is enclosed on its east side by a vast arc of sandy desert which broadens out into the two great dune-seas of Arabia, the Nafud in the north, and in the south the Empty Quarter. To the west, Najd is separated from the border hills of the Red Sea by fields of rough basaltic lava.

The peninsula is basically made up of a block of ancient rocks, tilted so that its high edge overlooks the Red Sea, and from there it slopes down in the direction of the Gulf. The high western edge of the country, known as the Hijaz (Barrier) in its northern section and as the Asir further south, attracts most of the country's rainfall. From the watershed the wadis divide, eastwards as long underground streams like the ar Rima-Batin and Dawasir that flow towards the Gulf, westwards in complex patterns of valleys and ravines, notably those of the Wadi Hamdh and its tributaries in the region of Medina, which emerge in the narrow coastal plain or Tihamah. Particularly in its southern section towards the border with Yemen, this coastal strip is quite well supplied with water, and a high storage dam has been built on the river Jizan. The hills of Asir which back the plain here benefit from the summer monsoon, and are extensively terraced to grow grain and orchard trees.

The eastern province of Saudi Arabia by the shores of the Gulf is known as the Hasa. Near its chief city of Hufuf in particular, the long underground seepage of water from the Hijaz breaks out in the artesian springs of the oases. This region contains the country's great oilfield. The oil port of Az Zahran is linked with the capital Riyadh by the country's only railway: plans to rebuild the 'pilgrim railway' to Medina from Damascus have not yet been put into effect.

Asphalt roads are the country's main means of communication. One crosses the central districts from east to west from Az Zahran to Riyadh, Mecca and Jiddah, the main Red Sea port. Another runs alongside the Trans-Arabian Oil Pipeline (TAP line) to Jordan, and is used to bring in fresh food. With the help of oil revenues, irrigation has been extended, plastics and fertilizer factories set up, the nomads settled, and the provincial towns linked by air.

An oasis in Bahrain.

The immense annual influx of pilgrims from all over the Moslem world is increasingly reliant on air transport. (WB)

THE COASTAL STATES

From the late eighteenth century, Britain had a powerful interest in maintaining safe travel along the seaways of the Gulf and South Arabia which lay on the main routes to India. To suppress piracy and protect and provision these lines of communication, Britain forged treaties and truces (hence the term 'Trucial States') with various shoreline sheikdoms, often undertaking to protect them after initial punitive expeditions. All have since become independent. Their frontiers, including those over the sea, which have never been clearly defined, have

The Bedouin

Hospitality plays an important role in Bedouin life and is valued highly.

The name signifies the dwellers in the *bayda* or desert, and refers to the wandering tribes of the Arabian interior. The earliest nomads of the peninsula kept donkeys rather than camels, as the Solubbi tinkers still do. The dromedary was domesticated about 3000 years ago, and with its help the overflow population from the oases of the south-west were able to live on the desert grazing grounds. Different pastures thrive at different seasons – the northern in winter, the southern in summer. So the Bedouin move not haphazardly, but with respect to well-known seasonal and territorial rights to water and fodder; disputes are settled by appeal to authority in the para-military pyramid of kin. Camel nomads are respected more than those with sheep or goats.

Oases are visited to trade and replenish supplies, and the tribes often own and harvest date-groves. Commerce comes naturally to these mobile tribes, and they may thereby become rich and settle again. There is thus a cycle from settled to nomadic and back once more to settled life, as in the story of Abraham, and town and desert are always in touch. To modern states with taxes, tariffs and customs posts the tribes are an embarrassment, and many Bedouin have succumbed to the easier existence of the cities: but the ascetic life and simple desert virtues of honour and hospitality are still widely respected among the Arabs. (WB)

become a matter of serious dispute since the discovery of oil.

The large natural harbour of **Kuwait** was a terminus of the route through Iraq, and was considered at one time as a possible base for a railway across northern Arabia. Now an oil port, Kuwait is a wealthy state which imports most needs. Water is acquired from wells or through distilling sea-water.

The island of **Bahrain** and the nearby peninsula of **Qatar** used to exist on pearling and dhow trading, but their economies now rely overwhelmingly on the mining and export of oil, through Manamah, Umm Said and several specialized terminals. Further east, **Abu Dhabi** draws oil both from inland and from offshore, and trades through the entrepôt of Dubay.

In spite of wide exploration, **Oman** has found oil only at one small field – that of Jebel Fahud on the western or desert slope of the mountains. The main Omani range, the Jebel Akhdar, an offshoot of the fold mountains of Makran on the other side of the Gulf of Oman, meets the coast between a series of deep inlets, on one of which lies the port of Muscat. The mountains trap a modest winter rainfall and grow winter grains and fruit trees. The high plateau edge that backs the bay of Dhufar on the south coast, by contrast, gets rain in summer from the monsoon winds, and grows a cover of shrubs, including the frankincense bush. On the plateau crest are summer meadows where the Qara and Mahra tribes graze cattle.

Further west along the south coast is the state of **South Yemen**, formerly the British Colony and Protectorate of Aden. Here too the plateau meets the Indian Ocean in a high edge where a moderate summer monsoon rain nourishes the myrrh bushes and supplies a number of coastal oases. Further inland lies the wide dust-covered plateau of the Jols, desolate and dissected by ravines. Beyond is the vale of Hadhramawt, watered by one of the few permanent streams of Arabia, where the inhabitants have close links through emigration with Malaysia. Aden, one of the great entrepôts of the Indian Ocean, has a large oil refinery.

North Yemen which, as **Yemen**, has been an independent state much longer than those described above, includes the highest part of the Arabian plateau, and its areas of highest rainfall, which here comes with the summer monsoon. The terraced slopes grow coffee and qat (a mild narcotic leaf), the higher valleys maize under irrigation and a depleted tree cover of willow and juniper. The oases of Shabwa, Ma'rib and Nejran, were once prosperous towns on the Spice Road to the Mediterranean. (WB)

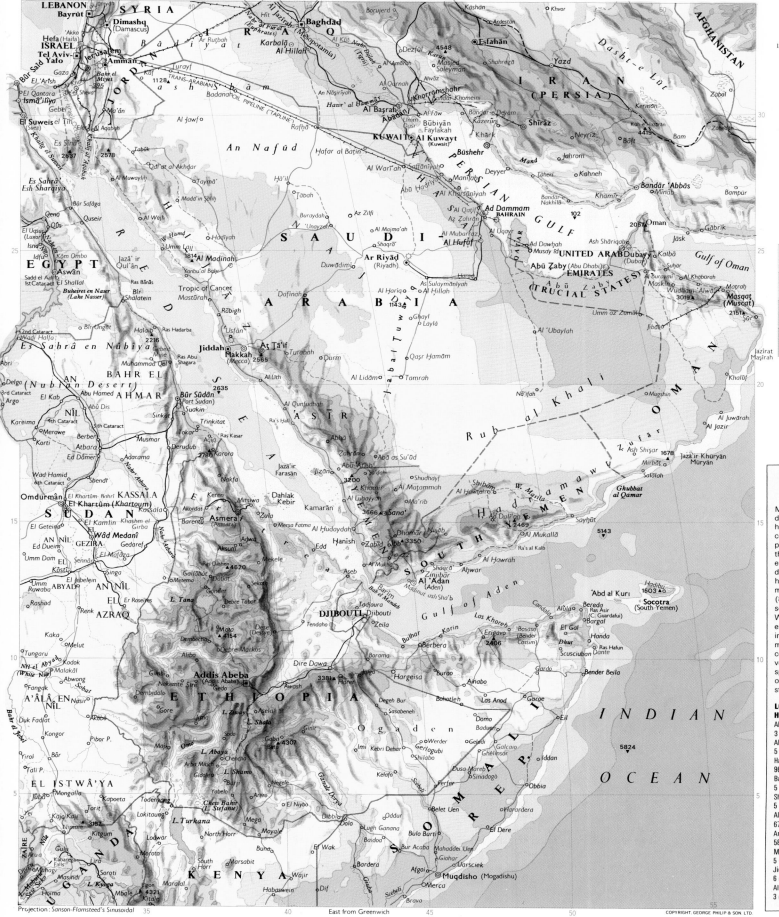

Climate

Much of the area is tropical desert or semi-desert. Intensely hot in summer, it forms the centre of a low-pressure area that pulls in dry winds, mostly from the north and west, often strongly enough to raise sand-storms and dust devils. Temperatures are highest June to August, with monthly means exceeding 30°C (86°F) everywhere except in the south-western mountains. Winters are surprisingly cool, especially in the mountains and in the north where temperatures may fall below freezing point. The central and western deserts are very dry; elsewhere winter or spring rains bring annual growth of vegetation, and heavy rain-storms can occur.

LOCALITY HEIGHT		JAN	JUL	YR
Abadan	°C	12.9	36.1	25.1
3 m	mm	20	0	144
Al Kuwayt	°C	12.8	34.7	25.0
5 m	mm	23	0	130
Ha'il	°C	10.3	30.6	21.1
968 m	mm	10	0	99
Bahrain	°C	16.9	33.3	25.8
5 m	mm	8	0	81
Sharjah	°C	17.8	32.8	25.8
5 m	mm	23	0	107
Al Madinah	°C	17.3	35.1	27.6
672 m	mm	0	0	37
Ar Riyad	°C	14.4	33.6	24.7
589 m	mm	3	0	81
Masqat	°C	21.9	33.3	28.6
5 m	mm	28	Tr	99
Jiddah	°C	23.9	31.7	28.1
6 m	mm	5	Tr	63
Al Adan	°C	25.5	32.2	28.9
3 m	mm	7	3	39

SOUTH ASIA

Southern Asia, often referred to as the Indian subcontinent, has an area of 4,460,000 km² (1,722,000 sq miles) – a small part of Asia as a whole yet almost continental in its impact on the traveller and in its share (nearly one-fifth) of the world's population. It extends from sub-equatorial coral beaches in the south to icy mountains overlooking the Vale of Kashmir in the north – approximately in the latitude of Greece.

Southern Asia is a subcontinent of unity and diversity. Binding it in unity is the annually occurring rhythm of human activities caused by the seasonal reversal of winds in the monsoon. Yet diversity arises from the same cause – the annual vagaries of the monsoon, that bring drought and near-famine to one region, flood and disease to another, in apparently random patterns. There is a cultural unity, too, to which the sensitive traveller reacts, from Kashmir to Cape Comorin (Kanya Kumari). Yet here again is the paradox of extraordinary diversity. Variety of race, language and religion all contribute, often related to invasions, trading connections or a colonial past. At the root of the culture of this subcontinent lies South Asia's millenial role as the cradle of Hinduism and Buddhism. (AL)

INDIA

India is a diamond-shaped country of area 3,287,580 km² (1,270,000 sq miles), bordered in the north-east by Nepal and the Himalaya, in the north-west by Pakistan and the valley of the Indus. It is bisected by the Tropic of Cancer, and extends south into the Indian Ocean almost to latitude 8°N. A population of about 640 million makes India the world's second-largest nation; only neighbouring China is bigger.

Landscape and Agriculture

Geographically India can be divided into three parts – the mountainous north, the great alluvial plain of the Brahmaputra and Ganga (Ganges), and the plateaux and lowlands that occupy the southern area, including most of the peninsula. Each provides an astonishing range of scenery, intensified by the variety of peoples, cultures and activities within them.

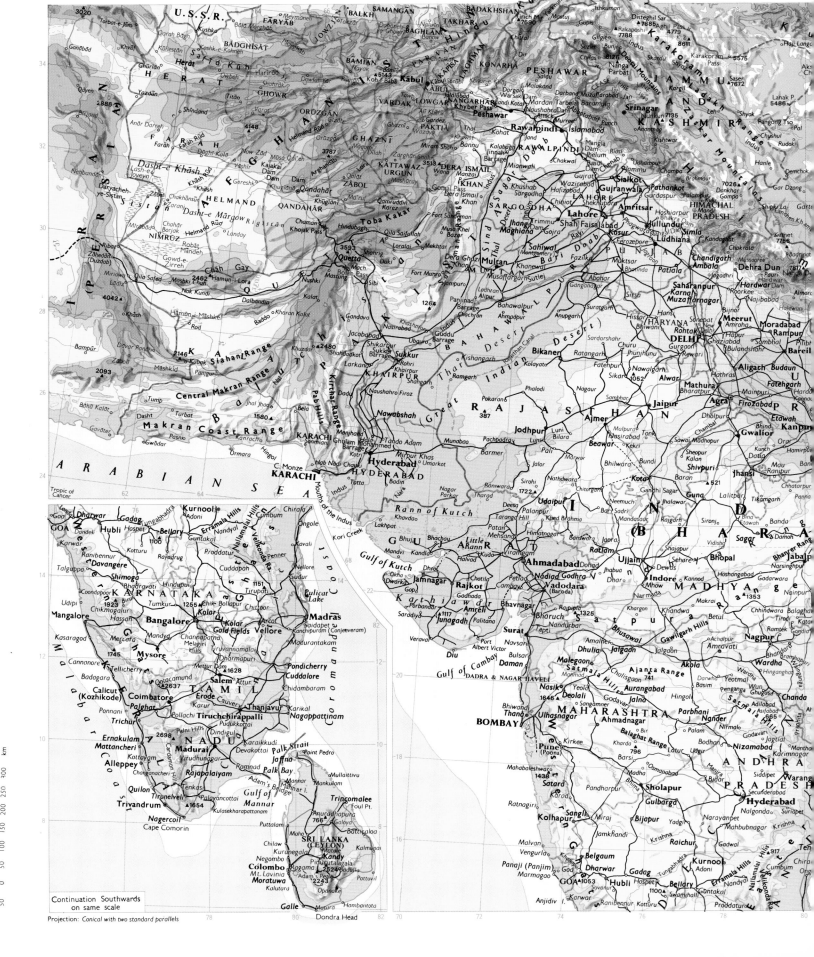

Continuation Southwards on same scale

Projection: Conical with two standard parallels

1:10 000 000

The mountainous north The Himalayan foothills make a backdrop for northern India, rising abruptly from the plains in towering ranks. Harsh dry highlands, sparsely occupied by herdsmen, stretch northward to the everlasting snows of the Karakoram. Below lie alpine meadows, lakes and woodlands, often grazed in summer by seasonally migrant flocks from lower villages. The fertile Vale of Kashmir has emerald-green rice-terraces, walnut and plane trees and apple and apricot orchards around half-timbered villages. It is crossed by ancient trackways once used as trade-routes by mule and yak trains, now military roads to the garrisons of the north. The wet, forested eastern Himalaya of Assam are ablaze with rhododendrons and magnolias, and terraced for buckwheat, barley and rice-growing. The high plateau of Meghalaya (abode of the clouds) is damp and cool; nearby Cherrapunji has one of the highest rainfalls in the world. Tropical oaks and teaks on the forest ridges of Nagaland, Manipur and Mizoram alternate with rice-patches and small towns; on the hilltops dry cultivation of rice is practised, in plots cleared for a few years' cultivation and then left fallow to recover.

The plains The great plains form a continuous strip from the Punjab eastward. Heavily irrigated by canals engineered in the late nineteenth century, the rich alluvial soils have provided prosperity for Sikh and Jat farmers of the Punjab and Haryana. Here are grown winter wheat and summer rice, cotton and cane sugar, with sorghum in the drier areas, and the successful agriculture forms a foundation for linked industrial development as well. Many small market towns are thriving. The fine plans for the joint state capital of Chandigarh, devised by Corbusier, have been fully realized.

The Vale of Kashmir, India. The valley is an ancient lake basin and has fertile alluvial soils.

Climate

Much of the Indian subcontinent lies in the north-east trade winds, which blow cool and mainly dry from November to February or March. From January through to April or May, as the sun approaches the Tropic of Cancer, the land warms steadily and the trade winds weaken. Then they reverse, often dramatically, as cooler, saturated air flows in from the oceans, bringing heavy monsoon rains especially to western coastal regions and the eastern uplands. Pakistan and central India miss the heavy rains and are generally dry to arid: southern India and Sri Lanka have a more equable maritime climate, rainy throughout the year.

LOCALITY HEIGHT		JAN	JUL	YR
Peshawar	°C	10.7	32.6	27.2
359 m	mm	39	7	363
Delhi	°C	14.3	31.2	25.3
216 m	mm	25	211	715
Katmandu	°C	10.0	24.4	18.6
1337 m	mm	15	373	1427
Cherrapunji	°C	11.7	20.3	17.4
1313 m	mm	20	2855	11437
Karachi	°C	18.9	29.3	25.8
4 m	mm	7	96	204
Calcutta	°C	20.2	29.1	26.8
6 m	mm	13	301	1582
Bombay	°C	24.3	27.5	27.3
11 m	mm	2	709	2078
Hyderabad (India)	°C	17.2	32.5	27.5
29 m	mm	4	69	157
Madras	°C	24.5	30.7	28.6
16 m	mm	24	83	1233
Trincomalee	°C	25.6	29.7	28.0
7 m	mm	211	54	1727

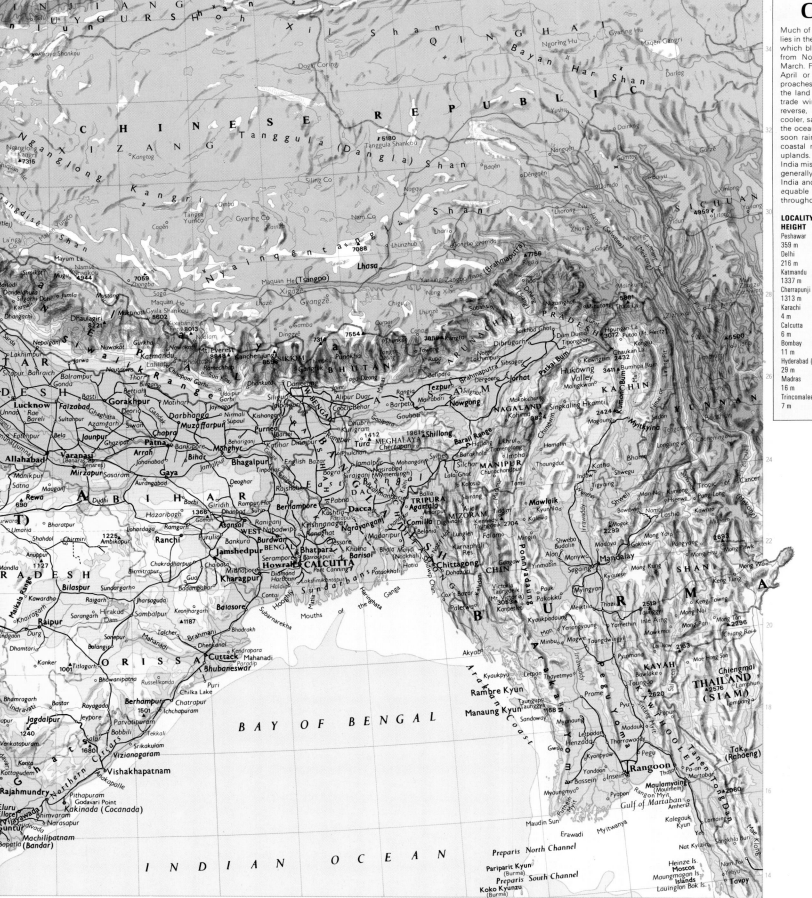

Pastoral landscape extends eastward to the broad plains surrounding Delhi, India's third largest city on the west bank of the Yamuna river. An ancient site, occupied for over 3,000 years, it now includes the Indian capital New Delhi, designed by Lutyens and built from 1912. Old city and new lie at a focal point of road and rail links, and are rapidly becoming overcrowded. To the east again lie the lowlands of Uttar Pradesh, criss-crossed by the Ganga and Yamuna rivers and their many tributaries. Slightly wetter, but less irrigated, these plains are farmed less for wheat and rice, more for spiked millet and sorghum, though maize and rice cultivation increase again in the wetter areas toward Bihar.

Among the most densely populated areas of India, these lowlands support many dozens of cities and smaller settlements – notably Aligarh with its university, historic Agra with its Red Fort and Taj Mahal, and Kanpur, a former colonial military centre, now an industrial metropolis. Allahabad is an administrative and cultural centre recently extended by development of textiles and light engineering industries and, under its Hindu name of Prayag, a focal point for millions of pilgrims, especially during its great festival every twelfth year. Varanasi (Banaras) is another sacred Hindu city, with many temples and burning ghats by the holy river Ganga, and an important Hindu university. Patna, the busy state capital of Bihar, is a centre of textiles and engineering, though no longer the important river port that it was. Along the Nepal border the *terai* or hillfoot plains, formerly malaria-infested swamp-forest, have now been cleared and made healthy for prosperous farming settlements.

Downstream from Tinpahar ('three hills') the Ganga begins its deltaic splitting into distributary streams, while still receiving tributaries from the north and west. West Bengal consists largely of the rice- and jute-growing lands flanking the distributary streams that flow south to become the Hooghly river, on which Calcutta is built. The Ganges-Kobadak barrage now provides irrigation for the north of this tract, while improving both water supply and navigation lower down the Hooghly. The Sunderbans – mangrove and swamp forests at the seaward margin of the Ganga delta – extend eastward into Bangladesh.

South-west from the Punjab plains lies the Thar or Great Indian Desert, its western fringes in Pakistan but with a broad tract of dunes in the north-eastern lowlands in Rajasthan. The desert ranges from perennially bone-dry wastelands of shifting sand to areas capable of cultivation in wet years. As the name Rajasthan implies, this state was until 1950 a land of rajahs and princes, palaces and temples; some of the buildings – including universities – endowed by these private benefactors remain important in Jodhpur, Jaipur, Ajmer, Udaipur and other cities. Rajasthan rises in a series of steps to a jagged, bare range of brightly-coloured sandstone ridges – the Aravallis, that extend north-eastward and end at New Delhi.

South and west of the Aravallis lie the cotton-growing lands of tropical Gujarat; Ahmadabad and the new state capital of Rajasthan – Gandhinagar – are its chief cities. Between the Gulfs of Cambay and Kutch is the low peninsular plateau of Kathiawar, whose declining deciduous forests still harbour small groups of tribal peoples, and indeed the last of India's native lions. Between this and the Pakistan border stretches the desert saltmarsh of the Rann of Kutch, once an arm of the Arabian sea, and still occasionally flooded by exceptionally heavy rains.

South-east of the Aravallis lies an area of transition between the great plains of the north and the uplands and plateaux of peninsular India. First come the Chambal badlands (wastelands south of Agra now partly reclaimed), then rough hill country extending south-eastward to Rewa. The river Sone provides a lowland corridor through the hills south of Rewa, and an irrigation barrage provides water for previously arid lands west of Gaya. Eastward again the hills are forested about Ambikapur and Lohardaga. Industrial development becomes important around the coalfields of the Damodar valley, centred on Asansol – with its rail-links to Hooghlyside – and the developing steel town of Jamshedpur-Tatanagar.

Peninsular India South of the Chambal river and of Indore (a princely capital until 1950) the sandy plateau of the north gives way to forested hills, split by the broad corridors of the Narmada and Tapti rivers. Tribal lands persist in the Satpura Range, and the Ajanta Range to the south is noted for primitive cave paintings near Aurangabad. From here south volcanic soils begin to predominate.

Bombay, India's largest city, lies on the coastal lowlands by a broad estuary, among emerald rice-fields dotted with low lava ridges; fishing villages with coconut palms line the shore, while inland rise the stepped, forested slopes and pinnacles of peninsular India's longest mountain chain, the Western Ghats.

East of the Ghats, on rich black soils well watered by the monsoons, stretch seemingly endless expanses of cotton and sorghum cultivation. Arid in late winter and spring, parched by May, they spring to life when the rains break in late May or June. The sleepy market towns follow a similar rhythm, full of activity when the agricultural cycle demands, and relaxing under the broiling sun when the time for activity is past.

South from the holiday beaches of Goa (formerly a Portuguese enclave, and still Portuguese in flavour), past busy Mangalore and Cochin to the state capital of Kerala, Trivandrum, the coast becomes a kaleidoscope of coconut groves and fishing villages,

Calcutta, capital of West Bengal, is seriously overcrowded.

ricefields, scrublands, cashew orchards and tapioca plantations. Here the Ghats are edged with granite, gneiss, sandstone and schist, and clad in heavy rain-forest. To the east the peninsula is drier, with rolling plateaux given over to the production of eleusine millet, pulses and other dry crops. Sugar, rice and spices are grown where simple engineering provides tanks, stopped with earth or masonry dams, to save the summer rains; now canals are performing the same task. Bangalore and Hyderabad-Secunderabad, once sleepy capitals of princely states, are now bustling cities, respectively capitals of Karnataka and Andhra-Pradesh.

History

India's earliest settlers were widely scattered across the subcontinent in Stone Age times. The first of its many civilizations developed in the Indus valley about 2600 BC, with centres at Mohenjo-Daro and Harappa, and in the Ganga valley from about 1500 BC. By the fourth and third centuries BC Pataliputra (modern Patna) formed the centre of a loosely-held empire that extended across the peninsula and beyond into Afghanistan. This first Indian empire broke up after the death of the Emperor Asoka in 232 BC, to be replaced by many others, both transient and lasting, during the centuries that followed. The Portuguese who crossed the Indian Ocean in the late fifteenth century, and the British, Danes, French and Dutch who quickly followed them, found a subcontinent divided in itself and ripe for plundering.

As a result of battles fought both in Europe and in India itself, Britain gradually gained ascendancy over both European rivals and local factions within the subcontinent; by 1805 the British East India Company was virtually in control, and the British Indian Empire (which included, however, many autonomous states) was gradually consolidated throughout the nineteenth and early twentieth centuries. Organized opposition to Britain's rule began before World War 1 and reached a climax after the end of World War 2. In August 1947 the Indian subcontinent became independent, but divided into the separate states of India, a mainly Hindu community, and Pakistan, where Moslems formed a majority. In the boundary disputes and reshuffling of minority populations that followed about half a million lives were lost; events since then have done little to promote good relations between the two states.

A Country of Diversity

India is a vast country with enormous problems of organization. It has over a dozen major languages, each with a rich literature, and many minor languages. Hindi, the national language, and the Dravidian languages of the south (Tamil, Telugu, Kannada and Malayalam) are Indo-European; in the north and east occur Sino-Tibetan tongues, and in forested hill refuges are found residual Austric languages. Racial stocks too are mixed, with dark tribal folk in forest remnants, Mongoloids in the north and east, and often lighter-coloured skins and eyes in the north-west – and in higher castes throughout the country.

The mosaic of religion also adds

variety to landscape and life. Hinduism is all-pervasive (though the state is officially secular), and Buddhism is slowly reviving in its country of origin (the Buddha was born on the border of India and Nepal about 563 BC). Buddhism's near-contemporary Mahavira and Jainism, with common elements including stress against destruction of any form of life, are strong in the merchant towns around Mt Abu in the Aravalli hills north of Ahmadabad. Islam contributes many mosques and tombs to the Indian scene; the Taj Mahal is the most famous, but there are many more. The forts of Delhi, Agra and many other northern cities, and the ghost city of Fatehpur Sikri, near Agra, are also Islamic relics of the Mogul period (1556–1707). Despite the formation of Pakistan, India retains a large Islamic minority of about 50 million.

Christian influences range from the elaborate Catholic churches and shrines remaining from Portuguese and French settlement, to the many schools and colleges set up by Christian denominations and still actively teaching; there are also notable church unions in both south and north India. Small Jewish minorities can also be found, providing local colour on a small scale.

The British period of rule left its own monuments; Bombay, for example, has some notable Victoriana, and New Delhi is a planned city of the Edwardian period.

Communications

A more vital memorial is the railway network – a strategic broad-gauge system fed by metre-gauge subsidiaries, with additional light railways, for example to the hill-stations of Simla, Darjeeling and

Ootacamund. Among developments since independence are the fast and comfortable inter-city diesel-electric trains but steam-engines remain the main work-horses – sensibly enough in a coal-rich country.

The road system also has strategic elements from the Mogul and British past, now rationalized into a system of national highways. Main roads are now passable all the year round, and feeder-roads are largely all-weather dirt roads taking traffic close to most of India's 650,000 villages.

The well-served international airports are linked with good, cheap internal services, widely used by passengers from a broad social spectrum. They include routes to tourist centres; India caters well for both her own tourists and for those from overseas.

Recent Development

At Independence India was already established as a partly-industrialized country, and has made great strides in further industrialization during a succession of five-year plans that provided explicitly for both nationalized and private industry. The Damodar coalfield around Asansol has been developed, and new fields opened. The Tata family's steel city of Jamshedpur-Tatanagar, itself now diversified by other industries, has been complemented by new state plants and

A Jain temple at Ranakpur. Jainism is a major Indian religion.

planned towns at Durgapur, Rourkela, Bhilai and Bokharo, with collaboration from Britain, West Germany and the USSR. Major engineering factories have been built at Bangalore, Bhopal, Chittaranjan, Vishakhapatnam and elsewhere, and oil refineries built at Barauni in the north-east, and near Bombay for new fields recently developed in the north-west. Several nuclear power stations are in operation. Irrigation reservoirs and canals have been commissioned, and hydro-electric power is fully exploited. Small-scale industry is also being encouraged. Industrial estates have had mixed success, but do well in places like Bangalore where there are enough related industries to achieve useful interactions.

In the countryside a generation of effort in community and rural development is starting to achieve results, most obviously where the Green Revolution of improved seeds and fertilizers has been successful, for example in the wheatlands of the Punjab and Haryana, or where irrigation has been newly applied and brought success. In such areas it can be argued that the gap between landless labourers and prosperous farmers widens when new methods bring greater yields; but this is one of many social problems that beset a complex society which – like India at present – is in the throes of a quiet but all-pervasive economic revolution. (AL)

A typical Indian village. Rural poverty is widespread.

Threshing grain, Pakistan. Modern farming methods are being introduced.

PAKISTAN

As Egypt is the gift of the Nile, so Pakistan is the gift of the Indus and its tributaries. Despite modern industrialization, irrigated farming is vital to this Islamic state, both in Punjab, the land of the five rivers Indus, Jhelum, Beas, Ravi and Sutlej, and downstream on the dry plains flanking the Indus in Khairpur and Hyderabad. West of the Indus delta the arid coastal plain of Makran rises first to the Coast Range, then in ridge after ridge to the north – stark, arid, deforested, and eroded. Between the ridges lie small desert basins, or larger ones like that containing the saltmarsh of Hamun-i-Mashkel on the Iranian border. Ridge and basin alternate through Baluchistan and Quetta, the damani-koh (skirts of the hills) still irrigated by the ancient tunnels called *karez* or *qanats*, for growing cereals and apricots.

North again stretches Peshawar district, flanking the towering Hindu Kush and Karakoram. East of Peshawar lies Kashmir, which Pakistan controls to the west of the 1947 ceasefire line, and India to the east. The ceasefire ended war and internecine slaughter that followed the grant of Independence from Britain, when the old Indian Empire was partitioned between India and Pakistan. Kashmir's problem was partly religious – a mainly Moslem population ruled by a Hindu Maharajah who acceded to Hindu India. But there was also an underlying strategic issue: five rivers rising in or passing through Kashmir or the neighbouring Indian state of Himachal Pradesh are vital to Pakistan's economy, and could not be left in the hands of possible enemies.

There were disputes, too, about the allocation of river waters to dry interfluves (*doabs*) at various levels for growing winter wheat, summer rice, sugar and cotton vital to both countries. A treaty of 1960 settled these issues, with international aid to re-engineer the canals from the colonial pattern to a two-nation scheme of integrated water use.

Like most developing countries, Pakistan has increased both mineral exploitation and manufacturing industry. To the small oil and coal fields near Rawalpindi has now been added a major resource of natural gas at Sui, between Sukkur and Multan. Karachi, formerly the capital and developed in the colonial period as a wheat port, is now a considerable manufacturing centre; so is the cultural centre, Lahore, in the north. The new, well-planned national capital, Islamabad, is growing east of Rawalpindi, with the serrated outline of the Murree Hills as a backdrop to the new architecture of the city. (AL)

BANGLADESH

Bangladesh broke away from Pakistan in 1972, having been the eastern wing of that country since Partition of the Indian Empire in 1947. Years of friction between Bengali speakers and Urdu-speaking officialdom, largely from West Pakistan, led to a war in which Indian forces attacked Pakistan and so helped the separatist movement. Bangladesh seceded, and a reduced Pakistan withdrew from the British Commonwealth.

Apart from a south-eastern fringe of forested ridges east of Chittagong, Bangladesh consists almost entirely of lowlands – mainly the eastern half of the great delta formed jointly by the Ganges (Ganga) and Brahmaputra. The western part (now West Bengal, India) is largely the 'dying delta' – its land a little higher and less often flooded, its deltaic channels seldom flushed by flood-waters. In contrast the heart of Bangladesh, following the main Ganges channel and the wide Brahmaputra, is the 'active delta'. Frequently flooded, with changing channels that are hazardous to life, health and property, the river also renews soil fertility with silt. The very low coastal fringe is liable to storm surges during hurricanes in the Bay of Bengal. Bangladesh has a dispute with India over water from the Ganges-Kobadak barrage.

The fertile silts of the 'active delta' yield the best jute, and high quality fibre is exported to India; jute and cotton are processed also in modern, post-Independence mills, for example at Narayanganj. There is a large hydro-electric plant at Karnaphuli reservoir, and a modern paper industry using bamboo from the hills. Crafts include boat-building. Chittagong is a busy seaport. The capital, Dacca, suffers from the problems of rapid growth. (AL)

Harvesting rice in the Katmandu valley. Crop yields are often low.

NEPAL AND BHUTAN

Nepal, Bhutan and Sikkim, three independent buffer states, formerly lay between India and Tibet. Now only Nepal and Bhutan retain their independence; Sikkim was incorporated into India in 1975, acquiring a democratic Assembly and representation in the Lok Sabha (Parliament) of New Delhi.

Nepal's mountain heartland lies between the towering Himalaya – the subject of an inconclusive boundary negotiation with China in 1961 – and the Siwalik Range, overlooking the Ganga plain. Its innumerable glens are the homes of a mosaic of peoples, of Indo-European and Tibetan stock, with a wide range of cultures and religions, and fierce clan loyalties.

This heartland, some 800 km (500 miles) from west to east, is divided between the basins of three main rivers, the Ghaghara, Gandak and Kosi. Between the last two, on a smaller river flanked by lake deposits, stands Katmandu, the royal and parliamentary capital, surrounded by emerald rice fields and orchards. The provincial centre of Pokhara is in a similar valley tributary to the Gandak, north of Nuwakot.

South of the Siwalik Range the formerly swampy and malarious *terai*, or hillfoot plain, is now an economic mainstay, with new farming settlements growing rice, wheat, maize, jute and sugar. Development is encouraged by the *terai* section of the Asian Highway. There are two short railways from India, Jaynagar-Janakpur and Raxaul-Amlekganj, where the railhead from the south meets the ropeway that takes goods up to Katmandu. Katmandu has air links to Indian and internal centres. As well as general development aid from the USA, USSR, Britain, New Zealand and Switzerland, China has built a road from Tibet to Katmandu, India one from near Nautanwa to Pokhara. Nepal's most famous assets are the mountains, now a considerable tourist attraction bringing revenue to the country. Everest (8,848 m, 29,000 ft) and Kanchenjunga (8,598 m, 28,200 ft) are the tallest peaks of a splendid mountain range, the greatest in the world, giving a backdrop that dominates every vista in Nepal.

Bhutan With a similar range of peoples, scenery and crops, Bhutan has a little hydro-electricity and light industry – relics of a phase of collaboration with India in the early 1970s, involving industrial and military development. However, in 1974 Bhutan decided not to renew Indian contracts, believing a policy of non-alignment would help her to maintain her role as a buffer state between India and her new northern neighbour, China. (AL)

SRI LANKA

Sri Lanka (formerly Ceylon) has been described as the pearl of the Indian Ocean; this island is also its crossroads. First inhabited by forest-dwelling negroid Veddas, it was settled later by brown-skinned Aryans from India. These are now dominant in the population although diluted by successive waves of incomers. Long-resident Tamils farm in the northern limestone peninsula of Jaffna; the Arab dhow sailors and merchants, who long ago used the monsoon winds to reach Ceylon (monsoon is an Arab word), settled in the ports. After Vasco da Gama's contact with India in the fifteenth century came new traders and colonists – first Portuguese, then Dutch, then British – and new immigrant Tamils were brought in from southeast India to farm the plantations of tea, rubber and coconuts.

From mountain core to coral strand stretches the 'wet zone' of south-western Sri Lanka, supporting cool, grassy downs, rain forests and tea gardens near the ancient religious centre of Kandy, and evergreen forest and palm-fringed beaches in the lowlands from Colombo to east of Galle. White Buddhist shrines and peasant cottages dot the cultivated lands, among coconut palms, rice paddies, sugar cane plantations and spice gardens. In contrast are the much drier zones of the north and east, with mean annual rainfall of 120 cm (50 in) or less. Here irrigation reservoirs were developed by an ancient urban civilization and abandoned in the face of advancing war, or malaria, or both. Since independence in 1948, the old reservoirs and canals are being re-engineered, and planned settlements established.

Traditional farming combines production of rice, sugar, spice and coconuts below irrigation 'tanks' or reservoirs, with millets and pulses on rain-fed fields. Some of the dry crops grow on *chenas* – patches in deciduous jungle where the trees are felled and burned, and the ground is tilled for a few years. Then the patches are abandoned for some time, allowing secondary forest to grow and bring back fertility while new patches are exploited.

Population has increased greatly in Sri Lanka since the successful control of malaria; industry is encouraged, for example round the seaport capital, Colombo. Tourism too is vital to the economy of this beautiful island. (AL)

THE MALDIVE ISLANDS

Divehi Raaje, or Republic of Maldives, comprises over 1,000 islands and atolls, some 200 of them inhabited, scattered along a broad north-south line starting 650 km (400 miles) west-south-west of Cape Comorin. The Maldives are coral reefs, probably built on a foundation of extinct submarine volcanoes. As mid-ocean islands, the Maldives are strategically significant.

The islands were settled from Sri Lanka about 500 BC. For a time under Portuguese, and later Dutch rule, the Maldives became a British protectorate in 1887, administered from Ceylon but retaining local sultanates. They achieved independence in 1965, and the last Sultan was deposed three years later.

Havadu, the principal island, and its neighbouring southern atolls are separated from the main chain by the $1\frac{1}{2}°$ Channel, just north of the Equator. Adequately watered and covered with tropical vegetation, the islands' crops are coconuts, bananas, mangoes, sweet potatoes and spices. Fish are plentiful in the lagoons and in the open sea; bonito and tuna are leading exports together with copra and coir. Japan is helping to develop the economically important fisheries. (AL)

Only since World War 2 has the term South-east Asia become widely used to describe the series of peninsulas and islands which lie east of India and south of China. The name was first employed around 1900 to designate a particular trade and shipping area, but the concept of a South-east Asian region goes back a long way. This was recognized by both the Chinese and the Japanese, who respectively called it the *Nan Yang* and the *Nanyo*, both meaning the 'southern seas'. Today the region includes Burma, Thailand, Cambodia (Kampuchea), Laos, Vietnam, Malaysia, Singapore, Brunei, Indonesia and the Philippines.

South-east Asia, which lies almost wholly in the humid tropics, is an area of rivers and seas. Each of the mainland states is focussed on one major river, with the Irrawaddy in Burma, the Chao Phraya in Thailand, the Mekong in Cambodia and South Vietnam, and the Hongha in North Vietnam. The maritime states, however, revolve around a series of seas and straits, from the highly strategic Strait of Malacca in the west to the Sulu, Celebes and Banda Seas in the east. Geologically, younger fold mountains pivot around an ancient and eroded core. **(PS)**

BURMA

Independent Burma came into being in 1948 with the end of British rule. The country includes many different ethnic and cultural groups, in particular the Burmans, the Shans, the Chins and the Mons. The present government has little control over some disaffected minority groups.

Geographically, the country has three main regions. The core area is a great structural depression drained by the Chindwin, Irrawaddy and Sittang rivers. Its coastal zone has a wet climate, but the inner region between Prome and Mandalay constitutes a 'dry zone', sheltered from the south-west monsoon and with a rainfall of less than 1,000 mm (40 in). In this 'dry zone', which was the original nucleus of the Burmese state, small-scale irrigation has long been practised in the narrow valleys. Important crops today are rice, cotton, jute and sugar-cane. To the west of this core region lie the fold mountains of the Arakan Yoma, while to the east rise the great Shan Plateau and the rugged

Climate

Like India, the great south-eastern peninsula of Asia lies in the north-east trade winds, which bring cool, dry air from China in winter – October to February. March and April are hot and mainly dry: late April and May mark the start of the south-westerly monsoon winds. These cool the air and bring heavy rain for the next five or six months. Within this general pattern the mountain ranges create many local pockets of climate. The valleys are generally drier and warmer than the hill slopes. Singapore has an almost uniform climate – hot and wet throughout the year.

LOCALITY HEIGHT		JAN	JUL	YR
Mandalay	°C	21.4	30.3	27.8
76 m	mm	1	72	871
Hanoi	°C	16.7	29.2	24.2
16 m	mm	18	323	1681
Chiengmai	°C	21.3	27.4	25.6
313 m	mm	7	188	1254
Vientiane	°C	21.5	27.7	25.9
170 m	mm	15	260	1683
Rangoon	°C	24.8	26.6	27.3
23 m	mm	3	580	2618
Quang Tri	°C	20.0	29.4	25.3
7 m	mm	170	89	2540
Krung Thep	°C	26.1	28.4	28.0
12 m	mm	9	178	1492
Saigon	°C	25.8	27.1	27.0
10 m	mm	6	242	1808
Kuala Lumpur	°C	26.8	27.1	27.1
38 m	mm	157	117	2499
Singapore	°C	26.1	27.4	27.1
10 m	mm	285	163	2282

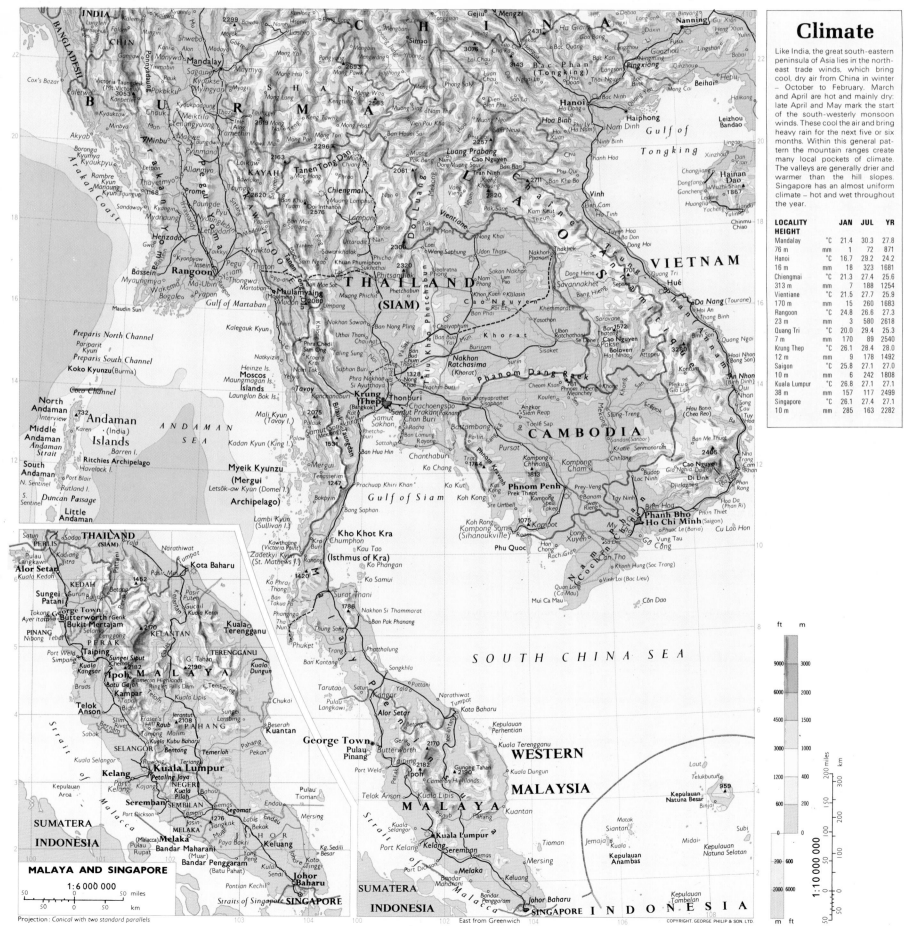

MALAYA AND SINGAPORE

1:6 000 000

50   0   50 miles
50   0   50 km

Projection: Conical with two standard parallels

1:10 000 000

COPYRIGHT. GEORGE PHILIP & SON. LTD.

ASIA SOUTH-EAST

uplands of the Tenasserim. These mountain regions are the home of many hill peoples.

Since 1962 and the declaration of the 'Burmese Way to Socialism', Buddhist Burma has been largely isolated and the economy has appeared to stagnate. (PS)

THAILAND

The Kingdom of Thailand – *Muang Thai* or 'Land of the Free' – has an area of 514,000 km² (198,457 sq miles), comparable with that of France or Spain. Known as Siam until 1939, it is the one South-east Asian country that has not been colonized, or occupied by foreign powers, except in war. Thailand is centred on the valley of the Chao Phraya River that flows across the central plain extending from the Gulf of Siam to the foothills of the northern mountains. Bounded in the west by the narrow mountain range that borders Burma, and in the east by lower hills separating the plain from the higher Khorat Plateau (Cao Nguyen Khorat), the central plain is Thailand's rice-bowl; it presents long vistas, with extensive rice fields, canals and rivers that provide the main routeways, and villages raised on stilts.

The capital city Bangkok (Krung Thep) stands at the southern edge of the plain, near the mouth of the Chao Phraya; with a seaport and international airport it is the transport centre of the country. Ornate Buddhist temples stand side by side with modern concrete buildings, and the growing population is already over a tenth of the total.

North Thailand is a region of fold mountains, with agriculturally-rich intermontane basins. The hill forests produce teak and other valuable timbers. Thailand's highest mountain, Doi Inthanon (2,576 m, 8,451 ft), and the high hills surrounding it are the home of many hill tribes who live by shifting cultivation of dry rice and opium poppies; Chiengmai, the beautiful northern capital, lies in this area. The Khorat Plateau to the east is a sandstone region of poor soils supporting savanna woodlands; glutinous rice, cassava and kenaf are its main produce. The long southern peninsula of Thailand is a forested region of rolling hills, producing tin ore and plantation rubber.

Thailand has long been famous for rice production; even today rice is still the largest earner of export income, despite the increasing importance of several other commodities including tapioca products, sugar, rubber and tin. Wolfram, forest products and fisheries are also being exploited; industries are underdeveloped, but local crafts in the villages help to provide overseas income, as does tourism. (PS)

Buddhist monks in Thailand. The temples are a focus of cultural life.

CAMBODIA

Cambodia (Kampuchea) has an area of 181,000 km² (69,900 sq miles) and a population of about 8.6 million. Its heartland is a wide basin drained by the Mekong River, in the centre of which lies the Tonlé Sap or 'Great Lake', a former arm of the sea surrounded by a broad plain. From November to June, when rains are meagre and the Mekong is low, the lake drains to the south and away to the sea. During the rainy season and period of high river water in June to October the flow reverses, and the lake more than doubles its area. To the south-west stand low mountain chains, including the Cardamom (Phnom Krávanh) and Elephant Mountains. The northern rim of the country is bounded by the Phanom Dang Raek uplands, with a prominent sandstone escarpment. Three-quarters of the country is forested. Nine-tenths of the population live on the fertile plains, mostly in small village settlements; Phnom Penh, the capital, is the only major city.

The Tonlé Sap lowlands were the cradle of the great Khmer Empire, which lasted from AD 802 to 1432; its zenith came in the reign of Suryavarman II (1113–1150), who built the great funerary temple of Angkor Wat. The wealth of the kingdom rested on abundant fish from the lake and rice from the flooded lowlands, for which an extensive system of irrigation channels and storage reservoirs was developed. Cambodia was under French rule from 1863 as part of

Transplanting rice on the Malay Peninsula.

Opium poppies. The drug comes from the immature fruit.

French Indo-China, achieving independence in 1954. In a short period of stability during the late 1950s and 1960s the country developed its small-scale agricultural resources and rubber plantations, remaining predominantly rural; with few workable minerals or sources of power, Cambodia had only minimal opportunities to develop industries, but achieved self-sufficiency in food production with some exports. Following several years of internal political struggles, involvement in the Vietnam war, a destructive civil war and a period of ruthless dictatorship, Cambodia is now devastated and at a very low ebb, unable even to maintain self-sufficiency in rice production, and with a high proportion of the population starving. (PS)

LAOS

Laos is a long, narrow country, sandwiched between Vietnam and Thailand, with an area of 237,000 km² (91,400 sq miles) and a population of about 3.5 million. The geographical nucleus of the country is the valley of the upper Mekong, the largest river of mainland South-east Asia, with a length of some 4,184 km (2,600 miles). It emerges from the Laos Plateau near Luang Prabang and flows for the next 960 km (600 miles) between the Khorat Plateau in the west and the Annamite Chain in the east. In the middle portion of the river there are a series of calm reaches which are interrupted by nine rapids. The most important of these is the Khone falls, the second

The old summer palace of Bang Pa In, Thailand.

greatest waterfall in the world.

The north of the country is made up of the Laos Plateau with an average height of about 915 m (3,000 ft). This is an intricately dissected plateau, with many deep river gorges and forested valleys, wooded ridges and lightly-vegetated areas of limestone. Communication between the isolated valleys is difficult in the broken terrain. The east of the country is dominated by the Annamite Chain, which tilts gradually towards the Mekong valley. Again the relief is complex and the surface of the land deeply dissected. Both these upland regions are the home of hill peoples, who account for over half the total population.

Laos has a long history of invasion and government by outsiders, including the Burmese and Siamese, and was a French protectorate from 1893 to 1954. Since independence Laos has acted uneasily as a buffer state, suffering involvement in the Vietnam war and destructive internal struggles that have left the country poor and undeveloped. About nine-tenths of the population live by subsistence agriculture. There are few industries, developed sources of power or exports. (PS)

VIETNAM

A country of mountains, coastal plains and deltas, Vietnam has an area of 329,550 km² (127,250 sq

Tropical Rain Forest

Rain forest in northern Borneo. Few undisturbed areas remain.

The tropical rain forests of South-east Asia are estimated to cover about 250,000,000 hectares (618,000,000 acres). They are the richest in species of all forest areas in the world. The South-east Asian region is thought to possess some 25,000 species of flowering plants, around 10 per cent of the world's flora.

The evergreen rain forest of the ever-wet, ever-hot tropics is a very complex community. In 20 hectares (49 acres) of forest, there can be as many as 350 different species of trees. These are usually arranged in at least three strata, with the top canopy being more than 40 m (131 ft) above the ground. In the forest, climbing and strangling plants are abundant. Many of the trunks are buttressed, and certain trees bear their flowers and fruits directly on the trunks and branches. The canopy is the home of a wide range of birds, bats and other mammals, including orang utan, the largest arboreal apes in the world.

Much of the rain forest has now been destroyed by shifting cultivators or felled for timber by extracting companies, and the remaining tracts are also under pressure. (PS)

miles) and a population of almost 50 million. In the north the coastal lands widen into the valley and delta of the Hongha and the valley of the Da River. This region has long been the main cultural focus of the country, and it was the original core of the Annamite empire which came into being with the revolt against Chinese rule in AD 939. In the south of the country, the coastal plains open out into the great delta of the Mekong River.

For most of their length the coastal lowlands are backed in the west by the steep and deeply dissected mountains of the Annamite Chain and to the north the country is dominated by the plateaux of Laos and Tongkin, which are often characterized by an intensely craggy, very inhospitable karstic (limestone) landscape. The mountain areas are the home of many different hill peoples.

Vietnam has a long and turbulent history. The name was first used when a southern ruler seized the northern capital of Hanoi and proclaimed himself emperor of a united Vietnam. Following a long period of missionary involvement and a military campaign lasting 25 years, Vietnam became a French protectorate in 1883, later joined by Laos and Cambodia in the French Indo-Chinese Union.

Freedom movements starting in the early twentieth century made little headway until the end of World War 2, when Communist-led guerillas under Ho Chi Minh declared Vietnam once again united and free. There followed a long war against the French (1946–54) which resulted in a Communist-dominated north centred on Hanoi and non-communist south, divided at the 17th parallel of latitude. A second and more ferocious war with strong US and Chinese involvement began in the early 1960s and ended with a

cease-fire in 1973. In 1975, after a relatively brief campaign between north and south, Vietnam was united under a Communist government.

Warfare lasting well over three decades has left Vietnam exhausted, though with considerable potential as a producer of rice, coffee, rubber and many other valuable cash crops. There are mineral deposits, including coal, in the north. (PS)

MALAYSIA

Malaysia is a federation of thirteen states; eleven form Western Malaysia in the Malay Peninsula, and the two states of Sarawak and Sabah make up Eastern Malaysia in northern Borneo. The regions are separated by some 650 km (400 miles) of the South China Sea. The Federation was established in 1963 from former British colonies; Singapore was originally a member but left in 1965. The total area is 329,750 km^2 (127,300 sq miles); the population about 13 million.

The Peninsula

The Malay Peninsula is dominated by fold mountains with a north-south axis. There are seven or eight major ranges, with frequently exposed granite cores. The most important is the so-called Main Range, which runs from the Thai border to the south-east of Kuala Lumpur, attaining 2,182 m (7,159 ft) at its highest point, Gunong Kerbau. The highest mountain, Gunong Tahan,

reaches 2,190 m (7,185 ft). South of the Main Range lies the flat and poorly-drained lowland of Johor, which is punctuated by isolated hills, often rising over 1,060 m (3,500 ft). The small rivers of Malaya have built up a margin of lowland around the coasts.

Northern Borneo

Northern Borneo has a mangrove-fringed coastal plain, up to 65 km (40 miles) wide, backed by hill country averaging 300 m (1,000 ft) in elevation. This is dominated by the east-west fold mountains of the interior, which rise from 1,400 m to 2,300 m (4,500 to 7,500 ft). The most striking is the granite peak of Mt Kinabalu (4,101 m, 13,455 ft) in Sabah, Malaysia's highest mountain. The natural vegetation of most of Malaysia is lowland rain forest and its montane variants. The Malaysian forests, which are dominated by the dipterocarp family of trees, are the richest in species of all forests in the world. Unfortunately, few undisturbed areas remain, mostly in such national parks as the Gunong Mulu in Sarawak and the Kinabalu in Sabah.

History and Economy

An early golden age of Malay political power came in the fifteenth century with the rise of the Kingdom of Malacca, which controlled the important sea routes and trade of the region. In 1414, the ruler of Malacca accepted the Islamic faith, which remains the official religion of Malaysia today. Malaysia is, however, characterized by great ethnic and cultural diversity, with Malays of many different origins, Chinese, Indians, Eurasians, Europeans and a number of aboriginal peoples.

The achievement of national unity and identity is not proving an easy process. Economically, Malaysia is the world's largest producer of natural rubber. Other important products are tin (more than one-third of the world's supply), timber, palm oil, rice and a wide range of tropical crops. Sarawak supplies much of the world's pepper. (PS)

SINGAPORE

The republic of Singapore comprises the island of Singapore and an additional fifty-four small islands lying within its territorial waters. The highest point on the main island is Bukit Timah (177 m, 581 ft). The position of Singapore, controlling the Strait of Malacca, is one of enormous strategic importance.

When Sir Stamford Raffles established British rule on the island in 1819, there were only 150 inhabitants. This had not always been so.

Singapura (the city of the lion) was an important settlement in the fourteenth century, but had been destroyed in the rivalry between the great kingdoms of Madjapahit (Java) and Siam. The modern city was originally laid out and planned by Raffles himself and remained under British rule until self-government was agreed on in 1958. In 1963, Singapore became part of the Federation of Malaysia, but disputes soon arose between Singapore and Malaysia, leading to separation and full independence in 1965.

Today, Singapore is one of the world's most remarkable commercial and industrial experiments. It is, in effect, a city-state, thick with skyscrapers, the most densely populated country in South-east Asia and a great *entrepôt* economy. Yet, the multi-racial population of predominantly Chinese, as well as Malay and Indians, still adheres to a medley of languages and cultures. (PS)

THE PHILIPPINES

The Republic of the Philippines received independence from the USA in 1946. It is a country of over 7,000 islands, about 1,000 of which are permanently inhabited. The two largest are Luzon in the north and Mindanao in the south.

The Philippines lack extensive areas of lowland and most of the islands are characterized by rugged interior mountains, the highest of which are Mt Apo (2,954 m, 9,691 ft) in Mindanao and Mt Pulog (2,929 m, 9,610 ft) in Luzon. There are over twenty active volcanoes in the islands, including Mt Apo and the powerful Mt Mayon in south-east Luzon. The latter erupted in 1814, partly destroying the city of Legazpi. The most important lowland region is the central plain of Luzon, a key rice producing area and a major zone of population concentration. The Manila Bay area is dominated by the urban complex of Metro Manila.

The most impressive man-made sight, however, is the spectacular series of irrigated rice terraces that contour the mountain slopes in the northern interior of Luzon. These have been constructed by Igorot tribesmen, descendants of some of the earliest people to colonize the Philippines. Elsewhere in the islands, and especially on Cebu, Leyte and Negros, maize is the staple foodstuff, reflecting the Philippines' former contacts with Spanish America. Another link is Roman Catholicism; 90 per cent of the population are Roman Catholic today. Most Philippine islanders are subsistence farmers; sugar, coconuts and tobacco are produced as cash crops. (PS)

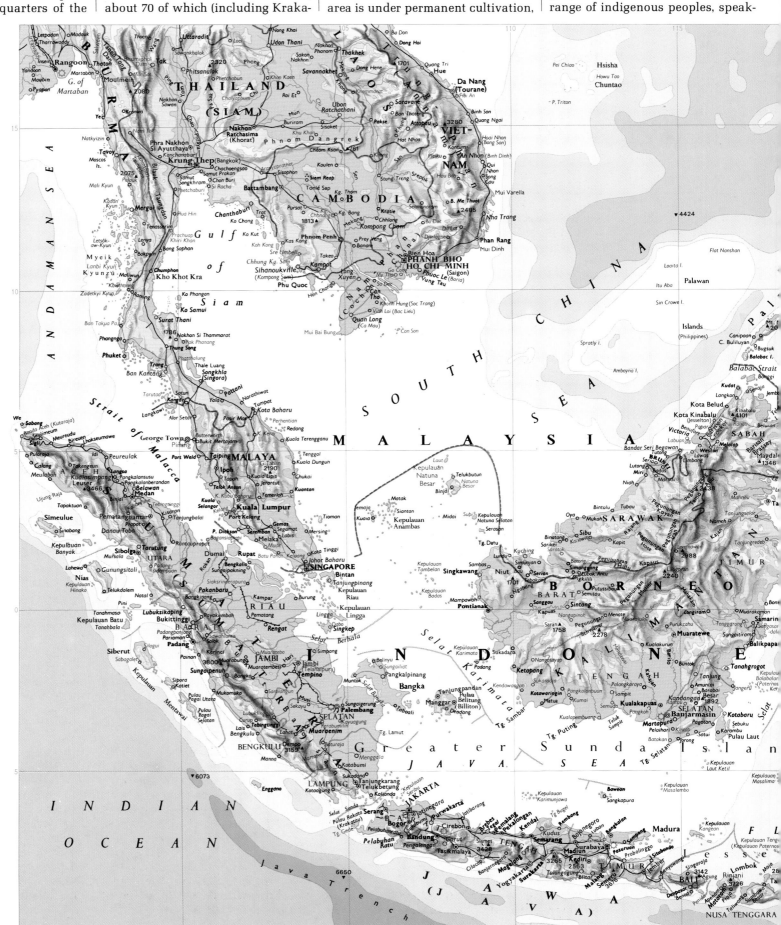

INDONESIA

Indonesia as a national entity covers most of the East Indies between the mainland of South-east Asia and Australia. With an area of 1,919,270 km² (741,030 sq miles), and a population of over 145 million, it includes more than 13,000 islands, scattered over an enormous area of tropical sea. However, three-quarters of the

area is included in the five main centres of Sumatra, Java, Kalimantan (southern Borneo), Sulawesi (Celebes) and Irian Jaya (the western end of New Guinea), which also include over four-fifths of the population; more than half the population is on Sumatra alone.

Most of the big islands stand on continental shelves and have extensive coastal lowlands though Sulawesi and the chain of islands between Java and Irian Jaya rise from deep water. All are mountainous, for this is an area of great crustal activity. Along the arc formed by Sumatra, Java and the Lesser Sunda Islands stand over 200 volcanoes, about 70 of which (including Kraka-

tau (Pulau Rakata) in the Sunda Strait) have erupted within the last two centuries, usually with memorable violence. Java alone has over 120 volcanoes, fourteen of which exceed 3,000 m (10,000 ft).

Vegetation and Agriculture

The natural vegetation of the tropical lowlands is rain forest (p. 93), which also spreads up into the hills. Much of this has now been cleared by shifting cultivators and replaced by secondary growth, though forest is still the dominant vegetation on most of the less populated islands. About one-tenth of the total land area is under permanent cultivation,

mostly of rice, maize, cassava and sweet potato; there are also large plantations of rubber, cane sugar, coffee and tea. Accessible parts of the rain forest are being exploited for their valuable timber; native forest in Sumatra is now virtually restricted to reserves and national parks. Mountain forests, less vulnerable because they are less accessible, still remain over wide areas. Many of the coasts are lined with mangrove swamps.

Peoples

The population of Indonesia is complex and varied. There is a wide range of indigenous peoples, speaking some 25 different languages and over 250 dialects; most numerous are the Javanese, Sundanese, Madurese, Malays, Bataks, Buginese and Balinese. Then there are Indians, Arabs, Chinese and European communities, many well-established after several generations of settlement. Four of the world's major religions – Islam, Hinduism, Christianity and Buddhism – are well represented with followers of Islam in the majority.

History and Development

The first important empire in the region was centred at Palembang in south-eastern Sumatra. This was the great maritime power of Sri Vijaya, which held sway from the eighth to the thirteenth centuries over the important trade routes of the Malacca and Sunda Straits. During the fourteenth century it was replaced by the kingdom of Madjapahit, centred on the fertile lands of east-central Java. From the sixteenth century onward European influences grew, the area coming progressively under the domination of the Dutch East India Company during the seventeenth to early nineteenth centuries. Freedom movements starting in the early twentieth century found their full expression under Japanese occupation in World War 2, and Indonesia declared its independence on the surrender of Japan in 1945. The independent state of Indonesia finally achieved full recognition in 1950.

Still largely agricultural, with most of the population engaged in subsistence farming, Indonesia has considerable potential for economic growth. Oil currently provides about half the national revenues; mining for tin, bauxite, coal, gold and other minerals is growing, and small-scale industries are developing to absorb the large number of unemployed. (PS)

Rice paddies on Bali. A quarter of agricultural land is irrigated.

Climate

Lying across the Equator, surrounded by warm ocean, Indonesia's islands are hot and generally rainy throughout the year. Temperatures near the coast seldom fall below 20°C (68°F) or rise far above 30°C (86°F): frost and snow are unknown except in the high mountains of Irian Jaya. Rainfall is heaviest from October to March, only in the south-eastern islands is there an almost rainless season from June to August. The Philippines are hot throughout the year, especially so during their dry months of March to June. Rain is heavy for the rest of the year, with typhoons prevalent in late summer.

LOCALITY HEIGHT		JAN	JUL	YR
Manila	°C	25.4	27.9	27.3
15 m	mm	18	253	1791
Zamboanga	°C	26.6	26.6	26.9
6 m	mm	51	120	1226
Medan	°C	25.6	26.9	26.4
23 m	mm	137	135	2029
Tarakan	°C	26.1	26.9	26.7
12 m	mm	277	262	3868
Padang	°C	26.2	26.9	26.9
7 m	mm	350	277	4427
Balikpapan	°C	26.1	25.6	26.1
7 m	mm	201	180	2228
Ambon	°C	27.8	25.3	26.7
4 m	mm	127	602	3459
Jakarta	°C	26.2	26.7	26.9
8 m	mm	335	61	1755
Pasuruan	°C	27.2	25.8	26.9
5 m	mm	226	25	1285
Kupang	°C	27.2	26.1	27.2
45 m	mm	388	5	1440

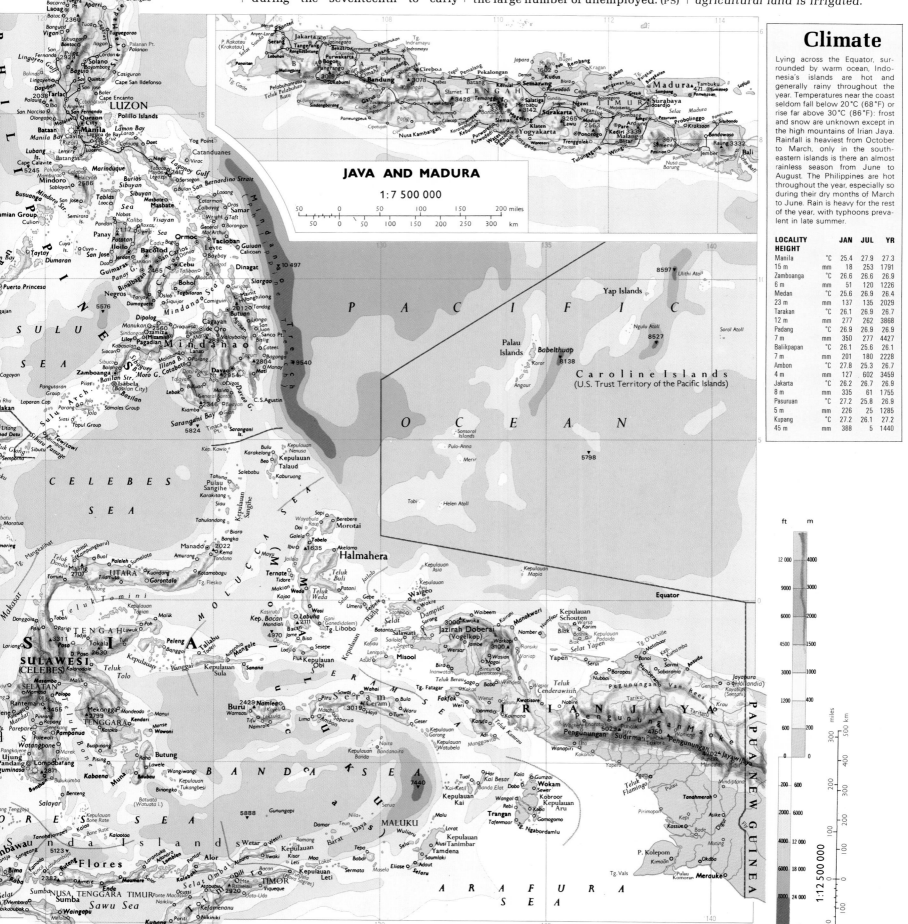

JAVA AND MADURA
1:7 500 000

COPYRIGHT. GEORGE PHILIP & SON. LTD.

EAST ASIA

East Asia comprises the lands to the east of the great mountain barrier which runs from south-western China, through the Himalaya, the Karakoram and the Tian Shan, to the Altai range on the borders of Mongolia, China and the USSR. With an area of 11,754,000 km² (4,538,220 sq miles), it occupies roughly 9 per cent of the land area of the globe, and exhibits a very great diversity of relief and climate. Altitudes vary from the high Tibetan plateau, where the average elevation is over 4,500 m (14,760 ft), to the floor of the Turfan (Turpan Hami) depression, 154 m (505 ft) below sea-level. East Asian climates range from the cold continental of northern Mongolia to the warm humid tropical climates of southern China and Hainan.

East Asia contains a population of over 1,150 million – well over one quarter of mankind. This population is unevenly distributed with the main concentrations in lowland areas open to the influence of the summer monsoon in eastern China, Korea, and Japan. Until recent times the whole area has been strongly dominated by the Chinese civilization. (JS)

Camels on the Mongolian steppes. Mongolia is a land of pastoralists.

MONGOLIA

With an area of 1,565,000 km² (604,270 sq miles), Mongolia covers a territory larger than France, Italy, Germany and the United Kingdom combined. It is, however, a thinly populated country, with an average of only one person per km².

Landscape and Agriculture

Mongolia may be broadly divided into two contrasting regions, respectively north and south of a line joining the Altai, Hangayn and Hentiyn mountains.

The southern half of Mongolia lies at an average height of 1,500 m (4,900 ft) and has a strongly continental climate. Temperatures may range from over 32°C (90°F) in the summer to −46°C (−50°F) in the winter, and rainfall is everywhere both meagre and variable, rarely amounting to more than 300 mm (12 in) per year. Apart from the north-east, where rivers flow into the Amur basin, inland drainage predominates. In the desert-steppelands of the south, salt lakes and salt pans occupy shallow depressions, and poor scrub eventually gives way to the arid wastes of the Gobi desert.

In northern Mongolia, high mountains alternate with river valleys and lake basins. In the north-west, where the Altai range rises to over 4,000 m (13,120 ft), boreal forests blanket the mountain slopes. Northern Mongolia receives an annual precipitation of 510 mm (20 in). Pastures are rich enough to support herds of cattle, and some wheat is grown, especially in areas where black earth soils occur. The Selenge and Orhon Gol river basins contain the most productive agricultural land and the main centres of population.

Mongolia is a land of nomadic pastoralists, and large herds of sheep, goats, camels and horses form the mainstay of the economy. Mongolian herdsmen inhabit gers – circular tents covered in felt – which are light and portable, but also weatherproof. The main foodstuffs of Mongolia include milk, cheese, mutton, and rancid butter.

Recent Development

Following the collapse of the Ch'ing dynasty in 1912, Mongolia broke away from China, but full independence was not gained until 1921. Thereafter the country fell increasingly under Soviet influence and in 1924 a communist People's Republic was proclaimed.

Since World War 2, textiles and food processing industries have been developed, with strong Soviet support. Aid from COMECON and the USSR has also been instrumental in the opening up of mineral deposits, which include copper, molybdenum, and coking coal.

Ulaanbaatar, the capital of Mon-

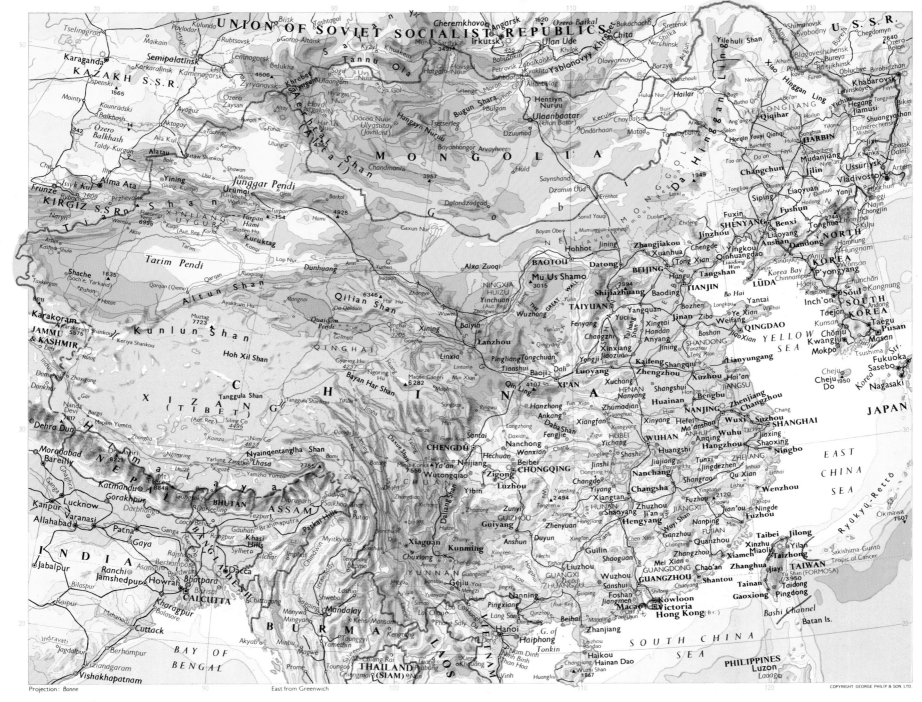

golia, is a modern city designed to some extent along Soviet Russian lines. (JS)

CHINA

With an area of 9,561,000 km² (3,691,500 sq miles), the People's Republic of China ranks as the world's third largest country, after the USSR and Canada. Before the development of modern forms of transport, the enormous size of China often hampered efficient communication between the centre of the country and the peripheries. Mileages are huge. By rail, the distances from Peking (Beijing) to Canton (Guangzhou) and Chungking (Chongqing) are 2,324 km (1,450 miles) and 2,567 km (1,600 miles) respectively.

One of the main determining influences on the evolution of Chinese civilization has been the geographical isolation of China from the rest of the world. Surrounded to the north, west and south by forests, deserts, and formidable mountain ranges, and separated from the Americas by the vast expanse of the Pacific Ocean, China until modern times was insulated from frequent contact with other civilizations, and her culture and society developed along highly individual lines.

Relief and Landscape

The Chinese landscape is like a chequerboard, in which mountains and plateaux alternate with basins and alluvial plains. There are two intersecting systems of mountain

The Great Wall of China dates from the fourth century BC.

chains, one trending from north-north-east to south-south-west, the other from east to west. The first system includes the mountains of Zhejiang and Fujian provinces, in south-eastern China, the Shandong peninsula, the mountains of Guizhou province, the Shanxi ranges, and the Da Hinggan Ling, close to the borders of Manchuria and Mongolia. The most important lowland areas of China – the Manchurian plain, the North China plain, and the lake basins of the central Yangtze (Chang Jiang) – occupy a zone of down-warping which also trends from north-east to south-west.

The east-west axes that transect these north-east to south-west trend lines are most prominent in the Daqing Shan and Qin Ling ranges; the southernmost axis, which underlies the watershed between the Yangtze and Si Kiang (Xi J.) river systems is less conspicuous.

Many mountain areas have been devastated by soil erosion through indiscriminate tree felling. The agricultural wealth of China is all in the lowlands.

The chequerboard pattern includes an extraordinary variety of landscapes. Manchuria, in the far north, comprises a wide area of gently undulating country, originally grassland, but now an important agricultural area. The loess lands of the north-west occupy a broad belt

from the great loop of the Hwang Ho (Huang He) into Shanxi and Henan provinces. Here, valley sides, hills and mountains are blanketed in loess – a fine-grained unstratified soil deposited by wind during the last glaciation. Within this region, loess deposits occur widely in the form of plateaux which are deeply incised by gorges and ravines.

By contrast with the loess lands, the landscape of the densely-populated North China plain is flat and monotonous. Settlement is concentrated in walled villages while large fields are the product of post-1949

High Plateau Life

The peaks and high plateaux of the Himalaya and central Asia are forested up to about 4,000 m (13,000 ft) with an open woodland of pines, cedars, cypresses, bamboos and rhododendrons. Above lies a zone of dwarf shrubs – willows, birches and junipers that spend half their year among swirling snow. This grades into a rough, semi-frozen tundra of coarse sedges and grasses, dotted with cushions of intensely-coloured alpine flowers; primulas, edelweiss and gentians become prominent as the snow retreats in early summer. Insects are surprisingly plentiful in the thin, cool air at 4,500 to 5,500 m (15,000 to 18,000 ft). Bees, wasps, flies, butterflies and moths are common, and grasshoppers, beetles and ants scurry over the sun-warmed ground.

At 6,000 m (19,500 ft) tundra turns to dry desert and both plants and animals become rare. Mites, small centipedes and jumping spiders have been found at this height, living in sunny corners among the rocks and feeding on plant debris and each other. Larger grazing animals – yaks, hangul deer and blue sheep, for example, emerge from the forest to feed on the high plateaux in summer, and mountain goats (tahr and markhor) and ibex find a living among the high, snow-encrusted crags. Wolves, snow leopards and high-flying eagles are their main predators. (BS)

Yaks grazing on high pastures.

Giant pandas inhabit bamboo forests in the mountains of Szechwan and nearby parts of Tibet.

Climate

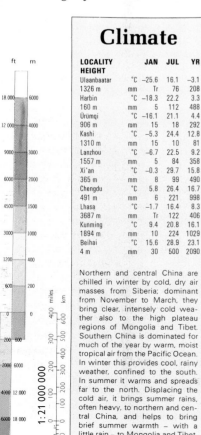

LOCALITY HEIGHT		JAN	JUL	YR
Ulaanbaatar	°C	−25.6	16.1	−3.1
1326 m	mm	Tr	76	208
Harbin	°C	−18.3	22.2	3.3
160 m	mm	5	112	488
Ürümqi	°C	−16.1	21.1	4.4
906 m	mm	15	18	292
Kashi	°C	−5.3	24.4	12.8
1310 m	mm	15	10	81
Lanzhou	°C	−6.7	22.5	9.2
1557 m	mm	5	84	358
Xi'an	°C	−0.3	29.7	15.8
365 m	mm	8	99	490
Chengdu	°C	5.8	26.4	16.7
491 m	mm	6	221	998
Lhasa	°C	−1.7	16.4	8.3
3687 m	mm	Tr	122	406
Kunming	°C	9.4	20.8	16.1
1894 m	mm	10	224	1029
Beihai	°C	15.6	28.9	23.1
4 m	mm	30	500	2090

Northern and central China are chilled in winter by cold, dry air masses from Siberia; dominant from November to March, they bring clear, intensely cold weather also to the high plateau regions of Mongolia and Tibet. Southern China is dominated for much of the year by warm, moist tropical air from the Pacific Ocean. In winter this provides cool, rainy weather, confined to the south. In summer it warms and spreads far to the north. Displacing the cold air, it brings summer rains, often heavy, to northern and central China, and helps to bring brief summer warmth – with a little rain – to Mongolia and Tibet.

The spectacular limestone scenery of parts of southern China.

Southern China China to the south of the Qin Ling ranges receives heavier and more reliable rainfall than the north, and winter temperatures are generally above freezing point. Summer weather, especially in the central Yangtze valley, is hot and humid. At Nanking, temperatures as high as 44°C (111°F) have been recorded. Inland, the mild climate and fertile soils of the Red Basin make this an important agricultural region. Rice production is dominant but at lower altitudes the climate is warm enough to allow the cultivation of citrus fruits, cotton, sugar-cane and tobacco.

The far south of China, including Guangdong province and the island of Hainan, lies within the tropics and enjoys a year-round growing season. Irrigated rice cultivation is the economic mainstay of southern China. Double cropping (rice as a main crop followed by winter wheat) is characteristic of the Yangtze valley; along the coast of Guangdong province two crops of rice can be grown each year, and in parts of Hainan island the annual cultivation of three crops of rice is possible. Crops such as tea, mulberry, and sweet potato are also cultivated, and in the far south, sugar cane, bananas, and other tropical crops are grown.

The interior While the Qin Ling ranges are an important boundary between the relatively harsh environments of the north and the more productive lands of the south, a second major line, which follows the Da Hinggan Ling mountains and the eastern edge of the high Tibetan plateau, divides the intensively cultivated lands of eastern China from the mountains and arid steppes of the interior. In the north, this

land consolidation schemes. Further south the Yangtze delta is a land of large lakes. Water is a predominant element of the landscape – the low-lying alluvial land with its irrigated rice fields is traversed by intricate networks of canals and other man-made water works, many of which date back several centuries.

Far inland in the Yangtze basin, and separated from the middle Yangtze valley by precipitous river gorges, lies the Red Basin of Szechwan (Sichuan). To north, west, and south, the basin is surrounded by high mountain ranges. The mountains of the Qin Ling ranges, in particular, protect the basin from cold winter winds. With its mild climate and fertile soils, the Red Basin is one of the most productive and densely populated regions of China. Rice fields, often arranged in elaborate terraces, dominate the landscape.

Other distinctive landscapes of southern China include those of north-eastern Guizhou province, where limestone spires and pinnacles rise vertically above small, intensively cultivated plains, and the Guangdong coastal lowlands, with their villages in groves of citrus, bananas, mangoes, and palms.

The Hwang Ho and Yangtze

The two major rivers of China are the Hwang Ho and the Yangtze. The Hwang Ho, or Yellow River (so called from the large quantities of yellowish silt which it transports) is 4,700 km (2,940 miles) long. Also known as 'China's Sorrow', the Hwang Ho throughout history has been the source of frequent and disastrous floods. In 1938, dykes along the Hwang Ho were demolished in order to hamper the advance of the Japanese army into northern China, and the river was diverted so as to enter the sea to the south of the Shandong peninsula. In the catastrophic floods which followed, nearly 900,000 lives were lost and 54,000 km² (21,000 sq miles) of land

was inundated. Since 1949, the incidence of flooding has declined sharply, largely as a result of state investment in flood prevention schemes.

The Yangtze, China's largest and most important river, is 5,520 km (3,450 miles) long, and its catchment basin is over twice as extensive as that of the Hwang Ho. Unlike the Hwang Ho, the Yangtze is navigable. During the summer months, ocean-going vessels of 10,000 tonnes may reach Wuhan, and 1,000 tonne barges may be taken as far upstream as Chungking. Despite the post-1949 improvement of roads and railways, the Yangtze remains an important transport artery.

Climate and Agriculture

Although the Chinese subcontinent includes a wide variety of relief and climate, it can be divided into three broad regions. Eastern China is divided into two contrasting halves, north and south of the Qin Ling ranges, while the third region comprises the mountains and arid steppes of the interior.

Northern China Throughout northern China, rainfall is light and variable, and is generally insufficient for irrigated agriculture. In winter, temperatures fall to between −1°C and −8°C (30°F and 18°F) and bitterly cold winds blow eastwards across the North China plain from the steppes of Mongolia. Summer temperatures, by contrast, are little different from those of southern China, and may reach a daily average of 28°C (82°F). The growing season diminishes northwards and in northern Manchuria only 90 days per year are free of frost. Despite advances in water conservation since World War 2, aridity and unreliability of rainfall restrict the range of crops that can be grown. Millet, maize and winter wheat are the staple crops of the North China plain, while coarse grains and soya beans are cultivated in Manchuria.

Tibet

Tibet, at the heart of Asia, forms the highest and most extensive area of plateau land in the world. Formidable mountain barriers – the Himalaya, the Karakoram, the ranges of the Kunlun Shan and Qilian Shan – surround the plateau, isolating Tibet from the rest of the world. In former times, the remote and inaccessible land of Tibet effectively separated the two great civilizations of Asia–India and China.

Within Tibet, high altitudes, thin soils, and a cold arid climate are the chief constituents of an unusually inhospitable physical environment. Tibet covers an area of 1,200,000 kms² (463,320 sq miles) but has an estimated population of under 2 million.

The Tibetan plateau lies mostly at an elevation of 4,500 m (14,760 ft) – an altitude only slightly lower than the summit of Mont Blanc in Europe. The plateau contains chains of hills and depressions choked with frost debris and gravel. Inland drainage predominates, with rivers and streams flowing into brackish lakes and salt marshes. The climate is extremely harsh, summer temperatures rarely rising above −1°C (30°F). Precipitation is generally less than 100 mm (4 in) and is mostly snow or sleet. Vegetation is limited to rough pasture.

Environmental conditions are less severe in the south of Tibet. In the sheltered valley of the Tsangpo (upper Brahmaputra), the climate is mild enough to allow the cultivation of highland barley. The valley contains the main centres of population, including Lhasa and Shigatse (Xigaze).

In the south-east of Tibet, the grain of the country is north to south. Here the upper waters of three great rivers – the Yangtze, the Mekong, and the Salween – flow in deep valleys separated by high parallel mountain ranges. This region is greener and more humid than elsewhere in Tibet. In the valleys below 3,000 m (9,800 ft), maize is cultivated, and ample pastureland covers the upper slopes.

The chief foodstuffs of Tibet include barley, butter, curds, and Chinese brick tea. Animals such as yak, sheep and cattle are kept, but most Tibetans are sedentary farmers, pastoral nomads accounting for only one-sixth of the population.

Tibet, formerly a theocratic state governed by Lamas, was assimilated by China after 1950, and is now administered by the People's Republic as an Autonomous Region. Tibetan refugees preserve the old culture. Lhasa, the capital of Tibet, is dominated by the Potala, formerly the monastery and palace of the Dalai Lama. (JS)

A Tibetan monastery. The Chinese now discourage religious life.

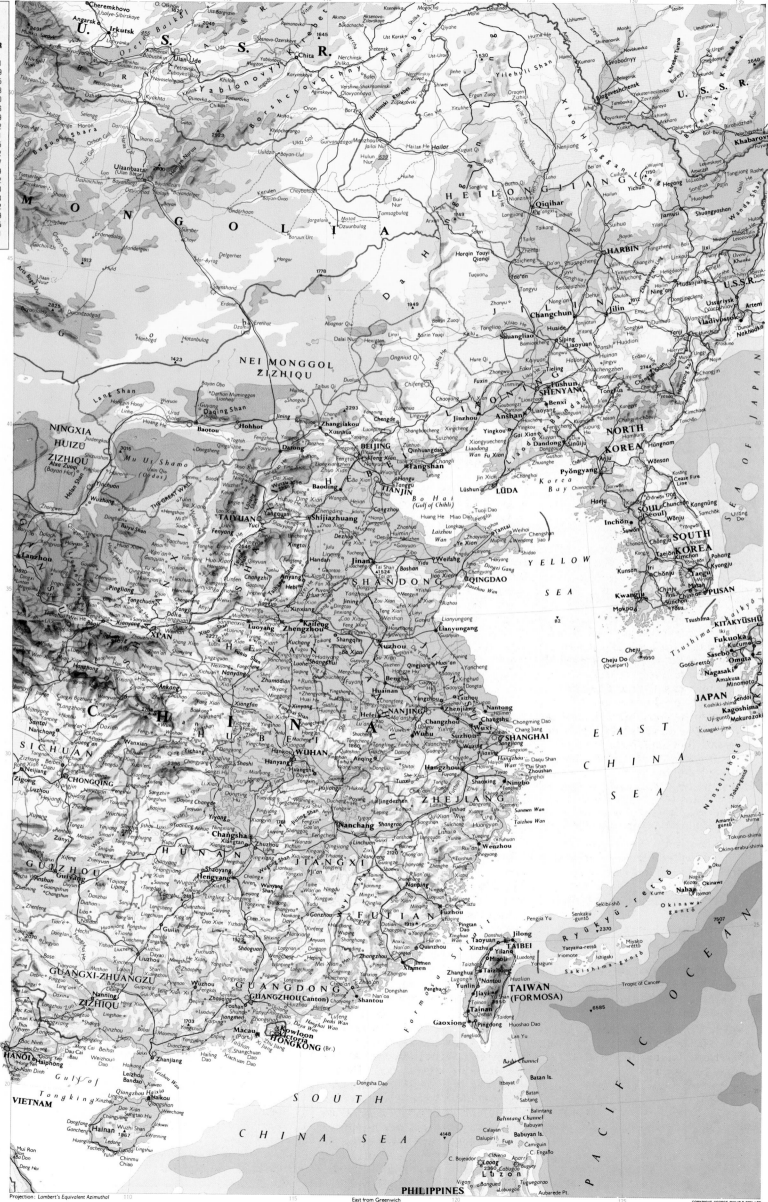

A fish-rearing commune in Guangdong Province.

boundary line is marked by the Great Wall of China, built to prevent incursions of steppe nomads. Western China includes the Dzungarian basin, the Turfan depression, the arid wastes of the Takla Makan desert, and the high plateau of Tibet.

In former centuries, the Dzungarian basin provided a corridor through which nomadic pastoralists were able to enter north-western China. Other important routes from Central Asia into China followed the northern and southern rims of the Takla Makan desert. Although aridity of climate has hampered the development of agriculture throughout most of western China, oasis crops are grown around the rim of the Takla Makan desert, and farming settlements also exist in the Gansu corridor to the north of the Qilian mountains.

History

Early Chinese civilization arose along the inland margins of the North China plain, in a physical setting markedly harsher (especially in terms of winter temperatures) than the environments of the other great civilizations of the Old World. The Shang dynasty, noted for its fine craftsmanship in bronze, flourished in northern China from 1630 to 1122 BC. Shang civilization was followed by many centuries of political fragmentation, and it was not until the third century BC that China was unified into a centrally-administered empire. Under the Ch'in dynasty (221 to 206 BC) the Great Wall of China was completed. This provided a continuous line of fortification running for a distance of 2,250 km (1,400 miles) from northern Gansu province to western Liaoning. Meanwhile, Chinese armies pushed southwards beyond the Yangtze, reaching the southern Chinese coast in the vicinity of Canton.

In succeeding centuries, there occurred a very gradual movement of population from the north to the warmer, moister, and more productive lands of the south. This slow migration was greatly accelerated by incursions of barbarian nomads into north China, especially during the Sung dynasty (AD 960 to 1279). By the late thirteenth century, the southern lands, including the Yangtze valley, probably contained be-

A farming commune near Nanking. Communes also run rural industry.

tween 70 and 80 per cent of the Chinese population.

During the Han, T'ang, and Sung dynasties, a remarkably stable political and social order evolved within China. The major distinguishing features of Chinese civilization came to include Confucianism, whereby the individual was subordinated to family obligations and to state service, the state bureaucracy, members of which were recruited by public examination, and the benign rule of the Emperor – the 'Son of Heaven'. Great advances were made in the manufacture of porcelain, silk, metals, and lacquerware, while gunpowder, the compass, and printing were among several Chinese inventions which found their way to the West in medieval times. Nevertheless, the economy of pre-modern China was overwhelmingly agricultural, and the peasant class accounted for most of the population.

Despite the geographical diversity and great size of her territory, China during pre-modern times experienced long periods of unity and cohesion, which were rarely disturbed by invasion from outside. Two important dynasties, the Yuan (1279–1368) and the Ch'ing (1644–1912), were established by the Mongols and Manchus respectively, but, almost invariably, alien rulers found it necessary to adopt Chinese methods of government, and the Chinese cultural tradition was preserved intact.

Another characteristic of pre-modern China was the tendency of Chinese rulers either to ignore the outside world, or to regard it with contempt. China was thought by her rulers to occupy a position of central importance, and all other countries were seen as essentially subordinate to the Chinese empire.

The Birth of the Republic

In the eighteenth century, China experienced a rapid acceleration in the rate of population growth, and standards of living began to fall. By the early nineteenth century, the government was weak and corrupt, and the country suffered frequent famines and political unrest. British victory in the Opium War (1839–42) was followed by the division of China into spheres of influence of the major Western imperialist powers, and by the establishment of treaty ports, controlled by Western countries, along the Chinese coast and the river Yangtze. Meanwhile, the disintegration of imperial China was hastened by peasant uprisings such as the Taiping rebellion (1850–64), and by the defeat of China in the Sino-Japanese War of 1894–5. Belated attempts were made to arrest the decline of the Chinese empire, but in 1912, and following an uprising in Wuhan, the last of the Chinese emperors abdicated and a republic was proclaimed.

Although the republican admin-

istration in Peking was regarded as the legitimate government, real power rested with army generals and with provincial governors. Rival generals, or warlords, raised private armies and plunged China into a long and disastrous period of internal disorder. Alternative solutions to China's problems were offered by two political parties – the Kuomintang (or Chinese Nationalist Party) formed by Sun Yat-sen and later led by Chiang Kai-shek, and the Communist Party. In 1931, Japan seized Manchuria, and in 1937 full-scale war broke out between the two countries. In the bitter fighting which followed, the Communists, under Mao Tse-tung, gained the support of the peasantry and proved adept practitioners of guerrilla warfare.

The defeat of Japan in 1945 was followed by a brief period of civil warfare in which the Communists routed the Kuomintang armies, forcing them to take refuge on the island of Taiwan. The People's Republic of China was officially proclaimed on 1 October 1949.

Under Communist rule, the mass starvation, malnutrition and disease which afflicted China before World War 2 have been virtually eliminated, and living standards have been greatly improved, especially in the countryside.

Recent Development

One of the salient features of the centrally-planned economy of post-1949 China has been the organization of the rural population into 50,000 communes – self-sufficient units of varying size which farm the land collectively. Communes also run rural industries, and are responsible for the administration of schools and clinics. Through the communes, labour has been organized on a vast scale to tackle public works schemes such as water conservation, flood control, and land reclamation.

Although food supply has generally kept abreast of population growth, the future size and growth rate of the Chinese population must give cause for concern. China's population, which amounts to about 933 million, is easily the largest in the world, and corresponds to roughly one quarter of mankind. By the late 1970s, the population was growing at 1.7 per cent per year, a rate which represents a net annual increase of about 15 million people.

Only 10 per cent of the total land area of China is cultivable, but environmental constraints are such that there is little prospect of meeting increased food demand by reclaiming land for agriculture. Future growth in food supply must come from continued intensification of land use, and from further gains in yields per hectare.

Although China is an agricultural country, government planners, especially since the death of Mao Tse-tung in 1976, have emphasized the need to industrialize. China has sufficient resources (coal, iron ore,

The morning rush hour in Peking.

crude oil) to support an industrial economy, but is deficient in capital and industrial technology. Sizeable centres of heavy industry exist in Manchuria (iron and steel at Anshan, engineering at Harbin, chemicals at Jilin) and in the environs of large cities such as Shanghai, Nanking, Wuhan, Chungking, and Tientsin.

Peking, the capital city of China, is a governmental and administrative centre of prime importance. Several buildings of outstanding architectural interest, such as the former imperial palace complex (once known as the Forbidden City) and the Temple and Altar of Heaven, have been carefully preserved and are now open to the public. Shanghai is China's largest city. In the nineteenth and early twentieth centuries, with a large community of foreign merchants, it grew rapidly as a major banking and trading centre. Since 1949, the city has lost its former commercial importance, but has emerged as a major centre for the manufacture of iron and steel, ships, textiles, and a wide range of engineering products.(JS)

TAIWAN

The island of Taiwan, also known as Formosa, lies 145 km (90 miles) east of the coast of Fujian province, China, and covers an area of 36,000 km² (13,900 sq miles). Since 1949, Taiwan has been occupied by the government of the Republic of China, which also administers the Pescadores and several small islands, including Quemoy (Jinmen) and Mazu, that lie close to the Chinese coast.

High mountain ranges, which extend for the entire length of the island, occupy the central and eastern parts of Taiwan, and only a quarter of the island's surface area is cultivated. The central mountain ranges rise to altitudes of over 3,000 m (10,000 ft), and carry dense forests of broadleaved evergreen trees such as camphor and Chinese cork oak. Above 1,500 m (5,000 ft), conifers such as pine, larch, and cedar predominate.

With its warm, moist, tropical climate, Taiwan provides a highly favourable environment for agricul-

ture, and the well-watered lands of the western coastal plain produce heavy rice crops. Sugar cane, sweet potatoes, bananas and pineapples are also grown.

Taiwan produces a wide range of manufactured goods, including colour television sets, electronic calculators, footwear, and ready-made clothing. Taibei, the capital, is a modern and affluent city, and an important administrative and cultural centre. (JS)

N AND
S KOREA

Mountains and rugged hills occupy most of the Korean peninsula – only 20 per cent of the surface area of 219,000 km² (84,560 sq miles) is suitable for cultivation.

The interior of North Korea is a harsh environment, characterized by long and severe winters. High forested mountains, cut by river gorges, lie along the borders of North Korea and Manchuria. Further south, a chain of bare, eroded mountains runs for almost the entire length of the peninsula, parallel with and close to the eastern coast.

The most productive land in the peninsula occurs along the southern coast, where winters are relatively mild. While South Korea contains the best rice lands in the peninsula, most mineral resources, including coal and iron ore, are concentrated in North Korea.

Since the Korean War (1950–53), South Korea has enjoyed rapid industrial growth, while Communist rule has been consolidated in North Korea. South Korea now contains over two-thirds of the peninsula's population of 54 million. Seoul, the capital of South Korea, is an increasingly affluent city, but suffers from acute traffic congestion, and from a housing shortage. (JS)

Hong Kong has one of the finest natural harbours in the world.

HONG KONG
AND MACAO

The British Crown Colony of Hong Kong, which consists of several islands together with a portion of

the Chinese mainland, lies on the southern coast of China, 130 km (80 miles) to the south-east of Canton. Hong Kong was acquired by Britain in three stages. The island of Hong Kong, which contains the city of Victoria, was ceded to Britain in 1842; Kowloon, on the mainland, and Lantao island were acquired in 1860; and the New Territories, which lie between Kowloon and the Chinese border, were obtained from China on a 99-year lease in 1898.

Described by Palmerston as 'a barren island with hardly a house upon it', Hong Kong now contains a population of over 4.6 million, and like Singapore constitutes a dynamic and densely crowded urban community, the fortunes of which are based on manufacturing, banking, and commerce. The sheltered waters between Victoria and Kowloon provide one of the finest natural harbours in the world, and Hong Kong has emerged as one of the busiest and most prosperous ports in Asia.

Macao lies across the estuary of the Pearl River, 64 km (40 miles) to the west of Hong Kong. Formerly an overseas province of Portugal, Macao was redefined in 1974 as a Chinese territory under Portuguese administration. The economy of Macao is based on tourism and on the manufacture of textiles. (JS)

HONG KONG map

CHINA · Shenchuan · Nantou · Lin Ma Hang · TAI PANG WAN (Mirs Bay) · HAU HOI WAN (Deep Bay) · Shek Wu Hui · Luen Wo Market · Plover Cove Res. · Ting Kok · Chek Mun Hoi Hap · Tap Mun Chau · Ping Shan · Kam Tin · Tai Po · Tai Po Hoi · Yuen Long · Shek Kong · Ma On Shan · High Island Res. · Tuen Mun (Castle Peak) · Tai Lam Chung Res. · NEW TERRITORIES 958 · Sha Kok Mei · Sha Tin · Sai Kung · Lower Shing Mun Res. · Ting Kau · Tsuen Wan Town · Ho Chung · Kau Sai Chau · Leung Shuen Wan Chau · So Kwun Wat · Sham Tseng · Urmston Road · Ma Wan · Tsing Yi · Kowloon · Hong Kong Airport · Ngau Mei Hoi · Chek Lap Kok I. · Ngong Shuen Chau · Yau Tong · Tseung Kwan · Tiu Keng Leng · Tai Wan Tau · Victoria · Victoria Pk. 554 · Peng Chau · Victoria Harbour · Chai Wan · Ninepin Group · TAI YUE SHAN (Lantau Island) · Tai O · Fung Wong Shan 934 · Shek Pik Res. · Cheung Sha · Cheung Chau I. · Pok Liu Chau (Lamma I.) · HONG KONG · Aberdeen · Tung Lung I. · Chek Chue · Stanley Pen. · Soko Islands · Po Toi I. · Lema Channel · 1 : 528 000

114°E · 114°10'E · 114°20'E · 22°30'N · 22°20'N · 22°10'N · 113°50'E

JAPAN

The Japanese archipelago lies off the Asian mainland in an arc extending from 45°N to 30°N, and thus occupies a latitudinal range comparable to the Atlantic seaboard of the USA from Maine to Florida. The Tsushima Strait (or Korea-Kaikyo), which separates Japan from Korea, is 180 km (112 miles) wide, and some 800 km (500 miles) of open sea lie between south-western Japan and the nearest point on the coast of China.

Geographical isolation has been a factor of major importance in shaping the course of Japanese history. In former times, the surrounding seas protected Japan from foreign invasion and, until the middle of the nineteenth century, Japan experienced only a few periods of direct contact with the outside world. Although initially inspired by Chinese influences, this comparatively remote island civilization developed many unique and distinctive features.

Four large and closely grouped islands (Hokkaido, Honshu, Shikoku, and Kyushu) constitute 98 per cent of the territory of Japan, the remainder being made up of a large number of smaller islands, including the Ryukyus, which lie between Kyushu and Taiwan. With a total area of 372,077 km² (143,660 sq miles), Japan may be regarded as a medium-sized country, smaller than France but slightly larger than Italy.

Landscape and Agriculture

Japan is a predominantly mountainous country and only 16 per cent of the surface area is cultivable. Although Japan lacks extensive areas of habitable land, her population, about 115 million, is the sixth largest in the world. Limited areas of agricultural land must therefore support very many people, and Japan is one of the most densely populated countries in the world.

The Japanese islands occupy a zone of instability in the earth's crust, and earthquakes and volcanic eruptions occur frequently. Throughout Japan, complex folding and faulting has produced an intricate mosaic of landforms, in which mountains and forested hills alternate with small inland basins and coastal

Climate

LOCALITY HEIGHT		JAN	JUL	YR
Wakkanai	°C	−5.9	16.7	6.2
3 m	mm	94	112	1161
Kushirogawa	°C	−7.2	15.8	5.3
33 m	mm	46	112	1090
Hakodate	°C	−3.6	19.4	8.3
33 m	mm	66	137	1184
Miyako	°C	−0.2	20.3	10.4
47 m	mm	57	132	1288
Niigata	°C	1.7	24.1	12.9
4 m	mm	194	193	1841
Tokyo	°C	3.7	25.1	14.7
6 m	mm	48	146	1563
Osaka	°C	4.5	26.6	15.5
8 m	mm	43	178	1359
Hiroshima	°C	4.2	25.4	14.7
30 m	mm	45	250	1596
Hachijo-Jima	°C	10.2	25.3	18.1
81 m	mm	192	180	3018
Kagoshima	°C	6.6	26.8	16.8
5 m	mm	75	343	2337

Japan has a moist temperate climate, cool in the north and warm in the south. In winter it stands in a cold airstream from Asia. Moistened by passage over the Sea of Japan, this deposits rain and snow over the western flanks of the islands: snow lies on the northern islands and on mountains in the south for several months each year. In summer south and easterly winds prevail, bringing much higher temperature and warm rains from the sea. Chilled by cold sea currents the northern islands remain cool, while the southern islands become subtropical. Typhoons, with strong winds and heavy rainfall, occur in late summer.

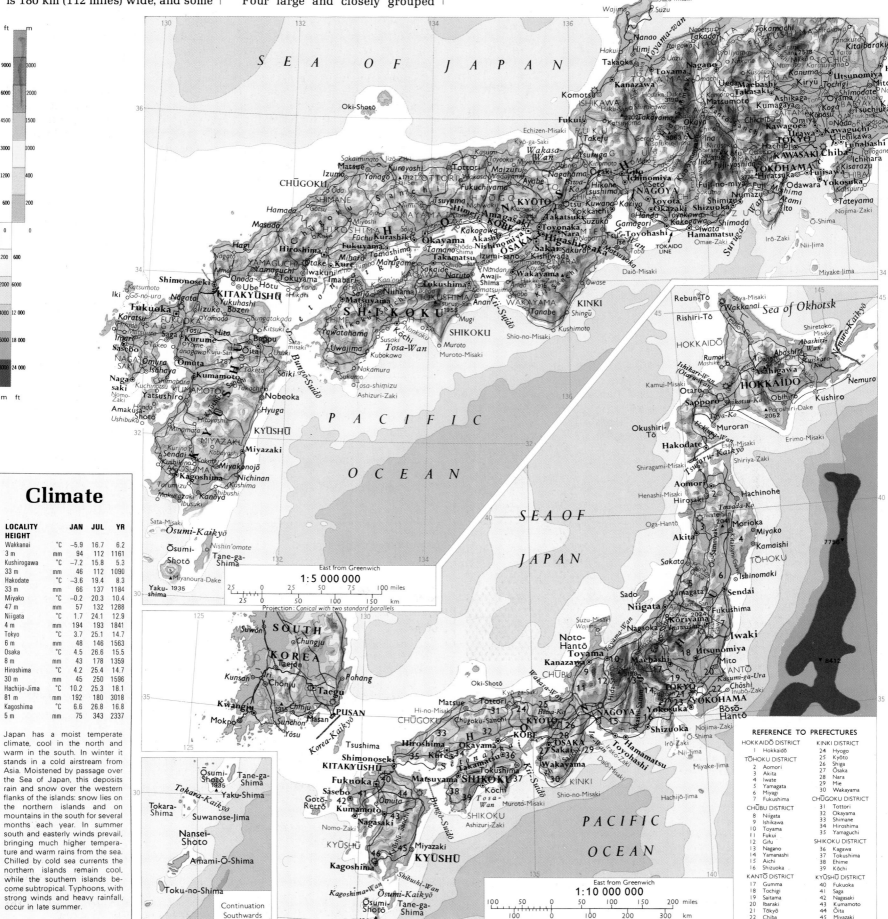

East from Greenwich
1:5 000 000
Projection: Conical with two standard parallels

East from Greenwich
1:10 000 000
Projection: Bonne

Continuation Southwards on same scale

REFERENCE TO PREFECTURES

HOKKAIDŌ DISTRICT
1 Hokkaidō

TŌHOKU DISTRICT
2 Aomori
3 Akita
4 Iwate
5 Yamagata
6 Miyagi
7 Fukushima

CHŪBU DISTRICT
8 Niigata
9 Ishikawa
10 Toyama
11 Fukui
12 Gifu
13 Nagano
14 Yamanashi
15 Aichi
16 Shizuoka

KANTŌ DISTRICT
17 Gumma
18 Tochigi
19 Saitama
20 Ibaraki
21 Tōkyō
22 Chiba
23 Kanagawa

KINKI DISTRICT
24 Hyogo
25 Kyōto
26 Shiga
27 Osaka
28 Nara
29 Mie
30 Wakayama

CHŪGOKU DISTRICT
31 Tottori
32 Okayama
33 Shimane
34 Hiroshima
35 Yamaguchi

SHIKOKU DISTRICT
36 Kagawa
37 Tokushima
38 Ehime
39 Kōchi

KYŪSHŪ DISTRICT
40 Fukuoka
41 Saga
42 Nagasaki
43 Kumamoto
44 Ōita
45 Miyazaki
46 Kagoshima

A tapestry of rice fields in southern Kyushu.

Assembling vehicles at the Honda car factory.

Hokkaido has large areas of coniferous forest.

Japanese Sea Foods

The Japanese eat more sea food per head than any other nation.

With a large population to feed and little agricultural land to spare for grazing animals, Japan has traditionally turned to the sea for much of her protein. Ringed by rich seas, with a long coastline and plenty of shallow inshore waters, the Japanese have always been inshore fishermen; they were also among the earliest deep-water hunters of fish and whales, and their modern factory-fishing fleets are seen today throughout the Pacific and other oceans. Each year, Japan takes the largest share – usually between 10 and 15 per cent – of the world's total catch. Consuming annually over 30 kg (70 lbs) of fish per head, the Japanese

eat more in their daily diet than any other nation. Also prominent in whaling, they keep a high proportion of the edible meat for human consumption.

The Japanese are likewise devoted to the squid, shrimps, king-crabs and many other kinds of sea food that are caught locally from small fishing boats. They have for long been pioneers of aqua-culture, farming oysters, mussels and shrimps and growing edible seaweeds in sheltered waters or tanks and ponds. This industry now provides a significant proportion of their total intake of sea foods, and is growing rapidly throughout the country. (BS)

plains. The pattern of landforms is further complicated by the presence of several volcanic cones and calderas. Active volcanoes include Bandai-san and Asama-san in central Honshu, and Aso-san and Sakurajima in Kyushu. The highest mountain in Japan, Fuji-san (3,776 m, 12,388 ft), is a long-dormant volcano which last erupted in 1707.

In the mountains, fast-flowing torrents, fed by snow-melt in the spring and by heavy rainfall during the summer, have carved out a landscape of deep valleys and sharp ridges. In central Japan, dense mixed forests of oak, beech and maple blanket mountain slopes to an altitude of 1,800 m (5,900 ft); further north in Hokkaido, boreal forests of fir and spruce predominate. In central Honshu, the Japan Alps with their high snow-capped ridges provide spectacular mountain scenery; the skyline in the coastal lowlands between Numazu and Shizuoka is by contrast dominated by the vast and majestic cone of Fuji-san.

Small intensively-cultivated coastal plains, separated from one another by rugged mountain spurs, make up most of the lowland of Japan. None of the plains is extensive: the Kanto plain, which is the largest, covers an area of only 13,000 km² (5,000 sq miles). Most of the coastal plains of Japan are formed of material deposited by rivers; their soils, however, have been altered and improved through centuries of careful cultivation.

History and Influences

Early Japan was peopled by immigrants arriving in successive waves from Korea and elsewhere on the Asian mainland. The earliest zone of settlement included northern Kyushu and the coastlands of the Setonaikai (Inland Sea). By the fifth century AD, Japan was divided amongst numerous clans, of which the largest and most powerful was the Yamato. Shinto, a polytheistic religion based on nature worship, had already emerged, as had the Japanese imperial dynasty.

During the sixth, seventh, and eighth centuries, Chinese cultural and political influences entered Japan. These included Buddhism, the Chinese script, and Chinese methods of government and administration. At a later stage, Confucianism was also imported. Early cities, modelled on the capital of T'ang dynasty China, were built at Nara (710) and at Kyoto (794); the latter city remained the seat of the imperial court until 1868.

The adoption of the Chinese system of centralized, bureaucratic government was relatively short-lived. From the early twelfth century onwards, political power passed increasingly to military aristocrats, and government was conducted in the name of the emperor by warrior leaders known as shoguns. Civil warfare between rival groups of feudal lords was endemic over long periods, but under the rule of the Tokugawa shoguns (1603–1867),

Japan enjoyed a hitherto unparalleled period of peace and prosperity. During this period, society was feudal and rigidly stratified, with military families (the feudal lords and their retainers, or samurai) forming a powerful elite. In the 1630s, Japan embarked on a lengthy phase of enforced isolation from the rest of the world.

This policy of seclusion could not be maintained indefinitely. In 1853, Commodore Perry of the US navy arrived in Japan and demanded that ports be opened to Western trade. The capitulation of the shogun to Perry's demands prepared the way for the overthrow of the Tokugawa government, and with the Meiji Restoration of 1868 imperial rule was resumed.

Under Western-style government, a thorough programme of modernization was set in train. Industrialization proceeded swiftly, and after victories in the Sino-Japanese War (1894–5) and the Russo-Japanese War (1904–5), Japan began to build up an overseas empire, which included the colonies of Taiwan and Korea. The growing strength of the Japanese military was demonstrated by the army's seizure of Manchuria in 1931. During the 1930s, and especially after the outbreak of war between Japan and China in 1937, militarist control of the government of Japan grew steadily. In 1941, the launching of a surprise attack on the American naval base of Pearl Harbour drew Japan into World War 2.

Recent Development

From her defeat in 1945 to 1952, Japan was administered by US forces. Many liberal and democratic reforms were enacted, and under the new constitution the power of the Emperor was much reduced and sovereignty formally vested in the people. The economic boom which accompanied the Korean War (1950–53) laid the basis for a remarkable period of industrial expansion, and by the late 1960s Japan had emerged as the world's third strongest industrial power, after the USA and the USSR.

Japanese industrial strength has been based on high rates of investment, on the adoption of modern technology, and on the efficient deployment of an industrious and highly skilled work force. At the same time, Japan's economic success has depended heavily on the use of imported minerals and fuels. Japan is strikingly deficient in fuel resources, and imported crude oil meets most of her energy needs.

The main centres of population and industry are concentrated within a narrow corridor stretching from the Kanto plain, through the coastlands of the Setonaikai, to northern Kyushu. This heavily urbanized zone contains nine cities with populations of over one million and three great industrial regions, centring respectively on Tokyo, Osaka, and Nagoya. Tokyo, the capital of Japan, forms the nucleus of a large and congested conurbation. (JS)

1 *Sydney, Australia. The great paradox of this huge continent is that most of the population is urban.*

2 *Mt Egmont, New Zealand.*

3 *Bora Bora, Polynesia. With its rugged interior, fringing reef and peaceful lagoon, Bora Bora eptiomizes the 'South Pacific' island.*

OCEANIA

**Summer Isles of Eden
lying in dark-purple spheres of sea.**

Tennyson, *Locksley Hall*, 1.164

OCEANIA

Oceania is a collective term for the islands of the Pacific Ocean, Australia, New Zealand and parts of Indonesia. The Pacific is the largest expanse of water in the world, occupying more than a third of the earth's surface; Magellan's first crossing in 1520–21 took no less than four months. Oceania is characterized by a seemingly bewildering array of islands, of varying origins. Some are coral islands, others volcanic and yet others, such as New Guinea, 'continental' islands.

Melanesia (the black islands) comprises New Guinea and the larger groups near to Australia. The name refers to the dark complexion of the fine-featured people with black, frizzy hair who are today the main indigenous coastal dwellers of the south-west Pacific. *Polynesia* (many islands) includes the many scattered islands in the central Pacific. The basically Caucasoid Polynesians, skilled in navigation, are sometimes termed 'the supreme navigators of history'. *Micronesia* (the small islands) includes the many minute coral islands north of Melanesia and a narrow Polynesian 'corridor' linking the Society Islands with South-east Asia. Micronesians today are markedly Polynesian, but in the west are more Malay or Mongoloid. (PS)

POLYNESIA

Four main groups of islands make up Polynesia. In the west lie the Tongan, Samoan and Tuvalu (Ellice) group; in the centre, the Cook, Society and Tubuai (Austral) group; in the east, the Marquesas and Tuamotu Archipelago; nearer to South America there are a number of isolated islands including Easter Island. Although there is much discussion of independence, most islands remain dependencies of the USA, New Zealand, Australia or France. Tonga and Western Samoa, among others, are now independent while the Cook Islands were granted internal self-government in 1965. (Tonga and Samoa are described more fully on p. 115.)

Most of the islands are basaltic; active vulcanicity is today confined to Hawaii and Western Polynesia, especially Tonga. With their rugged interiors, great gorge-like valleys, fringing barrier reefs and peaceful lagoons, these are picture-book 'South Pacific' islands. Others, like the Tuamotus, are coral atolls. All the islands except Rapa and Easter Island lie essentially within the

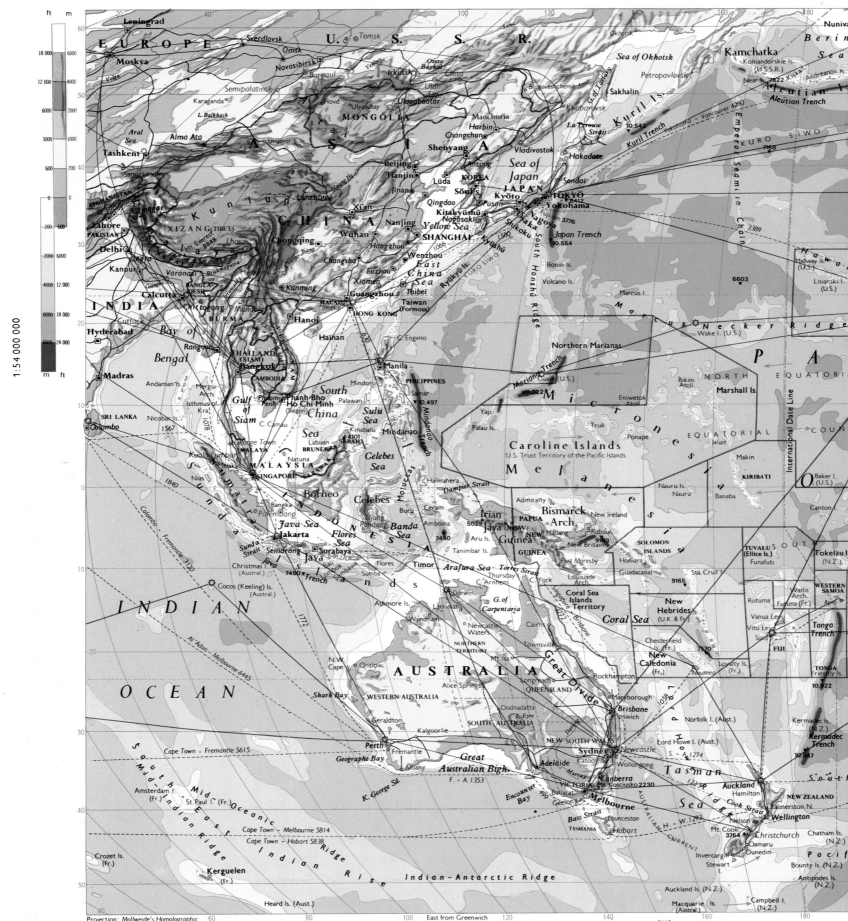

tropics, which accounts for their hot and mainly wet climates.

European exploration of Polynesia between 1760 and 1830 included the famous expeditions of Cook, Wallis, Bligh, Bougainville and Dumont d'Urville, who discovered an indigenous economy based on gardening and the resources of the sea. Shifting horticulture involved the clearing and burning of plots, which were then cultivated for two to three years, before being allowed to return to fallow. Ploughs were not used. The plants were set in *individual* holes made with a digging stick. The main crops were taro, yam, sweet potato, breadfruit, banana and coconut. The

Polynesians were fine navigators, guiding their canoes by the stars and the patterns of the waves. For long voyages they developed a double canoe of two equal hulls lashed together.

Between 1200 and 1800, the islands constituted separate chiefdoms. On the larger and more populous groups, such as Samoa and the Society Islands, society was highly stratified and capable of an advanced level of building construction. The poorer atolls, however, seem to have had more egalitarian societies.

One of the most remarkable islands is the isolated Easter Island, some 2,000 km (1,250 miles) from

Tahiti is the largest island of the Windward group and of the Society Islands. A narrow coastal plain fringes a jagged and mountainous interior. Vegetation includes coconut palms, hibiscus and tropical fruit trees.

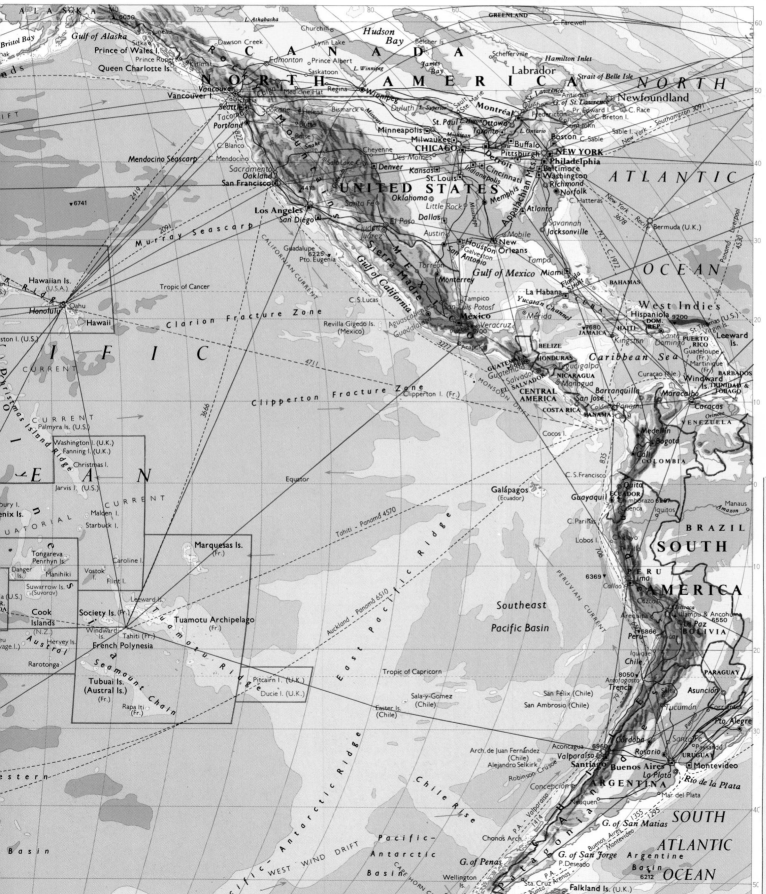

Climate

A generally stable pattern of north-east and south-east trade winds blows over central Pacific islands throughout the year, with no more than a 5° summer-to-winter shift. These winds bring equable, moist climates to most of the tropical islands, with little seasonal variation: rains are often slightly heavier in summer than in winter. Typhoons are common in the western Pacific, especially north of the equator in late summer and autumn. South of the tropics strong depressions bring cool, unsettled weather from the west, with heavy, constant cloud cover, persistent drizzle, and snow in winter.

LOCALITY HEIGHT		JAN	JUL	YR
Yap	°C	26.9	27.5	27.5
29 m	mm	165	429	3025
Jaluit	°C	27.5	28.1	27.8
6 m	mm	259	391	4033
Nauru	°C	27.2	27.5	27.5
27 m	mm	314	155	1908
Canton I	°C	29.2	29.4	29.2
4 m	mm	140	81	937
Malden I	°C	27.8	28.1	28.1
8 m	mm	89	48	696
Papeete (Tahiti)	°C	26.9	25.0	26.1
92 m	mm	251	53	1628
Rarotonga	°C	25.8	21.7	23.6
5 m	mm	234	112	2103
Noumea	°C	26.1	20.6	23.3
9 m	mm	94	91	1105
Pitcairn I	°C	24.7	20.0	22.5
73 m	mm	91	272	1699
Campbell I	°C	9.4	4.4	6.7
23 m	mm	84	157	1382

Principal Air Routes

West from Greenwich

COPYRIGHT, GEORGE PHILIP & SON, LTD.

OCEANIA

Pitcairn Island and 3,700 km (2,300 miles) from Chile, to whom it now belongs. This small dot in a vast ocean, only 25 km (16 miles) long, was first discovered by a Dutchman, Roggeveen, on Easter Sunday, 1722. It is world famous for its extraordinary assemblage of stone monuments and carvings. These monuments are stone platforms (*ahu*), often surmounted by striking statues, dourly massive and stylized in form. Yet, by the time of European contact, its civilization appears to have suffered a dramatic decline. Despite the evidence of Thor Heyerdahl, who is closely associated with the study of Easter Island, most specialists are convinced, on the basis of language and culture, that the ultimate origins of the Polynesians lie in South-east Asia rather than in South America.

The modern islanders of Polynesia have now recovered from the earlier population decline and by the year 2000 the Pacific population is expected to double. The old ways are retreating before a new commercial civilization, often based on tourism, which is seeking to develop this unique ocean realm. (PS)

MICRONESIA

Micronesia is a highly strategic area made up of more than 2,000 islands and islets, ranging from less than 0.13 km² (0.05 sq miles) to Guam, the largest, which is 583 km² (225 sq miles). The 'high' islands of the Marianas and parts of the Carolines are volcanic, the 'low' islands of the rest of the Carolines, the Marshalls and the Gilberts (Kiribati), are coralline, either low atolls or raised islands, up to 15 m (50 ft) above sea-level. Only the most northern of the Mariana group are volcanically active. The volcanic islands are the larger, with a more varied landscape and richer soils.

Micronesians appear to have come from the Philippines and Indonesia, and later from Melanesia. Indigenous cultures are particularly noted for their highly developed canoe and navigation technology, the single outrigger canoes of the Marshallese and Carolinians representing perhaps the highest achievement. Some of these possessed hulls more than 12 m (40 ft) long, held tightly together with coconut coir. Also impressive were the large meeting houses, thatched with palm leaves or pandans, characteristic of the Gilbert Islands, among others.

The main food crops are taro, coconuts, yams and breadfruit, and on some islands, sweet potatoes, cassava and maize. Protein comes primarily from fish, shellfish and sea turtles; pigs, chickens, dogs, wild birds and fruit bats are also eaten. The tropical maritime climate occasionally produces typhoons, especially in the Carolines, and unpredictable droughts, particularly in the

Easter Island's mysterious statues.

Gilbert Islands and on Nauru.

Since Magellan first discovered the Marianas in 1521, the colonial experience of the region has been very complex, with Spanish, German and Japanese administrations. The Gilbert Islands, administered by Britain from 1892, received their independence in 1979 and are now renamed Kiribati. Nauru, with its rich phosphate deposits, became independent in 1968, having been governed by Australia, New Zealand and Britain as a United Nations Trust Territory since World War 2. The Carolines, Marianas and Marshalls constitute a similar but, in their case, 'strategic trust' of the UN known as the Trust Territory of the Pacific Islands (TTPI) and administered by the USA. It is a matter for regret that some atolls have become nuclear testing sites, their indigenous peoples having been compulsorily moved. (PS)

MELANESIA

Melanesia is divided into a western part – New Guinea, the Bismarck Archipelago, the Solomon Islands and the islands of the Torres Straits – and an eastern part including the New Hebrides, New Caledonia, and sometimes Fiji. Fiji (1970), Papua New Guinea (1975) and the former British Solomons (1978) are now independent. The other islands remain dependencies of Australia, Britain and France. (Fiji is described more fully on p. 115.)

The double chain of islands forming the Solomons and the New Hebrides extends for some 2,250 km (1,400 miles) and represents the drowned outermost crustal fold on the borders of the ancient Australian continent. New Caledonia lies on an inner fold, nearer to Australia. The Solomons are the largest Pacific group outside New Guinea. Most islands are mountainous. Old coral terraces indicate periods of past uplift and there are active volcanoes and hot springs. Earth tremors are frequent. Some islands, for example

the Loyalty Islands, are raised coral atolls. The northern Solomons have a true hot and wet tropical oceanic climate; further south there tends to be an increasingly long cool season. In the wettest areas the vegetation is tropical rain forest, but where the rainfall is lower or more seasonal, savanna grasslands and scrub become dominant. The coastal plains are suitable for cultivation.

The food crops of Melanesia vary greatly with climate. Where the rainfall is regular and heavy, taro is the main starchy vegetable. In regions with freshwater swamps sago from the trunk of the sago palm (which can yield up to 300 kg (660 lb) of starch per palm) is important. Yams are cultivated in drier areas. In New Caledonia, taro production was based on irrigation. Commercial farming has been greatly improved recently. Traditional cash crops include coconuts, cocoa, coffee and rubber, with sugar cane important

Coconut Culture

Coconuts have many uses.

The Coconut (*Cocos nucifera*) is the most important palm of the humid tropics. Although its wild ancestor was probably of South American origin, it appears to have been first domesticated in Oceania, where to this day it remains both a vital local crop and a significant contributor to cash crop exports. The range of products it provides is remarkable. The fruits, which are large drupes, supply both food and drink. Coconut oil, extracted from the dried endosperm (copra), is invaluable for making soap, margarine and cosmetics. The fibrous husk provides coir, used to make mats, ropes and brushes. The leaves and trunks contribute a wide range of house-building materials, while the flower gives a sugary sap, called toddy, from which an intoxicating drink can be distilled. It is in every way an all-purpose plant.

In Oceania, with the arrival of Europeans, the coconut became an important plantation crop, especially in New Guinea, the Solomon Islands, New Hebrides and Fiji. Seedling palms were planted in rows, usually in large blocks of many hectares. Local labour was used to collect the nuts and dry the copra. Tall coconut palms begin to bear first after 6 or 7 years' growth and reach full maturity by 12 years. (PS)

on Fiji. Experiments are underway with irrigated rice-growing. The area also has important timber reserves and significant mineral resources, including phosphates on Bellona Island in the Solomons, and gold on Fiji.

One of the main characteristics of Melanesia is the enormous range of cultures and languages, some of which are spoken by fewer than a hundred people. This reflects the isolation of small local populations on islands, on mountains and in deep valleys. (PS)

AUSTRALIA

With a land area of 7,686,800 km² (2,967,900 sq miles), Australia is the smallest of the continents; primarily a land of low to medium altitude plateaux, these form monotonously flat landscapes extending for hundreds of kilometres. The edges of the plateaux are more diverse, particularly in the east where deep gorges and waterfalls create rugged relief between the Great Divide and the coast. In the north-west, impressive rugged gorge scenery is found in the Hamersley Range and Kimberley area.

The western half of Australia is formed of ancient rocks. Essentially an arid landscape of worn-down ridges and plateaux, with depressions occupied by sandy deserts and occasional salt lakes, this area has little surface water.

The eastern sixth of the continent, including Tasmania, forms the Eastern Highlands, the zone of greatest relief, greatest rainfall, most abundant vegetation and greatest population. High summits in this region include Mt Kosciusko, 2,230 m (7,314 ft), Round Mountain, 1,615 m (5,297 ft) and Bartle Frere, 1,611 m (5,287 ft). Much of this area shows signs of volcanic activity in the relatively recent geological past,

Bananas in northern Australia.

lava flows in western Victoria and near Atherton in North Queensland having occurred within the last two million years. These young basalts support nutrient-rich soils in contrast to the generally well weathered, nutrient-poor soils of nearly all the remainder of Australia.

Between the western plateaux and Eastern Highlands lie the Carpentaria, central and Murray lowlands. The central lowlands drain to the great internal river systems supplying Lake Eyre, or to the Bulloo system, or through great inland deltas to the Darling River. The parallel dune ridges of this area form part of a great continent-wide set of dune ridges extending in a huge anti-clockwise arc, eastwards through the Great Victoria Desert, northwards through the Simpson Desert and westwards in the Great Sandy Desert.

Australian deserts are. only moderately arid. No Australian climate station records a mean annual rainfall below 100 mm (4 in) despite great variations from year to year and season to season. This moderate aridity is illustrated by the widespread vegetation cover.

Vegetation and Wildlife

On the humid margins of the continent are luxuriant forests. These include the great jarrah forests of tall Eucalyptus hardwoods in the extreme south-west of Western Australia, the temperate rain forests with the Antarctic beech found in Tasmania and on humid upland sites north through New South Wales to the Queensland border, and the tropical and subtropical rain forests found in the wetter areas along the east coast, from the McIllwraith Range in the north to the vicinity of Mallacoota Inlet in the south. Some of these rain forest areas are maintained as managed forests, others are in national parks, but most of the original forest has been cleared for agriculture, particularly for dairying and cattle-fattening, and for sugar and banana cultivation north of Port Macquarie, and potatoes further south.

The most adaptable tree genus in Australia is the Eucalypts, which range from the tall flooded gum trees found on the edges of the rain forest, to the dry-living mallee species found on sand-plains and interdune areas. Acacia species, especially the bright-yellow flowered wattles, are also adapted to a wide range of environments. Associated with this adaptation of plants is the wide variety of animal adaptations, with about 277 different mammals, 400 species of reptiles and 700 of birds. Aborigines arriving from Asia over 40,000 years ago brought the dingo which rapidly replaced the thylacine or Tasmanian wolf, the largest marsupial predator, and preyed on smaller animals. Fires, lit for hunting and allowed to burn uncontrolled, altered much of the vegetation, probably allowing Eucalypt forests to expand at the expense of the rain forest. However, the Abo-

The Great Sandy Desert.

Much of Australia is grazing land.

rigines understood their environment, carefully protecting vital areas of natural food supply, restricting the use of certain desert waterholes which tradition taught would be reliable in a drought, and developing a resource-use policy which was aimed at living with nature. Although integration is now encouraged, Aborigines have as yet had little share in Australia's prosperity.

European settlement after 1788 upset this ecological balance, through widespread clearing of coastal forests, inadvertent overgrazing of inland pastures and introduction of exotic species, especially the rabbit. Europeans also brought the technology which enabled the mineral, water and soil resources of Australia to be developed. Agriculture around Esperance on the south coast of Western Australia, for example, depends on the treatment of trace element-deficient soils, while large areas, such as the Murrumbidgee Irrigation Area in New South Wales, rely on water regulation through large reservoirs. The most crucial water management issues are, however, the assurance of supplies to large cities, especially Sydney, Melbourne, Brisbane, Adelaide and Perth.

An Aborigine collecting turtle eggs.

Mineral Resources

Much of Australia's growth since the beginning of European settlement has been closely related to the exploitation of mineral resources, which has led directly to the founding, growth and often eventual decline of the majority of inland towns. Broken Hill and Mount Isa are copper, lead, zinc and silver producing centres, while Kalgoorlie, Bendigo, Ballarat and Charter Towers all grew in the middle and late nineteenth-century gold rushes. Today, less glamorous minerals support the Australian economy. In Western Australia, the great iron ore mines of Mount Tom Price, Mount Newman, and Mount Goldsworthy are linked by new railways to ports at Dampier and Port Hedland. Offshore are the oil and gas fields of the north-west shelf.

In the east, the coal-mines of central Queensland and eastern New South Wales are linked by rail to bulk loading facilities at Sarina, Gladstone, Brisbane, Newcastle, Sydney and Port Kemble, which enable this high grade coking coal to be shipped to markets throughout the world. Bauxite mining has led to new settlements at Nhulunby and

Weipa on the Gulf of Carpentaria, with associated refineries at Kwinana, Gladstone and Bell Bay.

Rum Jungle, south of Darwin, became well-known as one of the first uranium mines, but now deposits further east in Arnhem Land are being developed. Meanwhile new discoveries of ore bodies continue to be made in the ancient rocks of the western half of Australia. Natural gas from the Cooper Basin, just south of Innamincka on Cooper's Creek, is piped to Adelaide and Sydney, while oil and gas from the Bass Strait and brown coal from the Yallourn-Morwell area have been vital to the industrial growth of Victoria. Fossil fuels are supplemented by hydro-electric power from major schemes in western Tasmania and the Snowy Mountains and smaller projects near Cairns and Tully in north Queensland.

Agriculture and Rural Settlement

Rural Australia may be divided into extensive and intensive pastoral and agricultural zones. Apart from the empty and largely unusable desert areas in Western Australia and the Simpson Desert, extensive cattle or sheep production dominates all of Australia north and west of a line from Ceduna in South Australia, through Ivanhoe in New South Wales to Bundaberg in Queensland, and east of a line from Geraldton to Esperance in Western Australia. Cattle and sheep populations in this zone are sparse, individual pastoral holdings are large, some over 400,000 hectares (1 million acres), and towns are both small and far apart.

Some aborigines retain limited tracts of land in Arnhem Land and on the fringes of the deserts where they live by hunting and gathering, but nearly all aborigines now live close to government settlements or mission stations. Many are employed as stockmen and seasonal agricultural workers, while thousands of others have migrated to country towns and the major cities.

The intensive pastoral and agricultural zones support the bulk of the sheep and cattle of Australia, where wool, mutton and beef production is still the basic industry. Wheat is cultivated in combination with sheep raising over large tracts of the gentle inland slopes of the coastal ranges.

Along the east coast are important cattle fattening, dairy and sugar cane industries, the latter significant on the east coast from Grafton to Mossman. While the dairy industry has to be supported by government subsidies and has small and often uneconomic farms, the sugar industry has expanded to meet export markets, although the acres sown are strictly regulated. Irrigated areas support cotton, rice, fruit and vegetable crops, largely for consumption within Australia. Wine production around Perth, Adelaide, central Victoria and Newcastle has expanded recently. Australia is now more than self-sufficient in all foods. (ID)

OCEANIA

Political Development and Population

European settlement in Australia began in 1788 as a penal colony in New South Wales, spreading quickly to Queensland and Tasmania. During the nineteenth century the continent became divided into the states of New South Wales, Queensland (1859), South Australia (1836), Tasmania (1825), Victoria (1851) and Western Australia (1829), with the area now forming the Northern Territory being under the control of South Australia. During this colonial period the state sea-port capitals, Sydney, Brisbane, Adelaide, Hobart, Melbourne and Perth, became estab-

lished as the dominant manufacturing, commercial, administrative and legislative centres of their respective states.

In 1901, the states came together to create the Commonwealth of Australia with a federal constitution. Trade between the states became free, external affairs, defence and immigration policy became federal responsibilities, but health, education, transport, mineral, agricultural and industrial development remained firmly in the hands of each state. The new arrangements did little to alter the existing patterns of communications and commerce. Only gradually did federal powers of taxation come to give the federal

Government the opportunity to develop national policies.

The federal capital established at Canberra, in the new Australian Capital Territory, grew from a tiny settlement in 1911 to over 60,000 in 1966, and to over 200,000 now, becoming a great seat of administration and learning, and the largest inland regional commercial centre.

The federal government's territorial responsibilities also include the Northern Territory, self governing since 1978, Norfolk Island, the territory of Ashmore and Cartier Islands, the Australian Antarctic Territory, Heard Island, the McDonald Islands, Cocos (Keeling) Islands and Christmas Island. New

The gum is a species of Eucalypt.

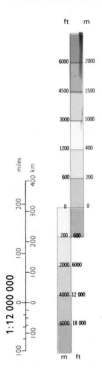

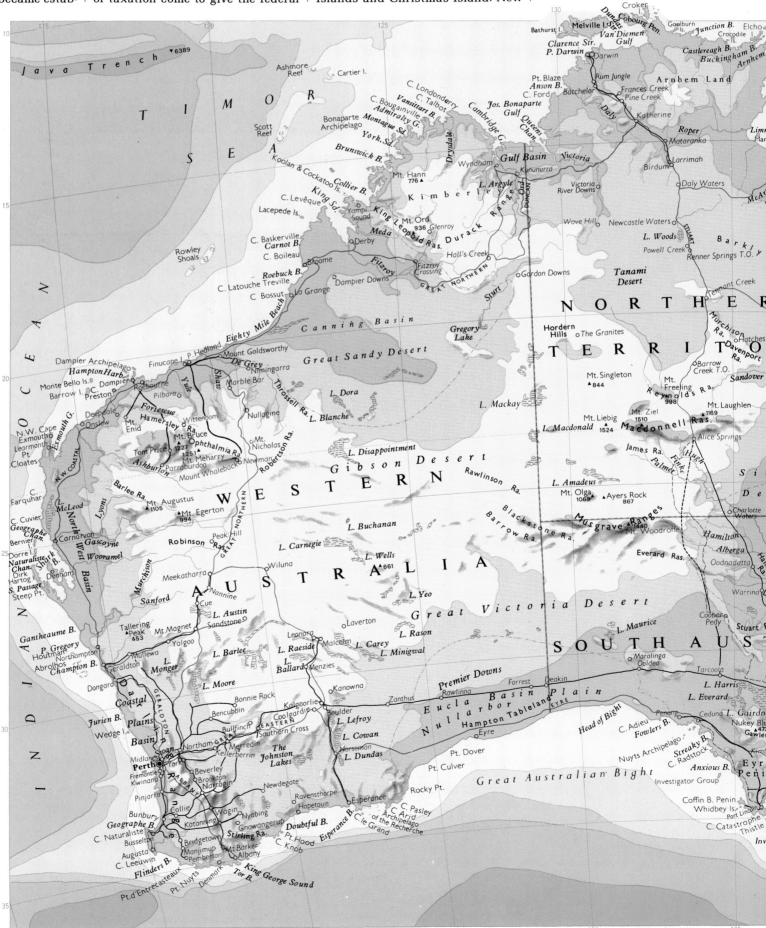

Projection: Bonne

Boundaries of the artesian basins

East from Greenwich

South Wales administers Lord Howe Island, while Tasmania is responsible for Macquarie Island.

Migration has changed the ethnic character of Australia since 1960. The multi-cultural Australian society now has Greek, Italian, Yugoslav, Turkish and Lebanese communities alongside the longer established Aboriginal, Chinese, British, Irish, Dutch and German communities. Almost 60 per cent of the total Australian population now live in Sydney, Melbourne, Adelaide, Brisbane, Perth and Hobart. Migration within the states from inland rural

Marsupials

Marsupials are mammals that give birth to their young at an early stage of development and attach them to their milk glands for a period, often inside a pouch (marsupium). Once widespread around the world, they have mostly been ousted by more advanced forms, but marsupials of many kinds continue to flourish in the isolation of Australia, New Guinea and South America.

Best known are the big red and grey kangaroos that range over the dry grasslands and forests of Australia. Standing up to 2 metres (6.5 ft) tall, they are browsers and grazers that now compete for food with cattle and sheep; many hundreds are killed each year. Bounding at speed they can clear fences of their own height, and travel tirelessly at 15 km (9–10 miles) per hour. Wallabies – smaller species of the same family – live in the forests and mountains. Australia has many other kinds of marsupials, though several have died out since the coming of Europeans. Tree-living koalas browse exclusively on eucalyptus leaves. Heavily-built wombats browse in the undergrowth like large rodents, and fierce-sounding Tasmanian Devils are mild scavengers of the forest floor. Then there are many tiny mouse-like, shrew-like, and mole-like species that feed on insects, seeds or honey. (BS)

The wombat.

Climate

LOCALITY HEIGHT		JAN	JUL	YR
Thursday I	°C	27.8	25.3	27.2
5 m	mm	462	5	1714
Darwin	°C	28.6	25.0	28.0
30 m	mm	386	3	1491
Daly Waters	°C	30.3	19.7	24.2
211 m	mm	165	3	663
Broome	°C	29.7	21.1	26.4
19 m	mm	160	5	581
Alice Springs	°C	28.6	11.7	20.6
580 m	mm	43	7	251
Carnarvon	°C	26.7	16.1	21.7
5 m	mm	10	41	231
Laverton	°C	28.1	11.4	20.3
460 m	mm	20	23	246
Kalgoorlie	°C	25.8	11.4	18.9
350 m	mm	10	23	246
Perth	°C	23.3	13.1	17.8
60 m	mm	8	170	881
Albany	°C	19.2	11.9	15.6
12 m	mm	36	152	1008

Western and central Australia are generally far drier than the east; most of the area west of 145 °E receives less than 75 cm (30 in) of rain annually, and much of the centre is arid desert with less than 25 cm (10 in) annually. This meagre rainfall is unpredictable and may fail altogether, producing droughts lasting several years. North of 17 °S heavy summer monsoon rains usually occur from October to April. Temperatures are high throughout the year in the north, moderating in winter in the centre and south, when clear skies may bring sharp night frosts. The south-western corner has a Mediterranean climate, with winter rains.

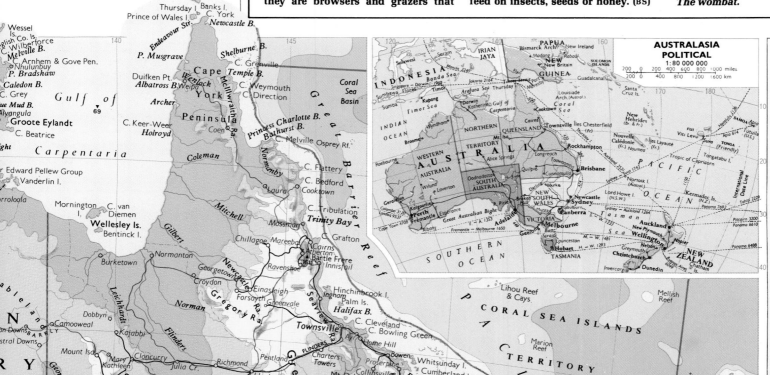

COPYRIGHT. GEORGE PHILIP & SON. LTD.

OCEANIA

areas to capital cities or coastal towns leaves many rural communities with an ageing population, while the new mining centres have young populations. The most rapid growth of population outside new mining centres is occurring in coastal towns through migration on retirement and deliberate attempts to establish an alternative life-style by leaving the big cities. (MD)

Industry and Urban Development

Soon after 1788, small-scale manufacturing began to supply domestic goods and machinery to the colonial community. Inevitably manufacturing grew in the colonial seaport capitals, especially Sydney and Melbourne which now have over 60 per cent of all Australian manufacturing industry. By 1971 27 per cent of the Australian workforce was engaged in manufacturing, 8 per cent in rural industries, 1 per cent in mining and 64 per cent in service industries. Rural industries contribute about 45 per cent of Australia's exports, mining 30 per cent and manufacturing about 20 per cent. Food, beverage and tobacco industries, transport equipment and general machinery are the largest sectors of manufacturing, much of which is concentrated into a few large firms.

This ownership concentration is matched by spatial concentration, less than a quarter of manufacturing being located outside the six state capitals, and most of that in three centres: Geelong with woollen mills, tanneries, an aluminium refinery and cement and paper works, and the steel-making towns of Newcastle and Wollongong. Some industry has been decentralized from the coastal cities, but generally attempts to develop industry outside capital cities have not been successful. State government decentralization policies assist industries to move to country towns, but most such moves tend to be to just outside the metropolitan area or to attractive coastal locations, such as Coffs Harbour in New South Wales.

The lack of industrial investment in country areas means that rural school-leavers find satisfying jobs hard to obtain in their home town and thus move to their state capital in search of work. In recent years, the farm labour force has become more urbanized, general farm workers being replaced by specialist contractors for building, fencing, shearing, well-digging, aerial spraying and truck driving. Some farmers prefer to live in town and drive out to their grazing or grain-growing properties whenever necessary. Small dairy farm owners often have second jobs in local sawmills or other urban industries and commute from their rural holdings.

These trends mean that small villages and towns have declined in importance. Rural children are taken several tens of kilometres by bus to large urban schools rather than attending small one-teacher local schools. Thus the larger regional centres grow, while the smallest towns decline. Australia's population is becoming even more urban.

Communications

Under the Australian Constitution the federal government has control over interstate and overseas transport and the state governments are each responsible for the regulation of transport within their own borders. Seven railway systems thus exist, each state system focussing on its capital city, with the Commonwealth Railways responsible for the Trans Australian, Central Australian and Northern Territory routes. The notorious differences in gauges between the states have been partially overcome by the construction of the standard-gauge links from Brisbane to Sydney, Sydney to Melbourne and Sydney to Perth via Broken Hill. The completion of the Tarcoola-Alice Springs route will provide the basic strategic standard-gauge rail network for Australia.

Railways are vital for bulk freight, especially mineral ores, coal and wheat. Among the busiest railways are the iron ore lines in the north-west of Western Australia. Busy

Eucalyptus macrocarpa blossom.

passenger traffic is concentrated in the electrified suburban systems of Sydney, Melbourne and Brisbane.

Although 89 per cent of all passenger transport is by private car, 7 per cent by rail and only 4 per cent by air, air services cope with much interstate travel. Airline competition is maintained and regulated by a two airline policy, one private and one government-owned for interstate traffic, mostly between the capital cities. Intrastate services to the capital city are supplied by state airlines, often subsidiaries of the two major internal airlines, with small airlines flying 'bus-stop' services between country towns.

Sydney is one of the most important ports of the South Pacific.

A rapidly improving highway system links all major cities and towns providing easy mobility for a largely car-owning population. Some journeys are still difficult, especially when floods wash away sections of road or sand drifts bury highways.

Australia is well served by local broadcasting and television. The radio remains a life-line for remote settlements dependent on the flying doctor or aerial ambulance and for many others when floods or bush fires threaten isolated properties. In the age of satellite communications few Australians are completely isolated save when emergencies emphasize the great contrast between life in the city and in the bush. (MD)

PAPUA NEW GUINEA

Papua New Guinea, forming part of Melanesia, comprises the eastern section of the Island of New Guinea, the Bismarck Archipelago and the northern part of the Solomon Islands, including the copper-rich island of Bougainville. The backbone of the main island is a high cordillera of rugged fold mountains which continue south-east as a chain of islands to the Louisiade Archipelago. About 2,400 km (1,500 miles) in length and averaging between 2,500 to 4,600 m (8,000 to 15,000 ft) in height, these mountains are covered with tropical montane 'cloud' forest. Isolated valleys, often more than 1 km (0.6 mile) in depth, and intermontane basins run parallel with the main ranges. Fertile with alluvium and volcanic materials, these are the sites of isolated settlements, even today linked only by light aircraft. The extreme remoteness of these regions still results in the occasional discovery of a hitherto unknown tribal group. The traditional garden crops of the 'Highlanders' include *kaukau* (sweet potato), sugar cane, bananas, maize, cassava and nut-bearing pandans. Pigs are kept mainly for status and ritual purposes. In the lowlands, taro is the staple food, although yams and sago are also important. The main cash crops are coconuts, coffee, cocoa and rubber.

Although the first European contact came as early as 1526, it was only in the late nineteenth century that permanent German and British settlements were established. After World War 2, the UN Trust Territory of New Guinea and the Territory of Papua were administered jointly by Australia. Self-government came in 1973 and full independence in 1975. The capital city, Port Moresby, is not linked by road to any other major centre, and communication with the Highlands depends essentially on the country's 400 airports and airstrips. (PS)

The Great Barrier Reef

The Great Barrier Reef is a maze of some 2,500 reefs exposed only at low tide, ranging in size from a few hundred hectares to 50 km^2 (20 sq miles), and extending over an area of 250,000 km^2 (100,000 sq miles). The section extending for about 800 km (500 miles) north of Cairns forms a discontinuous wall of coral through which narrow openings lead to areas of platform or patch reefs. South of Cairns, the reefs are less continuous, and extend further from the coast. Between the outer reef and the coast are many high islands, remnants of the mainland; coral cays, developed from coral sand on reefs and known locally as low islands, are usually small and uninhabited, exceptions being Green Island and Heron Island.

The modern reefs have developed in the last 20,000 years, over older foundations exposed to the atmosphere during former low sea-levels. Coral is susceptible to severe damage from tropical cyclones and to attack by the Crown-of-Thorns starfish. Much is now protected as the Great Barrier Reef Marine Park, but the existence of oil beneath the reef is a great threat to its ecological stability. (ID)

The underwater beauty of the reef.

Climate

LOCALITY HEIGHT		JAN	JUL	YR
Port Moresby	°C	28.1	25.6	26.9
38 m	mm	178	28	1011
Cairns	°C	27.8	20.8	24.7
5 m	mm	422	41	2253
Cloncurry	°C	31.1	17.8	25.6
193 m	mm	112	8	457
Longreach	°C	30.0	14.7	23.3
187 m	mm	53	20	417
Brisbane	°C	25.0	14.7	20.6
42 m	mm	163	56	1135
Port Augusta	°C	25.6	11.9	18.9
5 m	mm	15	18	239
Sydney	°C	21.9	11.7	17.2
42 m	mm	89	117	1181
Adelaide	°C	23.1	11.1	17.2
43 m	mm	20	171	536
Canberra	°C	20.3	5.8	13.3
560 m	mm	48	46	584
Launceston	°C	17.8	7.5	12.8
77 m	mm	46	46	716

North-eastern Australia, crossed by the Tropic of Capricorn, is hot throughout the year. Coastal regions are cooled and dampened by south-east trade winds, which bring year-round rain especially heavy in summer; Cairns receives over 120 cm (48 in) annually between January and March, and Brisbane and Sydney have their heaviest rains in summer or autumn. Further south, westerly winds prevail; summers are hot and winters are cool, with depressions bringing varied weather and most rain in winter. Inland regions are hotter and drier throughout the year. Papua New Guinea is hot and wet, with rains generally heaviest in summer.

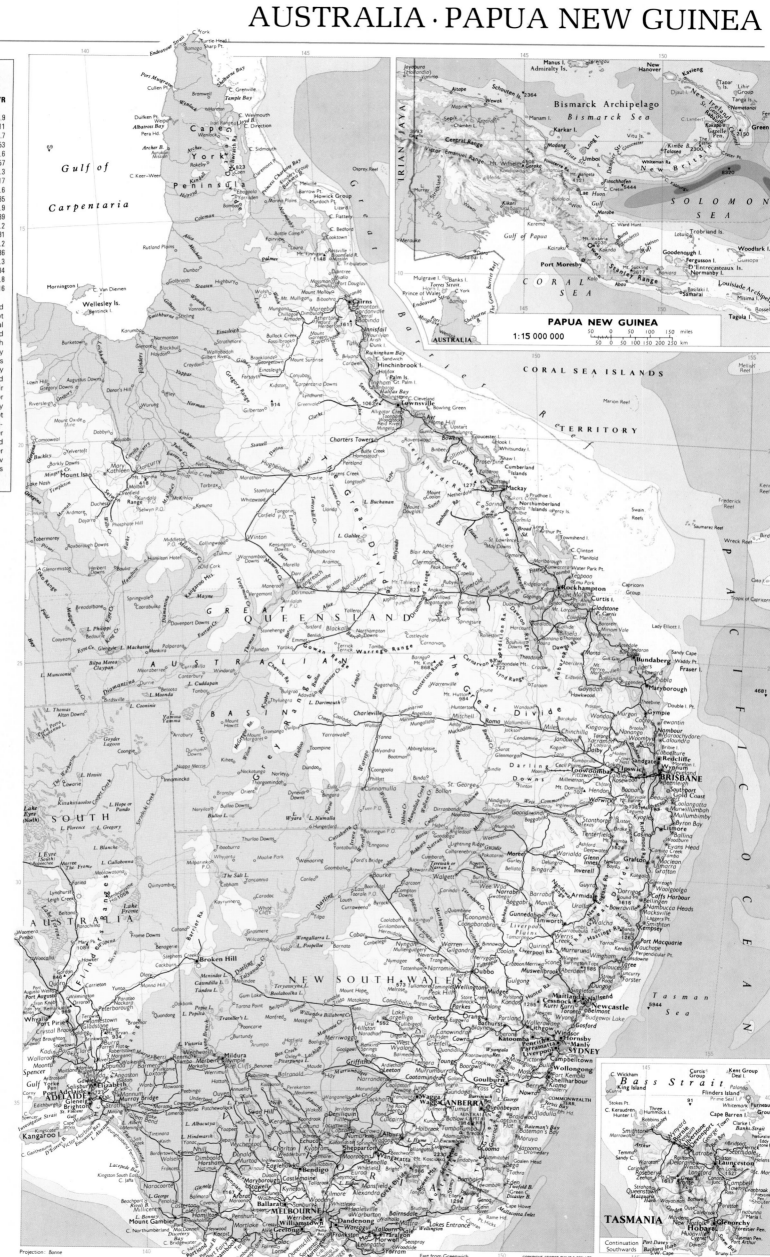

PAPUA NEW GUINEA
1:15 000 000

TASMANIA

Projection: Bonne

East from Greenwich

1:9 400 000

NEW ZEALAND

New Zealand lies in the south-western Pacific Ocean, 1,600 km (1,000 miles) east of Australia. The three main islands – North Island, South Island and Stewart Island – have a total area of 268,675 km² (103,736 sq miles). Geographically New Zealand also includes the out-lying Chatham Islands which are inhabited, the uninhabited Snares, Auckland, Bounty and Antipodes Islands, and southern Campbell Island occupied by a scientific team. Politically it includes the Kermadec and Tokelau Islands, and has two dependencies – the widely-scattered Cook Islands and Ross Dependency, Antarctica.

Landscape

Geologically part of the Circum-Pacific Mobile Belt of tectonic activity (pp. 8–9), New Zealand is moun-tainous and partly volcanic. Many of the highest mountains – the Southern Alps and Kaikoura Ranges of the South Island, for example – were thrust up from the sea bed in the past ten to fifteen million years, representing only the latest in a long series of orogenies. Much of the North Island was formed by volcanic action even more recently, mainly in the past one to four million years. Damaging earthquakes and volcanic eruptions have occurred in historic times; minor earthquakes are com-mon, and there are several areas of volcanic and geothermal activity, especially in North Island.

Newness makes New Zealand a rugged country, with mountains always in sight. About three-quarters of the total land area lies above the 200 m (650 ft) contour. The North Island has many spectacular but low ranges with peaks of 1,200 to 1,500 m (4,000 to 5,000 ft), made up of folded sedimentary rocks that form good soils. Folding and faulting give the eastern half of the island a strong north-east to south-west grain, especially in the south-east where the rivers have cut broad, fertile valleys between the ranges. The Coromandel Range and hilly Northland peninsula are softer and more worn, with few peaks over 800 m (12,600 ft).

Overlying these older rocks in the centre and north are massive spreads of lava, pumice and volcanic tuffs, formed during the past one to three

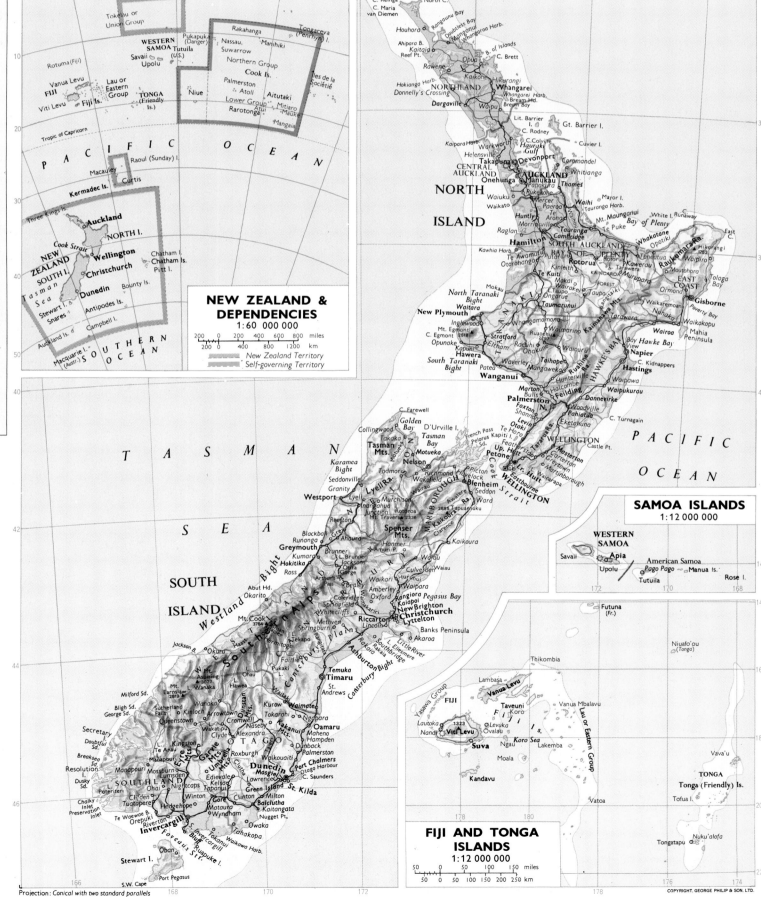

NEW ZEALAND & DEPENDENCIES
1:60 000 000

New Zealand Territory
Self-governing Territory

SAMOA ISLANDS
1:12 000 000

FIJI AND TONGA ISLANDS
1:12 000 000

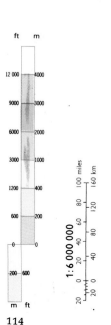

1:6 000 000

Projection: Conical with two standard parallels

COPYRIGHT. GEORGE PHILIP & SON. LTD.

million years. The great central Volcanic Plateau is dominated by three slumbering volcanoes – Ruapehu (2,796 m, 9,173 ft, the North Island's highest peak), and lesser Ngauruhoe and Tongariro. To the east stands the isolated cone of Mt Egmont (2,518 m, 8,261 ft), snow-capped and now dormant. Further north extensive fields of lava and ash cones lie across the base of the Northland peninsula, forming a firm, rolling site for Auckland, New Zealand's largest city.

South Island is mainly mountainous, with an alpine backbone extending obliquely from north-east to south-west. The highest peaks form a central massif, the Southern Alps, clustered about Mt Cook (3,764 m, 12,349 ft), New Zealand's highest mountain. From this massif, which is permanently ice-capped, glaciers descend on either flank. On the east, the outwash fans of rivers fed by the glaciers form the Canterbury Plains – South Island's only extensive lowland. The north end of the island has many high, rolling ranges, rising to the steeply folded and faulted Kaikoura Ranges of the north-east. In the far south – Fjord-land – the coast is indented by deep, steeply-walled sounds that wind far into the forested mountains.

The Maoris

A Maori farm manager.

'. . . strong, raw-boned, well-made, active people, rather above than under the common size . . . of a very dark brown colour, with black hair, thin black beards, and . . . in general very good features.' So Captain James Cook described the Maoris he met in New Zealand in 1770. Of Polynesian stock, the Maoris settled, mainly in North Island, from about AD 800 to 1350. A war-like people, living in small fortified settlements, they cultivated kumaras (sweet potatoes) and other crops, hunted seals and moas (large flightless birds, now extinct) and gathered seafoods.

The Maoris befriended the early European settlers; they readily accepted British sovereignty, Christianity and pacification, rebelling only as more and more of their communal land was bought for the settlers' use. Given parliamentary representation from 1876, they eventually integrated fully. Now Maoris form about eight per cent of New Zealand's population, living mostly in North Island. Though socially and politically equal in every way to whites, they are still over-represented in the poorer, unskilled sections of the population, and separated more by poverty than by colour from the mainstream of life. (BS)

Discovery and Settlement

New Zealand was discovered by Abel Tasman in 1642 and charted thoroughly by James Cook in 1769–70. Both explorers noted the presence of Maoris – Polynesians who hunted and farmed from well-defended coastal settlements, who were themselves relatively recent arrivals on the islands. Sealing gangs and whalers were New Zealand's first European inhabitants, closely followed by missionaries and farmers from Britain and Australia. By the early 1830s about 2,000 Europeans had settled.

In 1840 Britain rather reluctantly took possession, in the Treaty of Waitangi which gave rights and privileges of British subjects to the Maori people. The following decades saw the arrival of thousands of new settlers from Britain, and by mid-century there were over 30,000. Though their relationships with the Maoris (who at this stage outnumbered them two to one) were generally good, difficulties over land ownership led to warfare in the 1860s. Thereafter the Maori population declined while European numbers continued to increase.

British settlers found a climate slightly warmer than their own, with longer growing seasons but variable rainfall, sometimes with crippling drought in the dry areas. From 1844, when the first Merinos were introduced from Australia, New Zealand became predominantly a land of sheep, the grassy lowlands (especially in the South Island) providing year-round forage. Huge flocks were built up, mainly for wool and tallow production. From the lowlands they expanded into the hills – the 'high country' which was cleared of native bush and sown with European grasses for pasture. The North Island proved more difficult to turn into productive farmland, only later proving its value for dairying. New Zealand's early prosperity was finally established when the export of frozen mutton and lamb carcasses began in 1882. Soon a steady stream of chilled meat and dairy products – and later of fruit – was crossing the oceans to established markets in Britain. Wheat and other cereals were also grown.

High productivity was maintained by applications of fertilizers, mainly based on rock-phosphate mined on Nauru Island, in the Gilbert Islands group (now Kiribati).

Recent Development

Today New Zealand is a prosperous country, with a high standard of living for a multi-racial population of about 3 millions. Since 1907 a self-governing Dominion, New Zealand has for long relied on British markets for the export of agricultural produce, and has generally strong ties and affinities with Britain. Though agricultural products are still the main exports, the New Zealand economy has diversified considerably since World War 2. Iron ores, coal and small amounts of gold are among the few valuable minerals, recently boosted by natural gas and petroleum. Geothermal and hydro-electric power are well developed, and timber and forest products are finding valuable overseas markets. Despite the country's isolation, a prosperous tourist industry is also developing, based on the scenic beauty, abundance of game animals, and an as yet relatively peaceful and unhurried way of life. (BS)

SAMOA

A chain of three large and several small volcanic islands in the South Pacific Ocean, Samoa has a total area of about 3,100 km² (1,200 sq miles). Surrounded by coral reefs, the islands have a tropical maritime climate and a long history of Polynesian occupation. Europeans first called in the eighteenth century, establishing missions from about 1830. From 1899 Germany and the USA virtually split the group between them, forming Western and American Samoa.

In 1914 New Zealand seized Western Samoa, subsequently administering it as a dependency and later as a UN Trust Territory; it finally became independent in 1962. Western Samoa has a population of about 150,000 occupying four of the nine islands. Fish, copra, cocoa, bananas and timber are the main products. American Samoa has a population of about 30,000, mostly on the main island of Tutuila. The US Government is the main employer, with fish canning, tourism and agriculture the main industries. Many Samoans work overseas. (BS)

FIJI

Fiji was a port of call for whalers, sealers and other European voyagers throughout the eighteenth and nineteenth centuries. An extensive archipelago in the southern Pacific Ocean, Fiji includes two large islands, Viti Levu and Vanua Levu, and over 800 smaller ones, of which only about 100 are inhabited. The big islands are volcanic, the small ones mainly coral atolls; their total area is about 18,100 km² (7,000 sq miles), spread over an enormous area of ocean. The tropical maritime climate provides year-round warmth and heavy rainfall, covering the larger islands in dense rain forest, grading to savanna in drier areas. Mangrove swamps line the coasts.

Fiji is now a self-governing dominion. The population of about 600,000 is multi-racial; about two-fifths are of Fijian (mixed Melanesian and Polynesian) descent and about a half are of Indian descent, with small minorities of Europeans and Chinese. The islands export sugar and coconut products, gold from a mine on Viti Levu, and timber, and are developing tourism. (BS)

TONGA

South of Samoa and south-east of Fiji, the independent kingdom of Tonga forms a group of over 150 islands, with a land area of 700 km² (270 sq miles). Spread in a north-to-south arc over 700 km (440 miles) of the southern Pacific Ocean, it includes both volcanic and coral atoll islands; the largest island, Tongatapu, supports the capital Nuku'alofa. Set within the trade-wind belt of the tropics, the islands have a warm, moist climate throughout the year. Soils are fertile, and many of the islands were originally forested. They were discovered by Europeans in 1616.

Tongans are mainly small-holders who produce their own food and grow cash crops – notably copra and bananas – for export. Oil has recently been discovered in the group, and tourism is a growing source of revenue. (BS)

The lowlands of the South Island provide year-round pasture.

1 Toronto, capital of Ontario. It is Canada's second-largest city and a major commercial and financial centre.

2 The Capitol, Washington DC, USA.

3 The Canadian north includes huge areas of coniferous forest.

4 White Sands National Park, New Mexico, USA.

NORTH AMERICA

*America is so vast
that almost everything said about it is likely to be true,
and the opposite is probably equally true.*

James T Farrell, introduction to H L Mencken's *Prejudices: A Selection* (1958)

NORTH AMERICA

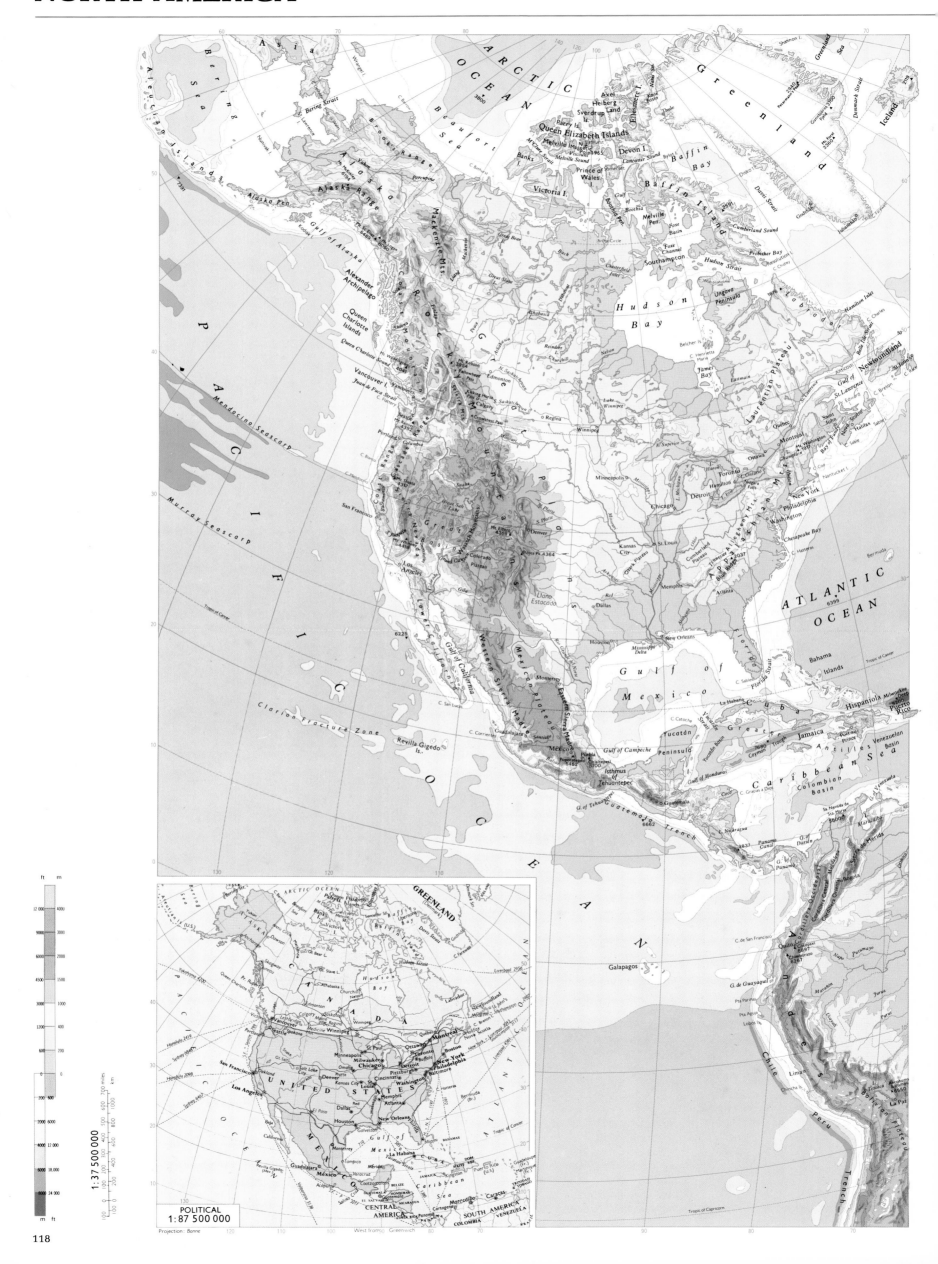

1:37 500 000

POLITICAL
1:87 500 000

Projection: Bonne

West from 0° Greenwich

Third largest of the world's continents, North America with its off-lying islands covers 24 million km² (9 million sq miles). From Newfoundland to Bering Strait it spans 116° of longitude, almost one third of the northern hemisphere; in latitude it extends from the tropical Gulf of Mexico in the south to the high Arctic, with its northern point only 7° (800 km, 500 miles) from the North Pole.

With a reputation for containing the biggest and best of everything, North America tends towards superlatives and extremes. Its highest peaks fall short of the highest in Asia and South America, but it includes the world's largest freshwater lake (Lake Superior) and greatest canyon (Grand Canyon, Arizona), its second largest bay (Hudson Bay), third longest river system (the Mississippi-Missouri) and fourth highest waterfall (Yosemite).

Climatic extremes are common, though some of its world records reflect little more than good coverage by an unusually complete network of stations. The world's highest-ever recorded shade temperature (56.9°C, 134°F) was logged in the Mexican desert, the longest continuous spell of high summer temperatures (six weeks with daily maxima over 49°C, 120°F) in Death Valley, California. The world record snowfall for one year (an astonishing 25 m, 82 ft) fell on Mt Rainier, Washington, and that for a single day (1.9 m, 6.2 ft) at Silver Lake, Colorado; the heaviest-ever rainfall in one minute (31.2 mm, 1.3 in) fell at Unionville, Maryland.

Topography and climate combine to provide an immense range of natural habitats across North America, from mangrove swamps and tropical forests in the south, through hot deserts, prairie, temperate and boreal forests, taiga and tundra to polar deserts in the far north. North America can claim both the largest-known living organisms (giant redwood cedars) and the oldest-known (bristlecone pines), both found in the western USA.

Standing at the edge of one of

the world's six great crustal plates (pp. 8–9), North America has been subject to pressure and uplift from its neighbouring Pacific plate, with results that show clearly on a physical map. Roughly one third of the continent, including the whole of the western flank, has been thrown into a spectacular complex of young mountains, valleys and plateaux – the Western Cordilleras. To the east lie much older mountains, longer-weathered and lower – the Appalachians in the south and the Laurentian Highlands in the north; these are separated from the western ranges by broad interior lowlands drained by the Mississippi-Missouri system.

The bleak northern plains, centred about Hudson Bay, rest on a shield or platform of ancient rocks that underlies most of central and eastern Canada. The Laurentian Shield, though warped and split by crustal movements, was massive enough to resist folding through the successive periods of mountain building that raised the Western Cordilleras. Planed by more than a million years of glaciation throughout the Ice Age, it is now free of permanent ice except on a few of the northern islands. Its surface remains littered with glacial debris that forms thin, waterlogged tundra or forest soils, and the once-glaciated region is fringed by a crescent of interlinked lakes and waterways, including the Great Bear Lake and the five Great Lakes.

From Stone Age times to the end of the fifteenth century North America was thinly populated with primitive hunting or farming populations, whose ways of life made little impact on its resources of minerals, energy and food. Today, with resources mobilized on a grand scale, it supports a population of over 250 million, a rate of increase unmatched by any other continent. Still running to superlatives, North America affords its millions – or anyway most of them – one of the highest material standards of living the world has ever seen. (BS)

CANADA

With a surface area of 9,976,139 km² (3,852,000 sq miles), Canada is the world's second largest country after the USSR; with a population of only 23½ million, it is one of the least-densely populated countries, including huge areas of virtually unoccupied mountains, forests, tundra and polar desert in the north and west.

Politically it is a confederation of ten provinces and two territories. To the east lie the Maritime provinces of Newfoundland, Nova Scotia, New Brunswick and Prince Edward Island, and the predominantly French-speaking province of Quebec; clustered about the Gulf of St Lawrence, they are based on ancient, worn-down mountains – the northern extension of the Appalachians – and the eastern up-tilted edge of the even older Canadian Shield. The central province of Ontario borders the Great Lakes, extending north across the Shield to Hudson Bay. Then come the prairie provinces of Manitoba, Saskatchewan and Alberta; like Quebec and Ontario, these include fertile farmlands in the south, where most of the population is to be found, and lake-strewn forest on the subarctic wastelands to the north.

South-western Alberta includes a substantial block of the Rocky Mountains, with peaks rising to over 4,000 m (13,120 ft) in Banff, Yoho and Kootenay National Parks. The westernmost province of British Columbia is entirely mountainous, a land of spectacular forests, lakes and fjords, and sheltered valleys with rich farmland. The northern territories include the relatively small and mountainous Yukon Territory in the west, bordering Alaska, and the much more extensive Northwest Territories stretching from the 60th parallel to the northern tip of Ellesmere Island.

The endless horizon of the prairies.

Exploration and Settlement

Norse voyagers and fishermen were probably the first Europeans briefly to visit Canada, but John Cabot's later discovery of North America, in 1497, began the race to annex lands and wealth. France and Britain were the main contenders.

Jacques Cartier's discovery of the St Lawrence River in 1534 gave France a head start; from their settlements near Quebec French explorers, trappers and missionaries pioneered routes deeply penetrating the northern half of North America. With possible routes to China and the Indies in mind, Frenchmen followed the St Lawrence and Niagara rivers deep into the heartland of the continent, hoping for the riches of another Eldorado and seeking to convert the natives as they went. Discovering the Great Lakes, they moved north, west and south in their search for trade. From the fertile valley of the upper St Lawrence French influence spread north beyond the coniferous forests and over the tundra. To the west and south they reached the prairies – potentially fertile farming country – exploring further to the Rockies and down the Ohio and Mississippi.

By 1763, after the series of wars that gave Britain brief control of the whole of North America, French-speaking communities were already scattered widely across the interior. Many of the southern settlements became American after 1776, when the USA declared independence from Britain. The northern ones became a British colony.

British settlers had for long been established on the Atlantic coast, farming where possible, with supplementary fishing. In the 1780s a new wave of English-speaking settlers – the United Empire Loyalists – moved north from the USA into Nova Scotia, New Brunswick and Lower Canada. With further waves of immigration direct from Britain, English speakers came to dominate the fertile lands between Lakes Huron and Erie. From there they gradually spread westward.

The Birth of Canada

Restricted to the north by intractable coniferous forests and tundra (virtually all that will grow on the barren, ice-scoured rocks and permafrost soils of the Canadian Shield), and to the south by the USA, the settlers spread through Quebec into Upper Canada – now Ontario, the only province along the Canadian shores of the Great Lakes. Mostly English-speaking and retaining British traditions, they continued westward to establish settlements across the narrow wedge of the northern prairie, finally crossing the Rockies to link with embryo settlements along the Pacific coast. So the fertile lowlands of the St Lawrence basin and the pockets of settlement on the Shield alone remained French in language and culture. The bulk of Canada to east and west became predominantly British, and remains so to this day.

Canada's varied topography and immense scale inhibited the development of a single nation; to promote Canadian unity across so wide a continent has been the aim of successive governments for more than two centuries. The union of British Upper Canada and French Lower Canada was sealed by the Confederation of 1867, when as the newly-named Provinces of Ontario and Quebec they were united with the Maritime core, Nova Scotia and New Brunswick. Three years later the settlement on the Red River entered the Confederation as Manitoba, and in the following year the Pacific colonies of Vancouver Island and British Columbia, now united as a single province, completed the link from sea to sea. Prince Edward Island joined in 1873, the prairie provinces of Alberta and Saskatchewan in 1905, Newfoundland in 1949.

Though self-governing in most respects from the time of the Confederation, Canada remained technically subject to the British Imperial Parliament until 1931, when the creation of the British Commonwealth made her a sovereign nation under the Crown.

A shrimp catch in Alaska.

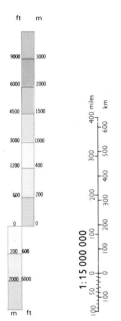

The Trans-Alaskan pipeline.

Alaska

In 1867, the year of the Canadian Confederation, the USA bought Alaska (the last Russian colony in North America) from the Tsarist Government for a mere $7 million. More extensive than the south-western lands acquired from Mexico, Alaska remained a territory for over 90 years, becoming America's largest state in 1959. Geographically it forms the north-western end of the Western Cordilleras; peaks in the main Alaska Range rise to over 6,000 m (20,000 ft), and the southern panhandle region is a drowned fjordland backed by ice-capped mountains. Earthquakes periodically raise and lower the shore, and have destroyed harbours and coastal settlements.

The panhandle, containing the state capital Juneau, reflected the interests of the original Russian settlements in water communication, pelts and fishing. Americans introduced salmon-canning and timber industries, but a gold-rush in the 1880s stimulated the later development of other mineral resources (notably copper and petroleum) and of a more varied economy in the main body of Alaska. Most modern developments are around Anchorage, Valdez and Fairbanks, and on the petroleum fields of the northern coast, which are linked to the Pacific ports by pipeline. Alaska is the first real test of the USA's resolve to balance development and preservation.

Farming is possible on the southern coastal lowlands; the interior table-lands are tundra-covered and rich in migrant birds and mammals. The volcanic Aleutian Islands, damp and fog-bound, have neither timber nor farming, but support small settlements of hunters, fishermen and military personnel. About one-seventh of the Alaskan population are of native Eskimo, Aleut or Indian stock; the rest are immigrants, mostly newcomers. Alaska is linked to Canada and the USA by the Alaska Highway, and by air and coastal shipping routes: pipelines are proposed to carry Alaskan natural gas to the main mass of the American market. (SFM)

Climate

LOCALITY HEIGHT		JAN	JUL	YR
Coppermine	°C	−28.6	9.3	−11.4
3 m	mm	13	34	246
Fairbanks	°C	−23.9	15.5	−3.1
134 m	mm	23	28	297
Nome	°C	−15.5	12.8	−3.3
4 m	mm	28	69	472
Yellowknife	°C	−27.8	15.8	−5.5
199 m	mm	13	28	213
Anchorage	°C	−11.1	13.9	1.7
40 m	mm	20	41	371
Whitehorse	°C	−15.0	13.3	−5.5
696 m	mm	15	41	267
Churchill	°C	−27.6	12.2	−7.0
35 m	mm	17	39	443
Port Harrison	°C	−25.0	8.9	−6.9
20 m	mm	14	51	395
Wrangell	°C	−0.8	14.2	6.7
11 m	mm	208	124	2189
Goose Bay	°C	−16.3	16.3	0.2
44 m	mm	72	84	837

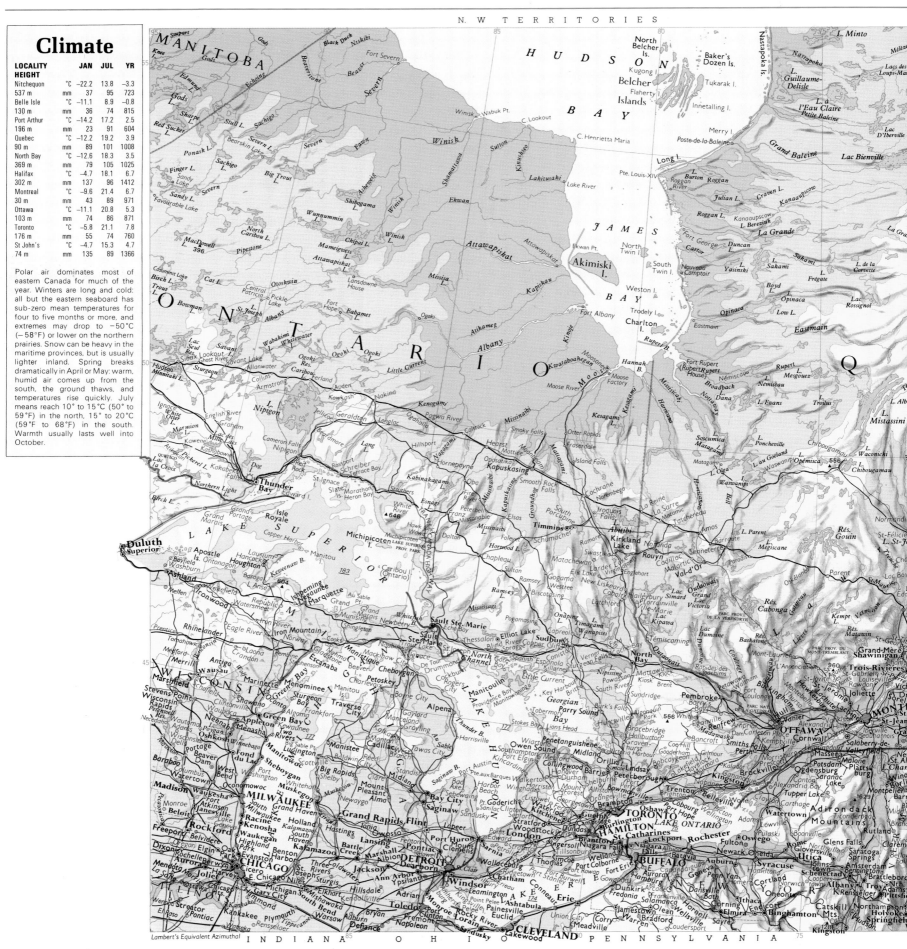

Climate

LOCALITY HEIGHT		JAN	JUL	YR
Nitchequon	°C	−22.2	13.8	−3.3
537 m	mm	37	95	723
Belle Isle	°C	−11.1	8.9	−0.8
130 m	mm	36	74	815
Port Arthur	°C	−14.2	17.2	2.5
196 m	mm	23	91	604
Quebec	°C	−12.2	19.2	3.9
90 m	mm	89	101	1008
North Bay	°C	−12.6	18.3	3.5
369 m	mm	79	105	1025
Halifax	°C	−4.7	18.1	6.7
302 m	mm	137	96	1412
Montreal	°C	−9.6	21.4	6.7
30 m	mm	43	89	971
Ottawa	°C	−11.1	20.8	5.3
103 m	mm	74	86	871
Toronto	°C	−5.8	21.1	7.8
176 m	mm	55	74	760
St John's	°C	−4.7	15.3	4.7
74 m	mm	135	89	1366

Polar air dominates most of eastern Canada for much of the year. Winters are long and cold: all but the eastern seaboard has sub-zero mean temperatures for four to five months or more, and extremes may drop to −50°C (−58°F) or lower on the northern prairies. Snow can be heavy in the maritime provinces, but is usually lighter inland. Spring breaks dramatically in April or May: warm, humid air comes up from the south, the ground thaws, and temperatures rise quickly. July means reach 10° to 15°C (50° to 59°F) in the north, 15° to 20°C (59°F to 68°F) in the south. Warmth usually lasts well into October.

With so much of the population spread out along a southern ribbon of settlement, 4,000 km (2,500 miles) long but rarely more than 480 km (300 miles) wide, Canada has struggled constantly to achieve unity. Trans-continental communications have played a critical role. From the eastern provinces the Canadian Pacific Railway crossed the Rockies to reach Vancouver in 1885. Later a second rail-route, the Canadian National, was pieced together, and the Trans-Canada Highway links the extreme east and west of the country symbolically as well as in fact. Trans-continental air routes link the major centres, and local air traffic is especially important over trackless forests, mountains and tundra. With radio and telephone communications, all parts of the confederation – even remote corners of the Arctic territories – are now firmly linked, though the sheer vastness of Canada remains. At noon in Vancouver it is already 3 pm in Toronto, and 4-30 pm in St Johns, Newfoundland.

A constant hazard to Canadian nationhood is the proximity of the USA. Though benign, with shared British traditions, the prosperous giant to the south has often seemed to threaten the very survival of Canada through cultural annexa-tion. A real and growing threat to unity is the persistence of French culture in Quebec Province – a last-ing political wedge between the western prairie and mountain pro-vinces and the eastern Maritimes.

Population and Urbanization

Though the population of Canada expanded rapidly from Confedera-tion onward, it remained predomi-nantly rural for many generations; only in recent decades have Canada's cities grown to match those of the USA. At Confederation in 1867 about 80 per cent of the population was rural. Only Montreal had passed the 100,000 population mark, with but six towns over 25,000. Not until the eve of World War 2 did the rural

The St Lawrence river.

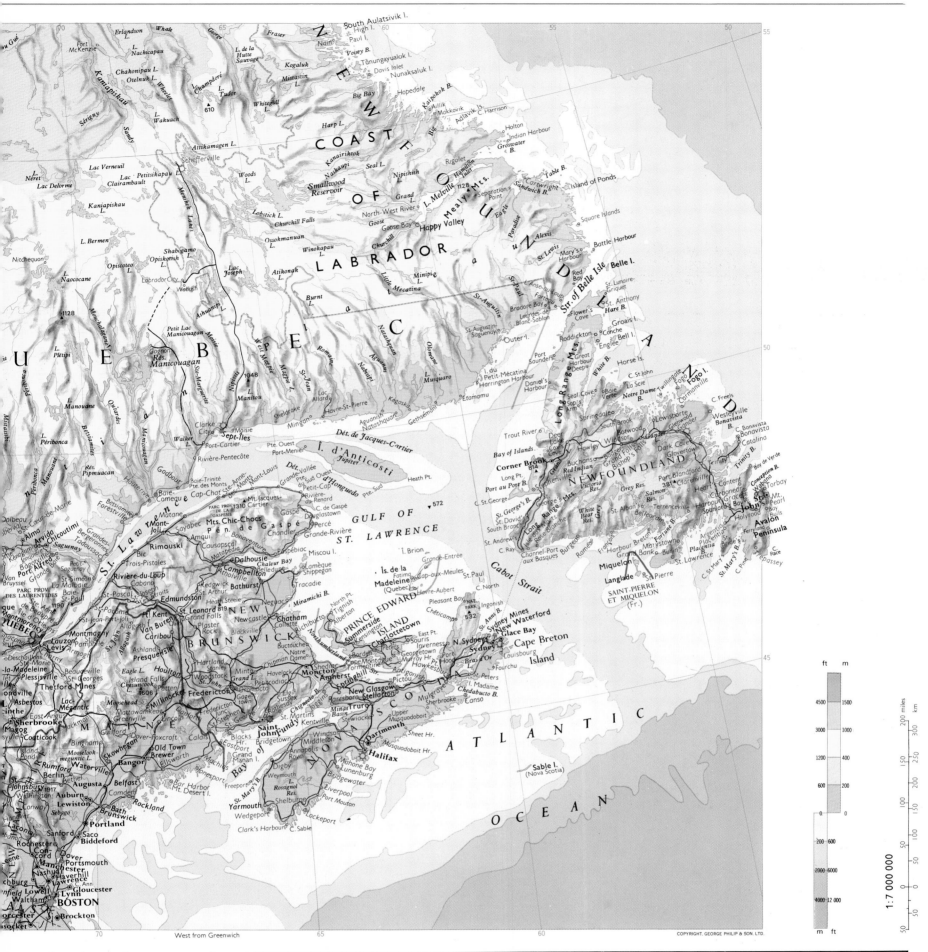

and urban elements stand in balance. In the 1941 census only 8 towns had over 100,000 inhabitants and a mere 21 had over 25,000. Thirty years later 76 per cent of Canada's population was urban.

The Tundra

Beyond their habitable southern rim the northlands of Canada and Alaska are bleak and bare; in the subarctic zone conifers stretch across the continent, but northward the boreal forest thins and dies out, to be replaced with tundra. This is a harsh environment, in which several factors combine to make life difficult for plants and animals. Glaciation has scoured the rocks bare, and soils have had insufficient time to form; the surface thaws in summer, but subsoils remain frozen. Winters are long and bitterly cold, summers brief and cool. Even in the south the season of

plant growth is only 70–80 days. Precipitation is light – usually less than 25 cm (10 in) per year, and most of it snow; except where it drifts, the snow seldom lies deep, but it provides important cover for vegetation and burrowing animals.

The tundra is covered with low grasses, lichens, mosses and spindly shrubs, providing food for migrating reindeer and resident hares, voles, lemmings and other small browsers and grazers. Their numbers are augmented each summer by hosts of migrant birds – ducks, geese, swans, waders, and many other kinds – that fly in from temperate latitudes to feed on the vegetation and insects. (SFM)

The tundra in autumn.

The national census of 1971 showed where the population of Canada – by then some 22 million – was accumulating. The metropolitan areas of Toronto and Montreal jointly contained one quarter of the total; together with Vancouver they accounted for over 30 per cent of the entire population. By contrast the urban centres of Newfoundland and the Maritimes had suffered relative stagnation.

Agriculture and Industry

Outside the big cities Canada remains rural; farming settlements still dominate the landscape, if not the economy. Abandonment of farm-land is a serious problem in the eastern provinces, where farming – except in such favoured areas as the Annapolis Valley, Nova Scotia – has always been marginal. Through the St Lawrence lowlands and Ontario peninsula farms are more prosperous and rural populations are denser, thinning again along the north shores of the Great Lakes. On the prairies mechanization of grain farming minimizes the need for labour, so population densities remain low; the mixed farming communities on the forest margins are often denser. Pacific coast population is concentrated in such rich farming areas as the Okanagan and lower Frazer River basins.

Industry, often dependent on local development of power resources, has transformed many remote and empty areas of Canada. Newfoundland's Labrador iron-ore workings around Shefferville are powered by the huge hydro-electric plant at Churchill Falls. Cheap hydro-electric power throughout Quebec and Ontario, coupled with improved transmission technology, has encouraged the development of wood-pulp and paper industries, even in distant parts of the northern forests, and stimulated industry and commerce in the south. Mining, too, has helped in the development of these provinces; Sudbury, Ontario, supplies most of the western world's nickel.

In the prairie provinces, small marketing, distribution and service centres have been transformed by the enormous expansion of the petro-chemical industry; the boom towns of Alberta, Edmonton and Calgary far outpaced the growth of the eastern cities during recent decades. Lacking hydrocarbons, depending mainly on farming, logging and pulping for their prosperity, the settlements of Pacific Canada have on the whole grown slowly, with the notable exception of Vancouver.

The northlands

Canada's northlands have an immense though localized potential

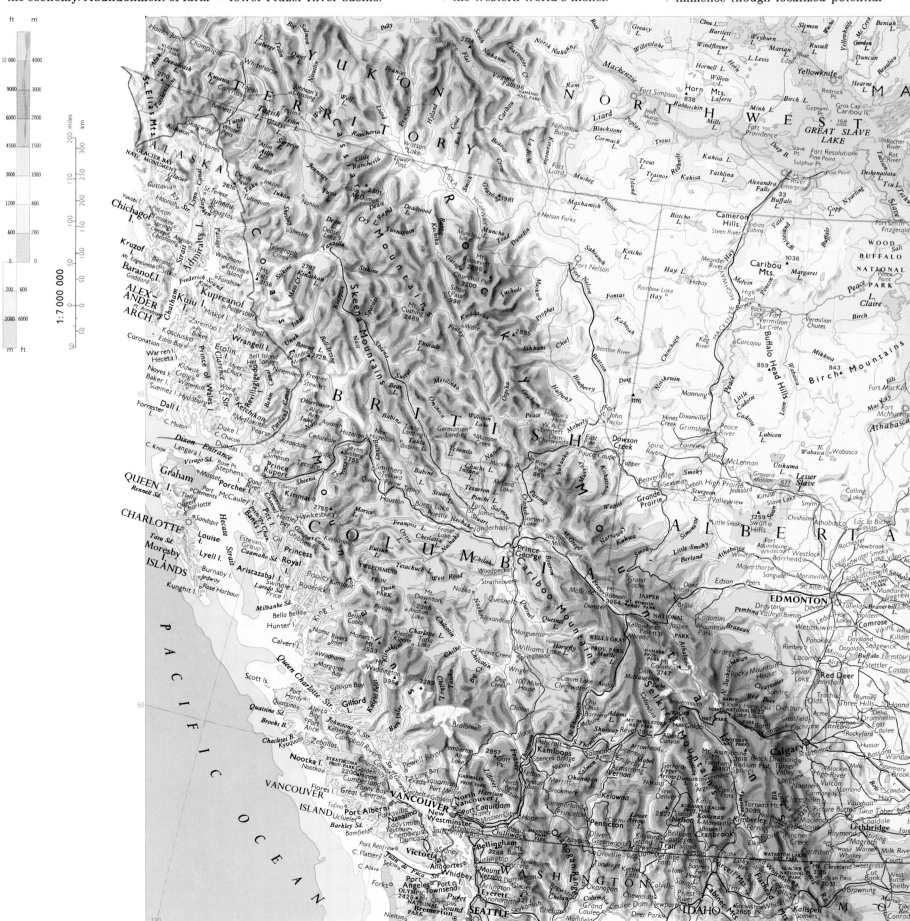

Projection: Lambert's Equivalent Azimuthal   West from Greenwich

CANADA

for development. Though the soils are poor and the climate is unyielding, mineral wealth is abundant under the permanently frozen subsoils. Already a major producer of zinc and nickel, the North also holds vast reserves of copper, molybdenum, iron, cadmium, uranium, and other metals of strategic importance; sulphur, potash and asbestos are currently exploited and natural gas and petroleum await development beyond the Mackenzie River delta.

Much of this immense mineral wealth will remain in the ground until the high costs of extraction and transportation can be justified. Also, legislation to protect the boreal forest and tundra against unnecessary or casual damage is growing.

Separatism

Canada's rapid development from a mainly rural to a predominantly urban society has brought its problems. In Quebec urbanization has fuelled a separatist movement that seeks to turn the province into an independent French-speaking republic. This issue to some extent obscures a wider and more fundamental division in Canadian politics, with the development of a Montreal-Toronto axis in the east, and a Vancouver-Winnipeg axis in the west. (SFM)

Vancouver, the industrial and commercial heart of British Columbia.

Climate

LOCALITY HEIGHT		JAN	JUL	YR
Fort Nelson	°C	-22.4	16.8	-1.1
375 m	mm	25	70	451
Grande Prairie	°C	-15.8	15.8	1.1
668 m	mm	33	63	427
Prince Rupert	°C	1.4	13.1	7.8
52 m	mm	249	122	2421
Prince George	°C	-10.4	15.2	3.6
676 m	mm	56	64	626
Edmonton	°C	-14.1	17.3	2.7
676 m	mm	24	85	474
Saskatoon	°C	-18.3	18.1	1.4
515 m	mm	23	61	371
Calgary	°C	-10.6	16.4	3.6
1079 m	mm	13	64	424
Winnipeg	°C	-17.7	20.2	2.5
240 m	mm	26	69	517
Lethbridge	°C	-8.2	18.9	5.4
903 m	mm	21	39	424
Vancouver	°C	2.3	17.6	9.8
4 m	mm	139	26	1048

The west coast and Rocky mountains receive year-round warm, moist air-streams, producing heavy coastal rainfall, especially in winter, and heavy rain or snow over the Rockies. January mean temperatures remain above freezing point even beyond the Alaska border: summers are warm and humid with means between 10° and 20°C (50° and 68°F). East of the Rockies dry polar air prevails. Winters are long and cold with sub-zero mean temperatures for three to five months in the south, six to eleven months in the north, and light snow. Summers are dry and warm, with July means of 15°C (59°F) even in the far north.

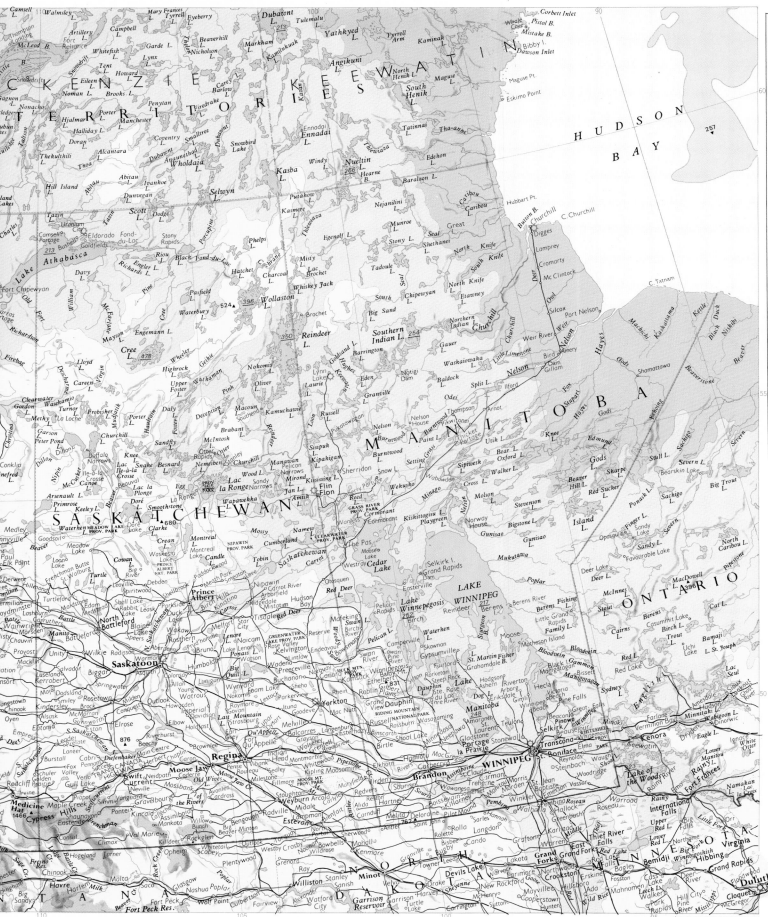

COPYRIGHT GEORGE PHILIP & SON LTD.

USA

The United States of America (USA), often known as the United States, or America, fills the North American continent between Canada and Mexico and also includes Alaska and the archipelago of Hawaii in a total area of 9,363,353 km² (3,615,200 sq miles). The population is about 218 million. The USA falls readily into an eastern section, including the Appalachian mountains and eastern coastal plain, a central section including the Mississippi basin and the broad prairie plains from the Dakotas to Texas, and a western section including the Rocky Mountains and Pacific coastlands.

THE EAST

Eastern North America is crossed by a band of low, folded mountains: though nowhere much above 2,000 m (6,500 ft), these for long formed a barrier to settlers. In the north are the Adirondacks, a southern extension of the ancient granite shield of Canada, rising to 1,629 m (5,344 ft). From Maine to Alabama runs a broad range of sedimentary mountains, the Appalachians. Younger than the Adirondacks (though much older than the Rockies) the Appalachians separate the Atlantic coastlands of the east from the Great Lakes and low plateaux of Ohio, Kentucky and Tennessee.

North-east of New York City lie the six New England states – the fertile wooded country that, at least in summer, made the early settlers feel at home. To the south the coastal plain widens, to be split by the drowned estuaries of the Susquehanna and Potomac rivers, draining into Chesapeake Bay. From Virginia to Florida smaller rivers drain eastwards, across a much broader plain, many of them entering coastal sounds with offshore sand-bars and islands.

In New York state a major spillway cuts through the mountains between the Adirondacks and Appalachians, linking the Great Lakes with the Hudson River valley and the Atlantic Ocean. This is the line of the famous Erie Canal route, the most used of several routes that gave the early settlers access to the Ohio country beyond the mountains. Other routes led to Pittsburgh and through the southern Appalachians into Tennessee. Central Ohio, Indiana and Illinois, that once formed America's North-west Territory, are rolling uplands and plains, smoothed by glaciation in the north but more rugged in the south, and drained by the rambling Ohio river.

Vegetation

The original vegetation of eastern America, on either flank of the mountains, was broadleaf deciduous forest of oak, ash, beech and maple, merging northwards into yellow birch, hemlock and pine. In the drier mid-west these immense woodlands turned to open country. Patchy grasslands covered northern Indiana and southern Illinois; central Illinois was forested along most watercourses, with prairie bluestem grasses on the drier interfluves. Around the southern Appalachians mixed oak, pine and tulip-tree dominated; pines covered the coastal plains to the south and east with bald cypress in northern Florida. Spruce blanketed the highlands from northern Maine to the Adirondacks; spruce, tamarack and balsam fir covered the high Appalachians. Most of this original forest is now gone, but there is still enough left – and some regenerating on abandoned farmland – to leave the mountains a blaze of colour each fall. Despite more than three hundred years of European settlement, the overall impression of eastern America, seen from the air, is still one of dense semi-continuous forests, except in the extensive farmlands north of the Ohio.

Autumn in Vermont, New England.

Manhattan Island, New York, with its famous skyscraper skyline.

Settlement and Development

The eastern USA is the heartland of many of America's rural and urban traditions. In the nineteenth century European immigrants poured through the ports of Boston, New York, Philadelphia and Baltimore. Many stayed to swell the cities, which grew enormously. Others moved in their thousands across the mountains, first on foot, later by river, canal and railway, to populate the interior and start the farms that fed the city masses. As raw materials of industry – coal and iron ore especially – were discovered and exploited, new cities grew up in the interior. Some were based on old frontier forts; Fort Duquesne became Pittsburgh and Fort Dearborn became Chicago. Railways spread over the booming farmlands, linking producer and consumer. Huge manufacturing cities, vast markets in their own right, developed along the Great Lakes as people continued to arrive, firstly from abroad, but latterly from the countryside where mechanization threw people off the land, into the cities and factories. In less than a hundred years between the late eighteenth and nineteenth centuries the Ohio country passed from Indian-occupied forests and plains to mechanized farmlands of unparalleled efficiency, becoming the granary of the western world, with some of its greatest and wealthiest industrial centres.

While the north boomed, the warmer southern states slipped into rural lethargy; becoming overdependent upon cotton cultivation, they remained backward and outside the mainstream of American prosperity. Though fortunes were made on the rich cotton estates of the south-east, Tennessee and the southern Appalachians spelled rural poverty for many generations of settlers. Today the pattern is much the same, though prosperity has increased throughout the east. The densest concentrations of industry and population lie in the north-east, especially in central New England. New York remains an important financial hub, and the most populous metropolis of the western hemisphere, while Washington DC, now part of a vast, sprawling megalopolis, loses none of its significance as the centre of federal government in the USA. The south-eastern states remain relatively rural and thinly populated although they are increasingly popular with the retired. (SFM)

The Niagara Falls, 50 m (167 ft) high, are a source of hydro-electricity as well as a tourist attraction.

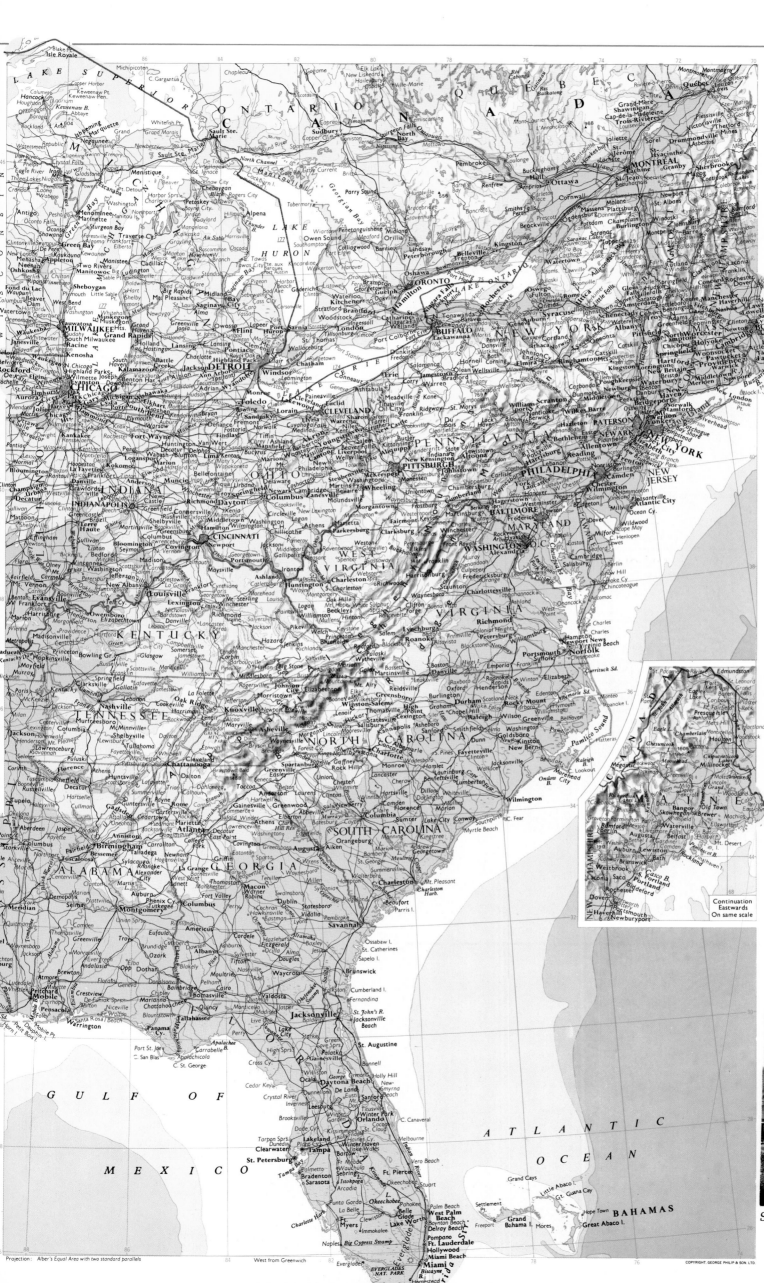

Climate

LOCALITY HEIGHT		JAN	JUL	YR
Boston	°C	-1.2	23.2	10.8
9 m	mm	100	73	1086
Chicago	°C	-3.3	24.3	10.5
190 m	mm	47	86	843
Scranton	°C	-2.5	21.7	9.3
228 m	mm	69	97	942
Washington (DC)	°C	2.7	25.7	13.9
20 m	mm	77	105	1036
Montgomery	°C	9.3	27.2	18.4
61 m	mm	130	119	1321
Asheville	°C	4.3	23.6	13.6
687 m	mm	81	109	962
Birmingham	°C	6.9	26.4	17.3
186 m	mm	137	132	1346
Charleston (S.Ca)	°C	10.2	26.7	18.3
15 m	mm	65	196	1249
Mobile	°C	11.0	27.5	19.5
3 m	mm	122	170	1577
Miami	°C	19.4	27.7	23.9
3 m	mm	52	171	1518

In the northern states winters are long and severe, dominated by cold air from the centre and northlands of the continent; depressions from the west bring heavy snow, which persists for several months. Short, late springs are followed by warm, humid summers with plentiful rain; autumn is usually long and colourful, with warm days and cold nights continuing into October or even later. Further south the winters ameliorate and shorten, though frosts may occur in the coldest months in all but the southernmost areas. The southern states are subtropical, with hot and humid summers, mild winters and a long growing season. Hurricanes are common along the southern coasts in summer and autumn.

1:7 500 000

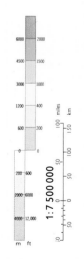

Steel plant, Pittsburgh.

127

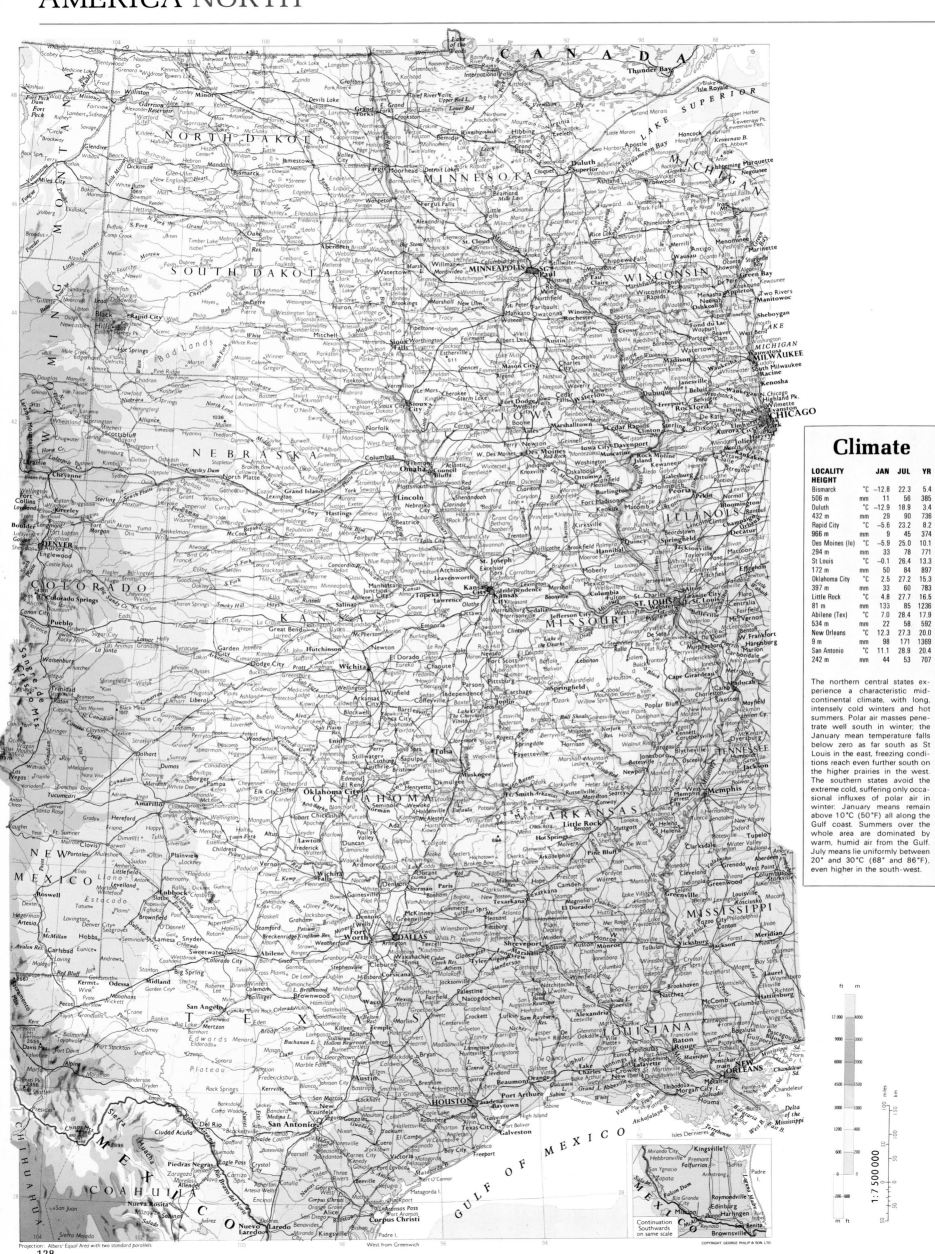

Climate

LOCALITY HEIGHT		JAN	JUL	YR
Bismarck	°C	-12.8	22.3	5.4
506 m	mm	11	56	385
Duluth	°C	-12.9	18.9	3.4
432 m	mm	29	90	736
Rapid City	°C	-5.6	23.2	8.2
966 m	mm	9	45	374
Des Moines (Io)	°C	-5.9	25.0	10.1
294 m	mm	33	78	771
St Louis	°C	-0.1	26.4	13.3
172 m	mm	50	84	897
Oklahoma City	°C	2.5	27.2	15.3
397 m	mm	33	60	783
Little Rock	°C	4.8	27.7	16.5
81 m	mm	133	85	1236
Abilene (Tex)	°C	7.0	28.4	17.9
534 m	mm	22	58	592
New Orleans	°C	12.3	27.3	20.0
9 m	mm	98	171	1369
San Antonio	°C	11.1	28.9	20.4
242 m	mm	44	53	707

The northern central states experience a characteristic mid-continental climate, with long, intensely cold winters and hot summers. Polar air masses penetrate well south in winter; the January mean temperature falls below zero as far south as St Louis in the east, freezing conditions reach even further south on the higher prairies in the west. The southern states avoid the extreme cold, suffering only occasional influxes of polar air in winter: January means remain above 10°C (50°F) all along the Gulf coast. Summers over the whole area are dominated by warm, humid air from the Gulf. July means lie uniformly between 20° and 30°C (68° and 86°F), even higher in the south-west.

Projection: Albers' Equal Area with two standard parallels

West from Greenwich

COPYRIGHT: GEORGE PHILIP & SON, LTD.

1:7 500 000

Continuation Southwards on same scale

THE CENTRAL STATES

Within the 1,400 km (875 miles) from the Mississippi River to the foothills of the Rocky Mountains, the land surface rises almost 3,000 m (9,850 ft), though the slope is often imperceptible to the traveller. From the Gulf of Mexico northward to Minnesota and the Dakotas the rise is even less perceptible, though the flatness is occasionally relieved by the outcrops of uplands – the Ozarks of northern Arkansas, for example. In summer nothing bars the northward movement of hot, moist air from the Gulf, nor in winter the southward movement of dry, cold air from the Arctic. These air masses produce great seasonal contrasts of climate, exacerbated by storms, blizzards and tornadoes. Westwards from the Mississippi the climate grows progressively drier.

The plains are crossed by a series of long, wide rivers, often of irregular flow, that drain off the Rockies: the Missouri, the Platte, the Arkansas, the Canadian and the Red Rivers. In contrast to the Ohio, which enabled travellers to pass downstream and so westwards to the Mississippi, these rivers of the plains provided little help to settlers moving westward, due to their seasonal variations in flow and the effort needed to move upstream when floods gave them depth.

Vegetation

West of the margins of the Mississippi tall blue-stem prairie grasses once extended from the Canadian border to southern Texas. Only along the watercourses were there trees – cottonwood and willow in the north, merging into oak and hickory further south. Westward the prairie grasslands thinned to the bunch grass and needle grass of the Great Plains in a belt from central North Dakota to western Oklahoma; locally-favoured areas such as western Nebraska had patches of broadleaf evergreens amidst shrubs and grasses. West of about meridian 100°W a variety of short grasses stretched from Montana and the Dakotas southwards to north-west Texas: in the far south on the Mexican border low xerophytic shrubs indicated increasing aridity. Higher ground, for example the Black Hills of south-western South Dakota, supported stands of pine.

Settlement and Development

Some thirty major tribes of native Indians used these vast and varied plains. Some – the Mandan, the Omaha and the Kansa along the Missouri River, for example – were settled farmers, while on the drier western plains the Blackfoot, Crow, Arapaho, Kiowa and Comanche were nomadic, following the buffalo,

Terracing and contour ploughing in Kansas.

the game and the pasture. European influences revolutionized their lives. By 1800 the horse, introduced from the south by the Spanish, made the Indian population (about 100,000) mobile as never before. Then English and French-speaking trappers and traders from the east brought firearms: the mounted Indian with a gun became too efficient a hunter, and rapidly depleted his food supply. Behind the traders came white settlers, killing off the buffalo, and crowding in other native peoples that they had driven from homelands in the south-east. As railways, cattle trails and the fences of the ranchers crossed the old hunting grounds, Indian farmers and hunters alike lost their traditional lands and livelihoods to the European intruders, and the plains settlement was virtually completed by the late nineteenth century.

The coming of the railways after the Civil War of the 1860s not only doomed the remnant Indian societies, but also introduced long and often bitter competition between different types of European farming. The dry grasslands that once supported the buffalo could just as well support herds of cattle on the open range, raised to feed the eastern cities. So the range lands often became crop-farms. In the dry years that followed soil deterioration and erosion began, becoming a major problem in the early decades of the present century.

With their markets in the cities of the east and in Europe, the plains farmers were caught in a vice between the desiccation of their farms and the boom and slump of their markets. By the 1930s agricultural depression led to massive foreclosing on mortgaged lands, and when the dust storms of eroded top-soil came the people were driven away – the 'Okies' of Guthrie and Steinbeck who fled to California. Much farmed land reverted to ranching.

Farming prospects improved during the later 1930s, when the New Deal brought better price structures. New approaches to farming practice, including dry farming (cropping only one year out of several), contour ploughing, diversification beyond basic grains, and widespread irrigation that was linked to the crea-

tion of a vast network of dams and reservoirs, transformed the plains. Nevertheless these areas are marginal to semi-desert, remaining highly susceptible to periodic changes in precipitation over a wide area: thus

French Influences

New Orleans street signs.

French influences in this region date from 1682, when the French explorer La Salle reached the great Mississippi delta and claimed it for his country, together with all the land drained by the Mississippi river and its tributaries. Called Louisiana after Louis XIV, this vast territory lay between New Spain in the west and a Spanish coastal strip to Florida to the east. New Orleans became the capital shortly after its foundation in 1718.

Though African slaves were imported and plantations founded in the south, Louisiana did not immediately flourish. The river and its tributaries, however, formed a great highway, linking the southern French settlements with fur-trading stations far to the north settled from Canada. The latter included Fort Crèvecoeur (1680, now Peoria) and Fort St Louis (1682, now La Salle), both on the Illinois river. Later followed Sainte Genevieve (1750), St Louis (1763) and Cape Girardeau (1795) – now mid-western towns with little but their names to indicate their French origins. Following the Seven Years War (1763) lands east of the Mississippi were ceded from France to Britain; lands west of the river passed to Spain, to be sold to the twenty-years-old USA in 1803 under the 'Louisiana Purchase'.
(SFM / BS)

A plantation house, Louisiana.

a poor snowfall on the Rockies may mean insufficient water for irrigation the following summer. Coupled with world-wide fluctuations in the cereals market (on which mid-west farmers still depend heavily) investment in farming on the plains remains very risky.

The Growth of Industry

In the Gulf Coast states, petroleum provides a radically different basis for prosperity. Since the exploitation of oil reserves in the early years of the century Oklahoma, Texas and Louisiana have shifted from a dependence upon agriculture (notably wheat, cattle, rice and sugar production) to the steadily developing refining and petro-chemical industries. Oil has transformed Dallas-Fort Worth into a major US conurbation, now larger than the twin-cities of Minneapolis-St Paul, which were once the chief urban focus of the agricultural economy of the upper Mississippi. At the meeting of the High Plains and the Rocky Mountains, mile-high Denver changed from a small railhead town to a wealthy state capital (and further to a smog-ridden metropolis) in response to mineral wealth and the growth of aero-space industries.

Further north the cities of the central USA are great trading centres, dependent upon local agriculture for their prosperity. Wholesaling and the trans-shipping of produce have been crucial since the days of the railheads, but cities like St Louis, Kansas City and Chicago have been able to diversify far beyond their original role, to become major manufacturing centres. Chicago, for example, is the main midwestern focus of the steel industries. Nowadays the interstate freeway system supplements and has partly replaced the railway networks, and air passenger traffic is increasing.

From the air the landscape between the Mississippi and the Rockies is one of quilted farmlands and vast reservoirs, blending into wheatlands with extensive grasslands. Almost all the original vegetation is long gone, and most people now live in the cities, but the landscape still reflects the critical importance of agriculture past and present. (SFM)

THE WEST

Here in the west is a complex mountain and plateau system, rich in scenic beauty and natural history, bordered by a rugged coast that starts in southern semi-deserts and ends in rain-soaked forests in the north. Americans appreciate their far west; for long the final frontier of a youthful, expanding nation, it is still the goal of tens of thousands of immigrants each year, and the vacation dream of many more: tourism is the most widespread industry.

Landscape

Topographically the west is a land of high mountain ranges divided by high plateaux and deep valleys. The grain of the country runs north-west to south-east, at a right-angle to the crustal pressures that produced it, and the highest mountains – the Rocky Mountains of a thousand legends – form a spectacular eastern flank. The southern Rockies of Colorado and New Mexico, remnants of an ancient granite plateau, are carved by weathering into ranges of spectacular peaks; Colorado alone has over 1,000 mountains of 3,000 m (10,000 ft) or more. Rising from dry, sandy, cactus-and-sagebrush desert, their lower slopes carry grey piñon pines and juniper scrub, with darker spruce, firs and pines above. At the timberline grow gnarled bristlecone pines, some 3,000 and more years old. Between the ranges 'parks' of mixed forest and grassland support deer and other game in summer grazing. To the south-west are the dry, colourful sandstones of the Colorado Plateau, dotted with cactus and deeply gouged by the Colorado River; to the north lies the Wyoming Basin, a rangeland of rich volcanic soil that once grazed herds of bison, and now supports sheep and cattle.

The central Rocky Mountains, towering over western Wyoming, Idaho and Montana, include many snow-capped peaks of 4,000 m (13,000 ft) and more; their eastern outliers, the Bighorn Mountains, rise a sheer 3,000 m (10,000 ft) above the surrounding grasslands. These are the Rockies of the tourists; each year thousands of people visit the many national parks and reserves in the splendid heartland of the Cordilleras. The scenery is matchless, the forests, grasslands, alpine tundras and marshes are ecologically fascinating, and the wild animals are reasonably accessible. There is every chance for tourists to see bison, wapiti, mule deer, moose, black and brown bears, beavers and a host of smaller mammals and birds in a day's safari.

West of the Rockies, beyond the dry plateau scrublands of Arizona, Utah and Nevada, a double chain of mountains runs parallel to the coast from Mexico to Canada. In the arid, sun-baked south they form the desert landscape on either side of the Gulf of California. At Los Angeles they merge, parting again to form the Sierra Nevada and the Coastal Ranges that face each other across the Great Valley of central California. They rejoin in the Klamath Mountains, then continue north on either side of a broad valley – to the west as a lowly coastal chain, to the east as the magnificently forested Cascade Range. By keeping rain from the interior, these mountains create the arid landscapes of the central Cordilleras.

Testing tomatoes in California.

Climate and Agriculture

In the damp winters and dry summers of southern California the coastal mountains support semi-desert scrub; the Sierra Nevada, rising far above them, is relatively well-watered and forested. In the early days of settlement the long, bone-dry summers made farming – even ranching – difficult in the central valley of California. But the peaks of Sierra Nevada, accumulating thick blankets of snow in winter, provided a reservoir for summer irrigation. Damming and water channelling have made the semi-deserts and dry rangelands bloom all over southern and central California, which now grows temperate and tropical fruits, vegetables, cotton and other thirsty crops in abundance.

Through northern California and Oregon, where annual rainfall is higher and summer heat less intense, the coastal mountains are clothed in forests of tall cedars and firs; notable among them are stands of giant redwood cedars, towering well over 100 m (330 ft). In coastal Washington Douglas firs, grand firs, Sitka spruce and giant *arborvitae* are the spectacular trees, rivalling the giant redwoods. Forests of giant conifers cover the Cascade Range too, providing the enormous stocks of timber on which the wealth of the north-west was originally based.

Settlement and Development

The Indian cultures of western America included hunting, fishing, seed-gathering and primitive irrigation farming. Some were semi-nomadic, others settled, living mostly in small, scattered communities. The first European colonists, spreading northward from New Spain (Mexico) in the 1760s, made little impact on the Indians. But their forts and missions (which included San Diego, Los Angeles and San Francisco) attracted later settlers who proved more exploitative. From the 1840s pressures increased with the arrival of land-hungry Americans, both by sea and along waggon trails from the east. After a brief struggle, the south-west was sold to the USA; almost immediately the gold rushes brought new waves of adventurers and immigrants.

The Oregon coast, though visited by Spanish, British and Russian mariners in search of furs from the sixteenth century onward, was first settled by American fur traders in 1811. Immigration began during the 1830s, the famous Oregon Trail across Wyoming and Idaho from the Mississippi coming into full use during the 1840s. After the establishment of the 49th parallel as the boundary between Canada and the USA, Oregon Territory (including Washington, Idaho and part of Montana) became part of the USA. Here in the north-west the forests and rangelands were equally vital to Indians and to settlers, and many battles were fought before the Indians were subdued and confined in tribal reserves.

Now the waggon trails are major highways; staging posts, mission stations and isolated forts are transformed into cities. Gold-mining, once the only kind of mining that mattered, has given way to the delving and processing of a dozen lesser metals, from copper to molybdenum. Fish-canning, food-processing, electronics and aerospace are major sources of employment. The movie industry, based near Los Angeles for the clarity of its atmosphere, has come and almost gone: this urban cluster now has a broad economy based on high-technology industries. The mountain states – once far behind in economic development – have caught up with the rest of the USA. But the enduring beauty of the western mountains remains. (BS)

The Grand Canyon

Sliced through the limestone of north-western Arizona, the Grand Canyon extends from Navajo Bridge near the Utah boundary to Lake Mead, an artificial reservoir on the Nevada-Arizona border. About 450 km (280 miles) long, dropping 660 m (2,165 ft) in its course, it carries the Colorado River down a winding, rocky staircase, through near-vertical cliffs of red, pink and grey strata. The rocks, mostly limestones, sandstones and shales, are marine and freshwater deposits up to 550 million years old; they stand on a much older crystalline basement that appears in the deeper sections.

The canyon formed during a period of earth movement in which the Colorado Plateau was forced upward, probably during the last ten million years. As the land rose, the river cut steadily downward through it. Lateral streams cut minor canyons on either side, carving crags, razor-back ridges and castle-like buttes, and adding the power of their torrents to the flow of the Colorado River. Still cutting, the water is estimated to be shifting half a million tonnes of debris each day from the canyon walls. In the semi-desert climate the cliffs stand firm and square-cut at the top; there is little rain to soften or erode them, though several metres of snow may pack the canyon rim in the depths of winter.

All the canyon and much of the nearby plateau is contained within a National Park. Almost unknown except to local Indians a century and a half ago, it now receives two million visitors each year. (BS)

The south rim of the Grand Canyon from Yaki Point.

A pueblo Indian village, New Mexico.

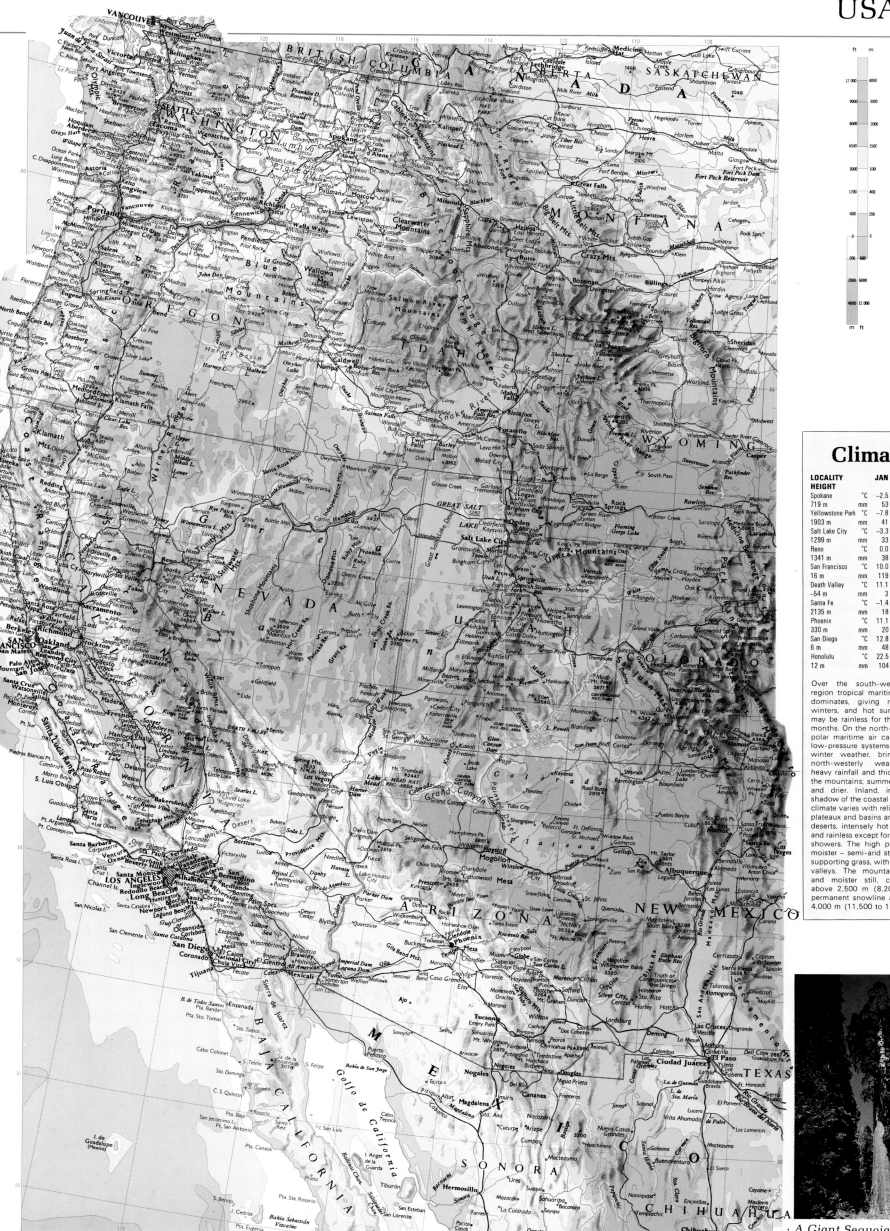

Climate

LOCALITY HEIGHT		JAN	JUL	YR
Spokane	°C	-2.5	21.1	9.4
719 m	mm	53	15	409
Yellowstone Park	°C	-7.8	16.4	3.6
1903 m	mm	41	33	445
Salt Lake City	°C	-3.3	24.7	10.6
1299 m	mm	33	15	414
Reno	°C	0.0	21.4	10.3
1341 m	mm	38	5	180
San Francisco	°C	10.0	15.0	13.6
16 m	mm	119	Tr	561
Death Valley	°C	11.1	38.6	24.4
-54 m	mm	3	8	41
Santa Fe	°C	-1.4	20.3	9.4
2135 m	mm	18	61	366
Phoenix	°C	11.1	32.5	21.1
330 m	mm	20	25	191
San Diego	°C	12.8	20.0	16.4
6 m	mm	48	3	259
Honolulu	°C	22.5	25.3	23.9
12 m	mm	104	23	643

Over the south-west coastal region tropical maritime air predominates, giving mild damp winters, and hot summers that may be rainless for three or four months. On the north-west coast polar maritime air caught up in low-pressure systems dominates winter weather, bringing mild north-westerly weather with heavy rainfall and thick snow on the mountains; summers are mild and drier. Inland, in the rain shadow of the coastal mountains, climate varies with relief. The low plateaux and basins are dry semi-deserts, intensely hot in summer and rainless except for occasional showers. The high plateaux are moister – semi-arid steppe-lands supporting grass, with trees in the valleys. The mountains, cooler and moister still, carry forest above 2,500 m (8,200 ft) to a permanent snowline at 3,500 to 4,000 m (11,500 to 13,000 ft).

A Giant Sequoia.

1:7 500 000

West from Greenwich

COPYRIGHT. GEORGE PHILIP & SON. LTD.

Industry near Houston, Texas. Much southern industry is oil-based.

THE UNITED STATES

Harvesting barley on the prairies of Colorado. Modern farming practices have transformed the plains.

North America's first settlers were natives of north-eastern Siberia who crossed the Bering Strait – then a marshy land-bridge – into Alaska some 20,000 to 30,000 years ago. Moving south down a corridor left open during the final advance of the northern ice sheet, they spread widely across North America. These were the ancestors of the brown-skinned 'Indians' who met the first settlers from northern Europe.

As Spanish settlers colonized South America, Mexico and Florida, French, British, Dutch and Swedish colonists established themselves in the east of North America from 1600 onward. The French penetrated westward through the Great Lakes and down the Mississippi River, reaching Fort Maurepas on the Gulf of Mexico in 1699. The British began to settle Virginia from 1607, New England (Maine, New Hampshire, Vermont, Massachusetts, Rhode Island and Connecticut) from 1620, Maryland from 1632 and Pennsylvania from 1681. Dutch and Swedish colonies established south of New England from 1623 became British by force of arms later in the century, renamed New York, New Jersey and Delaware.

By the mid-eighteenth century British North America consisted of the whole of the east coast from Florida to Nova Scotia, extending inland to the Allegheny Mountains. The French claimed much of Canada, and a wide swathe of central North America from the Mississippi delta to the Great Lakes and beyond. In 1763, following the Seven Years' War in Europe, all French possessions in North America were ceded to Britain, though the tiny islands of St Pierre and Miquelon reverted to France in 1816 and are French today.

Ill-feelings grew between the colonists and the British government over taxation and other interference, and the thirteen colonies fought and won their independence in 1775–81. So began the United States of America, a free, English-speaking society in the New World with boundaries extending to the Great Lakes in the north and the Mississippi in the west. Florida, which had remained loyal to Britain, was returned to Spain in 1783 and did not join the USA until 1821. Louisiana, the territory west of the Mississippi owned successively by France and Spain, was sold to the USA in 1803, more than doubling its area and opening up the whole of the Mississippi valley for settlement.

Westward Expansion

With a population of about three million and a predominantly rural economy, the United States began to expand westward across the Appalachians into the new territories (subsequently called the mid-west) beyond. Discovery of minerals and wide expanses of colonizable forest and range-lands increased the rate of expansion; soon new settlers were pouring across on well-established trails. Further stimuli for expansion came with the acquisition of Oregon in 1844, of northern Mexico, including Texas, in 1845, and finally of California, in 1848. The settlers poured westward, firstly into increasing opposition from the Indians, and later – after a long series of battles across the mid-west and into the mountains – past the broken, sullen remains of the tribes on reservation lands.

Between the 1860s and the end of the century no fewer than six cross-continental railways were established, with roads and chains of settlements branching out on either side of them. A vast supporting network of railways, roads and canals spread very quickly across the eastern and mid-western states, linking thousands of small settlements and transporting an ever-growing bulk of raw materials, agricultural produce and manufactured goods to and from the east coast ports.

Dissension and Union

The Civil War, bitterly fought over four years (1861–65), was a set-back to this forward march. The Federal Constitutional Convention of 1787 had provided for a firm but delicate balance between federal and state responsibilities. Foreign affairs, the protection of interstate commerce, and responsibilities for the new lands in the west (including their future admission to statehood) were vested in the federal government, while most other powers were exercised by strong state legislatures. Mid-century dissension between the mainly rural, slave-owning states of the south and the rapidly industrializing 'free' states of the north was exacerbated by the growing number of new states, carved from the western territories, that elected to be slaveless. Discontented by federal legislation that seemed to threaten their interests, in 1861 South Carolina, Georgia, Alabama, Florida, Mississippi, Louisiana and Texas seceded from the Union to form the Confederate States of America. They were shortly joined by Virginia, North Carolina, Tennessee and Arkansas. The Civil War resulted in victory for the North, emancipation of slaves, and a great strengthening of the federal element in the country's constitution.

The USA Today

The years following the Civil War saw the firm establishment of the USA as the world's leading industrial society. Still attracting enormous numbers of emigrants from Europe, her agricultural and industrial output grew at unprecedented rates to the end of the century and beyond. Stimulated by education, research and new, sophisticated machinery, agriculture developed into a highly mechanized industry for food production and processing. Chicago's agricultural machinery industries transformed the farmers' lives with mass-produced ploughs, tractors, seed-drills, reapers and binders. Only a generation after the pioneering days, farmers found themselves tightly integrated into an economic system with such factors as mortgages, availability of spare parts, freight prices and world markets at least as crucial to the success of their efforts as climate and soil.

Agriculture To the east of the western mountains farming was established in a zonal pattern which remains intact – though much modified – today, a pattern reflecting both the possibilities offered by climate and soils, and the inclinations and national origins of the settlers who first farmed the lands. In the north, from Minnesota to New England, lies a broad belt where dairy farming predominates, providing milk, butter and cheese for the industrial cities. Spring wheat is grown further west, where the climate is drier. The eastern and central states from Nebraska to Ohio form the famous 'corn belt' – immensely productive land, formerly prairie and forest, where corn (maize) is the main crop. Now much extended by the development of new, more tolerant strains, corn production has spread into neighbouring belts on either side. No longer principally human food, except in the poorer areas of the south, corn is grown mainly for feeding to cattle and pigs, which in turn supply the meat-packing industries of Chicago and the west. Soya beans, oats and other food and fodder crops grow in the corn belt, with wheat and dairy farming prominent along the northern border.

Southward again, from Oklahoma and Kansas to Virginia, stretches a broad belt of mixed farming where winter wheat and corn alternate as the dominant cereals. In the warmer southern states lies the former 'cotton-belt', where cotton and tobacco were once the most widespread crops; both are now concentrated into small, highly-productive areas where mechanical handling is possible, and the bulk of the land is used for a wide variety of other crops from vegetables to fruit and peanuts. Throughout American farming there has been a tendency to shift from small-scale operations to large, from labour-intensive to mechanized, and from low-capital to high-capital investment. The main centres of production are now concentrated in the western plains; much of the land originally farmed by the Pilgrim Fathers and other early settlers is now built over, or has reverted to attractive second-growth forest. By concentrating effort in this way, America has become a leading producer of meat, dairy foods, soya beans, corn, oats, wheat, barley, cotton, sugar and many other crops, both for home consumption and export.

Resources and Industry The spread of prosperity throughout a very broad spectrum of the community generated new consumer industries, to satisfy the demands of a large middle-class for ever-increasing standards of comfort and material welfare. America became the pioneer of massive-scale industrial production of everything from thumb-tacks to automobiles. With almost every material needed for production available within her own boundaries, or readily gained through trading with neighbours, her mining and extractive industries have been heavily exploited from the start.

For several generations coal formed the main source of power and the basis of industrial prosperity. Anthracite from eastern Pennsylvania, good bituminous and coking coals from the Appalachians, Indiana, Illinois, Colorado and Utah are still in demand, and enormous reserves remain. Oil, first drilled in Pennsylvania in 1859, was subsequently found in several major fields underlying the mid-west, the eastern and central mountain states, the Gulf of Mexico, California and Alaska. Home consumption of petroleum products has grown steadily; though the US remains a major producer, it is also by far the world's greatest consumer, and has for long been a net importer of oil. Natural gas too is found in abundance, usually in association with oil, and is moved to the main consumer areas through an elaborate, continent-wide network of pipes.

Today the USA is also a major producer of iron and steel, mica, molybdenum, uranium and many other primary materials, and a major consumer and exporter of a wide range of manufactured goods, from chemicals and industrial machinery, to paper and electronic equipment. The USA is the world's greatest economic power and the major influence on the world economy.

Population

The USA has one of the most diverse populations of any nation in the world. Until about 1860, with the exception of the native Indians and the southern negroes, the population was largely made up of immigrants of British origin, with small numbers of Spanish and French. After the Civil War, however, there was increasing immigration from the countries of central and south-eastern Europe – Italy, the Balkans, Poland and Russia. This vast influx of Europeans, numbering about 30,000,000 between 1860 and 1920, was markedly different in culture and language from the established population. More recently there have been lesser influxes of Japanese, Chinese, Filipinos and Puerto Ricans, with immigrants of Mexican origin from across the southern border. Although there are strong influences and pressures towards Americanization, these minority groups have tended to establish distinct social and cultural enclaves within US society as a whole.

The major westward movement of population through the last century was replaced after 1900 by more subtle but no less important shifts of population away from rural areas and into the cities. Today there is further movement from the old, grimy industrial centres and the tired, out-moded cities that flourished early in the century, away

Sugar-cane fields, Hawaii.

from the ageing buildings and urban dereliction, especially in the north and east, to new centres elsewhere.

The cities that gain population are mostly peripheral, on the Great Lakes and the coasts. The south is especially favoured for its warmth (particularly by retired folk) and its closeness to the major source of energy in the USA – petroleum. Development of southern petrochemical and electronic industries has helped to relieve rural poverty and given new economic life, though partly at the expense of the north. However, Chicago and the eastern conurbations – New York, Philadelphia, Baltimore and Washington – remain pre-eminent as centres of US commercial life.

Since her earliest inception from the thirteen colonies, the USA has led the world in industrial, economic and social innovation, creating problems through sheer ebullience and solving them – more or less – through inventiveness and enterprise, and with massive, wealth-bringing resources of energy and materials. Though currently beset by economic problems, America continues to enjoy one of the highest material standards of living ever known, and continues to produce what may well be her greatest asset of all – a highly skilled, literate and imaginative population. (BS, SFM)

HAWAII

The fiftieth state, the most recent and the most southerly of the United States, Hawaii is an archipelago of eight large and over one hundred smaller volcanic islands in mid-Pacific, 3,850 km (2,400 miles) southwest of California. Only on the main island are there currently active volcanoes. High rainfall, warmth and rich soils combine to provide a wealth of year-round vegetation; originally forested, the islands are still well covered with trees and shrubs, but now provide commercial crops of sugar-cane, cereals, forage for cattle, and a wide range of fruit and vegetables.

Originally settled by Polynesians possibly about AD 400, and visited by James Cook in 1778, Hawaii became a port-of-call for trans-Pacific shipping and a wintering station for New England whalers, but retained its independent status until annexed by the USA in 1898. Of its current population of just over 750,000, only about 2 per cent are full-blooded Polynesians; the rest are of Chinese, Japanese, Korean, Philippine and Caucasian origins, including many immigrants from mainland USA.

About 80 per cent of Hawaiians live on the island of Oahu, over half of them in the capital city of Honolulu. Agriculture, fishing and food processing are the main industries, though defence and tourism are also important to the economy. (BS)

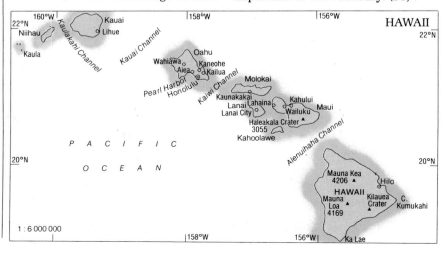

1

1 *Tropical forest on Costa Rica. These forests are highly productive and often have thousands of species of plant per hectare.*

2 *Rio de Janeiro, Brazil. The Sugar Loaf is in the background.*

3 *San Andrés Island, in the western Caribbean.*

SOUTH AMERICA

In a moment the ashes are made,
but a forest is a long time growing.

Seneca, *Naturales Quaestiones*, Book iii, Section 27

CENTRAL AMERICA

Central America is the narrow waistline of the Americas, known to the world for the canal that links the two great oceans in Panama. The backbone of the isthmus is mountainous, many of the volcanic vertebrae reaching heights of over 4,000 m (13,000 ft). It is the most tectonically active zone in the Americas with over 100 large volcanoes and frequent earthquakes. Flat land is at a premium; only on the Caribbean side does the coastal plain extend to any depth inland. The lowland vegetation is luxuriant and much of the Caribbean slope is still under tropical rain forest. The Pacific or lee side is much drier, particularly in the wider northern part of the isthmus. The mountains make their own climates and, to some extent, their own plant and animal life.

Overland travel remains difficult; no roadway as yet runs the length of the isthmus. The Pacific has been the main highway linking the various parts of Central America: it was on this side in the sixteenth century that the Spaniards established their ports, towns and seats of government, and it is the more important side of the isthmus today. (DJF)

MEXICO

Mexico (1,972,550 km², 761,600 sq miles) is one quarter the size of the USA, but much larger than the Central American countries to the south. The most populous Spanish-speaking country, and ranking tenth in the world, Mexico has a population of about 67 million. No other large country has a faster-growing population: between 1960 and 1980 it doubled, growing at an unprecedented 3.5 per cent per year. It is in consequence an astonishingly young society; the average Mexican is a seventeen-year-old, and three-quarters of the population is under thirty. The combination of a stable and very high birth rate (about 42 per thousand) and a declining and now very low death rate (about 6.5 per thousand) is the main cause of this population explosion. Legal and illegal permanent emigration to the USA was running at about a quarter of a million per year in the late 1970s. Mexico City (population in 1930 1 million, in 1960 4.9 million, estimated 1980 14 million) is the most populous city in the Americas. Matching economic expansion with population growth is a key political issue in the country today.

Landscape

Mexico is a land of great physical variety. The northern, emptier, half is open basin-and-range country of the Mesa Central. The land rises southwards from the Rio Grande (Rio Bravo del Norte) at the US border averaging about 2,600 m (8,500 ft) above sea-level in the middle where it is crowned by many snow-capped volcanic cones; Orizaba (5,750 m, 18,865 ft) in the east and Popocatepetl (5,452 m, 17,888 ft) and Ixtacihuatl (5,286 m, 17,340 ft) near Mexico City are the highest. Though a still-active earthquake zone, this is the most densely settled part of the country. The Mesa Central ends equally dramatically in the west, where the Sierra Madre Occidental rise to over 4,000 m (13,120 ft), and in the east where the Sierra Madre Oriental form a backcloth to the modest coastal plain bordering the Gulf of Mexico. In the far north-west is the isolated, 1,220 km (760 mile) long, mountain-cored peninsula of Baja California.

Mountains dominate southern Mexico, broken only by the low, narrow isthmus of Tehuantepec, which is crossed by railway and road and links the Gulf ports with Salina Cruz on the Pacific. The flat, low-lying limestone Yucatan peninsula in the south-east is an exception in a country where half the land is over 1,000 m (3,281 ft) above sea-level, and a quarter has slopes of over 25°. Deserts characterize the north-west, and tropical rain forest is the natural vegetation of Tehuantepec; 71 per cent of the country is arid or semi-arid and irrigation is mandatory for agriculture.

Economic Development

Agriculture occupies half the population but contributes less than a third of the economic product contributed by manufacturing. Crops include maize, coffee, cotton, sugar and henequen. Mexico City is the main industrial and commercial centre; Guadalajara and Monterrey are lesser centres. Petroleum discoveries during the 1970s in Tabasco and Campeche have turned Mexico into a major oil producer, exporting oil and gas to the USA. (DJF)

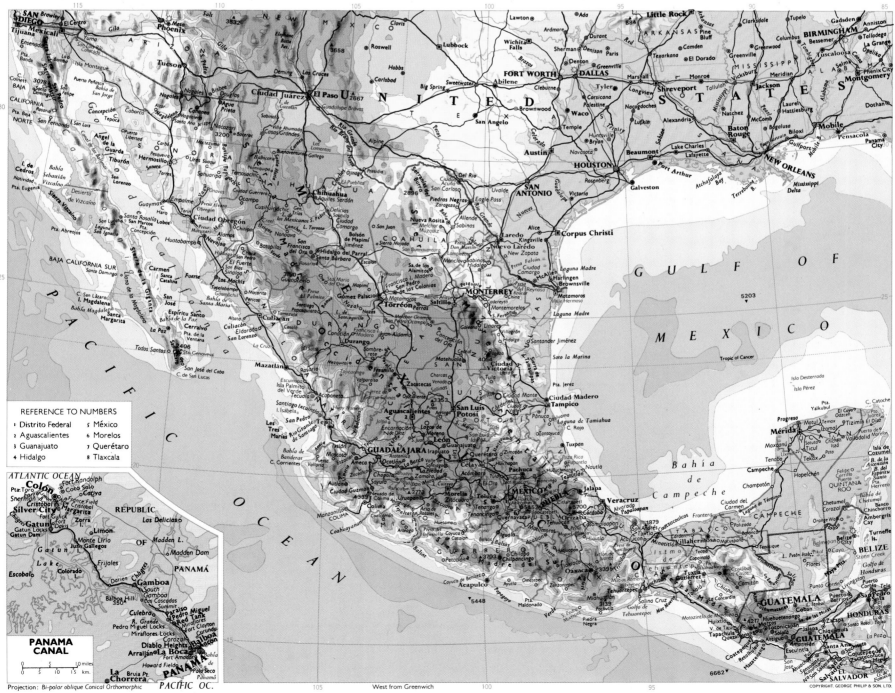

REFERENCE TO NUMBERS
1 Distrito Federal
2 Aguascalientes
3 Guanajuato
4 Hidalgo
5 México
6 Morelos
7 Querétaro
8 Tlaxcala

PANAMA CANAL

Projection: Bi-polar oblique Conical Orthomorphic

West from Greenwich

COPYRIGHT. GEORGE PHILIP & SON, LTD.

Fishermen on Lake Patzcuaro, Mexico. The main fish reserves are in the Gulfs of California and Mexico. They include shrimps, oysters, tuna and sardines.

Coffee beans. Coffee is an important crop throughout Central America.

GUATEMALA

Guatemala is the most populous Central American country (with a population of about 6.6 million), and the third largest (108,889 km², 42,042 sq miles). Her Pacific coastline, two and a half times longer than the Caribbean coast, is backed by broad alluvial plains, formed of material washed down from the towering volcanoes that front the ocean. These include extinct Tajumulco (4,217 m, 13,830 ft), the highest peak in Central America, and active Santiaguito – Santa Maria (3,768 m, 12,362 ft). A heavily-dissected plateau, the Altos, forms the core of the country; beautiful lakes such as the Atitlán mark its junction with the mountains. This area, with comfortable temperatures for living and maize cultivation, is both a focus of dense rural settlement and also the site of the current capital – earthquake-prone Guatemala City. The north-eastern third of the country is the Peten, a flat, low-lying limestone wilderness on Yucatan Peninsula. Once a centre of Mayan civilization, it contains many remarkable archaeological remains, in particular Tikal and Uaxactún.

The plains have been used for commercial-scale agriculture only since the 1950s, when malaria was brought under control and roads were built; cattle and cotton are now more important than the traditional banana crop. Lower mountain slopes, up to about 1,500 m (5,000 ft), yield most of the best coffee grown in Guatemala: coffee has been the most important export of the country in the twentieth century.

Indians make up half the population of Guatemala: the rest are mainly mestizos of mixed Indian and European stock. Society and government are run on autocratic lines, with the Indians wielding least influence. (DJF)

HONDURAS

Second largest of the Central American countries (112,088 km², 43,277 sq miles), Honduras has a small population (about 3.5 million). The state has a short (124 km, 80 mile) frontage on the Pacific in the Gulf of Fonseca. The limited lowlands around the Gulf form some of the prime cotton lands of the country.

Eighty per cent of Honduras is mountainous with peaks of more than 2,500 m (8,000 ft) in the west. The mountain ranges are metalliferous: lodes of gold drew the first Spanish conquistadors to found Tegucigalpa, the capital, in 1524, and silver is still an important export. Mining contributes more to the economy than it does in any other Central American state.

Most of Honduras has a seasonal climate, relatively dry between November and May. Traditional cattle-ranching, employing cowboys, is as much in evidence as agriculture. The aromatic pine forests of the east are being consumed by new paper mills on the hot, rain-soaked Caribbean coast. The lower alluvium-filled valleys of the rivers draining into the Caribbean have been reclaimed and the forest replaced by orderly banana plantations. Bananas account for over one-quarter of exports. Production is dominated by two large US companies. (DJF)

EL SALVADOR

The only Central American country without a Caribbean coast, El Salvador is also the smallest (21,040 km², 8,120 sq miles) with a dense population of about 4.5 million. Pressure on agricultural land has led to widespread emigration. The Pacific coastal plain is narrow and backed by a volcanic range averaging about 1,200 m (4,000 ft) in altitude. El Salvador has over twenty volcanoes, some still active, and crater lakes occupying a fertile central plain 400 to 800 m (1,300 to 2,600 ft) above sea-level. Here, in a densely populated belt, stand San Salvador, the capital, Santa Ana and Santa Tecla; urban and rural populations in this belt together account for 60 per cent of the country's population.

Within this fertile belt also is grown 90 per cent of the coffee and tobacco, and most of the maize and sugar – jointly the foundations of the agricultural economy. Coffee usually accounts for half the total value of the country's exports and one-third of her entire agricultural economy. The towns are centres of manufacturing for the domestic market. Inland the frontier with Honduras is marked by mountain ranges which reach heights of 2,000 m (6,560 ft): previously forested and empty, they are now attracting migrants desperate for agricultural land. (DJF)

Climate

Tropical Central America has intensely hot summers; July mean temperatures exceed 25°C (77°F) in the lowlands, though uplands are generally cooler. Warm winters are dominated by maritime air, with incursions of cold air from the north; January means exceed 20°C (68°F) in the lowlands. Trade winds and tropical storms bring frequent summer downpours to coasts and mountains of the south and east. Over 200 cm (80 in) of rain fall annually in parts of southern Mexico and the isthmus. Central, northern and western Mexico are dry, with less than 20 cm (8 in) of annual rain in the Gulf of California.

LOCALITY HEIGHT		JAN	JUL	YR
Guaymas	°C	17.6	30.25	24.5
8 m	mm	5	43	282
Monterrey	°C	14.3	26.7	21.5
528 m	mm	15	58	579
Mazatlan	°C	19.8	28.0	24.1
78 m	mm	12	174	805
Merida	°C	23.0	27.3	25.8
22 m	mm	31	133	930
Mexico City	°C	12.1	17.1	15.8
2310 m	mm	13	170	747
Veracruz	°C	21.1	27.5	25.1
16 m	mm	22	358	1672
Belize City	°C	23.5	27.6	26.6
1 m	mm	72	315	1648
Acapulco	°C	26.1	28.7	27.6
3 m	mm	8	230	1401
Guatemala City	°C	16.3	18.5	18.0
1502 m	mm	3	211	1281
San Salvador	°C	22.1	23.0	22.8
689 m	mm	5	304	1775

Pre-Columbian Civilizations

The Mayan temple of Chichen Itza in Yucatan.

The pre-Columbian civilizations of Central America flourished for centuries before the Spanish conquest and this heritage plays a strong role in fostering Mexican national identity today.

The Olmecs, the classical cultures of Teotihuacan, the Zapotecs and the Toltecs have all left remarkable architectural monuments in the Mexican landscape, but the two outstanding cultures were those of the Maya and the Aztecs. The Maya civilization was the most brilliant pre-Columbian civilization, flourishing in the third to the tenth centuries in an area extending from the Yucatan peninsula to Honduras. The Maya were mathematically advanced and had a sophisticated calendar.

The Aztec Empire was at its height when Mexico succumbed to the Spanish conquistadors in 1519. The Aztecs, originally an insignificant nomadic tribe, invaded the settled lands of Central Mexico in the thirteenth century and founded their island-city of Tenochtitlán in Lake Texcoco in 1325. During the fifteenth century they conquered the other states of Central Mexico and drew tribute from an empire which extended from the Pacific to the Gulf of Mexico and into northern Central America.

Many of the great pre-Columbian centres survive as archaeological sites today. The stepped pyramid, the rectangular courtyard and the symbolic ornamental masonry are particularly characteristic of the architecture. (DJF)

BELIZE

Belize is exceptional in Central America – a small country of 22,963 km² (8,866 sq miles) with only ten per cent under cultivation. Called British Honduras until 1973, it has a population of about 153,000, only one-fortieth that of neighbouring Guatemala, and a remarkably low population density of 7 per km² (17 per sq mile). Without a Pacific coast Belize remained a backwater in Spanish colonial times, and later as a British colony; still a colony today, the common language is English. Negroes are more numerous than the Mayan Indians of the interior, and cultural ties are as much with the former British West Indies as with South American neighbours.

The northern half of the country is low-lying, swampy and forested; the southern half is a high corrugated plateau with serrated peaks along its seaward edge. Most of the small population lives in the north, particularly along the coast and the navigable Belize river. Mahogany and chicle gum were staple exports until the 1950s, when sugar, citrus fruits and frozen shellfish began to find overseas markets. The world's second-largest coral barrier reef lies offshore, marked by a fringe of islands. The capital moved in 1970 from Belize City to a new interior site, Belmopan. (DJF)

NICARAGUA

Nicaragua is the largest of the Central American countries (130,000 km², 50,190 sq miles), and the least densely populated (about 2.5 million). The eastern half of the country is almost empty: on average each family of five has over a square kilometre at its disposal. The Caribbean plain is extensive, 80 km (50 miles) wide: the coast is a mixture of lagoons, sandy beaches and river deltas with shallow water and sand bars offshore. With over 750 cm (300 in) of rain in some years, it is forested and rich in a tropical fauna including crocodiles, turtles, deer, puma, jaguar, peccary and monkeys. Cut off from the populous west of Nicaragua, it was for two centuries the British protectorate of the Miskito Coast, with Bluefields (San Juan del Norte) as the largest settlement.

Inland the plain gives way gradually to mountain ranges (Pico Mogotán, 2,107 m, 6,913 ft) broken by basins and fertile valleys. In the west and south they overlook a great depression which runs from the Gulf of Fonseca south-eastwards and contains Lakes Managua and

Nicaragua. Lake Nicaragua (8,264 km², 3,191 sq miles) is the largest lake in Central America; though only 20 km (12.5 miles) from the Pacific, it drains to the Caribbean by the navigable San Juan river, and formed an important route across the isthmus before the Panama Canal was built. The capital city, Managua, and other major towns are here, as is much of Nicaragua's industrial development; so are the cotton fields and coffee plantations that provide the chief cash crops and exports of Nicaragua.

Forty volcanoes, many active, rise above the lakes and face the Pacific. San Cristóbal (1,745 m, 5,725 ft) is the highest, and still-smoking Momotombo is the most spectacular. Earthquakes are common; Managua was destroyed in 1931 and again in 1972. For over 40 years until 1979 the country was virtually ruled by the Somoza family. (DJF)

COSTA RICA

Costa Rica is small (50,700 km², 19,600 sq miles) and only 282 km (175 miles) across at the widest; the population is now over 2 million. With neither gold nor Indians the country was little developed during three centuries as a Spanish colony. Since independence (1821) Costa Rica has become the most European

of the Central American republics, with the best educational standards, longest life expectancy (67 years), most democratic system of government, highest per capita gross domestic product, and the least disparity between the poor and the rich.

Three mountain ranges form the skeleton of the country. In the southeast the Talamanca ranges rise to 3,837 m (12,585 ft) in Chirripo Grande; further north and west the Central Cordillera includes volcanic Irazú (3,432 m, 11,260 ft) and Poas (2,705 m, 8,875 ft), both active in recent decades; Miravalles (2,020 m, 6,627 ft) is one of four active volcanoes in the Cordillera de Guanacaste.

Coffee grown in the interior has been a corner-stone of the economy since 1850; in this century bananas have become a second, and together they supply half of Costa Rica's overseas earnings. The capital, San José, stands in the fertile Valle Central, in the economic heartland of the country. Drier Guanacaste, in the far north-west, is an important cattle-raising region. (DJF)

PANAMA

Panama links Central and South America; narrow and S-shaped, a total area of 75,650 km² (29,200 sq

miles) includes about 750 offshore islands and the formerly separate Canal Zone. 87 per cent of the country lies below 700 m (2,300 ft), sweltering permanently in tropical heat. Heavy downpours mark the May-to-December rainy season. The mountain ranges trend north-west to south-east, slightly athwart the lie of the country, and fragment the lowlands. In the west the Cordillera of Talamanca, of average height 900 m (3,000 ft) effectively blocked a possible road link with Central America until the 1960s. East of Colon, the lower San Blas cordillera runs towards Colombia, and a third volcanic range, the Baudo, extends into Colombia along the Pacific Coast.

Basins and valleys between the ranges support pockets of agriculture, though many lie uncultivated. In the west natural rain forest and savanna have been cleared for commercial banana production, coffee, cacao and sugar-cane plantations and cattle ranching, and for subsistence crops of rice, maize and beans. To the east in Darien the forest remains little disturbed, forming a refuge for indigenous Indians.

Much of Panama's small population (about 2 million) live within 20 km (12 miles) of the Canal, many in Panama City; 80 per cent of the gross domestic product of the country originates in this narrow zone. The Republic owes its very political existence to American recognition of a strategic situation between the two world oceans. It is remarkable that there is, as yet, no road linking Panama with the important South American mainland. (DJF)

The Panama Canal

Ships passing through a lock on the Panama Canal.

The Panama Canal is 82 km (51 miles) long from deep water at either end, 65 km (40 miles) long from coast to coast. Three sets of locks at either end lift vessels to the elevated central section 26 m (85 ft) above sea-level, which includes Gatun Lake and the 13 km (8 mile) Gaillard Cut through the continental divide.

An American-built railway crossed the isthmus in 1855. But it was a French company under de Lesseps that began cutting the canal in 1880. Engineering problems and disease stopped operations after ten years. In 1903 the province of Panama declared independence from Colombia

and granted the USA rights in perpetuity over a 16 km (10 mile) wide Canal Zone. Work on the present canal began one year later, and it was opened for shipping in 1914.

In the late 1970s there were about 13,000 transits through the canal – over 36 ships per day – carrying 118 tonnes of cargo, twice the amount for 1960. The canal, now running close to capacity, cannot take fully-laden ships of over about 80,000 tonnes (the size of many large tankers) and an alternative Panama Seaway is under discussion. From 1978 control of the Canal Zone reverted to Panama, and the Canal itself reverts in 1999. (DJF)

Climate

Tropical Western Atlantic and Caribbean surface water temperatures approach 30°C (86°F) in summer, and seldom fall below 21°C (70°F) in winter. Within this range lie the climates of most of the islands and mainland coasts of the area. Highlands are cooler, but frost is virtually unknown. Trade winds blow steadily for much of the year, bringing cool breezes to low-lying islands and shores, and rain to the uplands beyond, especially to eastern slopes of the highlands. Rainfall is heaviest in summer, boosted by cyclonic storms – sometimes violent – occurring mainly from August onward. Heaviest rainfall, exceeding 250 cm (100 in) annually, occurs in the Dominican Republic and Panama.

LOCALITY HEIGHT		JAN	JUL	YR
Hamilton	°C	17.2	26.1	21.4
46 m	mm	112	114	1463
Nassau	°C	20.3	27.4	24.3
10 m	mm	36	150	1216
La Habana	°C	22.2	27.8	25.0
24 m	mm	71	124	1224
San Juan	°C	23.6	26.9	25.6
19 m	mm	119	159	1631
Kingston	°C	25.4	28.3	27.1
12 m	mm	20	51	811
Montserrat	°C	24.5	27.2	26.4
40 m	mm	122	155	1638
Bridgetown	°C	24.7	26.7	25.9
55 m	mm	66	147	1275
Willemstad	°C	26.1	27.8	27.2
23 m	mm	53	38	582
Port of Spain	°C	25.6	26.4	26.4
20 m	mm	69	218	1631
San José	°C	19.0	20.6	20.4
1158 m	mm	8	230	1944

BAHAMAS

The Bahamas are an archipelago of over 600 islands, cays and reefs, centred on the Great Bahama Bank, a limestone reef extending off eastern Florida, Cuba and Hispaniola. The total area is 14,000 km² (5,405 sq miles); 22 of the islands are inhabited, with a population of about 225,000. The islands are low-lying.

The Bahamas became a source of slave labour for Hispaniola. Pirates used them as a base, and loyalists settled after the American Revolution to build up a slave-based cotton economy; in consequence 85 per cent of the population today are of African descent. The islands were for long a British colony, achieving independence in 1973. The thin calcareous soils of the south-eastern islands are cultivated by peasant farmers, but nearer to the USA agriculture and fishing have been largely superseded by tourism and associated activities; blockade-

Nassau, the capital of the Bahamas, situated on New Providence Island.

running during the Civil War (1861–5) and liquor-running during Prohibition (1920–33) were earlier industries based on the Bahamas' proximity to the USA. A benign winter climate, and the establishment of a tax-free tourist, commercial and industrial facility on Grand Bahama, enhance the islands' attractions. (DJF)

BERMUDA

Bermuda is a group of over one hundred small coral islands, straddling latitude 30°N in the Western Atlantic Ocean 917 km (570 miles) from Cape Hatteras, USA. The total island area is 53 km² (20 sq miles); only 20 of the islands are inhabited, and most of the population (about 58,000) live on Great Bermuda (Main Island). Island corals cap a submarine volcano that rises over 4,000 m (13,000 ft) from the ocean floor. The highest point is Town Hill (79 m, 260 ft).

Uninhabited when discovered by the Spaniard Juan Bermudez in 1503, the islands were taken over by the British six years later and slaves were introduced from nearby Virginia; today half the population is of African, the other half of British descent. The pleasant and fresh climate, coral sand beaches, historic buildings and pastel-coloured townships attract over 300,000 tourists each year, mainly from the USA; tourism is the mainstay of the economy, and the islands are also a tax haven for overseas companies. Bermuda remains a British colony with a long tradition of self-government; the parliament dates from 1603. Ties with the USA are also strong. (DJF)

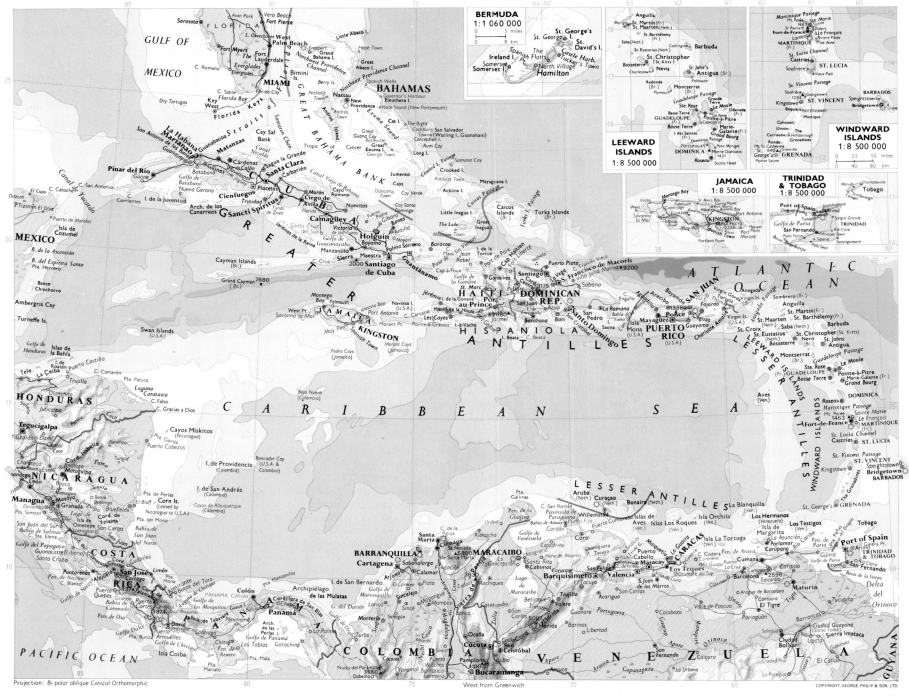

Projection: Bi-polar oblique Conical Orthomorphic

West from Greenwich

COPYRIGHT. GEORGE PHILIP & SON. LTD.

THE WEST INDIES

The West Indian islands form a small and scattered group, with a total land area of 233,000 km² (90,000 sq miles). They fall into two size categories – the Greater Antilles (Cuba, Hispaniola, Jamaica and Puerto Rico) and the Lesser Antilles (all the remaining smaller islands, including Aruba, Curaçao and Bonaire off the coast of Venezuela). Lying athwart the trade winds they have equable climates with tropical temperatures; mostly mountainous and volcanic, they are damp and fertile, with a wetter windward side and a drier lee. Their strategic position as stepping-stones to the New World gave them an early significance and coloured their subsequent history.

Few of the indigenous Indians survived early contacts with Columbus and his successors. African slaves, brought in to work mainly Spanish, British and French sugar plantations, were later augmented by East Indians and European immigrants, with the creation of a distinctive population mix. Lowland tropical forest was replaced by agriculture, and ports grew up from small settlements on the sheltered, leeward coasts of the islands. Today the economies of many of the island communities remain heavily dependent on primary agriculture, though mining and tourism are broadening their scope. Living standards are low, prospects for improvement are poor, and emigration is the escape route that many young West Indians are taking. (DJF)

Santiago and the US naval base at Guantanamo lie in the rain shadow of the Sierra behind them; the Sierra de Trinidad in the centre of the island and the Sierra del Rosario and Sierra de los Organos west of Havana are lower and less sheltering.

The undulating fringes of these mountain areas provide some of the best tobacco lands in Cuba: the very best cigar leaves are taken in the Vuelta regions around the Sierra de los Organos. The higher areas also produce coffee as a cash crop. Sugar, however, remains the outstanding cash crop of the island, as it has done throughout the twentieth century; it occupies over one million hectares (2.5 million acres), more than half the cultivated land of the island. Before the Cuban Revolution of 1959 the sugar was grown on large estates, many owned by US companies or individuals. Now the estates are nationalized, the focus of production has shifted eastward to Guayabal, and the USSR has replaced the USA as Cuba's main market for sugar. Cattle raising and rice cultivation are now being encouraged to diversify produce. Cuba is an exporter of several minerals, notably nickel.

A Spanish colony until 1898, Cuba received many Spanish and negro immigrants during early years of this century. Following the Castro revolution (1959), when 600,000 refugees left the island, Havana the chief port and capital was particularly depopulated. Since then rural development has been fostered in a relatively successful bid to make the quality of life more homogeneous throughout the island. (DJF)

to bauxite, an ore of aluminium. Bauxite overlies one-quarter of the island; mined since 1952, it supplies about one-sixth of the world's needs. Most is exported as ore, about one-fifth as alumina. Tourism and bauxite production, Jamaica's two most important industries, together account for almost two-thirds of foreign earnings.

Sugar, a staple product since the island became British in 1655, made Jamaica a prized imperial possession, and the African slaves imported to work the plantations were the forefathers of much of the present population. But the plantations disappeared and the sugar market collapsed in the nineteenth century; today sugar contributes only about 10 per cent of the country's foreign earnings. Unemployment and underemployment are currently rife, and many Jamaicans leave their country each year to work abroad, mainly in the USA and Canada. (DJF)

DOMINICAN REPUBLIC

The Dominican Republic shares the island of Hispaniola with Haiti; it occupies the eastern two-thirds, with an area of 48,700 km² (18,800 sq miles). Of the steep-sided mountain ranges that dominate the island, the Republic includes the northern Cordillera Septentrional, the huge Cordillera Central (rising to Pico Duarte, 3,175 m, 10,417 ft – the highest peak in the West Indies) and the southern Sierra de Bahoruco. Between them and to the east lie fertile valleys and lowlands, including the Vega Real and the coastal

Watering fields by hand in Haiti. Most of the population still lives by subsistence farming.

plains where both the main cugar plantations, and also the capital and chief port, Santo Domingo, are found. Typical of the area, the Dominican Republic is hot and humid close to sea-level, but cooler and fresher conditions prevail in the mountains; rainfall is heavy, especially in the north-east.

For long a Spanish colony, Hispaniola was initially the centrepiece but later the poor relation of the Empire. For a short time after 1795 it became French, then Spanish again in 1809, but in 1821 the Dominican Republic became independent. American interests grew, culminating in an occupation (1916-24), and a long period of corrupt dictatorship followed. Today the Dominican Republic is a moderately prosperous, Americanized, Spanish-speaking Latin-American democracy, with a largely white and mestizo population of about 5 million. The main exports are agricultural produce including sugar, tobacco, cacao, coffee and fruit, and there is considerable potential for the further development of hydroelectric power, mining, and industry, including tourism. (DJF)

CUBA

Cuba (114,500 km², 44,210 sq miles) is as large as all the other West Indian islands put together, with a population of about ten million. It is a narrow island, 193 km (120 miles) across at its widest, but stretches for over 1,200 km (750 miles) east-to-west.

Least mountainous of all the Greater Antilles, it is the one that is most suitable for modern mechanized agriculture. The plains run the length of the island from Guantánamo Bay in the south-east to Cape San Antonio in the west. They are broken by three sets of mountains which together occupy no more than one-quarter of the island. The highest, the Sierra Maestra and Sierra de Toar, form a 160 km (100 miles) long front to the Windward Passage (Paso de los Vientos): the highest point, Turquino, rises 1,974 m (6,476 ft) above sea-level. The Windward Passage provides a well-used route for hurricanes moving north. The port of

JAMAICA

Third-largest of the West Indian islands, Jamaica has an area of 10,960 km² (4,230 sq miles), and is the most populous island (over 2 million) in the English-speaking West Indies. 234 km (146 miles) long and up to 82 km (51 miles) wide, the island has a central range culminating in Blue Mountain Peak (2,256 m, 7,402 ft), from which it declines westward. Half the country lies above the 300 m (1,000 ft) contour line. Moist south-east trade winds bring rain to the mountains, windward slopes receiving up to 500 cm (200 in) in a normal year; hurricanes may bring exceptionally heavy rains during the later part of the wet season, which extends from May to October.

The 'cockpit country' in the north-west of the island is an inaccessible limestone area of steep broken ridges and isolated basins. These offered a refuge to escaped slaves prior to emancipation in 1838. Elsewhere the limestone has weathered

HAITI

Haiti occupies the western third of Hispaniola, with an area of 27,750 km² (10,700 sq miles) and a population of almost 5 million. It is mainly mountainous, with a long, deeply indented coast; most of the country is centred around the Massif du Nord (an extension of the Dominican Cordillera Central) and the long, narrow mountain range – Massif de la Hotte – forming the southern peninsula. In the deep bight between lies the chief port and capital, Port-au-Prince. Haiti is warm throughout the year, with high rainfall on the northern mountains but semi-arid conditions in their rain-shadow.

Haiti was ceded to France in 1697, a century before the rest of Hispaniola, and developed as a sugar-producing colony. A slave revolt in 1804 brought independence, but the 95 per cent black population, savagely misgoverned for generations, remains poor and backward, living by subsistence farming. (DJF)

PUERTO RICO

Puerto Rico is the smallest (8,897 km², 3,435 sq miles) of the Greater Antilles, with a population of about 3,320,000. The island was ceded by Spain to the USA in 1898 and is now a self-governing commonwealth in political association with the USA. Free access to the USA for goods manufactured in Puerto Rico, and for emigrants, has enriched the island's economy and relieved the pressures brought by one of the highest population densities in the Caribbean. Few families in Puerto Rico are without close relations living in the USA, most of them in New York.

The island is mountainous, with a narrow coastal plain; Cerro de Punta (1,338 m, 4,389 ft) is the highest peak. San Juan, the capital, was built originally around a fortified natural harbour where fleets of galleons once congregated. Flat ground suitable for cultivation is scarce, and mainly devoted to cash crops including sugar, coffee and, particularly since refugees settled from Cuba, tobacco. Copper is one of few exploitable minerals. The island's economic future seems largely to be linked with that of the USA. (DJF)

THE LEEWARD ISLANDS

The Leewards are the more northerly islands of the Lesser Antilles, extending from the Anegada Passage in the north to Marie-Galante, the southernmost island of the Guadeloupe group. The inner chain of islands – Saba, St Eustatius, St Kitts, Nevis, Montserrat and eastern Guadeloupe – are volcanic and steep, with damp, fertile soils. The outer islands – Anguilla, Barbuda, Antigua, western Guadeloupe and many smaller ones – are of limestone, and generally both lower and drier. Populations are mainly of African descent, and all the islands are – or have been until recently – fragments of French, British or Dutch empires, valued mainly for their spices and sugar.

The total area of the main islands – about 3,000 km² (1,160 sq miles) – supports a population of over half a million. Despite the fertility of many islands, and the intensive cultivation of their coastal lands, few seem large enough to support independent existence or provide more than mere subsistence for their dense populations. Most islands continue to export agricultural produce, including sugar, cotton and bananas; many are encouraging tourism. Guadeloupe benefits financially as an overseas département of France and France takes most exports. (DJF)

Banana plantations on Martinique, in the Windward Islands group.

THE WINDWARD ISLANDS

The Windwards are the southern islands of the Lesser Antilles chain. Martinique is French; the remainder – Dominica, St Lucia, St Vincent and Grenada – were British but have achieved levels of independence. Many of the islands changed hands often in colonial days, and show British, French and African traits.

All are volcanic islands, the highest peak, Morne Diablotins on Dominica, rising to 1,447 m (4,747 ft). Fumaroles, hot springs, lava outpourings and earthquakes indicate their tectonic instability; Mont Pelée on Martinique erupted in 1902, suffocating the 30,000 inhabitants of St Pierre with volcanic gas and debris. The climate is generally benign, but hurricanes often sweep in to destroy crops and housing. Most of the inhabitants of the Windwards are peasant farmers or agricultural labourers, the islands producing bananas, nutmegs and other spices, citrus fruits and sugar.

The total area of the five main islands is 3,188 km² (1,230 sq miles); with a total population of more than 750,000, the Windward Islands are densely peopled. Fortunately the rate of population growth is now lessening. (DJF)

BARBADOS

Barbados is a small island of 430 km² (166 sq miles), underlain with limestone and capped with coral. Mount Hillaby (340 m, 1,115 ft), the highest point, is fringed by marine terraces marking stages in the island's emergence from the sea. Soils are deep and fertile, and easily cultivated except in the eroded Scotland district of the north-east.

Barbados became British in 1642, and sugar production with African slave labour began almost immediately. The industry survived emancipation in 1834, mainly because there was little unused land to which freed slaves could withdraw, and it continues today to be the island's major crop. Cane plantations make up 90 per cent of the cropped land, and provide one half of the island's income from overseas. Together with tourism, sugar provides a precarious livelihood for a population of about 250,000, in what is probably the most densely populated rural country in the world. An independent state within the British Commonwealth, Barbados was early in adopting modern family planning methods, and emigration has also helped to keep the population down. (DJF)

NETHERLANDS ANTILLES

Though remote from the Antilles chains, the three islands of Aruba, Curaçao, and Bonaire, off the coast of Venezuela, are linked politically with the northern Leeward islands of St Eustatius, Saba and the southern half of St Maarten to form the Netherlands Antilles. Legally they form part of the Kingdom of the Netherlands. Their capital is at Willemstadt, on Curaçao. Their total area is 960 km² (370 sq miles), with an estimated population of 246,000. The offshore islands are dry and unproductive, though oranges have for long been grown on Curaçao and are the basis of the celebrated liqueur. Aruba is remarkable as one of the few West Indian islands with a substantial Arawak Indian population; from most other islands the Indians were long ago extirpated, usually as slave labour. Oil refineries are the mainstay of both islands, and oil products their major exports. The Leeward chain islands grow cotton, sugar cane and tropical fruits, and all are involved in a growing tourist industry. (BS)

TRINIDAD AND TOBAGO

Southernmost of the West Indian islands, Trinidad is a rectangular island lying a mere 16 km (10 miles) from the coast of Venezuela, off the Orinoco delta; an area of 5,100 km² (1,970 sq miles) includes three mountain ranges – the Northern, Central and Southern – aligned east to west and separated by lowlands. Tobago is a detached extension of the Northern Range lying 34 km (21 miles) to the north-east. Trinidad's highest point is Cerro Aripe (940 m, 3,085 ft) in the rugged, forest-covered Northern Range; the capital, Port of Spain, nestles behind the range on the sheltered west coast.

Both islands were discovered by Columbus in 1498. Trinidad was at first neglected, but later planted for sugar production by Spanish and French settlers. It became British in 1797. Negro slaves worked the plantations until emancipation, when Indian and Chinese indentured labourers were brought in. Indian influence is still strong in many Trinidad villages, while African influence remains strong in others. Tobago was settled earlier and struggled over by France, Spain and Holland before finally coming under British rule in 1802. Trinidad and Tobago joined to form a single British colony in 1899, receiving their independence in 1962.

Both islands are valued for their agricultural produce, including sugar, coffee, rubber, cacao, citrus fruits and other local or introduced crops, and Trinidad has one further product – naturally-occurring asphalt – that has for long been a major export. But throughout the twentieth century the life-blood of Trinidad's economy has been petroleum. Local crude oil, discovered in the south in the 1860s, and first exported in 1900, is today supplemented by offshore and imported supplies; refined petroleum products provide in value one-quarter of the islands' GDP, and over half their net exports. However, Trinidad and Tobago suffer the general West Indian problems of under-employment, overpopulation and poverty, which a developing tourist industry is helping to relieve. (DJF)

SOUTH AMERICA

South America occupies 12 per cent of the earth's land surface – 17.8 million km² (6.9 million sq miles). Structurally it has three parts – the Andes, the river basins and plains, and the ancient eastern highlands. The Andes run the length of the continent for about 8,000 km (5,000 miles). Glaciers and snowfields grace many of the peaks, some of which rise to over 6,500 m (21,000 ft). Aconcagua (6,960 m, 22,830 ft), in Argentina, is the highest mountain in the western hemisphere. West of the Andes lies a narrow coastal strip, except in the far south.

Three vast river basins lie to the east of the Andes; they are the llanos of Venezuela drained by the Orinoco, the Amazon basin (occupying 40 per cent of the continent) and the great Paraguay – Paraná – Uruguay basin that empties into the River Plate. The highlands are the rolling Guiana highlands of the north, and the more extensive Brazilian plateau that fills and gives shape to South America's eastern bulge. Both are of hard crystalline rock, geologically much older than the Andes, and their presence helps to explain the wanderings and meanderings of the great river systems.

South America has great climatic variety, due partly to the wide latitudinal extent but also to the great range in altitude. Eighty per cent of it falls within the tropics, but height may temper the tropical climate considerably – for example in the Altiplano of Bolivia (p. 146). The natural flora and fauna of the country are equally varied. Long isolation from the rest of the world allowed a great variety of plants and animals to evolve, and this natural variety has not yet been reduced significantly by human pressures. Electric eels, carnivorous piranha fish, manatees and river dolphins, amphibious boa constrictors, sloths, ant-eaters, armadillos, several kinds of marsupials, camel-like guanacos and llamas, rheas, Andean condors and humming birds are some of the many interesting animals indigenous to South America. Many of the plants found useful to man – potato, cassava, quinoa, squashes, cacao, sweet potato, pineapple and rubber, for example – were originally South American, and the vast forests of the Amazon and Andes may yet contain more. Pressures on the natural fauna and flora are growing, however, in a continent where ideas on conservation are shallow-rooted.

South America is prodigal,

Climate

LOCALITY HEIGHT		JAN	JUL	YR
Maracaibo	°C	26.5	28.5	27.8
48 m	mm	3	28	387
Georgetown	°C	26.3	26.2	27.0
1 m	mm	251	281	2418
Guayaquil	°C	25.5	23.5	24.9
6 m	mm	212	4	1100
Manaus	°C	25.9	26.9	26.7
83 m	mm	276	61	2102
Recife	°C	27.5	24.2	26.4
30 m	mm	53	254	1610
Lima	°C	21.5	15.3	18.2
155 m	mm	3	8	41
La Paz	°C	11.7	8.6	10.8
3660 m	mm	114	10	574
Asuncion	°C	28.8	18.2	23.7
64 m	mm	145	53	1340
Juan Fernandez I	°C	18.9	12.8	15.6
6 m	mm	20	147	937
Bahia Blanca	°C	23.9	8.9	16.1
29 m	mm	43	25	523

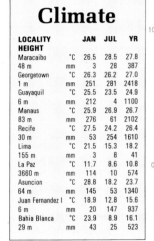

The Giant Toucan of the American tropics.

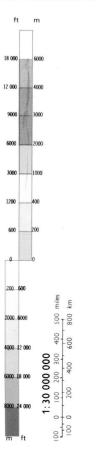

Projection: Lambert's Equivalent Azimuthal

too, with mineral wealth. Silver and gold were the first attractions but petroleum, iron, copper and tin are also plentiful, and many reserves have not yet been exploited. The people – who could yet prove Latin America's greatest resource – include a rich mix of original Amerindians, Spanish and Portuguese colonial immigrants, African slaves, and a later generation of immigrants and refugees from the turmoils of Europe. Though large (over 220 million) and growing faster than that of any other continent, the population is still small compared with the vast potential of South America itself. (DJF)

Tropical forest in the Amazon basin; possibly the world's oldest forest.

VENEZUELA

By South American standards Venezuela is a medium-sized country of 912,000 km² (352,000 sq miles); the population is small (about 13 million) but growing rapidly and predominantly urban. In the north and northwest, where 90 per cent of the population live, the Andes split to form two ranges separated from each other by the Maracaibo basin. Snow-capped Pico Bolivar (5,002 m, 16,411 ft) is the highest of several tall peaks in the area. Above 3,000 m (10,000 ft) are the *paramos* – regions of grassland vegetation where Indian villagers live; temperatures are mild and the land is fertile. Maracaibo swelters in tropical heat alongside the oilfields that for half a century have produced Venezuela's wealth.

The mountains running west to east behind the coast from Valencia to Trinidad have a separate geological history and gentler topography. Between the ranges are fertile alluvial basins, with many market towns of long-standing. Caracas, the capital, is one such town, now expanded and modernized to take a rapidly-swelling population, and fringed with the shanties of hopeful immigrants from poor rural areas.

South of the mountains are the llanos of the Orinoco – mostly a vast savanna of trees and grasslands that floods, especially in the west, during the April-to-October rains. This is now cattle-raising country. The Orinoco itself rises in the Guiana Highlands, a region of high dissected plateaux made famous as the site of Arthur Conan Doyle's *Lost World*. Mount Roraima, the highest peak, rises to 2,810 m (9,217 ft). Dense tropical forest makes this a little-known area. Not far to the north, however, lies Cerro Bolivar, where iron ore is mined and fed to the steel mills of Ciudad Guayana, a new industrial city built on the Orinoco since 1960; the smelting is powered by hydro-electricity from the nearby Caroni river, and a new deep-water port allows 60,000-tonne carriers to bring surplus ore to world markets. Modern developments in a primeval setting typify the changes that Venezuela is undergoing at present.

Oil has made Venezuela a rich country, at least in theory; the gross national product divided equally per capita would give each Venezuelan twice the mean income of South Americans as a whole. But wealth is distributed unevenly, and appears to be concentrated in the cities – hence the rapid urbanization that has made three out of every four Venezuelans a city dweller, leaving enormous areas of the country unpopulated. (DJF)

GUYANA

Guyana, formerly British Guiana, has been independent since 1966 and a republic since 1970. Although extensive (214,970 km², 83,000 sq miles), it is largely uninhabited: 95 per cent of the population of about 820,000 lives within a few kilometres of the coast, leaving the interior virtually empty. The coastal plain is mainly artificial, reclaimed from the sea by dykes and canals. The vast interior includes low forest-covered plateaux, the wooded Rupununi savannas, meandering river valleys, and the spectacular Roraima Massif on the Venezuela-Brazil border.

Land reclamation for sugar and cotton planting began in the eighteenth century under Dutch West India Company rule, using slave labour. It continued through the nineteenth century after the British took over, with indentured Asian labour replacing slaves after emancipation. Today sugar remains the main plantation crop, though production is largely nationalized and mechanized. Most comes from the lower Demerara river area, near the capital, Georgetown. The Asian community, who now make up half the total Guyanan population, are involved in rice-growing. Neither sugar nor rice provide year-round work, and unemployment is a problem. Bauxite mining and alumina production are well-established industries, combining with sugar production to provide two-thirds of the country's overseas earnings. (DJF)

SURINAM

Formerly Dutch Guiana, Surinam has an area of 163,260 km² (63,040 sq miles). The coastline of 350 km (218 miles) is of Amazonian mud and silt, fringed by extensive mangrove swamps. Behind lies an old coastal plain of sands and clays, bordering a stretch of sandy savanna. The heavily forested interior uplands are part of the Guiana Highlands, whose weathered soils form the basis of a new bauxite industry.

Surinam was first settled by British colonists in 1651, but in 1667 was ceded to Holland in exchange for Nieuw-Amsterdam, now New York. It was confirmed as a Dutch colony in 1816. Plantations were initially worked by African slaves, later by Chinese and East Indian indentured labour. The present-day population of about 375,000 reflects this history.

Surinam's hot, steamy climate grows an abundance of bananas, citrus fruits and coconuts for export, rice and many other tropical commodities for home consumption. Timber products, alumina and aluminium are the main industrial exports, and tourism is growing. (DJF)

FRENCH GUIANA

French Guiana, smallest of the three Guianas (91,000 km², 35,135 sq miles), is also the least populous and least developed. The narrow coastal plain consists of mangrove swamps and marshes, alternating with drier areas that can be cultivated; one such is the site of the capital, Cayenne. Inland a belt of sandy savanna rises to a forested plateau.

Settlement of French Guiana began in 1637 with a group of French merchant adventurers, but their effort and many successive ones failed; British and Dutch rivalries added to the natural problems of climate, terrain and health. From 1794 the struggling colony became a place of political exile, and from 1852 it became a convict settlement – with several mainland prisons and one on offshore Devil's Island. The prisons were finally closed in 1949.

Administered as an overseas département of France, French Guiana has a population of about 60,000, of whom about three-quarters live in Cayenne. Small amounts of fish, timber, bauxite and gold are exported, and substantial aid is received from France. (DJF)

Latin American Oil

Latin America currently produces more oil than it consumes. At the end of 1977 it yielded 4.6 million barrels of crude oil per day and consumed only 3.2 million; the balance, exported, represented revenue of US $4,500 million. For the last 50 years Venezuela has been the leading oil producer in Latin America. In the late 1970s, however, she was joined by Mexico.

While Venezuela has been husbanding her oil, reducing production to extend the life of reserves, Mexico's output has been expanding; the development of new finds have put her production level with Venezuela, and helped to maintain the surplus of production over consumption in Latin American countries. Prospects are bright for both countries; between them they share 90 per cent of Latin America's reserves of oil and natural gas, and there are good prospects for new finds on the Isthmus of Tehuantepec, the Gulf coast, the Venezuelan continental shelf and the Orinoco basin.

With other fuels (apart from wood) scarce, Latin America's need for oil will grow as her industries develop. Already Brazil spends one-third of her total bill for imports on oil, and is experimenting with alcohol as a possible alternative fuel. (DJF)

Oil rigs in Lake Maracaibo, Venezuela. Mexico also has major reserves.

COLOMBIA

Occupying the north-west corner of the continent, Colombia has an area of 1,138,914 km² (439,737 sq miles). The Andes cross the country from south to north, fanning out into three ranges with two intervening valleys. In the west the low Cordillera Occidental rises from the hot, forested Pacific coastal plain. Almost parallel to it, and separated by the Cauca river valley, is the much higher Cordillera Central; the high peaks of this range, many of them volcanic, rise to 5,000 m (16,400 ft) and over. To the east across the broad Magdalena river valley lies the more complex Cordillera Oriental, which includes high plateaux, plains, lakes and basins; the capital city, Bogotá, is situated on one of the plateaux, at a height of 2,610 m (8,563 ft). North-west of the mountains lies the broad Atlantic plain, crossed by many rivers. The Andean foothills to the east, falling away into the Orinoco and Amazon basins and densely covered with rain forest, occupy about two-thirds of the total area of the country.

Much of lowland Colombia is hot and steamy, with round-the-year temperatures of 20° to 25°C (68° to 77°F) and heavy rainfall, either constant or monsoonal. Of a total population of around 25.6 million, about 80 per cent live in the cooler climates of the Andes. Less than two per cent – a few cattle-rangers and Indians – live east of the mountains.

Colombia is a major producer of coffee, which grows mainly in the Andean uplands; bananas, sugar and rice are important lowland products. The wealth of the forests has yet to be exploited. Gold, silver, emeralds, iron, lead, zinc, mercury and many other minerals are plenti-

The Sierra Nevada de Santa Marta.

1:16 000 000

Projection: Sanson-Flamsteed's Sinusoidal

ful, and hydro-electric power is increasingly being developed. Petroleum is an important export and source of foreign exchange. (DJF)

BRAZIL

Fifth largest country in the world, Brazil has an area of 8,511,965 km² (3,286,473 sq miles), covering almost half of South America.

Landscape

Structurally, Brazil has two regions. In the north lies the vast Amazon basin, once an inland sea and now drained by a river system that carries one-fifth of the earth's running water. In the centre and south lies the sprawling bulk of the Brazilian highlands, a huge extent of hard crystalline rock deeply dissected into rolling uplands. This occupies the heartland (Matto Grosso), and the whole western flank of the country from the bulge to the border of Uruguay.

The Amazon river rises in the Peruvian Andes only 100 km (60 miles) from the Pacific Ocean, and many of its tributaries are of similar origin. Several are wide enough to take boats of substantial draught (6 m, 20 ft) from the Andean foothills all the way to the Atlantic – a distance of 5,000 km (3,000 miles) or more. Seven tributaries of the Amazon are over 1,600 km (1,000 miles) long; the vast Madeira is over 3,200 km (2,000 miles) long. Enormous masses of silt are carried, including sufficient fine material to discolour the surface waters of the Atlantic Ocean for 200 km (125 miles) off the mouth of the estuary. The largest area of river plain lies in the upper part of the basin, along the frontier with Bolivia and Peru. Downstream the flood plain is rela-

tively narrow, shrinking in width to a few kilometers where the basin drains between the Guiana Highlands in the north and the Brazilian Highlands in the south. Overall only 1 to 2 per cent of the Amazon valley is alluvial flood plain; away from this the soils are heavily leached and infertile, and liable to be washed away by tropical rainstorms if the protective canopy of forest is felled.

The undulating plateau of the northern highlands also carries poor soils; here rainfall is seasonal, and the typical natural vegetation is a thorny scrub forest, used as open grazing for poor cattle herds. Further south scrub turns to wooded savanna – the *campo cerrado* vege-

Climate

Crossed by the Equator, northern South America is hot throughout the year, with annual lowland temperatures exceeding 25°C (77°F) over wide areas of the north and west coasts, and the Amazon basin. Annual rainfall is heavy, exceeding 100 cm (40 in) across most of the equatorial region: over 300 cm (120 in) of rain falls year-round on French Guiana and parts of eastern Peru, over 800 cm (320 in) on northwestern Colombia. The Caribbean coast is drier, with 50 to 100 cm (20 to 40 in) annually. Seasonal warm climates occur near the Tropic, with winter means of 15 to 25°C (59 to 77°F). The west coast and mountains and the eastern Brazilian highlands are dry-to-arid.

LOCALITY HEIGHT		JAN	JUL	YR
Caracas	°C	19.6	21.9	21.6
865 m	mm	23	109	854
Merida	°C	17.5	18.7	18.7
1498 m	mm	55	125	1633
Cayenne	°C	25.1	25.1	25.5
9 m	mm	431	274	3744
Bogota	°C	14.2	13.9	14.5
2646 m	mm	58	51	1059
Seymour I,				
Galapagos	°C	26.1	23.9	25.0
11 m	mm	20	Tr	102
Quito	°C	13.0	12.9	13.0
2812 m	mm	119	20	1233
Fernando de				
Noronha I	°C	26.2	25.1	26.0
45 m	mm	35	174	1259
Cuzco	°C	13.6	10.3	12.8
3227 m	mm	163	5	813
Sucre	°C	13.1	9.5	12.2
2850 m	mm	185	5	706
Rio de Janeiro	°C	25.9	20.8	23.2
27 m	mm	137	43	1086

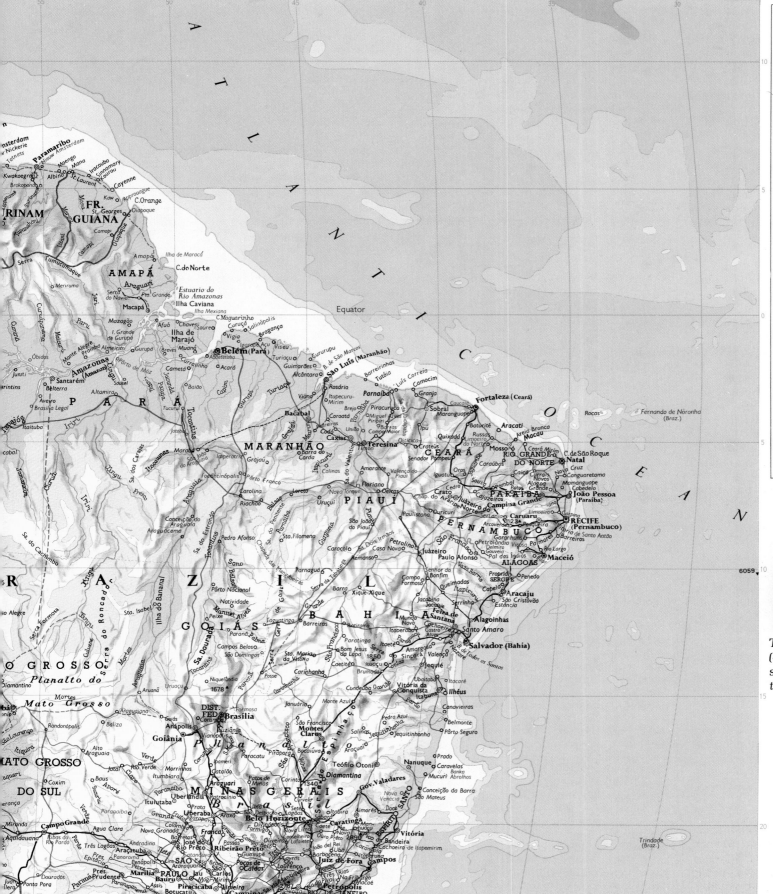

The Amazon, 6,516 km (4,072 miles) from source to mouth. Only the Nile is longer.

tation that covers 2 million km² (770,000 sq miles) of the interior plateau. It extends into the basin of the Paraná river and its tributaries, most of which start in the coastal highlands and flow east, draining ultimately into the Plate estuary. The Mato Grosso, on the frontier with Bolivia, is part of this area and still largely unexplored. The north-eastern uplands are poor farming country, with little alluvial land to be improved by irrigation; dry for at least half the year, they occasionally suffer long periods of drought.

Conditions are better in the south, with more reliable rainfall. The south-east includes a narrow coastal plain, swampy in places and with abundant rainfall throughout the year; behind rises the Great Escarpment (820 m, 2,700 ft) – first in a series of steps to the high eastern edge of the plateau. Over 60 per cent of Brazil's population lives in the four southern and south-eastern states (17 per cent of the total area).

Exploration and Settlement

Brazil was discovered by Pedro Alvarez Cabral in 1500, and gradually penetrated by Portuguese settlers, missionaries, explorers and prospectors during the seventeenth and eighteenth centuries. The semi-nomadic Indians indigenous to the country were enslaved for plantation work or driven into the interior, and African slaves were introduced, especially in the sugar-growing area of the north-east. For long little more than a group of rival provinces, Brazil began to unite in 1808 when the Portuguese royal court, seeking refuge from Napoleon, transferred from Lisbon to Rio de Janeiro. In 1822, shortly after the return of the King and court to Europe, Brazil declared independence. At first an Empire, it became a republic in 1889.

For many decades following the early settlements Brazil was mainly a sugar-producing colony, with most plantations centred on the rich coastal plains of the north-east. Later the same areas produced cotton, cacao, rice and other crops. In the south colonists penetrated the interior in search of slaves and minerals, especially gold and diamonds; the city of Ouro Prêto in Minas Gerais was built, and Rio de Janeiro grew as the port for the region. During the nineteenth century São Paulo state became the centre of a coffee-growing industry; while the fortunes made in mining helped to develop Rio de Janeiro, profits from coffee were invested in the city of São Paulo. Nineteenth-century immigrants from Italy and Germany settled in the south, introducing farming into the fertile valleys in coexistence with the cattle-ranchers and gauchos whose herds wandered the plains.

The second half of the nineteenth century saw the development of the wild rubber industry in the Amazon basin, where the city of Manaus, with its world-famous opera house, served as a centre and market; though Manaus lies 1,600 km (1,000

miles) upstream from the mouth of the Amazon, rubber collected from trees in the hinterland could be shipped out directly to world markets in ocean-going steamers. Brazil enjoyed a monopoly of the rubber trade until the early twentieth century, when Malaysian plantations began to compete.

Population and Economy

In 1872 Brazil had a population of about ten million. By 1972 this had increased almost ten-fold; 1978 saw about 115 million Brazilians, with a projected increase to 200 million by the end of the century. There are more Brazilians than Mexicans, Argentinians and Colombians put together, living within a political unity that has created South America's most powerful economy. In 1977 Brazil accounted for half the gross domestic product and over half the gross domestic investment in the continent. Much of the wealth is still centred in the cities, particularly those of the south-east; despite grandiose development plans aimed at spreading prosperity throughout the country, the interior remains poor and underpopulated.

The Altiplano

A reed boat on Lake Titicaca.

A high, rolling plateau 3,600 m (12,000 ft) above sea-level on the Peruvian border of Bolivia, the Altiplano stretches 400 km (250 miles) north to south between the eastern and western cordilleras of the Andes. Surrounded by high, snow-capped peaks, at its north end lies Lake Titicaca: to the south are smaller lakes, and extensive salt flats representing old lake beds. Though tropical in latitude the Altiplano is cold, windswept and bleak, and by any standards a harsh environment. Yet over half the population of Bolivia, including a high proportion of native Indians, make it their home.

The natural vegetation is grassland merging at high levels to *puna* – small bushes and trees forming a harsh scrubland. Summer rains and winter snows bring enough moisture to support grass, and the Altiplano is grazed by guanaco and vicuña as well as many smaller herbivores – chinchillas, viscachas and guinea-pigs. Llama and alpaca – domesticated from guanaco-like ancestors – are herded to provide meat and wool for the peasant farmers. The lakes attract enormous flocks of water birds, including ducks, geese, gulls and cormorants. The human inhabitants, small and tough, are physiologically adapted for life at high altitude, with more blood, more oxygen-carrying haemoglobin, and more efficient lungs than the Indians of the foothills. (BS)

The Iguaçu falls on the border between Brazil and Argentina.

Brazil's economy is still firmly based in agriculture, which employs the bulk of the work-force and provides 70 per cent of her overseas exports. Coffee, soya, cotton, cacao, sugar, rice, citrus fruits and bananas are among the main agricultural products. However, the standard of living among farmworkers is low, and many formerly prosperous agricultural areas (Recife and the north-east, for example) are in decline. Mineral production is strong; coal, iron, manganese, chrome and industrial diamonds are exported. Brazil produces a little petroleum, but buys in much more; her industries include iron and steel, motor car manufacture, plastics, pharmaceuticals, paper and textiles, and the potential for further development is enormous.

To a traditional network of rivers, that for long gave the only access to the interior, is now being added a network of arterial roads; the Amazon basin is gradually being opened for exploitation of forests and mines, with Santarém a new focus of agriculture in a frontier land. Further south the new capital of Brasilia, built from 1956 onward, in many ways encapsulates both the spirit and the problems of new

Rio de Janeiro, Brazil.

Brazil – a sparkling, dramatically planned modern city, deliberately planted in the interior as a gesture of faith, modern, practical and beautiful, but still surrounded by the shanties of poverty and – beyond them – the challenge of an untamed wilderness. (DJF)

ECUADOR

Ecuador's name comes from the Equator, which divides the country unequally; Quito, the capital, lies just within the southern hemisphere. There are three distinct regions – the coastal plain (Costa), the Andes, and the eastern alluvial plains of the Oriente – all on a small scale, for Ecuador, with an area of 283,560 km² (109,500 sq miles), is one of South America's smallest states.

The coastal plain, averaging 100 km (60 miles) wide, is a hot, fertile area of variable rainfall; recently cleared of forests and largely freed of malaria it is now good farmland. Banana farms, coffee and cacao plantations and fishing are the main sources of income, and Guayaquil is an improved and flourishing port. Of Ecuador's total population (7.8 million), about half now live in the Costa area, almost a million of them in Guayaquil. The Andes form three linked ranges across the country, with several of the central peaks rising above 5,000 m (16,400 ft). Quito, an old city rich in art and architecture from a colonial past, has a back-drop of snow-capped mountains, among them Cotopaxi (5,896 m, 19,340 ft – the world's highest active volcano) and Chimborazo (6,267 m, 20,556 ft). The Oriente, a heavily forested upland, is virtually unexploited except for recent developments of oil and natural gas. (DJF)

An agricultural landscape in the foothills of the Andes, Ecuador.

A Bolivian tin mine.

GALAPAGOS ISLANDS

Known officially to Ecuadorians as Archipiélago de Colón, the Galapagos group lies across the Equator 1,000 km (600 miles) west of Ecuador, the mother country. There are sixteen major islands and many smaller ones, with a total land area of about 8,000 km² (3,000 sq miles), widely scattered over seven times that area of ocean. All are volcanic, made up mainly of basaltic lava flows with shallow, cratered cones. Some cones are still active.

Discovered in 1535, the islands are thought to have arisen from the sea bed some five to seven million years ago. Though never linked directly to the mainland, the islands have acquired a unique flora and fauna mainly originating from South America, but showing evidence of rapid evolution and adaptation since their arrival on the islands. Interesting animals include the giant

BOLIVIA

Bolivia is a land-locked country of 1,098,600 km² (424,200 sq miles), made up of a wide stretch of the Andes (where 85 per cent of the population lives), and a long, broad Oriente – part of the south-western fringe of the Amazon basin. The western boundary is the High

tortoises (with different forms on the main islands), endemic lizards, penguins, cormorants and fur seals, and the celebrated Darwin's finches that have adapted to occupy many environmental niches. The endemic Galapagos species, though protected in law, are today endangered by introduced animals – for example, goats, dogs and cats. The Darwin Foundation sponsors research programmes on the islands.

Giant tortoises. The only other surviving species is in the Seychelles.

Cordillera Occidental, crowned by Sajama (6,520 m, 21,400 ft) and many other volcanic peaks. To the east lies the Altiplano, a high, treeless plateau which in prehistoric times was a great lake. Eastward again rises the majestic Cordillera Real, where Illimani, a glacier-covered peak 6,462 m (21,200 ft) high, forms a back-drop to La Paz, the capital city. In the transmontane region to north and east lies the huge expanse of the Oriente – foothills and plains extending from the semi-arid Chaco of the south-east, through the savanna-like llanos of the centre, to the high, wetter forests of the northern plains.

Climate is tempered by the cool Humboldt Current that sweeps past the islands from the south-east. Most rain falls on the peaks – the lowlands are dry to arid. Settled since about 1830, the islands now have a population of about 3,000, mostly Ecuadoreans, who live mainly by farming and fishing. (BS)

Marine iguanas, Fernandina Island.

Bolivia in pre-conquest days was the homeland of the Tiahuanaco culture (seventh to eleventh centuries AD) and was later absorbed into the Inca empire; Quechua the language of the Inca, is still spoken by large minorities in Bolivia today. Famous for its silver mines, the high Andean area was exploited ruthlessly by the Spanish conquistadors; the mine at Potosi, discovered in 1545, proved the richest in the world, and Upper Peru (today's highland Bolivia) was for two centuries one of the most densely populated of Spain's American colonies. In 1824 the local population seized their independence, naming their country after Simón Bolivar, hero of other South American wars of independence. When the era of silver passed the Bolivian economy flagged, and the country began to lose ground to its neighbours. The Pacific coast was lost to Chile and Peru in 1884, and large tracts of the Oriente were later ceded to Brazil in 1903 and Paraguay in 1935.

Today Bolivia is the poorest of the South American republics – an undeveloped country with most of the population (about 5 million) living in the most inhospitable part. Two-thirds of the wage-earners are engaged in agriculture, but wages and returns are low; Bolivia exports coffee, sugar, timber and cotton, but is an importer of wheat; irrigation schemes in the south-western Oriente may help to improve local production of staple foods. Mining contributes significantly to the country's wealth, and dominates export trade. Bolivia is a leading world producer of tin (normally accounting for over two-thirds of overseas income). Lead, zinc, antimony and sulphur are important exports; oil and gas are produced in small amounts. Industrial output is growing slowly with substantial help from foreign capital. (DJF)

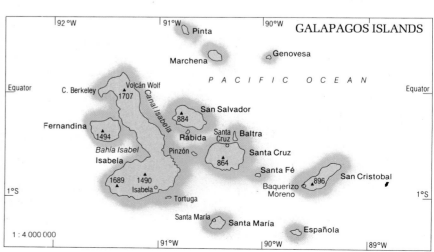

PERU

Peru is the largest of the Andean republics of South America, with an area of 1,285,216 km² (496,222 sq miles). Spread over coastal plain, mountains, and forested Amazon lowlands in the interior, Peru was formerly the homeland of Inca and other ancient civilizations, and has a long history of human settlement.

The coastal plain is narrow and generally arid, cooled by sea breezes from the offshore Humboldt current. Occasionally it suffers violent rainstorms, associated with shifts in the pattern of surface waters. Rivers that cut through the foothills provide water for irrigated agriculture, mainly of cotton, rice and sugar cane. The middle slopes of the Andes – the Quechua, at heights of 2,000 to 3,500 m (6,500 to 11,500 ft) – are warm-temperate and fairly well watered. These areas supported the main centres of Indian population in the Inca empire, and are just as well suited to densely-populated rural settlements today.

Above stand the higher reaches of the Andes, extending westward in cold, inhospitable tablelands at 4,000 to 4,800 m (13,000 to 15,700 ft), cultivated up to 4,200 m (13,700 ft) by peasant farmers and grazed by their alpacas, llamas and vicuñas. The snowy peaks of the high Andes rise to over 6,000 m (19,500 ft). Though close to the Pacific Ocean, most of the rivers that rise here eventually drain eastward into the Amazon. Their descent to the lowlands is through the montaña, a near-impenetrable maze of valleys, ridges and plains, permanently soaked by rain and thickly timbered. Beyond extend the Amazon lowlands, hot, wet, and mainly clad in tropical rain forest: occupying half the country, they are thinly inhabited by Indians.

Lima was developed as the Spanish colonial capital, and through its port of Callao passed much of the trade of Spanish settlers. Peru gained independence from Spain in 1824, but difficulties of travel and communication, political strife, earthquakes and other natural disasters, and a chronically unbalanced economy have dogged development. Nineteenth-century exports included guano (bird-droppings, valuable as an agricultural fertilizer) from the offshore islands, and wild rubber.

Today Peru faces many economic problems. Agricultural production has failed to keep up with popula-

Climate

Beyond latitude 20°S South America tapers rapidly; climates become more temperate and seasonal, and generally drier except in the south-west. On the plains east of the Andes mean January (summer) temperatures generally exceed 20°C (68°F), mean temperatures range between 5° and 15°C (41° and 59°F); the Andes themselves are cooler, with near-zero temperatures among their high peaks even in summer. Southern Chile, Patagonia and the Falkland Islands are chilled by cool currents. Central Chile is a cool, dry desert, merging into a cool Mediterranean climate around Santiago. Further south, rainfall increases rapidly, exceeding 300 cm (120 in) in the far south.

LOCALITY HEIGHT		JAN	JUL	YR
Bela Vista	°C	26.1	17.2	22.2
160 m	mm	168	33	1326
Antofagasta	°C	20.9	13.9	16.7
94 m	mm	0	5	13
Cordoba	°C	24.4	10.7	17.5
423 m	mm	101	8	680
Valparaiso	°C	17.8	11.9	14.7
41 m	mm	3	99	505
Santiago	°C	20.6	8.9	14.7
520 m	mm	3	76	358
Valdivia	°C	17.0	8.1	12.0
5 m	mm	66	394	2601
Sarmiento	°C	18.3	2.8	10.8
268 m	mm	5	15	130
Stanley	°C	8.7	2.2	5.5
2 m	mm	79	50	598
Punta Arenas	°C	10.8	1.9	6.7
8 m	mm	38	28	366
South Georgia	°C	4.4	−1.5	2.0
2 m	mm	118	113	1432

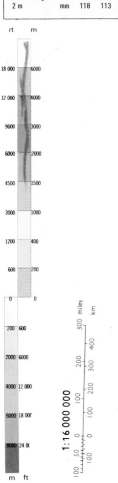

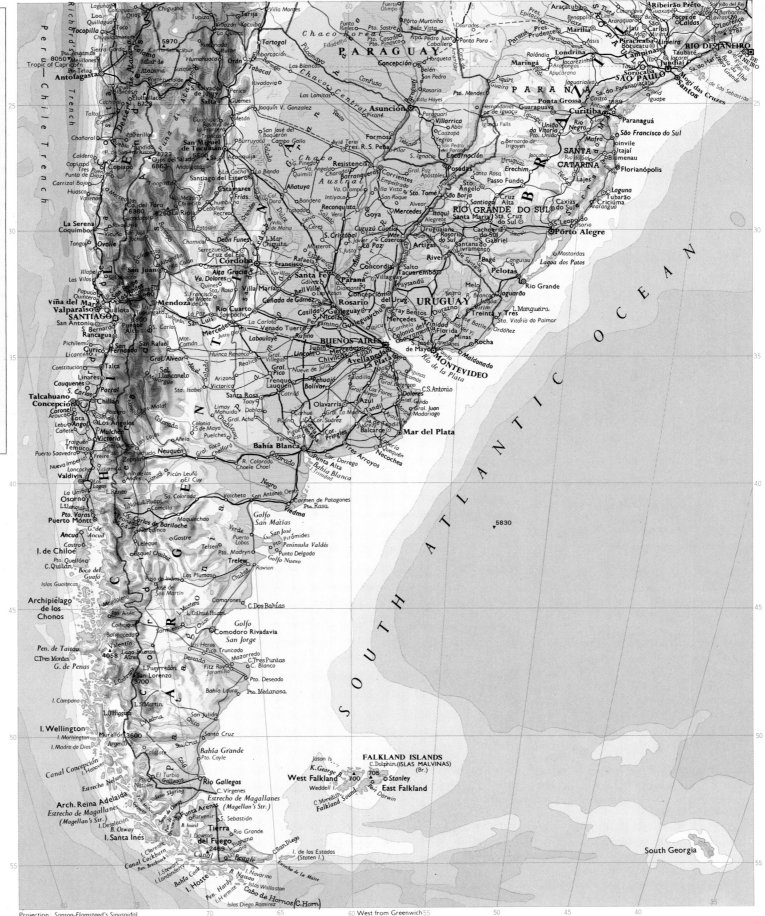

Projection: Sanson-Flamsteed's Sinusoidal

1:16 000 000

A smelting works in the Peruvian Andes, at 3,750 m (12,300 ft).

tion (nearly 17 million, and increasing rapidly), so Peru imports wheat, rice, meat and other staple foods. Cotton, coffee and sugar are exported. Offshore fishing in the rich Humboldt current supports canning and fish-meal industries — mainly for export, though many poor Peruvians lack dietary protein. Copper, lead, silver and other metals are exported, and Peru's exports of petroleum are growing, providing much-needed foreign capital for industrial development. (DJF)

PARAGUAY

A small country of area 406,752 km² (157,048 sq miles), Paraguay is bounded mainly by rivers – the Paraná (South America's second largest river) in the south and east, the Pilcomayo in the south-west, and the Paraguay and Apa rivers in the north-west. The middle reach of the Paraguay divides the country unequally. The eastern third, an extension of the Brazilian plateau at a height of 300 to 600 m (1,000 to 2,000 ft), is densely forested with tropical hardwoods. The western two-thirds is the Northern Chaco, a flat, alluvial plain rising gently from the damp, marshy Paraguay river valley to semi-desert scrubland along the western border.

Paraguay was settled early by the Spaniards, who were attracted by the labour supply of the native Guarani Indians. Asunción, the capital, was founded in 1537. Forming part of the Rio de la Plata Viceroyalty from 1766, Paraguay broke free in 1811 and achieved independence of Buenos Aires in 1813. For over a century Paraguay struggled for nationhood, torn by destructive internal combat and also conflict with neighbouring states. At a time when most other South American countries were attracting European settlers and foreign capital for development, Paraguay remained isolated and forbidding. Though poor and economically undeveloped, Paraguay exports agricultural produce (cotton, soy beans, manioc, maize), and is investing heavily in hydro-electric power. (DJF)

The Inca

Machu Picchu, ancient fortress city of the Inca, was discovered only in 1911.

The Inca empire centred upon Cuzco, in the Peruvian highlands. It developed from millennia of earlier Andean civilizations including the Chavin, the Nazca and the Tiahuanaco; the Inca began their conquests about AD 1350, and by the end of the fifteenth century their empire extended over 3,000 km (1,875 miles) from central Chile to Ecuador. Perhaps about ten million people owed allegiance to it when it fell, in 1532, to the Spanish conquistadors.

The empire was military and theo-cratic, with the sun as the focus of worship. Temples and shrines, built of massive, laboriously-shaped and closely-fitting blocks (the Inca had no metal tools) were created for sun worship; the Sun Temple at Cuzco had a circumference of 350 m (1,148 ft), and many other buildings were equally massive. The people were skilled farmers, using elaborate irrigation systems and terraced fields. Native potatoes and maize were the main crops, among many others, and llamas were the important domestic animals. The

Inca had a superb road network.

Gold and silver were particularly valued by the Inca for ornamentation. They were prized also by the conquistadors, who looted them from every corner of the empire and quickly set the Indians to mining more. The Inca had no written script. Buildings and terracing (notably those of Machu Picchu in Peru) and delicate ornaments form their main memorials, though fragments of Inca culture and beliefs remain among the Quechua-speaking Indians of Peru and Bolivia. (DJF)

URUGUAY

Tiny in comparison with her giant neighbours, Uruguay is the smallest independent South American state, with an area of 177,500 km² (68,530 sq miles). A low-lying, rolling country of tall prairie grasses and riparian woodlands, the highest land is less than 600 m (2,000 ft) above sea-level. The Atlantic coast and River Plate estuary are fringed with lagoons and sand dunes; the centre of the country is a low plateau, rising in the north toward the Brazilian border. The Uruguay river forms the western boundary, and is navigable as far as the falls at Salto, 300 km (186 miles) from the Plate.

Originally little more than the hinterland to the Spanish base of Montevideo, Uruguay formed a buffer area between northern Portuguese and western Spanish territories. Uruguay became independent in 1828, internal struggles and civil war intervening before the country developed a basis for prosperity. European immigrants settled the coast and the valley of the Uruguay river, farming the lowlands and leaving the highlands for stock-rearing. Meat processing, pioneered at Fray Bentos in the 1860s, was the start of a meat-and-hide export industry that, boosted by railways to Montevideo and later by refrigerated cargo ships established Uruguay's fortunes. Today a modern and moderately prosperous country, Uruguay still depends largely on exports of animal products – mostly meat, wool and dairy produce – for her livelihood. Farming is the main industry, though in a population of almost 2.9 million four out of five are urban-living and half live in the single large city of Montevideo. Poor in energy resources, Uruguay is developing hydro-electric power on the Uruguay river. (DJF)

The Atacama desert, northern Chile.

CHILE

Chile extends down the west coast of South America from latitude 17°30′S, well inside the tropics, to 55°50′S at Cape Horn – a narrow ribbon of a country twenty-five times longer than it is wide. A total area of 756,946 km² (292,257 sq miles) includes the tiny Juan Fernandez Islands and distant Easter Island in the south Pacific Ocean. Geographically Chile falls into three parallel zones, based on the longitudinal folding of the Andes. In the east are the Andean mountains themselves, their high peaks marking the boundary with Bolivia and Argentina. Along the coast runs a second, parallel range, Cordillera de la Costa; this merges with the Andes in the north but the mountains separate south of Santiago to form the third zone, a sheltered and fertile valley.

From the Bolivian border in the north down to 27°S runs an extension of the high plateau of Bolivia. San Pedro, a volcanic peak 6,159 m (20,206 ft) high is one of several marking the edge of the western cordilleras. South of Paso de San Francisco the ranges narrow and steepen; Ojos del Salado (6,863 m, 22,510 ft) and Aconcagua (6,960 m, 22,835 ft) stand sentinel at either end of this high central section of the Andes. South of 35°S the mountains fall away in height; south of 42°S the effects of glaciation become more marked, though the ranges are still spectacular and difficult to cross. In the far south the main line of the Andes curves eastward past Cape Horn, ending in Staten Island.

The coastal ranges create a rolling, hilly belt, rising to 3,000 m (10,000 ft) or more in the north but generally lower. Between this belt and the Andes runs the central valley, most clearly marked from Santiago south. Glacial and alluvial deposits divide the valley into a series of basins, and

Ushuaia, on the south coast of Tierra del Fuego, Argentina.

fast-flowing rivers cross it, cutting also through the coastal range to the sea. South of Puerto Montt the valley becomes a flooded channel and the coastal range breaks into a series of islands and archipelagos that lead down to Cape Horn.

Climate

Climatically Chile divides readily into a desert north, a warm-temperate centre and a cool-temperate south. The Atacama desert extends southward from Peru to about 27°S. Though rainless for long periods, cool, moist air from the offshore Humboldt current provides condensation and reduces temperatures below norms for the latitude. In central Chile reliable winter rains provide a Mediterranean climate; for agricultural purposes snow-melt water from the Andes is held back by dams, and used for summer irrigation. South of 40°S eastward-moving depressions bring rain throughout the year and strong, Roaring-Forties winds to the coasts; snow accumulates on the mountains, feeding glaciers that descend to sea-level in the far south.

Economic Development

A Spanish colony from the sixteenth century, Chile developed as a mining enterprise in the north and a series of vast ranches, haciendas, in the fertile central region. After the war of independence (1817) Chile united under Bernardo O'Higgins. Mining continued to flourish in the north; the discovery of caliche, an evaporite

rich in nitrates, brought new prosperity in the 1860s, and Chile expanded into the mineral-rich Atacama region in the War of the Pacific (1879–84). In the south Valparaiso developed as a port, the farmlands of the southern valley exporting produce to the new settlers of California and Australia. Economic patterns are similar today. Copper, mined and now smelted in the north, provides over half the total value of Chile's exports; agriculture continues to flourish in the fertile centre, and a new source of wealth – petroleum – is now being exploited in the far south. (DJF)

ARGENTINA

Largest of the Spanish-speaking countries of Latin America, Argentina forms a wedge from the tropic of Capricorn to Tierra del Fuego. Its area is 2,767,000 km² (1,068,300 sq miles). The western boundary lies high in the Andes, including basins, ridges, and peaks of 6,000 m (19,685 ft) in the north. South of latitude 27°S the ridges merge into a single high cordillera; south of 39°S the Patagonian Andes are lower, but including glaciers and volcanoes. Eastern Argentina is a series of alluvial plains, stretching from the Andean foothills to the sea. The Gran Chaco in the north slopes gradually toward the valley of the Paraná river, from high (1,000 m, 3,300 ft) desert in the foothills to

lowland swamp forest.

Further south are the extensive pampas grasslands, damp and fertile near Buenos Aires, drier but still productive elsewhere. Southward again the pampas give way to the much rougher and less hospitable plateaux of Patagonia, areas of mixed volcanic, alluvial and glacial debris, forming a harsh, wind-swept landscape. The climate varies from hot and humid in the north to bitterly cold, damp and stormy in the extreme south.

Only since the mid-nineteenth century has Argentina developed as a nation. Formerly a dependency of Peru, the country was settled first in the north-west around Salta and San Miguel de Tucumán, with strong links to Lima. This area is unusual today in retaining a largely mestizo (mixed Indian and Spanish) population, a remnant of colonial times. In 1776 Argentina, Uruguay, Paraguay and southern Bolivia were disengaged from Peru to form a separate viceroyalty, with administrative centre in Buenos Aires. After a long war of independence the United Provinces of the Rió de la Plata achieved self-government under Simón Bolivar, but Uruguay, Bolivia and Paraguay separated between 1814 and 1828; it took many years of warfare and turbulence before Argentina emerged as a nation (1816), united and centred on Buenos Aires. Early prosperity, based on stock-raising and farming, was boosted from 1870 by a massive influx of European immigrants, particularly Italians and Spaniards for whom the Argentine was a real alternative to the USA. They settled lands recently cleared of Indians and often organized by huge land companies. Britain provided much of the

Gauchos, South American cowboys, on the Argentinian pampas.

The Pampas

Pampa is a South American Indian word describing a flat, featureless expanse: the pampas of South America are the broad, grassy plains – equivalent to the North American prairies and the Russian steppes – that stretch between the eastern flank of the Andes and the sea, from southern Brazil to Argentina. Geologically they represent outwash fans of rubble, sand, silt and clay, washed down from the Andes by torrents and redistributed by wind and water. Fine soils cover huge expanses of pampas, providing good deep soils in the well-watered areas, and sandy desert where rainfall and ground-water are lacking. In the warm climate of eastern South America the grasses grow best with rainfall of 100 to 125 cm (40 to 50 in).

Originally the pampas were covered with indigenous bunch-grasses, with scattered stands of trees in the well-watered areas. Deer, guanaco, viscachas and cavys were the main grazers, and the pampas fauna included a wealth of bird life, including the ostrich-like rhea. Early Spanish settlers introduced horses and cattle, and later the best areas of pampas were enclosed for cattle ranching and cultivation. Now the pampas are almost entirely converted to rangelands growing imported turf-grasses, or to huge fields producing alfalfa, maize, wheat and flax. Tractors have mostly replaced the gauchos. (BS)

The volcano of Villarica, Chile.

capital and some of the immigrants. Families of English and Welsh sheep farmers, still speaking their own languages, are identifiable in Patagonia today. Development of a railway network to the ports, of steamship services to Europe and refrigerated vessels, all helped to create a strong meat-and-wheat economy that carried Argentina through the formative years and into the twentieth century.

Today Argentina is one of the wealthier countries of South America, with a population mainly of European stock, a strong middle class and an ebullient economy. Agriculture thrives; Argentina's efficient farming industry exports wheat, maize, sorghum and soy beans, and enormous quantities of meat, and produces sugar, oilseed, fruit and vegetables for home consumption. Minerals are present but largely undeveloped; coal and natural gas are exploited, and the country is approaching self-sufficiency in petroleum production, mainly from Patagonia and the north-west. Manufacturing industries are strong, but heavily centralized around Buenos Aires. Of the total population of Argentina (estimated 26.4 million) about one-third live in the capital; Buenos Aires is South America's most populous and most affluent city. (DJF)

THE FALKLAND ISLANDS

A low-lying group of over 200 islands, the Falklands lie 480 km (300 miles) from South America. Windswept, virtually treeless, covered with peat moorland and tussock grass, they have a total area

King penguins, moulting, S. Georgia.

of 16,000 km² (6,177 sq miles), mostly contained in two major islands, East and West Falkland, separated by Falkland Sound. The rolling landscape rises to two high points of about 700 m (2,300 ft) – Mount Usborne in East Falkland, Mount Adam in West Falkland. The 2,000 Falkland Islanders are English-speaking and mainly of British descent: over half live in Stanley, the capital, in a sheltered inlet on East Falkland. The islands are rich in subantarctic wildlife, including penguins, seals and sea lions.

Discovered in 1592, the Falklands were occupied by British and French settlements in 1764–5. The French interest, bought by Spain in 1770, passed ultimately to Argentina, which retained settlements in East Falkland. The British withdrew in 1774 without, however, relinquishing their claim to the islands. Returning in 1833 they dispossessed the Argentine settlers, starting a settlement of their own that became a Crown Colony in 1892. Sheep farming is the islanders' main source of revenue. Argentina maintains a claim to the Falklands. (BS)

SOUTH GEORGIA

An island of the Antarctic fringe, South Georgia lies 1,300 km (820 miles) east and slightly south of the Falkland Islands. 170 km (106 miles) long, with an area of 3,755 km² (1,450 sq miles), this island of steep mountains and deeply-incised fjords forms part of the Scotia Arc – an underwater extension of the Andes. Its mountain spine rises centrally to over 2,700 m (8,800 ft). Though in similar latitude to the Falkland Islands and Cape Horn, South Georgia lies in a broad tongue of very much colder Antarctic water. Its climate is correspondingly colder; ice covers its mountains and descends in glaciers to the sea, and snow covers the ground from May to October. Summers are mild and damp at sea-level, and thick tussock grass covers the coastal plains and the foothills of the mountains.

Discovered by James Cook in 1775, South Georgia has never had permanent human residents. But it stands in a rich patch of ocean, and is the home and breeding ground of fur seals, elephant seals, penguins, and over a dozen species of petrels including albatrosses, prions and storm petrels. From 1904 it was an important whaling centre, but its stations are now abandoned and derelict. South Georgia is administered as a Dependency of the Falkland Islands. (BS)

ISLANDS OF THE ATLANTIC OCEAN

ATLANTIC OCEAN

THE AZORES

Part of the mid-Atlantic Ridge, the Azores are a group of ten large and several small islands, all of volcanic origin, with a total area of 2,344 km^2 (905 sq miles). Of relatively recent origin, the islands are mostly mountainous and steep sided, with high cliffs and narrow beaches of shell gravel or dark volcanic sand. The highest mountain is Pico, a volcanic cone of 2,351 m (7,713 ft). Earthquakes are often felt and minor eruptions happen occasionally.

Well-watered, with an equable, temperate climate and fertile soils, the islands grow food crops and vines; all flat or slightly-sloping land is cultivated. The islands support a population of about 300,000, mostly of Portuguese stock. Small-scale farming and fishing are the main occupations; sperm whaling (from open boats) provides oil and other whale products for export, and canned fish, fruit and wines are also exported, mainly to Portugal. The Azores are governed as three districts of Portugal; Horta, on Fayal, is the main administrative centre. (BS)

MADEIRA

Madeira, the largest of a group of volcanic islands, lies 550 km (350 miles) from the Moroccan coast. Porto Santo and the uninhabited Ilhas Selvagens and Desertas make up the group, with total area 800 km^2 (308 sq miles). With a warm temperate climate, adequate rain and good soils, Madeira was originally forested, but early settlers cleared the uplands for plantations. Now farming is the main occupation; produce includes cane sugar, wines, vegetables and both temperate and tropical fruit. Tourism and handicrafts are additional sources of revenue. The islands are administered as part of Portugal. The population is about 270,000. (BS)

CAPE VERDE ISLANDS

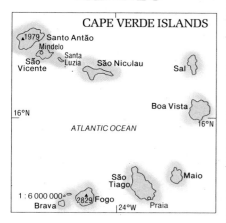

An archipelago of ten large and many small islands, the Cape Verdes lie 560 km (350 miles) off Dakar; northern Windward and southern

Leeward islands together total 4,033 km^2 (1,557 sq miles). They are volcanic and mainly mountainous, with steep cliffs and rocky headlands; the highest, Fogo, rises to 2,829 m (9,281 ft) and is volcanically active. The islands are tropical, hot for most of the year, and mainly dry at sea-level. Higher ground is damp and fertile, producing good crops of maize, groundnuts, coffee, cane sugar, beans, potatoes and tropical fruit; droughts, however, are common and crops often fail. The population of about 314,000 are mainly Negro or Creole, descended from African slaves. The islands, formerly an overseas province of Portugal, became an independent republic in 1975. (BS)

CANARY ISLANDS

A group of seven large and many small volcanic islands, the Canaries (Islas Canarias) lie off south Morocco, the nearest within 100 km (60 miles). Inshore islands Lanzarote and Fuerteventura are low-lying. The western group, including Tenerife and Gran Canaria, are more mountainous; Pico de Teide in Tenerife exceeds 4,000 m (12,200 ft). The islands have a subtropical climate, dry at sea-level but damp on higher ground. Soils are fertile, supporting farming and fruit-growing mostly by large-scale irrigation. Bananas, sugar, coffee and citrus fruits are the main crops at lower levels; temperate cereals, potatoes, tomatoes and vines grow in the cooler, damper air above. Much of the produce is exported to Europe for the early spring market. With a population of about 1.2 million the islands are administratively two provinces of Spain; their capitals are Las Palmas and Santa Cruz. (BS)

ASCENSION ISLAND

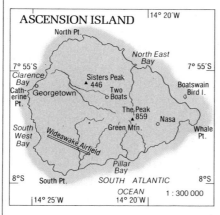

Standing in isolation on the Mid-Atlantic Ridge, Ascension is a triangular volcanic island of area 88 km^2 (34 sq miles), with a single high peak, Green Mountain (859 m, 2,817 ft), surrounded by low-lying ash and lava plains. The lowland is hot and arid throughout the year. The mountain climate is cool and damp enough to support a farm, which supplies vegetables for the local community of about 1,200. Ascension has no native population. Administered from St Helena, its inhabitants are British, St Helenian or American, involved in telecommunication or satellite research. (BS)

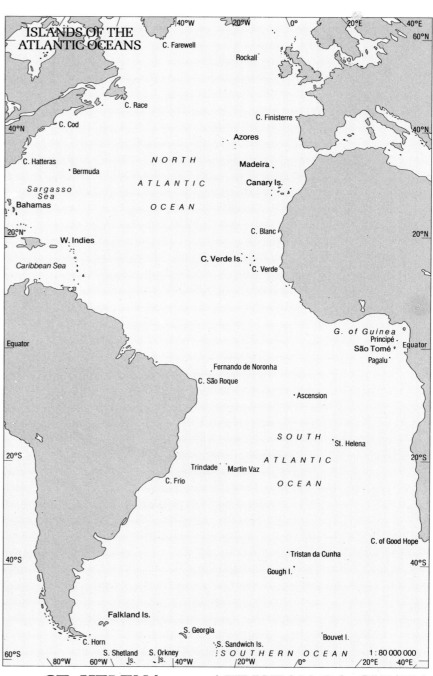

ISLANDS OF THE ATLANTIC OCEANS

ST HELENA

An isolated island of 122 km^2 (47 sq miles), St Helena is a rectangular, slab-sided island of old volcanic rocks, well off the main line of the Mid-Atlantic Ridge. A tableland deeply dissected by valleys, it has steep cliffs and ridges. There is relatively little flat ground available. Standing in the trade winds, St Helena has a cool tropical maritime climate, dry at sea-level but moist enough for farming on the heights. The population of about 5,000, mainly of East Indian descent, produce potatoes and other vegetables and raise cattle, sheep and goats on small-holdings. Cultivable land is scarce and many are unemployed. St Helena is a British colony, heavily dependent on subsidies. (BS)

TRISTAN DA CUNHA

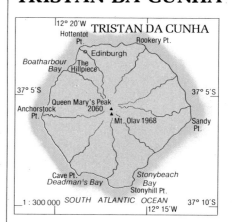

One of four scattered islands toward the southern end of the Mid-Atlantic Ridge, Tristan da Cunha is a volcanic cone 2,060 m (6,760 ft) high, ringed by a lava plain that drops steeply to the sea; a narrow strip of flat ground 8 km (5 miles) long accommodates the settlement of about 300 inhabitants. The climate is mild and damp with frequent storms; the islanders grow potatoes and rear sheep and cattle for their own use. The island was evacuated 1961–63 following a volcanic eruption. Nightingale and Inaccessible Islands are small, uninhabited islands nearby; Gough Island, 400 km (250 miles) to the south-east, is a steep, craggy forest-covered island some 13 km (8 miles) long; its only

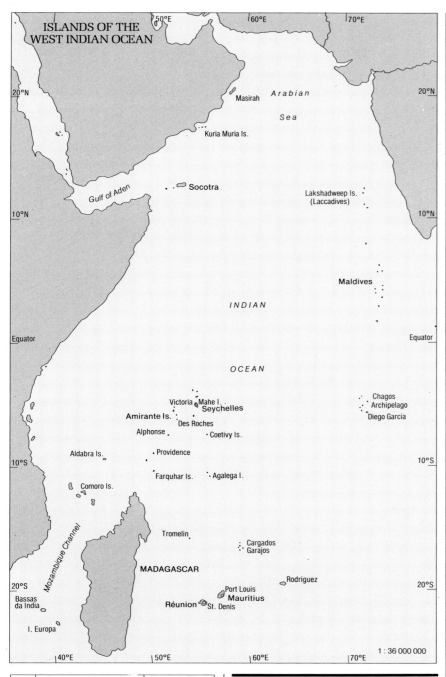

ISLANDS OF THE WEST INDIAN OCEAN

1 : 36 000 000

GOUGH ISLAND

1 : 250 000

9° 55'W

settlement is a weather-station. All are administered as dependencies of St Helena. (BS)

INDIAN OCEAN

THE SEYCHELLES

The Seychelles include a compact group of 4 large and 36 small granitic islands, and a wide scattering of coralline islands (14 of them inhabited) lying mainly to south and west; of the total land area of about 280 km² (108 sq miles), 82 per cent lies in the four main islands – Mahé, Praslin, Silhouette and La Digue; these also include 98 per cent of the population of about 62,000. Mahé is mountainous, rising to 906 m (2,971 ft). With a tropical oceanic climate the Seychelles are warm and humid; they produce copra, cinnamon and tea and grow food for local consumption; fishing and tourism are important industries. Formerly a British colony, the islands became independent in 1976. The capital, Victoria, is on Mahé. (BS)

BRITISH INDIAN OCEAN TERRITORY

An administrative unit formed in 1965, BIOT includes the Chagos Archipelago and the distant islands of Farquhar, Desroches and Aldabra in the Seychelles group. These are small coralline atolls rising from shallow plateaux of the Indian Ocean, with a total land area of about 230 km² (90 sq miles). The tropical marine climate supports coconut plantations; the population of about 300 are imported seasonally to work copra and guano deposits. Aldabra houses a scientific base, for study of the giant tortoises and other unique fauna and flora. (BS)

COMORO ISLANDS

Lying between Mozambique and Madagascar, the Comoros include four large volcanic islands and several smaller coral islands; their total land area is 2,236 km² (863 sq miles). The large islands are mountainous, with high plateaux and crags. Grande Comoro, the largest, rises to 2,361 m (7,746 ft) and is volcanically active. Hot and well watered, with fertile though porous soils, the islands were originally forested; now cultivated, they are mostly under subsistence agriculture and produce coconuts, spices, coffee and cocoa for export. The population of about 320,000 are of mixed Malay, Arab and Malagasy stock. Formerly French, the islands now form an independent republic. (BS)

MASCARENE ISLANDS

These include the volcanic islands of Réunion, Mauritius and Rodriguez; the Cargados Carajos and Agalega atolls are associated dependencies.

Réunion is an ovate mountainous island of 2,512 km² (970 sq miles); the tallest peak, Piton de Neiges, 3,071 m (10,070 ft) high, is sporadically active. It lies within cool southeast trade winds in winter, receiving heavy rainfall on the weather side; summers are calm and oppressively hot. Heavily populated (about 500,000) with people of mixed Arab, Negro, European and East Indian stock, it is mainly agricultural, producing cane sugar, spices and fruit for export. Formerly a French colony, it is now an overseas département of France. The population is growing, and there is substantial emigration to Madagascar and France.

Mauritius, a slightly smaller island of 2,000 km² (772 sq miles) lies 700 km (440 miles) north-east of Réunion. Fringed with coral reefs, it has a high lava plateau rising to a southern massif with a peak of 826 m (2,711 ft). Similar to Réunion in climate and soils, it produces cane sugar (accounting for 90 per cent of exports), tea and tobacco, also vegetables and livestock mainly for home consumption. The population (about 925,000) includes many of Indian stock, with Africans, Chinese, Malagasys and Europeans. Originally a French possession, Mauritius became a British colony in 1810, and achieved independence within the British Commonwealth in 1968. Unemployment is a major problem among the large and growing population.

Rodriguez, a much smaller island of 110 km² (42 sq miles), is a dependency of Mauritius lying 560 km (350 miles) to the east. Its population of about 25,000, mainly of African and Indian stock, are mostly subsistence farmers and fishermen. Cargados Carajos (St Brandon's Rocks), 400 km (250 miles) north of Mauritius, are also administered as dependencies. They are mainly coral atolls used as bases for commercial fishing. The Agalega Islands, a further 550 km (340 miles) north, are atolls used for copra production. (BS)

THE COCOS (KEELING) ISLANDS

These consist of two coral atolls with some 28 islands of total land area 14 km² (5.5 sq miles), isolated in the eastern Indian Ocean. Settled since 1826 and a British colony from 1857, they have a tropical maritime climate with rainfall adequate for coconut growing. Many of the islands are coconut plantations, in the care of about 600 inhabitants, mostly of Malayan or British stock. Only Home, Direction and West Islands are permanently inhabited. The islands became external territories of Australia in 1955. (BS)

THE SOUTHERN ISLANDS

In the southern Indian Ocean lie six isolated groups of grassy and heath-covered islands, uninhabited except for scientific bases. Mainly volcanic, they stand in the west wind belt, with cool, overcast and stormy climates throughout the year. Most are snow-covered for at least part of winter; Kerguelen and Heard Island are mountainous enough to have permanent ice-caps. Surrounded by rich seas, they have immense populations of breeding seals, and of sea birds including penguins, albatrosses and storm petrels. Amsterdam, St Paul, Kerguelen and Iles Crozet are overseas territories of France. Marion and Prince Edward Islands are South African, and McDonald and Heard Islands are external territories of Australia. (BS)

Climate

Small, low-lying oceanic islands have stable temperature regimes controlled by the surface temperatures of their oceans. Cool-temperate and temperate islands, lying in the belt of westerly winds, are cool and stormy in winter, warmer and more placid in summer; only the highest ones carry permanent ice or snow on their mountains. Subtropical and tropical islands lie mostly in the trade wind belts. Those that are low-lying tend to be dry at sea-level, but wet enough to support natural forest or agriculture on higher ground, where damp air forced upward yields its moisture as rain. Tropical storms bring additional rains to many islands.

LOCALITY HEIGHT		JAN	JUL	YR
ATLANTIC ISLANDS				
Azores (Horta)	°C	14.4	21.6	17.7
60 m	mm	125	32	1028
Madeira (Funchal)	°C	16.1	21.4	18.6
25 m	mm	63	Tr	546
Canary Is (Tenerife)	°C	17.4	24.2	20.8
46 m	mm	36	0	252
Cape Verde Is (Porto de Praia)	°C	22.5	26.1	24.7
34 m	mm	3	5	259
Ascension I (Georgetown)	°C	26.1	25.6	26.1
17 m	mm	5	13	132
St Helena (Jamestown)	°C	23.6	19.7	21.7
12 m	mm	8	8	137
Tristan da Cunha	°C	17.0	11.5	14.2
23 m	mm	89	155	1679

LOCALITY HEIGHT		JAN	JUL	YR
INDIAN OCEAN ISLANDS				
Seychelles (Port Victoria)	°C	26.4	25.6	26.4
5 m	mm	386	84	2350
Comoro Is (Moroni)	°C	27.0	23.6	25.6
59 m	mm	424	295	2883
Cocos (Keeling) I	°C	27.5	26.1	27.1
5 m	mm	137	221	1986
Rodriguez I	°C	27.0	22.2	24.7
43 m	mm	140	86	1323
Mauritius I	°C	26.4	20.3	23.3
55 m	mm	216	58	1285
Amsterdam I	°C	16.5	10.9	13.5
27 m	mm	109	116	1157
Marion I	°C	6.7	3.7	5.1
26 m	mm	194	228	2451
Iles Kerguelen	°C	7.2	1.1	3.9
16 m	mm	81	63	925
Heard I	°C	3.3	-0.8	1.1
5 m	mm	147	91	1379

1 *Children poling a native dug-out canoe in Okavango Swamp, Botswana. The swamp is an area of inland drainage.*
2 *Lake Nakuru, Kenya and (5) Lake Abayita, Ethiopia are two examples of the chain of elongated lakes in the African rift valley system.*
3 *The foliage of the coconut palm, and the papaya (centre), Kenya.*
4 *Namaqualand in flower, north-west Cape Province, South Africa.*

AFRICA

5

There is always something new out of Africa.

Pliny the Elder, *Natural History*, Book viii, Section 17

AFRICA

Lying athwart the Equator, but extending to some 35° north and south, the vast continent of Africa covers a wide range of environments. The Sahara Desert stretches across northern Africa from west to east, containing the mountain massifs of Hoggar and Tibesti; lowlands to the east are threaded through from south to north by the Nile river valley. Mediterranean Africa, lying north of the Sahara, includes the sharply folded and eroded Atlas Mountains; the coastal and Nile valley lands were the home of the ancient civilization of Egypt, with rich evidence of early Phoenician, Greek, Roman and Moslem contacts.

South of the Sahara, Africa may be divided by the 1,000 m (3,000 ft) contour line running from the south-west (Angola) to the north-east (Ethiopia). North of this line the low plateaux of central and west Africa surround the great basins of the Congo and Niger rivers and the inland basin of Lake Chad. Here are Africa's major areas of tropical rain forest with savanna dominant on the inner and higher ground. East and south of the 1,000 m (3,000 ft) contour lie Africa's highest plateaux and mountain massifs, and the complex rift-valley systems of north-eastern and eastern Africa.

The rift valleys of east Africa are part of the most extensive fissure in the earth's crust, extending south from the Dead Sea, down the Red Sea, across the Ethiopian Highlands, through Kenya to reach the sea again near the mouth of the Zambezi. Both this main rift and its principal branch to the west of Lake Victoria contain deep, long lakes of which Tanganyika, Turkana (formerly Rudolf), and Nyasa are the largest. The rift valleys are also associated with great snow-capped peaks – notably Kilimanjaro and Mt Kenya. Here also are the high, open and grassy savanna plains with most of Africa's famous wild life game parks. South and west of the Zambezi river system lie the arid uplands of the Kalahari and Namib deserts, and the dry highlands of Namibia. In the far south a damper climate brings Mediterranean conditions to the plains of South Africa, and to the Drakensberg and Cape Ranges.

The Sahara Desert formed a

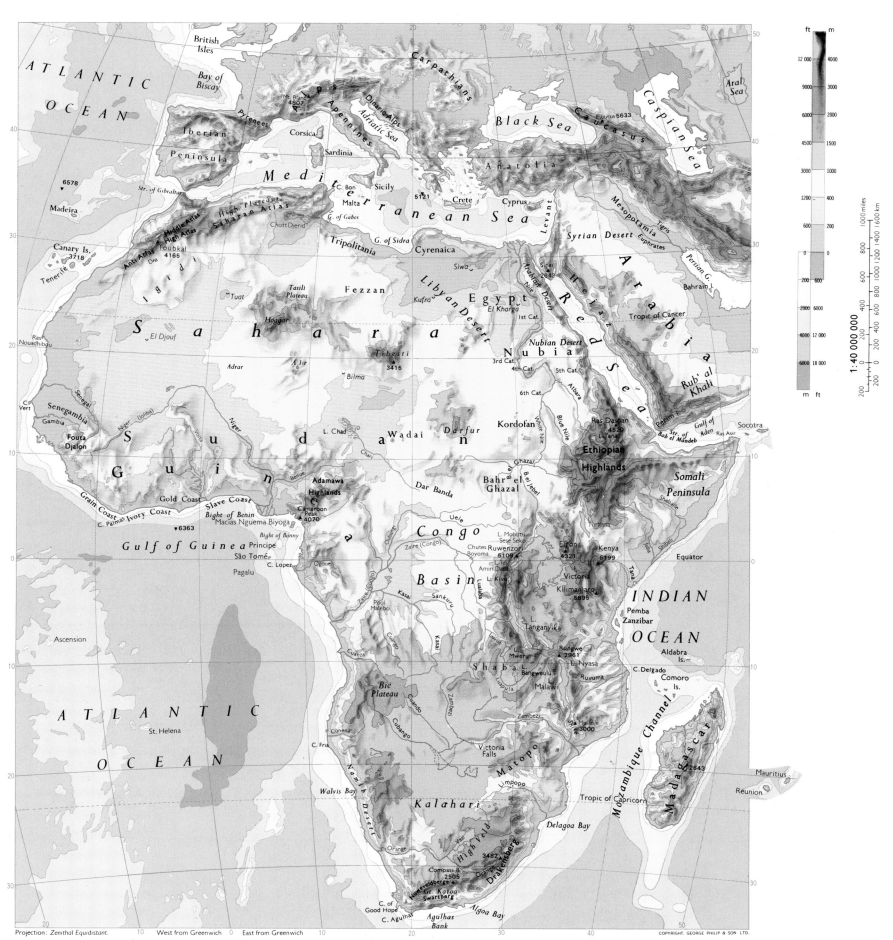

Projection: Zenithal Equidistant.   West from Greenwich   East from Greenwich   COPYRIGHT. GEORGE PHILIP & SON LTD.

barrier that was at least partly responsible for delaying European penetration; Africa south of the Sahara remained the 'Dark Continent' for Europeans until well into the nineteenth century. The last fifteen years of the century saw the final stages of the European 'scramble for Africa', that resulted in most of the continent being partitioned between and colonized by Britain, France, Germany, Belgium, Portugal and Spain. Today almost all of the fifty-odd states of Africa are independent, though traces of their recent colonial history are still evident in their official languages, administrative institutions, legal and educational systems, architecture, transport networks and economics: even the very crops they grow were in many cases introduced by Europeans.

The colonial pattern, and the current political pattern succeeding it, were superimposed on a very complex and fluid system of indigenous states and cultures, many of which have proved to be remarkably resilient. There are many hundreds of ethnic groups, languages and religions; indeed the peoples of Africa themselves are of many physical types, at many different levels of economic, social and political development, and they have reacted in differing ways to the impact of European colonial rule. Just as there is no such thing as a typical African landscape, so there is no such person as a typical African: the peoples of Africa are culturally just as heterogeneous as (and certainly no more 'backward' than) the indigenous peoples of any other continent. The pattern is complicated still further by the infusion of European, Asian, Arab and 'mixed' minorities – the British, Dutch and other 'Whites' of South Africa, the Asians of Kenya and the Lebanese of West Africa are typical examples of these groups.

To the outside world today Africa is a continent wracked by the internal conflicts of its states – racial, ethnic and political conflicts, intractable economic problems, and outside political interference. Each state is now striving with varying degrees of success and in its own way to meet and overcome these problems and challenges. (BH)

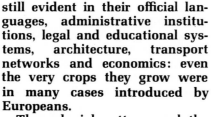

MOROCCO

The name Morocco is derived from the Arabic *Maghreb-el-Aksa* (the Farthest West). Over the centuries the country's high mountains have acted as a barrier to penetration, so that Morocco has been much less affected by outside influences than Algeria and Tunisia. Morocco was the last North African territory to succumb to European colonialism; not until 1912 did the Sultan of Morocco accept the French protectorate, in a settlement that also gave Spain control of the Rif mountains, but not the city of Tangier (Tanger), which was later internationalized.

In 1956 France and Spain gave up their protectorate, and by 1958 the Tangier zone was incorporated in a unified Morocco, which became an independent kingdom.

Economic Development

Of the total Moroccan population of about 19 million, some two-thirds speak Arabic and one-third Berber. Since independence a large proportion of the once-important European and Jewish communities have departed. Independence brought many problems. To the difficulties accompanying reunification were added the burdens of a fast-growing population, high unemployment and lack of trained personnel and capital. Yet Morocco has considerable potential for economic development. The country possesses large cultivable areas, abundant water supplies for irrigation and hydro-electric power, and diverse mineral resources.

Two principal ways of life exist in the mountains – peasant cultivation and semi-nomadic pastoralism. In contrast to these modern economic development is found in the Atlantic plains and plateaux. The major irrigation schemes created during the colonial period are situated here – on the Wadis Sebou, Oum er Rbia and N'fis. Phosphates, of which Morocco is the world's leading exporter, are mined around Khouribga, and the country's modern industry is concentrated in the Atlantic ports, particularly in Casablanca which is the largest city, chief port and major manufacturing centre. (RL)

Western Sahara

Western Sahara occupies a coastal strip between Mauritania and Morocco. After the withdrawal of the Spanish in 1975, the administration of this desert territory and a population of under 140,000 people was divided between Morocco, which annexed the northern two-thirds, and Mauritania. In 1979, after the withdrawal of the Mauritanian administration, Morocco occupied the southern portion of the former colony as well. However a resistance movement, the Polisario Front, which is supported by Algeria, is actively opposed to the annexation and in 1976 they proclaimed the Saharan Arab Democratic Republic. The United Nations has recognized the right of the people of Western Sahara to self-determination and independence, and the Moroccan occupation is not recognized by the international community. (On the map the boundary between Mauritania and Morocco divides Western Sahara between them, the northern two-thirds appearing in Morocco.)

Western Sahara is entirely desert and the population density is extremely low (1 person per 5 km², 2 sq miles). (DC)

ALGERIA

With an area of 2,381,741 km² (919,600 sq miles) Algeria is the largest of the three Maghreb countries and, after Sudan, the biggest political unit in the Middle East and Africa. However over nine-tenths of the country's 18.5 million inhabitants live in the northern coastlands. The vast Saharan territories, covering over 2 million km² (772,200 sq miles) or about 85 per cent of the total area, are very sparsely populated; most of the inhabitants are concentrated in the oases, which form densely-populated islands separated by vast empty areas. The majority of the population speak Arabic, but there is a significant Berber-speaking minority in the mountainous north-east.

Like her neighbours Morocco and Tunisia, Algeria experienced French colonial rule and settler colonization. Algeria was the first Maghreb country conquered by France and the last to receive independence. European settlers acquired over a quarter of the cultivated land, mainly in north-western Algeria, and rural colonization transformed the plains, producing cash crops.

Recent Economic Development

Oil was discovered in the Algerian Sahara in 1956 and Algeria's natural gas reserves are among the largest in the world. Since independence in 1962 revenues from oil and gas, which provide over 90 per cent of the country's exports, have enabled the government to embark on an ambitious economic development programme, with rapid industrialization, but neglect of agriculture. (RL)

The Atlas Mountains

December in a cultivated valley in the High Atlas near Marrakech.

Extending from Morocco into northern Algeria and Tunisia, the Atlas is a prominent range of fold mountains. Its highest peak, Jebel Toubkal (4,165 m, 13,670 ft) is one of a jagged row – the High Atlas – in central Morocco; the lesser ranges cluster on either side and to the east, generally with a north-east to south-west trend. Heavily glaciated during the Ice Age, the highest Atlas ranges are now capped with alpine tundra and patches of permanent snow. North-facing slopes receive good winter rainfall, especially on the seaward side of the western ranges, and are forested with pines, cedars, and evergreen and cork oaks.

Tablelands between the ranges provide high pastures and rich soils for farming. The southern and eastern ranges are drier and covered with semi-desert scrub, providing rough pastures and poor cultivation.

Formerly linked to Spain during short spells of geological history, the Atlas Mountains support both European and African plants and animals. The Algerian bear and wild ass and the Barbary lion, once plentiful, are now extinct. Small populations of deer, closely akin to European Red deer, graze with Barbary sheep and Dorcas gazelles among the high peaks, and Barbary apes steal crops. (BS)

LIBYA

Libya covers a total area of 1,760,000 km² (680,000 sq miles). Rainfall averages less than 50 mm (2 in) a year for 90 per cent of the country, and desert landscapes predominate with extensive sand seas in the south and east. Only the two uplands in the north, the Jebel Nafusah and the Jebel Akhdar, are relatively well-watered. These two upland areas, together with the Jefara plain between the Jebel Nefusah and the sea, contain the most important agricultural areas, as well as most of the country's inhabitants and the two major cities – Tripoli, the capital, and Benghazi.

After a period of considerable prosperity under Roman rule, Libya was conquered by the Arabs in the seventh century AD and in the sixteenth century came under Ottoman rule. In 1912 the country became an Italian colony, and much of the best agricultural land in the coastlands was expropriated and granted to Italian settlers. At independence in 1951 Libya was considered to be one of the poorest countries in the world, with few known natural resources, a difficult environment and a population which was largely nomadic, poor and backward in almost every respect. This bleak picture changed dramatically with the discovery and development of the country's oil resources after 1959. With growing revenues from petroleum exports, important new highways have been built to link the different regions, and considerable investment has been made in education, housing and health provision. Since the Revolution in 1969, emphasis has been given to agricultural development and industrialization, and Libya has become heavily dependent on foreign workers. (RL)

A livestock market in Tunisia. Sheep, goats and cattle are reared.

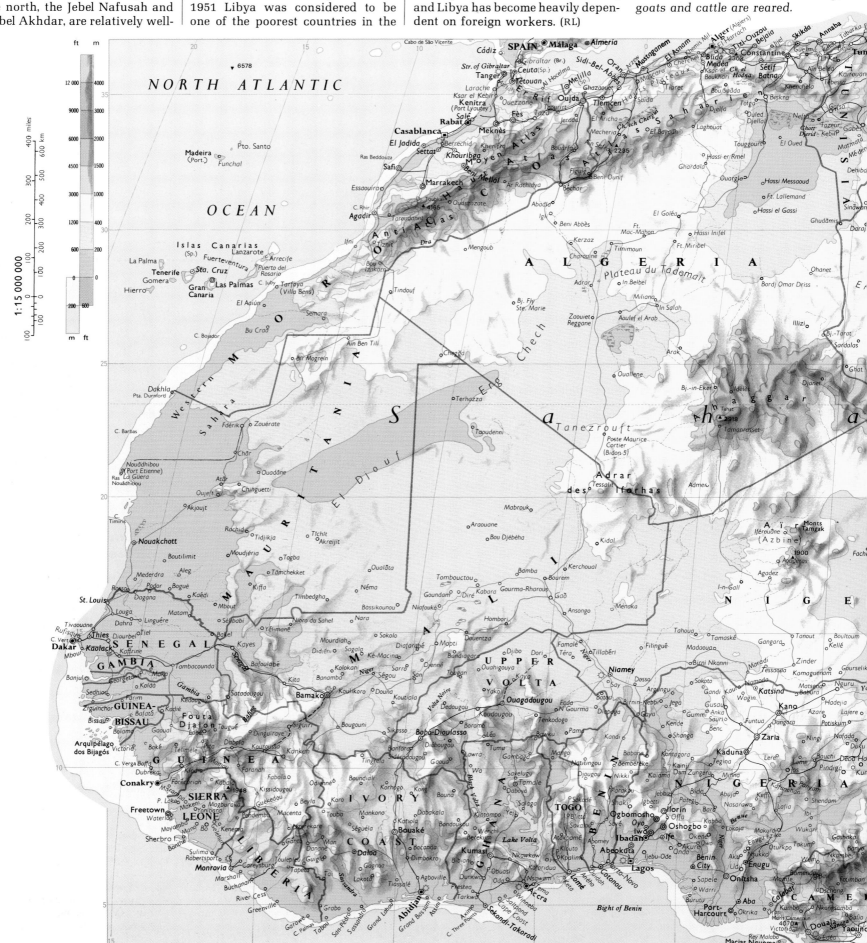

TUNISIA

Tunisia, 164,150 km² (63,400 sq miles), is the smallest of the three countries that comprise north-west Africa, but it has a long and rich history. It was the first part of the region to be conquered by the Phoenicians, Romans and later the Arabs, and each successive civilization has left a marked impression on the country. Consequently Tunisia has acquired a distinct national identity, and has a long tradition of urban life. Close contacts with Europe have always existed, and France established a protectorate in 1881.

The country possesses only a few modest resources, and since independence has faced severe economic and social problems. Nevertheless the government has embarked upon ambitious programmes to modernize agriculture, introduce industries, improve social services and reduce the high level of unemployment.

Tunisia consists of the eastern end of the Atlas Mountains together with the central steppelands to the south which are separated from the country's Saharan sector by the vast Chott el Djerid. In the north the lower Medjerda valley and the low-lying plains of Bizerta and Tunis were densely colonized. Major irrigation schemes have been carried out in recent years and these lowlands, which produce cereals, vines, citrus fruits and vegetables, represent the country's most important agricultural area. New industries, sometimes coupled with tourism, have transformed a number of coastal towns, for example, Sfax, Monastir and Sousse. By comparison the interior has been neglected. (RL)

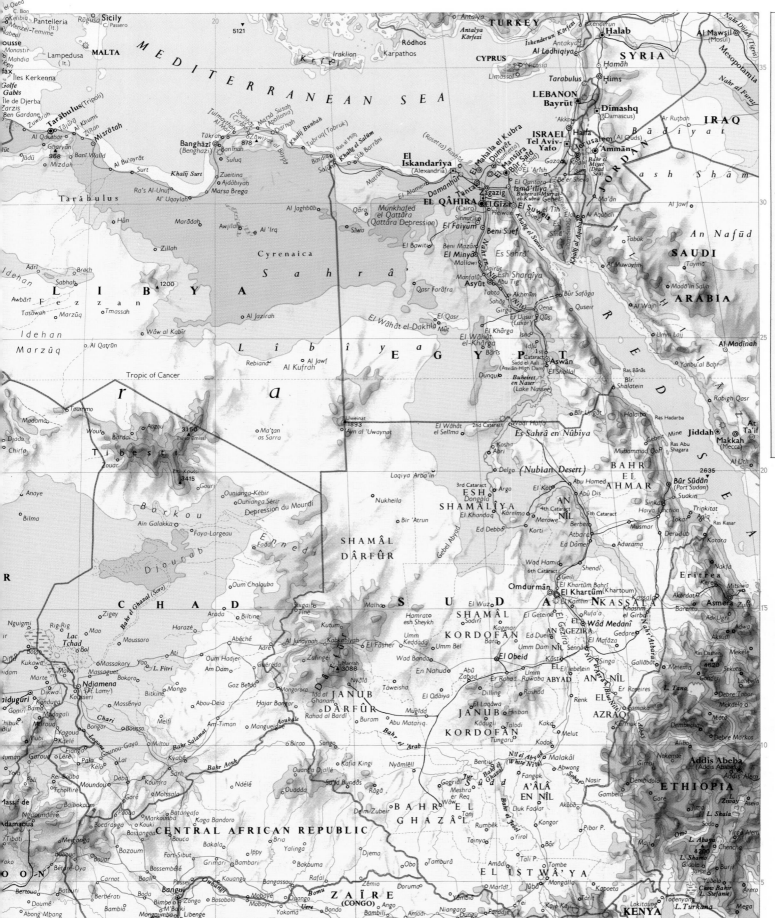

Climate

The northern third of Africa, crossed by the Tropic of Cancer, lies squarely under the influence of a dry continental air mass throughout the year. Annual rainfall is less than 40 cm (16 in) over most of the area, and very much less throughout the Sahara core. Mean monthly temperatures exceed 24°C (75°F) over most of the Sahara and 36°C (97°F) over the hottest parts in July; winters are cool (8° to 10°C, 46.5° to 50°F) in the north, but approach summer means in the south. The Atlas region, cooled by trade winds, has a gentler climate with plentiful winter rains. The Sahel, bounding the southern Sahara, has unreliable summer rains that may fail altogether over several years.

LOCALITY HEIGHT		JAN	JUL	YR
Tunis	°C	11.0	25.9	18.3
4 m	mm	70	1	466
Casablanca	°C	12.4	22.5	17.6
58 m	mm	66	0.	426
Béchar	°C	9.2	34.0	21.1
806 m	mm	7	0	90
El Qâhira	°C	14.0	28.9	22.0
74 m	mm	4	0	22
Nouadhibou	°C	19.5	22.2	21.7
4 m	mm	3	Tr	36
Tessalit	°C	20.1	34.5	28.7
494 m	mm	1	23	118
Bûr Sûdân	°C	24.4	33.7	28.3
2 m	mm	4	9	110
Kaduna	°C	23.5	24.2	25.02
644 m	mm	Tr	216	1273
Freetown	°C	26.7	25.9	26.7
11 m	mm	13	894	3434
Lagos	°C	26.7	24.4	26.2
6 m	mm	40	150	1625

MAURITANIA

Two-thirds of the Islamic Republic of Mauritania consist of rocky and sandy desert wastes. Less than 10 per cent of the population live in towns. Apart from the main north-south highway and routes associated with mineral developments, surface communications consist of rough tracks.

Only in the southern third of the country and along the Atlantic Coast is precipitation sufficient to support sahelian thorn bush and grasslands. Apart from oasis settlements such as Atar and Tidjikdja the only permanent arable agriculture is in the south, where it is concentrated in a narrow strip along the Senegal river. Crops of millet, sorghum, beans, peanuts and rice are grown, often using the natural late summer floods for irrigation. When the Senegal River Project is complete large areas should be developed for irrigated crops of rice, cotton, and sugar cane.

About three-quarters of the population are cattle herders who drive their herds from the Senegal river through the Sahel steppelands in step with the seasonal rains. In good years the country's livestock outnumber the human population by about five to one, but during periods of drought overgrazing is widespread and more than half may die.

Off the Atlantic coast the cold Canaries Current is associated with a rich fishing ground. However the national fishing industry is still evolving and only about 30,000 tonnes of fish are landed each year at the major fishing port of Nouadhibou (Port Etienne).

As the Atlantic coast in the south of the country lacks good harbours, a port and capital city have been constructed at Nouakchott. This now handles a growing proportion of the country's trade, including exports of copper which are mined near Akjoujt. Exported minerals, particularly high-grade iron ores which are worked near F'Dérik, provide the country with most of its foreign revenue, though animal products, gum arabic, and dates are also exported. (DC)

MALI

Mali is a large sparsely populated country consisting mainly of desert plains. Water dominates the life of the people and most of the population is concentrated along the Senegal and Niger rivers, which besides providing water for stock and irrigation, serve as much needed communication routes. The Niger and its tributaries support a fishing industry that exports dried fish to Ivory Coast, Upper Volta and Ghana. With the exception of small areas in the south of the country, irrigation is necessary for all arable crops. The Sudan savanna grasslands and highland areas in the south-east are often tsetse-free, and large numbers of sheep and cattle are traditionally kept in the area, though periodic drought may severely reduce their numbers. The northern portion of the country is barren desert.

Millet, cotton and groundnuts are important crops on the unirrigated lands of the south, while rice is intensively grown with irrigation. A large irrigation scheme has been developed near Ségou which produces rice, cotton and sugar cane, and there are many smaller schemes. Strict socialist policies disrupted agricultural development in the decade after independence (1959); though these have been relaxed, the embryonic manufacturing industries producing shoes, matches, beer and textiles are still largely state controlled. (DC)

UPPER VOLTA

Land-locked Upper Volta is the successor to Mossi, one of West Africa's earliest states dating from AD 1100. As large as Italy, and with only about 6.5 million inhabitants, it is nevertheless over-populated; low, seasonal and erratic rainfall, thin, eroded and mainly lateritic soils, and dearth of other resources combine to keep Upper Volta one of the poorest states in the world.

The Mossi people, who are the majority tribe, live around Ouagadougou, the capital; another major group, the Bobo, dwell around Bobo Dioulasso. Both grow cotton and millet, guinea corn (sorghum) and groundnuts for food, and collect shea nuts for cooking oil. Nomadic Fulani keep cattle. Small surpluses of all these products are sold overseas and to the better-off countries to the south, especially the Ivory Coast; however, remittances sent home by migrants working in those countries probably provide most of Upper Volta's income from overseas. Manganese mining could be developed at Tambao in the far northeast, though this would necessitate a 340 km (210 mile) extension to the railway from Abidjan (Ivory Coast), which is already 1,145 km (715 miles) long. Another hope lies in eliminating the simulium fly, whose bite causes blindness. This would permit settlement and farming of the valleys, where the most fertile and best watered lands are found. (RH-C)

NIGER

Most of the northern portion of this large, mid-continental, land-locked country consists of hot, arid, sandy or stony basins, lateritic plateaux and isolated hills. Occasionally in areas such as the Aïr Mountains, where the rainfall is more reliable, or where groundwater lies near to the surface, patches of thorn scrub may occur. Only in the most southerly portion of the country is rainfall adequate for arable agriculture, and less than 5 per cent of the country is cultivated. Irrigation schemes are being developed along the Niger, to produce rice, maize and cotton, but about three-quarters of the population are still dependent on crops of millet, sorghum and groundnuts, grown by slash-burn cultivation techniques. About one-fifth of the population are herdsmen who keep large numbers of cattle in the areas of grassland and thorn scrub.

Zinder and Maradi are the main markets for groundnuts and probably the most important centres for commerce, though the capital Niamey is growing in importance. Deposits of tin and tungsten are mined in the Aïr Mountains and large uranium deposits are worked by the French Atomic Energy Commission and the Niger government. Apart from the development of these minerals, the country has little industry except for the processing of agricultural produce and building materials. (DC)

CHAD

Chad is a sprawling land-locked state with poor communications, few urban settlements and virtually no industries except for the processing of agricultural products. Ninety per cent of the population make a living from crop cultivation, or by herding animals.

In the north a sparse nomadic Arabic population live in a harsh, hot desert which contains extensive tracts of mobile dunes (Erg du Djourab), and the volcanic Tibesti mountains.

The wetter southern portions of the country are covered by wooded savanna and crops of cotton, groundnuts, millet and sorghum are grown by settled black cultivators. A wide band of sahelian thorn bush occupies the greater part of the central area of the country and provides pasturage for large numbers of migratory cattle and considerable herds of game and wildlife.

Lake Chad, a large shallow body of water which fluctuates greatly in size, is the focal point of much of the country's drainage. Most water feeding the Lake comes from the rivers Chari and Logone which are the only large perennial water courses in the country. Agriculture and population are concentrated along their valleys and in the vicinity of Lake Chad. Fishing is locally important. Dried fish is exported, but sales of cotton, meat and other animal products provide most exports. (DC)

EGYPT

Egypt, with the longest-known history of any country in Africa, has an area of 1,001,450 km² (386,660 sq miles), most of which is desert. But for the River Nile, that brings the waters of the East African and Ethiopian Highlands to the Mediterranean, Egypt would scarcely be populated, for 96 per cent of the present population lives in the Nile valley and its rich delta. Egypt was nominally under Turkey for much of

A phosphate mine in Niger. Traces of several minerals have been found, but to date exploitation of tin, tungsten and uranium is most important.

the time from the first century AD to the nineteenth century, and a British protectorate from 1882 to 1922. Sultan Mohammed Ali established a dynasty in 1841 which continued until 1952–3, when a revolutionary government led by General Neguib and Colonel Nasser took over and made Egypt a republic.

The Desert

Egypt's deserts are not uniform, but offer varied landscapes. Beyond the Gulf of Suez and the Suez Canal the Sinai Peninsula in the south is mountainous and rugged. It contains the highest of Egypt's mountains (Jebel Katherina, 2,637 m, 8,650 ft) and is almost entirely uninhabited. The Eastern Desert, between the Nile and the Red Sea, is a much dissected area and parts of the Red Sea Hills are over 2,000 m (6,560 ft). Water is obtained from the light rainfall, from occasional springs, and from beneath dry stream beds. Except for a few mining settlements along the coast this area is not suitable for permanent settlement and is occupied only by nomads.

The Western Desert includes almost three-quarters of Egypt and consists of low vales and scarps, mainly of limestones. Over its stony and sandy surfaces great tank battles were fought in World War 2. A number of depressions in the desert surface fall below sea level, the most notable being the Qattara Depression (−133 m, −435 ft), a waste of salt lakes and marshes. There are a number of oases, the most important being Khârga, Dakhla, Farâfra, Baharîya and Siwa. By drawing on deep-seated artesian waters it is hoped to expand the farming area of the first four as a contribution to the solution of Egypt's present population problem. Except at the oases the desert is uninhabited.

The Nile

The Nile Valley was one of the cradles of civilization. The dependable annual flooding of the great river each summer and the discovery of the art of cultivating wheat and barley fostered simple irrigation techniques and favoured cooperation between the farmers. Stability and leisure developed arts and crafts, city life began and the foundations were laid of writing, arithmetic, geometry and astronomy. Great temples and pyramid tombs within the valley remain today as memorials of this early civilization.

Today, even more than in the past, the Egyptian people, living within a desert, depend almost entirely on the waters of the Nile. These are extremely seasonal, and control and storage have become essential during this century. For seasonal storage the Aswan Dam (1902) and the Jebel Awliya Dam in Sudan (1936) were built. The Aswan High Dam (1967) sited 6.4 km (4 miles) above the Aswan Dam, is the greatest of all. It holds back twenty-five times as much as the older Aswan Dam and permits year-round storage. Through

The Nile, the longest river in the world (6,648 km, 4,155 miles).

this dam the Egyptian Nile is now regulated to an even flow throughout the year. The water that has now accumulated behind the dam, in Lake Nasser, is making possible the reclamation of more desert land, the intensification of agriculture and the cultivation of crops that need more water, such as rice for export. The dam is also a source of hydro-electric power and aids the expansion of industry.

Industry

The traditional Egypt of the gallabyia-clad peasant toiling on his tiny plot of land is slowly changing. Pressure of population on the limited amount of farmland is leading to an expansion of industry as an alternative way of life. Today Egypt is the second most industrialized country of Africa (after the Republic of South Africa). Most of this industrial development has come about since World War 2. Textiles, including spinning, weaving, dyeing and printing of cotton, wool, silk and man-made fibres form by far the largest industry. Other manufactures derive from local agricultural and mineral raw materials, and include sugar-refining, milling, oilseed pressing, and the manufacture of chemicals, glass and cement. There are iron and steel, oil-refining and car-assembly industries and many consumer goods such as radios, TV sets and refrigerators are made. The cities of Cairo and Alexandria are the major industrial centres. (AH, AM)

SUDAN

The Sudan, formerly an Anglo-Egyptian Condominium, has been an independent republic since 1956. With an area of 2,505,800 km^2 (967,500 sq miles), this is the largest state of Africa. It consists essentially of vast clay plains and sandy areas, parts of the Nile basin and the Sahara, but it presents two very different landscapes. The extreme north is virtually uninhabited desert; to the south, where the desert gives way to semi-desert, nomads move over age-old tribal areas.

The belt across the centre of the country holds most of the population. Here low rainfall, supplemented by wells and small reservoirs for irrigation, allows subsistence farming, but the bulk of the population lives by or near the Blue and White Niles. This is the Arab part of the Sudan where 70 per cent of the population live, nearly all being Moslems. Near these rivers, and relying on them for irrigation, are a number of modern mechanized farming schemes, headed by the famous Gezira Scheme, one of the first of its kind in the world. Crops grown are cotton and oilseeds for export, sugar cane and sorghum for local consumption. Khartoum stands at the junction of the Blue and White Niles.

Southern Sudan presents a very different landscape. Much of it is a great clay plain, upland fringed and experiencing a heavy annual rainfall. During the rainy season the plain becomes a vast reed-covered swamp and the Nilotic cattle-rearing tribes (Shilluk and Dinka) move to the dry ridges and islands until the floods abate. (AH, AM)

The Sahara

Only about 15 per cent of the Sahara is sand; stony desert is more common.

This is a vast desert of 9,000,000 km^2 (3,500,000 sq miles) that stretches almost 5,000 km (over 3,000 miles) across northern Africa from the Atlantic coast to the Red Sea. Its northern borders abut the Atlas Mountains and the Mediterranean Sea; in the south the desert merges into the poorly-watered steppelands of the Sahel. Dominated by bone-dry air masses, most of it receives less than 10 cm (4 in) of rain per year. Shade temperatures are high, reaching over 50°C (122°F) during the day but falling dramatically, sometimes to freezing point or lower, at night. Vegetation is sparse except at oases, where ground-water rises or is pumped to the surface. Coarse gravel covers 70 per cent of the ground, and shifting sand about 15 per cent. High mountains of volcanic origin break the monotony of the interior, including the Ahaggar of south-eastern Algeria, and the much higher Tibesti of north Chad which rise to 3,300 m (11,000 ft).

The Sahara is far from lifeless. Its human population of about two million are mostly oasis farmers, with a minority of nomadic herdsmen. Mining and drilling for oil and natural gas are recently-developed industries. The patchy vegetation supports a meagre desert fauna of scorpions, beetles, locusts, snakes and skinks. Addax antelopes are among the few large mammals; smaller species include jerboas, that avoid the heat by burrowing, and long-eared fennecs that prey on them. (BS)

GAMBIA

This small low-lying state forms a narrow strip on either side of the river Gambia. Except for the capital Banjul, which is also the major port, no town has a population of more than ten thousand. All the large settlements are on the river, which provides the principal means of communication.

Ninety per cent of the population is rural. Rice is grown in swamps and on the floodplains of the river, while millet, sorghum and cassava are grown by shifting cultivation on the higher ground. Groundnuts are grown by almost every arable farmer, dominating the economy and providing nine-tenths of export earnings. A successful tourist industry has been developed. (DC)

SENEGAL

At independence in 1960 Senegal had a well-planned capital and a top-heavy administration, both legacies from a former role as the administrative centre for French West Africa. One-fifth of the country's population lives in Dakar and the adjacent Cap Vert area. Dakar has large modern docks with bunkering and ship repair facilities and is the major industrial centre.

In the north-east of the country Fulani tribesmen eke out a spartan existence by keeping herds of cattle on the scrub and semi-desert vegetation. In contrast in the south the savanna bushlands are cultivated; cassava, sorghum and rice crops are grown. About half of the cultivated land produces groundnuts, a crop which dominates the country's economy and exports. The only other major exports are phosphates.

In an attempt to diversify and stabilize the economy the government is encouraging tourism, and is involved with Mali and Mauritania in a major scheme to increase irrigated crop production. (DC)

GUINEA

Guinea is a country of varied landscapes, ranging from the grasslands and scattered woodland of the in-

terior highlands and Upper Niger plains, to the swampy mangrove-fringed plains of the Atlantic coast. Dense forests occupy the western foothills of the Fouta Djalon.

Two-thirds of the population are employed in agriculture and food processing. Bananas, palm-oil, pineapples and rice are important crops on the wet coastal plain, whilst in the drier interior cattle are kept by nomadic herdsmen.

After independence Guinea became a socialist state. The large bauxite deposits are partially developed and, with alumina, provide important exports. There is great potential for iron ore mining and hydro-electric power. (DC)

GUINEA-BISSAU

Guinea-Bissau is a land largely composed of swamps and riverine estuaries. On gaining independence in 1974 the country possessed few basic services and agriculture had been severely dislocated by the war of independence. There appear to be no mineral deposits and industrial output is negligible.

About 85 per cent of the active population are subsistence farmers, and a small surplus of groundnuts is exported. Large numbers of livestock are kept on the grasslands in the east, and there is considerable potential for growing irrigated rice and sugar cane. A fishing industry is developing. (DC)

SIERRA LEONE

Freetown, the capital of Sierra Leone, has the best natural harbour in West Africa, and was established as a settlement for freed slaves.

At independence in 1961 three-quarters of the population were employed in subsistence agriculture, yet rice had to be imported, and only small surpluses of palm kernel, coffee and ginger were produced.

Revenues from diamond and iron ore mining, of major importance since the thirties, and other minerals, provide funds for education and agricultural developments, whilst overseas aid has provided a skeletal network of new roads to serve all but the less populated north.

The main centres for the production of coffee, cocoa, and timber products are in the south-east of the

country near Kenema. Rice and palm oil are produced throughout Sierra Leone, except in the drier north, where groundnuts and cattle herding are more important. The Government has established large scale mechanized rice cultivation in the bolilands of the north-west, the seasonally-flooded riverine grasslands of the south-east and the mangrove swamps near Port Loko, in an effort to boost rice production.

In the mid-1970s the iron mine closed, and illicit workings severely affected the alluvial diamond mining industry, which has produced a concentration of population in the Yengema-Koidu area. Fortunately, bauxite production is expanding and production of rutile from large reserves in the Southern Province has begun.

Apart from mills processing oil palm and rice, most factories are in or near Freetown, where there is a concentration of population and the port facilities assist import and export of materials. The Government is aiding a tourist industry and modern hotels have been established on the coast near Freetown. (DC)

LIBERIA

Liberia, which gained independence in 1847, is the oldest independent West African state and lacks a legacy of colonial administration. A sparsely-populated country with large tracts of inaccessible tropical rain forest, Liberia is popularly known for her 'flag of convenience' (used by about one-sixth of the world's commercial shipping), and for large American-owned rubber plantations.

There has been an open door policy towards foreign entrepreneurs, and the economy has developed rapidly following the exploitation of large iron ore deposits by foreign companies. Though diamonds and gold have long been worked, iron ore accounts for about half the value of all exports. The economy is a mixture of large foreign-

owned corporations operating mines and plantations, and of indigenous peoples who still exist largely as shifting subsistence cultivators. The rural economy is dominated by six major rubber companies, pre-eminent amongst which are Firestone, Uniroyal and B.F. Goodrich. These companies produce two-thirds of the rubber, though in 1974 the Government set up state latex processing plants to stimulate local rubber production. Government agreements with foreign companies are being revised to bring direct benefits to the country.

Schemes to increase the production of rice, coffee and palm kernels are being established with the objective of founding a prosperous agricultural economy before the mineral deposits are depleted. The forest resources are being developed by foreign companies, and there are substantial exports of timber, mainly in the form of logs.

There are few manufacturing or processing industries, partly because of the small local market. The establishment of a Customs Union with Sierra Leone should help expand the market and stimulate the small-scale processing plants which currently manufacture a range of items such as plywood, beer, soft drinks, soap and furniture. (DC)

IVORY COAST

Except for Nigeria, the Ivory Coast is the largest Guinea coastal land (322,460 km^2, 124,500 sq miles) – a little larger than Italy. Again except for Nigeria, it lies closest to the Equator, and has substantial forest in the south where the basic resources of coffee, cocoa and timber are produced, and also the lesser crops of bananas and pineapple. The Guinea savanna lands of the centre and north are much less fertile, producing small amounts of sugar, cotton and tobacco that now support developing industries, and food crops important to a rapidly growing market in the capital, Abidjan. Like

Weighing diamonds in Sierra Leone. Diamonds are a major source of income.

Kenya, which is economically comparable, the Ivory Coast has few worked minerals, but manufacturing industries are developing.

In terms of such indices as GNP and international trade figures, the Ivory Coast is one of Africa's most prosperous countries. This show of prosperity was initiated by the Vridi canal, opened in 1950, that made Abidjan a spacious and sheltered deep-water port – a rarity in Africa. Then the Ivory Coast's *laissez-faire* economy has proved attractive to foreign firms, especially French firms, and France has given much aid, particularly for basic services and education. Lastly, on achieving independence, the Ivory Coast freed herself economically from support of seven other countries in the French West African Federation.

Outward prosperity is visually expressed in Abidjan, whose skyline is a minor Manhattan, and where most of the 44,000 French live. However, the cost of living for Ivoriens is high; almost everything is centralized in Abidjan, and there are great human and regional inequalities. Nevertheless, a second port has been developed since 1971 at San Pedro, and efforts are being made to develop other towns and the relatively backward north. (RH-C)

GHANA

Formerly known appropriately as the Gold Coast, the present name was adopted on independence. It recalls the state of Ghana which lay north of the upper Niger from the eighth to the thirteenth centuries, from whose population some of modern Ghana's peoples may be descended. Ghana in 1957 was the first tropical African country to become independent of colonial rule, and until 1966 was led by Dr Nkrumah, prominent in movements for African liberation. Under him the Akosombo dam was completed, providing power to smelt imported alumina into aluminium, and for the main towns, mines and industries in the Takoradi-Kumasi-Tema triangle, the most developed part of the country. To build the dam, a second deep-water port was built at Tema, east of Accra, the capital. Tema is now Ghana's main port for imports and for cocoa export.

Cocoa has been the leading export since 1924, and until the late 1970s Ghana was the world's leading producer. However, neighbouring Ivory Coast is overtaking Ghana both in this and in forestry production.

Unlike the Ivory Coast, Ghana has long been a producer of minerals – gold has been exploited for a thousand years. However, production of most minerals is currently static or

A lake-side village in Togo.

declining. The few remaining gold mines, with the notable exception of Obuasi, are now scarcely economic. Manganese production was recently revived to meet a new demand in battery manufacture; the substantial reserves of bauxite remain undeveloped while imported alumina is used in the Tema aluminium smelter. Industrial diamonds contribute modestly to Ghana's economy.

Ghana thus has diversified resource development, although cocoa production remains dominant. Aluminium manufacture, which is merely refining an import with local power for re-export, has not proved especially advantageous, and Ghana has fallen far behind the neighbouring Ivory Coast in pace of development. (RH-C)

TOGO

Togo is a small country nowhere more than 120 km (75 miles) wide, though it stretches inland from the Gulf of Guinea for some 500 km (312 miles) between Ghana to the west and Benin to the east. The Togo-Atacora Mountains cross the country from south-west to north-east. In the south-west the major forests and cash crops are found.

The railway inland from the coast stops at Blitta, in central Togo, and the road is the only means of keeping the poorer, drier northern parts of this awkwardly shaped country in touch with the more developed areas of the south, including the capital and main port of Lomé and the important phosphate mining area with its port of Kpémé. Phosphates, coffee and cocoa are the important exports, but major food crops are cassava, yams, maize and sorghum-millets. (BH)

BENIN

Formerly known as Dahomey (the name of an old kingdom centred on Abomey), Benin extends some 620 km (390 miles) north to south, although the coastline is a mere 100 km (62 miles) long.

After the Dutch expelled the Portuguese from the Gold Coast in 1642, they established their West African head-quarters at Ouidah where, until 1961, there was a tiny Portuguese enclave. Several million slaves were shipped from here, mainly to Brazil, where Dahomean customs survive among negroes. Because of early European contact, and through returned ex-slaves, coastal Benin early acquired an educated élite, as did Senegal, Sierra Leone and Gabon. Once prominent as clerks and teachers in former French West Africa, many of these are now unemployed. Benin has little to sell except oil palm produce; fees from Niger's transit trade through Cotonou are an important additional source of revenue. (RH-C)

NIGERIA

Four times the size of the United Kingdom (923,770 km², 356,670 sq miles), Nigeria is tropical Africa's most important country. Ranking seventh as a world producer of oil, there are many other resources (albeit dwarfed in exports by oil),

including cocoa in the south-west, timber, rubber and oil palm in the south-centre and east, and cotton and groundnuts in the north. These reflect the latitudinal (4–14°N) and altitudinal extent of the country; highlands rise to over 1,830 m (6,000 ft). There are over 70 million Nigerians, making it by far the most populous African state; one in every six Africans is Nigerian. Nigeria is also the second or third most populated country of the Commonwealth, and in the world's top ten. Natural wealth and substantial armed forces give Nigeria a commanding position in Africa, and the oil reserves are a focus of world-wide interest.

Nigeria is unique in Africa south of the Sahara for the numerous pre-colonial towns of the south-west (for example, Ibadan) and the north (for example, Kano). Domestic trade between these and Nigeria's very varied regions was developed in pre-colonial days, and is now intense.

Nigeria is a federation of nineteen states, many of which are larger than most independent African states. It includes many tribal groups, the largest being the Yoruba of the south-west, the Igbo (Ibo) of the east, and the Hausa, Fulani and Kanuri of the north. The north is Islamic, and Islam is increasing in the south, where most people are Pagan or Christian. With so many diversities, including those of religion and a developing social system, Nigeria suffers internal stresses and national unity is often strained. (RH-C)

CAMEROON

Half the size of neighbouring Nigeria, Cameroon has only one-ninth the population. The mountainous borderlands between them lie on a line of crustal weakness dating from the break-up of the super-continent, Gondwanaland (pp. 8–9). The mountains, mostly volcanic, include Mt Cameroun (4,070 m, 13,350 ft) which is occasionally active.

The word 'Cameroon' is derived from the Portuguese *camarões* – prawns fished by Portuguese explorers' seamen in coastal estuaries. However European contact dates mainly from German rule. Begun in 1884, this was superseded by a French mandate over most of the country from 1916 to 1960. South-western Cameroon was formerly part of a British mandate. The extensive plantations of oil palm, rubber, bananas, and other crops date from colonial times. Douala is Cameroon's main port for exports of cocoa, coffee and aluminium, and for transit trade of neighbours. Kribi exports timber. Aluminium is produced at Edéa, using hydro-electric power from the Sanaga river, and a railway is being built to the north. (RH-C)

CENTRAL AFRICAN REPUBLIC

This poor, land-locked country, extending from 30° to 11°N, is as large as France (623,000 km², 240,540 sq miles) but with only about 2.5 million inhabitants. It lies on an undulating plateau between the Chad and Congo basins; the numerous rivers drain to both, and natural erosion has been accentuated by unwise planting of trees in rows on foreign plantations. Rain forest is confined to the south-west. The rest of the country is savanna, often with lateritic soils, and was much depopulated for the European and Arab slave trades, and later for forced labour. Most farming is for subsistence, but coffee, cotton and groundnuts are exported, as well as significant amounts of timber, diamonds and uranium. (RH-C)

EQUATORIAL GUINEA

At the turn of the fifteenth century the Papacy awarded Africa and Asia to Portugal, and the Americas west of 50°W to Spain. The latter sought a source of slaves in Africa, and in 1778 the Portuguese ceded Fernando Poó (Macias Nguema Biyoga) and Annobon (Pagalu), together with rights on the mainland, against Spanish agreement to Portuguese advance west of 50°W in Brazil. Plantations of coffee and cocoa were established on these mountainous and volcanic islands, similar to many Caribbean islands.

Mainland Mbini is very different, lower and thinly peopled, less developed, and with fewer foreign enterprises, except in forestry (especially okoume and mahogany production) and the oil palm. Coffee and cocoa are also grown. (RH-C)

SÃO TOMÉ and PRINCIPE

These mountainous and volcanic islands, Portuguese until 1975, comprise Africa's second smallest state,
little more than twice the area of Andorra. They are akin to neighbouring Fernando Poó and Annobon (see Equatorial Guinea). São Tomé is the larger and more developed island; both have coastal coconut plantations, with oil palm and cocoa plantations in the interior. (RH-C)

GABON

The name Gabon is derived from one given by a Portuguese explorer in the sixteenth century to an estuary which he thought resembled a hooded and sleeved cloak, gabão in Portuguese. In the nineteenth century the French navy suppressed the local slave trade, and landed freed slaves at the base called Libreville where, as in the British counterpart (Freetown, Sierra Leone), an educated élite arose.

Gross National Product figures suggest that Gabon is one of Africa's richest states, but this is misleading: though rich in resources, the country has a low population (just over half a million in an area larger than the United Kingdom), to whom the wealth has not yet spread.

Most of the country is forested, and valuable timbers were the main export until 1962. Since then minerals have been developed, as usual in Africa by foreign companies whose profits leave the country. First came oil and gas from near Port Gentil. Then the world's largest deposit of manganese was mined at Moanda, near Franceville, although the ore has to be exported through the Congo by a branch of the Congo-Ocean railway. Lastly, there is uranium from nearby Mounana. Gabon, with the Central African Republic and Niger, are France's main sources of uranium. A railway is being built across Gabon to provide the country's own outlet for the manganese and uranium, and to open new areas to forestry.

Apart from cocoa and coffee grown in the north near Mbini, farming of all kinds is rare, the Gabonese preferring to work in other economic activities and the towns. Much food is imported. (RH-C)

CONGO

This former French colony, half the area of France, has about 1.5 million inhabitants. Although astride the Equator, only the near-coastal Mayombe ridges and the east-central and northern parts of the Congo basin have truly equatorial climate
and vegetation. They are the sources of the most valuable exports of timber and oil palm produce. The areas around Brazzaville, the capital, and those north and west of it are drier, with savanna vegetation except where tributaries of the Congo flood widely.

The Congo-Ocean railway from Brazzaville to Pointe Noire (Congo's only port) has spectacular engineering. It is a major artery, not just for Congo but for Gabon, the Central African Republic and Chad. Transit traffic on the railway is an important source of revenue. There are small oil-fields near Pointe Noire, but few other minerals. (RH-C)

ZAIRE

Formerly made up of several African kingdoms, more recently a Belgian colony, Zaire and her peoples suffered successively from the slave trade, and then from the sadistic methods and corruption of the Congo Free State (1884–1908). Belgium then assumed administration until independence was granted in 1960. The country's huge size (seventy-seven times that of Belgium) and small population stretched Belgium's modest resources; in colonial days oil palm and rubber plantations were developed in the equatorial Congo basin, mining on the Congo-Zambezi watershed, and coffee-growing on the Congo-Nile watershed in the north-east. The Congo river was developed as a major artery, its rapids and falls by-passed by railways, and an important railway built from the river port of Kinshasa to the coastal port of Matadi.

Minerals from the far south-eastern Shaba Province (formerly Katanga), refined on the spot, provide much of Zaire's export income, though shortages of skilled workers and spare parts, mis-government, and dislocation of railway links through Angola, Zimbabwe and
Mozambique, have affected revenues. Most outstanding of many minerals are copper and cobalt (normally two-thirds of all exports), manganese, tin, gold and diamonds. Industry was substantial at independence, and the massive hydro-electric power developments at Inga, below Kinshasa, provide for further expansion in the future. (RH-C)

ANGOLA

Angola is one of Africa's largest states (1,246,700 km², 481,350 sq miles), twice the area of Texas. Extending through 13° of latitude, the altitudinal range is from sea-level to 2,619 m (8,592 ft). There is a strong cooling effect from the cold offshore Benguela Current, and climate and vegetation range from desert on the south coast to equatorial and montane conditions in the centre and north. Thus Angola normally has exceptionally varied agricultural output; the coastal waters are rich in fish, and extensive mineral resources include oil.

Portugal established Luanda in 1575, the oldest European-founded city in Africa south of the Sahara. As a centre of the slave trade, some three million captives from Angola passed through it to the Americas, and the depopulation dislocated local life for many generations. More recently, as a Portuguese colony, Angola's development was hampered by the small population (now about 6.7 million), by Portugal's economic weakness, centralized rule and mercantilist theories, and latterly by thirteen years of guerrilla war between three rival nationalist groups. Potentially it is a rich country. Oil reserves are important both on the coast and offshore near Luanda and Cabinda, and hydro-electric power and irrigation developments are substantial. Diamonds, a major export, come from the north-east, near the Zaire border. (RH-C)

Heavily-eroded countryside in Zaire.

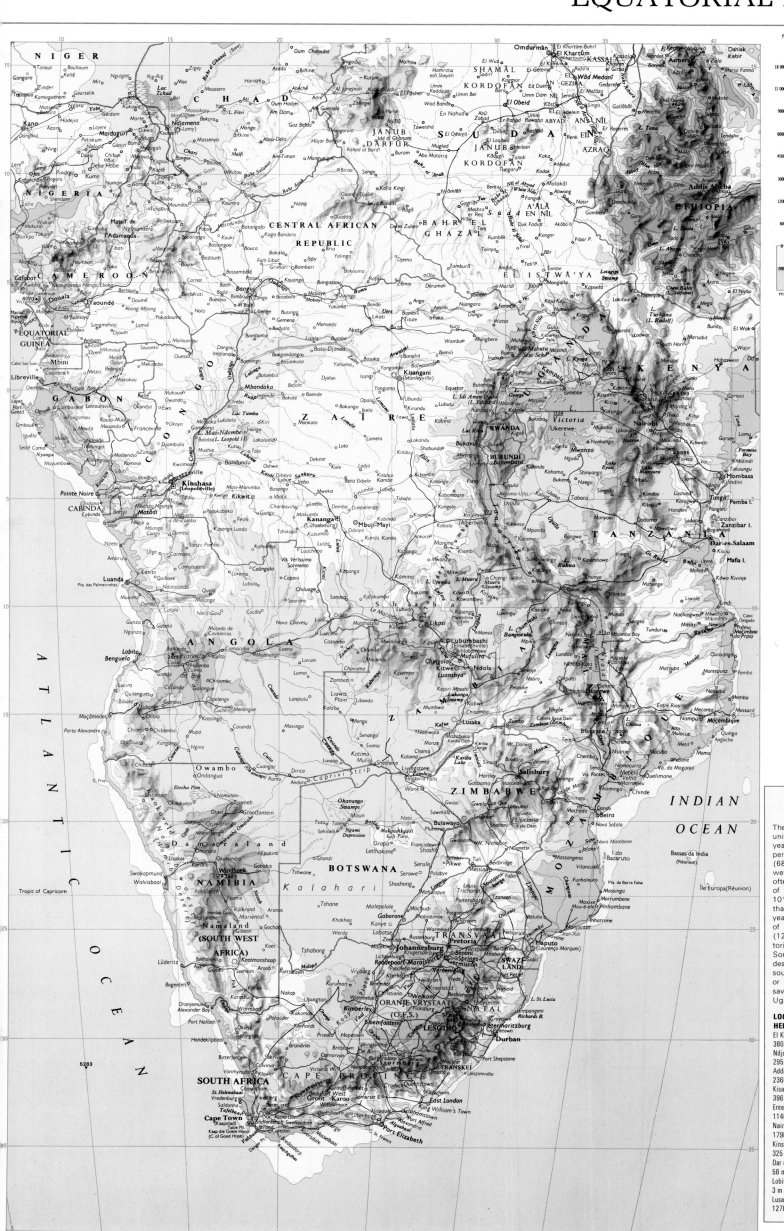

Climate

The equatorial zone of Africa is uniformly hot throughout the year, with mean monthly temperatures between 20° and 28°C (68° and 82°F). It is also mainly wet, with round-the-year rainfall often intensified seasonally. Most of the zone between latitudes 10°N and 10°S receives more than 100 cm (40 in) of rain per year; the wettest coastal areas of West Africa receive 300 cm (120 in) or more. Eastern equatorial lands are much drier. Somali and northern Kenya are deserts or semi-deserts; further south monsoon winds bring single or double seasonal rains to the savanna-lands of southern Kenya, Uganda and Tanzania.

LOCALITY HEIGHT		JAN	JUL	YR
El Khartûm	°C	22.5	30.8	28.7
380 m	mm	0	48	164
Ndjamena	°C	23.5	27.5	27.9
295 m	mm	0	156	646
Addis Abeba	°C	16.1	15.1	16.8
2360 m	mm	24	228	1089
Kisangani	°C	25.9	24.2	25.3
396 m	mm	53	132	1704
Entebbe	°C	22.0	20.6	21.5
1146 m	mm	79	73	1574
Nairobi	°C	17.8	14.9	17.5
1798 m	mm	45	19	926
Kinshasa	°C	25.9	22.5	25.3
325 m	mm	713	3	1354
Dar es Salaam	°C	27.3	23.3	25.7
58 m	mm	58	21	1043
Lobito	°C	25.0	19.7	23.7
3 m	mm	8	0	221
Lusaka	°C	21.4	16.1	20.6
1278	mm	231	Tr	836

Projection: Sanson Flamsteed's Sinusoidal

East from Greenwich

COPYRIGHT. GEORGE PHILIP & SON. LTD.

165

ETHIOPIA

Ethiopia, larger than Benelux, France, Spain and Portugal combined (1,221,900 km², 471,776 sq miles) spans almost 15° of latitude and longitude. The main feature is a massive block of volcanic mountains, rising to 4,620 m (15,150 ft) and divided into Eastern and Western Highlands by the Great Rift Valley. Steep escarpments face each other across the rift, opening northwards to form the southern and western boundaries of the high Welo plateau. The Eastern Highlands fall away gently to the south and east. The Western.Highlands, generally lower but far more extensive and deeply trenched, are the sources of the Blue Nile and its tributaries. Off their north-eastern flank, close to the Red Sea, lies the Danakil Depression, an extensive desert that falls to 116 m (381 ft) below sea-level.

In the lower areas of both highlands tropical cereals, oil seeds, coffee and cotton are dominant crops, while at higher altitudes temperate cereals, pulses and fruits are produced. Giant thistles, red hot poker and lobelia are characteristic of the montane vegetation. In the desert of the Rift Valley the Danakil tend their herds, as do the Somali pastoralists on the dry Ogaden plain to the south-east.

Coptic Christianity reached the northern Kingdom of Aksum in the fourth century, surviving there and in the mountains to the south when Islam spread through the rest of north-east Africa. These core areas also survived colonial conquest. Indeed Ethiopia itself became a colonial power between 1897 and 1908, taking Somali and other peoples into her feudal Empire. Invaded by Italy in 1935, Ethiopia became independent again six years later. In 1974 a revolutionary military government deposed Haile Selassie, the last emperor. The new government established collective farms and allocated some land to former semi-serfs, but political unrest – including a strong separatist movement for Eritrea – has continued. Ethiopia has substantial potential, but its realization seems far off. (RH-C)

DJIBOUTI

Independent since 1977, this state lies in the Afro-Asian rift valley system. Larger than Wales, it forms a hinterland to the Gulf of Tadjoura. Part of Djibouti lies below sea-level;

much of the low ground is hot, arid and unproductive. Mt Goudah, the principal mountain, rises to 1,783 m (5,848 ft), and is covered with juniper and box forest.

Djibouti is important because of the railway link with Addis Ababa, which forms Ethiopia's main artery for overseas trade. Also a general and refuelling port, it developed as a French naval base paralleling the former British port at Aden. Djibouti was previously the French territory of the Afars and Issas. Afars also live in adjacent Ethiopia and are better known by the Arabic word 'Danakil', while the Issas (or Ishaak) are Somali. Both Ethiopia and Somali have claimed this country. The railway and port lie in the Issa region. (RH-C)

SOMALI REPUBLIC

Twice as large as Italy (which formerly ruled the eastern part), Somali became independent in 1960. The northern section, formerly British Somaliland, is the highest and most arid, rising to 2,408 m (7,900 ft); the mountains are an easterly projection of the Ethiopian Highlands, wooded with box and cedar. The east and south has some 500 mm (20 in) rainfall on the coast. Dunes have diverted the Webbe Shibeli river to the south, making it available for irrigation: bananas are a major export from this area, especially to Italy. Inland is low plain or plateau, arid, with grass and thorn bush.

The Somali, though belonging to separate tribes or clans, are conscious of being one nation and members of one of Africa's rare nation states. Expatriate Somali living in southern Djibouti, Ogaden (eastern Ethiopia) and north-east Kenya are mostly pastoralists, who move across borders in search of pasture and water. The Somali are also seafarers, and the Somali Republic has a flag of convenience. (RH-C)

KENYA

Bisected by the Great Rift Valley, the Kenya Highlands are formed by volcanoes and lava flows rising from 1,500 m (4,900 ft) to the glacier-capped peaks of Mt Kenya at 5,199 m (17,000 ft). The greater part of the country, however, comprises plains cut across old crystalline rocks, except where sedimentary strata extend across the Tana Basin and

into the Somali Republic.

The land area of the Republic of Kenya is 582,650 km² (225,000 sq miles) but 80 per cent of the people crowd into about 15 per cent of the country in the south-west corner where average rainfalls of over 750 mm (30 in) a year support dense farming populations. The Kikuyu and others practise small-scale farming on the fertile volcanic soils on the eastern flanks of the Highlands from Limuru to Nyeri, Meru and Embu.

The western Highlands descend to the equally populous Lake Victoria basin around Kakamega and Kisii, focussing on Kisumu. Nakuru and Eldoret are farming centres originally settled by Europeans. The modern capital city of Nairobi is within this core area of Kenya, from which derive most of the exports of coffee, tea, pyrethrum and sisal, with soda ash from the Magadi alkaline lake.

A second concentration of population occurs along the coast adjacent to Mombasa, which is Kenya's second city and a port that also serves Uganda. There are ancient towns and ruins, and an Islamic Swahili culture. These now coexist with an international tourist industry. By contrast the extensive semi-arid interior plains contain widely scattered pastoral peoples (Masai, Turkana, Galla). (WM)

UGANDA

Extending from Lake Victoria to the western arm of the Great Rift Valley and beyond, Uganda is a land of lakes (sources of the White Nile) originating from the tilting and faulting associated with the rift valley system. On the west the Ruwenzori block has been uplifted to 5,109 m (16,762 ft), while the eastern frontier bisects the large extinct volcano of Mt Elgon.

In the south rainfall is abundant in two seasons, and small patches of the original rain-forest remain. However, most of the forest has been cleared from the densely-settled areas, notably in the historic kingdoms of Buganda and Busoga. Here the banana is a staple of diet, and coffee, tea and sugar are grown for sale. Here too are the capital Kampala, and the industrial centre of Jinja, adjacent to the Owen Falls hydro-electric station. The western former kingdoms of Bunyoro, Toro and Ankole depend more on cattle.

To the north, one rainy season

Game Herds

Zebra and wildebeest in Amboseli National Park, Kenya.

The savanna grasslands of East Africa support immense numbers of grazing and browsing animals, of all kinds from grasshoppers and ostriches to zebras and elephants. The commonest mammals are mainly or exclusively grass-eaters; they include zebras and several kinds of antelopes – hartebeest, wildebeest, topi, Thompson's gazelle and oribi – which often feed in mixed herds and drink together at the waterholes in the evenings. Elephants, impala, steenbok and buffalo graze on grasses too – mostly the longer ones – but also browse on shrubs and trees. Giraffes, black rhinoceroses, gerenuk and eland are mainly browsers.

The life cycles of all these animals are determined largely by rainfall. During the wet season (November to June in the neighbourhood of Serengeti, Tanzania, where all may be found) they straggle widely across the short-grass upland plains; this is the time when most of the young are born, and grazing is richest. As the dry season approaches they migrate to lower and damper land, feeding among the longer, deeper-rooted grasses. The bigger species – zebra, buffalo and wildebeest – graze first, mainly on the tops of the grasses, and the elephants tread down the shoulder-high growth. This lets in the smaller species, which nibble at the stems and bases of the grass, and still leaves plenty on the trees and shrubs for browsers. (BS)

each year supports a savanna of trees and grassland. Population is generally less dense, and farmers grow finger-millet and sorghum, with cotton and tobacco as cash crops. Tsetse fly inhibits cattle-keeping in some areas, which have become game parks, but the dry north-east (Karamoja) supports nomadic pastoralists. (WM)

RWANDA

Uplift on the flank of the western arm of the Great Rift Valley has raised much of Rwanda to well over 2,000 m (6,000 ft). On the northern border are the perfectly shaped but extinct volcanoes of the Mfumbiro Range rising to 4,507 m (14,786 ft), a last reserve of the mountain gorilla. A small country of 26,330 km² (10,166 sq miles), Rwanda is very densely populated and the steep slopes are intensively cultivated. Exports include coffee, cassiterite (copper ore) and tungsten, and when conditions permit there is a large movement into Zaire and Uganda for employment. As in Burundi, there are deep social and cultural divisions between the farming majority and the traditional, nomadic owners of cattle. (WM)

BURUNDI

From the capital of Bujumbura on Lake Tanganyika a great escarpment rises to the rift highlands, reaching 2,670 m (8,760 ft), which make up most of Burundi. Cool and healthy, the highlands support a dense but dispersed farming population, the Hutu, and a minority of the unusually tall cattle-keeping Tutsi. This is similar to Rwanda and being also a small country of 27,834 km² (10,747 sq miles) and overpopulated, employment is sought in neighbouring countries. Coffee is widely grown for export throughout the uplands and cotton is grown on the rift valley floor in the Ruzizi valley. (WM)

TANZANIA

From the islands of Zanzibar and Pemba, Tanzania extends across the high plateau of eastern Africa, mostly

Zanzibar, Tanzania.

above 1,000 m (3,000 ft), to the rift valleys filled by lakes Tanganyika and Nyasa (Malawi), whose deepest waters reach below sea level. The Northern Highlands flank branches of the eastern rift valley, containing the strongly alkaline lake Natron and lakes Eyasi and Manyara, and dominated by the giant and ice-capped extinct volcano of Kilimanjaro, 5,895 m (19,340 ft), the highest mountain in Africa. The Southern Highlands overlook Lake Nyasa in the southern end of the rift system.

The land area of Tanzania is 945,000 km² (365,000 sq miles) but the population is dispersed into several concentrations mostly on the margins of the country, separated by sparsely inhabited savanna woodland (*miombo*), often infested with tsetse fly. This poses problems of communication and Dodoma is therefore a more central location for a capital than Dar es Salaam.

Along the coast and on Zanzibar and other islands are old cities and ruins of the historic Swahili-Arab culture, and the major ports and railway termini of Dar es Salaam and Tanga. Local products include sisal and cashew nuts with cloves from Pemba and there are some beach resorts. The Northern Highlands centre on Moshi and support intensive agriculture exporting coffee and tea. This contrasts with the nomadic Masai pastoralists of the surrounding plains. Tea also comes from the Southern Highlands. South of Lake Victoria is an important cotton-growing and cattle-rearing area focussing on Mwanza but including the Williamson diamond mine at Mwadui, near Shinyanga, and gold mines at Geita and elsewhere, now of diminished importance. Attempts to develop the *miombo* woodlands have been hindered by sleeping sickness, drought and poor soils, and traditional settlement is based on shifting cultivation.

Rail connections enable Dar es Salaam to act as a port for Zambia and, by ferry across Lake Tanganyika, for eastern Zaire. (WM)

ZAMBIA

Zambia occupies a vast expanse of high plateaux in the interior of south-central Africa. Most of it is

drained by the Zambezi and two of its major tributaries, the Kafue and the Luangwa. The latter and the central section of the Zambezi occupy a low-lying rift valley (part of the east African rift system), bounded by rugged escarpments. Lake Kariba, formed by damming in 1960, occupies part of the floor of this rift valley; like the hydro-electric power generated from it, the lake is shared by Zambia and Zimbabwe. The magnificent Victoria Falls are similarly shared. Power generated from the Kafue River now supplements supplies from Kariba. Much of north-eastern Zambia is drained to the Atlantic Ocean by headwaters of the Congo – the Chambeshi, which loses itself within the vast swamps of the Bangweulu depression, and the Luapula which flows into Lake Mweru, one of the smaller rift-valley lakes of eastern Africa.

Zambia is a leading producer of copper; despite efforts to diversify, the economy remains stubbornly dependent on this one mineral. The Copperbelt, centred on Kitwe, is the major urban region while the capital, Lusaka, provides another major growth pole. Rural development has proved elusive, and tribal societies continue to subsist in traditional fashion. Rural-urban migration has increased markedly since independence in 1964 and work is scarce. Shanty towns and a variety of small-scale enterprises provide an alternative urban life style. Commercial farming, concentrated in central regions astride the railway, frequently fails to meet the needs of the growing urban population. As a land-locked country heavily dependent upon international trade, Zambia relies on her neighbours for access to ports. In the colonial era the principal outlets were via Rhodesia (Zimbabwe) and Mozambique or South Africa. Alternatives, notably a railway, highway and oil pipeline to Dar es Salaam, have been developed but Zambia continues to have serious transport problems. (GK)

MALAWI

Malawi is a small, hilly if not mountainous country with an extraordinary shape derived from association with a nineteenth-century missionaries' and traders' route up the Zambezi, Shire and Lake Nyasa. Malawi is relatively poor in natural resources; and compared with neighbouring countries has a high population density and excessive pressure upon the land. Most of Malawi's economic activity centres upon agriculture, which supports most of the population and provides over 90 per cent of the domestic exports. Tea and tobacco, mostly from large estates, are the principal export crops while basic foodstuffs

are largely derived from small, quasi-subsistence peasant holdings which occupy most of the farmland.

Industrial and urban development are extremely limited. Malawi has a long history as an exporter of labour migrants, and large numbers of Malawians still work or seek work abroad. It is therefore not surprising that Malawi is classified as one of the least developed of the developing countries. This status, together with political stability and conservative policies since independence in 1964, have gained access to foreign capital, aid and sympathy which have stimulated economic and especially rural development. Nevertheless the basic problems of poverty, overpopulation and unemployment continue unresolved. (GK)

MOZAMBIQUE

Mozambique, like other ex-Portuguese African countries, arose from the search for a route round Africa to the riches of Asia; Vasco da Gama and his successors established forts at Beira (Sofala), Quelimane and Mozambique Island. Dutch conquest of Portuguese Asia in the seventeenth century, and concentration by the Portuguese on the slave trade from western Africa to the Americas, resulted in decay of Mozambique settlements. However, being so little affected by the slave trade, and acting as a refuge in wars, Mozambique was never depopulated to the extent of Angola, and now maintains a higher population on a smaller area (about 12 million on 783,000 km², 302,320 sq miles).

Mozambique forms a transit route for much of the overseas trade of Swaziland, the Transvaal, Zimbabwe, Zambia and Zaire, involving the ports of Maputo, Beira and Nacala-Velha. Rail, port and handling services provide substantial employment and revenues. Mozambique workers also work on contract in South African mines.

The country is as elongated as western Europe, narrowing southward. Because of the warm offshore Mozambique current all the country is tropical; there is little commercial fishing, and coral reefs lie offshore. The only natural harbours are Maputo and Nacala. Here is southern Africa's widest coastal plain, with plantations of coconut and sisal with sugar on the alluvial flats. As in the northern foothills, farmers grow maize, groundnuts, cotton and cashew. Only the inner borderlands are high; because of this and remoteness from Portugal, Mozambique attracted few European settlers. At the limit of navigation on the Zambezi is Africa's largest dam, Cabora Bassa, whose power goes largely to South Africa. (RH-C)

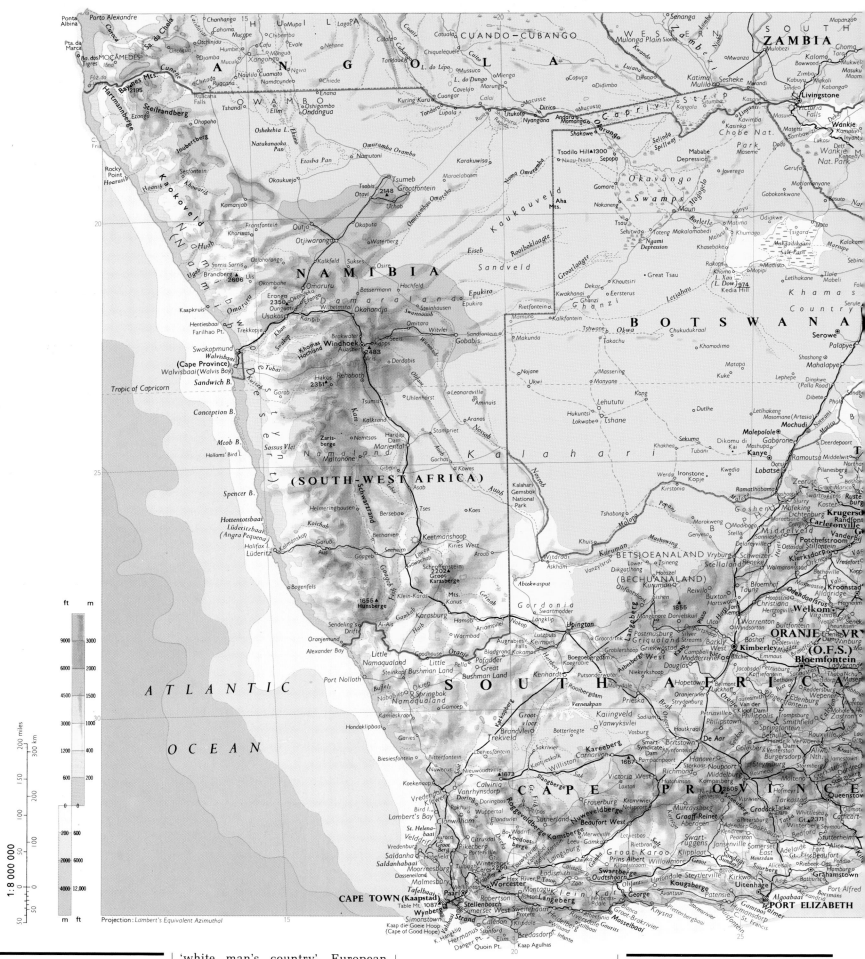

ZIMBABWE

Zimbabwe (formerly Rhodesia) is a compact, land-locked state which lies astride the high plateaux between the Zambezi and Limpopo valleys. Occupied in 1890 by the British South African Company, it was subsequently developed as a

'white man's country'. European immigration was encouraged and the white population reached a peak of 278,000 in 1975. A large proportion of the land, including most mineral-rich areas and all the main towns, was reserved for European or government ownership. Africans were admitted to limited rights within this European Area, mostly as employees and their dependents; and there has been careful control of population movements to minimize the occurrence of shanty towns and squatter settlements. Originally dependent upon gold and tobacco, the economy is now markedly diverse.

Many Africans have been drawn into the money economy, but a majority continue to live in tribal homelands where poverty is widespread and would be acute but for support provided by absentee workers. The African population, doubling in less than twenty years, exerts severe and growing pressures on all resources and services. As the country develops under African majority rule, racial laws relating to land ownership and residential rights are being changed. Marked adjustments in population patterns are likely to follow. (GK)

BOTSWANA

Formerly the British Protectorate of Bechuanaland, Botswana became an independent state in 1966. The physical environment is discouraging for a new country seeking economic viability. Botswana occupies the Kalahari Basin, a sandy

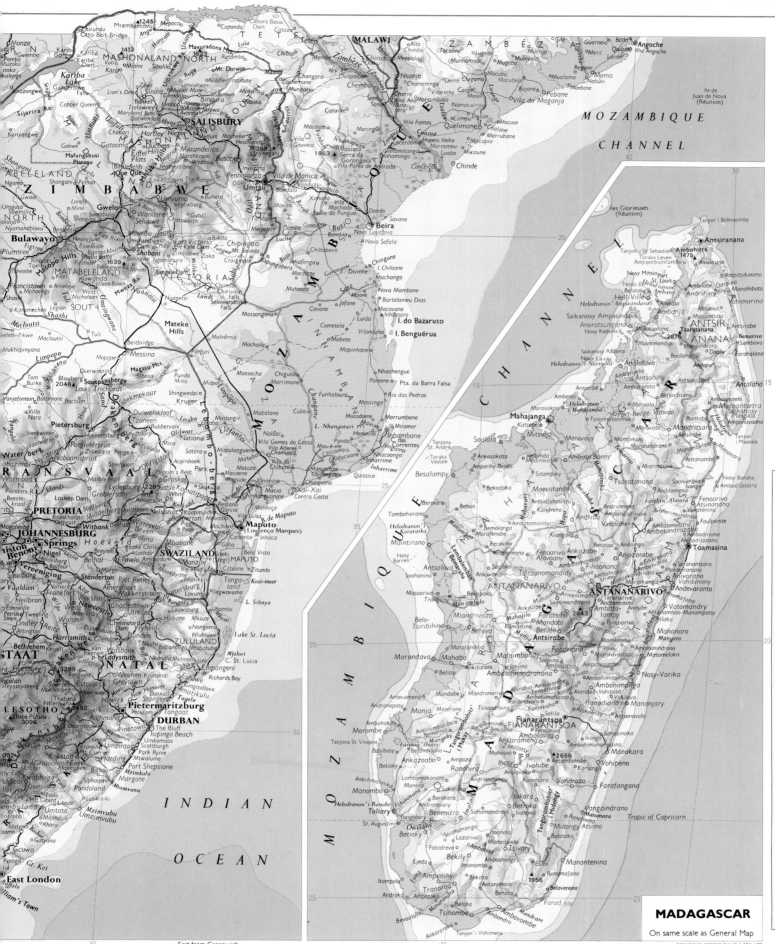

Climate

Southward from the 15th parallel African climates become progressively drier and more seasonal. With the sun overhead in January the summers remain hot. Mean January temperatures over much of the high central core (including the Kalahari Basin) and eastern coastal flank stand above 24°C (75°F); only in the Drakensberg highlands are they less than 16°C (61°F). Winter means are 10° to 15°C (17.5° to 26°F) lower in the interior, 5° to 10°C (9° to 17.5°F) lower on the coast. The high interior is arid and the western coastal strip a desert; eastern and south-eastern coastal regions have moderate rainfall (75 cm, 30 in annually) with most falling in summer. The southern tip has a Mediterranean climate with most rain in winter.

LOCALITY HEIGHT		JAN	JUL	YR
Salisbury	°C	20.0	13.6	18.2
1479 m	mm	216	1	863
Tananarive	°C	19.3	13.0	16.8
1310 m	mm	286	10	1270
Bulawayo	°C	20.9	13.6	18.7
1345 m	mm	134	Tr	589
Windhoek	°C	22.9	13.0	19.0
1700 m	mm	77	1	370
Walvisbaai	°C	18.9	14.7	17.0
7 m	mm	Tr	Tr	23
Fort Dauphin	°C	25.6	19.7	22.8
44 m	mm	160	107	1660
Pretoria	°C	21.0	10.3	16.7
1400 m	mm	125	10	746
Johannesburg	°C	20.0	10.6	16.1
1666 m	mm	114	8	709
Durban	°C	23.4	16.3	20.2
4 m	mm	119	29	1044
Capetown	°C	20.6	12.2	16.7
17 m	mm	15	89	508

MADAGASCAR
On same scale as General Map

COPYRIGHT. GEORGE PHILIP & SON. LTD.

East from Greenwich

desert and focus of inland drainage.

Subsistence farming, in which cattle-keeping plays a prominent role, is the main occupation. Along the railway line, there is commercial dairying and arable farming. The country relies on South Africa for much of its trade and also for the tourists who visit the wildlife reserves of Makgadikgadi and Okavango. The opening of rich diamond deposits at Orapa in 1971 and of copper at Selibe-Pikwe in 1974, have given the economy a boost, but the country is poor in natural resources and the economic outlook is unpromising. (GW)

The Kalahari

The Kalahari Basin, a dry upland region of roughly 250,000 km² (100,000 sq miles), lies mainly in Botswana but extends across the borders of Namibia and South Africa. Level or slightly undulating, with only occasional rock outcrops to break the relief, most of it lies between 1,000 and 1,200 m (3,300 to 4,000 ft) above sea level. Thin sandy soil covers much of the ground, with shifting, crescent-shaped dunes where over-grazing has destroyed the vegetation, but the Kalahari is by no means a uniform desert. Annual rainfall of 30 to 45 cm (12 to 18 in), most effective in the cooler season, allows growth of grasses, thorn scrub and spindly

Bushmen hunting with arrows.

woodland, especially in the damper north. Summers, however, are searingly hot, and most of the plants dry out or shed their leaves. Insects, snakes and birds are plentiful, and large herds of game – notably springbok and wildebeest – graze with their attendant lions, hyaenas and other predators.

Kalahari has a human population of about 100,000, most of them semi-nomadic Bantu herdsmen. There are also some 17,000 bushmen – short, copper-skinned aboriginals who for generations have lived successfully as nomadic hunter-gatherers in the Kalahari heartlands. (BS)

AFRICA SOUTH

NAMIBIA

Born out of the late nineteenth century scramble for Africa, Namibia is a country of diversity, physically and socially. Fringing the southern Atlantic is the arid Namib Desert, virtually uninhabited. This area is separated by a major escarpment from a north-south spine of mountains, which culminate in the Khomas Highlands near the capital of Windhoek. This rugged spine, built of very thick schists and quartzites, rises to 2,483 m (8,150 ft) in the peak Moltkeblik. To the east the country occupies the fringes of the Kalahari Desert.

Formerly a German colony, Namibia came under a South African mandate in 1920 and took on the trappings of Afrikaner racial attitudes (now receding). The population consists of many different groups, including the traders, farmers and professional men of European origins, the Herero who are Hamitic cattle herders, and the Owambo–negroid farmers in the well-watered north. Rich in minerals, the country has attracted large-scale investment by multi-national companies, for example at Tsumeb which is linked to the meagre rail network. The main outlet of the country is Walvisbaai, but this is South African territory; if Namibia achieves independence it may have to rely on the less adequate port at Lüderitz for maritime trade. At present the country is in political limbo; South Africa's mandate is not recognized by the United Nations, and South Africa has gone against world opinion in granting virtual independence to a government elected under her aegis. (GW)

LESOTHO

The Kingdom of Lesotho consists mainly of a high mountainous plateau which is deeply fretted by the headwaters of the Orange river. The country declines altitudinally from east to west, with the highest ridges, over 3,000 m (9–10,000 ft), developed on basaltic lavas. This treeless zone with its steep valleys has an excess of water, making it boggy in summer, and in winter a frozen tundra. It is also over-populated. All of this contrasts with the lower narrow western belts of the foothills and lowlands, stretching southwards from Butha-Buthe to Mohale's Hoek. Here the dominant rock is sandstone.

The difficult physical environment and the fact of being surrounded by South African territory provide major economic and political problems for the country. Most of the population are involved in subsistence agriculture, but the steep slopes and thin soils make this an unrewarding occupation. The only urban and industrial development lies in the west at Maseru, the capital. The present trend is for people to drift to the small towns or to find employment in South Africa. The country's scenery is conducive to tourism and the altitude allows winter sports; however, to develop this potential massive capital investment, especially in roads, would be necessary. (GW)

SWAZILAND

Among the smallest countries in Africa, 17,000 km^2 (6,564 sq miles), Swaziland nevertheless reveals strong scenic contrasts. From west to east the country descends in three altitudinal steps; the Highveld, average altitude 1,200 m (4,000 ft), and the Middleveld, lying between 350 and 1,000 m (1,000 and 3,500 ft) are made of old, hard rocks; the Lowveld, average height 270 m (900 ft) is of softer shales and sandstones in the west, and basalts in the east. Shutting the country in on the east are the 800 m (2,600 ft) high Lebombo Mountains. Rivers rising in South Africa completely traverse these belts; their valleys provide communication lines and are sources of perennial water, important for irrigation. Although the wild animal population has been greatly reduced, there are still numbers of hippopotamus, wildebeest, zebra and antelope. Lions, baboons and monkeys are less numerous.

In the late nineteenth century European colonists settled and today the main economic features result from basic differences in occupational structures between black and white Swazi. Those derived from European stock are involved in commerce, industry and, predominantly, large-scale farming of cash crops, especially sugar, fruit, cattle and cereals. The indigenous Swazi are still mostly engaged in subsistence farming based on maize, with fragmented land-holdings and a dispersed settlement pattern. As a result there are few large towns.

Swaziland is part of a custom's union which includes South Africa. For overseas trade the country relies on the Mozambique port of Maputo to which it is linked by the only railway. Thus politically it is sandwiched between Apartheid and Marxism, which partly accounts for the substitution of government by Royal Decree for the former Parliamentary Rule (1973–8). (GW)

SOUTH AFRICA

Geologically very ancient, South Africa has only scant superficial deposits of sediments less than six hundred million years old. Geological history has had a great effect on all aspects of the country's development – on its landforms, patterns of population, industrial growth and agricultural potential.

Landscape

South Africa is divisible into two major natural zones – the interior and the coastal fringe. The interior in turn consists of two major parts. Most of Cape Province, the Transvaal and the Orange Free State are drained by the Orange River and its important right-bank tributaries which flow with gentle gradients over level plateaux, varying in height from 1,200–2,000 m (4,000–6,000 ft). The northern Transvaal is occupied by the Bushveld, an area of granites and igneous intrusions, drained by rivers which flow northwards to the Limpopo. The coastal fringe is divided from the interior by the Fringing Escarpment, a feature that makes communication within the country very difficult. In the east the massive basalt-capped rock wall of the Drakensberg, at its most majestic near Mont-aux-Sources and rising to over 3,000 m (over 10,000 ft), overlooks the Natal and Transkei coastlands. In the west there is a similar divide between the interior plateau and the coastlands though this is less well developed. The Fringing Escarpment also runs along the south coast, where it is fronted by many independent mountain ranges with an east-west alignment.

Immigration and Development

South Africa's economic and political development is closely related to these physical components. The country was peopled by negroids from the north, who introduced a cattle-keeping, grain-growing culture. Entering by the plateaux of the north-east, they continued southwards into the well-watered zones below the Fringing Escarpment of present-day Natal and Transkei. Moving into country occupied by Bushmanoid peoples they absorbed some of the latter's cultural features, especially the clicks so characteristic of the modern Zulu and Xhosa languages. By the eighteenth century these Bantu-speaking groups had penetrated to the south-east in the region of the Kei and Fish rivers.

Simultaneously with this advance, a group of Europeans was establishing a victualling point for the Dutch East India Company on the site of modern Cape Town. These Company employees, augmented by Huguenot refugees, eventually spread out from Cape Town, beginning a movement of European farmers throughout southern Africa and bringing about the development of the Afrikaners. Their advance was channelled in the south by the parallel coastal ranges, so that eventually black and white met near the Kei River. To the north, once the Fringing Escarpment had been overstepped, the level surface of the plateaux allowed a rapid spread. From this colonizing process, aided by an implanting of British people in the south-east and near Durban, the present-day disposition of black-dominated and white-dominated lands arose.

The Homelands

Stretching from the Transvaal's western border with Botswana, running in a horseshoe to the north of Pretoria and then southward through Natal and the Transkei, are the so-called Homelands – territories occupied almost exclusively by Africans. From the outset the Africans operated a form of mixed agriculture, giving them subsistence but little more. The men were cattle keepers and warriors, the women tilled the plots, in a culture based on extensive holdings of communal land. European farming was also based on extensive holdings but incorporated individual land-holding rights. Not surprisingly, conflict arose from the juxtapositioning of the two groups. However, with the discovery of valuable minerals (gold in the Banket

deposits of the Witwatersrand, diamonds in the Kimberlite pipes of the Cape, platinum in the Bushveld and coal in the Transvaal and Natal) both groups were drastically affected.

Urbanization

Exploitation of southern Africa's minerals led to trade with overseas markets and the development of major urban complexes. Johannesburg, founded rather improbably on a continental watershed, grew the fastest; its growth encouraged the expansion of Durban and to a large extent caused Cape Town and Port Elizabeth to flourish. The appearance of a capitalist-based, market-oriented economy caused even greater divergence between white and black. The politically-dominant whites reproduced a European economy and, after the transfer of political power, developed strong links with Britain.

The African farmers gained little from the mineral boom. With their constant needs for new grazing grounds frustrated by the white farmers, and with taxes to pay, they had little alternative but to seek employment in the cities and mines, and on European-owned farms. Thus the African areas became labour pools. Migrant labour became the normal way of life for many men, agriculture in the Native Reserves (so designated early in the twentieth century) stagnated and even regressed, with yields decreasing

The Royal Natal National Park, looking towards the Drakensberg.

and soil erosion becoming rampant.

Small groups of Africans took up urban life in 'locations' which became a typical feature of all towns whatever their size. Separated by a *cordon sanitaire* of industry, a river or the railway line from the white settlement, these townships with their rudimentary housing, often supplemented by shanty dwellings and without any real services, mushroomed during World War 2 and left South Africa with a major housing problem in the late 1940s. Nowhere was this problem greater than in the Johannesburg area, where it was solved by the building of a vast complex of brick boxes, the South Western Townships (SOWETO).

The contrast in prosperity, between South African whites and blacks, which has increased steadily, is nowhere more visibly expressed than in their respective urban areas. The white areas could be Anytown in North America; skyscrapers, multi-track roads, large department stores and well-tended suburbs. The black towns could only be South African: though rudimentary in what they offer, they are rigidly planned.

'Separate Development'

The discrepancy in numbers between the two groups, and the lasting differences of life styles, led the whites to formalize the differences in the doctrine of Separate Development (Apartheid). As part of this scheme the predominantly African areas (the former Reserves) are encouraged to work toward an independent national status, based on language difference. Despite being fragmented into many separate units, some areas have declared their independence of South Africa. Thus the Tswana people of the northern Transvaal occupy the state of Bophuthatswana, an entity of nineteen separate parts, totally unrecognized by the rest of the world.

The political future of South Africa will not be solved, however, by merely carving independent countries out of the territory, for there are millions of black Africans living outside their Homelands, with little expectation of work or a reasonable standard of living if they return. A further problem is posed by the Coloured peoples – descendants of mixed-race marriages – and the Asiatics, who are mainly descendants of Indians brought in several generations ago to work in the sugar-cane fields of Natal; neither of these groups has the full rights of citizenship enjoyed by the white ruling majority, and neither has a 'homeland' other than South Africa. (GW)

MADAGASCAR

The island of Madagascar is a semi-continent, larger than France, and immensely varied both physically and culturally. Almost all geological eras are represented, and made more vivid by steep faulting, volcanic outpourings, and deeply-trenched valleys. There are extensive, rugged lateritic areas, so that soils are often poor and farming unrewarding. The coasts are rugged and hostile, with little natural shelter; Diego Suarez, a naval base in the far north, is difficult to reach overland. The north and east are hot and wet, and subject to cyclones. The west is drier, and the south and south-west are arid.

Immigration and Population

Also unique to the island is its mixture of peoples, drawn from several continents. Those on the west side are of Bantu origin, drawn from southern Africa via the Comoro Islands 'bridge'. Those of the centre and east (the Merina or Hova people) came first from Indonesia. The earliest immigrations date from two thousand years ago, but later waves arrived during the seventh to the fifteenth centuries, sailing to Madagascar from south-east Asia with the Equatorial Current, helped by the monsoons. Other Asians followed, all rice-growers, reverent to cattle, with language and funeral rites similar to those in Indonesia. They had a monarchy until French occupation in 1895–96. In the south-centre, the Betsileo are more mixed Bantu-Indonesian, as are other groups, yet all feel 'Malagasy' rather than African or Asian. Many other immigrant groups have also settled.

Wildlife of Madagascar

A Madagascan lemur.

Separated from mainland Africa for at least 50 million years, Madagascar developed a distinct flora and fauna of its own. Before the coming of man, some 3,000 years ago, nearly all of the island was forested, with several different kinds of forest that varied according to local climates. Only the south-western corner was semi-desert, dotted with strange, cactus-like plants of a family (*Didieraceae*) unique to the island. Now much of the forest is cleared for agriculture, but within the remnants lives a strange collection of mammals and reptiles – descendants of Madagascar's original stocks that have evolved in isolation.

Among the many colourful reptiles are some forty species of chameleons – half the world's total. Up to 60 cm (2 ft) long, they crawl slowly among the branches, popping out their sticky, telescopic tongues to catch insects; the bigger ones catch birds and mice too. Most striking of the mammals are lemurs – primates related closely to bush-babies and more distantly to monkeys. Formerly widespread in Africa, but now found only in Madagascar, in the absence of competition from other tree-living animals they have diversified into twenty of more species, filling many of the forest niches occupied on the mainland by monkeys and apes. (BS)

Agriculture and Industry

Landscapes and agriculture (dominantly rice with cattle and pigs) in the central highlands are south Asian in character; the east coast and northern highlands are more African, with fallow-farming of food crops and cultivation of coffee, sugar, spices and essential oil plants for export, mostly from foreign-owned plantations. In the dry west and south nomadic pastoralism is important, and rice is grown by irrigation. Significant minerals are graphite, chromite and mica. Because of the rough terrain and size of the country air transport is important, with a network of over sixty airports. Many roads become impassable in the wet season. (RH-C)

THE ARCTIC

'Arctic' implies the cold regions of the north. There is no generally-agreed definition or boundary, but the limit to the Arctic accepted by most geographers and ecologists is the tree-line – the boundary within which trees will not grow to the height of a man. This coincides satisfactorily with the climatologists' view that a polar climate is one in which the mean temperature of the warmest month does not exceed 10°C (50°F). Whichever definition is used, the Arctic includes the northern shores of Europe, Canada and the USSR, Greenland, northern Iceland, many islands of the Arctic and North Pacific Oceans, and the Arctic Ocean itself.

Alaskan and Canadian Arctic lands are mostly low-lying, though the Brooks Range and some of the northern islands – especially Baffin and southern Ellesmere Islands – are mountainous with permanent ice-caps. Greenland is three large islands completely buried under a permanent capping of ice except for the extreme north and south-west. Iceland has only a small remnant of the ice-cap that formerly covered it; Jan Mayen Island, Svalbard (including Bear Island), Franz Josef Land (Frantsa Iosifa) and Novaya Zemlya have glaciers and permanent ice on their mountains, with narrow coastal strips that thaw in summer.

The Eskimo culture is disappearing.

All are warmed to varying degrees by the North Atlantic Drift, a current that carries Atlantic surface waters northward between Iceland and Norway and into the heart of the Arctic basin. The Kola peninsula and much of the Siberian Arctic shores are low-lying, snow-covered in winter and marshy in summer. The great rivers of Siberia carry warmth from central Asia to the Arctic Ocean, softening the harshness of winter along the northern shore. The Taymyr Peninsula and north-eastern Siberia are mountainous and snow-capped, with narrow coastal plains that thaw briefly in summer.

Though much of the Arctic Ocean is covered with floating pack ice, especially in winter, only Greenland and a few of the northern islands now carry permanent land ice, and many areas of the Arctic are completely clear of snow for two or three months each summer. Some parts – the cold desert areas of north Greenland, for example – see little snow even in winter. The Arctic is generally colder than the sub-arctic and temperate zones surrounding it, but it is by no means uniformly cold – nor is it the coldest part of the northern hemisphere throughout the year.

In winter, when the sun disappears for several months and there is no incoming radiation, air temperatures fall as both land and sea ice give up their heat. Over much of the area January mean temperatures reach −20°C (−4°F) to −30°C (−22°F) or lower. But in north-eastern Siberia, far from any warming effects of the oceans, they fall even further, to −40°C (−40°F) and below. Though technically in the subarctic, this is the coldest region of the north in winter. With spring the sun returns, and land and sea ice warm gradually. Temperatures rise to freezing point, then higher as the snow disappears, so that mean monthly temperature for two or three summer months may reach 5° to 10°C (41° to 50°F) or higher in the subarctic. With long days which are often sunny and warm, the Arctic can be surprisingly pleasant.

Arctic Vegetation

Summer temperatures are sufficient to thaw the ground to a depth of half a metre (1½ ft) or more; though the soil and groundwater beneath are permanently frozen (permafrost), the surface may be marshy and warm enough to encourage growth of a wide range of plants. So the ground is partly or completely covered with vegetation – the characteristic, low-lying tundra vegetation which is especially adapted to thrive in short seasons at low temperature, and to survive, living but inactive, for many months under winter snows. Tundra soils are generally poor, tending to be acid, waterlogged and low in available nutrients. But a surprising wealth of species grows on them, including mosses, lichens, algae, sedges, rushes, grasses, shrubs, and small flowering herbs. Many are tufted or compact, shaped to combat the strong, biting winds that blow across the tundra. Often they are slow-growing, producing only millimetres of new shoots each year. The flowering plants – poppies, dwarf lupins, saxifrages, campions, bluebells and many others – put on a brilliant show in early summer, and berries, red leaves and tufted cotton grasses bring colour in autumn.

Arctic Land Animals

Arctic plants support a wide range of insects, spiders, snails and other invertebrates. Butterflies, moths, bumble-bees, beetles and dragonflies are common in milder parts of the tundra, and mosquitos and black-flies, including many biting species, can make life miserable for birds and mammals, including humans, in summer. The tundra supports many herbivorous mammals, most of which are resident throughout winter. The smallest – mice, lemmings and voles – live in snow tunnels just above ground in winter. There they are protected from predators and extreme cold, and can find plenty of food. Arctic and Snow-shoe hares are larger and live more in the open; many change colour to match their changing

Arctic Marine Animals

Polar bears spend most of their lives at sea.

Though Arctic lands are poor and unproductive, Arctic seas are comparatively rich, especially in summer. Fish and zooplankton (small surface-living animals) are plentiful, providing food for many kinds of sea-birds and mammals. Cliffs on Arctic islands are often the home of thousands of gulls, guillemots, puffins and fulmars, while the beaches and pack ice below are thronged with seals.

Ten species of seals live in the Arctic. Largest of all are walruses, up to 4 m (13 ft) long; they use their tusks to dig the sea bed for food – mainly clams. Like all other seals they come ashore (or onto the sea ice) to produce their pups and rest; clumsy on land, they are graceful and efficient swimmers. Sea lions and fur seals (distinguished by their small pointed ears) breed in huge colonies of hundreds or thousands on islands in the north Pacific Ocean. Fur seals, valued for their soft, silky fur, are hunted commercially under international control. Bearded seals and Ringed seals live mostly in the Arctic Ocean and are the main prey of Eskimos.

Polar bears too prey on seals. Up to 2.5 metres (8 ft) long from nose to tail, they spend most of their lives at sea, swimming or riding the ice floes in search of their next meal. (BS)

The Jacobshaun glacier, Greenland.

background, from brown in summer to snow-white in winter. Still larger herbivores – musk oxen, moose, caribou and reindeer – are nomadic or migratory. Wolves, Arctic and red foxes, weasels, stoats and occasional lynx are the predatory mammals of the tundra. A few species of birds, snow buntings, ptarmigan and snowy owls, for example, are resident through the winter, but each spring sees an enormous influx of migratory birds – swans, ducks, geese, waders and many smaller species, moving in to take advantage of the summer abundance of food.

Man in the Arctic

Despite the inhospitable climate and long hours of winter darkness, man has lived in the Arctic for at least 20,000 years as a hunter and gatherer of food. Early nomads probably spread first along the rivers from central Siberia, perhaps at a time when the Arctic was milder. Some, like the Lapps, took to migrating with the reindeer. Others, like the Eskimo, lived mainly by the sea, moving out onto the fast ice in winter to hunt bears and seals, and returning to land in summer. Others again hunted and trapped mainly on land and in the estuaries; immigrants to southern Greenland and Iceland even farmed and raised stock successfully during warm spells in the climatic cycle. Curiously, however, the most valuable commercial products that the Arctic has yielded – whalebone and whale oil, fur seal skins, coal and a few other minerals, and most recently of all petroleum – have been gained with little help from, and even less benefit to, indigenous populations.

Left to themselves, Arctic people have often been able to carve out hard but successful livelihoods, and even produce small surpluses of furs, skins and artifacts for markets in the south. However, their cultures – many of them rich in folk-lore, arts and spare-time skills – are now fast disappearing as the northlands, for economic, social and strategic reasons, come increasingly under the control of the societies to the south of them. In recent decades over many parts of the Arctic, the shift from traditional to modern living, brought about by the influx of money and goods from the south, has been fast and brutal. Communities once self-sufficient have been destroyed or disoriented, left in their harsh environments with some of the comforts of civilization, but little sense of purpose. Optimists see this as a sad but inevitable and short-lived phase in the process of integrating Arctic lands and peoples with the rest of the world. (BS)

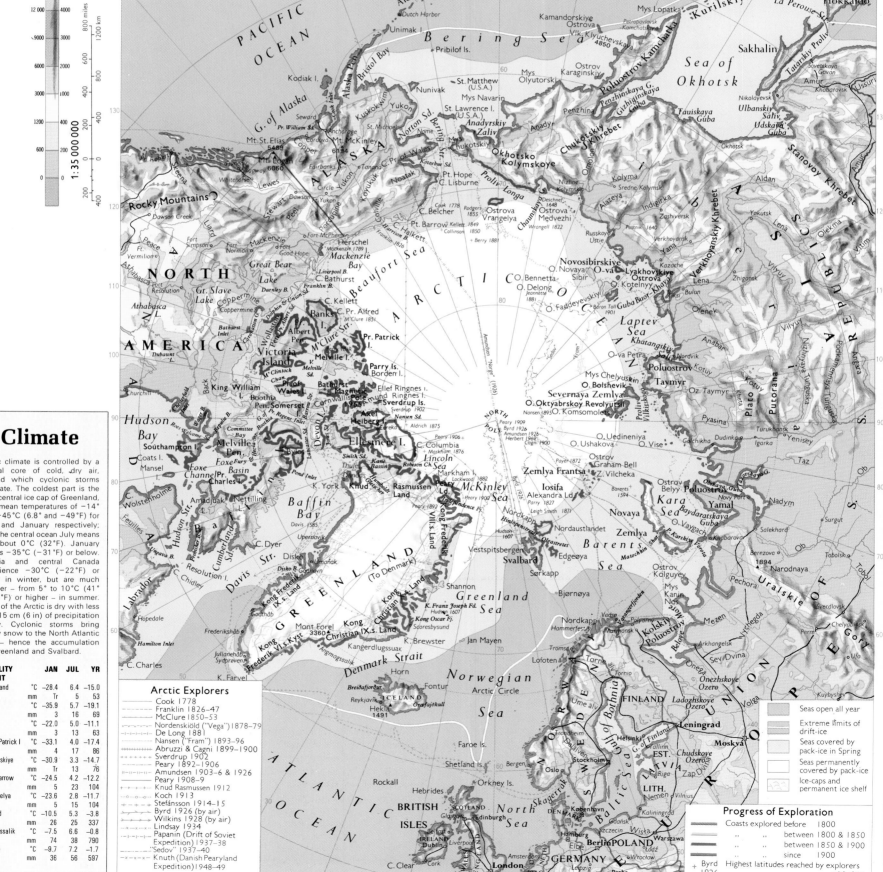

Climate

Arctic climate is controlled by a central core of cold, dry air, around which cyclonic storms circulate. The coldest part is the high central ice cap of Greenland, with mean temperatures of −14° and −45°C (6.8° and −49°F) for July and January respectively; over the central ocean July means are about 0°C (32°F). January means −35°C (−31°F) or below. Siberia and central Canada experience −30°C (−22°F) or lower in winter, but are much warmer – from 5° to 10°C (41° to 50°F) or higher – in summer. Most of the Arctic is dry with less than 15 cm (6 in) of precipitation yearly. Cyclonic storms bring heavy snow to the North Atlantic area – hence the accumulation on Greenland and Svalbard.

LOCALITY HEIGHT		JAN	JUL	YR
Peary Land	°C	−28.4	6.4	−15.0
9 m	mm	Tr	5	53
Eureka	°C	−35.9	5.7	−19.1
11 m	mm	3	16	69
Thule	°C	−22.0	5.0	−11.1
37 m	mm	3	13	63
Prince Patrick I	°C	−33.1	4.0	−17.4
15 m	mm	4	17	86
Lyakhovskiye	°C	−30.9	3.3	−14.7
7 m	mm	Tr	13	76
Point Barrow	°C	−24.5	4.2	−12.2
7 m	mm	5	23	104
O Vrangelya	°C	−23.6	2.8	−11.7
3 m	mm	5	15	104
Svalbard	°C	−10.5	5.3	−3.8
7 m	mm	26	25	337
Angmagssalik	°C	−7.5	6.6	−0.8
35 m	mm	74	38	790
Godthab	°C	−9.7	7.2	−1.7
20 m	mm	36	56	597

Arctic Explorers

Cook 1778
Franklin 1826–47
McClure 1850–53
Nordenskiöld ("Vega") 1878–79
De Long 1881
Nansen ("Fram") 1893–96
Abruzzi & Cagni 1899–1900
Sverdrup 1902
Peary 1892–1906
Amundsen 1903–6 & 1926
Peary 1908–9
Knud Rasmussen 1912
Koch 1913
Stefánsson 1914–15
Byrd 1926 (by air)
Wilkins 1928 (by air)
Lindsay 1934
Papanin (Drift of Soviet Expedition) 1937–38
"Sedov" 1937–40
Knuth (Danish Pearyland Expedition) 1948–49

Projection: Zenithal Equidistant

Progress of Exploration

Coasts explored before 1800
" " between 1800 & 1850
" " between 1850 & 1900
" " since 1900
+ Byrd 1926 Highest latitudes reached by explorers with date

Seas open all year
Extreme limits of drift-ice
Seas covered by pack-ice in Spring
Seas permanently covered by pack-ice
Ice-caps and permanent ice shelf

1:35 000 000

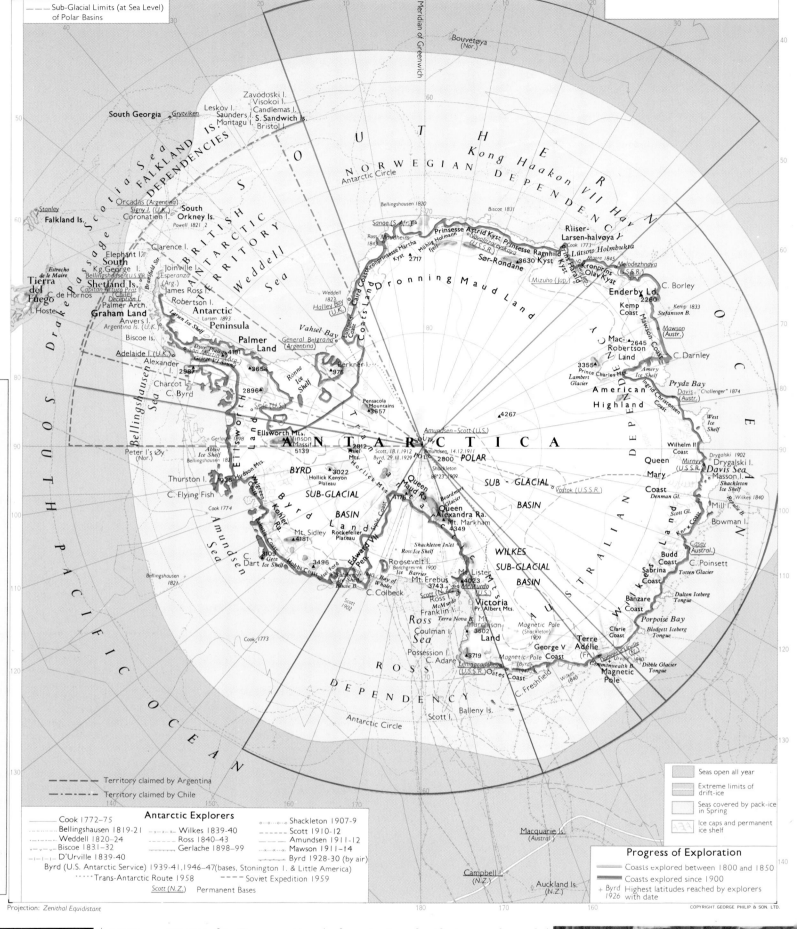

Sub-Glacial Limits (at Sea Level) of Polar Basins

Projection: *Zenithal Equidistant*

Territory claimed by Argentina
Territory claimed by Chile

Antarctic Explorers

Cook 1772–75
Bellingshausen 1819–21 — Wilkes 1839–40 — Shackleton 1907–9
Weddell 1820–24 — Ross 1840–43 — Scott 1910–12
Biscoe 1831–32 — Gerlache 1898–99 — Amundsen 1911–12
D'Urville 1839–40 — Mawson 1911–14
Byrd (U.S. Antarctic Service) 1939–41,1946–47(bases, Stonington I. & Little America) — Byrd 1928–30 (by air)
Trans-Antarctic Route 1958 — Soviet Expedition 1959
Scott (N.Z.) Permanent Bases

Seas open all year
Extreme limits of drift-ice
Seas covered by pack-ice in Spring
Ice caps and permanent ice shelf

Progress of Exploration

Coasts explored between 1800 and 1850
Coasts explored since 1900
Byrd 1926 Highest latitudes reached by explorers with date

COPYRIGHT GEORGE PHILIP & SON. LTD.

Climate

Antarctica has many climates, all of them cold. On the high plateau mean annual temperatures range from −40° to −50°C (−40° to −58°F) with light winds, little cloud and very light snowfall. Lower down at the edge of the plateau mean temperatures are 15° to 20° higher, with stronger winds and more cloud and snow. Coastal stations are often affected by depressions, bringing relatively warm air from the sea with thick clouds, strong variable winds and heavy snowfall; however, much of the continent is dry desert, with less than 15 cm (6 in) of rain-equivalent per year. Mean annual coastal temperatures range from −10° to −25°C (14° to −13°F) according to latitude. At northern stations, especially in the Maritime Antarctic (Peninsula and Scotia Sea), summer temperatures often rise above freezing point, sleet and rain replace snow, and there is a thaw of several weeks.

LOCALITY HEIGHT		JAN	JUL	YR
Vostok	°C	−32.8	−65.3	−55.6
3420 m	mm	—	—	—
South Pole	°C	−28.6	−59.7	−49.5
2800 m	mm	—	—	—
Eights Station	°C	−7.4	−34.0	−25.5
494 m	mm	—	—	—
Ellesworth	°C	−8.3	−32.4	−22.9
42 m	mm	—	—	—
Scott Base	°C	−5.8	−30.8	−20.8
16 m	mm	—	—	—
Mirny	°C	−1.9	−16.7	−11.6
30 m	mm	13	77	625
Mawson	°C	−0.3	−17.8	−11.2
14 m	mm	—	—	—
Stonington I	°C	−0.1	−11.7	−7.3
9 m	mm	10	33	317
Deception I	°C	1.6	−8.3	−2.9
8 m	mm	58	15	564
Laurie I	°C	0.0	−11.1	−4.7
4 m	mm	36	33	399

THE ANTARCTIC

Antarctica is an ice-covered continent 13.9 million km² (5.4 million sq miles) in area, surrounding the South Pole and isolated from the rest of the world by the Southern Ocean. Its ice cap, of estimated volume 24 million km³ (5.9 million miles³), has a mean thickness of 1,880 m (6,160 ft), in places reaching depths of 4,000 m (13,000 ft). Representing about 90 per cent of the world's ice, its mean elevation of 2,000 m (6,560 ft) makes Antarctica by far the highest continent with the lowest surface temperatures. The ice-cap overspreads the rocky core of the continent, spreading out to sea in floating ice shelves and glacier tongues. Over 90 per cent of the coastline is ice cliff, much of it more than 50 m (164 ft) high and descending to great depths.

Seismic surveys show a mountainous continent of about 8 million km² (3 million sq miles) beneath the ice, in two distinct blocks. East Antarctica includes a massive block of ancient rocks that once formed part of the Gondwanaland complex (pp. 8–9). These appear at the surface in scattered exposures, notably in the Transantarctic mountains of Victoria Land. Huge ranges of mountains lie beneath the ice, especially under the dome of Wilkes and Princess Elizabeth Lands, which rises unbroken to over 4,000 m (13,000 ft). By contrast the South Pole, at an elevation of 2,800 m (9,200 ft), overlies a wide rocky basin which is almost at sea-level. The great block of East Antarctica stands alongside an archipelago of steep mountainous islands, mostly hidden under the lower ice-cap of West

Antarctica. Subglacial topography includes deep channels falling well below sea-level. Exposed groups of peaks stand clear of the ice mantle, notably Vinson Massif (5,120 m, 16,800 ft), the highest point of the continent. West Antarctica spreads northward into Antarctic Peninsula, a rugged finger of partly-buried mountains pointing toward South America. Fold mountains of similar structure occur in the South Shetland and South Orkney Islands and South Georgia.

The East Antarctica block formerly lay alongside Australia in subtropical latitudes, separating some forty million years ago and cooling gradually. With only 4 to 5 per cent of continental rocks visible at the surface, the fossil record is meagre, but coal deposits in Victoria Land show that subtropical swamps existed only a few hundred km from where the South Pole is today. In them lived insects, fishes, amphibians, reptiles, and almost certainly birds and marsupials as well — creatures whose descendants are found in Australia and South America today. West Antarctica, too, had a subtropical past, though much of the fossil record has been destroyed by earth movements and volcanic activity.

Permanent ice may have started to gather on the Antarctic highlands thirty to forty million years ago. By four million years ago there was glacier ice at sea-level, and two million years ago the ice-cap was probably complete. Since then only mosses, lichens, algae and fungi, with just two species of flowering plants, manage to grow on Antarctica, and the land fauna includes only insects, mites and other tiny invertebrates. Though the land is poor, the seas around it are rich; all the big Antarctic animals — birds and seals, for example — feed in the sea. Continental Antarctica has no exploitable crops and no permanent human populations. Mineral deposits are plentiful, especially in West Antarctica, but costs of exploiting them are prohibitive.

Climate

Antarctica lies almost entirely within the polar circle, receiving long hours of daylight in summer but very little in winter. At its coldest station — Vostok, a permanently-manned

Scott at base camp during his ill-fated expedition to the South Pole in 1910–12.

The Antarctic peninsula, a rugged, mountainous finger pointing towards South America.

Soviet base high on the polar plateau in latitude 78°S – the world's lowest temperature of −88.3°C (−126.9°F) has been recorded, and temperatures seldom rise above −25°C (−13°F) even in summer. The South Pole, with a permanent American base, is lower and slightly warmer throughout the year. Coastal Antarctica has more tolerable living conditions; at nearly all shore stations temperatures rise to within a few degrees of freezing point for two or three months each summer, and at some of the warmer stations there may be a thaw lasting several days or weeks.

At a few points along the coast 'oases' form; these are very dry, ice-free areas where the rocks, warmed by the sun, heat the air to 10°C (50°F) and more, and fresh-water ponds and lakes may form. But an Antarctic oasis is seldom green — there is too little soil or ground moisture to support vegetation, though clumps of algae and moss may grow near the lake edges. Antarctic Peninsula and the neighbouring South Orkney and South Shetland Islands have the mildest and dampest climates. In sheltered corners where melt-water collects, the ground may be damp enough to support extensive mats of mosses, and even clumps of grass. Though in latitudes similar to their northern namesakes, the South Orkneys and South Shetlands are far colder, with permanent ice-caps and glaciers sweeping down to the sea.

Antarctica's cold spreads outward to freeze the sea surface in winter, in places to thicknesses of 3 m (10 ft) or more, and forming continuous sheets extending several hundred km from the shore. In summer the ice sheets break up, dispersing north and eastward about the continent as a belt of floes – pack ice – that persists locally from year to year. Tabular and angular bergs calve from the ice cliffs and glaciers; the largest ones, several km long, drift well beyond the pack ice into the Southern Ocean, melting slowly over several years. The immense white reflective surface of the ice-cap, and the pack ice covering so much of the polar region, ensure that, latitude for latitude, this is by far the colder hemisphere.

Discovery and Exploration

Pack ice, polar cold and dearth of resources kept the Antarctic region inviolate long after the Arctic was fully explored. Captain James Cook narrowly missed discovering the continent in 1773. Seal hunters were the first to see it in 1820. Considerable stretches of coast were charted during the 1840s by French, British and American expeditions, though no landing was made on the continent itself until 1895. 'Heroic age' explorations of Scott, Shackleton, Amundsen, Mawson and Byrd began with the present century, continuing with breaks up to World War 2.

Since then Antarctica has been explored thoroughly from the ground and by air, mainly by nationally-sponsored expeditions with permanent coastal and inland bases. Several thousand Soviet, U S, French, British, Argentinian, Chilean, Commonwealth and other scientists visit each summer, with much smaller numbers overwintering. Some thirteen nations are currently involved in Antarctic research, bound voluntarily by an international Antarctic Treaty, which was signed in 1959 and runs for 30 years. Though sectors of the continent are formally claimed by Britain, Chile, Argentina, Norway, France, Australia and New Zealand, all claims are currently shelved in the interests of international cooperation. (BS)

Antarctic Animals

Chinstrap penguins feeding chicks.

Antarctic birds and mammals feed at sea, using the land and sea ice for resting and producing their young. Polar seas, rich in nutrients and oxygen, support vast summer blooms of phytoplankton (tiny surface-living plant cells) that in turn supports zooplankton (small crustaceans, fish larvae and other surface-feeding animals); these become the food of fish, squid, sea birds, seals and whales. Though plentiful in summer, plankton grows scarce and descends to deep water in autumn; many of the birds and mammals that depend on it migrate away at the end of the summer and return in spring.

About forty species of sea birds breed in the Antarctic region and on Southern Ocean islands; they include petrels, gulls, skuas, terns, cormorants, and six species of penguins. Nearly all breed during the three months of summer when temperatures are warmest and food is plentiful. Emperor penguins, the largest species, breed in winter, incubating in blizzards at −50°C (−58°F) and lower; this allows their chicks time to grow and be ready for the sea by summer. Feeding flocks of petrels numbering hundreds of thousands, and penguin colonies of over a million nests, are reported from Antarctica. Six species of seals inhabit the region, feeding entirely at sea and producing their pups either on stony beaches or on sea ice. Many kinds of whales move south each summer into Antarctic waters, including Blue, Fin, Sei and Sperm whales; hunted since the early days of the century, these are now becoming rare. (BS)

STATISTICAL INFORMATION

The countries selected for inclusion in this section have been chosen on the basis of size of population or value of production. The following notes should be referred to for explanations of the entries.

Column one
1. Form of government.
2. Principal languages.
3. Currency. The CFA franc is a currency used in some African countries that have been associated with France. CFA = Communauté Financière Africaine.
4. Currency exchange rate.

   Units of national currency per £ sterling and $ US.

   In recent years the exchange rates have fluctuated more than previously. The figures quoted refer to March 1980. They have been rounded and are intended only as a rough guide. If the current rate is needed, most newspapers quote the exchange rates of the principal currencies on a day-to-day basis, and the financial newspapers give a weekly list of nearly all the world's currencies. In some countries, particularly those with socialist regimes, there are two different exchange rates, one for tourists and the other for general commerce. The latter is quoted in this table.
5. The area of the country in square kilometres and miles including inland water.

Column two
1. Total population, in millions (M = millions). Density of population per square kilometre and per square mile.

   The population total is at least that estimated by the United Nations for mid-year 1978; in some cases later figures have become available and these have been quoted.
2. The proportion of the population under 15 and over 65 years. LE = life expectancy at birth.

   The life expectancy of females tends to be greater than that of males, but the figure quoted is an average of the male and female figures.
3. The Birth Rate (BR) and Death Rate (DR), that is the number of births/deaths per thousand total population. The Annual Increase in Population (AI) is the average for the years 1970–77 and includes emigration and immigration as well as the natural change brought about by births and deaths.
4. The proportion of the population living in cities and towns is given as the urban population (Urb. pop.).
5. The name of the capital with its population in thousands.
6. Any significant divisions in the population on the grounds of tribe, religion, language or colour. (Trad. = Traditional beliefs, RC = Roman Catholic.)

Column three
Gross Domestic Product (GDP) is an approximate measure of the total value of a country's production. In socialist countries there is a different measure, the Net Material Product (NMP). The GDP and NMP are not comparable. Moreover, because methods of calculating GDP vary, any comparison based on these figures should be made cautiously.

The total GDP/NMP is quoted first, in millions of $ US. The second figure in dollars is the GDP/NMP divided by the population, the GDP or NMP per capita. These figures are usually those for 1978 but in some cases the latest available figures are in the period 1975–77. The percentages in parentheses following each of these figures show the average annual rate of change in the period 1970–77.

The second line shows the percentage contribution of agriculture and industry to the total GDP or NMP.

The next few lines are concerned with Foreign Trade. The figures for Exports and Imports are in millions of $ US. The total figures are followed by the principal commodities concerned and by a list of the principal trading partners. The final item in this column is the amount of aid given or received. It is given in millions of $ US.

AFGHANISTAN
1. Republic
2. Pashto, Persian
3. Afghani (100 puli)
4. £1 = 98
   $1 = 43
5. Area: 647,497 km²
   250,000 sq miles

1. 15.11M; 23/km²; 60/sq mile
2. −15 45%; +65 3%; LE 40
3. BR 43.0; DR 21.0; AI 2.5%
4. Urb. pop. 8%
5. Kabul 588
6. Pashtun 59%; Tadzhik 30%

GDP $2,616 (2.8%), $153 (0.4%)
Agric. 49% Indust. 17% Others 34%
Exp. $313 Skins, natural gas
Imp. $491 Food, textiles, petroleum
USSR, US, India, UK, Japan, W. Germany
Aid received: $63.2

ALGERIA
1. Republic
2. Arabic, French
3. Dinar (100 centimes)
4. £1 = 8.7
   $1 = 3.8
5. Area: 2,381,741 km²
   919,595 sq miles

1. 18.51M; 8/km²; 20/sq miles
2. −15 47%; +65 3%; LE 53
3. BR 47.8; DR 15.4; AI 3.2%
4. Urb. pop. 52%
5. Algiers 1,503
6. Arab 80%; Berber 19%

GDP $16.497 (−), $954 (−)
Agric. 8% Indust. 39% Others 53%
Exp. $5,809 Crude petroleum, wine, natural gas
Imp. $7,126 Machinery, iron and steel, food
France, W. Germany, USSR, USA, Italy, UK
Aid received: $131.2

ANGOLA
1. Republic
2. Portuguese
3. Kwanza (100 lwei)
4. £1 = 63
   $1 = 28
5. Area: 1,246,700 km²
   481,350 sq miles

1. 6.73M; 5/km²; 14/sq mile
2. −15 42%; +65 3%; LE 39
3. BR 47.2; DR 24.5; AI 2.4%
4. Urb. pop. 15%
5. Luanda 475

GDP $2,701 (−), $434 (−)
Exp. $1,227 Coffee, diamonds, crude petroleum
Imp. $625 Machinery, textiles, metals
USA, Portugal, Canada, W. Germany
Aid received: $16.9

ARGENTINA
1. Republic
2. Spanish
3. Peso (100 centavos)
4. £1 = 3,850
   $1 = 1,690
5. Area: 2,766,889 km²
   1,068,300 sq miles

1. 26.39M; 10/km²; 25/sq mile
2. −15 29%; +65 8%; LE73
3. BR 22.7; DR 9.4; AI 1.3%
4. Urb. pop. 81%
5. Buenos Aires 8,436

GDP $49.088 (2.8%), $1.934 (1.5%)
Agric. 12% Indust. 35% Others 53%
Exp. $5,650 Meat, wool, cereals, metals, textiles, leather, machinery
Imp. $4,162 Machinery, chemicals, iron and steel, non-ferrous metals
W. Germany, USA, Brazil, Japan, UK, Chile
Aid received: $27.5

AUSTRALIA
1. Federal state
2. English
3. Dollar (100 cents)
4. £1 = 2.1
   $1 = 0.9
5. Area: 7,686,810 km²
   2,967,894 sq miles

1. 14.25M; 2/km²; 5/sq mile
2. −15 29%; +64 8%; LE71
3. BR 15.7; DR 7.6; AI 1.5%
4. Urb. pop. 86%
5. Canberra 215

GDP $100,765 (3.3%), $7,239 (1.6%)
Agric. 5% Indust. 25% Others 70%
Exp. $17,420 Wool, cereals, metals, meat, coal, chemicals
Imp. $18,460 Machinery, vehicles, textiles, crude petroleum
Japan, USA, UK, New Zealand, W. Germany, China
Aid given: $550

AUSTRIA
1. Republic
2. German
3. Schilling (100 groschen)
4. £1 = 29
   $1 = 13
5. Area: 83,849 km²
   32,374 sq miles

1. 7.51M; 90/km²; 232/sq mile
2. −15 23%; +65 15%; LE 72
3. BR 11.3; DR 12.5; AI 0.2%
4. Urb. pop. 52%
5. Vienna 1,590

GDP $47,954 (4.0%), $6,377 (3.8%)
Agric. 5% Indust. 33% Others 62%
Exp. $12,205 Machinery, textiles, iron and steel
Imp. $16,013 Machinery, food, textiles, vehicles, chemical products
W. Germany, Italy, Switzerland, UK
Aid given: $230

BANGLADESH
1. Republic
2. Bengali
3. Taka (100 paisas)
4. £1 = 35
   $1 = 15
5. Area: 143,998 km²
   55,598 sq miles

1. 84.66M; 588/km²; 1,523/sq mile
2. −15 46%; +65 3%; LE 36
3. BR 49.5; DR 28.1; AI 2.4%
4. Urb. pop. 9%
5. Dacca 1,730
6. Moslem 80%; Hindu 15%

GDP $7,663 (7.3%), $93 (4.8%)
Agric. 54% Indust. 8% Others 38%
Exp. $576 Jute, hides and skins, tea
Imp. $1,294 Machinery, vehicles, food, chemicals
USA, UK, China, W. Germany
Aid received: $689.5

BELGIUM
1. Kingdom
2. French, Flemish, German
3. Franc (100 centimes)
4. £1 = 65
   $1 = 29
5. Area: 30,513 km²
   11,781 sq miles

1. 9.84M; 323/km²; 835/sq mile
2. −15 22%; +65 14%; LE 71
3. BR 12.4; DR 11.7; AI 0.4%
4. Urb. pop. 95%
5. Brussel 1,042
6. Flemish 56%; Walloon 43%

GDP $79,205 (3.7%), $8,058 (3.4%)
Agric. 2% Indust. 30% Others 68%
Exp. $44,300 Iron and steel, vehicles, machinery, non-ferrous metals, textiles
Imp. $46,391 Machinery, vehicles, non-ferrous metals, diamonds, petroleum
W. Germany, France, Netherlands, UK, USA
Aid given: $949

BOLIVIA
1. Republic
2. Spanish
3. Peso (100 centavos)
4. £1 = 57
   $1 = 25
5. Area: 1,098,581 km²
   424,165 sq miles

1. 5.14M; 5/km²; 12/sq mile
2. −15 43%; +65 4%; LE 47
3. BR 46.6; DR 18.0; AI 2.7%
4. Urb. pop. 29%
5. La Paz 655

GDP $2,334 (5.8%), $415 (3.1%)
Agric. 18% Indust. 24% Others 58%
Exp. $641 Tin ore, crude petroleum lead, zinc, tungsten
Imp. $618 Lard, flour, cooking oil, iron and steel, machinery
UK, USA, Japan, W. Germany
Aid received: $72

BRAZIL
1. Federal Republic
2. Portuguese
3. Cruzeiro (100 centavos)
4. £1 = 103
   $1 = 45
5. Area: 8,511,965 km²
   3,286,488 sq miles

1. 115.40M; 14/km²; 35/sq mile
2. −15 44%; +65 3%; LE 59
3. BR 37.1; DR 8.8; AI 2.8%
4. Urb. pop. 61%
5. Brasilia 763

GDP $155,331 (9.8%), $1,384 (6.8%)
Agric. 10% Indust. 26% Others 64%
Exp. $12,055 Iron ore, coffee, sugar, cotton, pinewood
Imp. $13,230 Machinery, fuel and lubricants, chemicals, wheat
USA, W. Germany, Netherlands, UK, Japan, Argentina
Aid received: $119.3

BULGARIA
1. Republic
2. Bulgarian
3. Lev (100 stotinki)
4. £1 = 1.9
   $1 = 0.8
5. Area: 110,912 km²
   42,823 sq miles

1. 8.81M; 79/km²; 206/sq mile
2. −15 22%; +65 11%; LE 71
3. BR 16.1; DR 10.7; AI 0.5%
4. Urb. pop. 59%
5. Sofia 965
6. Bulgarian 88%; Turkish 10%

GDP $15,965 (7.6%), $1,814 (7.0%)
Agric. 18% Indust. 52% Others 30%
Exp. $7,448 Food products, tobacco, non-ferrous metals, textiles
Imp. $7,617 Machinery, oil, natural gas, steel, cellulose
USSR, E. Germany, Libya, W. Germany
Aid given: $10

BURMA
1. Republic
2. Burmese
3. Kyat (100 pyas)
4. £1 = 15
   $1 = 8
5. Area: 678,033 km²
   261,790 sq miles

1. 32.21M; 48/km²; 123/sq mile
2. −15 40%; +65 4%; LE 50
3. BR 39.5; DR 15.8; AI 2.2%
4. Urb. pop. 16%
5. Rangoon 1,586
6. Burmese 72%; Karen 8%; Shan 7%

GDP $3,786 (2.6%), $120 (0.3%)
Agric. 47% Indust. 10% Others 43%
Exp. $243 Rice, rubber, jute, pulses
Imp. $309 Machinery, textiles
UK, India, W. Germany, Japan
Aid received: $76.6

CAMBODIA (KAMPUCHEA)
1. Republic
2. Cambodian, French
3. Riel (100 sen)
4. £1 = 2,732
   $1 = 1,200
5. Area: 181,035 km²
   69,898 sq miles

1. 8.57M; 47/km²; 123/sq mile
2. −15 46%; +65 3%; LE 46
3. BR 46.7; DR 19.0; AI 2.9%
4. Urb. pop. 12%
5. Phnom Penh (?)50

GDP $718 (2.8%), $102 (2.4%)
Agric. 41% Indust. 17% Others 42%
Exp. $10 Rubber, rice, cattle
Imp. $101 Machinery, textiles, iron and steel, petroleum
USSR, Japan, Thailand
Aid received: $27.7

CAMEROON
1. Federal Republic
2. French, English
3. CFA Franc (100 centimes)
4. £1 = 470
   $1 = 206
5. Area: 475,442 km²
   183,569 sq miles

1. 8.06M; 17/km²; 44/sq mile
2. −15 42%; +65 3%; LE 36
3. BR 40.4; DR 22.0; AI 1.9%
4. Urb. pop. 20%
5. Yaoundé 314
6. RC 20%; Christian 13%; Moslem 12%

GDP $3,309 (3.7%), $427 (1.8%)
Agric. 31% Indust. 12% Others 57%
Exp. $705 Cocoa, coffee
Imp. $784 Manufactured goods, machinery
France, W. Germany, USA, UK
Aid received: $139.2

CANADA
1. Commonwealth
2. English, French
3. Dollar (100 cents)
4. £1 = 2.6
   $1 = 1.2
5. Area: 9,976,139 km²
   3,851,800 sq miles

1. 23.50M; 2.3/km²; 6/sq mile
2. −15 26%; +65 8%; LE 74
3. BR 15.5; DR 7.3; AI 1.3%
4. Urb. pop. 76%
5. Ottawa 693
6. English 60%; French 27%

GDP $200,149 (4.7%), $8,583 (3.4%)
Agric. 4% Indust. 25% Others 71%
Exp. $230,040 Vehicles, woodpulp, paper, metal ores, wheat
Imp. $189,340 Machinery, iron and steel, textiles, petroleum, fruit
USA, UK, Japan, W. Germany
Aid given: $2,147

CHILE
1. Republic
2. Spanish
3. Peso (100 centesimos)
4. £1 = 89
   $1 = 39
5. Area: 756,946 km²
   292,257 sq miles

1. 10.86M; 14/km²; 37/sq mile
2. −15 38%; +65 5%; LE 63
3. BR 23.9; DR 7.8; AI 1.9%
4. Urb. pop. 79%
5. Santiago 3,595
6. Mestizo 66%; Spanish 25%

GDP $9,221 (−0.1%), $865 (−1.7%)
Agric. 10% Indust. 25% Others 65%
Exp. $2,152 Copper, paper, iron ore, nitrate, timber
Imp. $2,035 Industrial equipment, fuels, chemicals, food
USA, W. Germany, UK, France, Netherlands
Aid received: $48.4

CHINA
1. Popular Republic
2. Chinese
3. Yuan (10 tsjao, 100 fyng)
4. £1 = 3.4
   $1 = 1.5
5. Area: 9,561,000 km²
   3,691,500 sq miles

1. 933.03M; 98/km²; 252/sq mile
2. −15 36%; +65 6%; LE 62
3. BR 26.9; DR 10.3; AI 1.7%
4. Urb. pop. 18%
5. Peking 7,570

Agric. 29% Indust. 38% Others 33%
Exp. $7,700 Agricultural products, textiles, minerals
Imp. $6,300 Grain, cotton, fertilizer, aircraft
Japan, Hong Kong, W. Germany
Aid given: $210

COLOMBIA
1. Republic
2. Spanish
3. Peso (100 centavos)
4. £1 = 102
   $1 = 45
5. Area: 1,138,914 km²
   439,737 sq miles

1. 25.64M; 23/km²; 58/sq mile
2. −15 45%; +65 3%; LE 61
3. BR 40.6; DR 8.8; AI 2.9%
4. Urb. pop. 60%
5. Bogotá 2,855
6. Mestizo 50%; Mulatto 25%; White 20%

GDP $13,574 (6.5%), $568 (3.5%)
Agric. 27% Indust. 24% Others 49%
Exp. $2,302 Coffee, emeralds, cotton, food
Imp. $1,563 Machinery, vehicles, organic chemicals, metals
USA, W. Germany, Sweden, Japan, Netherlands
Aid received: $71.3

COSTA RICA
1. Republic
2. Spanish
3. Colón (100 centimos)
4. £1 = 20
   $1 = 8.6
5. Area: 50,700 km²
   19,575 sq miles

1. 2.11M; 42/km²; 108/sq mile
2. −15 44%; +65 4%; LE 63
3. BR 31.1; DR 4.5; AI 2.6%
4. Urb. pop. 41%
5. San José 234

GDP $3,066 (6.0%), $1,481 (3.4%)
Agric. 22% Indust. 22% Others 56%
Exp. $798 Bananas, coffee, manufactures
Imp. $1,026 Machinery, transport equipment, chemicals, paper
USA, Japan, W. Germany
Aid received: $26.7

CUBA
1. Socialist Republic
2. Spanish
3. Peso (100 centavos)
4. £1 = 1.6
   $1 = 0.7
5. Area: 114,524 km²
   44,218 sq miles

1. 9.73M; 85/km²; 220/sq mile
2. −15 37%; +65 6%; LE 70
3. BR 19.8; DR 5.6; AI 1.5%
4. Urb. pop. 60%
5. Havana 1,861

NMP $8,943 (2.5%), $973 (−)
Exp. $3,525 Sugar, minerals, tobacco, fish, nickel, coffee
Imp. $4,188 Chemicals, machinery, vehicles
USSR, Japan, China
Aid received: $32.1

CZECHOSLOVAKIA
1. Socialist Republic
2. Czech, Slovak
3. Koruna (100 halers)
4. £1 = 12
   $1 = 5.2
5. Area: 127,869 km²
   49,370 sq miles

1. 15.14M; 118/km²; 307/sq mile
2. −15 24%; +65 12%; LE 70
3. BR 18.4; DR 11.5; AI 0.7%
4. Urb. pop. 67%
5. Prague 1,176
6. Czech 65%; Slovak 29% RC 48%

NMP $36,741 (4.2%), $2,444 (3.6%)
Agric. 10% Indust. 61% Others 29%
Exp. $10,818 Machinery, manufactured goods
Imp. $12,560 Machinery, raw materials, fuel
USSR, E. Germany, Poland, W. Germany
Aid given: $429

DENMARK
1. Kingdom
2. Danish
3. Krone (100 oerer)
4. £1 = 12
   $1 = 5.5
5. Area: 43,069 km²
   16,629 sq miles

1. 5.10M; 118/km²; 307/sq mile
2. −15 23%; +65 13%; LE 79
3. BR 12.2; DR 10.4; AI 0.5%
4. Urb. pop. 67%
5. Copenhagen 1,251
6. Lutheran 90%

GDP $46,017 (2.8%), $9,041 (2.4%)
Agric. 6% Indust. 19% Others 75%
Exp. $10,117 Machinery, bacon, other meat, fish, dairy products
Imp. $14,810 Machinery, vehicles, iron and steel, textiles, petroleum
W. Germany, Sweden, UK
Aid given: $354

DOMINICAN REPUBLIC
1. Republic
2. Spanish
3. Peso (100 centavos)
4. £1 = 2.3
   $1 = 1
5. Area: 48,734 km²
   18,816 sq miles

1. 5.12M; 105/km²; 272/sq mile
2. −15 48%; +65 3%; LE 58
3. BR 42; DR 10.7; AI 2.9%
4. Urb. pop. 47%
5. Santo Domingo 818
6. Mulatto 73%; Whites 16%; Negro 10%

GDP $4,467 (8.4%), $897 (5.2%)
Agric. 21% Indust. 23% Others 56%
Exp. $604 Sugar, iron ore, cocoa
Imp. $860 Petroleum, machinery, yarns, vehicles
USA, Venezuela, Japan, Netherlands
Aid received: $32.3

ECUADOR
1. Republic
2. Spanish
3. Sucre (100 centavos)
4. £1 = 57
   $1 = 25
5. Area: 283,561 km²
   109,484 sq miles

1. 7.81M; 28/km²; 71/sq mile
2. −15 44%; +65 4%; LE 56
3. BR 41.8; DR 9.5; AI 3.4%
4. Urb. pop. 42%
5. Quito 600
6. Indian 40%; Mestizo 40%; White 10%; Negro 5%

GDP $6,152 (10.5%), $814 (6.8%)
Agric. 20% Indust. 28% Others 52%
Exp. $1,258 Bananas, coffee, cocoa, sugar
Imp. $1,508 Machinery, chemical products, vehicles
USA, W. Germany, Japan, UK, Venezuela
Aid received: $67.4

EGYPT
1. Republic
2. Arabic
3. Pound (100 piasters)
4. £1 = 1.6
   $1 = 0.7
5. Area: 1,001,449 km²
   386,659 sq miles

1. 41M; 41/km²; 106/sq mile
2. −15 41%; +65 3%; LE 53
3. BR 37.7; DR 11.8; AI 2.2%
4. Urb. pop. 44%
5. Cairo 5,921
6. Moslem 93%; Christian 6%

GDP $18,775 (4.2%), $485 (1.9%)
Agric. 24% Indust. 22% Others 54%
Exp. $1,726 Cotton, rice, cotton fabric, fruit, vegetables
Imp. $4,808 Machinery, manufactured goods, wheat, vehicles
USA, W. Germany, Italy, France, USSR
Aid received: $1,032.1

EL SALVADOR
1. Republic
2. Spanish
3. Colón (100 centavos)
4. £1 = 5.7
   $1 = 2.5
5. Area: 21,041 km²
   8,124 sq miles

1. 4.35M; 207/km²; 535/sq mile
2. −15 46%; +65 3%; LE 58
3. BR 41.7; DR 7.8; AI 3.3%
4. Urb. pop. 39%
5. San Salvador 366
6. Mestizo 89%; Indian 10%

GDP $2,619 (5.1%), $615 (2.0%)
Agric. 30% Indust. 16% Others 54%
Exp. $629 Coffee, cotton
Imp. $1,025 Machinery, vehicles, petroleum, fertilizers
USA, Guatemala, W. Germany, Japan
Aid received: $38.6

ETHIOPIA
1. Republic
2. Amharic
3. Birr (100 cents)
4. £1 = 4.7
   $1 = 2.0
5. Area: 1,221,900 km²
   471,776 sq miles

1. 29.71M; 24/km²; 63/sq mile
2. −15 45%; +65 3%; LE 38
3. BR 49.4; DR 25.8; AI 2.3%
4. Urb. pop. 12%
5. Addis Ababa 1,133
6. Orthodox 55%; Moslem 35%

GDP $2,669 (2.8%), $97 (0.6%)
Agric. 46% Indust. 10% Others 44%
Exp. $333 Coffee, pulses, oilseed, hides and skins
Imp. $349 Textiles, foodstuffs, vehicles, machinery
USA, W. Germany, Japan, Italy
Aid received: $133.6

FINLAND
1. Republic
2. Finnish, Swedish
3. Markka (100 pennia)
4. £1 = 8.5
   $1 = 3.7
5. Area: 337,009 km²
   130,120 sq miles

1. 4.75M; 14/km²; 36/sq mile
2. −15 22%; +65 10%; LE 72
3. BR 13.5; DR 9.2; AI 0.4%
4. Urb. pop. 59%
5. Helsinki 825
6. Finnish 92%; Swedish 7%

GDP $30,171 (3.4%), $6,365 (2.9%)
Agric. 10% Indust. 28% Others 62%
Exp. $8,618 Machinery, ships, paper, timber, pulp, clothing
Imp. $7,864 Machinery, crude petroleum, iron and steel, textiles
USSR, Sweden, W. Germany, UK
Aid given: $64

FRANCE
1. Republic
2. French
3. Franc (100 centimes)
4. £1 = 9.4
   $1 = 4.1
5. Area: 547,026 km²
   211,208 sq miles

1. 53.40M; 98/km²; 253/sq mile
2. −15 23%; +65 14%; LE 73
3. BR 14.0; DR 10.1; AI 0.6%
4. Urb. pop. 70%
5. Paris 9,863
6. RC 86%; Protestant 2%

GDP $380,692 (3.8%), $7,172 (3.2%)
Agric. 5% Indust. 28% Others 67%
Exp. $76,609 Machinery, vehicles, iron and steel, textiles, cereals, wine, chemicals
Imp. $81,715 Machinery, petrol, iron and steel, non-ferrous metals, vehicles, textiles, meat
W. Germany, Belg.-Lux., Italy, Netherlands, USA, UK
Aid given: $4,452

GAMBIA
1. Republic
2. English
3. Dalasi (100 butut)
4. £1 = 4
   $1 = 1.8
5. Area: 11,295 km²
   4,361 sq miles

1. 0.57M; 50/km²; 131/sq mile
2. −15 41%; +65 2%; LE 40
3. BR 43.3; DR 24.1; AI 2.6%
4. Urb. pop. 16%
5. Banjul 48
6. Moslem 70%

GDP $118 (−), $226 (−)
Agric. 56% Indust. 3% Others 41%
Exp. $44 Groundnuts, vegetable oils, fish
Imp. $103 Cotton fabric, cereals
UK, France, China, Netherlands
Aid received: $13.0

GERMANY (EAST)
1. Socialist Republic
2. German
3. Ostmark (100 pfennigs)
4. £1 = 4.0
   $1 = 1.8
5. Area: 108,174 km²
   41,766 sq miles

1. 16.76M; 155/km²; 401/sq mile
2. −15 19%; +65 16%; LE 72
3. BR 13.9; DR 13.9; AI −0.2%
4. Urb. pop. 76%
5. Berlin (East) 1,101
6. Protestant 80%; RC 11%

NMP $72,190 (5.1%), $4,304 (5.4%)
Agric. 10% Indust. 62% Others 28%
Exp. $13,267 Machinery, vehicles, consumer goods, fuels
Imp. $14,572 Machinery, crude petroleum, coal, iron ore
USSR, Czechoslovakia, Poland
Aid given: $153

GERMANY (WEST)
1. Federal Republic
2. German
3. Deutschmark (100 pfennigs)
4. £1 = 4.0
   $1 = 1.8
5. Area: 248,343 km²
   95,886 sq miles

1. 61.31M; 247/km²; 639/sq mile
2. −15 21%; +65 15%; LE 72
3. BR 9.4; DR 11.8; AI 0.2%
4. Urb. pop. 82%
5. Bonn 285

GDP $516,150 (2.4%), $8,406 (2.3%)
Agric. 3% Indust. 41% Others 56%
Exp. $142,090 Machinery, vehicles, iron and steel, textiles, organic chemicals
Imp. $120,668 Manufactured goods, machinery, crude petroleum, non-ferrous metals
France, Netherlands, USA, Italy, Belgium
Aid given: $4,218

GHANA
1. Republic
2. English
3. Cedi (100 pesewas)
4. £1 = 6.3
   $1 = 2.8
5. Area: 238,537 km²
   92,100 miles

1. 10.97M; 46/km²; 119/sq mile
2. −15 46%; +65 4%; L E 38
3. B R 48.8; D R 21.9; A I 2.8%
4. Urb. pop. 31%
5. Accra 738
6. Trad. 38%; Protestant 29%; R C 14%; Moslem 12%

G D P $4,912 (3.0%), $498 (0.3%)
Agric. 51% Indust. 13% Others 36%
Exp. $811 Cocoa, timber, gold
Imp. $862 Food, mineral fuels, chemicals, manufactured goods, vehicles
U K, U S A, W. Germany, France, Japan
Aid received: $95.6

GREECE
1. Republic
2. Greek
3. Drachma (100 lepta)
4. £1 = 89
   $1 = 39
5. Area: 131,944 km²
   50,944 miles

1. 9.36M; 71/km²; 184/sq mile
2. −15 24%; +65 12%; L E 69
3. B R 15.9; D R 8.8; A I 0.7%
4. Urb. pop. 65%
5. Athens 2,101

G D P $26,208 (4.6%), $2,824 (3.9%)
Agric. 15% Indust. 19% Others 66%
Exp. $2,724 Manufactured goods, textiles, tobacco, chemicals, foodstuffs
Imp. $6,778 Machinery, vehicles, crude petroleum, iron and steel, W. Germany, Italy, U K, Netherlands, France

GUATEMALA
1. Republic
2. Spanish
3. Quetzal (100 centavos)
4. £1 = 2.3
   $1 = 1
5. Area: 108,889 km²
   42,042 sq miles

1. 6.62M; 61/km²; 157/sq mile
2. −15 44%; +65 3%; L E 49
3. B R 42.6; D R 9.8; A I 2.9%
4. Urb. pop. 36%
5. Guatemala 717

G D P $5,593 (6.0%) $869 (3.0%)
Agric. 26% Indust. 16% Others 58%
Exp. $1,160 Sugar, cotton, bananas, beef, timber, vegetable oil
Imp. $1,084 Chemicals, food, vehicles, textiles, petroleum
U S A, W. Germany, Costa Rica, El Salvador
Aid received: $56.4

GUYANA
1. Republic
2. English
3. Dollar (100 cents)
4. £1 = 5.8
   $1 = 2.5
5. Area: 214,969 km²
   83,000 sq miles

1. 0.82M; 4/km²; 10/sq mile
2. −15 47%; +65 3%; L E 61
3. B R 26.7; D R 7.1; A I 2.4%
4. Urb. pop. 40%
5. Georgetown 182
6. East Indian 51%; African 31%; Hindu 33%; Anglican 20%; R C 15%

G D P $438 (3.9%), $562 (2.0%)
Agric. 21% Indust. 25% Others 54%
Exp. $289 Sugar, bauxite, rice, alumina, rum, timber
Imp. $279 Flour, textiles, manufactured goods, vehicles
U S A, U K, U S S R, Canada, Trinidad and Tobago
Aid received: $11.5

HAITI
1. Republic
2. French
3. Gourde (100 centimes)
4. £1 = 11
   $1 = 5
5. Area: 27,750 km²
   10,714 sq miles

1. 4.83M; 174/km²; 451/sq mile
2. −15 42%; +65 4%; L E 50
3. B R 42.7; D R 17.4; A I 1.7%
4. Urb. pop. 24%
5. Port-au-Prince 703

G D P $1,166 (4.6%), $250 (2.9%)
Agric. 41% Indust. 15% Others 44%
Exp. $149 Coffee, bauxite, manufactures
Imp. $225 Machinery, petroleum, cereals
U S A, Surinam, France, Japan, Canada
Aid received: $73.2

HONDURAS
1. Republic
2. Spanish
3. Lempira (100 centavos)
4. £1 = 4.6
   $1 = 2
5. Area: 112,088 km²
   43,277 sq miles

1. 3.44M; 31/km²; 79/sq mile
2. −15 48%; +65 2%; L E 54
3. B R 49.3; D R 14.6; A I 3.8%
4. Urb. pop. 31%
5. Tegucigalpa 274

G D P $1,074 (3.6%), $506 (0.7%)
Agric. 29% Indust. 18% Others 53%
Exp. $596 Bananas, coffee, timber, meat
Imp. $693 Manufactured goods, machinery, vehicles, chemicals
U S A, U K, Japan, W. Germany, Guatemala, Nicaragua
Aid received: $49.7

HONG KONG
1. British Colony
2. English, Chinese
3. Hong Kong Dollar (100 cents)
4. £1 = 11.4
   $1 = 5
5. Area: 1,045 km²
   400 sq miles

1. 4.61M; 4,411/km²; 11,525/sq mile
2. −15 36%; +65 6%; L E 71
3. B R 17.5; D R 5.1; A I 1.9%
4. Urb. pop. 89%
5. Victoria 849
6. 60% of pop. born in H.K.

G D P $10,737 (8.0%), $2,381 (5.9%)
Agric. 1% Indust. 23% Others 76%
Exp. $11,499 Manufactured goods, toys and games, electrical goods
Imp. $13,452 Machinery, textiles, food, chemicals
U K, U S A, Japan, W. Germany, Australia
Aid received: $1.7

HUNGARY
1. Popular Republic
2. Hungarian
3. Forint (100 filler)
4. £1 = 76
   $1 = 33
5. Area: 93,030 km²
   35,919 sq miles

1. 10.69M; 115/km²; 298/sq mile
2. −15 21%; +65 13%; L E 69
3. B R 15.7; D R 13.1; A I 0.4%
4. Urb. pop. 51%
5. Budapest 2,082
6. R C 48%; Protestant 23%

N M P $23,260 (6.2%), $2,184 (5.2%)
Agric. 16% Indust. 47% Others 37%
Exp. $6,350 Machinery, clothing, medical supplies, fruit and vegetables
Imp. $7,898 Machinery, vehicles, non-ferrous metals, crude petroleum
U S S R, E. Germany, W. Germany, Czechoslovakia
Aid given: $91

ICELAND
1. Republic
2. Icelandic
3. Krona (100 aurar)
4. £1 = 915
   $1 = 402
5. Area: 103,000 km²
   39,768 sq miles

1. 0.22M; 2/km²;6/sq mile
2. −15 29%; +65 9%; L E 76
3. B R 18.0; D R 6.5; A I 1.2%
4. Urb. pop. 87%
5. Reykjavik 83

G D P $1,917 (4.6%), $8,715 (3.2%)
Exp. $641 Fish, fish products
Imp. $674 Fuel oil, vehicles, food, paper and cardboard
U S A, U K, U S S R, Norway, Sweden, W. Germany

INDIA
1. Federal Republic
2. Hindi, English
3. Rupee (100 paisa)
4. £1 = 18
   $1 = 8
5. Area: 3,287,580 km²
   1,269,335 sq miles

1. 638.39M; 194/km²; 503/sq mile
2. −15 41%; +65 3%; L E 41
3. B R 35.2; D R 15.9; A I 2.2%
4. Delhi 3,647
6. Hindu 83%; Moslem 11%; Christian 3%

G D P $86,152 (2.5%), $141 (0.4%)
Agric. 36% Indust. 16% Others 48%
Exp. $6,415 Jute products, tea, iron ore, iron and steel, cotton goods
Imp. $7,405 Petroleum, machinery, wheat, raw cotton, fertilizers
U S A, Japan, U S S R, U K, W. Germany
Aid received: $1,317.1

INDONESIA
1. Republic
2. Bahasa Indonesian
3. Rupiah (100 sen)
4. £1 = 1,422
   $1 = 625
5. Area: 1,919,270 km²
   741,030 sq miles

1. 145.10M; 76/km²; 196/sq mile
2. −15 43%; +65 2%; L E 48
3. B R 42.9; D R 16.9; A I 2.6%
4. Urb. pop. 18%
5. Jakarta 4,576
6. Moslem 89%; Protestant 5%; R C 2%

G D P $45,896 (7.8%), $320 (5.0%)
Agric. 31% Indust. 29% Others 40%
Exp. $11,643 Coffee, rubber, palm-oil, tin ore, tea, petroleum
Imp. $6,690 Rice, petroleum, manufactured goods, machinery
Japan, Singapore, U S A, W. Germany
Aid received: $614.6

IRAN
1. Islamic Republic
2. Persian
3. Rial (100 dinars)
4. £1 = 161
   $1 = 70
5. Area: 1,648,000 km²
   636,296 sq miles

1. 35.21M; 21/km²; 55/sq mile
2. −15 46%; +65 3%; L E 58
3. B R 42.5; D R 11.5; A I 2.8%
4. Urb. pop. 47%
5. Tehran 4,496
6. Indo-European 66%; Turk 25%; Kurd 5%; Arab 4%

G D P $66,777 (10.2%), $1,988 (7.4%)
Agric. 9% Indust. 48% Others 43%
Exp. $22,457 Petroleum, carpets, cotton
Imp. $14,968 Machinery, chemicals, vehicles
W. Germany, U S A, U K, Japan
Aid received: $3.7

IRAQ
1. Republic
2. Arabic
3. Dinar (10 riyals)
4. £1 = 0.7
   $1 = 0.3
5. Area: 434,924 km²
   167,925 sq miles

1. 12.33M; 28/km²; 73/sq mile
2. −15 48%; +65 3%; L E 53
3. B R 48.1; D R 14.6; A I 3.4%
4. Urb. pop. 66%
5. Baghdad 2,969
6. Arab 78%; Kurd 18%

G D P $13,635 (8.7%), $1,226 (5.2%)
Agric. 7% Indust. 60% Others 33%
Exp. $11,008 Crude petroleum, dates
Imp. $3,898 Manufactured goods, machinery, foods
U K, U S S R, Italy, France, Czechoslovakia
Aid received: $40.2

IRELAND
1. Republic
2. Irish, English
3. Irish pound (100 pence)
4. £1 = 1.1
   $1 = 0.5
5. Area: 70,283 km²
   27,136 sq miles

1. 3.37M; 48/km²; 124/sq mile
2. −15 31%; +65 11%; L E 71
3. B R 22.1; D R 10.5; A I 1.2%
4. Urb. pop. 52%
5. Dublin 544

G D P $9,389 (3.4%), $2,943 (2.2%)
Agric. 17% Indust. 15% Others 68%
Exp. $5,678 Cattle, dairy products, non-ferrous metals
Imp. $7,097 Machinery, textiles, vehicles, iron and steel
U K, U S A, W. Germany, France

ISRAEL
1. Republic
2. Hebrew, Arabic
3. Shekel (100 agorot)
4. £1 = 9
   $1 = 4
5. Area: 20,700 km²
   7,992 sq miles

1. 3.69M; 178/km²; 462/sq mile
2. −15 33%; +65 8%; L E 72
3. B R 25.2; D R 6.8; A I 2.8%
4. Urb. pop. 82%
5. Jerusalem 336
6. Jewish 85%; Moslem 11%; Christian 3%

G D P $14,724 (5.4%), $4,079 (2.4%)
Agric. 7% Indust. 26% Others 67%
Exp. $3,716 Fruit, diamonds, clothing, chemicals, food
Imp. $5,582 Machinery, diamonds, iron and steel
U S A, W. Germany, U K, Netherlands, Italy
Aid received: $636.8

ITALY
1. Republic
2. Italian
3. Lira (100 centesimi)
4. £1 = 1,855
   $1 = 815
5. Area: 301,225 km²
   116,304 sq miles

1. 56.70M; 188/km²; 496/sq mile
2. −15 24%; +65 12%; L E 72
3. B R 12.5; D R 9.4; A I 0.7%
4. Urb. pop. 53%
5. Rome 2,898

G D P $170,767 (3.0%), $3,040 (2.2%)
Agric. 8% Indust. 35% Others 57%
Exp. $56,055 Fruit, clothing, machinery, textiles, vehicles
Imp. $56.446 Cereals, wood, vehicles, meat, petroleum
U S A, France, W. Germany, Netherlands, U K
Aid given: $1,646

IVORY COAST
1. Republic
2. French
3. CFA Franc (100 centimes)
4. £1 = 470
   $1 = 206
5. Area: 322,463 km²
   124,504 sq miles

1. 7.61M; 24/km²; 61/sq mile
2. −15 43%; +65 3%; L E 44
3. B R 45.6; D R 20.6; A I 2.6%
4. Urb. pop. 32%
5. Abidjan 850
6. Trad. 65%; Moslem 23%; Christian 12%

G D P $6,441 (10.3%), $1,251 (7.5%)
Agric. 23% Indust. 12% Others 65%
Exp. $2,322 Timber, coffee, cocoa
Imp. $2,325 Metalwork, cement, wine, machinery
France, U S A, W. Germany, Italy, Netherlands
Aid received: $106.2

JAMAICA
1. Republic
2. English
3. Dollar (100 cents)
4. £1 = 4.1
   $1 = 1.8
5. Area: 10,962 km²
   4,232 sq miles

1. 2.13M; 194/km²; 503/sq mile
2. −15 43%; +65 6%; L E 65
3. B R 29.8; D R 7.1; A I 1.6%
4. Urb. pop. 37%
5. Kingston 573
6. African 77%; Afro-European 15%

G D P $2,045 (−0.5%), $1,471 (−2.2%)
Agric. 9% Indust. 29% Others 62%
Exp. $710 Alumina, bauxite, sugar
Imp. $872 Manufactured goods, machinery, textiles
U S A, U K, Canada, Norway
Aid received: $29.2

JAPAN
1. Constitutional monarchy
2. Japanese
3. Yen (100 sen)
4. £1 = 566
   $1 = 248
5. Area: 372,077 km²
   143,660 sq miles

1. 114.90M; 309/km²; 800/sq mile
2. −15 24%; +65 8%; L E 75
3. B R 15.4; D R 6.1; A I 1.3%
4. Urb. pop. 76%
5. Tokyo 11,684
6. Buddhist 85M; Shinto 83M

G D P $564,041 (5.1%), $5,002 (3.8%)
Agric. 5% Indust. 30% Others 65%
Exp. $97,501 Machinery, iron and steel, textiles, chemicals, vehicles
Imp. $78,731 Crude petroleum, foods, machinery, textile fibres, iron ore
U S A, Saudia Arabia, Australia, Indonesia, S. Korea
Aid given: $3,936

JORDAN
1. Constitutional monarchy

1. 2.98M; 30/km²; 79/sq mile

G D P $1,452 (−), $697 (−)
Agric. 9% Indust. 16% Others 75%

2. Arabic
3. Dinar (1000 fils)
4. £1 = 0.7
   $1 = 0.3
5. Area: 97,740 km²
   37,737 sq miles

2. −15 48%; +65 3%; LE 53
3. BR 47.8; DR 14.7; AI 3.2%
4. Urb. pop. 42%
5. Amman 672

Exp. $297 Fertilizers, fruit
Imp. $1,499 Machinery, vehicles, aircraft, steel, textiles, petroleum, food
USA, W. Germany, Saudi Arabia, UK
Aid received: $134.9

KENYA
1. Republic
2. Swahili, English
3. Shilling (100 cents)
4. £1 = 17
   $1 = 7.3
5. Area: 582,645 km²
   224,961 sq miles

1. 14.86M; 26/km²; 66/sq mile
2. −15 48%; +65 3%; LE 49
3. BR 48.7; DR 16.0; AI 3.6%
4. Urb. pop. 10%
5. Nairobi 776
6. Kikuyu 20%; Luo 14%; Lukya 13%; Kamba 11% Protestant 36%; RC 22%; Moslem 4%

GDP $4,427 (4.6%), $309 (1.1%)
Agric. 34% Indust. 13% Others 53%
Exp. $1,025 Coffee, tea, petroleum products, pyrethrum
Imp. $1,710 Machinery, vehicles, iron and steel, petroleum
UK, W. Germany, Netherlands, USA, Japan
Aid received: $151.7

KOREA (NORTH)
1. Republic
2. Korean
3. Won (100 jon)
4. £1 = 1.9
   $1 = 0.8
5. Area: 120,538 km²
   46,540 sq miles

1. 17.07M; 142/km²; 367/sq mile
2. −15 42%; +65 4%; LE 61
3. BR 35.7; DR 9.4; AI 2.6%
4. Urb. pop. 48%
5. Pyongyang 1,500

Agric. 8% Indust. 54% Others 38%
Exp. Metals, minerals
Imp. Fuels, machinery, chemicals
USSR, Japan

KOREA (SOUTH)
1. Republic
2. Korean
3. Won (100 chon)
4. £1 = 1,315
   $1 = 577
5. Area: 98,477 km²
   38,022 sq miles

1. 37.02M; 376/km²; 974/sq mile
2. −15 39%; +65 4%; LE 65
3. BR 28.8; DR 8.9; AI 1.8%
4. Urb. pop. 48%
5. Seoul 6,879
6. Buddhist 15%; Confucian 14%; Protestant 9%; RC 2%

GDP $34,615 (9.9%), $950 (8.0%)
Agric. 21% Indust. 30% Others 49%
Exp. $12.713 Clothing, wigs, timber, machinery
Imp. $15,074 Machinery, chemicals, petroleum
USA, Japan, Saudi Arabia, Kuwait
Aid received: $227

KUWAIT
1. Emirate
2. Arabic, English
3. Dinar (1000 fils)
4. £1 = 0.6
   $1 = 0.3
5. Area: 17,818 km²
   6,880 sq miles

1. 1.20M; 67/km²; 174/sq mile
2. −15 44%; +65 2%; LE 69
3. BR 41.5; DR 4.8; AI 6.1%
4. Urb. pop. 57%
5. Kuwait 775

GDP $11,307 (−), $11,307 (−)
Agric. 0% Indust. 77% Others 23%
Exp. $10,464 Petroleum products, crude petroleum, chemicals
Imp. $4,617 Machinery, manufactured products, food
USA, W. Germany, UK, Japan, France
Aid received: $1.9

LAOS
1. Kingdom
2. Lao, French
3. Kip (100 at)
4. £1 = 910
   $1 = 400
5. Area: 236,800 km²
   91,429 sq miles

1. 3.55M; 15/km²; 39/sq mile
2. −15 42%; +65 3%; LE 40
3. BR 44.6; DR 22.8; AI 2.3%
4. Urb. pop. 15%
5. Vientiane 177

GDP $203 (−), $69 (−)
Exp. $5 Tin, timber, raw cotton
Imp. $64 Agricultural products, petroleum products, machinery
Thailand, Malaysia, USA, Japan, Indonesia
Aid received: $25

LEBANON
1. Republic
2. Arabic, French
3. Pound (100 piastres)
4. £1 = 7.8
   $1 = 3.3
5. Area: 10,400 km²
   4,015 sq miles

1. 3.01M; 289/km²; 750/sq mile
2. −15 44%; +65 5%; LE 63
3. BR 39.8; DR 9.9; AI 3.1%
4. Urb. pop. 60%
5. Beirut 702
6. Christian 35%; Moslem 22%

GDP $1,488 (−), $603 (−)
Agric. 10% Indust. 16% Others 74%
Exp. $497 Foods, machinery, jewellery
Imp. $1,224 Precious stones, machinery
Saudi Arabia, Switzerland, UK, Kuwait, Syria, USA
Aid received: $26.4

LIBYA
1. Republic
2. Arabic
3. Dinar (100 dirhams)
4. £1 = 0.7
   $1 = 0.3
5. Area: 1,759,540 km²
   679,360 sq miles

1. 2.75M; 2/km²; 4/sq mile
2. −15 49%; +65 4%; LE 53
3. BR 45.0; DR 14.7; AI 3.9%
4. Urb. pop. 30%
5. Tripoli 551

GDP $19,363 (17.5%), $7,422 (12.8%)
Agric. 2% Indust. 58% Others 40%
Exp. $9,561 Crude petroleum
Imp. $3,782 Machinery, vehicles
W. Germany, Italy, UK, USA, Netherlands
Aid received: $27.1

LUXEMBOURG
1. Grand Duchy
2. Luxembourgeois, French, German
3. Franc (100 centimes)
4. £1 = 65
   $1 = 29
5. Area: 2,586 km²
   998 sq miles

1. 0.36M; 139/km²; 360/sq mile
2. −15 20%; +65 13%; LE 70
3. BR 11.4; DR 11.8; AI 0.7%
4. Urb. pop. 68%
5. Luxembourg 78

GDP $2,788 (2.8%), $7,717 (1.4%)
Agric. 3% Indust. 37% Others 60%
Trade included under Belgium

MADAGASCAR
1. Republic
2. Malagasy, French
3. Franc (100 centimes)
4. £1 = 470
   $1 = 206
5. Area: 587,041 km²
   226,658 sq miles

1. 8.29M; 14/km²; 37/sq mile
2. −15 46%; +65 3%; LE 38
3. BR 46; DR 25; AI 30%
4. Urb. pop. 14%
5. Antananarivo 378
6. Trad. 50%+; RC 17%; Protestant 15%

GDP $1,859 (−), $232 (−)
Agric. 41% Indust. 15% Others 44%
Exp. $338 Foodstuffs, textiles, animal products
Imp. $347 Metalware, chemicals, wines, food
France, USA, W. Germany, Réunion
Aid received: $71.0

MALAWI
1. Republic
2. Bantu, English
3. Kwacha (100 tambala)

1. 5.67M; 48/km²; 124/sq mile
2. −15 44%; +65 3%; LE 43

GDP $723 (12.3%), $140 (9.5%)
Agric. 49% Indust. 11% Others 40%
Exp. $174 Tobacco, tea, sugar.

---

4. £1 = 1.8
   $1 = 0.8
5. Area: 118,484 km²
   45,747 sq miles

3. BR 50.5; DR 26.5; AI 3.2%
4. Urb. pop. 10%
5. Lilongwe 103
6. RC 18%; Presbyterian 15%

groundnuts
Imp. $339 Machinery, textiles, vehicles
UK, USA, Netherlands, Zimbabwe
Aid received: $67.7

MALAYSIA
1. Federation
2. Malay, Chinese, English
3. Ringgit (100 cents)
4. £1 = 5.0
   $1 = 2.2
5. Area: 329,749 km²
   127,316 sq miles

1. 12.96M; 39/km²; 101/sq mile
2. −15 45%; +65 3%; LE 68
3. BR 38.7; DR 9.9; AI 2.8%
4. Urb. pop. 27%
5. Kuala Lumpur 452
6. Malay 51%; Chinese 35%; Indian 11%

GDP $9,297 (9.3%), $781 (6.6%)
Agric. 28% Indust. 23% Others 49%
Exp. $8,058 Rubber, tin, wood, fish, palm oil
Imp. $6,508 Machinery, crude petroleum, vehicles, textiles, rice, iron and steel
Japan, USA, USSR, UK, W. Germany, Australia
Aid received: $73.2

MALI
1. Republic
2. French
3. Franc (100 centimes)
4. £1 = 941
   $1 = 413
5. Area: 1,240,000 km²
   47,876 sq miles

1. 6.29M; 5/km²; 131/sq mile
2. −15 49%; +65 2%; LE 38
3. BR 49.0; DR 23.2; AI 2.5%
4. Urb. pop. 17%
5. Bamako 400
6. Bambara 20%; Fulani 10%; Senufo 8%

GDP $507 (−), $89 (−)
Agric. 45% Indust. 7% Others 48%
Exp. $107 Cotton, groundnuts, cattle
Imp. $219 Petroleum, machinery, vehicles, sugar
France, Ivory Coast, Senegal, China
Aid received: $101.4

MEXICO
1. Federal Republic
2. Spanish
3. Peso (100 centavos)
4. £1 = 52
   $1 = 23
5. Area: 1,972,547 km²
   761,605 sq miles

1. 66.94M; 34/km²; 88/sq mile
2. −15 48%; +65 3%; LE 65
3. BR 42.0; DR 6.5; AI 3.5%
4. Urb. pop. 64%
5. Mexico City 11,943
6. Mestizo 55%; Indian 29%; White 15%

GDP $74,248 (5.5%), $1,150 (1.9%)
Agric. 9% Indust. 30% Others 61%
Exp. $5,772 Manufactured products, petroleum, coffee, sugar, cotton
Imp. $7,786 Cereals, machine tools, iron and steel, machinery, vehicles
USA, W. Germany, Japan, France, UK, Canada
Aid received: $57.9

MOROCCO
1. Kingdom
2. Arabic, French, Spanish
3. Dirham (100 centimes)
4. £1 = 8.5
   $1 = 3.7
5. Area: 446,550 km²
   172,414 sq miles

1. 18.91M; 42/km²; 110/sq mile
2. −15 46%; +65 2%; LE 53
3. BR 46.2; DR 15.7; AI 3.1%
4. Urb. pop. 38%
5. Rabat 597

GDP $8,083 (4.6%), $453 (1.5%)
Agric. 24% Indust. 24% Others 52%
Exp. $1,511 Citrus fruit, phosphates, minerals
Imp. $4,955 Machinery, manufactured products
France, W. Germany, Italy, USA
Aid received: $179.4

MOZAMBIQUE
1. Republic
2. Portuguese, Bantu
3. Escudo (100 centavos)
4. £1 = 69
   $1 = 30
5. Area: 783,030 km²
   302,330 sq miles

1. 11.76M; 15/km²; 39/sq mile
2. −15 45%; +65 3%; LE 44
3. BR 43.1; DR 20.1; AI 2.3%
4. Urb. pop. 6%
5. Maputo 384
6. Trad. 70%; Christian 15%; Moslem 13%

GDP $2,722 (−), $295 (−)
Exp. $129 Sugar, cotton, copra, nuts, sisal, tea
Imp. $278 Machinery, iron and steel, vehicles, petroleum
Portugal, South Africa, UK, India, W. Germany
Aid received: $56.4

NEPAL
1. Constitutional monarchy
2. Nepali
3. Rupee (100 pice)
4. £1 = 28
   $1 = 12
5. Area: 140,798 km²
   54,362 sq miles

1. 13.42M; 95/km²; 247/sq mile
2. −15 40%; +65 3%; LE 44
3. BR 42.9; DR 20.3; AI 2.3%
5. Katmandu 210
6. Hindu 90%; Buddhist 9%

GDP $1,340 (2.0%), $106 (−0.2%)
Agric. 67% Indust. 10% Others 83%
Exp. Food and live animals
Imp. Manufactured goods
India
Aid received: $55.8

NETHERLANDS
1. Kingdom
2. Dutch
3. Guilder (100 cents)
4. £1 = 4.4
   $1 = 1.9
5. Area: 40,844 km²
   15,769 sq miles

1. 13.99M; 343/km²; 887/sq mile
2. −15 25%; +65 11%; LE 74
3. BR 12.6; DR 8.2; AI 0.9%
4. Urb. pop. 77%
5. The Hague 673
6. RC 40%; Dutch Reformed Church 28%

GDP $106,406 (3.2%), $7,683 (2.3%)
Agric. 6% Indust. 32% Others 62%
Exp. $50,280 Machinery, textiles, chemical products, petroleum, iron and steel, vegetables
Imp. $53,812 Machinery, crude petroleum, textiles, vehicles, clothing, non-ferrous metals
W. Germany, Belgium-Lux., France, Italy, UK, USA
Aid given: $1,596

NEW ZEALAND
1. Commonwealth
2. English
3. Dollar (100 cents)
4. £1 = 2.3
   $1 = 1.0
5. Area: 268,675 km²
   103,736 sq miles

1. 3.11M; 12/km²; 30/sq mile
2. −15 29%; +65 9%; LE 72
3. BR 16.3; DR 7.9; AI 1.4%
4. Urb. pop. 81%
5. Wellington 329
6. European 91%; Maori 8%

GDP $13,136 (−), $4,251 (−)
Exp. $3,752 Meat, wool, butter, cheese
Imp. $3,500 Machinery, textiles, vehicles, iron and steel, petroleum products
USA, Japan, Australia, UK
Aid given: $65

NICARAGUA
1. Republic
2. Spanish
3. Córdoba (100 centavos)
4. £1 = 23
   $1 = 10
5. Area: 130,000 km²
   50,193 sq miles

1. 2.40M; 18/km²; 48/sq mile
2. −15 50%; +65 3%; LE 53
3. BR 48.3; DR 13.9; AI 3.4%
4. Urb. pop. 49%
5. Managua 500
6. Mestizo and Mulatto 70%; White 20%; Black 10%

GDP $2,233 (5.9%), $967 (2.4%)
Agric. 23% Indust. 21% Others 56%
Exp. $628 Cotton, meat, coffee, sugar
Imp. $755 Machinery, vehicles, chemicals, crude oil, food
USA, Venezuela, W. Germany, Japan, Costa Rica
Aid received: $39.2

NIGER
1. Republic
2. Arabic, French
3. C F A Franc (100 centimes)
4. £1 = 470
   $1 = 206
5. Area: 1,267,000 km² 489,190 sq miles

1. 4.99M; 4/km²; 10/sq mile
2. −15 44%; +65 3%; LE 39
3. B R 52.2; D R 25.5; A I 2.7%
4. Urb. pop. 8%
5. Niamey 130

G D P $599 (−), $130 (−)
Agric. 51% Indust. 7% Others 42%
Exp. $134 Groundnuts
Imp. $127 Manufactured products
France, Nigeria
Aid received: $121.2

NIGERIA
1. Federal Republic
2. English
3. Naira (100 kobo)
4. £1 = 1.3
   $1 = 0.5
5. Area: 923,768 km² 356,667 sq miles

1. 72.22M; 78/km²; 202/sq mile
2. −15 44%; +65 2%; LE 37
3. B R 49.3; D R 22.7; A I 2.8%
4. Urb. pop. 23%
5. Lagos 1,477
6. Hausa 21%; Ibo 18%; Yoruba 18%; Fulani 10% Moslem 47%

G D P $25,120 (7.8%), $399 (5.0%)
Agric. 26% Indust. 38% Others 36%
Exp. $9,483 Petrol, cocoa, groundnuts, tin
Imp. $12,857 Machinery, textiles, vehicles, iron and steel
USA, UK, France, Japan, Netherlands
Aid received: $58.1

NORWAY
1. Kingdom
2. Norwegian
3. Krone (100 øre)
4. £1 = 11
   $1 = 4.9
5. Area: 324,219 km² 125,182 sq miles

1. 4.06M; 13/km²; 32/sq mile
2. −15 23%; +65 14%; LE 75
3. B R 12.7; D R 9.8; A I 0.6%
4. Urb. pop. 45%
5. Oslo 645

G D P $35,589 (4.8%), $8,809 (4.1%)
Agric. 6% Indust. 27% Others 67%
Exp. $10,037 Machinery, ships, crude oil, paper, non-ferrous metals
Imp. $11,429 Machinery, ships, vehicles, iron and steel, non-ferrous minerals, fuel oil
UK, Sweden, Denmark, W. Germany, USA, Japan, France
Aid given: $401

PAKISTAN
1. Islamic Republic
2. Urdu, Bengali, English
3. Rupee (100 paisas)
4. £1 = 22
   $1 = 9.9
5. Area: 803,943 km² 310,400 sq miles

1. 76.77M; 95/km²; 247/sq mile
2. −15 44%; +65 3%; LE 51
3. B R 36; D R 12; A I 3.2%
4. Urb. pop. 26%
5. Islamabad 77
6. Punjabi 66%; Sindhi 13%; Pashto 9%; Urdu 8%

G D P $14,510 (3.6%), $200 (0.9%)
Agric. 31% Indust. 16% Others 53%
Exp. $1,442 Cotton, leather, rice, textiles, carpets
Imp. $3,275 Manufactured goods, machinery, iron and steel, vehicles, fuel oil
Japan, Hong Kong, UK, W. Germany, Italy
Aid received: $471.4

PANAMA
1. Republic
2. Spanish
3. Balboa (10 centesimos)
4. £1 = 23
   $1 = 10
5. Area: 75,650 km² 29,208 sq miles

1. 1.87M; 25/km²; 64/sq mile
2. −15 44%; +65 4%; LE 66
3. B R 28.2; D R 7.1; A I 3.1%
4. Urb. pop. 50%
5. Panama 428
6. Mulatto 72%; African Negro 14%; European 12%

G D P $2,213 (3.4%), $1,250 (0.3%)
Agric. 17% Indust. 17% Others 66%
Exp. $228 Petroleum products, bananas, sugar, fish
Imp. $861 Machinery, manufactured goods, petroleum
USA, UK, Venezuela, Japan, W. Germany
Aid received: $37

PAPUA NEW GUINEA
1. Commonwealth
2. English, Papuan
3. Kina (100 toea)
4. £1 = 1.6
   $1 = 0.7
5. Area: 461,691 km² 178,260 sq miles

1. 3.0M; 5/km²; 14/sq mile
2. −15 45%; +65 4%; LE 48
3. B R 40.6; D R 17.1; A I 2.2%
4. Urb. pop. 13%
5. Port Moresby 113

G D P $1,518 (4.8%), $536 (2.6%)
Agric. 34% Indust. 32% Others 42%
Exp. $779 Coffee, gold, coconut oil, cocoa
Imp. $675 Machinery, foodstuffs, petroleum products
UK, Australia, Japan, Singapore, USA, W. Germany
Aid received: $267.6

PARAGUAY
1. Republic
2. Guarani, Spanish
3. Guarani (100 centimos)
4. £1 = 284
   $1 = 125
5. Area: 406,752 km² 157,048 sq miles

1. 2.89M; 7/km²; 18/sq mile
2. −15 44%; +65 3%; LE 62
3. B R 39.8; D R 8.9; A I 2.9%
4. Urb. pop. 40%
5. Asunción 565
6. Mestizo 74%; White 21%

G D P $2,092 (7.0%), $745 (3.9%)
Agric. 34% Indust. 19% Others 47%
Exp. $257 Cotton, vegetable oil, meat, timber
Imp. $319 Machinery, vehicles, fuel oil, foodstuffs, iron
Brazil, Argentina, W. Germany, USA, UK
Aid received: $42.1

PERU
1. Republic
2. Spanish
3. Sol (100 centavos)
4. £1 = 576
   $1 = 253
5. Area: 1,285,216 km² 496,222 sq miles

1. 16.82M; 13/km²; 34/sq mile
2. −15 44%; +65 3%; LE 54
3. B R 41.0; D R 11.9; A I 3.0%
4. Urb. pop. 43%
5. Lima 3,303
6. Mestizo and Indian 88%; European 12%

G D P $10,572 (4.6%), $646 (1.7%)
Agric. 13% Indust. 36% Others 51%
Exp. $1,433 Copper, fish meal, sugar, cotton, coffee, wool, petroleum, silver, iron ore
Imp. $1,614 Machinery, tobacco, chemicals, food, vehicles
USA, W. Germany, Japan, UK, Argentina
Aid received: $81.0

PHILIPPINES
1. Republic
2. Tagalog, English
3. Peso (100 centavos)
4. £1 = 17
   $1 = 7.3
5. Area: 300,000 km² 115,831 sq miles

1. 46.35M; 154/km²; 400/sq mile
2. −15 46%; +65 3%; LE 58
3. B R 43.8; D R 10.5; A I 2.9
4. Urb. pop. 32%
5. Manila 1,438

G D P $20,675 (6.4%), $459 (3.4%)
Agric. 28% Indust. 27% Others 45%
Exp. $1,442 Sugar, coconut oil, copra, copper, wood, bananas
Imp. $5,143 Petroleum products, iron and steel, machinery, vehicles
Japan, USA
Aid received: $182.8

POLAND
1. People's Republic
2. Polish
3. Złoty (100 groszy)
4. £1 = 66
   $1 = 29
5. Area: 312,677 km² 120,725 sq miles

1. 35.01M; 112/km²; 290/sq mile
2. −15 24%; +65 9%; LE 71
3. B R 19.0; D R 9.3; A I 0.9%
4. Urb. pop. 56%
5. Warsaw 2,080

N M P $87,150 (8.8%), $2,512 (7.8%)
Agric. 16% Indust. 52% Others 32%
Exp. $13,361 Coal, fertilizers, ships, meat, timber, clothes
Imp. $15,121 Iron ore, petroleum products, fertilizers, wheat, machinery
USSR, E. Germany, France, USA, UK
Aid given: $69

PORTUGAL
1. Republic
2. Portuguese
3. Escudo (100 centavos)
4. £1 = 109
   $1 = 48
5. Area: 91,641 km² 35,382 sq miles

1. 9.79M; 107/km²; 276/sq mile
2. −15 28%; +65 10%; LE 69
3. B R 16.8; D R 9.8; A I 0.9%
4. Urb. pop. 37%
5. Lisbon 1,612

G D P $14,724 (4.5%), $1,580 (2.4%)
Agric. 13% Indust. 34% Others 53%
Exp. $2,393 Cork, wine, wood pulp, sardines, resin
Imp. $4,791 Iron and steel, vehicles, raw cotton, oil seeds, coffee, sugar, wheat, petroleum
France, UK, USA, W. Germany

PUERTO RICO
1. Commonwealth in assoc. with USA
2. Spanish, English
3. US Dollar (100 cents)
4. £1 = 2.3
5. Area: 8,897 km² 3,435 sq miles

1. 3.32M; 373/km²; 966/sq mile
2. −15 35%; +65 7%; LE 72
3. B R 22.6; D R 6.0; A I 2.8%
4. Urb. pop. 58%
5. San Juan 515

G D P $10,902 (3.2%), $3,304 (0.4%)
Agric. 3% Indust. 38% Others 59%
Exp. Clothing, chemicals, tobacco, electrical machinery
Imp. Machinery, textiles, petroleum, vehicles
USA, Venezuela, Japan, Virgin Is, Canada

ROMANIA
1. Socialist Republic
2. Romanian
3. Leu (100 bani)
4. £1 = 10
   $1 = 4
5. Area: 237,500 km² 91,700 sq miles

1. 21.85M; 92/km²; 238/sq mile
2. −15 25%; +65 10%; LE 70
3. B R 19.5; D R 9.6; A I 1.0%
4. Urb. pop. 48%
5. Bucharest 1,934
6. Romanian 88%; Hungarian 9%; German 2%

N M P $26,450 (10.8%), $1,240 (9.8%)
Agric. 16% Indust. 61% Others 23%
Exp. $7,021 Petroleum products, cement, cereals, vehicles
Imp. $7,018 Iron ore, coke, non-ferrous metals, vehicles
USSR, E. Germany, W. Germany, Poland, USA, Czechoslovakia
Aid given: $334

SAUDI ARABIA
1. Kingdom
2. Arabic
3. Ryal (100 nilalas)
4. £1 = 7.6
   $1 = 3.4
5. Area: 2,149,600 km² 829,961 sq miles

1. 7.87M; 4/km²; 9/sq mile
2. −15 45%; +65 3%; LE 45
3. B R 49.5; D R 20.2; A I 3.0%
4. Urb. pop. 25%
5. Riyadh 667

G D P $56,870 (12.3%), $6,155 (9.1%)
Agric. 1% Indust. 69% Others 30%
Exp. $39,208 Crude petroleum, petroleum products
Imp. $14,651 Machinery, vehicles, food
UK, USA, Japan, Italy, France, Netherlands, W. Germany

SENEGAL
1. Republic
2. French, West African
3. C F A Franc (100 centimes)
4. £1 = 470
   $1 = 206
5. Area: 196,192 km² 75,750 sq miles

1. 5.38M; 27/km²; 71/sq mile
2. −15 42%; +65 3%; LE 45
3. B R 55.4; D R 23.9; A I 2.4%
4. Urb. pop. 32%
5. Dakar 799

G D P $1,646 (−), $331 (−)
Agric. 34% Indust. 22% Others 44%
Exp. $476 Groundnuts, phosphates, preserved fish
Imp. $640 Rice, sugar, petroleum products, machinery, textiles
France, USA, Mauritania
Aid received: $125.6

SIERRA LEONE
1. Republic
2. English, West African
3. Leone (100 cents)
4. £1 = 2.4
   $1 = 1.0
5. Area: 71,740 km² 27,699 sq miles

1. 3.29M; 46/km²; 119/sq mile
2. −15 37%; +65 3%; LE 44
3. B R 44.7; D R 20.7
4. Urb. pop. 14%
5. Freetown 214
6. Trad. 66%; Moslem 28%

G D P $666 (1.4%), $214 (−0.1%)
Agric. 38% Indust. 17% Others 45%
Exp. $91 Diamonds, iron ore
Imp. $181 Foodstuffs, manufactured goods
UK, Japan, W. Germany, Netherlands, USA
Aid received: $18.9

SINGAPORE
1. Republic
2. English, Chinese, Malay, Tamil
3. Dollar (100 cents)
4. £1 = 4.9
   $1 = 2.2
5. Area: 581 km² 224 sq miles

1. 2.33M; 4,010/km²; 10,402/sq mile
2. −15 32%; +65 4%; LE 68
3. B R 17.0; D R 5.2; A I 1.5%
4. Urb. pop. 60%
5. Singapore 2,308
6. Chinese 76%; Malay 15%; Indian 7%

G D P $5,915 (9.0%), $2,594 (7.3%)
Agric. 2% Indust. 27% Others 71%
Exp. $10,134 Rubber, petroleum products, machinery
Imp. $13,049 Machinery, textiles, rubber
Malaysia, USA, Japan, UK, China
Aid received: $12.7

SOMALI REPUBLIC
1. Republic
2. Italian, English
3. Shilling (100 centisimis)
4. £1 = 14
   $1 = 6
5. Area: 637,657 km² 246,201 sq miles

1. 3.44M; 5/km²; 14/sq mile
2. −15 45%; +65 2%; LE 41
3. B R 47.2; D R 21.7; A I 2.7%
4. Urb. pop. 20%
5. Mogadishu 230
6. Somali 76%; Sab 19%; Bantu 4%

G D P $492 (−), $155 (−)
Exp. $106 Livestock, bananas
Imp. $167 Foodstuffs, machinery
USSR, USA, UK, Saudi Arabia, Italy, China
Aid received: $77.8

SOUTH AFRICA
1. Republic
2. English, Afrikaans
3. Rand (100 cents)
4. £1 = 1.8
   $1 = 0.8
5. Area: 1,221,037 km²

1. 27.70M; 23/km²; 59/sq mile
2. −15 42%; +65 4%; LE 52
3. B R 42.9; D R 15.5; A I 2.5%
4. Urb. pop. 48%

G D P $39,793 (4.0%), $1,436 (1.4%)
Agric. 8% Indust. 38% Others 54%
Exp. $7,182 Manufactured goods, gold, machinery, vehicles, tobacco, diamonds

471,445 sq miles

5. Pretoria 562
6. Bantu 70%; White 18%; Coloured 9%; Asian 3%

Imp. $7,193 Machinery, vehicles, textiles, petroleum, petroleum products, chemicals
U K, Japan, U S A, W. Germany

SPAIN
1. Monarchy
2. Spanish
3. Peseta (100 centimos)
4. £1 = 152
   $1 = 67
5. Area: 504,750 km²
   194,884 sq miles

1. 37.11M; 74/km²; 190/sq mile
2. −15 28%; +65 10%; L E 72
3. B R 17.2; D R 7.9; A I 1.1%
4. Urb. pop. 61%
5. Madrid 3,520
6. Spanish 73%; Catalan 16%; Galician 8%; Basque 2%

G D P $115,590 (4.7%), $3,152 (3.5%)
Agric. 9% Indust. 39% Others 52%
Exp. $13,115 Manufactured goods, food, tobacco
Imp. $18,708 Manufactured goods, fuel oils, vegetable oil, foodstuffs
U S A, W. Germany, France, U K, Italy

SRI LANKA
1. Republic
2. Sinhalese, English, Tamil
3. Rupee (100 cents)
4. £1 = 35
   $1 = 15
5. Area: 65,610 km²
   25,332 sq miles

1. 14.35M; 218/km²; 566/sq mile
2. −15 39%; +65 4%; L E 66
3. B R 29.9; D R 7.8; A I 1.6%
4. Urb. pop. 22%
5. Colombo 592
6. Sinhalese 72%; Tamil 20%

G D P $3,412 (4.5%), $244 (2.8%)
Agric. 39% Indust. 14% Others 47%
Exp. $847 Tea, rubber, copra, coconut oil, coconut fibre
Imp. $940 Foodstuffs, machinery, petroleum products, textiles, rice
China, W. Germany, Italy, India, Australia, U K, Saudi Arabia
Aid received: $154.5

SUDAN
1. Republic
2. Arabic, Hamitic, English
3. Pound (100 piastres)
4. £1 = 0.9
   $1 = 0.4
5. Area: 2,505,813 km²
   967,500 sq miles

1. 17.38M; 7/km²; 18/sq mile
2. −15 47%; +65 3%; L E 49
3. B R 47.8; D R 17.5; A I 3.1%
4. Urb. pop. 20%
5. Khartoum 334
6. Arab 49%; Dinka 12%; Nubian 8%

G D P $4,689 (−), $298 (−)
Agric. 39% Indust. 11% Others 50%
Exp. $661 Sheep, groundnuts, sesame, cotton, gum Arabic
Imp. $1,060 Fertilizers, tobacco, sugar, machinery
U K, U S A, India, W. Germany, China
Aid received: $130.4

SURINAM
1. Dutch Colony
2. Dutch
3. Guilder (100 cents)
4. £1 = 4.1
   $1 = 1.8
5. Area: 163,265 km²
   63,037 sq miles

1. 0.37M; 2/km²; 6/sq mile
2. −15 46%; +65 4%; L E 64
3. B R 36.9; D R 7.2; A I 2.7%
4. Urb. pop. 38%
5. Paramaribo 151
6. Indian 37%; Creole 31%; Indonesian 15%; Negro 10%

G D P $503 (−), $1,194 (−)
Agric. 9% Indust. 27% Others 64%
Exp. $330 Alumina, bauxite, rice, citrus fruit, wood, bananas
Imp. $292 Vehicles, foodstuffs, petroleum products
U S A, Netherlands, W. Germany, Trinidad
Aid received: $82.1

SWEDEN
1. Kingdom
2. Swedish
3. Krona (100 oerer)
4. £1 = 9.6
   $1 = 4.2
5. Area: 449,750 km²
   173,649 sq miles

1. 8.28M; 18/km²; 48/sq mile
2. −15 21%; +65 15%; L E 75
3. B R 11.2; D R 10.8; A I 0.4%
4. Urb. pop. 83%
5. Stockholm 1,375

G D P $78,259 (2.0%), $9,474 (1.6%)
Agric. 4% Indust. 27% Others 69%
Exp. $21,560 Machinery, iron and steel, wood-pulp, paper, vehicles, ships, iron ore
Imp. $20,123 Machinery, petroleum products, vehicles, textiles, non-ferrous metals
U K, Denmark, W. Germany, Norway
Aid given: $1,075

SWITZERLAND
1. Federal republic
2. German, French, Italian, Romansch
3. Franc (100 rappen or centimes)
4. £1 = 3.8
   $1 = 1.7
5. Area: 41,288 km²
   15,941 sq miles

1. 6.34M; 155/km²; 399/sq mile
2. −15 22%; +65 13%; L E 73
3. B R 11.3; D R 9.0; A I 0.3%
4. Urb. pop. 55%
5. Bern 284
6. German 65%; French 18%; Italian 12%
   Protestant 48%; R C 49%

G D P $60,578 (0.2%), $9,570 (−0.1%)
Agric. 6% Indust. 40% Others 54%
Exp. $23,561 Machinery, watches, textiles, medicines, chemical products
Imp. $23,804 Machinery, vehicles, iron and steel, textiles, petroleum products
W. Germany, France, U S A, Italy, U K
Aid given: $1,860

SYRIA
1. Republic
2. Arabic
3. Pound (100 piastres)
4. £1 = 8.9
   $1 = 3.9
5. Area: 185,180 km²
   71,498 sq miles

1. 8.09M; 44/km²; 113/sq mile
2. −15 49%; +65 3%; L E 57
3. B R 45.4; D R 15.4; A I 3.3%
4. Urb. pop. 48%
5. Damascus 1,097
6. Moslem 88%; Christian 12%

G D P $6,581 (9.8%), $839 (6.4%)
Agric. 20% Indust. 19% Others 61%
Exp. $1,053 Cotton, crude petroleum, livestock, phosphates
Imp. $2,437 Machinery, chemicals, vehicles, textiles, iron and steel
W. Germany, Italy, China, U S S R, France
Aid received: $62.3

TAIWAN
1. Republic
2. Chinese
3. New Dollar (100 cents)
4. £1 = 82
   $1 = 36
5. Area: 35,961 km²
   13,885 sq miles

1. 17.2M; 478/km²; 1,239/sq mile
2. −15 36%; +65 4%; L E 70
3. B R 26; D R 5; A I 2.1%
4. Urb. pop. 62%
5. Taipei 3,050

Agric. 14% Indust. 38% Others 48%
Exp. $9,500 Textiles, machinery, bananas, laminates
Imp. $9,000 Machinery, textiles, iron and steel, cereals
U S A, Japan, Hong Kong

TANZANIA
1. Federal Republic
2. Swahili, English
3. Shilling (100 cents)
4. £1 = 19
   $1 = 8.1
5. Area: 945,087 km²
   364,900 sq miles

1. 16.55M; 18/km²; 45/sq mile
2. −15 44%; +65 2%; L E 40
3. B R 47; D R 22; A I 2.8%
4. Urb. pop. 7%
5. Dar es Salaam 752
   Dodoma (being

G D P $3,417 (4.5%), $212 (1.7%)
Agric. 44% Indust. 10% Others 46%
Exp. $470 Coffee, cotton, diamonds, sisal, nuts
Imp. $1,150 Machinery, vehicles, textiles, petroleum products, iron and steel

developed)
6. Trad. 35%; Christian 31%; Moslem 31%

U K, Zambia, India, Hong Kong, W. Germany, Japan
Aid received: $299.5

THAILAND
1. Kingdom
2. Thai
3. Baht (100 satangs)
4. £1 = 46
   $1 = 20
5. Area: 514,000 km²
   198,457 sq miles

1. 45M; 88/km²; 227/sq mile
2. −15 44%; +65 3%; L E 56
3. B R 25.3; D R 10.8; A I 2.8%
4. Urb. pop. 13%
5. Bangkok 4,702
6. Thai 75%; Chinese 18%; Malay 3%

G D P $18,159 (6.7%), $412 (3.8%)
Agric. 28% Indust. 22% Others 50%
Exp. $4,093 Rice, rubber, maize, tin, timber
Imp. $5,360 Foodstuffs, machinery, vehicles, iron and steel, petroleum
Japan, U S A, W. Germany, U K, Malaysia
Aid received: $93.7

TOGO
1. Republic
2. Bantu languages, Hamitic, French
3. C F A Franc (100 centimes)
4. £1 = 470
   $1 = 206
5. Area: 56,000 km²
   21,622 sq miles

1. 2.41M; 43/km²; 111/sq mile
2. −15 50%; +65 3%; L E 35
3. B R 50.6; D R 23.3; A I 2.6%
4. Urb. pop. 15%
5. Lomé 135
6. Trad. 56%; R C 18%; Moslem 9%; Protestant 7%

G D P $599 (−), $269 (−)
Agric. 34% Indust. 16% Others 50%
Exp. $159 Cocoa, cotton, coffee, phosphates
Imp. $284 Cotton, machinery, food, vehicles
Netherlands, France, W. Germany, U K
Aid received: $48.9

TRINIDAD AND TOBAGO
1. Parliamentary state
2. English
3. Dollar (100 cents)
4. £1 = 5.5
   $1 = 2.4
5. Area: 5,128 km²
   1,979 sq miles

1. 1.13M; 220/km²; 571/sq mile
2. −15 39%; +65 4%; L E 66
3. B R 25.3; D R 6.5; A I 1.6%
4. Urb. pop. 49%
5. Port-of-Spain 350
6. Negro 43%; East Indian 36%; Mixed 16%; White 2%

G D P $3,509 (10.7%), $3,147 (9.4%)
Agric. 3% Indust. 54% Others 43%
Exp. $2,039 Petroleum, sugar, tar
Imp. $1,963 Machinery, crude petroleum, textiles, vehicles
U S A, Saudi Arabia, U K, Indonesia, Iran
Aid received: $5.2

TUNISIA
1. Republic
2. Arabic, French
3. Dinar (1000 millimes)
4. £1 = 0.9
   $1 = 0.4
5. Area: 164,150 km²
   63,379 sq miles

1. 6.03M; 37/km²; 95/sq mile
2. −15 44%; +65 4%; L E 54
3. B R 36.4; D R 13.8; A I 2.3%
4. Urb. pop. 44%
5. Tunis 944

G D P $4,981 (9.4%), $821 (6.8%)
Agric. 17% Indust. 17% Others 66%
Exp. $1,090 Iron ore, crude petroleum, phosphates, olive oil
Imp. $2,119 Machinery, wheat, textiles, iron and steel
France, Italy, U S A, W. Germany
Aid received: $174.7

TURKEY
1. Republic
2. Turkish
3. Lira (100 kurus)
4. £1 = 160
   $1 = 70
5. Area: 780,576 km²
   301,382 sq miles

1. 43.21M; 55/km²; 143/sq mile
2. −15 40%; +65 4%; L E 54
3. B R 39.6; D R 14.6; A I 2.7%
4. Urb. pop. 45%
5. Ankara 1,701
6. Turkish 90%; Kurds 7%

G D P $41,051 (7.4%), $999 (4.3%)
Agric. 27% Indust. 21% Others 52%
Exp. $2,288 Cotton, fruit, tobacco
Imp. $4,597 Machinery, petroleum, medicines, iron and steel, vehicles
W. Germany, U S A, U K, Italy, France

UGANDA
1. Republic
2. English, Bantu
3. Shilling (100 cents)
4. £1 = 17
   $1 = 7.4
5. Area: 236,036 km²
   91,134 sq miles

1. 12.78M; 54/km²; 140/sq mile
2. −15 46%; +65 3%; L E 50
3. B R 45.2; D R 15.9; A I 3.4%
4. Urb. pop. 7%
5. Kampala 331
6. Christian 60%; Trad. 33%; Moslem 5%

G D P $3,075 (−0.1%), $266 (−3.3%)
Agric. 53% Indust. 10% Others 37%
Exp. $659 Coffee, raw cotton, tea, copper
Imp. $158 Manufactured products, machinery, textiles
U S A, U K, W. Germany, Japan
Aid received: $18.8

UNITED KINGDOM
1. Kingdom
2. English, Welsh
3. Pound (100 pence)
4. $1 = 0.4
5. Area: 244,796 km²
   94,516 sq miles

1. 55.82M; 228/km²; 591/sq mile
2. −15 23%; +65 14%; L E 73
3. B R 12.3; D R 11.7; A I 0.1%
4. Urb. pop. 75%
5. London 6,970
6. England 82.9%; Scotland 9.3%; Wales 4.9%; N. Ireland 2.8%

G D P $244,457 (1.8%), $4,377 (1.7%)
Agric. 3% Indust. 30% Others 67%
Exp. $71,691 Machinery, vehicles, textiles, iron and steel, non-ferrous metals
Imp. $78,557 Cereals, machinery, petroleum, chemicals, foodstuffs, textiles
U S A, W. Germany, France, Ireland, Netherlands
Aid given: $3,426

UPPER VOLTA
1. Republic
2. French
3. C F A Franc (100 centimes)
4. £1 = 470
   $1 = 206
5. Area: 274,200 km²
   105,869 sq miles

1. 6.55M; 24/km²; 62/sq mile
2. −15 43%; +65 3%; L E 32
3. B R 47.9; D R 23.2; A I 2.3%
5. Ouagadougou 169
6. Trad. 75%; Moslem 20%; R C 5%

G D P $547 (−), $91 (−)
Agric. 42% Indust. 12% Others 46%
Exp. $55 Cattle, cotton, groundnuts
Imp. $209 Machinery, vehicles, petroleum, food
France, Ivory Coast, U S A, W. Germany
Aid received: $92.1

URUGUAY
1. Republic
2. Spanish
3. Peso (100 centésimos)
4. £1 = 20
   $1 = 8.6
5. Area: 177,508 km²
   68,536 sq miles

1. 2.86M; 16/km²; 42/sq mile
2. −15 27%; +65 9%; L E 69
3. B R 20.9; D R 10.2; A I 1.2%
4. Urb. pop. 83%
   Montevideo 1,230

G D P $3,693 (1.1%), $1,319 (0.1%)
Agric. 10% Indust. 27% Others 63%
Exp. $608 Meat, wool, textiles, leather
Imp. $730 Machinery, vehicles, crude petroleum
W. Germany, Spain, Italy, Brazil, U S A
Aid received: $11.5

USA
1. Federal Republic
2. English
3. Dollar (100 cents)
4. £1 = 2.3
5. Area: 9,363,353 km²
3,615,200 sq miles

1. 218.06M; 23/km²; 60/sq mile
2. −15 28%; +65 11%; L E 73
3. B R 15.3; D R 8.8; A I 0.8%
4. Urb. pop. 74%
5. Washington 3,022
6. White 88%; Black 11% Protestant 34%; R C 24%; Jewish 3%

G D P $1,878,835 (2.8%), $8,665 (1.9%)
Agric. 3% Indust. 29% Others 68%
Exp. $141,154 Machinery, vehicles, cereals, aircraft, chemical products, iron and steel
Imp. $182,787 Vehicles, machinery, iron and steel, crude petroleum, clothing, textiles
Canada, Japan, U K, W. Germany, Mexico
Aid given: $12,456

USSR
1. Socialist Republic
2. Russian and others
3. Rouble (100 kopeks)
4. £1 = 1.5
$1 = 0.6
5. Area: 22,402,200 km²
8,649,500 sq miles

1. 264.5M; 12/km²; 31/sq mile
2. −15 26%; +65 9%; L E 69
3. B R 18.1; D R 9.6; A I 0.9%
4. Urb. pop. 62%
5. Moscow 8,011
6. Russian 53%; Ukrainian 17%; Uzbek 4%; Byelorrusian 4%

N M P $540,214 (5.7%), $2,086 (4.8%)
Agric. 17% Indust. 52% Others 31%
Exp. $52,176 Machinery, iron and steel, crude petroleum, non-ferrous metals
Imp. $50,546 Machinery, shoes, clothing, ships, iron and steel, railway stock
E. Germany, Poland, Bulgaria, Hungary
Aid given: $1,924

VENEZUELA
1. Republic
2. Spanish
3. Bolivar (100 centimes)
4. £1 = 9.8
$1 = 4.3
5. Area: 912,050 km²
352,144 sq miles

1. 13.12M; 14/km²; 37/sq mile
2. −15 45%; +65 3%; L E 66
3. B R 36.1; D R 7.0; A I 3.1%
4. Urb. pop. 75%
5. Caracas 2,576
6. Mestizo 70%; White 20%; Negro 8%; Indian 2%

G D P $35,592 (5.6%), $2,794 (2.4%)
Agric. 6% Indust. 39% Others 55%
Exp. $9,548 Crude petroleum, petroleum products, iron ore, coffee
Imp. $9,003 Machinery, vehicles, cereals, iron and steel, manufactured products
U S A, Netherlands, Canada, Japan, Antilles, W. Germany
Aid received: $5.8

VIETNAM
1. Democratic Republic
2. Vietnamese, French
3. Dong (100 xu)
4. £1 = 4.9
$1 = 2.2
5. Area: 329,556 km²
127,242 sq miles

1. 49.89M; 151/km²; 392/sq mile
2. −15 41%; +65 4%; L E 45
3. B R 41.5; D R 20.5; A I 2.9%
4. Urb. pop. 24%
5. Hanoi 1,444

G D P — (2.8%), — (0%)
Agric. 29% Indust. 7% Others 64%
Exp. Coal, food, fish
Imp. Machinery, raw materials
U S S R, Japan, Singapore, Hong Kong

YUGOSLAVIA
1. Federal Republic
2. Serbian, Croatian
3. Dinar (100 paras)
4. £1 = 46
$1 = 20
5. Area: 255,804 km²
98,766 sq miles

1. 21.91M; 86/km²; 222/sq mile
2. −15 25%; +65 8%; L E 68
3. B R 17.4; D R 8.7; A I 0.9%
4. Urb. pop. 39%
5. Belgrade 775
6. Serb 42%; Croat 23%; Slovene 9%; Macedonian 6%; Moslem 5%; Albanian 5%

N M P $27,637 (5.8%), $1,294 (4.8%)
Agric. 17% Indust. 40% Others 43%
Exp. $5,659 Non-ferrous metals, machinery, timber, textiles, ships, wine
Imp. $9,987 Chemicals, machinery, textiles, iron and steel, crude petroleum
Italy, U S S R, W. Germany

ZAÏRE
1. Democratic Republic
2. French, Lingala
3. Zaïre (100 makuta)
4. £1 = 3.7
$1 = 1.6
5. Area: 2,345,409 km²
905,560 sq miles

1. 27.75M; 12/km²; 31/sq mile
2. −15 41%; +65 3%; L E 44
3. B R 45.2; D R 20.5; A I 2.5%
4. Urb. pop. 30%
5. Kinshasa 2,008

G D P $3,695 (3.8%), $148 (1.0%)
Agric. 19% Indust. 22% Others 59%
Exp. $925 Copper, diamonds, cobalt, coffee, palm oil
Imp. $588 Machinery, vehicles, petroleum products, cotton fabric, cereals
Belgium, Angola, Italy, U K, W. Germany
Aid received: $215.2

ZAMBIA
1. Republic
2. English
3. Kwacha (100 ngwee)
4. £1 = 1.8
$1 = 0.8
5. Area: 752,614 km²
290,586 sq miles

1. 5.65M; 7/km²; 19/sq mile
2. −15 47%; +65 3%; L E 45
3. B R 51.5; D R 20.3; A I 3.6%
4. Urb. pop. 36%
5. Lusaka 401

G D P $2,687 (4.2%), $523 (0.9%)
Agric. 13% Indust. 35% Others 52%
Exp. $898 Copper, zinc, lead, cobalt, tobacco
Imp. $671 Machinery, vehicles, textiles, iron and steel, petroleum products
U K, Japan, W. Germany, Italy, South Africa
Aid received: $83.8

ZIMBABWE
1. Commonwealth
2. English
3. Dollar (100 cents)
4. £1 = 1.5
$1 = 0.7
5. Area: 390,581 km²
150,804 sq miles

1. 6.93M; 18/km²; 46/sq mile
2. −15 46%; +65 2%; L E 52
3. B R 47.9; D R 14.4; A I 3.5%
4. Urb. pop. 19%
5. Salisbury 564
6. African 95%; European 4%

G D P $3,569 (3.5%), $530 (0%)
Exp. $650 Tobacco, chrome, asbestos, copper
Imp. $541 Petroleum, manufactures, vehicles
South Africa, France, W. Germany
Aid received: $5.7

INDEX TO TEXT

The entries in this index give both page and column references: **159.**4 is a reference to page 159, column 4. The italicized entries are references to illustrations.

INDEX TO MAPS

The number in bold type which precedes each name in the index refers to the number of the page where that feature or place will be found.

The geographical co-ordinates which follow the place name are sometimes only approximate but are close enough for the place name to be located. The first co-ordinate indicates latitude i.e. distance north or south of the Equator. The second coordinate indicates longitude i.e. distance east or west of the meridian of Greenwich in England (shown as 0° longitude). Both latitude and longitude are measured in degrees and minutes (with 60 minutes in a degree), and appear on the map as horizontal and vertical grid lines respectively. Thus the entry for Bristol in England reads:

21 Bristol, England 51 26N 2 35W

This entry indicates that Bristol is on page 21, at latitude 51 degrees 26 minutes north (approximately half way between horizontal gridlines 51 and 52 marked on either side of the map), and at longitude 2 degrees 35 minutes west (approximately half the distance between vertical grid lines 2 and 3, marked at top and bottom of the map). Where lines extended from these two points cross on the page, the location of Bristol is marked.

An open square □ signifies that the name refers to an administrative division of a country while a solid square ■ follows the name of a country.

Rivers have been indexed to their mouth or to their confluence.

The alphabetical order of names composed of two or more words is governed primarily by the first word and then by the second. This is an example of the rule:

West Wyalong
West Yorkshire
Westbrook
Westbury
Westerland
Western Australia

Names composed of a proper name (Gibraltar) and a description (Strait of) are positioned alphabetically by the proper name. All river names are followed by R. If the same word occurs in the name of a town and a geographical feature, the town name is listed first followed by the name of the geographical feature.

Names beginning with M', Mc are all indexed as if they were spelled Mac.

If the same place name occurs two or more times in the index and all are in the same country, each is followed by the name of the administrative subdivision in which it is located. The names are placed in the alphabetical order of the subdivisions. For example:

Stour, R., Dorset
Stour, R., Hereford and Worcester
Stour, R., Kent
Stour, R., Suffolk

If the same place name occurs twice or more in the index and the places are in different countries they will be followed by the country names and the latter in alphabetical order.

Sheffield, U.K.
Sheffield, U.S.A.

If there is a mixture of these situations, the primary order is fixed by the alphabetical sequence of the countries and the secondary order by that of the country subdivisions. In the latter case the country names are omitted.

Rochester, U.K.
Rochester,Minn. (U.S.A.) are omitted
Rochester, N.H. (U.S.A.) from the
Rochester, N.Y. (U.S.A.) index

Former names of certain towns are referenced to the names in current use: Stalingrad = Volgograd. English conventional name forms for certain towns are referenced to the local spelling of that town name: Florence = Firenze.

Abbreviations in Map Index

A.S.S.R. – *Autonomous Soviet Socialist Republic*
Ala. – *Alabama*
Alas. – *Alaska*
Ang. – *Angola*
Arch. – *Archipelago*
Arg. – *Argentina*
Ariz. – *Arizona*
Ark. – *Arkansas*
B. – *Baie, Bahia, Bay, Boca, Bucht, Bugt*
B.C. – *British Columbia*
Br. – *British*
C. – *Cabo, Cap, Cape*
C.A.R. – *Central African Republic*
C. Prov. – *Cape Province*
Calif. – *California*
Chan. – *Channel*
Col. – *Colombia*
Colo. – *Colorado*
Conn. – *Connecticut*
Cord. – *Cordillera*
D.C. – *District of Columbia*
Del. – *Delaware*
Dep. – *Dependency*
Des. – *Desert*
Dist. – *District*
Dom. Rep. – *Dominican Republic*
E. – *East*
Eng. – *England*
Fd. – *Fjord*
Fed. – *Federal, Federation*
Fla. – *Florida*
Fr. – *France, French*
G. – *Golfe, Golfo, Gulf, Guba*
Ga. – *Georgia*
Gt. – *Great*
Hants. – *Hampshire*
Hd. – *Head*
Hts. – *Heights*
I.(s) – *Île, Ilha, Insel, Isla, Island (s)*
Id. – *Idaho*
Ill. – *Illinois*
Ind. – *Indiana*
J. – *Jezero (L.)*
K. – *Kap, Kapp*
Kans. – *Kansas*
Kep. – *Kepulauan (I.)*
Kól. – *Kólpos (B.)*
Ky. – *Kentucky*
L. – *Lac, Lacul, Lago, Lagoa, Lake, Limni, Loch, Lough*
La. – *Louisana*
Ld. – *Land*
Mad. P. – *Madhya Pradesh*
Man. – *Manitoba*
Mass. – *Massachusetts*
Md. – *Maryland*
Me. – *Maine*
Mich. – *Michigan*
Minn. – *Minnesota*
Miss. – *Mississippi*
Mo. – *Missouri*
Mont. – *Montana*
Mt.(s) – *Mont, Monte, Monti, Muntii, Montaña, Mountain (s)*
Mys. – *Mysore*
N. – *North, Northern*
N.B. – *New Brunswick*
N.C. – *North Carolina*
N.D. – *North Dakota*
N.H. – *New Hampshire*
N. Ire. – *Northern Ireland*
N.J. – *New Jersey*
N. Mex. – *New Mexico*
N.S.W. – *New South Wales*
N.Y. – *New York*
N.Z. – *New Zealand*
Nat. Park – *National Park*
Nebr. – *Nebraska*
Neth. – *Netherlands*
Nev. – *Nevada*
Newf. – *Newfoundland*
Nic. – *Nicaragua*
Nig. – *Nigeria*
O.F.S. – *Orange Free State*
Okla. – *Oklahoma*
Ont. – *Ontario*
Oreg. – *Oregon*
Os. – *Ostrov (I.)*
Oz – *Ozero (L.)*
P. – *Pass, Passo, Pasul*
P.N.G. – *Papua New Guinea*
Pa. – *Pennsylvania*
Pak. – *Pakistan*
Pass. – *Passage*
Pen. – *Peninsula*
Pk. – *Peak*
Plat. – *Plateau*
Pol. – *Poluostrov*
Port. – *Portugal, Portuguese*
Prov. – *Province, Provincial*
Pt. – *Point*
Pta. – *Ponta, Punta*
Pte. – *Pointe*
Que. – *Quebec*
Queens. – *Queensland*
R. – *Rio, River*
R.S.F.S.R. – *Russian Soviet Federal Socialist Republic*
Ra.(s) – *Range(s)*
Reg. – *Region*
Rep. – *Republic*
Res. – *Reserve, Reservoir*
S. – *South*
S. Africa – *South Africa*
S.C. – *S. Carolina*
S.D. – *South Dakota*
S. Leone – *Sierra Leone*
S.S.R. – *Soviet Socialist Republic*
Sa. – *Serra, Sierra*
Sask. – *Saskatchewan*
Scot. – *Scotland*
Sd. – *Sound*
Sp. – *Spain, Spanish*
St. – *Saint*
Str. – *Strait, Stretto*
Switz. – *Switzerland*
Tanz. – *Tanzania*
Tas. – *Tasmania*
Tenn. – *Tennessee*
Terr. – *Territory*
Tex. – *Texas*
U.K. – *United Kingdom*
U.S.A. – *United States of America*
U.S.S.R. – *Union of Soviet Socialist Republics*
Ut. P. – *Uttar Pradesh*
Va. – *Virginia*
Vdkhr. – *Vodokhranilishche (Res.)*
Ven. – *Venezuela*
Vic. – *Victoria*
Vt. – *Vermont*
W. – *West*
W. Va. – *West Virginia*
Wis. – *Wisconsin*
Wyo. – *Wyoming*
Yorks. – *Yorkshire*
Yug. – *Yugoslavia*

Aldershot Avezzano

21 Aldershot 51 15 N 0 43 W
158 Aleg 17 3 N 13 55 W
76 Aleisk 52 40 N 83 0 E
75 Aleksandrov Gai 50 15 N 48 35 E
77 Aleksandrovsk-Sakhalinskiy 50 50 N 142 20 E
76 Aleksandrovskoye 60 35 N 77 50 E
60 Aleksinac 43 31 N 21 12 E
38 Ålen 62 49 N 11 17 E
28 Alençon 48 27 N 0 4 E
80 Aleppo 36 10 N 37 15 E
31 Aléria 42 5 N 9 30 E
124 Alert Bay 50 30 N 127 35 W
31 Alès 44 9 N 4 5 E
62 Alessandria 44 54 N 8 37 E
30 Alet-les-Bains 43 0 N 2 20 E
106 Aleutian Is. 52 0 N 175 0 W
124 Alexander Arch. 57 0 N 135 0 W
127 Alexander City 32 56 N 85 57 W
174 Alexander I. 69 0 S 70 0 W
159 Alexandria = El Iskandarîya 31 0 N 30 0 E
168 Alexandria, S. Africa 33 38 S 26 28 E
128 Alexandria, La. 31 20 N 92 30 W
128 Alexandria, Minn. 45 50 N 95 20 W
127 Alexandria, Va. 38 47 N 77 1 W
127 Alexandria Bay 44 20 N 75 52 W
68 Alexandroúpolis 40 50 N 25 24 E
55 Alfaro 42 10 N 1 50 W
61 Alfatar 43 59 N 27 13 E
45 Alfeld 52 0 N 9 49 E
63 Alfonsine 44 30 N 12 1 E
24 Alford 53 16 N 0 10 E
21 Alfreton 53 6 N 1 22 W
76 Alga 49 46 N 57 20 E
53 Algarve 36 58 N 8 20 W
53 Algeciras 36 9 N 5 28 W
55 Algemesí 39 11 N 0 27 W
158 Alger 36 42 N 3 8 E
158 Algeria ■ 35 10 N 3 0 E
158 Algiers = Alger 36 42 N 3 8 E
168 Algoabaai 33 50 S 25 45 E
122 Algonquin Prov. Park 45 35 N 78 35 W
55 Alhama de Almería 36 57 N 2 34 W
55 Alhama de Aragón 41 18 N 1 54 W
55 Alhama de Murcia 37 51 N 1 25 W
55 Alhambra, Sp. 38 54 N 3 4 W
131 Alhambra, U.S.A. 34 0 N 118 10 W
55 Aliaga 40 40 N 0 42 W
68 Aliákmon, R. 40 30 N 22 36 E
55 Alicante 38 23 N 0 30 W
55 Alicante □ 38 30 N 0 37 W
128 Alice 27 47 N 98 1 W
124 Alice Arm 55 29 N 129 23 W
110 Alice Springs 23 40 S 135 50 E
165 Alicedale 33 15 S 26 4 E
53 Alijó 41 16 N 7 27 W
41 Alingsås 57 56 N 12 31 E
87 Alipur Duar 26 30 N 89 35 E
127 Aliquippa 40 38 N 80 18 W
53 Aljezur 37 18 N 8 49 W
53 Aljustrel 37 55 N 8 10 W
34 Alkmaar 52 37 N 4 45 E
87 Allahabad 25 25 N 81 58 E
125 Allan 51 53 N 106 4 W
123 Allard Lake 50 40 N 63 10 W
30 Allassac 45 15 N 1 29 E
118 Allegheny Mts. 38 0 N 80 0 W
127 Allegheny, R. 40 27 N 80 0 W
30 Allègre 45 12 N 3 41 E
137 Allende 28 20 N 100 50 W
127 Allentown 40 36 N 75 30 W
86 Alleppey 9 30 N 76 28 E
45 Aller, R. 52 57 N 9 11 E
31 Allevard 45 24 N 6 5 E
30 Allier, R. 46 58 N 3 4 E
30 Allier □ 46 25 N 3 0 E
113 Alligator Creek 19 23 S 146 58 E
24 Alloa 56 7 N 3 49 W
31 Allos 44 15 N 6 38 E
122 Alma, Canada 48 35 N 71 40 W
123 Alma, U.S.A. 43 25 N 84 40 W
76 Alma Ata 43 15 N 76 57 E
113 Almaden 17 22 S 144 40 E
53 Almagro 38 50 N 3 45 W
55 Almansa 38 51 N 1 5 W
53 Almanzor, P. de 40 15 N 5 18 W
55 Almanzora, R. 37 14 N 1 46 W
60 Almaș, Mt. 44 49 N 22 12 E
55 Almazán 41 30 N 2 30 W
55 Almazora 39 57 N 0 3 W
145 Almeirim, Brazil 1 30 S 52 0 W
53 Almeirim, Port. 39 12 N 8 37 W
34 Almelo 52 22 N 6 42 E
55 Almenar 41 43 N 2 12 W
55 Almenara, Sa. de 37 34 N 1 32 W
55 Almeria 36 52 N 2 32 W
55 Almeria, G. de 36 40 N 2 30 W
139 Almirante 9 10 N 82 30 W
68 Almirós 39 11 N 22 45 E
53 Almodóvar 37 11 N 8 2 W
53 Almodóvar del Campo 38 43 N 4 10 W
53 Almogia 36 50 N 4 32 W
55 Almoradi 38 7 N 0 46 W
53 Almorox 40 14 N 4 24 W
53 Almuñécar 36 43 N 3 41 W
21 Alnwick 55 25 N 1 42 W
87 Alon 22 12 N 95 5 E
125 Alonsa 50 50 N 99 0 W
95 Alor, I. 8 15 S 124 30 E
53 Alora 36 49 N 4 46 W
53 Alosno 37 33 N 7 7 W
53 Alpedrinha 40 6 N 7 27 W
31 Alpes-Maritimes □ 43 55 N 7 10 E
31 Alpes-de-Haute-Provence □ 44 8 N 6 10 E
113 Alpha 24 8 S 146 39 E
62 Alpi Atesine, Mts. 46 55 N 11 30 E
45 Alpi Lepontine, Mts. 46 22 N 8 27 E
62 Alpi Orobie, Mts. 46 7 N 10 0 E
45 Alpi Pennine, Mts. 46 0 N 7 30 E
53 Alpiarça 39 15 N 8 35 W
128 Alpine 30 35 N 103 35 W
16 Alps, Mts. 47 0 N 8 0 E
110 Alroy Downs 19 20 S 136 5 E
29 Alsace, Reg. 48 15 N 7 25 E
55 Alsasua 42 54 N 2 10 W
45 Alsfeld 50 44 N 9 19 E
21 Alston 54 48 N 2 26 W
148 Alta Gracia 31 40 S 64 30 W
124 Alta Lake 50 10 N 123 0 W
37 Altaelv, R. 69 57 N 23 17 E
144 Altagracia 10 45 N 71 30 W
73 Altai, Mts. 48 0 N 90 0 E
96 Altai = Aerht'ai Shan, mts 46 40 N 92 45 E
65 Altamura 40 50 N 16 33 E
45 Altdorf 46 52 N 8 36 E
55 Altea 38 38 N 0 2 W
45 Altenberg 50 46 N 13 47 E
48 Altenmarkt 47 43 N 14 39 E
53 Alter do Châo 39 12 N 7 40 W
29 Altkirch 47 37 N 7 15 E
145 Alto Araguaia 17 15 S 53 20 W
21 Alton, U.K. 51 8 N 0 59 W
128 Alton, U.S.A. 38 55 N 90 5 W
45 Altona 53 32 N 9 56 E
127 Altoona 40 32 N 78 24 W
45 Altstätten 47 22 N 9 33 E
96 Altun Shan, mts. 39 0 N 89 0 E
85 Alùla 11 50 N 50 45 E
95 Alusi 7 35 S 131 40 E
55 Alustante 40 36 N 1 40 W
53 Alvaiázere 39 49 N 8 23 W
137 Alvarado 18 40 N 95 50 W
41 Alvdalen, R. 59 23 N 13 30 E
53 Alverca 38 56 N 9 1 W
113 Alvie 38 15 S 143 30 E
53 Alvito 38 15 N 8 0 W
41 Alvsborgs □ 58 30 N 12 30 E
37 Älvsbyn 65 39 N 20 59 E
86 Alwar 27 38 N 76 34 E
75 Alyat Pristan 39 59 N 49 28 E
24 Alyth 56 38 N 3 15 W
159 Am-Timan 11 0 N 20 10 E
121 Amadjuak 64 0 N 72 50 W
121 Amadjuak L. 65 0 N 71 0 W
102 Amagasaki 34 42 N 135 20 E
102 Amakusa-Shotō, Is. 32 15 N 130 10 E
41 Åmål 59 2 N 12 40 E
68 Amaliás 37 47 N 21 22 E
148 Amambay □ 23 0 S 56 0 W
76 Amangeldy 50 10 N 65 10 E
65 Amantea 39 8 N 16 3 E
145 Amapá 2 5 N 50 50 W
145 Amapá □ 1 40 N 52 0 W
145 Amarante, Brazil 6 14 S 42 50 W
53 Amarante, Port. 41 16 N 8 5 W
53 Amaraleja 38 12 N 7 13 W
128 Amarillo 35 14 N 101 46 W
63 Amaro, Mt. 42 5 N 14 6 E
80 Amasya 40 40 N 35 50 E
145 Amazon = Amazonas, R. 2 0 S 53 30 W
145 Amazonas, R. 2 0 S 53 30 W
144 Amazonas □ 4 20 S 64 0 W
77 Ambarchik 69 40 N 162 20 E
169 Ambatolampy 19 20 S 47 35 E
45 Amberg 49 25 N 11 52 E
137 Ambergris Cay 18 0 N 88 0 W
31 Ambérieu 45 57 N 5 20 E
30 Ambert 45 33 N 3 44 E
21 Ambleside 54 26 N 2 58 W
95 Ambon 3 35 S 128 20 E
131 Amboy 34 33 N 115 51 W
113 Amby 26 30 S 148 11 E
137 Ameca 20 30 N 104 0 W
63 Amélia 42 34 N 12 25 E
30 Amèlie-les-Bains-Palalda 42 29 N 2 41 E
131 American Falls 42 46 N 112 56 E
174 American Highland 73 0 S 75 0 E
114 American Samoa, I. 14 20 S 170 0 W
34 Amersfoort 52 9 N 5 23 E
125 Amery 56 45 N 94 0 W
68 Amfípolis 40 48 N 23 52 E
68 Amfissa 38 32 N 22 22 E
68 Amflokhía 38 52 N 21 9 E
77 Amga, R. 62 38 N 134 32 E
87 Amherst, Burma 16 0 N 97 40 E
123 Amherst, Canada 45 48 N 64 8 W
63 Amiata, Mte. 42 54 N 11 40 E
29 Amiens 49 54 N 2 16 E
68 Amindaion 40 42 N 21 42 E
153 Amirantes, Is. 6 0 S 53 0 E
21 Amlwch 53 24 N 4 21 W
80 'Ammān 32 0 N 35 52 E
29 Amnéville 49 16 N 6 9 E
53 Amorebieta 43 13 N 2 44 W
122 Amos 48 35 N 78 5 W
99 Amoy = Xiamen 24 25 N 118 4 E
123 Amqui 48 28 N 67 27 W
86 Amritsar 31 35 N 74 57 E
45 Amrum, I. 54 37 N 8 21 E
34 Amsterdam, Neth. 52 23 N 4 54 E
127 Amsterdam, U.S.A. 42 58 N 74 10 W
48 Amstetten 48 7 N 14 51 E
76 Amu Darya, R. 43 40 N 59 1 E
120 Amukta Pass. 52 25 N 172 0 W
120 Amundsen G. 70 30 N 123 0 W
174 Amundsen Sea 72 0 S 115 0 W
77 Amur, R. 52 56 N 141 10 E
53 Amurrio 43 3 N 3 0 W
68 Amvrakíkos Kól. 39 0 N 20 55 E
80 An Najaf 32 3 N 44 15 E
80 An Nāsirīyah 31 0 N 46 15 E
27 An Uaimh 53 39 N 6 40 W
131 Anaconda 46 7 N 113 0 W
53 Anadia 40 26 N 8 27 W
80 Anadolu, Reg. 38 0 W 39 0 E
77 Anadyr 64 35 N 177 20 E
77 Anadyr, R. 64 55 N 176 5 E
124 Anahim Lake 52 28 N 125 18 W
113 Anakie 23 32 S 147 45 E
94 Anambas, Kep. 3 20 N 106 30 E
102 Anan 33 54 N 134 40 E
86 Anantnag 33 45 N 75 10 E
145 Anápolis 16 15 S 48 50 W
81 Anār 30 55 N 55 13 E
80 Anatolia, Reg. = Anadolu, Reg. 38 0 N 39 0 E
148 Añatuya 28 20 S 62 50 W
28 Ancenis 47 21 N 1 10 W
120 Anchorage 61 10 N 149 50 W
53 Anciāo 39 56 N 8 27 W
144 Ancohuma, Mt. 16 0 S 68 50 W
63 Ancona 43 37 N 13 30 E
148 Ancud 42 0 S 73 50 W
38 Andalsnes 62 35 N 7 43 E
53 Andalucía, Reg. 37 35 N 5 0 W
127 Andalusia 31 51 N 86 30 W
91 Andaman Is. 12 30 N 92 30 E
91 Andaman Sea 13 0 N 96 0 E
45 Andernach 50 24 N 7 25 E
30 Andernos-les-Bains 44 44 N 1 6 W
127 Anderson, Ind. 40 5 N 85 40 W
127 Anderson, S.C. 34 32 N 82 40 W
142 Andes, Mts. 20 0 S 68 0 W
86 Andhra Pradesh □ 15 0 N 80 0 E
68 Andikíthira, I. 35 52 N 23 15 E
68 Andíparos, I. 37 0 N 25 3 E
81 Andkhvoy 36 52 N 65 8 E
55 Andorra ■ 42 30 N 1 30 E
21 Andover 51 13 N 1 29 W
120 Andreanof Is. 51 0 N 178 0 W
50 Andrespol 51 45 N 19 34 E
65 Ándria 41 13 N 16 17 E
139 Andros, I. 24 30 N 78 4 W
68 Ándros I. 37 50 N 24 50 E
139 Andros Town 24 43 N 77 47 W
49 Andrychów 49 51 N 19 18 E
53 Andújar 38 3 N 4 5 W
139 Anegada Pass. 18 15 N 63 45 W
158 Aného 6 12 N 1 34 E
77 Angara, R. 58 6 N 93 0 E
113 Angaston 34 30 S 139 8 E
41 Ange 62 31 N 15 35 E
137 Angel de la Guarda, I. 29 30 N 113 30 W
95 Angeles 15 9 N 120 35 E
41 Ängelholm 56 15 N 12 58 E
131 Angels Camp 38 8 N 120 30 W
37 Angermanälven, R. 62 48 N 17 56 E
28 Angers 47 30 N 0 35 E
29 Angerville 48 19 N 2 0 E
55 Anglés 41 57 N 2 38 E
21 Anglesey, I. 53 17 N 4 20 W
29 Anglure 48 35 N 3 50 E
173 Angmagssalik 65 40 N 37 20 W
165 Ango 4 10 N 26 5 E
165 Angola ■ 12 0 S 18 0 E
30 Angoulême 45 39 N 0 10 E
30 Angoumois, Reg. 45 30 N 0 25 E
139 Anguilla, I. 8 14 N 63 5 W
111 Angurugu 14 0 S 136 25 E
24 Angus, Braes of 56 51 N 3 0 W
41 Anholt, I. 56 42 N 11 33 E
99 Anhui □ 33 15 N 116 15 E
51 Anina 45 5 N 21 51 E
28 Anjou, Reg. 47 20 N 0 15 W
99 Ankang 32 38 N 109 5 E
80 Ankara 40 0 N 32 54 E
127 Ann Arbor 42 17 N 83 45 W
158 Annaba 36 50 N 7 46 E
91 Annam, Reg. = Trung-Phan, Reg. 16 30 N 107 30 E
91 Annamitique, Chaîne, Mts. 17 0 N 106 0 E
24 Annan 54 59 N 3 16 W
24 Annan, R. 54 59 N 3 16 W
127 Annapolis 38 59 N 76 30 W
123 Annapolis Royal 44 44 N 65 32 W
31 Annecy 45 55 N 6 8 E
31 Annecy, L. d' 45 52 N 6 10 E
31 Annonay 45 15 N 4 40 E
68 Ano Viánnos 35 2 N 25 21 E
99 Anqing 30 30 N 117 3 E
45 Ansbach 49 17 N 10 34 E
99 Anshan 41 3 N 122 58 E
55 Ansó 42 51 N 0 48 W
110 Anson, B. 13 20 S 130 6 E
122 Ansonville 48 46 N 80 43 W
95 Ansuda 2 11 S 139 22 E
80 Antakya 36 14 N 36 10 E
80 Antalya 36 52 N 30 45 E
80 Antalya Körfezi 36 15 N 31 30 E
174 Antarctica 90 0 S 0 0
174 Antarctic Pen. 67 0 S 60 0 W
31 Antibes 43 34 N 7 6 E
31 Antibes, C. d' 43 31 N 7 7 E
123 Anticosti, I. 49 20 N 62 40 W
28 Antifer, C. d' 49 41 N 0 10 E
128 Antigo 45 8 N 89 5 W
137 Antigua 14 34 N 90 41 W
139 Antigua, I. 17 0 N 61 50 W
131 Antimony 38 7 N 112 0 W
30 Antioche, Pertuis d' 46 5 N 1 30 W
106 Antipodes Is. 49 45 S 178 40 E
148 Antofagasta 23 50 S 70 30 W
148 Antonina 25 26 S 48 42 W
165 António Enes = Angoche 16 8 S 40 0 E
28 Antrain 48 28 N 1 30 W
27 Antrim 54 43 N 6 13 W
34 Antwerp = Antwerpen 51 13 N 4 25 E
34 Antwerpen 51 13 N 4 25 E
34 Anvers = Antwerpen 51 13 N 4 25 E
120 Anvik 62 40 N 160 12 W
99 Anyang 36 7 N 114 26 E
95 Anyer-Lor 6 6 S 105 56 E
76 Anzhero Sudzhensk 56 10 N 83 40 E
64 Ánzio 41 28 N 12 37 E
102 Aomori 40 45 N 140 45 E
62 Aosta 45 43 N 7 20 E
95 Aparri 18 22 N 121 38 E
60 Apatin 45 40 N 19 0 E
137 Apatzingán 19 0 N 102 20 W
34 Apeldoorn 52 13 N 5 57 E
45 Apen 53 12 N 7 47 E
94 Apenam 8 35 S 116 13 E
17 Apennines, Mts. = Appennini, Mts. 41 0 N 15 0 E
137 Apizaco 19 26 N 98 9 W
45 Apolda 51 1 N 11 30 E
159 Apollonia = Marsa Susa 32 52 N 21 59 E
128 Apostle Is. 47 0 N 90 30 W
144 Apoteri 4 2 N 58 32 W
118 Appalachian Mts. 38 0 N 80 0 W
63 Appennini, Mts. 41 0 N 15 0 E
62 Appenino Ligure, Mts. 44 30 N 9 0 E
63 Appiano 46 27 N 11 27 E
21 Appleby 54 35 N 2 29 W
65 Apricena 41 47 N 15 25 E
31 Apt 43 53 N 5 24 E
148 Apucarana 23 55 S 51 33 W
81 Aq Chah 37 0 N 66 5 E
80 'Aqaba 29 31 N 35 0 E
80 'Aqaba, Khalîj al 28 15 N 33 20 E
159 Aqîq 18 14 N 38 12 E
80 Ar Raqqah 35 56 N 39 1 E
80 Ar Riyād 24 41 N 46 42 E
80 Ar Rutbah 33 0 N 40 15 E
159 Arab, Bahr el, R. 9 2 N 29 28 E
73 Arabia, Reg. 25 0 N 45 0 E
156 Arabian Des. 28 0 N 32 30 E
73 Arabian Sea 15 0 N 65 0 E
145 Aracajú 10 55 S 37 4 W
145 Aracati 4 30 S 37 44 W
145 Araçatuba 21 10 S 50 30 W
53 Aracena, Sa. de 37 48 N 6 40 W
145 Araçuai 16 52 S 42 4 W
51 Arad 46 10 N 21 20 E
55 Aragón, R. 42 13 N 1 44 W
55 Aragon, Reg. 41 0 N 1 0 W
145 Araguacema 8 50 S 49 20 W
145 Araguari 18 38 S 48 11 W
80 Arāk 34 0 N 49 40 E
87 Arakan Coast 19 0 N 94 0 E
75 Araks, R. 40 1 N 48 28 E
76 Aral Sea = Aralskoye More 44 30 N 66 0 E
76 Aralsk 46 50 N 61 20 E
76 Aralskoye More 44 30 N 60 0 E
27 Aran, I. 55 0 N 8 30 W
27 Aran Is. 53 5 N 9 42 W
128 Aransas P. 28 0 N 97 9 W
148 Arauca 7 0 N 70 40 W
145 Araxá 19 35 S 46 55 W
144 Araya, Pen. de 10 40 N 64 0 W
80 Arbīl 36 15 N 44 5 E
41 Arboga 59 24 N 15 52 E
31 Arbois 46 55 N 5 46 E
24 Arbroath 56 34 N 2 35 W
64 Arborea 39 46 N 8 34 E
29 Arc 47 28 N 5 34 E
30 Arcachon 44 40 N 1 10 W
30 Arcachon, Bassin d' 44 42 N 1 10 W
128 Arcadia 44 13 N 91 29 W
131 Arcata 40 55 N 124 4 W
63 Arcévia 43 29 N 12 58 E
75 Archangel = Arkhangelsk 64 40 N 41 0 E
55 Archena 38 9 N 1 16 W
64 Arci, Mte. 39 47 N 8 44 E
29 Arcis-sur-Aube 48 32 N 4 10 E
125 Arcola 49 40 N 102 30 W
55 Arcos 41 12 N 2 16 W
53 Arcos de los Frontera 36 45 N 5 49 W
145 Arcoverde 8 25 S 37 4 W
121 Arctic Bay 73 2 N 85 11 W
173 Arctic Ocean 78 0 N 160 0 W
120 Arctic Red River 67 15 N 134 0 W
80 Ardabīl 38 15 N 48 18 E
53 Ardales 36 53 N 4 51 W
31 Ardeche, R. 44 16 N 4 39 E
31 Ardèche □ 44 42 N 4 16 E
34 Ardennes, Reg. 49 30 N 5 10 E
29 Ardennes □ 49 35 N 4 40 E
29 Ardentes 46 45 N 1 50 E
24 Ardgour, Reg. 56 45 N 5 25 W
128 Ardmore, Australia 21 39 S 139 11 E
128 Ardmore, U.S.A. 34 10 N 97 5 W
27 Ardnacrusha 52 43 N 8 38 W
29 Ardres 50 50 N 2 0 E
24 Ardrossan 55 39 N 4 50 W
27 Ards □ 54 35 N 5 30 W
27 Ards Pen. 54 30 N 5 25 W
139 Arecibo 18 29 N 66 42 W
53 Arenas 40 17 N 5 6 W
38 Arendal 58 28 N 8 46 E
55 Arenys de Mar 41 35 N 2 33 E
144 Arequipa 16 20 S 71 30 W
165 Arero 4 41 N 38 50 E
30 Arès 44 47 N 1 8 E
53 Arévalo 41 3 N 4 43 W
55 Arga, R. 42 18 N 1 47 W
53 Argamasilla de Alba 39 8 N 3 5 W
30 Argelès-Gazost 43 0 N 0 6 W
30 Argelès-sur-Mer 42 34 N 3 1 E
29 Argent 47 33 N 2 25 E
63 Argenta 44 37 N 11 50 E
28 Argentan 48 45 N 0 1 W
63 Argentário, Mte. 42 23 N 11 11 E
31 Argentera, Mt. de l' 44 10 N 7 18 E
62 Argentera, P. 44 11 N 7 17 E
29 Argenteuil 48 57 N 2 14 E
123 Argentia 47 18 N 53 58 W
64 Argentiera, C. dell' 40 44 N 8 8 E
142 Argentine Basin, Reg. 44 0 S 51 0 E
148 Argentina ■ 35 0 S 66 0 W
148 Argentino, L. 50 10 S 73 0 W
30 Argenton Château 46 59 N 0 27 W
30 Argenton-sur-Creuse 46 36 N 1 30 E
51 Arges, R. 44 10 N 26 45 E
159 Argo 19 28 N 30 30 E
68 Argolikós Kól. 37 20 N 22 52 E
68 Argolis □ 37 38 N 22 50 E
29 Argonne, Mts. 49 0 N 5 20 E
68 Árgos 37 40 N 22 43 E
68 Argostólion 38 12 N 20 33 E
77 Argun, R. 43 22 N 45 55 E
41 Århus 56 8 N 10 11 E
65 Ariano Irpino 41 10 N 15 4 E
144 Arica, Chile 18 32 S 70 20 W
144 Arica, Col. 1 30 S 75 30 W
110 Arid, C. 34 1 S 123 10 E
102 Arida 33 29 N 135 44 E
30 Ariège, R. 43 31 N 1 32 E
30 Ariège □ 42 56 N 1 30 E
24 Arisaig 56 50 N 5 40 W
55 Ariza 41 19 N 2 3 W
131 Arizona □ 34 20 N 111 30 W
144 Arjona 10 14 N 75 22 W
68 Arkadhía □ 38 48 N 21 3 E
24 Arkaig, L. 56 58 N 5 10 W
128 Arkansas, R. 33 48 N 91 4 W
128 Arkansas □ 35 0 N 92 30 W
128 Arkansas City 37 4 N 97 3 W
75 Arkhangelsk 64 40 N 41 0 E
27 Arklow 52 48 N 6 10 W
45 Arkona, C. 54 41 N 13 26 E
30 Arlanc 45 25 N 3 42 E
48 Arlberg P. 49 9 N 10 12 E
31 Arles 43 41 N 4 40 E
128 Arlington 44 25 N 97 4 W
34 Arlon 49 42 N 5 49 E
41 Arlöy 55 38 N 13 5 E
27 Armagh 54 22 N 6 40 W
30 Armagnac, Reg. 43 44 N 0 10 E
29 Armançon, R. 47 57 N 3 30 E
144 Armenia 4 35 N 75 45 W
75 Armenian S.S.R. □ 40 0 N 41 10 E
51 Armeniș 45 13 N 22 17 E
29 Armentières 50 40 N 2 50 E
113 Armidale 30 30 S 151 40 E
29 Arnay-le-Duc 47 10 N 4 27 E
55 Arnedo 42 12 N 2 5 W
34 Arnhem 51 58 N 5 55 E
111 Arnhem, B. 12 20 S 136 10 E
62 Arno, R. 43 31 N 10 17 E
45 Arnstadt 50 50 N 10 56 E
53 Aroche 37 56 N 6 57 E
53 Arosa, Ria de 42 28 N 8 57 W
61 Arpașul de Jos 45 45 N 24 38 E
64 Arpino 41 40 N 13 35 E
113 Arrabury 26 45 S 141 0 E
53 Arraiolos 38 44 N 7 59 W
24 Arran, I. 55 34 N 5 12 W
29 Arras 50 17 N 2 46 E
30 Arrats, R. 44 6 N 0 52 E
28 Arrée, Mts. d' 48 26 N 3 55 W
30 Arros, R. 43 30 N 0 2 W
124 Arrowhead 50 40 N 117 55 W
114 Arrowtown 44 57 S 168 50 E
30 Ars 46 13 N 1 30 W
61 Arsache 43 47 N 25 45 E
63 Arsiero 45 49 N 11 22 E
29 Ars-sur-Moselle 49 5 N 6 4 E
55 Artá 39 40 N 3 20 E
68 Arta 39 8 N 21 2 E
121 Artemovsk 48 35 N 37 55 E
29 Artenay 48 5 N 1 50 E
128 Artesia 32 55 N 104 25 W
113 Arthur, Pt. 22 7 S 150 3 E
148 Artigas 30 20 S 56 30 W
29 Artois, Reg. 50 20 N 2 30 E
80 Artvin 41 14 N 41 44 E
95 Aru, Kep. 6 0 S 134 30 E
165 Arua 3 1 N 30 58 E
145 Aruanã 15 0 S 51 10 W
139 Aruba, I. 12 30 N 70 0 W
87 Arunachal Pradesh □ 28 0 N 95 0 E
165 Arusha 3 20 S 36 40 E
131 Arvada 44 43 N 106 6 W
31 Arve, R. 46 12 N 6 8 E
123 Arvida 48 16 N 71 14 W
41 Arvika 59 40 N 12 36 E
76 Arys 42 26 N 68 48 E
75 Arzamas 55 27 N 43 55 E
158 Arzew 35 50 N 0 23 W
38 Aš 50 13 N 12 12 E
80 As Salt 32 2 N 35 43 E
80 As Samāwah 31 15 N 45 15 E
80 As Sulaimānīyah 24 8 N 47 10 E
80 As Sulaymānīyah 35 35 N 45 29 E
81 As Suwayh 22 10 N 59 33 E
80 As Suwaydā' 32 40 N 36 30 E
80 As Șuwayrah 32 55 N 45 0 E
81 As Zarqā' 25 0 N 53 30 E
102 Asahigawa 43 45 N 142 30 E
87 Asansol 23 40 N 87 1 E
123 Asbestos 45 47 N 71 58 W
137 Ascensión, B. de la 19 50 N 87 20 W
152 Ascension, I. 8 0 S 14 15 W
48 Aschach 48 23 N 14 0 E
45 Aschaffenburg 49 58 N 9 8 E
65 Áscoli Satriano 41 11 N 15 32 E
131 Ash Fork 35 14 N 112 32 W
80 Ash Shāmiyah 31 55 N 44 35 E
81 Ash Shāriqah 25 23 N 55 26 E
114 Ashburton 43 53 S 171 48 E
110 Ashburton, R. 37 52 S 145 5 E
21 Ashby-de-la-Zouch 52 45 N 1 29 W
127 Asheville 35 39 N 82 30 W
21 Ashford 51 8 N 0 53 E
21 Ashington 55 12 N 1 35 W
76 Ashkhabad 38 0 N 57 50 E
127 Ashland, Ky. 38 25 N 82 40 W
127 Ashland, Pa. 40 45 N 76 22 W
128 Ashland, Wis. 46 40 N 90 52 W
80 Ashquelon 31 42 N 34 55 E
127 Ashtabula 41 52 N 80 50 W
131 Ashton 44 6 N 111 30 W
21 Ashton-under-Lyne 53 30 N 2 8 W
73 Asia 40 0 N 90 0 E
64 Asinara, G. dell' 41 0 N 8 30 E
64 Asinara, I. 41 5 N 8 15 E
85 Asīr, Ras 11 55 N 51 0 E
85 Asīr, Reg. 18 40 N 42 30 E
38 Askim 59 35 N 11 10 E
81 Asmār 35 10 N 71 27 E
41 Asnen, L. 56 35 N 15 45 E
62 Ásola 45 12 N 10 25 E
114 Aspiring, Mt. 44 23 S 168 46 W
31 Aspres 44 32 N 5 44 E
87 Assam □ 25 45 N 92 30 E
34 Asse 50 54 N 4 6 E
34 Assen 53 0 N 6 35 E
125 Assiniboia 49 40 N 106 0 W
124 Assiniboine, Mt. 50 52 N 115 39 W
125 Assiniboine, R. 49 53 N 97 8 W
145 Assis 22 40 S 50 20 W
63 Assisi 43 4 N 12 36 E
24 Assynt, L. 58 25 N 5 10 W
75 Astārā 38 30 N 48 50 E
62 Asti 44 54 N 8 11 E
53 Astorga 42 29 N 6 8 W
131 Astoria 46 16 N 123 50 W
41 Astorp 56 6 N 12 55 E
75 Astrakhan 46 25 N 48 5 E
53 Asturias, Reg. 43 15 N 6 0 W
148 Asunción 25 21 S 57 30 W
159 Aswân 24 4 N 32 57 E
159 Aswân High Dam 24 5 N 32 54 E
80 At Ṭā'if 21 5 N 40 27 E
148 Atacama Des. 24 0 S 69 20 W
148 Atacama, Salar de 24 0 S 68 20 W
68 Atalándi 38 39 N 22 58 E
102 Atami 35 0 N 139 55 E
158 Atâr 20 30 N 13 5 W
77 Atara 63 10 N 129 10 E
159 Atbara 17 42 N 33 59 E
159 'Atbara, Nahr, R 17 40 N 33 56 E
128 Atchison 39 40 N 95 0 W
55 Ateca 41 20 N 1 49 W
34 Ath 50 38 N 3 47 E
124 Athabasca 54 45 N 113 20 W
125 Athabasca, L. 59 10 N 109 30 W
125 Athabasca, R. 58 40 N 110 50 W
27 Athboy 53 37 N 6 55 W
27 Athenry 53 18 N 8 45 W
127 Athens, Ala. 34 49 N 86 58 W
127 Athens, Ga. 33 56 N 83 24 W
127 Athens, Ohio 39 52 N 82 64 W
128 Athens, Tex. 32 11 N 95 48 W
68 Athens = Athínai 37 58 N 23 46 E
113 Atherton 17 17 S 145 30 E
68 Athínai 37 58 N 23 46 E
27 Athlone 53 26 N 7 57 W
68 Athos, Mt. 40 9 N 24 22 E
27 Athy 53 0 N 7 0 W
120 Atka I. 52 15 N 174 30 W
127 Atlanta 33 50 N 84 24 W
128 Atlantic 41 25 N 95 0 W
127 Atlantic City 39 25 N 74 25 W
152 Atlantic Ocean 10 0 N 30 0 W
158 Atlas, Anti, Mts. 30 0 N 8 0 W
158 Atlas, Moyen, Mts. 37 0 N 5 0 W
158 Atlas Saharien, Mts. 34 10 N 3 30 E
124 Atlin 59 31 N 133 41 W
127 Atmore 31 2 N 87 30 W
53 Atouguia 39 20 N 9 20 W
63 Atri 42 35 N 14 0 E
122 Attawapiskat 53 0 N 82 30 W
122 Attawapiskat L. 52 20 N 88 0 W
48 Attersee 47 55 N 13 31 E
48 Attersee, L. 47 52 N 13 33 E
68 Attikí □ 38 10 N 23 40 E
86 Attock 33 52 N 72 20 E
120 Attu I. 52 55 N 173 0 E
86 Attur 11 35 N 78 30 E
128 Atwood 39 52 N 101 3 W
29 Aube, R. 48 34 N 3 43 E
29 Aube □ 48 15 N 4 0 E
31 Aubenas 44 37 N 4 24 E
30 Aubrac, Mts. d' 44 38 N 2 58 E
127 Auburn, Ala. 32 57 N 85 30 W
131 Auburn, Calif. 38 50 N 121 10 W
127 Auburn, Me. 44 6 N 70 14 W
127 Auburn, N.Y. 42 57 N 76 39 W
30 Auch 43 39 N 0 36 E
29 Auchel 50 30 N 2 39 E
114 Auckland 36 52 S 174 46 E
30 Aude □ 44 13 N 3 15 E
122 Auden 50 17 N 87 54 W
28 Audierne 48 1 N 4 34 W
45 Aue 50 34 N 12 43 E
45 Auerbach 50 30 N 12 25 E
28 Auffay 49 43 N 1 7 E
45 Augsburg 48 22 N 10 54 W
65 Augusta, Italy 37 14 N 15 12 E
110 Augusta, U.S.A. 33 29 N 81 59 W
127 Augusta 44 20 N 69 46 W
50 Augustów 53 51 N 23 0 E
110 Augustus, Mt. 24 20 S 116 50 E
113 Augustus Downs 18 35 S 139 55 E
28 Aulne, R. 48 17 N 4 16 W
29 Aulnoye 46 2 N 0 22 W
30 Aunis, Reg. 46 0 N 0 50 W
28 Auray 47 40 N 3 0 W
45 Aurich 53 28 N 7 30 E
30 Aurillac 44 55 N 2 26 E
128 Aurora, Colo. 39 44 N 104 55 W
127 Aurora, Ill. 41 42 N 88 20 W
128 Austin, Minn. 43 37 N 92 59 W
131 Austin, Nev. 39 30 N 117 1 W
128 Austin, Tex. 30 20 N 97 45 W
110 Australia ■ 23 0 S 135 0 E
113 Australian Alps, Mts. 36 30 S 148 8 E
113 Australian Capital Terr. □ 35 15 S 149 8 E
174 Australian Dependency □ 73 0 S 90 0 E
48 Austria ■ 47 0 N 14 0 E
29 Authie, R. 50 21 N 1 38 E
137 Autlán 19 40 N 104 30 W
148 Autofagasta 23 50 S 70 30 W
31 Autun 46 58 N 4 17 E
30 Auvergne, Mts. 45 20 N 2 45 E
30 Auvergne, Reg. 45 30 N 3 20 E
30 Auvézère, R. 45 12 N 0 51 E
29 Auxerre 47 48 N 3 32 E
31 Auxonne 47 10 N 5 20 E
30 Auzat 45 27 N 3 19 E
29 Avallon 47 30 N 3 53 E
68 Ávas 40 57 N 25 56 E
145 Aveiro, Brazil 3 10 S 55 5 W
53 Aveiro, Port. 40 37 N 8 38 W
65 Avellino 40 54 N 14 46 E
38 Averøya, I. 63 0 N 7 35 E
144 Aves, Is. de 12 0 N 67 40 W
29 Avesnes 50 8 N 3 55 E
41 Avesta 60 9 N 16 10 E
30 Aveyron, R. 44 5 N 1 16 E
30 Aveyron □ 44 22 N 2 45 E
63 Avezzano 42 2 N 13 24 E

Aviemore Béthune

24	Aviemore	57 11 N	3 50W
65	Avigliano	40 44 N	15 41 E
31	Avignon	43 57 N	4 50 E
53	Ávila	40 39 N	4 43W
53	Ávila, Sa. de	40 40 N	5 0W
53	Avilés	43 35 N	5 57W
113	Avoca, R.	52 48 N	6 10W
124	Avola, Canada	51 45 N	119 30W
65	Avola, Italy	36 56 N	15 7 E
65	Avola	36 56 N	15 7 E
21	Avon, R., Avon	51 30 N	2 43W
21	Avon, R., Dorset	50 43 N	1 46W
21	Avon, R., Gloucester	51 59 N	2 10W
21	Avon □	51 30 N	2 40W
21	Avonmouth	51 30 N	2 42W
28	Avranches	48 40 N	1 20W
165	Awash	9 1 N	40 10 E
118	Axel Heiberg Ld.	80 0 N	90 0W
30	Ax-les-Thermes	42 44 N	1 50 E
21	Axminster	50 47 N	3 1W
29	Ay	49 3 N	4 0 E
77	Ayan	56 30 N	138 16 E
81	Aybak	36 15 N	68 5 E
68	Ayía Paraskevi	39 14 N	26 16 E
68	Ayíos Evstrátios	39 34 N	24 58 E
125	Aylesbury, Canada	50 55 N	105 53W
21	Aylesbury, U.K.	51 48 N	0 49W
120	Aylmer, L.	64 0 N	109 0W
80	'Ayn al Mubārak	24 10 N	38 10 E
24	Ayr	55 28 N	4 37W
24	Ayr, R.	55 29 N	4 28W
21	Ayre, Pt. of	54 27 N	4 21W
61	Aytos	42 47 N	27 16 E
80	Az Zahrān	26 10 N	50 7 E
80	Az Zilfi	26 12 N	44 52 E
80	Az Zubayr	30 20 N	47 50 E
53	Azambuja	39 4 N	8 51W
80	Azarbāījān □	37 0 N	44 30 E
158	Azare	11 55 N	10 10 E
158	Azbine = Aïr	18 0 N	8 0 E
75	Azerbaijan S.S.R. □	40 20 N	48 0 E
53	Aznalcóllar	37 32 N	6 17W
16	Azores, Is.	38 44 N	29 0W
75	Azov	47 3 N	39 25 E
75	Azov Sea = Azovskoye More	46 0 N	36 30 E
76	Azovy	64 55 N	64 35 E
131	Aztec	36 54 N	108 0W
139	Azua	18 25 N	70 44W
53	Azuaga	38 16 N	5 39W
53	Azuer, R.	39 8 N	3 36W
148	Azul	36 42 S	59 43W

B

91	Ba Don	17 45 N	106 26 E
53	Baamonde	43 7 N	7 44W
81	Baba, Koh-i-, Mts.	34 40 N	67 20 E
51	Babadag	44 53 N	28 48 E
113	Babinda	17 27 S	146 0 E
95	Babo	2 30 S	133 30 E
81	Bābol	36 40 N	52 50 E
81	Babol Sar	36 45 N	52 45 E
95	Babuyan Chan.	18 58 N	122 0 E
80	Babylon	32 40 N	44 30 E
91	Bac Ninh	21 13 N	106 4 E
91	Bac-Phan, Reg.	22 0 N	105 0 E
145	Bacabal	5 20 S	56 45W
95	Bacan, I.	1 0 S	127 30 E
51	Bacau	46 35 N	26 55 E
29	Baccarat	48 28 N	6 42 E
45	Bacharach	50 3 N	7 46 E
76	Bachelina	57 45 N	67 20 E
120	Back, R.	67 15 N	95 15W
45	Backnang	48 57 N	9 26 E
49	Bacs-Kiskun □	46 43 N	19 30 E
49	Bácsalmás	46 8 N	19 17 E
45	Bad Driburg	51 44 N	9 0 E
45	Bad Ems	51 22 N	7 44 E
45	Bad Godesberg	50 41 N	7 4 E
45	Bad Hersfeld	50 52 N	9 42 E
45	Bad Honnef	50 39 N	7 13 E
48	Bad Ischl	47 44	13 38 E
45	Bad Kissingen	50 11 N	10 5 E
45	Bad Lauterberg	51 38 N	10 29 E
48	Bad Leonfelden	48 31 N	14 18 E
45	Bad Mergentheim	49 29 N	9 47 E
45	Bad Nauheim	50 24 N	8 45 E
45	Bad Oldesloe	53 56 N	10 17 E
45	Bad Pyrmont	51 59 N	9 5 E
45	Bad Segeberg	53 58 N	10 16 E
45	Bad Tölz	47 43 N	11 34 E
45	Bad Wildungen	51 7 N	9 10 E
53	Badajoz	38 50 N	6 59W
81	Badakhshan □	36 30 N	71 0 E
55	Badalona	41 26 N	2 15 E
80	Badanah	30 58 N	41 30 E
49	Baden, Austria	48 1 N	16 13 E
45	Baden, Switz.	47 28 N	8 18 E
45	Baden-Baden	48 45 N	8 14 E
45	Baden Württemberg □	48 40 N	9 0 E
24	Badenoch, Reg.	57 0 N	4 0W
48	Badgastein	47 7 N	13 9 E
81	Bādghīsāt □	35 0 N	63 0 E
63	Badia Polèsine	45 6 N	11 30 E
53	Baena	37 37 N	4 20W
53	Baeza	37 57 N	3 25W
121	Baffin B.	72 0 N	65 0W
121	Baffin I.	68 0 N	77 0W
80	Bafra	41 34 N	35 54W
81	Bāft	29 15 N	56 38W
77	Bagdarin	54 26 N	113 36 E
148	Bagé	31 20 S	54 15W
80	Baghdād	32 20 N	44 30 E
64	Bagheira	38 5 N	13 30 E
81	Baghīn	30 12 N	56 45 E
81	Baghlān	36 12 N	69 0 E
65	Bagnara Cálabria	38 16 N	15 49 E
30	Bagnères-de-Luchon	42 47 N	0 38 E
62	Bagni di Lucca	41 1 N	10 37 E
63	Bagno di Romagna	43 50 N	11 59 E
31	Bagnols-sur-Cèze	44 10 N	4 36 E
123	Bagotville	48 22 N	70 54W
60	Bagrdan	44 5 N	21 11 E
95	Baguio	16 26 N	120 34 E
53	Bahabòn de Esgueva	41 52 N	3 43W
139	Bahamas ■	24 0 N	74 0W
91	Bahau	2 48 N	102 26 E
86	Bahawalpur	29 37 N	71 40 E
145	Bahia = Salvador	13 0 S	38 30W
139	Bahia, Is. de la	16 45 N	86 15W
148	Bahia Blanca	38 35 S	62 13W
144	Bahia de Caráquez	0 40 S	80 27W
148	Bahia Laura	48 10 S	66 30W
144	Bahia Negra	20 5 S	58 5W
81	Bahrain ■	26 0 N	50 35 E
51	Baia Mare	47 40 N	23 37 E
145	Baião	2 50 S	49 15W
51	Baicoi	45 3 N	25 52 E
123	Baie Comeau	49 12 N	68 10W
123	Baie T. Paul	47 28 N	70 32W
80	Ba 'iji	35 0 N	43 30 E
27	Baile Atha Cliath = Dublin	53 20 N	6 18W
53	Bailén	38 8 N	3 48W
127	Bainbridge	30 53 N	84 34W
120	Baird Mts.	67 10 N	160 15W
49	Baja	46 12 N	18 59 E
113	Bajimba, Mt.	29 17 S	152 6 E
131	Baker	36 16 N	116 2W
106	Baker I.	0 10 N	176 35 E
120	Baker L.	64 0 N	97 0W
131	Baker, Mt.	48 50 N	121 49W
120	Baker Lake	64 20 N	96 10W
122	Baker's Dozen Is.	57 30 N	79 0W
131	Bakersfield	35 25 N	119 0W
80	Bakhtīāri □	32 0 N	49 0 E
75	Bakinskikh Komissarov	39 20 N	49 15 E
49	Bakony Forest = Bakony Hegyseg, Reg.	47 10 N	17 30 E
75	Baku	40 25 N	49 45 E
21	Bala, L.	52 53 N	3 38W
94	Balabac Str.	7 53 N	117 5 E
86	Balaghat	21 49 N	80 12 E
86	Balaghat Ra.	18 50 N	76 30 E
113	Balaklava, Australia	34 7 S	138 22 E
75	Balaklava, U.S.S.R.	44 30 N	33 30 E
75	Balakovo	52 4 N	47 55 E
75	Balashov	51 30 N	43 10 E
87	Balasore	21 35 N	87 3 E
49	Balaton, L.	46 50 N	17 40 E
55	Balazote	38 54 N	2 9W
137	Balboa	9 0 N	79 30W
148	Balcarce	38 0 S	58 10W
61	Balchik	43 28 N	28 11 E
114	Balclutha	46 15 S	169 45 E
131	Baldy Pk.	33 55 N	109 35W
55	Baleares, Is.	39 30 N	3 0 E
113	Balfe's Creek	20 12 S	145 55 E
94	Bali, I.	8 20 S	115 0 E
80	Balikesir	39 35 S	27 58 E
94	Balikpapan	1 10 S	116 55 E
91	Baling	5 41 N	100 55 E
145	Baliza	16 0 S	52 20W
17	Balkan Pen.	42 0 N	22 0 E
81	Balkh □	36 30 N	67 0 E
76	Balkhash	46 50 N	74 50 E
76	Balkhash, Oz.	46 0 N	74 50 E
24	Ballachulish	56 40 N	5 10W
24	Ballater	57 2 N	3 2W
113	Ballerat	37 39 S	143 59 E
113	Ballina, Australia	28 50 S	153 31 E
27	Ballina, Mayo	54 7 N	9 10W
27	Ballina, Tipperary	52 49 N	8 27W
27	Ballinasloe	53 20 N	8 12W
128	Ballinger	31 45 N	99 58W
27	Ballinrobe	53 36 N	9 13W
27	Ballycastle	55 12 N	6 15W
27	Ballymena	54 53 N	6 18W
27	Ballymoney	55 5 N	6 30W
27	Ballyshannon	54 30 N	8 10W
24	Balmoral	57 3 N	3 13W
51	Bals	44 22 N	24 5 E
137	Balsas, R.	17 55 N	102 10W
17	Baltic Sea	56 0 N	20 0 E
27	Baltimore, Eire	51 29 N	9 22W
127	Baltimore, U.S.A.	39 18 N	76 37W
86	Balūchistān, Reg.	27 30 N	65 0 E
158	Bamako	12 34 N	7 55W
165	Bambari	5 40 N	20 35 E
113	Bambaroo	18 50 S	146 10 E
45	Bamberg	49 54 N	10 53 E
81	Bāmīān □	35 0 N	67 0 E
81	Bampur	27 15 N	60 21 E
91	Ban Bua Yai	15 33 N	102 26 E
91	Ban Mae Sot	16 40 N	98 30 E
91	Ban Nong Pling	15 40 N	100 10 E
91	Ban Phai	16 4 N	102 44 E
91	Ban Takua Pa	8 55 N	98 25 E
106	Banaba	0 45 S	169 50 E
165	Banalia	1 32 N	25 5 E
158	Banamba	13 29 N	7 22W
113	Banana	24 32 S	150 12 E
145	Bananal, I. de	11 30 S	50 30W
159	Bânâs, Ras	23 57 N	35 50 E
27	Banbridge	54 26 N	6 16W
21	Banbury	52 4 N	1 21W
24	Banchory	57 3 N	2 30W
122	Bancroft	45 3 N	77 51W
86	Banda	25 30 N	80 26 E
94	Banda Aceh	5 35 N	95 20 E
95	Banda Sea	6 0 S	130 0 E
81	'Bandār Abbās	27 15 N	56 15 E
81	Bandar-e Chārak	26 45 N	54 20 E
81	Bandar-e Nakhīlū	26 58 N	53 30 E
91	Bandar Maharani	2 2 N	102 34 E
94	Bandar Seri Begawan	4 52 N	115 0 E
81	Bandar-e Bushetir	28 55 N	50 55 E
80	Bandar-e Ma'shūr	30 35 N	49 10 E
81	Bandar-e Rig	29 30 N	50 45 E
81	Bandar-e Sháh	37 0 N	54 10 E
80	Bandar-e Shahpur	30 30 N	49 5 E
165	Bandawe	11 58 S	34 5 E
145	Bandeira, Pico da	20 26 S	41 47W
80	Bandirma	40 20 N	28 0 E
27	Bandon	51 44 N	8 45W
27	Bandon, R.	51 40 N	8 35W
165	Bandundu	3 15 S	17 22 E
95	Bandung	6 36 S	107 48 E
55	Bañeres	38 44 N	0 38W
139	Banes	20 58 N	75 43W
124	Banff, Canada	51 20 N	115 40W
24	Banff, U.K.	57 40 N	2 32W
124	Banff Nat. Park	51 38 N	116 22W
169	Bangala Dam	21 7 S	31 25 E
86	Bangalore	12 59 N	77 40 E
165	Bangassou	4 55 N	23 55 E
159	Banghāzī	32 11 N	20 3 E
95	Bangil	7 36 S	112 50 E
94	Bangka, I., Selatan	3 30 S	105 30 E
95	Bangka, I., Utara	1 50 N	12 S 5 E
95	Bangkalan	7 2 S	112 46 E
91	Bangkok = Krung Thep	13 45 N	100 31 E
87	Bangladesh ■	24 0 N	90 0 E
21	Bangor, Gwynedd	53 13 N	4 9W
27	Bangor, N. Down	54 40 N	5 40W
127	Bangor, Me.	44 48 N	68 42W
165	Bangui	4 23 N	18 35 E
165	Bangweulu, L.	11 0 S	30 0 E
139	Bani	18 16 N	70 22W
159	Banīnah	32 0 N	20 12 E
60	Banja Luka	44 49 N	17 26 E
95	Banjar	7 24 S	108 30 E
94	Banjarmasin	3 20 S	114 35 E
95	Banjarnegara	7 24 S	109 42 E
158	Banjul	13 28 N	16 40W
118	Banks I.	73 30 N	120 0W
114	Banks, Pen.	43 45 S	173 15 E
27	Bann, R.	55 2 N	6 35W
28	Bannalec	47 57 N	3 42W
131	Banning	48 44 N	91 56W
24	Bannockburn	56 5 N	3 55W
53	Baños de Molgas	42 15 N	7 40W
49	Banská Bystrica	48 46 N	19 14 E
49	Banská Stiavnica	48 25 N	18 55 E
95	Banten	6 5 S	106 8 E
27	Bantry	51 40 N	9 28W
27	Bantry, B.	51 35 N	9 50W
95	Bantul	7 55 S	110 19 E
30	Banyuls	42 29 N	3 8 E
99	Baoding	30 50 N	115 28 E
99	Baoji	34 20 N	107 5 E
99	Baotou	40 32 N	110 2 E
87	Bapatla	15 55 N	80 30 E
60	Bar	42 8 N	19 8 E
76	Barabinsk	55 20 N	78 20 E
128	Baraboo	43 28 N	89 46W
139	Barahona, Dom. Rep.	18 13 N	71 7W
53	Barahona, Sp.	41 17 N	2 39W
87	Barail Ra.	25 15 N	93 20 E
102	Barak □	38 20 N	140 0 N
86	Baramula	34 15 N	74 20 E
124	Baranof I.	57 0 N	135 10W
49	Baranya □	46 0 N	18 15 E
95	Barat□, Java	7 0 S	107 0 E
94	Barat□, Kalimantan	0 0 S	111 0 E
145	Barbacena	21 15 S	43 56W
144	Barbacoas	1 45 N	78 0W
139	Barbados ■	13 0 N	59 30W
55	Barbastro	42 2 N	0 5 E
53	Barbate	36 13 N	5 56W
169	Barberton, S. Africa	25 42 S	31 2 E
127	Barberton, U.S.A.	41 0 N	81 40W
139	Barbuda, I.	17 30 N	61 40W
113	Barcaldine	22 33 S	145 13 E
159	Barce = Al Marj	32 25 N	20 40 E
55	Barcelona, Sp.	41 21 N	2 10 E
144	Barcelona, Ven.	10 10 N	64 40W
65	Barcellona Pozzo di Gotto	38 8 N	15 15 E
31	Barcelonnette	44 23 N	6 40 E
144	Barcelos	1 0 S	63 0W
159	Bardaī	21 25 N	17 0 E
85	Bardera	2 20 N	42 0 S
159	Bardia	31 45 N	25 0 E
21	Bardsey I.	52 46 N	4 47W
86	Bareilly	28 22 N	79 27 E
28	Barentin	49 33 N	0 58 E
173	Barents Sea	73 0 N	39 0 E
28	Barfleur	49 40 N	1 17W
28	Barfleur, Pte. de	49 42 N	1 17W
62	Barga	44 5 N	10 30 E
85	Bargal	11 25 N	51 0 E
77	Barguzin	53 37 N	109 37 E
87	Barhi	24 15 N	85 25 E
65	Bari	41 6 N	16 52 E
86	Bari Doab, Reg.	30 20 N	73 0 E
85	Barīm	12 39 N	43 25 E
144	Barinas	8 36 N	70 15W
159	Bârîs	24 42 N	30 31 E
94	Barisan, Bukit, Mts.	3 30 S	102 15 E
94	Barito, R.	4 0 S	114 50 E
81	Barkā	24 30 N	58 0 E
110	Barkly Tableland	19 50 S	138 40 E
29	Bar-le-Duc	48 47 N	5 10 E
65	Barletta	41 20 N	16 17 E
113	Barmera	34 15 S	140 28 E
21	Barmouth	52 44 N	4 3W
21	Barnard Castle	54 33 N	1 55W
76	Barnaul	53 20 N	83 40 E
128	Barnesville	33 6 N	84 9W
21	Barnet	51 37 N	0 15W
34	Barneveld	52 7 N	5 36 E
28	Barneville	49 23 N	1 46W
21	Barnsley	53 33 N	1 29W
21	Barnstaple	51 5 N	4 3W
86	Baroda = Vadodara	22 20 N	73 10 E
144	Barquisimeto	9 58 N	69 13W
145	Barra	11 5 S	43 10W
24	Barra, I.	57 0 N	7 30W
145	Barra do Piraí	22 30 S	43 50W
113	Barraba	30 21 S	150 35 E
65	Barrafranca	37 22 N	14 10 E
144	Barranca	10 45 S	77 50W
144	Barrancabermeja	7 0 N	73 50W
144	Barrancas	8 55 N	62 5W
53	Barrancos	38 10 N	6 58W
144	Barranquilla	11 0 N	74 50W
145	Barras	1 45 S	73 13W
122	Barraute	47 30 N	76 50W
53	Barreiro	38 40 N	9 6W
145	Barretos	20 30 S	48 35W
124	Barrhead	54 10 N	114 30W
21	Barrow, U.K.	54 8 N	3 15W
120	Barrow, U.S.A.	71 16 N	156 50W
110	Barrow, I.	20 45 S	115 20 E
27	Barrow, R.	52 46 N	7 0W
110	Barrow Creek	21 30 S	133 55 E
53	Barruelo	42 54 N	4 17W
21	Barry	51 23 N	3 19W
122	Barry's Bay	45 30 N	77 40W
131	Barstow	34 58 N	117 2W
29	Bar-sur-Aube	48 14 N	4 40 E
128	Bartlesville	36 50 N	95 58W
21	Barton-upon-Humber	53 41 N	0 27W
127	Bartow	27 53 N	81 49W
29	Bas Rhin □	48 40 N	7 30 E
45	Basel	47 35 N	7 35 E
65	Basento, R.	40 25 N	16 40 E
75	Bashkir A.S.S.R. □	54 0 N	57 0 E
95	Basilan City = Lamitan	6 37 N	122 0 E
95	Basilan Str.	13 10 S	122 0 E
21	Basildon	51 34 N	0 29 E
65	Basilicata □	40 30 N	16 0 E
21	Basingstoke	51 15 N	1 5W
122	Baskatong Res.	46 46 N	75 50W
45	Basle = Basel	47 35 N	7 35 E
165	Basoka	1 16 N	23 40 E
24	Bass Rock	56 5 N	2 40W
113	Bass, Str.	39 15 S	146 30 E
63	Bassano del Grappa	45 45 N	11 45 E
165	Bassas da India, I.	22 0 S	39 0 E
139	Basse Terre	16 0 N	61 40W
87	Bassein	16 45 N	94 30 E
139	Basseterre	17 17 N	62 43W
29	Bassigny, Reg.	48 0 N	5 10 E
87	Basti	26 52 N	82 55 E
31	Bastia	42 40 N	9 30 E
34	Bastogne	50 1 N	5 43 E
51	Bata	1 57 N	9 50 E
95	Bataan, Pen.	14 38 N	120 30 E
139	Barabanó, G. de	22 30 N	82 30W
77	Batagoy	67 38 N	134 38 E
77	Batamay	63 30 N	129 15 E
95	Batangas	13 35 N	121 10 E
127	Batavia	43 0 N	78 10W
21	Bath	51 22 N	2 22W
24	Bathgate	55 54 N	3 38W
158	Bathurst = Banjul	13 28 N	16 40W
113	Bathurst, Australia	33 25 S	149 31 E
123	Bathurst, Canada	47 37 N	65 43W
120	Bathurst, C.	70 30 N	128 30W
118	Bathurst I.	76 30 N	130 10W
81	Batinah, Reg.	24 0 N	57 0 E
158	Batna	35 34 N	6 15 E
128	Baton Rouge	30 30 N	91 5W
165	Batouri	4 30 N	14 25 E
91	Battambang	13 7 N	103 12 E
65	Battipáglia	40 38 N	15 0 E
21	Battle	50 55 N	0 30 E
125	Battle, R.	52 45 N	108 15W
127	Battle Creek	42 20 N	85 10W
123	Battle Harbour	52 13 N	55 42W
125	Battleford	52 45 N	108 15W
49	Battonya	46 16 N	21 03 E
94	Batu, Kep.	0 30 S	98 25 E
75	Batumi	41 30 N	41 30 E
145	Baturité	4 28 S	38 45W
95	Baubau	5 25 S	123 50 E
158	Bauchi	10 22 N	9 48 E
28	Baud	47 52 N	3 1W
28	Baugé	47 31 N	0 8W
45	Baunatal	51 19 N	9 15 E
145	Baus	18 22 S	52 47½
45	Bautzen	51 11 N	14 25W
87	Bawdwin	23 5 N	97 50 E
94	Bawean, I.	5 46 S	112 35 E
87	Bawlake	19 11 N	97 21 E
127	Bay City, Mich.	43 35 N	83 51W
128	Bay City, Tex.	28 59 N	95 55W
114	Bay View	39 25W	176 50 E
139	Bayamón	18 24 N	66 10W
76	Bayanaul	50 45 N	75 45 E
45	Bayerischer Wald, Reg.	49 0 N	13 0 E
45	Bayern □	49 7 N	11 30 E
28	Bayeux	49 17 N	0 42W
77	Baykal, Oz.	53 0 N	108 0 E
77	Baykal, L. = Baykal, Oz.	53 0 N	108 0 S
77	Baykir	61 50 N	95 50 E
76	Baykonur	47 48 N	65 50 E
29	Bayon	48 30 N	6 20 E
30	Bayonne	43 30 N	1 28 E
45	Bayreuth	49 56 N	11 35 E
80	Bayrūt	33 53 N	35 31 E
128	Baytown	29 42 N	94 57W
55	Baza	37 30 N	2 47W
30	Bazas	44 27 N	0 13W
125	Beach	46 57 N	104 0W
21	Beachy Hd.	50 44 N	0 16 E
148	Beagle	55 0 S	68 30W
114	Bealey	43 2 S	171 36 E
122	Beardmore	49 36 N	87 59W
128	Beardstown	40 0 N	90 25W
30	Béarn, Reg	43 28 N	0 36W
30	Béarn, R.	43 40 N	0 47W
55	Beas de Segura	38 15 N	2 53W
55	Beasain	43 3 N	2 11W
31	Beaucaire	43 48 N	4 39 E
113	Beaudesert	27 59 S	153 0 E
94	Beaufort, Malaysia	5 30 N	115 40 E
127	Beaufort, U.S.A.	34 45 N	76 40W
118	Beaufort Sea	70 30 N	146 0W
168	Beaufort West	32 18 S	22 36 E
122	Beauharnois	45 20 N	73 20W
31	Beaulieu	43 45 N	7 20 E
24	Beauly	57 29 N	4 27W
21	Beaumaris	53 16 N	4 7W
28	Beaumont, Fr.	44 45 N	0 46 E
128	Beaumont, U.S.A.	30 5 N	94 8W
29	Beaumont-sur-Oise	49 9 N	2 17 E
31	Beaune	47 2 N	4 50 E
125	Beausejour	50 5 N	96 35 E
29	Beauvais	49 25 N	2 8 E
125	Beauval	55 9 N	107 35W
30	Beauvoir-sur-Mer	46 55 N	2 1W
30	Beauvoir-sur-N.	46 12 N	0 30W
120	Beaver	66 40 N	147 50W
86	Beawar	26 3 N	74 18 E
21	Beccles	52 27 N	1 33 E
53	Becerreá	42 51 N	7 10W
158	Béchar	31 38 N	2 18 E
127	Beckley	37 50 N	81 8W
28	Bécon	47 30 N	0 50W
55	Bédar	37 11 N	1 59W
21	Bedford, U.K.	52 8 N	0 29W
127	Bedford, Pa.	40 1 N	78 30W
127	Bedford, Ind.	38 50 N	86 30W
49	Bedzin	50 19 N	19 7 E
45	Beelitz	52 14 N	12 58 E
113	Beenleigh	27 43 S	153 10 E
80	Be'er Sheva	31 15 N	34 48 E
21	Beeston	52 55 N	1 11W
128	Beeville	28 27 N	97 44W
60	Bega, Canalul	45 37 N	20 46 E
28	Bégard	48 38 N	3 18W
81	Behshahr	36 45 N	53 35 E
99	Beijing	39 45 N	116 25 E
34	Beilen	52 52 N	6 27 E
45	Beilngries	49 1 N	11 27 E
169	Beira	19 50 S	34 52 E
80	Beirut = Bayrut	33 53 N	35 31 E
169	Beitbridge	22 12 S	30 0 E
53	Beja, Port.	38 2 N	7 53W
158	Béja, Tunisia	36 10 N	9 0 E
53	Beja □	37 55 N	7 55W
158	Bejaia	36 42 N	5 2 E
53	Béjar	40 23 N	5 46W
49	Békés	46 47 N	21 9 E
49	Békéscsaba	46 40 N	21 10 E
91	Bekok	2 20 N	103 7 E
87	Bela, India	25 50 N	82 0 E
86	Bela, Pak.	26 12 N	66 20 E
60	Bela Crkva	44 55 N	21 27 E
60	Bela Palanka	43 13 N	22 17 E
94	Belawan	3 33 N	98 32 E
75	Belaya Tserkov	49 45 N	30 10 E
122	Belcher Is.	56 20 N	79 20W
55	Belchite	41 18 N	0 43W
75	Belebey	54 72 N	54 7 E
145	Belém	1 20 S	48 30W
148	Belén	27 40 S	67 5W
131	Belen	34 40 N	106 50W
61	Belene	43 39 N	25 10 E
85	Belet Uen	4 30 N	45 5 E
27	Belfast, U.K.	54 35 N	5 56W
127	Belfast, U.S.A.	44 30 N	69 0W
27	Belfast, L.	54 40 N	5 50W
29	Belfort	47 38 N	6 50 E
29	Belfort, Terr. de □	47 38 N	6 52 E
86	Belgaum	15 55 N	74 35 E
34	Belgium ■	51 30 N	5 0 E
27	Belgooly	51 44 N	8 30W
75	Belgorod	50 35 N	36 35 E
75	Belgorod-Dnestrovskiy	46 11 N	30 23 E
60	Belgrade = Beograd	44 50 N	20 37 E
94	Belitung, Pulau, I.	3 10 S	107 50 E
137	Belize ■	17 0 N	88 30W
137	Belize City	17 25 N	88 0W
148	Bella Vista	28 33 S	59 0W
62	Bellágio	45 59 N	9 15 E
113	Bellata	29 53 S	149 46 E
28	Belle I.	47 20 N	3 10W
123	Belle I, Str. of	51 30 N	56 30W
128	Belle Fourche	44 43 N	103 52W
31	Belledonne, Mts.	45 11 N	6 0 E
31	Bellegarde-sur-V.	46 4 N	3 49 E
31	Belleville, Fr.	46 7 N	4 45 E
128	Belleville, Ill.	38 30 N	90 0W
124	Bellevue, Can.	46 35 N	84 10W
31	Belley	45 46 N	5 41 E
121	Bellin	60 0 N	70 0W
113	Bellingen	30 25 S	152 50 E
174	Bellingshausen Sea	66 0 S	80 0W
45	Bellinzona	46 11 N	9 1 E
55	Bellpuig	41 37 N	1 1 E
63	Belluno	46 8 N	12 6 E
53	Bélmez	38 17 N	5 17W
145	Belmonte, Brazil	16 0 S	39 0W
53	Belmonte, Port.	40 21 N	7 20W
137	Belmopan	17 18 N	88 30W
27	Belmullet	54 13 N	9 58W
145	Belo Horizonte	19 55 S	43 56W
77	Belogorsk	51 0 N	128 20 E
128	Beloit	42 35 N	89 0W
75	Belomorsk	64 35 N	34 30 E
75	Beloretsk	53 58 N	58 24 E
75	Beloye, Oz.	60 10 N	37 35 E
75	Beloye More	66 0 N	38 0 E
65	Belpasso	37 37 N	15 0 E
64	Belsito	37 50 N	13 47 E
113	Beltana	30 48 S	138 25 E
145	Belterra	2 45 S	55 0W
27	Belturbet	54 6 N	7 28W
65	Belvedere Marittimo	39 37 N	15 52 E
128	Belvidere	42 15 N	88 55W
53	Bembézar, R.	38 0 N	5 20W
128	Bemidjī	47 30 N	94 50W
24	Ben Cruachan, Mt.	56 26 N	5 8W
24	Ben Hope, Mt.	58 24 N	4 36W
24	Ben Lawers, Mt.	56 33 N	4 13W
113	Ben Lomond, Mt., Australia	30 1 S	151 43 E
24	Ben Lomond, Mt., U.K.	56 12 N	4 39W
24	Ben Macdhui, Mt.	57 4 N	3 40W
24	Ben More, Mt.	56 26 N	6 2W
24	Ben More Assynt, Mt.	58 7 N	4 51W
24	Ben Nevis, Mt.	56 48 N	5 0W
24	Ben Wyvis, Mt.	57 40 N	4 35W
165	Bena Dibele	4 4 S	22 50 E
53	Benagalbón	36 45 N	4 15W
53	Benavente	38 59 N	8 49W
53	Benavides	42 30 N	5 54W
24	Benbecula, I.	57 26 N	7 20W
113	Benbonyathe Hill	30 25 S	139 11 E
131	Bend	44 2 N	121 15W
85	Bender Beila	9 30 N	50 48 E
75	Bendery	46 50 N	29 50 E
48	Benešov	49 46 N	14 41 E
29	Bénestroff	48 54 N	6 45 E
65	Benevento	41 7 N	14 45 E
29	Benfeld	48 22 N	7 34 E
87	Bengal, B. of	18 0 N	89 0 E
159	Benghazi = Banghazī	32 11 N	20 3 E
94	Bengkalis	1 30 N	102 10 E
94	Bengkulu	3 50 S	102 12 E
125	Bengough	49 25 N	105 10W
165	Benguela	12 37 S	13 25 E
165	Beni	32 11 S	148 43 E
159	Beni Mazâr	28 32 N	30 44 E
158	Beni Mellal	32 21 N	6 21W
159	Beni Suef	29 5 N	31 6 E
55	Benidorm	38 33 N	0 9W
158	Benin ■	10 0 N	2 0 E
158	Benin, B. of	5 0 N	3 0 E
158	Benin City	6 20 N	5 31 E
55	Benisa	38 43 N	0 3 E
113	Benlidi	24 35 S	144 50 E
127	Bennettsville	34 38 N	79 39W
28	Bénodet	47 53 N	4 7W
169	Benoni	26 11 S	28 18 E
45	Bensheim	49 40 N	8 38 E
131	Benson	31 59 N	110 19W
95	Benteng	6 10 S	120 30 E
127	Benton Harbor	42 10 N	86 28W
91	Bentong	3 31 N	101 55 S
158	Benue, R.	7 47 N	6 45 E
99	Benxi	41 20 N	123 48 E
60	Beograd	44 50 N	20 37 E
68	Berati	40 43 N	19 59 E
159	Berber	18 0 N	34 0 E
85	Berbera	10 30 N	45 2 E
55	Berberia, C.	38 39 N	1 24 E
62	Berceto	44 30 N	10 0 E
45	Berchtesgaden	47 37 N	13 1 E
29	Berck	50 25 N	1 36 E
75	Berdichev	49 57 N	28 30 E
76	Berdsk	54 47 N	83 2 E
75	Berdyansk	46 45 N	36 50 E
158	Berekum	7 29 N	2 34W
49	Berettyóújfalu	47 13 N	21 33 E
75	Berezniki	59 24 N	56 46 E
76	Berezovo	64 0 N	65 0 E
55	Berga	42 6 N	1 48 E
62	Bérgamo	45 42 N	9 40 E
53	Bergantiños	43 20 N	8 40W
45	Bergen, E. Germany	50 24 N	13 26 E
34	Bergen, Neth.	52 40 N	4 42 E
38	Bergen, Norway	60 23 N	5 27 E
34	Bergen-op-Zoom	51 30 N	4 18 E
30	Bergerac	44 51 N	0 30 E
45	Bergheim	50 57 N	6 38 E
45	Bergisch-Gladbach	50 59 N	7 9 E
29	Bergues	50 58 N	2 24 E
34	Bergum	53 13 N	5 59 E
87	Berhampore	24 2 N	88 27 E
87	Berhampur	19 15 N	84 54 E
120	Bering Sea	66 0 N	170 0W
173	Bering Str.	65 0 N	168 0W
55	Berja	36 50 N	2 56W
131	Berkeley	38 0 N	122 20W
61	Berkovitsa	43 16 N	23 8 E
21	Berkshire □	51 30 N	1 20W
53	Berlanga	38 17 N	5 50W
45	Berleburg	51 3 N	8 22 E
53	Berlenga, I.	39 25 N	9 30W
45	Berlin, Germany	52 32 N	13 24W
127	Berlin, U.S.A.	44 29 N	71 10W
53	Bermeja, Sa.	36 45 N	5 11W
55	Bermeo	43 25 N	2 47W
139	Bermuda, I.	32 45 N	65 0W
45	Bern	46 57 N	7 28 E
65	Bernalda	40 24 N	16 44 E
131	Bernalilo	35 17 N	106 37W
148	Bernardo de Irigoyen	26 15 S	53 40W
45	Bernau	47 53 N	12 20 E
28	Bernay	49 5 N	0 35 E
48	Berndorf	47 59 N	16 1 E
45	Berne = Bern	46 57 N	7 28 E
45	Berner Alpen, Mts.	46 27 N	7 35 E
45	Bernina, Piz	46 20 N	9 54 E
48	Beroun	49 57 N	14 5 E
48	Berounka, R.	50 0 N	13 47 E
31	Berre	43 28 N	5 11 E
31	Berre, Étang de	43 27 N	5 5 E
113	Berri	34 14 S	140 35 E
29	Berry, Reg.	47 0 N	2 0 E
45	Bersenbrück	52 33 N	7 56 E
45	Berthoud	47 3 N	7 37 E
29	Bertincourt	50 5 N	2 58 E
165	Bertoua	4 30 N	13 45 E
127	Berwick	41 4 N	76 17W
21	Berwick-upon-Tweed	55 47 N	2 0W
21	Berwyn Mts.	52 54 N	3 26W
29	Besançon	47 9 N	6 0 E
31	Bessèges	44 18 N	4 8 E
127	Bessemer	46 27 N	90 0W
28	Bessin, Reg.	49 21 N	1 0W
28	Bessines-sur-Gartempe	46 6 N	1 22 E
53	Betanzos	43 15 N	8 12W
165	Bétaré-Oya	5 40 N	14 5 E
55	Betera	39 35 N	0 28W
168	Bethanien	26 31 S	17 8 E
169	Bethlehem, S. Africa	28 14 S	28 18 E
127	Bethlehem, U.S.A.	40 39 N	75 24W
29	Béthune	50 30 N	2 38 E

Béthune, R. **Cabruta**

28	Béthune, R.	49 56 N	1 5 E
29	Betan Bazoches	48 42 N	3 15 E
113	Betoota	25 40 S	140 42 E
62	Béttola	44 46 N	9 35 E
102	Betung	2 0 S	103 10 E
51	Beuca	44 14 N	24 56 E
31	Beuil	44 6 N	7 0 E
125	Beulah	50 16 N	101 2W
45	Bevensen	53 5 N	10 34 E
110	Beverley, Australia	32 9 S	116 56 E
21	Beverley, U.K.	53 52 N	0 26W
124	Beverly	53 36 N	113 21W
131	Beverly Hills	34 4 N	118 29W
34	Beverwijk	52 28 N	4 38 E
45	Bex	46 15 N	7 0 E
158	Beyla	8 30 N	8 38W
21	Bexhill	50 51 N	0 29 E
76	Beyneu	45 10 N	55 3 E
80	Beypazari	40 10 N	31 48 E
80	Beyşehir Gólú, L.	37 40 N	31 45 E
60	Bezdan	45 28 N	18 57 E
75	Bezhitsa	53 19 N	34 17 E
30	Béziers	43 20 N	3 12 E
87	Bhadrakh	21 10 N	86 30 E
86	Bhadravati	13 49 N	76 15 E
87	Bhamo	24 15 N	97 15 E
86	Bhanrer Ra.	23 40 N	79 45 E
86	Bharatpur	27 15 N	77 30 E
87	Bhatpara	22 50 N	88 25 E
86	Bhilwara	25 25 N	74 38 E
86	Bhima, R.	17 20 N	76 30 E
86	Bhiwandi	19 15 N	73 0 E
86	Bhiwani	28 50 N	76 9 E
86	Bhopal	23 20 N	77 53 E
87	Bhubaneswar	20 15 N	85 50 E
86	Bhusaval	21 1 N	75 56 E
87	Bhutan ■	27 25 N	89 50 E
49	Biała, R.	49 46 N	17 40 E
50	Biała Piska	53 37 N	22 5 E
50	Biała Podłaska	52 4 N	23 6 E
50	Białogard	54 2 N	15 58 E
50	Białystok	53 10 N	23 10 E
65	Biancaville	37 39 N	14 50 E
30	Biarritz	43 29 N	1 33W
45	Biasca	46 22 N	18 58 E
45	Biberach	48 5 N	9 49 E
53	Bibey, R.	42 24 N	7 13W
158	Bibiani	6 30 N	2 8W
123	Bic	48 20 N	68 41W
65	Bîccari	41 23 N	15 12 E
158	Bida	9 3 N	5 58 E
21	Bicester	51 53 N	1 9W
86	Bidar	17 55 N	77 35 E
127	Biddeford	43 30 N	70 28 E
21	Bideford	51 1 N	4 13W
91	Bidor	4 6 N	101 15 E
131	Bieber	41 4 N	121 6W
45	Biel	47 8 N	7 14 E
49	Bielé Karpaty, Mts.	49 5 N	18 0 E
45	Bielefeld	52 2 N	8 31 E
50	Bielsk Podlaski	52 47 N	23 12 E
49	Bielsko-Biała	49 50 N	19 8 E
91	Biên Hoa	10 57 N	106 49 E
45	Bienne = Biel	47 8 N	7 14 E
55	Biescas	42 37 N	0 20W
65	Biferno, R.	41 40 N	14 38 E
122	Big Beaver House	52 59 N	89 50W
128	Big Bend Nat. Park	29 15 N	103 15W
120	Big Delta	64 15 N	145 0W
127	Big Rapids	43 42 N	85 27W
125	Big River	53 50 N	107 0W
120	Big Salmon	61 50 N	136 0W
128	Big Spring	32 10 N	101 25W
127	Big Stone Gap	36 52 N	82 45W
30	Biganos	44 39 N	0 59W
125	Biggar, Canada	52 10 N	108 0W
24	Biggar, U.K.	55 38 N	3 31W
113	Biggenden	25 31 S	152 4 E
131	Bighorn Mts.	44 30 N	107 20W
30	Bigorre, Reg.	43 5 N	0 2 E
131	Bigtimber	45 33 N	110 0W
63	Bihaí	44 49 N	15 57 E
87	Bihar	25 5 N	85 40 E
87	Bihar □	25 0 N	86 0 E
51	Bihor □	47 0 N	22 10 E
158	Bijagos, Arquipélago dos	11 15 N	16 10W
60	Bijeljina	44 46 N	19 17 E
86	Bikaner	28 2 N	73 18 E
77	Bikin	46 50 N	134 20 E
106	Bikini Atoll, I.	12 0 N	167 30 E
91	Bilauk Taungdan, Ra.	13 0 N	99 0 E
53	Bilbao	43 16 N	2 56W
60	Bileća	42 53 N	18 27 E
80	Bilecik	40 5 N	30 5 E
68	Bilishti	40 37 N	20 59 E
21	Billingham	54 36 N	1 18W
131	Billings	45 43 N	108 29W
30	Billom	45 43 N	3 20 E
159	Bilma	18 50 N	13 30 E
60	Bilo Gora	45 53 N	17 15 E
113	Biloela	24 34 S	150 31 E
128	Biloxi	30 30 N	89 0W
159	Biltine	14 40 N	20 50 E
95	Bima	8 22 S	118 49 E
95	Binalbagan	10 12 N	122 50 E
94	Binatang	2 10 N	111 40 E
113	Binbee	20 19 S	147 56 E
34	Binche	50 26 N	4 10 E
169	Bindura	17 18 S	31 18 E
45	Bingen	49 57 N	7 53 E
131	Bingham Canyon	40 31 N	112 10W
91	Binh Dinh = An Nhon	13 55 N	109 7 E
94	Binjai	3 50 N	98 30 E
63	Biograd	43 56 N	15 29 E
60	Biokovo	43 23 N	17 0 E
159	Bir 'Atrun	18 15 N	26 40 E
80	Bi'r Mubayrīk	23 22 N	39 8 E
159	Bîr Shalatein	23 5 N	35 25 E
111	Bird, I.	22 20 S	155 20 E
113	Birdsville	25 51 S	139 20 E
110	Birdum	15 50 S	133 0 E
94	Bireuen	5 14 N	96 39 E
81	Bīrjand	32 57 N	59 10 E
21	Birkenhead	53 24 N	3 1W
48	Birkfeld	47 21 N	15 45 E
21	Birmingham, U.K.	52 30 N	1 55W
127	Birmingham, U.S.A.	33 31 N	86 50W
158	Birnin-Kebbi	12 32 N	4 12 E
27	Birr	53 7 N	7 55W
125	Birtle	50 30 N	101 5W
30	Biscay, B. of	45 0 N	2 0W
65	Biscéglie	41 14 N	16 30 E
29	Bischwiller	48 47 N	7 50 E
131	Bishop	37 20 N	118 26W
21	Bishop Auckland	54 40 N	1 40W
123	Bishop's Falls	49 2 N	55 24W
21	Bishop's Stortford	51 52	0 11 E
50	Biskupiec	53 53 N	20 58 E
128	Bismarck	46 49 N	100 49W
106	Bismark Arch.	3 30 S	148 30 E
158	Bissau	11 45 N	15 45W
60	Bitola	41 5 N	21 21 E
45	Bitterfeld	51 36 N	12 20 E
168	Bitterfontein	31 0 S	18 32 E
131	Bitterroot Ra.	46 0 N	114 20W
102	Biwa-Ko, L.	35 15 N	135 45 E
76	Biysk	52 40 N	85 0 E
158	Bizerte = Binzerte	37 15 N	9 50 E
41	Bjärka	58 16 N	15 44 E
60	Bjelašnica, Mt.	43 11 N	18 21 E
173	Bjørnøya, I	74 25 N	19 0 E
41	Bjuv	56 7 N	12 56 E
128	Black Hills, Mts	44 0 N	103 50W
21	Black Mts.	51 52 N	3 50W
51	Black Sea	43 30 N	35 0 E
158	Black Volta, R.	8 41 N	1 33W
113	Blackall	24 26 S	145 27 E
113	Blackbull	18 0 S	141 7 E
21	Blackburn	53 44 N	2 30W
131	Blackfoot	43 13 N	112 12W
21	Blackpool	53 48 N	3 3W
123	Blacks Harbour	45 3 N	66 49W
123	Blackville	47 5 N	65 58W
113	Blackwater	23 35 S	149 0 E
27	Blackwater, R., Cork	51 51 N	7 50W
27	Blackwater, R., Dungannon	54 31 N	6 34W
27	Blackwater, R., Meath	53 39 N	6 43W
128	Blackwell	36 55 N	97 20W
21	Blaenau Ffestiniog	53 0 N	3 57W
60	Blagoevgrad	42 2 N	23 5 E
77	Blagoveshchensk	50 20 N	127 30 E
125	Blaine Lake	52 51 N	106 52W
113	Blair Atholl, Australia	22 42 S	147 31 E
24	Blair Atholl, U.K.	56 46 N	3 50W
24	Blairgowrie	56 36 N	3 20W
29	Blamont	48 35 N	6 50 E
158	Blanc, C. = Ras Nouadhibou	37 15 N	9 56 E
31	Blanc, Mt.	45 50 N	6 52 E
131	Blanca Pk.	37 35 N	105 29W
55	Blanco, C.	39 21 N	2 51 E
21	Blandford	50 52 N	2 10W
55	Blanes	41 40 N	2 48 E
29	Blangy	49 14 N	0 17 E
165	Blantyre	15 45 S	35 0 E
27	Blarney	51 57 N	8 35W
21	Blaydon	54 56 N	1 47W
30	Blaye	45 8 N	0 40W
45	Bleckede	53 18 N	10 43 E
63	Bled	46 27 N	14 7 E
48	Bleiburg	46 35 N	14 49 E
41	Blekinge □	56 15 N	15 15 E
21	Bletchley	51 59 N	0 54W
158	Blida	36 30 N	2 49 E
95	Blitar	8 5 S	112 11 E
168	Bloemfontein	29 6 S	26 14 E
28	Blois	47 35 N	1 20 E
50	Błonie	52 12 N	20 37 E
128	Bloomington, Ill.	40 25 N	89 0W
127	Bloomington, Ind.	39 10 N	86 30W
48	Bludenz	47 10 N	9 50 E
127	Blue Island	41 40 N	87 41W
111	Blue Mud, B.	13 30 S	136 0 E
127	Blue Mts.	45 15 N	119 0W
159	Blue Nile, R. = Nîl el Azraq, R.	10 30 N	35 0 E
118	Blue Ridge, Mts	36 30 N	80 15W
127	Bluefield	37 18 N	81 14W
139	Bluefields	12 0 N	83 50W
113	Bluff, Australia	23 40 S	149 0 E
114	Bluff, N.Z.	46 36 S	168 21 E
148	Blumenau	27 0 S	49 0W
21	Blyth	55 8 N	1 32W
131	Blythe	33 40 N	114 33W
158	Bo	7 55 N	11 50W
99	Bo Hai	39 0 N	120 0 E
152	Boa Vista	2 48 N	60 30W
139	Boaco	12 29 N	85 35W
165	Boali	4 48 N	18 7 E
53	Boatman	27 16 S	146 55 E
158	Bobo-Dioulasso	11 8 N	4 13W
51	Boboc	45 13 N	26 59 E
50	Bobr R.	52 4 N	15 4 E
75	Bobruysk	53 10 N	29 15 E
145	Bocaiuva	17 7 S	43 49W
53	Boceguillas	41 20 N	3 39W
49	Bochnia	49 58 N	29 27 E
45	Bocholt	51 50 N	6 35 E
45	Bochum	51 28 N	7 12 E
31	Bocognano	42 5 N	9 3 E
51	Boçsa	45 21 N	21 47 E
165	Boda	4 19 N	17 26 E
77	Bodaybo	57 50 N	114 0 E
37	Boden	65 50 N	21 42 E
45	Bodensee, L.	47 35 N	9 25 N
21	Bodmin	50 28 N	4 44W
21	Bodmin Moor, Reg.	50 33 N	4 36W
37	Bodø	67 17 N	14 27 E
49	Bodva, R.	48 19 N	20 45 E
128	Bogalusa	30 50 N	89 55W
113	Bogantungan	23 41 S	147 17 E
113	Boggabri	30 45 S	150 0 E
21	Bognor Regis	50 47 N	0 40W
95	Bogor	6 36 S	106 48 E
77	Bogorodskoye	52 22 N	140 30 E
144	Bogota	4 34 N	74 0W
76	Bogotal	56 15 N	89 50 E
87	Bogra	24 26 N	89 22 E
29	Bohain	49 59 N	3 28 E
45	Böhmerwald, Mts.	49 30 N	12 40 E
95	Bohol, I.	9 58 N	124 20 E
85	Bohotleh	8 20 N	46 25 E
123	Boiestown	46 27 N	66 26W
131	Boise	43 43 N	116 9W
45	Boizenburg	55 16 N	13 36 E
95	Bojonegoro	7 9 S	111 52 E
158	Boké	10 56 N	14 17W
165	Bokote	0 12 S	21 8 E
81	Bol, Kuh-e	30 40 N	52 45 E
158	Bolama	11 30 N	15 30W
144	Bolívar, Arg.	36 2 S	60 53W
148	Bolívar, Col.	2 0 N	77 0W
144	Bolivia ■	17 6 S	64 0W
142	Bolivian Plat.	19 0 S	69 0W
31	Bollène	44 18 N	4 45 E
41	Bollnäs	61 22 N	16 28 E
41	Bolmen, L.	56 57 N	13 45 E
63	Bologna	44 30 N	11 20 E
29	Bologne	48 10 N	5 8 E
91	Boloven, Cao Nguyen, Mts.	15 10 N	106 30 E
63	Bolsena, L. di	42 35 N	11 55 E
77	Bolshevik, Os.	78 30 N	102 0 E
75	Bo'shoy Kavkas	42 50 N	44 0 E
76	Bolshoy Atlym	62 25 N	66 50 E
21	Bolton	53 35 N	2 26W
63	Bolzano	46 30 N	11 20 E
165	Boma	5 50 S	13 4 E
113	Bomaderry	34 52 S	150 37 E
113	Bombala	36 56 S	149 15 E
86	Bombay	18 55 N	72 50 E
159	Bon, C.	37 1 N	11 2 E
139	Bonaire, I.	12 10 N	68 15W
110	Bonaparte Arch.	15 0 S	124 30 E
123	Bonaventure	48 5 N	63 32W
123	Bonavista	48 40 N	53 5W
123	Bonavista B.	48 58 N	53 25W
63	Bondeno	44 53 N	11 22 E
158	Bondoukou	8 2 N	2 47W
95	Bondowoso	7 56 S	113 49 E
95	Bone, Teluk, G.	4 10 S	120 50 E
24	Bo'ness	56 0 N	3 38W
159	Bongor	10 35 N	15 20 E
128	Bonham	33 30 N	96 10W
31	Bonifacio	41 24 N	9 10 E
64	Bonifacio, Bouches de	41 23 N	9 10 E
106	Bonin Is.	27 0 N	142 0 E
45	Bonn	50 43 N	7 6 E
131	Bonners Ferry	48 38 N	116 21W
28	Bonneval	48 11 N	1 24 E
31	Bonneville	46 5 N	6 24 E
110	Bonnie Rock	30 29 S	118 22 E
156	Bonny, B. of	4 0 N	8 0 E
125	Bonnyville	54 20 N	110 45W
64	Bonorva	40 25 N	8 47 E
94	Bontang	0 10 N	117 30 E
34	Boom	51 6 N	4 20 E
113	Boonah	28 0 S	152 35 E
128	Boone	42 5 N	93 46W
121	Boothia, G. of	70 0 N	90 0W
120	Boothia Pen.	70 30 N	95 0W
21	Bootle	53 28 N	3 1W
165	Booué	0 5 S	11 55 E
113	Bopeechee	29 35 S	137 30 E
60	Bor	44 5 N	22 7 E
41	Borås	57 42 N	13 1 E
144	Borba	4 12 S	59 34W
30	Bordeaux	44 50 N	0 36W
123	Borden	46 18 N	63 47W
24	Borders □	55 30 N	3 0W
62	Bordighera	43 47 N	7 40 E
34	Borger, Neth.	52 54 N	7 33 E
128	Borger, U.S.A.	35 40 N	101 20W
62	Borgo	46 3 N	11 27 E
62	Borgomanera	45 41 N	8 28 E
62	Borgosésia	45 43 N	8 9 E
75	Borisoglebsk	51 27 N	42 5 E
75	Borisov	54 17 N	28 28 E
144	Borja	4 20 S	77 40W
45	Borken	51 3 N	9 21 E
45	Borkum, I.	53 35 N	6 41 E
41	Borlänge	60 28 N	14 33 E
174	Borley, C.	66 15 S	52 30 E
45	Borna	51 8 N	12 31 E
94	Borneo, I.	1 0 N	115 0 E
41	Bornholm, I.	55 8 N	14 55 E
53	Bornos	36 48 N	5 42W
55	Borriol	40 4 N	0 4W
30	Bort-les-Orgues	45 24 N	2 29 E
80	Borujerd	33 55 N	48 50 E
77	Borzya	50 24 N	116 31 E
60	Bosanska Gradiška	45 9 N	17 15 E
63	Bosanska Kostajnica	45 11 N	16 33 E
63	Bosanski Novi	45 2 N	16 22 E
21	Boscasble	50 42 N	4 42W
60	Bosna, R.	45 4 N	18 29 E
63	Bosna i Hercegovina □	44 0 N	18 0 E
61	Bosporus, Str. = Karadeniz Boğazi, Str.	41 10 N	29 10 E
128	Bossier City	32 28 N	93 38W
21	Boston, U.K.	52 59 N	0 2W
127	Boston, U.S.A.	42 20 N	71 0W
61	Botevgrad	42 55 N	23 47 E
37	Bothnia, G.	63 0 N	21 0 E
168	Botswana ■	23 0 S	24 0 E
145	Botucatu	22 55 S	48 30W
123	Botwood	49 6 N	55 23W
158	Bou Saâda	35 11 N	4 9 E
165	Bouar	6 0 N	15 40 E
158	Bouârfa	32 32 N	1 58 E
110	Bougainville, C.	13 57 S	126 4 E
158	Bougouni	11 30 N	7 20W
110	Boulder	40 3 N	105 10W
131	Boulder City	36 0 N	114 58W
29	Bouligny	49 17 N	5 45 E
29	Boulogne-sur-Mer	50 42 N	1 36 E
30	Bourbon-Lancy	46 37 N	3 45 E
30	Bourbonnais, Reg.	46 28 N	3 0 E
30	Bourg	45 3 N	0 34W
31	Bourg en Bresse	46 13 N	5 12 E
30	Bourg Madame	42 29 N	1 58 E
31	Bourg-de-Péage	45 2 N	5 3 E
30	Bourges	47 5 N	2 22 E
41	Bourget, L. du	45 44 N	5 52 E
28	Bourgneuf, B. de	47 3 N	2 10W
28	Bourgneuf-en-Retz	47 2 N	1 58W
29	Bourgogne, Reg.	47 0 N	4 30 E
31	Bourgoin-Jallieu	45 36 N	5 17 E
113	Bourke	30 8 S	145 55 E
21	Bournemouth	50 43 N	1 53W
30	Boussac	46 22 N	2 13 E
30	Boussens	43 12 N	1 2 E
152	Bouvet, Øya.	55 0 S	3 30 E
113	Bowen	20 0 S	148 16 E
131	Bowie	32 15 N	109 30W
21	Bowland Forest	54 0 N	2 30W
113	Bowling Green, C.	19 19 S	147 25 E
128	Bowman	46 12 N	103 21W
24	Bowmore	55 45 N	6 18W
124	Bowness	50 55 N	114 25W
125	Bowsman	52 15 N	101 12W
34	Boxtel	51 36 N	5 9 E
27	Boyle	53 58 N	8 19W
27	Boyne, R.	53 40 N	6 34W
131	Bozeman	45 40 N	111 0W
165	Bozoum	6 25 N	16 35 E
62	Bra	44 41 N	7 50 E
34	Brabant □	49 15 N	5 20 E
63	Brac, I.	43 20 N	16 40 E
63	Bracciano, L. di	42 6 N	12 10 E
41	Bräcke	62 42 N	15 32 E
51	Brad	46 10 N	22 50 E
65	Brádano, R.	40 41 N	16 20 E
21	Bradford, U.K.	53 47 N	1 45W
127	Bradford, U.S.A.	41 58 N	78 41W
123	Bradore Bay	51 27 N	57 18W
128	Brady	31 8 N	99 25W
53	Braga	41 35 N	8 32W
53	Bragança □	41 30 N	6 45W
87	Brahmanbaria	23 50 N	91 15 E
87	Brahmaputra, R.	24 2 N	90 59 E
21	Braich-y-Pwll, Pt.	52 47 N	4 46W
51	Brăila	45 19 N	27 59 E
21	Braintree,	51 53 N	0 34 E
45	Brake	53 19 N	8 30 E
45	Brakel	51 43 N	9 10 E
122	Brampton, Canada	43 42 N	79 46W
122	Brampton, U.S.A.	46 0 N	97 46W
144	Branco, R.	1 30 N	61 15W
41	Brande	55 47 N	9 7 E
45	Brandenburg	52 24 N	12 33 E
125	Brandon	49 50 N	100 0W
48	Brandýs	50 10 N	14 40 E
122	Brantford	43 15 N	80 15W
30	Brantôme	45 22 N	0 39 E
145	Brasília	15 55 S	47 40W
145	Brasilia Legal	3 45 S	55 40W
51	Braşov	45 7 N	25 39 E
34	Brasschaat	51 19 N	4 27 E
49	Bratislava	48 10 N	17 7 E
77	Bratsk	56 10 N	101 3 E
51	Bratul Sulina, R.	45 10 N	29 20 E
48	Braunau	48 15 N	13 3 E
45	Braunschweig	52 17 N	10 28 E
21	Braunton	51 6 N	4 9W
131	Brawley	32 58 N	115 30W
27	Bray	53 12 N	6 6W
29	Bray, Reg.	49 40 N	1 40 E
127	Brazil	39 30 N	87 8W
145	Brazil ■	11 0 S	54 0W
142	Brazilian Highlands, Mts.	18 0 S	46 30W
165	Brazzaville	4 9 S	15 12 E
60	Brčko	44 54 N	18 46 E
113	Breadalbane	23 48 S	139 33 E
24	Breadalbane, Reg.	56 30 N	4 15W
114	Bream, B.	35 56 S	174 35 E
95	Brebes	6 52 S	109 3 E
24	Brechin	56 44 N	2 40W
21	Breckland, Reg.	52 30 N	0 40 E
49	Breclav	48 46 N	16 53 E
21	Brecon	51 57 N	3 23W
21	Brecon Beacons, Mts.	51 53 N	3 27W
34	Breda	51 35 N	4 45 E
168	Bredasdorp	34 33 S	20 2 E
48	Bregenz	47 30 N	9 45 E
37	Breidafjördur	65 20 N	23 0W
31	Breil	43 56 N	7 31 E
45	Bremen	53 4 N	8 47 E
45	Bremerhaven	53 34 N	8 35 E
53	Brenes	37 32 N	5 54W
128	Brenham	30 5 N	96 27W
48	Brenner P.	47 0 N	11 30 E
122	Brent, Canada	46 0 N	78 30W
21	Brent, U.K.	51 33 N	0 18W
21	Brentwood	51 37 N	0 19W
62	Bréscia	45 33 N	10 13 E
50	Breslau = Wrocław	51 5 N	17 5 E
29	Bresles	49 25 N	2 13 E
63	Bressanone	46 43 N	11 40 E
24	Bressay, I.	60 10 N	1 5W
31	Bresse, Plaine de	46 20 N	5 10 E
30	Bressuire	46 51 N	0 30W
28	Brest, Fr.	48 24 N	4 31W
75	Brest, U.S.S.R.	52 10 N	23 40 E
28	Bretagne, Reg.	48 0 N	3 0W
29	Breteuil	49 38 N	2 18 E
30	Breton, Pertuis	46 16 N	1 22W
114	Brett, C.	35 10 S	174 20 E
113	Brewarrina	30 0 S	146 51 E
127	Brewton	31 9 N	87 2W
49	Brezno	48 50 N	19 40 E
31	Briançon	44 54 N	6 39 E
29	Briare	47 38 N	2 45 E
29	Bricon	48 5 N	5 0 E
21	Bridgend	51 30 N	3 35W
127	Bridgeport	41 12 N	73 12W
127	Bridgeton	39 29 N	75 10W
110	Bridgetown, Australia	33 58 S	116 7 E
139	Bridgetown, Barbados	13 0 N	59 30W
123	Bridgetown, Can.	44 55 N	65 12W
113	Bridgewater, Australia	36 36 S	143 59 E
123	Bridgewater, Can.	44 25 N	64 31W
21	Bridgnorth	52 33 N	2 25W
21	Bridgwater	51 7 N	3 0W
21	Bridlington	54 4 N	0 10W
21	Bridport	50 43 N	2 45W
29	Brie, Plaine de la	48 35 N	3 10 E
29	Brie-Comte Robert	48 40 N	2 35 E
45	Brienzersee, L.	46 44 N	7 53 E
21	Brigg	53 33 N	0 30W
131	Brigham City	41 30 N	112 1W
113	Brighton, Australia	35 1 S	138 30 E
122	Brighton, Canada	44 3 N	77 44W
21	Brighton, U.K.	50 50 N	0 9W
28	Brignogan-Plages	48 40 N	4 20W
31	Brignoles	43 25 N	6 5 E
65	Bríndisi	40 39 N	17 55 E
30	Brioude	45 18 N	3 23 E
113	Brisbane	27 25 S	152 54 E
21	Bristol	51 26 N	2 35W
120	Bristol B.	58 0 N	159 0W
21	Bristol Chan.	51 18 N	3 30W
174	British Antarctic Terr.	66 0 S	45 0W
124	British Columbia □	55 0 N	125 15W
19	British Is.	55 0 N	4 0W
168	Britstown	30 37 S	23 30 E
128	Britton	45 50 N	97 47W
30	Brive-la-Gaillarde	45 10 N	1 32 E
53	Briviesca	42 32 N	3 19W
113	Brixton	23 32 S	144 52 E
49	Brno	49 10 N	16 35 E
24	Broad Law, Mt.	55 30 N	3 22W
21	Broads, The	52 30 N	1 15 E
125	Brock	51 27 N	108 42W
121	Brodeur Pen.	72 0 N	88 0W
24	Brodick	55 34 N	5 9W
50	Brodnica	53 15 N	19 25 E
128	Broken Bow	41 25 N	99 35W
113	Broken Hill	31 58 S	141 29 E
21	Bromley	51 20 N	0 5 E
41	Bromölla	56 5 N	14 25 E
41	Brønderslev	57 17 N	9 55 E
113	Bronte Pk.	42 8 S	146 30 E
128	Brookfield	39 50 N	92 50W
128	Brookhaven	31 40 N	90 25W
120	Brooks Ra.	68 40 N	147 0W
110	Brookton	32 22 N	116 57 E
24	Broom, L.	57 55 N	5 15W
24	Brora	58 0 N	3 50W
41	Brösarp	55 44 N	14 8 E
27	Brosna, R.	53 8 N	8 0W
121	Broughton I.	67 35 N	63 50W
24	Broughty Ferry	56 29 N	2 50W
21	Brown Willy, Mt.	50 35 N	4 34W
128	Brownfield	33 10 N	102 15W
131	Browning	48 35 N	113 10W
125	Brownlee	50 43 N	105 59 N
128	Brownsville	25 54 N	97 30W
128	Brownwood	31 45 N	99 0W
29	Bruay	50 29 N	2 33 E
122	Bruce Mines	46 20 N	83 45W
45	Bruchsal	49 9 N	8 39 E
21	Brue, R.	51 10 N	2 50W
45	Brugg	47 29 N	8 11 E
34	Brugge	51 13 N	3 13 E
124	Brule	53 15 N	117 38W
29	Brumath	48 43 N	7 40 E
94	Brunei ■	4 52 N	115 0 E
41	Brunflo	63 4 N	14 50 E
63	Brunico	46 48 N	11 56 E
38	Brunkeberg	59 25 N	8 30 E
125	Bruno	52 20 N	105 30W
45	Brunsbüttelkoog	53 52 N	9 13 E
45	Brunswick, W. Germany = Braunschweig	52 17 N	10 28 E
127	Brunswick, Ga.	31 10 N	81 30W
127	Brunswick, Me.	43 53 N	69 50W
60	Brusartsi	43 40 N	23 5 E
148	Brusque	27 5 S	49 0W
34	Brussel	50 51 N	4 21 E
34	Bruxelles = Brussel	50 51 N	4 21 E
29	Bruyères	48 10 N	6 40 E
50	Brwinow	52 9 N	20 40 E
127	Bryan, Ohio	41 30 N	84 30W
128	Bryan, Tex.	30 40 N	96 27W
75	Bryansk	53 13 N	34 25 E
60	Brzava, R.	45 21 N	20 45 E
49	Brzeg	50 52 N	17 30 E
50	Brzeg Din	51 16 N	16 41 E
144	Bucaramanga	7 0 N	73 0W
24	Buchan, Reg.	57 32 N	2 8W
24	Buchan Ness, Pt.	57 29 N	1 48W
125	Buchanan, Canada	51 40 N	102 45W
158	Buchanan, Liberia	5 57 N	10 2W
45	Buchholz	53 19 N	9 51 E
45	Bückeburg	52 16 N	9 2 E
131	Buckeye	33 28 N	112 40W
24	Buckie	57 40 N	2 58W
21	Buckingham, U.K.	52 0 N	0 59W
122	Buckingham, U.S.A.	45 37 N	75 24W
21	Buckinghamshire □	51 50 N	0 55W
123	Buctouche	46 30 N	64 45W
51	Bucureşti	44 27 N	26 10 E
127	Bucyrus	40 48 N	83 0W
49	Budafok	47 26 N	19 2 E
87	Budalin	22 20 N	95 10 E
49	Budapest	47 29 N	19 5 E
21	Bude	50 49 N	4 33W
51	Budeşti	44 13 N	26 30 E
63	Búdrio	44 31 N	11 31 E
60	Budva	42 17 N	18 50 E
144	Buenaventura	29 15 S	69 40W
55	Buendia, Pantano de	40 25 N	2 43W
148	Buenos Aires	34 30 S	58 20W
148	Buenos Aires, L.	46 35 S	72 30W
125	Buffalo, Canada	50 49 N	110 42W
127	Buffalo, U.S.A.	42 55 N	78 50W
125	Buffalo Narrows	55 52 N	108 28W
50	Bug, R.	51 20 N	23 40 E
144	Buga	4 0 N	77 0W
75	Bugulma	54 38 N	52 40 E
21	Builth Wells	52 10 N	3 26W
53	Bujalance	37 54 N	4 23W
165	Bujumbura	3 16 S	29 18 E
165	Bukavu	2 20 S	28 52 E
165	Bukene	4 15 S	32 48 E
76	Bukhara	39 50 N	64 10 E
91	Bukit Mertajam	5 22 N	100 28 E
94	Bukittinggi	0 20 S	100 20 E
165	Bukoba	1 20 S	31 49 E
169	Bulawayo	20 7 S	28 32 E
61	Bulgaria ■	42 35 N	25 30 E
85	Bulhar	10 25 N	44 30 E
113	Bullock Creek	17 40 S	144 30 E
114	Bulls	40 10 S	175 24 E
29	Bully-les-Mines	50 27 N	2 44 E
85	Bulo Burti	3 50 N	45 33 E
77	Bulun	70 37 N	127 30 E
165	Bumba	2 13 N	22 30 E
51	Bumbeşti Jiu	45 10 N	23 22 E
87	Bumhpa Bum, Mt.	26 40 N	97 20 E
27	Buncrana	55 8 N	7 28W
113	Bundaberg	24 54 S	152 22 E
86	Bundi	25 30 N	75 35 E
81	Buraymī	24 15 N	55 53 E
21	Bure, R.	52 38 N	1 38 E
45	Burg	54 25 N	11 10 E
61	Burgas	42 33 N	27 29 E
61	Burgaski Zaliv, B.	42 30 N	27 39 E
45	Burgdorf	52 27 N	10 0 E
49	Burgenland □	47 20 N	16 20 E
123	Burgeo	47 36 N	57 34W
53	Burgo de Osma	41 35 N	3 4W
53	Burgos	42 21 N	3 41W
53	Burgos □	42 21 N	3 41W
45	Burgstädt	50 55 N	12 49 E
45	Burgsteinfurt	52 9 N	7 23 E
95	Burias, I.	13 5 N	122 55 E
139	Burica, Pta	8 3 N	82 51W
113	Burketown	17 45 S	139 33 E
131	Burley	42 37 N	113 55W
122	Burlington, Canada	43 25 N	79 45W
128	Burlington, Colo.	39 21 N	102 18W
127	Burlington, N.C.	36 7 N	79 27W
131	Burlington, Wash.	48 29 N	122 19W
76	Burlyu-Tyube	46 30 N	79 10 E
87	Burma ■	21 0 N	96 30 E
113	Burnie	41 4 S	145 56 E
21	Burnley	53 47 N	2 15W
131	Burns	43 40 N	119 4W
124	Burns Lake	54 20 N	125 45W
125	Burntwood, L.	55 35 N	99 40W
113	Burra	33 40 S	138 55 E
55	Burriana	39 50 N	0 4W
21	Burry Port	51 41 N	4 17W
80	Bursa	40 15 N	29 5 E
21	Burton-on-Trent	52 48 N	1 39W
95	Buru, I.	3 30 S	126 30 E
165	Burundi ■	3 15 S	30 0 E
94	Burung	0 21 N	108 25 E
21	Bury	53 36 N	2 19W
21	Bury St. Edmunds	52 15 N	0 42 E
77	Buryat A.S.S.R. □	53 0 N	110 0 E
41	Buskerud □	60 20 N	9 0 E
29	Bussang	47 50 N	6 50 E
34	Bussum	52 16 N	5 10 E
53	Busto, C.	43 34 N	6 28W
62	Busto Arsizio	45 38 N	8 50 E
165	Busu-Djanoa	1 50 N	21 5 E
45	Büsum	54 7 N	8 50 E
165	Buta	2 50 N	24 53 E
165	Butare	2 31 S	29 52 E
24	Bute, I.	55 48 N	5 2W
165	Butembo	0 9 N	29 18 E
65	Butera	37 10 N	14 10 E
24	Butt of Lewis, Pt.	58 30 N	6 20W
131	Butte, Mont.	46 0 N	112 31W
128	Butte, Neb.	42 56 N	98 54W
91	Butterworth	5 24 N	100 23 E
95	Butuan	8 52 N	125 36 E
95	Butung, I.	5 0 S	122 45 E
45	Butzbach	50 24 N	8 40 E
21	Buxton	53 16 N	1 54W
77	Buyaga	59 50 N	127 0 E
102	Buzen	33 35 N	131 5 E
63	Buzet	45 24 N	13 58 E
75	Buzuluk	52 48 N	52 12 E
61	Byala Slatina	43 26 N	23 55 E
50	Bydgoszcz	53 10 N	18 0 E
75	Byelorussian S.S.R. □	53 30 N	27 0 E
131	Bylas	33 11 N	110 9W
121	Bylot I.	73 0 N	78 0W
165	Byrd Ld.	79 30 S	125 0W
174	Byrd Sub-Glacial Basin	82 0 S	120 0W
113	Byrock	30 40 S	146 27 E
113	Byron Bay	28 30 S	153 30 E
37	Byske	64 59 N	21 17 E
77	Byrranga, Gory	75 0 N	100 0 E
49	Bytom	50 25 N	19 0 E
50	Bytôw	54 10 N	17 30 E

C

91	Ca Mau, Mui, Pt.	8 35 N	104 42 E
148	Caazapá	26 9 S	56 24W
123	Cabana	8 25 S	78 5W
55	Cabanes	40 9 N	0 2 E
53	Cabeza del Buey	38 38 N	3 12W
144	Cabimas	10 30 N	71 25W
165	Cabinda	5 40 S	12 11 E
131	Cabinet Mts.	48 8 N	115 46W
148	Cabo Blanco	47 56 S	65 47W
145	Cabo Frio	22 51 S	42 3W
122	Cabonga Res.	47 35 N	76 40W
113	Caboolture	27 5 S	152 47 E
169	Cabora Bassa Dam	15 30 S	32 40 E
137	Caborca	30 40 N	112 10W
123	Cabot Str.	47 15 N	59 40W
53	Cabrera, Sa.	42 12 N	6 40W
144	Cabruta	7 50 N	66 10W

Espíritu Santo

Ghazipur

145	Espíritu Santo □	19 30 S	40 30W
55	Espluga de Francolí	41 24 N	1 7 E
55	Espuña, Sa.	37 51 N	1 35W
158	Essaouira	31 32 N	9 42W
34	Essen, Belgium	51 28 N	4 28 E
45	Essen, W. Germany	51 28 N	6 59 E
21	Essex □	51 48 N	0 30 E
45	Esslingen	48 43 N	9 19 E
29	Essonne □	48 30 N	2 20 E
148	Estados, I. de los	54 40 S	64 30W
145	Estância, Brazil	11 15 S	37 30W
131	Estancia, U.S.A.	34 50 N	106 1W
139	Estelí	13 9 N	86 22W
55	Estella	42 40 N	2 0W
53	Estepa	37 17 N	4 52W
53	Estepona	36 24 N	5 7W
125	Esterhazy	50 37 N	102 5W
29	Esternay	48 44 N	3 33 E
125	Estevan	49 10 N	103 0W
75	Estonian S.S.R. □	48 30 N	25 30 E
53	Estoril	38 42 N	9 23W
53	Estrêla, Sa. da	40 10 N	7 45W
53	Estrella, Mt.	38 25 N	3 35W
145	Estrondo, Sa. de	7 20 S	48 0W
28	Étables-s.-Mer	48 38 N	2 51W
29	Étampes	48 26 N	2 10 E
31	Étang	46 52 N	4 10 E
29	Étaples	50 30 N	1 39 E
86	Etawah	26 48 N	79 6 E
125	Ethelbert	51 32 N	100 25W
85	Ethiopia ■	8 0 N	40 0 E
156	Ethiopian Highlands, Mts.	10 0 N	37 0 E
24	Etive, L.	56 30 N	5 12W
65	Etna, Mt.	37 45 N	15 0 E
168	Etosha Pan	18 40 S	16 30 E
28	Étretat	49 42 N	0 12 E
45	Ettlingen	48 58 N	8 25 E
24	Ettrick, R.	55 31 N	2 55W
127	Euclid	41 32 N	81 31W
113	Eucumbene, L.	36 2 S	148 40 E
127	Eufaula	31 55 N	85 11W
131	Eugene	44 0 N	123 8W
128	Eunice	30 35 N	92 28W
34	Eupen	50 37 N	6 3 E
80	Euphrates, R. = Furat, Nahr al	33 30 N	43 0 E
28	Eure, R.	49 18 N	1 12 E
28	Eure □	49 6 N	1 0 E
131	Eureka, Calif.	40 50 N	124 0W
131	Eureka, Nev.	39 32 N	116 2W
131	Eureka, Utah	40 0 N	112 0W
16	Europe	50 0 N	15 0 E
165	Europa, Île	22 20 S	40 22 E
53	Europa, Picos de	43 10 N	5 0W
34	Europoort	51 57 N	4 10 E
45	Euskirchen	50 40 N	6 45 E
127	Evanston, Ill.	42 0 N	87 40W
131	Evanston, Wyo.	41 10 N	111 0W
127	Evansville	38 0 N	87 35W
30	Evaux	46 12 N	2 29 E
87	Everest, Mt.	28 5 N	86 58 E
131	Everett	48 0 N	122 10W
127	Everglades Nat. Park	25 50 N	80 40W
21	Evesham	52 6 N	1 57W
31	Evian	46 24 N	6 35W
28	Évreux	49 0 N	1 8 E
68	Evritania □	39 5 N	21 30 E
28	Évron	48 23 N	1 58W
68	Évros □	41 10 N	26 0 E
68	Evvoia □	38 40 N	23 40 E
24	Ewe, L.	57 49 N	5 38W
21	Exe, R.	50 37 N	3 25W
21	Exeter	50 43 N	3 31W
21	Exmoor, Reg.	51 10 N	3 55W
110	Exmouth, Australia	22 6 S	114 0 E
21	Exmouth, U.K.	50 37 N	3 24W
110	Exmouth, G.	22 15 S	114 15 E
53	Extremadura, Reg.	39 30 N	6 5W
165	Eyasi, L.	3 30 S	35 0 E
24	Eye Pen.	58 20 N	0 51 E
24	Eyemouth	55 53 N	2 5W
30	Eymoutiers	45 45 N	1 45 E
113	Eyre, L.	28 30 S	136 45 E
110	Eyre, Pen.	33 30 S	137 17 E

F

41	Fåborg	55 6 N	10 15 E
63	Fabriano	43 20 N	12 52 E
49	Fadd	46 28 N	18 49 E
63	Faenza	44 17 N	11 53 E
53	Fafe	41 27 N	8 11W
51	Făgăraş	45 48 N	24 58 E
51	Făgăraş, Mt.	45 40 N	24 40 E
38	Fagernes	61 0 N	9 16 E
41	Fagersta	61 1 N	15 46 E
148	Fagnano, L.	54 30 S	68 0W
81	Fahraj	29 0 N	59 0 E
81	Fahud	22 18 N	56 28 E
120	Fairbanks	64 59 N	147 40W
128	Fairbury	40 5 N	97 5W
127	Fairfield, Ala.	33 30 N	87 0W
131	Fairfield, Calif.	38 14 N	122 1W
128	Fairfield, Ill.	38 20 N	88 20W
128	Fairfield, Iowa	41 0 N	91 58W
128	Fairfield, Tex.	31 40 N	96 0W
128	Fairmont, Minn.	43 37 N	94 30W
127	Fairmont, W. Va.	39 29 N	80 10W
127	Fairport	43 8 N	77 29W
113	Fairview, Australia	15 31 S	144 17 E
124	Fairview, Canada	56 5 N	118 25W
120	Fairweather, Mt.	58 55 N	137 45W
87	Faizabad	26 45 N	82 10 E
139	Fajardo	18 20 N	65 39W
21	Fakenham	52 50 N	0 51 E
28	Falaise	48 54 N	0 12W
68	Falakrón Óros, Mt.	41 15 N	23 58 E
63	Falconara Marittima	43 37 N	13 23 E
128	Falfurrias	27 8 N	98 8 E
41	Falkenberg	56 54 N	12 30 E
45	Falkensee	52 35 N	13 6 E
45	Falkenstein	50 27 N	12 24 E
24	Falkirk	56 0 N	3 47W
148	Falkland, Sd.	52 0 S	60 0W
148	Falkland Is. □	51 30 S	59 0W
41	Falköping	58 12 N	13 33 E
128	Falls City	40 0 N	95 40W
139	Falmouth, Jamaica	18 30 N	77 40W
21	Falmouth, U.K.	50 9 N	5 5W
55	Falset	41 7 N	0 50 E
139	Falso, C.	17 45 N	71 40W
41	Falster, I.	54 48 N	11 58 E
41	Falsterbo	55 23 N	12 50 E
41	Falun	60 37 N	15 37 E
80	Famagusta	35 8 N	33 55 E
107	Fanning I.	3 51 N	159 22W
63	Fano	43 50 N	13 0 E
41	Fanø, I.	55 25 N	8 25 E
158	Faranah	10 2 N	10 45W
81	Farar	32 30 N	62 17 E
21	Fareham	50 52 N	1 11W
114	Farewell, C.	39 36 S	143 55 E
128	Fargo	47 0 N	97 0W
128	Faribault	44 15 N	93 19W
87	Faridpur	18 14 N	79 34 E
113	Farina	30 3 S	138 15 E
21	Farnborough	51 17 N	0 46W
21	Farne Is.	55 38 N	1 37W
145	Faro, Brazil	2 0 S	56 45W
53	Faro, Port.	37 2 N	7 55W
40	Faroe Is.	62 0 N	7 0W
110	Farquhar, C.	23 38 S	113 36 E
81	Farrashband	28 57 N	52 5 E
81	Fars □	29 30 N	55 0 E
38	Farsund	58 5 N	6 55 E
173	Farvel, R.	59 48 N	43 55W
81	Fāryāb □	36 0 N	65 0 E
65	Fasano	40 50 N	17 20 E
27	Fastnet Rock	51 22 N	9 27W
86	Fatehgarh	27 25 N	79 35 E
86	Fatehpur, Rajasthan	28 0 N	75 4 E
86	Fatehpur, Ut.P.	27 8 N	81 7 E
53	Fátima	39 37 N	8 39W
29	Faucilles, Mts.	48 5 N	5 50 E
29	Faulquemont	49 3 N	6 36 E
51	Faurei	45 6 N	27 19 E
37	Fauske	67 17 N	15 25 E
64	Favara	37 19 N	13 39 E
31	Favone	41 47 N	9 26 E
128	Fayetteville, Ark.	36 0 N	94 5W
127	Fayetteville, N.C.	35 0 N	78 58W
158	Fdérik	22 40 N	12 45 E
27	Feale, R.	52 26 N	9 28W
127	Fear, C.	33 45 N	78 0W
114	Featherston	41 6 S	175 20 E
28	Fécamp	49 45 N	0 22 E
45	Fehmarn, I.	54 26 N	11 10 E
114	Feilding	40 13 S	175 35 E
145	Feira de Santana	12 15 S	38 57W
49	Fejér □	47 9 N	18 30 E
55	Felanitx	39 27 N	3 7 E
48	Feldbach	46 57 N	15 52 E
137	Felipe Carillo Puerto	19 38 N	88 3W
21	Felixstowe	51 58 N	1 22W
21	Fens, Reg.	52 45 N	0 2 E
75	Feodosiya	45 2 N	35 28 E
76	Fergana	40 23 N	71 46 E
122	Fergus	43 43 N	80 24W
128	Fergus Falls	46 25 N	96 0W
60	Feričanci	45 32 N	18 0 E
48	Ferlach	46 32 N	14 18 E
122	Ferland	50 19 N	88 27W
27	Fermanagh □	54 21 N	7 40W
63	Fermo	43 10 N	13 42 E
53	Fermoselle	41 19 N	6 27W
27	Fermoy	52 4 N	8 18W
145	Fernando de Noronha, Is.	4 0 S	33 10W
86	Ferozepore	30 55 N	74 40 E
68	Férrai	40 53 N	26 10 E
63	Ferrara	44 50 N	11 36 E
64	Ferrato, C.	39 18 N	9 39 E
53	Ferreira do Alentejo	38 4 N	8 6W
30	Ferret, C.	44 38 N	1 15W
158	Fès	34 0 N	5 0W
51	Fetesti	44 22 N	27 51 E
24	Fetlar, I.	60 36 N	0 52W
31	Feurs	45 45 N	4 13 E
81	Feyzābad	37 7 N	70 33 E
159	Fezzan	27 0 N	15 0 E
168	Fianarantsoa	21 26 S	47 5 E
45	Fichtelgebirge, Mts.	50 10 N	12 0 E
169	Ficksburg	28 51 S	27 53 E
62	Fidenza	44 51 N	10 3 E
24	Fife □	56 13 N	3 2W
30	Figeac	44 37 N	2 2 E
55	Figueras	42 18 N	2 58 E
158	Figuig	32 5 N	1 11W
68	Fieri	40 43 N	19 33 E
114	Fiji ■	17 20 S	179 0 E
55	Filabres, Sa. de los	37 13 N	2 20W
174	Filchner Ice Shelf	78 0 S	60 0W
21	Filey	54 13 N	0 10W
131	Fillmore	34 23 N	118 58W
62	Finale Lígure	44 10 N	8 21 E
63	Finale nell 'Emilia	44 50 N	11 18 E
24	Findhorn	57 30 N	3 45W
127	Findlay	41 0 N	83 41W
28	Finistère □	48 20 N	4 20W
53	Finisterre, C.	42 50 N	9 19W
110	Finke	25 34 S	134 35 E
37	Finland ■	70 0 N	27 0 E
75	Finland, G. of	60 0 N	26 0 E
113	Finley	35 38 S	145 35 E
113	Finniss, C.	33 38 S	134 51 E
37	Finnmark □	69 30 N	25 0 E
41	Finspång	58 45 N	15 43 E
45	Finsteraarhorn, Mt.	46 31 N	8 10 E
45	Finsterwalde	51 37 N	13 42 E
62	Fiorenzuola	44 56 N	9 54 E
63	Firenze	43 47 N	11 15 E
31	Firminy	45 23 N	4 18 E
86	Firozabad	27 10 N	78 25 E
51	Fîrtanesti	45 48 N	27 59 E
81	Frūzābād	28 52 N	52 35 E
81	Fīrūzkūh	35 50 N	52 40 E
21	Fishguard	51 59 N	4 59W
127	Fitchburg	42 35 N	71 47W
55	Fitero	42 4 N	1 52W
148	Fitz Roy	47 10 S	67 0W
110	Fitzroy Crossing	18 9 S	125 38 E
62	Fivizzana	44 14 N	10 8 E
38	Fla	60 25 N	9 26 E
131	Flagstaff	35 10 N	111 40W
37	Flåm	60 52 N	7 14 E
21	Flamborough Hd.	54 8 N	0 4W
131	Flaming Gorge L.	41 15 N	109 30W
34	Flandre Occidentale □	51 0 N	3 0 E
34	Flandre Orientale □	51 0 N	4 0 E
34	Flandres, Plaines des	51 10 N	3 15 E
24	Flannan Is.	58 9 N	7 52W
113	Flattery, C., Australia	14 58 S	145 21 E
131	Flattery, C., U.S.A.	48 21 N	124 31W
21	Fleetwood	53 55 N	3 1W
38	Flekkefjord	58 18 N	6 39 E
45	Flensburg	54 46 N	9 28 E
28	Flers	48 47 N	0 33W
125	Flin Flon	54 46 N	101 53W
110	Flinders, B.	34 19 S	114 9 E
113	Flinders, I.	40 0 S	148 0 E
113	Flinders, Ras.	31 30 S	138 30 E
21	Flint, U.K.	53 15 N	3 7W
127	Flint, U.S.A.	43 0 N	83 40W
107	Flint I.	11 26 S	151 48W
55	Flix	41 14 N	0 32 E
29	Flixecourt	50 0 N	2 5 E
21	Flodden	55 37 N	2 8W
38	Flora	38 40 N	88 30W
63	Florence, Italy = Firenze	43 47 N	11 15 E
127	Florence, Ala.	34 50 N	87 50W
131	Florence, Ariz.	33 0 N	111 25W
131	Florence, Oreg.	44 0 N	124 3W
127	Florence, S.C.	34 5 N	79 50W
144	Florencia	1 36 N	75 36W
137	Flores	16 50 N	89 40W
95	Flores, I.	8 35 S	121 0¼
95	Flores Sea	6 30 S	124 0 E
148	Florida	34 7 S	56 10W
127	Florida □	28 30 N	82 0W
118	Florida Str.	25 0 N	80 0W
49	Floridsdorf	48 15 N	16 25 E
68	Flórina	40 48 N	21 26 E
55	Flumen, R.	41 50 N	0 25W
64	Flumendosa, R.	39 30 N	9 25 E
34	Flushing = Vlissingen	51 26 N	3 34 E
174	Flying Fish, C.	72 30 S	103 0W
51	Focşani	45 41 N	27 15 E
65	Fóggia	41 28 N	15 31 E
152	Fogo	49 43 N	54 17W
48	Fohnsdorf	47 12 N	14 40 E
45	Föhr, I.	54 40 N	8 30 E
30	Foix	42 58 N	1 38 E
68	Fokís □	38 30 N	22 15 E
68	Folégandros, I.	36 37 N	24 55 E
122	Foleyet	48 15 N	82 25W
21	Folkestone	51 5 N	1 11 E
62	Follónica, G. di	42 54 N	10 53 E
125	Fond du Lac, Canada	59 20 N	107 10W
128	Fond-du-Lac, U.S.A.	43 46 N	88 26W
64	Fondi	41 21 N	13 25 E
29	Fontainebleau	48 24 N	2 40 E
144	Fonte Boa	2 25 S	66 0W
30	Fontenay-le-Comte	46 28 N	0 48W
99	Foochow = Fuzhou	26 5 N	119 18 E
29	Forbach	49 10 N	6 52 E
113	Forbes	33 22 S	148 0 E
173	Forel, Mt.	66 52 N	36 55W
124	Forest Lawn	51 4 N	114 0W
124	Forestburg	52 35 N	112 1W
123	Forestville	48 48 N	69 20W
30	Forez, Mts. du	45 40 N	3 50 E
24	Forfar	56 40 N	2 53W
29	Forges-les-Eaux	49 37 N	1 30 E
63	Forlí	44 14 N	12 2 E
21	Formby Pt.	53 33 N	3 7W
55	Formentera, I.	38 40 N	1 30 E
55	Formentor, C.	39 58 N	3 13 E
64	Fórmia	41 15 N	13 34 E
148	Formosa, Arg.	26 15 S	58 10W
145	Formosa, Brazil	15 32 S	47 20W
99	Formosa = Taiwan ■	24 0 N	121 0 E
145	Formosa, Sa.	12 0 S	55 0W
99	Formosa Str.	24 40 N	124 0 E
53	Fornos de Algodres	40 48 N	7 32W
24	Forres	57 37 N	3 38W
128	Forrest City	35 1 N	90 47W
113	Forsayth	18 33 S	143 34 E
131	Forsyth	46 14 N	106 37W
122	Fort Albany	52 15 N	81 35W
159	Fort-Archambault	9 5 N	18 23 E
124	Fort Assinboine	54 20 N	114 45W
24	Fort Augustus	57 9 N	4 40W
131	Fort Bridger	41 22 N	110 20W
121	Fort Chimo	58 9 N	68 12W
125	Fort Chipewyan	58 46 N	111 9W
128	Fort Collins	40 30 N	105 4W
122	Fort Coulonge	45 50 N	76 45W
128	Fort Dodge	42 29 N	94 10W
125	Fort Frances	48 35 N	93 25W
120	Fort Franklin	65 30 N	123 45W
122	Fort George	53 40 N	79 0W
124	Fort Graham	56 38 N	124 35W
131	Fort Hancock	31 19 N	105 56W
122	Fort Hope	51 30 N	88 10W
123	Fort Kent	47 12 N	68 30W
159	Fort-Lamy = Ndjamena	12 4 N	15 8 E
128	Fort Laramie	42 15W	104 30W
127	Fort Lauderdale	26 10 N	80 5W
124	Fort Liard	60 20 N	123 30W
124	Fort Mackay	57 12 N	111 41W
123	Fort McKenzie	56 50 N	69 0W
124	Fort Macleod	49 45 N	113 30W
158	Fort MacMahon	29 51 N	1 45 E
120	Fort McPherson	67 30 N	134 55W
128	Fort Morgan	40 10 N	103 50W
127	Fort Myers	26 30 N	82 0W
124	Fort Nelson	58 50 N	122 30W
120	Fort Norman	64 57 N	125 30W
127	Fort Payne	34 25 N	85 44W
131	Fort Peck	47 1 N	105 30W
131	Fort Peck Res.	47 40 N	107 0W
127	Fort Pierce	27 29 N	80 19W
165	Fort Portal	0 40 N	30 20 E
124	Fort Providence	61 20 N	117 30W
125	Fort Qu'Appelle	50 45 N	103 50W
124	Fort Resolution	61 10 N	114 40W
122	Fort Rupert	51 30 N	78 40W
124	Fort St. James	54 30 N	124 10W
124	Fort St. John	56 15 N	120 50W
86	Fort Sandeman	31 20 N	69 25 E
124	Fort Saskatchewan	53 40 N	113 15W
122	Fort Severn	56 0 N	87 40W
124	Fort Simpson	61 45 N	121 30W
128	Fort Smith	35 25 N	94 25W
128	Fort Stockton	30 48 N	103 2W
128	Fort Sumner	34 24 N	104 8W
127	Fort Valley	32 33 N	83 52W
124	Fort Vermilion	58 30 N	115 57W
169	Fort Victoria	20 8 S	30 55 E
122	Fort William, Canada = Thunder Bay	48 20 N	89 10W
24	Fort William, U.K.	56 48 N	5 8W
128	Fort Worth	32 45 N	97 25W
120	Fort Yukon	66 35 N	145 12W
145	Fortaleza	3 35 S	38 35W
139	Fort-de-France	14 36 N	61 5W
110	Fortescue, R.	21 20 S	116 5 E
24	Forth, Firth of	56 5 N	2 55W
24	Fortrose	57 35 N	4 10W
131	Fortuna	48 38 N	124 8W
31	Fos	43 20 N	4 57 E
99	Foshan	23 4 N	113 5 E
62	Fossano	44 39 N	7 40 E
174	Fossil Bluff	71 15 S	69 0W
28	Fougères	48 21 N	1 14W
24	Foula, I.	60 10 N	2 5W
21	Foulness, I.	51 26 N	0 55 E
30	Fourchambault	47 0 N	3 3 E
29	Fourmies	50 1 N	4 2 E
68	Foúrnoi, I.	37 36 N	26 32 E
158	Fouta Djalon, Mts.	11 20 N	12 10W
114	Foveaux, Str.	46 42 S	168 10 E
21	Fowey	50 20 N	4 39W
110	Fowlers, B.	31 59 S	132 34 E
125	Fox Valley	50 30 N	109 25W
121	Foxe Chan.	66 0 N	80 0W
121	Foxe Pen.	65 0 N	76 0W
27	Foyle, L.	55 6 N	7 18W
27	Foynes	52 37 N	9 6W
53	Foz	43 33 N	7 20W
148	Foz do Iguaçu	25 30 S	54 30W
55	Fraga	41 32 N	0 21 E
28	France ■	47 0 N	1 0 E
165	Franceville	1 38 S	13 35 E
29	Franche Comté, Reg.	46 30 N	5 50 E
123	Francis Harbour	52 34 N	55 44W
169	Francistown	21 11 S	27 32 E
45	Frankenberg	51 3 N	8 47 E
45	Frankenwald, Mts.	50 18 N	11 36 E
127	Frankfort, Ind.	40 20 N	86 33W
127	Frankfort, Ky.	38 12 N	85 44W
45	Frankfurt am Main	50 7 N	8 40 E
45	Frankfurt an der Oder	52 50 N	14 31 E
45	Fränkishe Alb.	49 20 N	11 30 E
128	Franklin, Nebr.	40 9 N	98 55W
127	Franklin, N.H.	43 28 N	71 39W
127	Franklin, N.J.	41 9 N	74 38W
127	Franklin, Pa.	41 22 N	79 45W
127	Franklin, Tenn.	35 54 N	86 53W
127	Franklin, W. Va.	38 38 N	79 21W
131	Franklin D. Roosevelt L.	48 30 N	118 16W
120	Franklin Mts.	66 0 N	125 0W
120	Franklin Str.	72 0 N	96 0W
113	Frankston	38 8 S	145 8 E
76	Frantsa Iosifa, Zemlya, Is.	76 0 N	62 0 E
113	Fraser, I.	25 15 S	153 10 E
124	Fraser, R.	49 9 N	123 12W
124	Fraser Lake	54 0 N	124 50W
24	Fraserburgh	47 41 N	2 0W
91	Fraser's Hill	3 43 N	101 43 E
61	Frăteşti	43 59 N	25 59 E
45	Frauenfeld	47 34 N	8 54 E
148	Fray Bentos	33 10 S	58 15W
41	Fredericia	55 34 N	9 45 E
127	Frederick, Md.	39 25 N	77 23W
128	Frederick, Okla.	34 22 N	99 0W
127	Fredericksburg	38 16 N	77 29W
123	Fredericton	45 57 N	66 40W
41	Frederiksborg □	55 50 N	12 10 E
173	Frederikshåb	62 0 N	49 30W
41	Frederikshavn	57 28 N	10 31 E
41	Frederikssund	55 50 N	12 3 E
38	Fredrikstad	59 13 N	10 57 E
139	Freeport, Bahamas	26 30 N	78 35W
128	Freeport, Ill.	42 18 N	89 40W
127	Freeport, N.Y.	40 39 N	73 35W
128	Freeport, Tex.	28 55 N	95 22W
158	Freetown	8 30 N	13 10W
45	Freiburg	48 0 N	7 50 E
148	Freire	39 0 S	72 50W
45	Freising	48 24 N	11 27 E
48	Freistadt	48 30 N	14 30 E
45	Freital	51 0 N	13 40 E
31	Fréjus	43 25 N	6 44 E
128	Fremont, Nebr.	41 30 N	96 30W
127	Fremont, Ohio	41 20 N	83 5W
145	French Guiana ■	4 0 N	53 0W
145	Fresco, R.	6 39 S	51 59W
137	Fresnillo	23 10 N	103 0W
131	Fresno	36 47 N	119 50W
110	Frewena	19 50 S	135 50 E
165	Fria, C.	18 0 S	12 0 E
148	Frías	28 40 S	65 5W
45	Fribourg	46 49 N	7 9 E
45	Friedrichshafen	47 39 N	9 29 E
48	Friesach	46 57 N	14 24 E
34	Friesland □	53 5 N	5 50 E
45	Fritzlar	51 8 N	9 19 E
63	Friuli Venezia Giulia □	46 0 N	13 0 E
121	Frobisher B.	63 0 N	67 0W
21	Frome	51 16 N	2 17W
127	Front Royal	38 55 N	78 10W
53	Fronteira	39 3 N	7 39W
137	Frontera	18 30 N	92 40W
30	Frontignan	43 27 N	3 45 E
41	Frôvi	59 28 N	15 24 E
51	Frumoasa	46 28 N	25 48 E
76	Frunze	42 54 N	74 36 E
68	Fthiótis □	38 50 N	22 25 E
102	Fuchu	34 34 N	133 14 E
53	Fuengirola	36 32 N	4 41W
53	Fuente Ovejuna	38 15 N	5 25W
53	Fuentes de Andalucia	37 28 N	5 20W
55	Fuentes de Ebro	31 31 N	0 38W
53	Fuentes de León	38 5 N	6 32W
158	Fuerteventura, I.	28 30 N	14 0W
81	Fuhūd	22 18 N	56 28 E
102	Fuji	35 9 N	138 39 E
99	Fujian □	26 0 N	118 0 E
102	Fuji-san, Mt.	35 22 N	138 44 E
102	Fuji-no-miya	35 20 N	138 40 E
102	Fujisawa	35 22 N	139 29 E
102	Fukuchiyama	35 25 N	135 9 E
102	Fukui	36 0 N	136 10 E
102	Fukui □	36 0 N	136 12 E
102	Fukuoka	33 30 N	130 30 E
102	Fukuoka □	33 30 N	131 0 E
102	Fukushima	37 30 N	140 15 E
102	Fukushima □	37 30 N	140 15 E
102	Fukuyama	34 35 N	133 20 E
45	Fulda	50 32 N	9 41 E
128	Fulton, Mo.	38 50 N	91 55W
127	Fulton, N.Y.	43 20 N	76 22W
29	Fumay	50 0 N	4 40 E
30	Fumel	44 30 N	0 58 E
102	Funabashi	35 45 N	140 0 E
106	Funafuti, I.	8 30 S	179 0 E
158	Funchal	32 45 N	16 55W
123	Fundy, B. of	45 0 N	66 0W
158	Funtua	11 31 N	7 17 E
80	Furat, Nahr al, R.	33 30 N	43 0 E
21	Furness	54 14 N	3 8W
45	Furstenwalde	52 20 N	14 3 E
45	Fürth	49 29 N	11 0 E
121	Fury & Hecla Str.	69 40 N	81 0W
144	Fusagasugá	4 21 N	74 22W
99	Fushun	42 0 N	123 59 E
45	Füssen	47 12 N	121 33 E
106	Futuna, I.	14 25 S	178 20 E
99	Fuzhou	26 5 N	119 16 E
21	Fylde, R.	53 47 N	2 56W
41	Fyn, I.	55 20 N	10 30 E
24	Fyne, L.	56 0 N	5 20W
41	Fyns □	55 15 N	10 30 E

G

158	Gabès	33 53 N	10 2 E
165	Gabon ■	0 10 S	10 0 E
168	Gaborone	24 37 S	25 57 E
61	Gabrovo	42 52 N	25 27 E
81	Gach-Sārān	30 15 N	50 45 E
60	Gacko	43 10 N	18 33 E
86	Gadag	15 30 N	75 45 E
55	Gádor, Sa. de	36 57 N	2 45W
127	Gadsden, Ala.	34 1 N	86 0W
131	Gadsden, Ariz.	32 35 N	114 47W
86	Gadwal	16 10 N	77 50 E
51	Găesti	44 48 N	25 14 E
64	Gaeta	41 12 N	13 35 E
64	Gaeta, G. di	41 0 N	13 25 E
158	Gafsa	34 24 N	8 51 E
123	Gagetown	45 46 N	66 29W
158	Gagnoa	6 4 N	5 55W
30	Gah	43 12 N	0 27W
48	Gail, R.	46 36 N	13 53 E
30	Gaillac	43 54 N	1 54 E
28	Gaillon	49 10 N	1 20 E
21	Gainsborough	53 23 N	0 46W
113	Gairdner, L.	32 0 S	136 0 E
24	Gairloch, L.	57 43 N	5 45W
147	Galápagos, Is.	0 0 N	89 0W
24	Galashiels	55 37 N	2 50W
51	Galaţi	45 27 N	28 2 E
65	Galátone	40 8 N	18 3 E
68	Galaxídhion	38 22 N	22 23 E
55	Galera	37 45 N	2 33W
75	Galich	58 23 N	42 18 E
53	Galicia, Reg.	42 43 N	8 0W
62	Gallarte	45 40 N	8 48 E
127	Gallatin	36 24 N	86 27W
86	Galle	6 5 N	80 10 E
55	Gállego, R.	41 39 N	0 51W
144	Gallinas, Pta.	12 28 N	71 40W
65	Gallipoli	40 8 N	18 0 E
127	Gallipolis	38 50 N	82 10W
37	Gällivare	67 7 N	20 32 E
24	Galloway, Reg.	55 0 N	4 25W
24	Galloway, Mull of	54 38 N	4 50W
131	Gallup	35 30 N	108 54W
48	Galtür	46 58 N	10 11 E
128	Galveston	29 15 N	94 48W
128	Galveston B.	29 30 N	94 50W
27	Galway	53 16 N	9 4W
27	Galway, B.	53 10 N	9 20W
27	Galway □	53 16 N	9 3W
102	Gamagori	34 50 N	137 14 E
158	Gambia ■	13 20 N	15 45W
158	Gambia, R.	13 28 N	16 34W
137	Gamboa	9 8 N	79 42W
131	Gamerco	35 33 N	108 56W
122	Gananoque	44 20 N	76 10W
87	Gandak, R.	25 32 N	85 5 E
123	Gander	49 1 N	54 33W
55	Gandesa	41 3 N	0 26 E
55	Gandía	38 58 N	0 9W
87	Ganga, Mouths of the	21 30 N	90 0 E
87	Ganga, R.	23 22 N	90 32 E
87	Gangaw	22 5 N	94 15 E
87	Ganges, R. = Ganga, R.	23 22 N	90 32 E
30	Gannat	46 7 N	3 11 E
49	Ganserdorf	48 20 N	16 43 E
99	Gansu	36 0 N	104 0 E
158	Gaò	18 0 N	1 0 E
158	Gaoual	11 45 N	13 25W
99	Gaoxing	22 38 N	102 18 E
31	Gap	44 33 N	6 5 E
131	Garberville	40 11 N	123 50W
31	Gard □	44 2 N	4 10 E
62	Garda, L. di	45 40 N	10 40 E
45	Gardelegen	52 32 N	11 21 E
128	Garden City	38 0 N	100 45W
81	Gardēz	33 31 N	68 59 E
131	Gardiner	45 3 N	110 53W
85	Gardo	9 18 N	49 20 E
131	Garfield	47 3 N	117 8W
68	Gargaliánoi	37 4 N	21 38 E
65	Gargano, Testa del, Pt.	41 49 N	16 12 E
64	Garigliano, R.	41 13 N	13 45 E
76	Garm	39 0 N	70 20 E
45	Garmisch-Partenkirchen	47 30 N	11 5 E
81	Garmsār	35 20 N	52 25 E
30	Garonne, R.	45 2 N	0 36W
30	Garrigues, Reg.	43 40 N	3 30 E
131	Garrison	46 37 N	112 56W
128	Garrison Res.	47 30 N	102 0W
120	Garry, L.	65 40 N	100 0W
30	Gartempe, R.	46 48 N	0 50 E
45	Gartz	54 17 N	13 21 E
95	Garut	7 14 S	107 53 E
53	Garvão	37 42 N	8 21W
127	Gary	41 35 N	87 20W
144	Garzón	2 10 N	75 40W
30	Gascogne, Reg.	43 45 N	0 20 E
158	Gashaka	7 20 N	11 29 E
123	Gaspé	48 52 N	64 30W
123	Gaspesian Prov. Park	49 0 N	66 45W
127	Gastonia	35 17 N	81 10W
68	Gastoúri	39 34 N	19 54 E
55	Gata, C. de	36 41 N	2 13W
53	Gata, Sa. de	40 20 N	6 20W
60	Gătaia	45 26 N	21 30 E
24	Gatehouse of Fleet	54 53 N	4 10W
21	Gateshead	54 57 N	1 37W
29	Gatinais, Reg.	48 5 N	2 40 E
30	Gâtine, Hauteurs de	46 40 N	0 50W
122	Gatineau Nat. Park	45 30 N	75 52W
169	Gatooma	18 21 S	29 55 E
53	Gaucín	36 31 N	5 19W
87	Gauhati	26 5 N	91 55 E
174	Gaussberg, Mt.	66 45 S	89 0 E
55	Gavá	41 18 N	2 0 E
81	Gavater	25 10 N	61 23 E
68	Gávdhos, I.	34 50 N	24 6 E
41	Gavle	60 41 N	17 13 E
41	Gävleborgs □	61 20 N	16 15 E
62	Gavorrano	42 55 N	10 55 E
28	Gavray	49 55 N	1 20W
113	Gawler	34 30 S	138 42 E
87	Gaya	24 47 N	85 4 E
113	Gayndah	25 35 S	151 39 E
80	Gaza	31 30 N	34 28 E
80	Gaziantep	37 6 N	37 23 E
50	Gdańsk	54 22 N	18 40 E
50	Gdansk □	54 10 N	18 30 E
50	Gdynia	54 35 N	18 33 E
159	Gebeit Mine	21 3 N	36 29 E
30	Gèdre	42 47 N	0 2 E
41	Gedser	54 35 N	11 55 E
113	Geelong	38 2 S	144 20 E
34	Geeraadsbergen	50 45 N	3 53 E
45	Geesthacht	53 25 N	10 20 E
159	Geili	16 1 N	32 37 E
38	Geilo	60 32 N	8 14 E
165	Geita	2 48 S	32 12 E
96	Gejiu	23 20 N	103 10 E
65	Gela	37 3 N	14 15 E
65	Gela, G. di	37 0 N	14 8 E
34	Gelderland □	52 5 N	6 10 E
80	Gelibolu	40 28 N	26 43 E
45	Gelnhausen	50 12 N	9 12 E
45	Gelsenkirchen	51 30 N	7 5 E
45	Gelting	54 43 N	9 53 E
91	Gemas	2 37 N	102 36 E
165	Gemena	3 20 N	19 40 E
63	Gemona del Fruiuli	46 16 N	13 7 E
45	Gemünden	50 3 N	9 43 E
30	Gençay	46 23 N	0 23 E
148	General Alvear	36 0 S	60 0W
148	General Juan Madariaga	37 0 S	57 0W
148	General Pico	35 45 S	63 50W
148	General Pinedo	27 15 S	61 30W
61	General Toshevo	43 42 N	28 6 E
148	General Villegas	35 0 S	63 0W
45	Geneva = Genève, Switz.	46 12 N	6 9 E
127	Geneva, U.S.A.	42 53 N	77 0W
45	Geneva, L. = Léman, L.	46 26 N	6 30 E
45	Genève	46 12 N	6 9 E
53	Genil, R.	37 42 N	5 19W
34	Genk	50 58 N	5 32 E
62	Genova	44 24 N	8 56 E
62	Génova, G. di	44 0 N	9 0 E
34	Gent	51 2 N	3 37 E
45	Genthin	52 24 N	12 10 E
168	George	33 58 S	22 29 E
113	George, L.	43 30 N	73 30W
121	George R. = Port Nouveau-Quebec	58 30 N	65 50W
113	George Town, Australia	41 5 S	148 55 E
91	George Town, Malaysia	5 25 N	100 19 E
113	Georgetown, Australia	18 17 S	143 33 E
122	Georgetown, Ont.	43 40 N	80 0W
158	Georgetown, Gambia	13 30 N	14 47W
144	Georgetown, Guyana	6 50 N	58 12W
127	Georgetown, U.S.A.	33 22 N	79 15W
127	Georgia □	32 0 N	82 0W
124	Georgia Str.	49 20 N	124 0W
122	Georgian B.	45 15 N	81 0W
75	Georgian S.S.R. □	41 0 N	45 0 E
75	Georgiu-Dezh	51 3 N	39 20 E
75	Georgiyevsk	44 12 N	43 28 E
45	Gera	50 53 N	12 5 E
45	Gera □	50 45 N	11 30 E
110	Geraldton, Australia	28 48 S	114 32 E
122	Geraldton, Canada	49 44 N	86 59W
29	Gérardmer	48 3 N	6 50 E
80	Gerede	40 45 N	32 10 E
55	Gérgal	37 7 N	2 31W
45	Gerlafingen	47 10 N	7 34 E
169	Germiston	26 15 S	28 5 E
102	Gero	35 48 N	137 14 E
49	Gerlachovka, Mt.	49 11 N	20 7 E
55	Gerona	41 58 N	2 46 E
55	Gerona □	42 11 N	2 30 E
30	Gers □	43 35 N	0 38 E
45	Geseke	51 38 N	8 29 E
53	Getafe	40 18 N	3 44W
30	Gevaudan, Reg.	44 40 N	3 40 E
60	Gevgelija	41 9 N	22 30 E
131	Geyser	47 17 N	110 30W
37	Geysir	64 19 N	20 18W
87	Ghaghara, R.	25 45 N	84 40 E
158	Ghana ■	6 0 N	1 0W
158	Ghardaïa	32 31 N	3 37 E
80	Ghat	24 59 N	10 19 E
159	Ghazal, Bahr el, R.	9 31 N	30 25 E
86	Ghaziabad	28 42 N	77 35 E
87	Ghazipur	25 38 N	83 35 E

Ghaznī Heinsburg

81 Ghaznī 33 30 N 68 17 E
62 Ghedi 45 24 N 10 16 E
31 Ghisonaccia 42 1 N 9 26 E
81 Ghowr □ 34 0 N 64 20 E
158 Ghudāmis 30 11 N 9 29 E
81 Ghūrīān 34 17 N 61 25 E
27 Giant's Causeway 55 15 N 6 30W
62 Giaveno 45 3 N 7 20 E
139 Gibara 21 0 N 76 20W
64 Gibellina 37 48 N 13 0 E
53 Gibraléon 37 23 N 6 58W
53 Gibraltar 35 55 N 5 40W
29 Gien 47 40 N 2 36 E
45 Giessen 50 34 N 8 40 E
45 Gifhorn 52 29 N 10 32 E
102 Gifu 35 30 N 136 45 E
102 Gifu □ 36 0 N 137 0 E
137 Giganta, Sa. de la 25 30 N 111 30W
24 Gigha, I. 55 42 N 5 45W
62 Giglio, I. 42 20 N 10 52 E
30 Gignac 43 39 N 3 32 E
53 Gijón 43 32 N 5 42W
131 Gila, R. 32 43 N 114 33W
131 Gila Bend 32 57 N 112 43W
80 Gīlān □ 37 0 N 49 0 E
106 Gilbert Is. = Kiribati ■ 1 0 N 176 0 E
125 Gilbert Plains 51 9 N 100 28W
113 Gilbert River 18 9 S 142 50 E
113 Gilgandra 31 42 S 148 39 E
86 Gilgit 35 50 N 74 15 E
125 Gillam 56 20 N 94 40W
21 Gillingham 51 23 N 0 34 E
122 Gilmour 44 48 N 77 37W
131 Gilroy 37 10 N 121 37W
113 Gindie 23 45 S 148 10 E
68 Gióna, Mt. 38 38 N 22 14 E
95 Giong, Teluk, B. 4 50 N 118 20 E
31 Giovi, P. del 44 30 N 8 55 E
65 Giovinazzo 41 10 N 16 40 E
49 Giraltovce 49 7 N 21 32 E
144 Girardot 4 18 N 74 48W
24 Girdle Ness 57 9 N 2 2W
80 Giresun 40 45 N 38 30 E
159 Girga 26 17 N 31 55 E
87 Giridih 24 10 N 86 21 E
30 Gironde, R. 45 30 N 1 0W
30 Gironde □ 44 45 N 0 30W
55 Gironella 42 2 N 1 53 E
24 Girvan 55 15 N 4 50W
29 Gisors 49 15 N 1 40 E
63 Giulianova 42 45 N 13 58 E
51 Giurgiu 43 52 N 25 57 E
29 Givet 50 8 N 4 49 E
31 Givors 45 35 N 4 45 E
77 Gizhiginskaya, Guba 61 0 N 158 0 E
50 Giżycko 54 2 N 21 48 E
68 Gjirokastra 40 7 N 20 16 E
120 Gjoa Haven 68 20 N 96 0W
123 Glace Bay 46 11 N 59 58W
131 Glacier Nat. Park 48 40 N 114 0W
113 Gladstone, Queens. 23 52 S 151 16 E
113 Gladstone, S. Australia 33 17 S 138 22 E
125 Gladstone, Canada 50 20 N 99 0W
38 Glåma, R. 59 12 N 10 57 E
45 Glarus 47 3 N 9 4 E
24 Glasgow, U.K. 55 52 N 4 14W
127 Glasgow, U.S.A. 37 2 N 85 55W
21 Glastonbury 51 9 N 2 42W
45 Glauchau 50 50 N 12 33 E
48 Gleisdorf 47 6 N 15 44 E
24 Glen Affric 57 15 N 5 0W
24 Glen Coe 56 40 N 5 0W
24 Glen Garry 57 3 N 5 7W
24 Glen More 57 12 N 4 30 E
28 Glénan, Îs. de 47 42 N 4 0W
114 Glenbrook 33 46 S 150 37 E
128 Glendive 47 7 N 104 40W
113 Glenelg 34 58 S 138 30 E
113 Glenelg, R. 38 3 S 141 9 E
27 Glengariff 51 45 N 9 33W
113 Glenn Innes 29 44 S 151 44 E
113 Glennies Creek 32 30 S 151 8 E
113 Glenore 17 50 S 141 12 E
113 Glenormiston 22 55 S 138 50 E
131 Glenrock 42 53 N 105 55W
24 Glenrothes 56 12 N 3 11W
127 Glens Falls 43 20 N 73 40W
27 Glenties 54 48 N 8 18W
124 Glenwood, Canada 49 21 N 113 24W
128 Glenwood, U.S.A. 45 38 N 95 21W
131 Glenwood Springs 39 39 N 107 15W
49 Gliwice 50 22 N 18 41 E
48 Glödnitz 46 53 N 14 7 E
48 Gloggnitz 47 41 N 15 56 E
50 Głogów 51 37 N 16 5 E
21 Glossop 53 27 N 1 56W
113 Gloucester, Australia 32 0 S 151 59 E
21 Gloucester, U.K. 51 52 N 2 15W
21 Gloucestershire □ 51 44 N 2 10W
49 Glubczyce 50 13 N 17 52 E
45 Glücksburg 54 48 N 9 34 E
45 Glückstadt 53 46 N 9 28 E
48 Gmünd, Kärnten 46 54 N 13 31 E
48 Gmünd, Niederösterreich 48 45 N 15 0 E
48 Gmunden 47 55 N 13 48 E
50 Gniezno 52 30 N 17 35 E
91 Gô Công 10 12 N 107 0 E
86 Goa 15 33 N 73 59 E
87 Goalpara 26 10 N 90 40 E
24 Goat Fell, Mt. 55 37 N 5 11W
168 Goba 7 1 N 39 59 E
45 Goch 51 40 N 6 9 E
87 Godavari, R. 16 37 N 82 18 E
123 Godbout 49 20 N 67 38W
122 Goderich 43 45 N 81 41W
139 Golfito 8 41 N 83 5W
173 Godhavn 69 15 N 53 38W
49 Gödöllö 47 38 N 19 25 E
125 Gods L. 54 40 N 94 10W
173 Godthåb 64 10 N 51 46W
168 Goei Hoop, K.die = Good Hope, C. of 34 24 S 18 30 E
34 Goeree 51 50 N 4 0 E
34 Goes 51 30 N 3 55 E
122 Gogama 47 35 N 81 35W
113 Gogango 23 40 S 150 2 E
50 Gogolin 50 30 N 18 0 E
159 Gogriâl 8 30 N 28 0 E
145 Goias □ 12 10 S 48 0W
48 Goisern 47 38 N 13 38 E
102 Gojo 34 21 N 135 42 E
87 Gokteik 22 26 N 97 0 E
41 Göl 57 4 N 9 42 E
156 Gold Coast 4 0 N 1 40W
50 Gołdap 54 19 N 22 19 E
124 Golden, Canada 51 20 N 117 0W
128 Golden, U.S.A. 39 42 N 105 30W
125 Goldfields 37 45 N 117 13W
127 Goldsboro 35 24 N 77 59W
53 Golega 39 24 N 8 29W
50 Goleniów 53 35 N 14 50 E
139 Golfito 8 41 N 83 5W
31 Golo, R. 42 31 N 9 32 E
24 Golspie 57 58 N 3 58W
165 Goma 1 37 S 29 10 E
75 Gomel 52 28 N 31 0 E
158 Gomera, I. 28 10 N 17 5W
137 Gómez Palacio 25 40 N 104 40W
81 Gonābād 34 15 N 58 45 E
139 Gonaïves 19 20 N 72 50W
87 Gonda 27 9 N 81 58 E
53 Gondomar, Port 41 10 N 8 35W
53 Gondomar, Sp. 42 7 N 8 45W
29 Gondrecourt 48 26 N 5 30 E
128 Gonzales 29 30 N 97 30W
168 Good Hope, C. of 34 24 S 18 30 E
21 Goole 53 42 N 0 52W
113 Goondiwindi 28 30 S 150 21 E
34 Goor 52 13 N 6 33 E
123 Goose Bay 53 15 N 60 20W
45 Göppingen 48 42 N 9 40 E
55 Gor 37 23 N 2 58W
87 Gorakhpur 26 47 N 83 32 E
60 Goražde 43 40 N 18 56 E
53 Gorbea, Peña 43 1 N 2 50W
139 Gorda, Pta. 14 10 N 83 10W
128 Gordon 42 49 N 102 6W
113 Gordonvale 17 5 S 145 50 E
27 Gorey 52 41 N 6 18W
144 Gorgona, I. 3 0 N 78 10W
75 Goris 39 31 N 46 23 E
63 Gorízia 45 56 N 13 37 E
50 Gorka 51 39 N 16 58 E
75 Gorki = Gorkiy 56 20 N 44 0 E
75 Gorkiy 56 20 N 44 0 E
75 Gorkovskoye Vdkhr 57 2 N 43 4 E
49 Gorłice 49 35 N 21 11 E
45 Görlitz 51 10 N 14 59 E
75 Gorlovka 48 25 N 37 58 E
61 Gorna Oryakhovitsa 43 7 N 25 40 E
75 Gornyatski 67 49 N 64 20 E
95 Gorontalo 0 35 N 123 13 E
27 Gort 53 4 N 8 50W
75 Goryn, R. 52 8 N 27 17 E
50 Gorzów Wielkopolski 52 43 N 15 15 E
50 Gorzów Wielkopolski □ 52 40 N 15 20 E
127 Goshen 41 36 N 85 46W
45 Goslar 51 55 N 10 23 E
21 Gosport 50 48 N 1 8W
60 Gostiva 41 48 N 20 57 E
50 Gostyń 51 50 N 17 3 E
41 Göteborg 57 43 N 11 59 E
41 Göteborgs och Bohus □ 58 30 N 11 30 E
41 Götene 58 33 N 13 30 E
45 Gotha 50 56 N 10 42 E
37 Gotland, I. 57 30 N 18 30 E
61 Gotse Delchev 41 43 N 23 46 E
102 Gōtsu 35 0 N 132 14 E
45 Göttingen 51 31 N 9 55 E
49 Gottwaldov 49 14 N 17 40 E
34 Gouda 52 1 N 4 42 E
153 Gough, I. 40 10 S 9 45W
122 Govin Res. 48 35 N 74 40W
113 Goulburn 32 22 S 149 31 E
159 Gounou-Gaya 9 38 N 15 31 E
30 Gourdon 44 44 N 1 23 E
29 Gournay 49 29 N 1 44 E
30 Gouzon 46 12 N 2 14 E
21 Gower, Pen. 51 35 N 5 10W
58 Gozo, I. 36 1 N 14 15 E
168 Graaff-Reinet 32 13 S 24 32 E
45 Grabow 53 17 N 11 31 E
63 Gračac 44 18 N 15 57 E
63 Grado, Italy 45 40 N 13 20 E
53 Grado, Sp. 43 23 N 6 4W
113 Grafton, Australia 29 35 S 152 0 E
128 Grafton, U.S.A. 48 30 N 97 25W
122 Graham, Canada 49 20 N 90 30W
127 Graham, N.C. 36 5 N 79 22W
128 Graham, Tex. 33 7 N 98 38W
124 Graham I. 53 40 N 132 30W
174 Graham Ld. 65 0 S 64 0W
125 Grahamdale 51 30 N 98 34W
168 Grahamstown 33 19 S 26 31 E
31 Graie, Alpi, Mts. 45 30 N 7 10 E
145 Grajaú 5 50 S 46 30W
30 Gramat 44 48 N 1 43 E
24 Grampian □ 57 20 N 2 45W
24 Grampian Highlands, Mts. 56 50 N 4 0W
68 Gramshi 40 52 N 20 12 E
158 Gran Canaria, I. 27 55 N 15 35W
148 Gran Chaco, Reg. 25 0 S 61 0W
62 Gran Paradiso, Mt. 49 33 N 7 17 E
63 Gran Sasso d'Italia, Mts. 42 25 N 13 30 E
139 Granada, Nic. 11 58 N 86 0W
53 Granada, Sp. 37 10 N 3 35W
53 Granada □ 37 5 N 4 30W
27 Granard 53 47 N 7 30W
122 Granby 45 25 N 72 45W
139 Grand Bahama I. 26 40 N 78 30W
123 Grand Bank 47 6 N 55 48W
158 Grand Bassam 5 10 N 3 49W
139 Grand Bourg 15 53 N 61 19W
131 Grand Canyon 36 10 N 112 45W
131 Grand Canyon Nat. Park 36 15 N 112 20W
139 Grand Cayman, I. 19 20 N 81 20W
131 Grand Coulee Dam 48 0 N 118 50W
123 Grand Falls 47 2 N 67 46W
124 Grand Forks, Canada 49 0 N 118 30W
128 Grand Forks, U.S.A. 48 0 N 97 3W
128 Grand Island 40 59 N 98 25W
122 Grand' Mère 46 36 N 72 40W
125 Grand Rapids, Canada 53 12 N 99 19W
127 Grand Rapids, Mich. 42 57 N 85 40W
128 Grand Rapids, Minn. 47 19 N 93 29W
45 Grand St-Bernard, Col. du 45 53 N 7 11 E
131 Grand Teton, Mt. 43 45 N 110 57W
148 Grande, B. 50 30 S 68 20W
123 Grand Baie 48 19 N 70 52W
123 Grande-Entrée 47 30 N 61 40W
124 Grande Prairie 55 15 N 118 50W
123 Grande Rivière 48 26 N 64 30W
53 Grândola 38 12 N 8 35W
24 Grangemouth 56 1 N 3 43W
41 Grängesberg 60 6 N 15 1 E
131 Grangeville 45 57 N 116 4W
114 Granity 41 39 S 171 51 E
145 Granja 3 17 S 40 50W
53 Granja de Moreruela 41 48 N 5 44W
21 Grantham 52 55 N 0 39W
24 Grantown-on-Spey 57 19 N 3 36W
131 Grants 35 14 N 107 57W
55 Grao de Gandía 39 0 N 0 27W
131 Grass Valley 39 18 N 121 0W
31 Grasse 43 38 N 6 56 E
30 Graulhet 43 45 N 1 58 E
55 Graus 42 11 N 0 20 E
29 Gravelines 51 0 N 2 10 E
113 Gravesend, Australia 29 35 S 150 20 E
21 Gravesend, U.K. 51 25 N 0 22 E
21 Grays 51 28 N 0 23 E
125 Grayson 50 45 N 102 40W
48 Graz 47 4 N 15 27 E
53 Grazalema 36 46 N 5 23W
60 Grdelica 42 55 N 22 3 E
139 Great Abaco I. 26 15 N 77 10W
113 Great Australian Basin 24 30 S 143 0 E
110 Great Australian Bight 33 30 S 130 0 E
139 Great Bahama Bank 23 15 N 78 0W
114 Great Barrier I. 37 12 S 175 25 E
113 Great Barrier Reef 19 0 S 149 0 E
131 Great Basin 40 0 N 116 30W
120 Great Bear L. 65 0 N 120 0W
128 Great Bend 38 25 N 98 55W
159 Great Bitter Lake 30 15 N 32 40 E
27 Great Blasket, I. 52 5 N 10 30W
16 Great Britain, I. 54 0 N 2 15W
113 Great Dividing Range 25 0 S 147 0 E
139 Great Exuma I. 23 30 N 75 50W
131 Great Falls 47 27 N 111 12W
139 Great Inagua I. 21 0 N 73 20W
86 Great Indian Des. 28 0 N 72 0 E
21 Great Orme's Hd. 53 20 N 3 52W
21 Great Ouse, R. 52 47 N 0 22 E
118 Great Plains 42 0 N 100 0W
165 Great Ruaha, R. 7 56 S 37 52 E
131 Great Salt L. 41 0 N 112 30W
131 Great Salt Lake Des. 40 20 N 113 50W
110 Great Sandy Des. 21 0 S 124 0 E
124 Great Slave L. 61 30 N 114 20W
99 Great Wall of China 38 30 N 109 30 E
122 Great Whale, R. 55 20 N 77 45 E
21 Great Whernside, Mt. 54 9 N 1 59W
21 Great Yarmouth 52 40 N 1 45 E
139 Greater Antilles 20 0 N 74 0W
21 Greater Manchester □ 53 35 N 2 15W
94 Greater Sunda Is. 4 30 S 113 0 E
68 Greece ■ 40 0 N 23 0 E
128 Greeley 40 30 N 104 40W
127 Green Bay 44 30 N 88 0W
127 Green B. 45 0 N 87 30W
114 Green Island 45 54 S 170 27 E
131 Green River, Utah 39 0 N 110 10W
131 Green River, Wyo. 41 32 N 109 28W
127 Greencastle 39 40 N 86 48W
173 Greenland ■ 66 0 N 45 0W
173 Greenland Sea 73 0 N 10 0W
24 Greenock 55 57 N 4 45W
27 Greenore 54 2 N 6 8W
127 Greensboro 36 7 N 79 46W
127 Greensburg, Ind. 39 20 N 85 30W
127 Greensburg, Pa. 40 18 N 79 31W
158 Greenville, Liberia 5 7 N 9 6W
127 Greenville, Mich. 43 12 N 85 14W
128 Greenville, Miss. 33 25 N 91 0W
127 Greenville, N.C. 35 37 N 77 26W
127 Greenville, Pa. 41 23 N 80 22W
127 Greenville, S.C. 34 54 N 82 24W
128 Greenville, Tex. 33 5 N 96 5W
21 Greenwich 51 28 N 0 0
128 Greenwood, Miss. 33 30 N 90 4W
127 Greenwood, S.C. 34 13 N 82 13W
113 Gregory Downs 18 35 S 138 45 E
45 Greiffenberg 53 6 N 13 57 E
45 Greifswald 54 6 N 13 23 E
48 Grein 48 14 N 14 51 E
45 Greiz 50 39 N 12 12 E
41 Grenå 56 26 N 10 53 E
128 Grenada 33 45 N 89 50W
139 Grenada, I. 12 10 N 61 40W
31 Grenoble 45 12 N 5 42 E
95 Gresik 9 13 S 112 38 E
128 Gretna 30 0 N 90 2W
24 Gretna Green 55 0 N 3 3W
45 Greven 52 7 N 7 36 E
68 Grevenà □ 40 2 N 21 25 E
45 Grevenbroich 51 6 N 6 32 E
34 Grevenmacher 49 41 N 6 26 E
41 Grevie 56 22 N 12 46 E
114 Grey, R. 42 27 S 171 12 E
123 Grey Res. 48 20 N 56 30W
114 Greymouth 42 29 S 171 13 E
169 Greytown 29 1 S 30 36 E
131 Gridley 39 27 N 121 47W
127 Griffin 33 15 N 84 16W
125 Griffith Mine 50 47 N 93 25W
21 Grimsby 53 35 N 0 5W
37 Grimsey, I. 66 33 N 18 0W
38 Grimstad 58 22 N 8 35 E
45 Grindelwald 46 38 N 8 2 E
128 Grinnell 41 45 N 92 50W
63 Grintavec, Mt. 46 21 N 14 32 E
29 Gris Nez, C. 50 50 N 1 35 E
30 Grisolles 43 49 N 1 19 E
75 Grodno 53 42 N 23 52 E
50 Grodzisk Mazowiecki 52 7 N 20 37 E
28 Groix, I. de 47 38 N 3 28W
45 Gronau 52 13 N 7 2 E
34 Groningen 53 15 N 6 35 E
34 Groningen □ 53 16 N 6 40 E
168 Groot Karoo, Reg. 32 35 S 23 0 E
165 Groot Namakwaland = Namaland, Reg. 26 0 S 18 0 E
168 Grootfontein 19 31 S 18 6 E
55 Grosa, Pta. 39 6 N 1 36 E
48 Gross Glockner, Mt. 47 5 N 12 40 E
45 Gross Ottersleben 52 5 N 11 33 E
45 Grossenbrode 54 21 N 11 4 E
45 Grossenhain 51 17 N 13 32 E
48 Grossgerungs 48 34 N 14 57 E
65 Grottáglie 40 32 N 17 25 E
63 Grožnjan 45 22 N 13 43 E
75 Groznyy 43 20 N 45 45 E
61 Grudovo 42 21 N 27 10 E
50 Grudziadz 53 30 N 18 47 E
41 Grums 59 22 N 13 5 E
45 Gruyères 46 35 N 7 4 E
75 Gryazi 52 30 N 39 58 E
174 Grytviken 53 50 S 37 10W
45 Gstaad 46 28 N 7 18 E
137 Guadalajara, Mexico 20 40 N 103 20W
53 Guadalajara, Sp. 40 37 N 3 12W
53 Guadalcanal 38 5 N 5 52W
106 Guadalcanal, I. 9 32 S 160 12 E
53 Guadalén, R. 38 5 N 3 32W
53 Guadalete, R. 36 35 N 6 13W
53 Guadalmez, R. 38 46 N 5 4W
55 Guadalope, R. 41 15 N 0 3W
53 Guadalupe, Sp. 39 27 N 5 17W
131 Guadalupe, U.S.A. 34 59 N 120 33W
53 Guadalupe, Sa. de 39 26 N 5 25W
128 Guadalupe Pk. 31 50 N 105 30W
53 Guadarrama, Sa. de 41 0 N 4 0W
139 Guadeloupe, I. 16 20 N 61 40W
139 Guadeloupe Pass. 16 50 N 68 15W
53 Guadiana, R. 37 14 N 7 22W
55 Guadiana Menor, R. 37 56 N 3 15W
55 Guadiela, R. 40 22 N 2 49W
55 Guadix 37 18 N 3 11W
148 Guafo, B. del 43 35 S 74 0W
148 Guaíra 24 5 S 54 10W
148 Guaitecas, Is. 44 0 S 74 30W
144 Guajira, Pen. de la 12 0 N 72 0W
63 Gualdo Tadino 43 14 N 12 46 E
106 Guam, I. 13 27 N 144 45 E
144 Guanare 8 42 N 69 12W
99 Guangdong □ 23 0 N 113 0 E
99 Guangxi-Zhuangzu Zizhiqu □ 24 0 N 109 0 E
99 Guangzhou 23 5 N 113 10 E
144 Guaqui 16 41 S 68 54W
55 Guara, Sa. de 42 19 N 0 15W
148 Guarapuava 25 20 S 51 30W
53 Guarda 40 32 N 7 20W
53 Guarda □ 40 40 N 7 20W
55 Guardamar del Segura 38 5 N 0 39W
53 Guardo 42 47 N 4 50W
144 Guasaualito 7 15 N 70 44W
137 Guatemala 14 38 N 90 31W
137 Guatemala ■ 15 40 N 90 30W
144 Guaviare, R. 4 3 N 67 44W
139 Guayama 17 59 N 66 7W
144 Guayaquil 2 15 S 79 52W
63 Gúbbio 43 20 N 12 34 E
50 Gubin 51 58 N 14 45 E
38 Gudbrandsdalen 62 0 N 9 14 E
29 Guebwiller 47 55 N 7 12 E
53 Guecho 43 21 N 2 59W
158 Guékedou 8 40 N 10 5W
158 Guelma 36 25 N 7 29 E
122 Guelph 43 35 N 80 20W
28 Guéméné-sur-Scorff 48 4 N 3 13W
28 Guérande 47 20 N 2 26W
30 Guéret 46 11 N 1 51 E
29 Guérigny 47 6 N 3 10 E
53 Guernica 43 19 N 2 40W
21 Guernsey, I. 49 30 N 2 35W
137 Guerrero □ 17 30 N 100 0W
31 Gueugnon 45 36 N 4 3 E
63 Guglionesi 51 55 N 14 54 E
142 Guiana Highlands, Mts. 5 0 N 60 0W
53 Guijo de Coria 40 6 N 6 28W
21 Guildford 51 14 N 0 34W
99 Guilin 25 18 N 110 15 E
28 Guilvinec 47 48 N 4 17W
145 Guimarães 2 9 S 44 35W
53 Guimarãis 41 28 N 8 24W
156 Guinea, Reg. 9 0 N 3 0 E
158 Guinea ■ 10 20 N 10 0W
156 Guinea, G. of 3 0 N 2 30 E
158 Guinea-Bissau ■ 12 0 N 15 0W
139 Güines 22 50 N 82 0W
28 Guingamp 48 34 N 3 10W
28 Guipavas 48 26 N 4 29W
55 Guipuzcoa □ 43 12 N 2 15W
144 Guiria 10 32 N 62 1iW
29 Guiscard 49 40 N 3 0 E
29 Guise 49 52 N 3 35 E
53 Guitiriz 43 11 N 7 50W
95 Guiuan 11 2 N 125 44 E
99 Guiyang 26 32 N 106 40 E
99 Guizhou □ 27 0 N 107 0 E
86 Gujarat □ 23 20 N 71 0 E
86 Gujranwala 32 10 N 74 12 E
86 Gujrat 32 40 N 74 2 E
128 Gulfport 30 28 N 89 3W
125 Gull Lake 50 10 N 108 55W
76 Gulshad 46 45 N 74 25 E
38 Gulsvik 60 24 N 9 38 E
165 Gulu 2 48 N 32 17 E
113 Gumla 23 2 N 84 32 E
102 Gumma □ 36 30 N 138 20 E
45 Gummersbach 51 2 N 7 32 E
158 Gummi 12 4 N 5 9 E
86 Guna 24 40 N 77 19 E
113 Gunnedah 30 59 S 150 15 E
86 Guntakal 15 11 N 77 27 E
125 Gunworth 51 20 N 108 10W
80 Gūrchān 34 55 N 49 25 E
113 Gurley 29 45 S 149 48 E
91 Gurun 5 49 N 100 27 E
76 Guryer 47 5 N 52 0 E
158 Gusau 12 18 N 6 31 E
64 Gúspini 39 32 N 8 38 E
49 Güssing 47 3 N 16 20 E
45 Güstrow 53 47 N 12 12 E
45 Gütersloh 51 54 N 8 25 E
49 Gutu = Kalárovo 47 54 N 18 0 E
144 Guyana ■ 5 0 N 59 0W
30 Guyenne, Reg. 44 30 N 0 40 E
113 Guyra 30 15 S 151 40 E
87 Gwa 17 30 N 94 40 E
86 Gwādar 25 10 N 62 18 E
86 Gwalior 26 12 N 78 10 E
169 Gwanda 20 55 S 29 0 E
50 Gwda, R. 53 4 N 16 44 E
27 Gweedore 55 4 N 8 15W
169 Gwelo 19 27 S 29 49 E
21 Gwent □ 51 45 N 3 0W
21 Gwynedd □ 53 0 N 4 0W
113 Gympie 26 11 S 152 38 E
49 Gyoma 46 56 N 20 58 E
49 Gyöngyös 47 48 N 20 15 E
49 Györ 47 41 N 17 40 E
49 Györ Sopron □ 47 40 N 17 20 E
125 Gypsumville 51 45 N 98 40W

H

91 Ha Dong 20 58 N 105 46 E
45 Haag 48 11 N 12 12 E
34 Haarlem 52 23 N 4 39 E
86 Hab Nadi Chauki 25 0 N 66 50 E
102 Hachinohe 40 30 N 141 29 E
102 Hachiōji 33 3 N 139 55 E
24 Haddington 55 57 N 2 48W
158 Hadejia 12 30 N 9 59 E
41 Haderslev 55 17 N 9 30 E
85 Hadhramawt, Reg. 15 30 N 49 30 E
21 Hadrian's Wall 55 0 N 2 30 E
80 Hafar al Bāṭin 28 25 N 46 50 E
87 Haflong 25 10 N 93 5 E
37 Hafnarfjörđur 64 3 N 21 55W
45 Hagen 51 21 N 7 29 E
30 Hagetmau 43 39 N 0 37W
41 Hagfors 60 3 N 13 45 E
28 Hague, C. de la 49 43 N 1 57W
29 Haguenau 48 49 N 7 47 E
99 Haikou 20 1 N 107 0 E
99 Hailar 49 10 N 119 34 E
131 Hailey 43 30 N 114 15W
122 Haileybury 47 30 N 79 38W
34 Hainaut □ 50 30 N 4 0 E
99 Hainan 19 0 N 109 30 E
49 Hainburg 48 9 N 16 56 E
124 Haines Junction 60 45 N 137 30W
48 Hainfeld 48 3 N 15 48 E
91 Haiphong 20 55 N 105 42 E
139 Haiti ■ 19 0 N 72 30W
49 Hajdu-Bihar □ 47 30 N 21 30 E
49 Hajdúböszörmény 47 40 N 21 30 E
49 Hajdúdurog 47 48 N 21 30 E
49 Hajdúhadház 47 40 N 21 40 E
49 Hajdúszoboszló 47 27 N 21 22 E
50 Hajnówka 52 45 N 23 36 E
81 Hajr, Reg. 24 0 N 56 34 E
41 Håkantorp 58 18 N 12 55 E
102 Hakodate 41 45 N 140 44 E
102 Hakui 36 53 N 136 47 E
80 Halab 36 10 N 37 15 E
159 Halaib 22 5 N 36 30 E
45 Halberstadt 51 53 N 11 2 E
114 Halcombe 40 8 S 175 30 E
45 Haldensleben 52 17 N 11 30 E
86 Haldwani 29 25 N 79 30 E
85 Hali 18 40 N 41 15 E
123 Halifax, Canada 44 38 N 63 35W
21 Halifax, U.K. 53 43 N 1 51W
48 Hall 47 17 N 11 30 E
34 Halle, Belgium 50 44 N 4 13W
45 Halle, E. Germany 51 29 N 12 0 E
41 Hällefors 59 46 N 14 30 E
48 Hallein 47 40 N 13 5 E
113 Hallett 33 25 S 138 55 E
174 Halley Bay 76 30 S 27 0W
37 Hällnäs 64 18 N 19 40 E
41 Hallsberg 59 5 N 15 7 E
41 Hallstahammar 59 38 N 16 15 E
95 Halmahera, I. 0 40 N 128 0 E
41 Halmstad 56 37 N 12 56 E
159 Halq el Oued 36 53 N 10 10 E
45 Haltern 51 44 N 7 10 E
80 Hamāh 35 5 N 36 40 E
102 Hamada 34 50 N 132 10 E
80 Hamadān 34 52 N 48 32 E
80 Hamadān □ 35 0 N 48 40 E
102 Hamamatsu 34 45 N 137 45 E
45 Hamburg 53 32 N 9 59 E
37 Häme □ 61 30 N 24 30 E
37 Hämeenlinna 61 3 N 24 26 E
45 Hameln 52 7 N 9 24 E
110 Hamersley Ra. 22 0 S 117 45 E
113 Hamilton, Australia 37 37 S 142 0 E
139 Hamilton, Bermuda 32 15 N 64 45W
122 Hamilton, Canada 43 20 N 79 50W
114 Hamilton, N.Z. 37 47 S 175 19 E
24 Hamilton, U.K. 55 47 N 4 2W
131 Hamilton, Mont. 46 20 N 114 6W
127 Hamilton, Ohio 39 20 N 84 35W
125 Hamiota 50 11 N 100 38W
127 Hamlet 34 56 N 79 40W
45 Hamm 51 40 N 7 58 E
41 Hammarö, I. 59 20 N 13 30 E
37 Hammerfest 70 33 N 23 50 E
127 Hammond, Ind. 41 40 N 87 30W
128 Hammond, La. 30 30 N 90 28W
21 Hampshire □ 51 3 N 1 20W
127 Hampton 37 4 N 76 8W
41 Hamrångefjarden 60 59 N 17 5 E
99 Handan 36 35 N 114 28 E
165 Handeni 5 25 S 38 2 E
49 Handlová 48 45 N 18 35 E
124 Haney 49 12 N 122 40W
131 Hanford 36 25 N 119 45W
37 Hangö 59 59 N 22 57 E
99 Hangzhou 30 18 N 120 11 E
99 Hangzhou wan 30 15 N 120 40 E
114 Hanmer 42 32 S 172 50 E
124 Hanna 51 40 N 112 0W
45 Hannover 52 23 N 9 43 E
41 Hanö, B. 55 45 N 14 60 E
41 Hanö, I. 56 0 N 14 50 E
91 Hanoi 21 5 N 150 40 E
148 Hanover, I. 50 58 S 74 40W
86 Hansi 29 10 N 75 57 E
99 Hangyang 30 35 N 114 2 E
37 Haparanda 65 52 N 24 8 E
86 Hapur 28 45 N 77 45 E
80 Harad 24 15 N 49 0 E
99 Harbin 45 48 N 126 40 E
123 Harbour Breton 47 29 N 55 50W
123 Harbour Deep 50 25 N 56 30W
123 Harbour Grace 47 40 N 53 22W
45 Harburg 53 27 N 9 58 E
38 Hardanger Fd. 60 15 N 6 0 E
168 Hardap Dam 24 28 S 17 48 E
34 Harderwijk 52 21 N 5 36 E
86 Hardwar 29 58 N 78 16 E
148 Hardy, Pen. 55 30 S 68 20W
85 Harer 9 20 N 42 8 E
28 Harfleur 49 30 N 0 10 E
21 Harlech 52 52 N 4 7W
131 Harlem 48 29 N 108 39W
34 Harlingen, Neth. 53 11 N 5 25 E
128 Harlingen, U.S.A. 26 30 N 97 50W
21 Harlow 51 47 N 0 9 E
41 Härnösand 62 38 N 18 5 E
53 Haro 42 35 N 2 55W
127 Harriman 36 0 N 84 35W
123 Harrington Harbour 50 31 N 59 30W
24 Harris, I. 57 50 N 6 55W
127 Harrisburg 37 42 N 88 30W
128 Harrison 36 10 N 93 4W
122 Harriston 43 57 N 80 53W
21 Harrogate 53 59 N 1 32W
21 Harrow 51 35 N 0 15W
127 Hartford 41 47 N 72 41W
21 Hartland Pt. 51 2 N 4 32W
21 Hartlepool 54 42 N 1 11W
124 Hartley Bay 46 4 N 80 45W
127 Hartsville 34 23 N 80 2W
127 Harvey 41 40 N 87 40W
21 Harwich 51 56 N 1 18 E
86 Haryana □ 29 0 N 76 10 E
45 Harz, Mts. 51 40 N 10 40 E
21 Haslemere 51 5 N 0 41W
86 Hassan 13 0 N 76 5 E
34 Hasselt 50 56 N 5 21 E
158 Hassi er Rmel 32 35 N 3 24 E
158 Hassi Messaoud 31 15 N 6 35 E
114 Hastings, N.Z. 39 39 S 176 52 E
21 Hastings, U.K. 50 51 N 0 36 E
127 Hastings, Mich. 42 40 N 85 20 E
128 Hastings, Neb. 40 34 N 98 22W
131 Hatch 32 45 N 107 8W
86 Hathras 27 36 N 78 6 E
127 Hatteras, C. 35 10 N 75 30W
128 Hattiesburg 31 20 N 89 20W
49 Hatvan 47 40 N 19 45 E
38 Haugesund 59 23 N 5 13 E
61 Hauntii Sebeșului, Mt. 45 30 N 23 30 E
48 Hausruck, Mts. 48 6 N 13 30 E
29 Haut-Rhin □ 48 0 N 7 15 E
31 Haute-Corse □ 42 30 N 9 20 E
30 Haute-Garonne □ 43 28 N 1 30 E
29 Haute-Marne □ 48 10 N 5 20 E
29 Hautmont 50 15 N 3 55 E
31 Haute-Savoie □ 46 0 N 6 20 E
30 Haute-Vienne □ 45 50 N 1 10 E
31 Hautes-Alpes □ 44 40 N 6 30 E
30 Hautes-Pyrénées □ 43 0 N 0 10 E
21 Havant 50 51 N 0 59W
122 Havelock 44 26 N 77 53W
21 Haverfordwest 51 48 N 4 59W
127 Haverhill 42 50 N 71 2W
21 Havering 51 33 N 0 20 E
48 Havlíckuv Brod 49 36 N 15 33 E
131 Havre 48 40 N 109 34W
123 Havre St. Pierre 50 18 N 63 33W
80 Havza 41 0 N 35 35 E
133 Hawaii □ 20 0 N 155 0W
133 Hawaii, I. 20 0 N 155 0W
24 Hawick 55 25 N 2 48W
122 Hawk Junction 48 5 N 84 35W
114 Hawke, B. 39 25 S 177 20 E
113 Hawker 31 59 S 138 22 E
114 Hawke's Bay □ 39 45 S 176 35 E
123 Hawke's Harbour 53 2 N 55 50W
123 Hawkesbury, Nova Scotia 45 40 N 61 10W
122 Hawkesbury, Ont. 45 35 N 74 40W
131 Hawthorne 38 37 N 118 47W
113 Hay, Australia 34 30 S 144 51 E
21 Hay, U.K. 52 4 N 3 9W
29 Hayange 49 20 N 6 2 E
131 Hayden 40 30 N 107 22W
120 Hayes, Mt. 63 37 N 146 43W
125 Hayes, R. 57 3 N 92 9W
21 Hayling I. 50 40 N 1 0W
21 Haywards Heath 51 0 N 0 5W
81 Hazārān, Kuh-e, Mt. 29 35 N 57 20 E
127 Hazard 37 18 N 83 10W
29 Hazebrouck 50 42 N 2 31 E
21 Heanor 53 1 N 1 20W
122 Hearst 49 40 N 83 41W
123 Heart's Content 47 54 N 53 27W
123 Heath Steele 48 30 N 66 20W
99 Hebei □ 39 0 N 116 0 E
113 Hebel 28 59 S 147 48 E
123 Hebertville 47 0 N 71 30W
24 Hebrides, Inner, Is. 57 20 N 6 40W
24 Hebrides, Outer, Is. 57 50 N 7 25W
121 Hebron 58 10 N 62 50W
124 Hecate Str. 53 10 N 130 30W
41 Hedemora 60 18 N 15 58 E
41 Hedmark □ 61 45 N 11 0 E
34 Heemstede 52 19 N 4 37 E
34 Heerde 52 24 N 6 2 E
34 Heerenveen 52 57 N 5 55 E
99 Hefei 31 52 N 117 18 E
34 Heerlen 50 55 N 6 0 E
45 Heide 54 10 N 9 7 E
45 Heidelberg 49 23 N 8 41 E
45 Heidenheim 48 40 N 10 10 E
169 Heilbron 27 16 S 27 59 E
45 Heilbronn 49 8 N 9 13 E
45 Heiligenstadt 51 22 N 10 9 E
99 Heilongjiang □ 48 0 N 126 0 E
37 Heinola 61 13 N 26 10 E
125 Heinsburg 53 50 N 110 30W

Jihočeský

Korhogo

48	Jihočeský □	49 8 N	14 35 E
158	Jijel	36 52 N	5 50 E
85	Jijiga	9 20 N	42 50 E
55	Jijona	38 34 N	0 30W
99	Jilin	43 55 N	126 30 E
55	Jiloca, R.	41 21 N	1 39W
99	Jilong	25 8 N	121 42 E
60	Jimbolia	45 47 N	20 57 E
53	Jimena de la Frontera	36 27 N	5 24W
137	Jiménez	27 10 N	105 0W
99	Jinan	36 38 N	117 1 E
48	Jindřichuv Hradec	49 10 N	15 2 E
165	Jinja	0 25 N	33 12 E
99	Jinmen, I.	24 25 N	118 25 E
139	Jinotega	13 6 N	85 59W
139	Jinotepe	11 50 N	86 10W
99	Jinzhou	41 5 N	121 3 E
80	Jisr ash Shughūr	35 49 N	36 18 E
85	Jīzān	16 57 N	42 3 E
148	Joaçaba	27 5 S	51 31W
145	João Pessoa	7 10 S	34 52W
53	Jodar	37 50 N	3 21W
86	Jodhpur	26 23 N	73 2 E
29	Joeuf	49 12 N	6 1 E
123	Joggins	45 42 N	64 27W
169	Johannesburg	26 10 S	28 8 E
24	John O'Groats	58 39 N	3 3W
124	Johnson's Crossing	60 33 N	133 27W
107	Johnston I.	17 10 N	169 8 E
91	Johore, R.	1 39 N	103 57 E
127	Johnstown, N.Y.	43 1 N	74 20W
127	Johnstown, Pa.	40 19 N	78 53W
91	Johor Baharu	1 45 N	103 47 E
91	Johore □	2 5 N	103 20 E
29	Joigny	48 0 N	3 20 E
29	Joinville	48 27 N	5 10 E
37	Jokkmokk	66 35 N	19 50 E
127	Joliet	41 30 N	88 0W
95	Jolo, I.	6 0 N	121 0 E
95	Jombang	7 32 S	112 12 E
122	Jones, C.	54 33 N	79 35W
41	Jönköping	57 45 N	14 10 E
41	Jonsered	57 45 N	12 10 E
30	Jonzac	45 27 N	0 28W
80	Jordan ■	31 0 N	36 0 E
80	Jordan, R.	31 46 N	35 33 E
81	Jorm	36 50 N	70 45 E
37	Jörn	65 5 N	20 12 E
158	Jos	9 53 N	8 51 E
110	Joseph Bonaparte, G.	14 0 S	29 0 E
28	Josselin	47 57 N	2 33W
38	Jotunheimen, Mts.	61 30 N	9 0 E
50	Jozefow	52 9 N	21 12 E
148	Juárez	37 40 S	59 43W
145	Juàzeiro	9 30 S	40 30W
158	Juby, C.	28 0 N	12 59W
55	Júcar, R.	39 40 N	2 18W
48	Judenburg	47 12 N	14 38 E
45	Juist, I.	53 40 N	7 0 E
144	Juli	16 10 S	69 25W
113	Julia Creek	20 40 S	141 55 E
173	Julianehåb	60 43 N	46 0W
63	Julijske Alpe, Mts.	46 15 N	14 1 E
86	Jullundur	31 20 N	75 40 E
34	Jumet	50 27 N	4 25 E
55	Jumilla	38 28 N	1 19W
86	Junagadh	21 30 N	70 30 E
128	Junction City, Kans.	39 4 N	96 55W
131	Junction City, Oreg.	44 20 N	123 12W
113	Jundah	24 46 S	143 2 E
124	Juneau	58 26 N	134 30W
113	Junee	34 49 S	147 32W
45	Jungfrau, Mt.	46 32 N	7 58 E
96	Junggar Pendi	44 0 N	87 0 E
148	Junín	34 33 S	60 57W
148	Junin de los Andes	39 45 S	71 0W
80	Jūniyah	33 59 N	35 30 E
148	Juquiá	24 19 S	47 38W
24	Jura, I.	56 0 N	5 50W
31	Jura □	46 47 N	5 45 E
144	Jurado	7 7 N	77 46W
144	Juruá, R.	2 37 S	65 44W
145	Juruti	2 9 S	56 4W
29	Jussey	47 50 N	5 55 E
148	Justo Daract	33 52 S	65 12W
45	Jüterbog	51 59 N	13 6 E
139	Juventud, I.de la	21 40 N	82 40W
29	Juvisy	48 43 N	2 23 E
41	Jylland, Reg.	56 25 N	9 30 E
37	Jyväskylä	62 12 N	25 47 E

K

86	K2, Mt.	36 0 N	77 0 E
168	Kaap Plato	28 30 S	24 0 E
168	Kaapstad = Cape Town	33 55 S	18 22 E
95	Kabaena, I.	5 15 S	122 0 E
165	Kabale	9 38 N	11 37W
165	Kabarega Falls	2 15 S	31 38 E
158	Kabba	7 57 N	6 3 E
165	Kabinda	6 23 S	24 38 E
165	Kabongo	7 22 S	25 33 E
113	Kabra	23 25 S	150 25 E
81	Kābul	34 28 N	69 18 E
165	Kabwe	14 30 S	28 29 E
87	Kachin □	26 0 N	97 0 E
76	Kachiry	53 10 N	75 50 E
113	Kadina	34 0 S	137 43 E
158	Kaduna	10 30 N	7 21 E
68	Kafirévs, Ákra	38 9 N	24 8 E
165	Kafue, R.	15 56 S	28 55 E
165	Kago Bandoro	7 8 N	19 8 E
76	Kagan	39 43 N	64 33 E
102	Kagawa □	34 15 N	134 0 E
102	Kagoshima	31 36 N	130 40 E
114	Kaiapoi	42 24 S	172 40 E
99	Kaifeng	34 48 N	114 21 E
114	Kaikohe	35 25 S	173 49 E
114	Kaikoura	42 25 S	173 43 E
158	Kainji Dam	10 1 N	4 40 E
158	Kairouan	35 45 N	10 5 E
45	Kaiserslautern	49 30 N	7 43 E
114	Kaitaia	35 8 S	173 17 E
114	Kaitangata	46 17 S	169 51 E
91	Kajang	2 59 N	101 48 E
102	Kake	34 6 N	132 19 E
102	Kakegawa	34 45 N	138 1 E
75	Kakhovka	46 46 N	34 28 E
102	Kakogawa	34 46 N	134 51 E
86	Kalabagh	33 0 N	71 28 E
95	Kalabahi	8 13 S	124 31 E
75	Kalach	50 22 N	41 0 E
87	Kaladan, R.	20 9 N	92 57 E
168	Kalahari, Des.	24 0 S	22 0 E
77	Kalakan	55 15 N	116 45 E
68	Kalamariá	40 33 N	22 55 E
68	Kalamata	37 3 N	22 10 E
127	Kalamazoo	42 20 N	85 35W
80	Kalan	39 7 N	39 32 E
49	Kalárovo	47 54 N	18 0 E
86	Kalat	29 8 N	66 31 E
68	Kalávrita	38 3 N	22 8 E
165	Kalemie	5 55 S	29 9 E
87	Kalewa	22 41 N	95 32 E
110	Kalgoorlie	30 40 S	121 22 E
94	Kalimantan □	0 0	115 0 E
68	Kálimnos, I.	37 0 N	27 0 E
75	Kalinin	56 55 N	35 55 E
75	Kaliningrad	54 44 N	20 32 E
41	Kållandsö, I.	58 40 N	13 5 E
41	Källby	58 30 N	13 0 E
68	Kallithéa	37 55 N	23 41 E
68	Kallonís, Kól.	39 10 N	26 10 E
41	Kalmar	56 40 N	16 20 E
75	Kalmyk A.S.S.R. □	46 5 N	46 1 E
76	Kalmykovo	49 0 N	51 35 E
49	Kalocsa	46 32 N	19 0 E
61	Kalofer	42 37 N	24 59 E
75	Kaluga	54 35 N	36 10 E
86	Kalutara	6 35 N	80 0 E
75	Kama, R.	55 45 N	52 0 E
77	Kamchatka Pol.	57 0 N	160 0 E
76	Kamen	53 50 N	81 30 E
75	Kamenets Podolskiy	48 40 N	26 30 E
63	Kamenjak, Rt.	44 46 N	13 55 E
75	Kamenka	65 58 N	44 0 E
61	Kameno	42 35 N	27 18 E
75	Kamensk Shakhtinskiy	48 23 N	40 20 E
76	Kamensk Uralskiy	56 28 N	61 54 E
77	Kamenskoye	62 45 N	165 30 E
102	Kameoka	35 0 N	135 35 E
48	Kamienna Góra	50 48 N	16 2 E
165	Kamina	8 45 S	25 0 E
124	Kamloops	50 40 N	120 20W
165	Kampala	0 20 N	32 30 E
91	Kampar	4 18 N	101 9 E
91	Kampong Chhnang	12 15 N	104 20 E
91	Kampot	10 36 N	104 10 E
125	Kamsack	51 35 N	101 50W
75	Kamskoye Vdkhr.	58 0 N	56 0 E
75	Kamyshin	50 10 N	45 30 E
131	Kanab	27 3 N	112 29W
165	Kananga	5 55 S	22 18 E
75	Kanash	55 48 N	47 32 E
68	Kanastraíon, Akra	39 54 N	23 40 E
102	Kanazawa	36 30 N	136 38 E
91	Kanchanaburi	14 8 N	99 31 E
87	Kanchenjunga, Mt.	27 50 N	88 10 E
86	Kanchipuram	12 52 N	79 45 E
76	Kandagach	49 20 N	57 15 E
75	Kandalaksha	67 9 N	32 30 E
75	Kandalakshskiy Zaliv	66 0 N	35 0 E
94	Kandangan	2 50 S	115 20 E
114	Kandavu, I.	19 0 S	178 15 E
86	Kandy	7 18 N	80 43 E
127	Kane	41 39 N	78 53W
113	Kangaroo, I.	35 45 S	137 0 E
80	Kangāvar	34 40 N	48 0 E
87	Kangto, Mt.	27 50 N	92 35 E
60	Kanjiža	46 3 N	20 4 E
127	Kankakee	41 6 N	87 50W
127	Kannapolis	35 32 N	80 37W
86	Kannauj	27 3 N	79 26 E
158	Kano	12 2 N	8 30 E
102	Kanoya	31 23 N	130 51 E
87	Kanpetlet	21 10 N	93 59 E
86	Kanpur	26 35 N	80 20 E
128	Kansas, R.	39 7 N	94 36W
128	Kansas □	38 40 N	98 0W
128	Kansas City, Kans.	39 0 N	94 40W
128	Kansas City, Mo.	39 3 N	94 30W
77	Kansk	56 20 N	96 37 E
102	Kantō □	36 0 N	120 0 E
168	Kanye	25 0 S	25 28 E
158	Kaolack	14 5 N	16 8W
165	Kapiri Mposha	13 59 S	28 43 E
81	Kāpīsā □	34 45 N	69 30 E
48	Kaplice	48 42 N	14 30 E
94	Kapuas, R.	0 25 S	109 24 E
113	Kapunda	34 20 S	138 56 E
122	Kapuskasing	49 25 N	82 30W
76	Kara	69 10 N	65 25 E
76	Kara Bogaz Gol, Zaliv	41 0 N	53 30 E
76	Kara Kalpak A.S.S.R. □	43 0 N	59 0 E
76	Kara Sea	75 0 N	70 0 E
80	Karabük	41 12 N	32 37 E
86	Karachi	24 53 N	67 0 E
86	Karad	17 54 N	74 10 E
80	Karadeniz Boğazi	41 10 N	29 5 E
76	Karaganda	49 50 N	73 0 E
86	Karaikkudi	10 0 N	78 45 E
81	Karaj	35 4 N	51 0 E
76	Karakas	48 20 N	83 30 E
86	Karakoram P.	35 33 N	77 46 E
80	Karaköse	39 44 N	43 3 E
94	Karambu	3 53 S	116 6 E
168	Karasburg	28 0 S	18 44 E
76	Karasino	66 50 N	86 50 E
37	Karasjok	69 27 N	25 30 E
76	Karasuk	53 44 N	78 2 E
76	Karatau	43 10 N	70 28 E
102	Karatsu	33 30 N	130 0 E
48	Karawanken, Mts.	46 30 N	14 40 E
76	Karazhal	48 2 N	70 49 E
80	Karbalā	32 47 N	44 3 E
49	Karcag	47 19 N	21 1 E
68	Kardhítsa	39 23 N	21 54 E
159	Kareima	18 30 N	21 40 E
75	Karelian A.S.S.R. □	65 30 N	32 30 E
76	Kargat	55 10 N	80 15 E
86	Kargil	34 32 N	76 12 E
75	Kargopol	61 30 N	38 58 E
169	Kariba L.	16 40 S	28 25 E
86	Karikal	10 59 N	79 50 E
86	Karimnagar	18 26 N	79 10 E
102	Kariya	34 58 N	137 1 E
76	Karkaralinsk	49 30 N	75 10 E
75	Karkinitskiy Zaliv	45 36 N	32 35 E
45	Karl-Marx-Stadt	50 50 N	12 55 E
48	Karlovy Vary	50 13 N	12 51 E
41	Karlshamn	56 10 N	14 51 E
41	Karlskoga	59 22 N	14 33 E
41	Karlskrona	56 10 N	15 35 E
45	Karlsruhe	49 3 N	8 23 E
41	Karlstad	59 23 N	13 30 E
120	Karluk	57 30 N	155 0W
86	Karnataka □	13 15 N	77 0 E
48	Karnische Alpen, Mts.	46 36 N	13 0 E
48	Kärnten □	46 52 N	13 30 E
165	Karonga	9 57 S	33 55 E
68	Kárpathos, I.	35 37 N	27 10 E
75	Karpogory	63 59 N	44 27 E
80	Kars	40 40 N	43 5 E
76	Karsakpay	47 55 N	66 40 E
76	Kartaly	53 3 N	60 40 E
165	Karungu	0 50 S	34 10 E
86	Karur	10 59 N	78 2 E
49	Karviná	49 53 N	18 25 E
91	Kas Kong	11 27 N	102 12 E
165	Kasai, R.	3 2 S	16 57 E
165	Kasama	10 16 S	31 9 E
165	Kasese	0 15 N	30 3 E
81	Kāshān	34 5 N	51 30 E
96	Kashi	39 30 N	76 2 E
72	Kashmir □	34 0 N	78 0 E
75	Kasimov	54 55 N	41 20 E
68	Kásos, I.	35 20 N	26 55 E
68	Kassándra, Pen.	40 0 N	23 30 E
45	Kassel	51 19 N	9 32 E
165	Kassinga	15 5 S	16 23 E
95	Kassue	6 58 S	139 21 E
80	Kastamonu	41 25 N	33 43 E
68	Kastélli	35 29 N	23 38 E
68	Kastoría	40 30 N	21 19 E
68	Kástron	39 53 N	25 8 E
86	Kasur	31 5 N	74 25 E
77	Kata	58 46 N	102 40 E
68	Kateríni	40 18 N	22 37 E
87	Katha	24 10 N	96 30 E
110	Katherine	14 27 S	132 20 E
86	Kathiawar, Reg.	22 0 N	71 0 E
94	Katiet	2 21 S	99 14 E
168	Katima Mulilo	17 28 S	24 13 E
120	Katmai Mt.	58 20 N	154 59W
87	Katmandu	27 45 N	85 12 E
113	Katoomba	33 41 S	150 19 E
49	Katowice	50 17 N	19 5 E
49	Katowice □	50 30 N	19 0 E
24	Katrine, L.	56 15 N	4 30 E
41	Katrineholm	59 9 N	16 12 E
158	Katsina	7 10 N	9 20 E
41	Kattegat, Str.	57 0 N	11 20 E
34	Katwijk-aan-Zee	52 12 N	4 22 E
133	Kauai, I.	19 30 N	155 30W
75	Kaunas	54 54 N	23 54 E
158	Kaura Namoda	12 37 N	6 33 E
37	Kautokeino	69 0 N	23 4 E
77	Kavacha	60 16 N	169 51 E
60	Kavadarci	41 26 N	22 3 E
86	Kavali	14 55 N	80 1 E
68	Kavàlla	40 57 N	24 28 E
61	Kavarna	43 26 N	28 22 E
145	Kaw	4 30 N	52 15W
102	Kawagoe	35 55 N	139 29 E
102	Kawaguchi	35 52 N	138 45 E
165	Kawambwa	9 48 S	29 3 E
102	Kawanoe	34 1 N	133 34 E
87	Kawardha	22 0 N	81 17 E
102	Kawasaki	35 35 N	138 42 E
122	Kawene	48 45 N	91 15W
114	Kawerau	38 7 S	176 42 E
114	Kawhia Harbour	38 4 S	174 49 E
87	Kawnro	22 48 N	99 8 E
91	Kawthaung	10 5 N	98 36 E
87	Kawthoolei □	18 0 N	97 30 E
87	Kayah □	19 15 N	97 15 E
131	Kayenta	36 46 N	110 15 E
158	Kayes	14 25 N	11 30W
80	Kayseri	38 45 N	35 30 E
94	Kayuagung	3 28 S	104 46 E
77	Kazachye	70 52 N	135 58 E
76	Kazakh S.S.R. □	50 0 N	58 0 E
75	Kazan	55 48 N	49 3 E
61	Kazanlŭk	42 38 N	25 35 E
75	Kazbek, Mt.	42 30 N	44 30 E
81	Kāzerūn	29 38 N	51 40 E
49	Kazincbarcika	48 17 N	20 36 E
76	Kazym, R.	63 54 N	65 50 E
68	Kéa, I.	37 30 N	24 22 E
85	Kebri Dehar	6 45 N	44 17W
49	Kecskemet	46 57 N	19 35 E
91	Kedah □	5 50 N	100 40 E
95	Kediri	7 51 S	112 1 E
168	Keetmanshoop	26 35 S	18 8 E
125	Keewatin	47 23 N	93 0W
120	Keewatin, Reg.	63 20 N	94 40W
68	Kefallinía, I.	38 28 N	20 30 E
95	Kefamenanu	9 28 S	124 38 E
158	Keffi	8 55 N	7 43 E
37	Keflavik	64 2 N	22 35W
45	Kehl	48 34 N	7 50 E
21	Keighley	53 52 N	1 54W
113	Keith, Australia	36 0 S	140 20 E
24	Keith, U.K.	57 33 N	2 58W
77	Kël	69 30 N	124 10 E
91	Kelang	3 2 N	101 26 E
91	Kelantan, R.	6 11 N	102 16 E
159	Kelibia	36 50 N	11 3 E
110	Kellerberrin	31 36 S	117 38 E
131	Kellogg	47 30 N	116 5W
124	Kelowna	49 50 N	119 25W
114	Kelso, N.Z.	45 54 S	169 15 E
24	Kelso, U.K.	55 36 N	2 27W
131	Kelso, U.S.A.	46 10 N	122 57W
91	Keluang	2 3 N	103 18 E
125	Kelvington	52 20 N	103 30W
75	Kem	65 0 N	34 38 E
75	Kem, R.	64 57 N	34 41 E
76	Kemerovo	55 20 N	85 50 E
37	Kemi	65 47 N	24 32 E
37	Kemijärvi	66 43 N	27 22 E
37	Kemijoki, R.	65 47 N	24 30 E
45	Kempten	47 42 N	10 18 E
122	Kemptville	45 0 N	75 38W
95	Kendal, Indonesia	6 56 S	110 14 E
21	Kendal, U.K.	54 19 N	2 44W
95	Kendari	3 50 S	122 30 E
120	Kendi	60 30 N	151 0W
87	Kendrapara	20 35 N	86 30 E
158	Kenema	7 50 N	11 14W
87	Keng Tawng	20 45 N	98 18 E
87	Keng Tung	21 0 N	99 30 E
158	Kenitra	34 15 N	6 40W
27	Kenmare	51 52 N	9 35W
127	Kennedy, C. = Canaveral, C.	28 28 N	80 31W
21	Kennet, R.	51 28 N	0 57W
125	Kenora	49 50 N	94 35W
127	Kenosha	42 33 N	87 48W
123	Kensington	46 25 N	63 34W
127	Kent	41 8 N	81 20W
21	Kent □	51 12 N	0 40 E
120	Kent Pen.	68 30 N	107 0W
76	Kentau	43 32 N	68 36 E
127	Kenton	40 40 N	83 35W
127	Kentucky □	37 20 N	85 0W
123	Kentville	45 6 N	64 29W
165	Kenya ■	2 20 N	38 0 E
165	Kenya, Mt.	0 10 S	37 18 E
128	Keokuk	40 25 N	91 30W
50	Kępno	51 18 N	17 58 E
86	Kerala □	11 0 N	76 15 E
113	Kerang	35 40 S	143 55 E
81	Kerāy	26 15 N	57 30 E
75	Kerch	45 20 N	36 20 E
106	Kerguelan, I.	48 15 S	69 10 E
165	Kericho	0 22 S	35 15 E
94	Kęrinci, Mt.	2 5 S	101 0 E
159	Kerkenna, Is.	34 48 N	11 1 E
68	Kerkintis, L.	41 12 N	23 10 E
68	Kérkira	39 38 N	19 50 E
34	Kerkrade	50 53 N	6 4 E
106	Kermadec Is.	31 8 S	175 16W
81	Kermān	30 15 N	57 1 E
80	Kermānshāhān	34 23 N	47 0 E
128	Kermit	31 56 N	103 3W
125	Kerrobert	52 0 N	109 11W
128	Kerrville	30 1 N	99 8W
27	Kerry □	52 7 N	9 35W
37	Keski-Suomen □	63 0 N	25 0 E
21	Keswick	54 35 N	3 9W
49	Keszthely	46 50 N	17 15W
158	Keta	5 49 N	1 0 E
94	Ketapang	1 55 S	110 0 E
124	Ketchikan	55 25 N	131 40W
50	Kętrzyn	54 7 N	21 22 E
21	Kettering	52 24 N	0 44W
128	Kewanee	41 18 N	90 0W
128	Keweenaw B.	47 0 N	88 0W
127	Keyser	39 26 N	79 0W
76	Khabarovo	69 30 N	60 30 E
77	Khaborovsk	48 20 N	135 0 E
86	Khairpur □	23 30 N	69 8 E
81	Khalij-e Fars	28 20 N	51 45 E
68	Khálki	39 26 N	22 30 E
68	Khalkidhikí □	40 25 N	23 20 E
68	Khalkís	38 27 N	23 42 E
75	Khalmer Yu	67 58 N	65 1 E
75	Khalturin	58 40 N	48 50 E
85	Khalūf	20 30 N	57 56 E
81	Khānābād	36 45 N	69 5 E
86	Khandwa	21 49 N	76 22 E
77	Khandyga	62 30 N	134 50 E
86	Khanewal	30 20 N	71 55 E
68	Khaniá	35 30 N	24 4 E
77	Khanka, Oz.	45 0 N	132 30 E
76	Khanty-Mansiysk	61 0 N	69 0 E
87	Kharagpur	22 20 N	87 25 E
86	Kharda	18 40 N	75 40 E
86	Khargon	21 45 N	75 40 E
75	Kharkov	49 58 N	36 20 E
75	Kharovsk	59 56 N	40 13 E
159	Khartoum = El Khartûm	15 31 N	32 35 E
81	Khāsh Rūd	28 15 N	61 5 E
61	Khaskovo	41 56 N	25 30 E
77	Khatanga	72 0 N	102 20 E
159	Khatanga, R.	73 30 N	109 0 E
80	Khavāri □	37 20 N	46 0 E
158	Khemis Miliana	36 11 N	2 14 E
158	Khenifra	32 58 N	5 46W
75	Kherson	46 35 N	32 35 E
68	Khersónisos Akrotíri	35 30 N	24 10 E
77	Khilok	51 30 N	110 45 E
68	Khíos	38 27 N	26 9 E
76	Khiva	41 30 N	60 18 E
75	Khmelnitisky	49 23 N	27 0 E
91	Khmer Rep. = Cambodia ■	12 15 N	105 0 E
86	Khojak P.	30 55 N	66 30 E
77	Kholmsk	35 5 N	139 48 E
91	Khong, R.	14 7 N	105 51 E
75	Khoper, R.	52 0 N	43 20 E
68	Khóra Sfakion	35 15 N	24 9 E
81	Khorāsān □	34 0 N	58 0 E
91	Khorat, Cao Nguyen	15 30 N	102 50 E
91	Khorat = Nakhon Ratchasima	14 59 N	102 12 E
80	Khorramābād	33 30 N	48 25 E
80	Khorramshahr	30 29 N	48 15 E
81	Khūgīanī	31 28 N	66 14 E
87	Khulna	22 45 N	89 34 E
86	Khushab	32 20 N	72 20 E
80	Khūzestan □	31 0 N	50 0 E
81	Khvor	33 45 N	55 0 E
80	Khvoy	38 35 N	45 0 E
81	Khyber P.	34 10 N	71 8 E
113	Kiama	34 40 S	150 50 E
165	Kibombo	3 57 S	25 53 E
60	Kičevo	41 34 N	20 59 E
124	Kicking Horse P.	51 27 N	116 25W
21	Kidderminster	52 24 N	2 13W
45	Kiel	54 16 N	10 8 E
45	Kiel Canal = Nord Ostsee Kanal	54 15 N	9 40 E
49	Kielce	50 58 N	20 42 E
75	Kiev = Kiyev	50 30 N	30 28 E
68	Kifisiá	38 4 N	23 49 E
165	Kigali	1 5 S	30 4 E
165	Kigoma-Ujiji	5 30 S	30 0 E
102	Kii-Suido, Chan.	33 0 N	134 50 E
60	Kikinda	45 50 N	20 30 E
68	Kiklàdhes, Is.	37 20 N	24 30 E
41	Kil	59 30 N	13 20 E
113	Kilcoy	26 59 S	152 30 E
27	Kildare	53 10 N	6 50W
165	Kilimanjaro	3 7 S	37 20 E
165	Kilindini	4 4 S	39 40 E
80	Kilis	36 50 N	37 10 E
27	Kilkee	52 41 N	9 40W
27	Kilkenny	52 40 N	7 17W
68	Kilkís	40 58 N	22 57 E
27	Killala	54 13 N	9 12W
27	Killaloe	52 48 N	8 28W
125	Killarney, Canada	49 10 N	99 40W
27	Killarney, Eire	52 2 N	9 30W
24	Killiecrankie, P. of	56 44 N	3 46W
24	Killin	56 27 N	4 20W
68	Killíni, Mt.	37 54 N	22 25 E
27	Killybegs	54 38 N	8 26W
24	Kilmarnock	55 36 N	4 30W
113	Kilmore	37 25 S	144 53 E
165	Kilosa	6 48 S	37 0 E
27	Kilrush	52 39 N	9 30W
128	Kimball	41 17 N	103 20W
110	Kimberley, Canada	49 40 N	116 10W
168	Kimberley, S. Africa	28 43 S	24 46 E
131	Kimberly	42 33 N	114 25W
94	Kinabalu, Mt.	6 0 N	116 0 E
125	Kincaid	49 40 N	107 0W
122	Kincardine	44 10 N	81 40W
165	Kindu	2 55 S	25 50 E
75	Kineshma	57 30 N	42 5 E
113	King, I.	39 50 S	144 0 E
113	King, Mt.	25 10 S	147 31 E
148	King George B.	51 30 S	60 30W
121	King George Is.	53 40 N	80 30W
110	King Leopold, Ras.	17 20 S	124 20 E
110	King Sd.	16 50 S	123 20 E
120	King William I.	69 0 N	98 0W
168	King William's Town	32 51 S	27 22 E
113	Kingaroy	26 32 S	151 51 E
131	Kingman	35 12 N	114 2W
110	Kingoonya	30 54 N	135 18 E
131	Kings Canyon Nat. Park	37 0 N	118 45W
21	Kings Lynn	52 45 N	0 25 E
21	Kingsbridge	50 14 N	3 46W
27	Kingscourt	53 55 N	6 48W
122	Kingston, Canada	44 20 N	76 30W
139	Kingston, Jamaica	18 0 N	76 50W
114	Kingston, N.Z.	45 20 S	168 43 E
127	Kingston, N.Y.	41 55 N	74 0W
127	Kingston, Pa.	41 19 N	75 58W
127	Kingston, R.I.	41 29 N	71 30W
21	Kingston, U.K.	51 30 N	0 20W
139	Kingstown	13 10 N	61 10W
24	Kingussie	47 5 N	4 2W
165	Kinkala	4 18 S	14 49 E
102	Kinki □	33 30 N	136 0 E
114	Kinloch	44 51 S	168 20 E
41	Kinna	57 32 N	12 42 E
24	Kinross	56 13 N	3 25W
27	Kinsale	51 42 N	8 31W
165	Kinshasa	4 20 S	15 15 E
127	Kinston	35 18 N	77 35W
24	Kintyre, Pen.	55 30 N	5 35W
68	Kiparissía	37 15 N	21 40 E
68	Kiparissiakós Kól.	37 25 N	21 25 E
122	Kipawa Reserve Prov. Park	47 0 N	78 30W
45	Kirchheim	48 38 N	9 20 E
77	Kirensk	57 50 N	107 55 E
76	Kirgiz S.S.R. □	42 0 N	75 0 E
106	Kiribati ■	1 0 N	176 0 E
24	Kirkcaldy	56 7 N	3 10W
24	Kirkcudbright	54 50 N	4 3W
37	Kirkenes	69 40 N	30 5 E
24	Kirkintilloch	55 57 N	4 10W
122	Kirkland Lake	48 15 N	80 0W
128	Kirksville	40 8 N	92 35W
80	Kirkūk	35 30 N	44 21 E
24	Kirkwall	58 59 N	2 59W
75	Kirov	58 35 N	49 40 E
75	Kirovabad	40 45 N	46 10 E
75	Kirovograd	48 35 N	32 20 E
75	Kirovsk	67 48 N	33 50 E
24	Kirriemuir	56 41 N	3 0W
75	Kirsanov	52 35 N	42 40 E
86	Kirthar Ra.	27 0 N	67 0 E
37	Kiruna	67 50 N	20 20 E
102	Kiryū	36 25 N	139 20 E
41	Kisa	57 58 N	15 37 E
165	Kisangani	0 35 N	25 15 E
94	Kisaran	2 47 N	99 29 E
102	Kisarazu	35 25 N	139 59 E
86	Kishangarh	27 50 N	70 30 E
75	Kishinev	47 0 N	28 50 E
102	Kishiwada	34 28 N	135 22 E
165	Kisii	0 40 S	34 45 E
120	Kiska I.	52 0 N	177 30 E
49	Kiskörös	46 37 N	19 20 E
49	Kiskundorozsma	46 16 N	20 5 E
75	Kislovodsk	43 50 N	42 45 E
102	Kiso-Gawa, R.	35 2 N	136 45 E
49	Kispest	47 27 N	19 9 E
158	Kissidougou	9 5 N	10 0W
49	Kisújszállzás	47 12 N	20 50 E
165	Kisumu	0 3 S	34 45 E
49	Kisvárda	48 14 N	22 4 E
102	Kitakyūshū	33 50 N	130 50 E
165	Kitale	1 0 N	35 12 E
68	Kíthira	36 9 N	23 0 E
68	Kíthnos, I.	37 26 N	24 27 E
124	Kitimat	53 55 N	129 0W
127	Kittanning	40 49 N	79 30W
127	Kittery	43 7 N	70 42W
165	Kitwe	12 54 S	28 7 E
48	Kitzbühel	47 27 N	12 24 E
165	Kivu, L.	1 48 S	29 0 E
75	Kiyev	50 30 N	30 28 E
75	Kiyevskoye, Vdkhr.	51 0 N	30 0 E
75	Kizel	59 3 N	57 40 E
75	Kizlyar	43 51 N	46 40 E
76	Kizyl-Arvat	38 58 N	56 15 E
60	Kladanj	44 14 N	18 42 E
48	Kladno	50 10 N	14 7 E
48	Klagenfurt	46 38 N	14 20 E
75	Klaipeda	55 43 N	21 10 E
131	Klamath Falls	42 20 N	121 50W
63	Klanjec	46 3 N	15 45 E
95	Klaten	7 43 S	110 36 E
48	Klatovy	49 23 N	13 18 E
124	Klawak	55 35 N	133 0W
124	Kleena Kleene	52 0 N	124 50W
63	Klekovača, Mt.	44 25 N	16 32 E
168	Klerksdorp	26 51 S	26 38 E
45	Kleve	51 46 N	6 10 E
41	Klippan	56 8 N	13 10 E
49	Kłodzko	50 28 N	16 38 E
120	Klondike	64 0 N	139 40W
49	Klosterneuburg	48 18 N	16 19 E
120	Kluane, L.	61 25 N	138 50W
21	Knaresborough	54 1 N	1 29W
61	Knezha	43 30 N	23 56 E
21	Knighton	52 21 N	3 2W
34	Knokke	51 20 N	3 17 E
128	Knoxville, Iowa	41 20 N	93 5W
127	Knoxville, Tenn.	35 58 N	83 57W
173	Knud Rasmussen Ld.	80 0 N	55 0W
49	Knurów	50 13 N	18 38 E
121	Koartac	61 5 N	69 36W
102	Kobe	34 45 N	135 10 E
41	København	55 41 N	12 34 E
45	Koblenz	50 21 N	7 36 E
50	Kobyłka	52 21 N	21 10 E
60	Kočani	41 55 N	22 25 E
63	Kočevje	45 39 N	14 50 E
102	Kōchi	33 30 N	133 35 E
120	Kodiak	57 48 N	152 23W
120	Kodiak I.	57 30 N	152 45 E
159	Kodok	9 53 N	32 7 E
158	Koforidua	6 3 N	0 17W
102	Kōfu	35 40 N	138 30 E
41	Køge	55 27 N	12 11 E
86	Kohat	33 40 N	71 29 E
87	Kohima	25 35 N	94 10 E
174	Kohler Ra.	77 0 S	110 0W
76	Kokand	40 30 N	70 57 E
37	Kokkola	63 50 N	23 8 E
127	Kokomo	40 30 N	86 6W
121	Koksoak, R.	58 30 N	68 10W
169	Kokstad	30 32 S	29 29 E
75	Kola	68 45 N	33 8 E
86	Kolar	13 12 N	78 15 E
61	Kolarovgrad	43 27 N	26 42 E
60	Kolašin	42 50 N	19 31 E
95	Kolepom, I.	8 0 S	138 30 E
75	Kolguyev	69 20 N	48 30 E
86	Kolhapur	16 43 N	74 15 E
48	Kolín	50 2 N	15 9 E
45	Köln	50 56 N	9 58 E
50	Koło	52 14 N	18 40 E
50	Kołobrzeg	54 10 N	15 35 E
75	Kołomna	55 8 N	38 45 E
75	Kolomyya	48 31 N	25 2 E
87	Kolosib	24 15 N	92 45 E
76	Kolpashevo	58 20 N	83 5 E
75	Kolskiy Zaliv	69 23 N	34 0 E
165	Kolwezi	10 40 S	25 25 E
77	Kolyma, R.	64 40 N	153 0 E
49	Komárno	47 49 N	18 5 E
49	Komárom	47 43 N	18 7 E
102	Komatsu	36 25 N	136 30 E
75	Komi A.S.S.R.	64 0 N	55 0 E
49	Komló	46 15 N	18 16 E
102	Komoro	36 19 N	138 26 E
68	Komotiri	41 9 N	25 26 E
91	Kompong Som	10 38 N	103 30 E
77	Komsomolets, Os.	80 30 N	95 0 E
77	Komsomolsk	50 30 N	137 0 E
81	Konarha	35 15 N	71 0 E
77	Kondakovo	69 20 N	151 30 E
158	Koudougou	12 10 N	2 20W
87	Konglu	27 13 N	97 57 E
165	Kongolo	5 22 S	27 0 E
38	Kongsberg	59 39 N	9 39 E
75	Königsberg = Kaliningrad	54 42 N	20 32 E
50	Konin	52 12 N	18 15 E
60	Konjic	43 42 N	17 58 E
75	Konosha	61 0 N	40 5 E
50	Konstantynów Lódźki	51 45 N	19 20 E
45	Konstanz	47 39 N	9 10 E
158	Kontagora	10 23 N	5 27 E
80	Konya	37 52 N	32 35 E
110	Koonibba	31 58 S	133 27 E
124	Kootenay Nat. Park	51 0 N	116 0W
60	Kopaonik, Mts.	43 10 N	21 0 E
38	Kopervik	59 17 N	5 17 E
76	Kopeysk	55 7 N	61 37 E
41	Köping	59 31 N	16 3 E
41	Kopparbergs □	61 20 N	14 15 E
60	Korab, Mt.	41 44 N	20 40 E
68	Korça	40 37 N	20 50 E
63	Korčula, I.	42 57 N	17 0 E
80	Kordestān □	36 0 N	47 0 E
99	Korea ■	39 0 N	124 0 E
158	Korhogo	9 29 N	5 28 E

Korinthiakós Kól. | Lîbîya, Sahrâ'

68	Korinthiakós Kól.	38 16 N	22 30 E
68	Korinthía □	37 50 N	22 35 E
68	Kórinthos	37 26 N	22 55 E
102	Kōriyama	37 24 N	140 23 E
63	Kornat, I.	43 50 N	15 20 E
114	Koro Sea	17 30 S	179 45W
50	Koronowo	53 19 N	17 55 E
49	Körös, R.	46 30 N	142 42 E
77	Korsakov	46 30 N	142 42 E
41	Korsør	55 20 N	11 9 E
50	Korsze	54 11 N	21 9 E
34	Kortrijk	50 50 N	3 17 E
77	Koryakskiy Khrebet, Mts.	61 0 N	171 0 E
68	Kos, I.	36 50 N	27 15 E
50	Koscierzyna	54 8 N	17 59 E
124	Kosciusko I.	56 0 N	133 40W
49	Košice	48 42 N	21 15 E
60	Kosjerić	44 0 N	19 55 E
60	Kosovska-Mitrovica	42 54 N	20 52 E
63	Kostajnica	45 17 N	16 30 E
61	Kostenets	42 15 N	23 52 E
159	Kôstî	13 8 N	32 43 E
75	Kostroma	57 50 N	41 58 E
50	Kostrzyn	52 24 N	17 14 E
50	Koszalin	54 12 N	16 8 E
49	Köszeg	47 23 N	16 33 E
86	Kota	25 14 N	75 49 E
91	Kota Baharu	6 7 N	102 14 E
94	Kota Kinabalu	6 0 N	116 12 E
94	Kotabaru	3 20 S	116 20 E
94	Kotabumi	4 49 S	104 46 E
94	Kotawaringin	2 28 S	111 27 E
45	Köthen	51 44 N	11 59 E
37	Kotka	60 28 N	26 55 E
75	Kotlas	61 15 N	47 0 E
60	Kotor	42 25 N	18 47 E
86	Kotri	25 22 N	68 22 E
68	Kótronas	36 38 N	22 29 E
48	Kotschach Mauthern	46 40 N	13 0 E
86	Kottayam	9 35 N	76 33 E
120	Kotzebue	66 53 N	162 39W
68	Koufonísi, I.	34 56 N	26 8 E
165	Koula-Moutou	1 15 S	12 25 E
113	Koumala	21 38 S	149 15 E
76	Kounradskiy	47 20 N	75 0 E
145	Kourou	5 9 N	52 39W
158	Kouroussa	10 45 N	9 45W
60	Kovačica	45 5 N	20 38 E
75	Kovel	51 10 N	25 0 E
101	Kowloon	22 20 N	114 15 E
120	Koyukuk, R.	64 56 N	157 30W
68	Kozáni	40 19 N	21 47 E
60	Kozara, Mts.	45 0 N	17 0 E
86	Kozhikode = Calicut	11 15 N	75 43 E
75	Kozhva	65 10 N	57 0 E
50	Kozmin	51 48 N	17 27 E
50	Kozuchów	51 45 N	15 35 E
158	Kpalimé	6 57 N	0 37 E
158	Kpandu	7 2 N	0 18 E
91	Kra, Isthmus of = Kra, Kho Khot	10 15 N	99 30 E
91	Kra, Kho Khot	10 15 N	99 30 E
91	Kra Buri	10 22 N	98 46 E
60	Kragujevac	44 2 N	20 56 E
49	Krakow	50 5 N	20 0 E
75	Kramatorsk	48 50 N	37 30 E
41	Kramfors	62 55 N	17 48 E
63	Kranj	46 16 N	14 22 E
63	Krapina	46 10 N	15 52 E
49	Krapkowice	50 29 N	17 55 E
75	Krasavino	60 58 N	46 26 E
77	Kraskino	42 45 N	130 58 E
48	Kraslice	50 19 N	12 31 E
49	Krasnik	50 55 N	22 5 E
75	Krasnodar	45 5 N	38 50 E
75	Krasnokamsk	58 0 N	56 0 E
76	Krasnouralsk	58 0 N	60 0 E
76	Krasnovodsk	40 0 N	52 52 E
75	Krasnovishersk	60 23 N	56 59 E
77	Krasnoyarsk	56 8 N	93 0 E
50	Krasnystaw	50 57 N	23 5 E
75	Krasnyy Yar	46 43 N	48 23 E
45	Krefeld	51 20 N	6 22 E
68	Kremaston, L.	38 52 N	21 30 E
75	Kremenchug	49 5 N	33 25 E
75	Kremenchugskoye, Vdkhr.	49 20 N	32 30 E
60	Kremenica	40 55 N	21 25 E
48	Krems	48 25 N	15 36 E
86	Krishna, R.	15 43 N	80 55 E
87	Krishnanagar	23 24 N	88 33 E
38	Kristiansand	58 5 N	7 50 E
41	Kristianstad	56 5 N	14 7 E
38	Kristiansund	63 10 N	7 45 E
37	Kristinestad	62 18 N	21 25 E
68	Kriti, I.	35 15 N	25 0 E
68	Kritsá	35 10 N	25 41 E
60	Kriva Palanka	42 11 N	22 19 E
75	Krivoy Rog	47 51 N	33 20 E
60	Križevci	46 3 N	16 32 E
63	Krk, I.	45 5 N	14 56 E
63	Krka, R.	45 50 N	15 30 E
48	Krkonoše, Mts.	50 50 N	15 30 E
49	Krnov	50 5 N	17 40 E
50	Krobia	51 47 N	16 59 E
48	Kročehlavy	50 8 N	14 9 E
49	Kroměríz	49 18 N	17 21 E
41	Kronobergs □	56 45 N	14 30 E
75	Kronshtadt	60 5 N	29 35 E
168	Kroonstad	27 43 S	27 19 E
77	Kropotkin	58 50 N	115 10 E
50	Krośniewice	52 15 N	19 11 E
49	Krosno	49 35 N	21 56 E
50	Krotoszyn	51 42 N	17 23 E
63	Krsko	45 57 N	15 30 E
169	Krugersdorp	26 5 S	27 46 E
61	Krumovgrad	41 29 N	25 38 E
91	Krung Thep	13 45 N	100 35 E
49	Krupinica, R.	48 5 N	18 53 E
60	Kruševac	43 35 N	21 28 E
50	Krzyz	52 52 N	16 0 E
158	Ksar El Boukhari	35 5 N	2 52 E
158	Ksar el Kebir	35 0 N	6 0W
94	Kuala	2 46 N	105 47 E
91	Kuala Kangsar	4 49 N	100 57 E
91	Kuala Kubu Baharu	3 35 N	101 38 E
91	Kuala Lumpur	3 9 N	101 41 E
91	Kuala Selangor	3 20 N	101 15 E
91	Kuala Terengganu	5 20 N	103 8 E
94	Kualakapuas	2 55 S	114 20 E
94	Kualapembuang	3 14 S	112 38 E
91	Kuantan	3 49 N	103 20 E
75	Kuba	41 21 N	48 22 E
75	Kuban, R.	45 20 N	37 30 E
102	Kubokawa	33 12 N	133 8 E
48	Kuchenspitze, Mt.	47 3 N	10 14 E
94	Kuching	1 33 N	110 25 E
102	Kuchinotsu	32 36 N	130 11 E
95	Kudus	6 48 N	110 51 E
159	Kufra, El Wâhât et	24 17 N	23 15 E
48	Kuhnsdorf	46 37 N	14 38 E
81	Kūhpāyeh	32 44 N	52 20 E
165	Kuito	12 22 S	16 55 E
68	Kukësi □	42 15 N	20 15 E
91	Kulai	1 44 N	103 35 E
110	Kulgera	25 50 S	133 18 E
76	Kulsary	46 59 N	54 1 E
76	Kulunda	52 45 N	79 15 E
76	Kulyab	37 55 N	69 50 E
94	Kumai	2 52 S	111 45 E
102	Kumamoto	32 45 N	130 45 E
114	Kumara	42 37 S	171 12 E
158	Kumasi	6 41 N	1 38 E
158	Kumba	4 36 N	9 24 E
113	Kumbarilla	27 15 S	150 55 E
102	Kumagaya	36 9 N	139 22 E
41	Kumla	59 8 N	15 10 E
158	Kumo	10 1 N	11 12 E
87	Kumon Bum, Mts.	26 0 N	97 15 E
86	Kunch	26 0 N	79 10 E
81	Kunduz	36 50 N	68 50 E
76	Kungrad	43 6 N	58 54 E
41	Kungsbacka	57 30 N	12 7 E
95	Kuningan	6 59 S	108 29 E
87	Kunlong	23 20 N	98 50 E
73	Kunlun Shan, Mts.	36 0 N	82 0 E
96	Kunming	25 1 N	102 41 E
110	Kununurra	15 40 S	128 39 E
113	Kunwarara	22 25 S	150 7 E
37	Kuopio	62 53 N	27 35 E
95	Kupang	10 19 S	123 39 E
124	Kupreanof I.	56 50 N	133 30W
60	Kupres	44 1 N	17 15 E
75	Kura, R.	39 24 N	49 24 E
102	Kurashiki	34 40 N	133 50 E
102	Kure	34 14 N	132 32 E
76	Kurgaldzhino	50 35 N	70 20 E
76	Kurgan	55 30 N	65 0 E
77	Kurilskiye Os.	45 0 N	150 0 E
102	Kurino	31 57 N	130 43 E
86	Kurnool	15 45 N	78 0 E
113	Kurri Kurri	32 50 S	151 28 E
75	Kursk	51 42 N	36 11 E
102	Kurume	33 15 N	130 30 E
77	Kurya	61 15 N	108 10 E
102	Kushima	31 29 N	131 14 E
102	Kushimoto	33 28 N	135 47 E
102	Kushiro	43 0 N	144 30 E
87	Kushtia	23 55 N	89 5 E
120	Kuskokwim, R.	60 17 N	162 27W
120	Kuskokwim B.	59 45 N	162 25W
76	Kustanai	53 20 N	63 45 E
80	Kütahya	39 25 N	29 59 E
75	Kutaisi	42 19 N	42 40 E
94	Kutaraja = Banda Aceh	5 35 N	95 20 E
86	Kutch, G. of.	22 50 N	69 15 E
60	Kutina	45 29 N	16 48 E
48	Kutná Hora	49 57 N	15 16 E
50	Kutno	52 15 N	19 23 E
113	Kuttabul	21 5 S	148 48 E
159	Kutum	14 20 N	24 10 E
80	Kuwait ■	29 30 N	47 30 E
102	Kuwana	35 0 N	136 43 E
75	Kuybyshev, Kuyb. Obl.	53 12 N	50 9 E
75	Kuybyshev, Tatar A.S.S.R.	54 57 N	49 5 E
77	Kuyumba	61 10 N	97 10 E
75	Kuyto, Oz.	64 40 N	31 0 E
80	Kuzey Anadolu Dağlari	41 30 N	35 0 E
75	Kuznetsk	53 12 N	46 40 E
75	Kuzomen	66 22 N	36 50 E
63	Kvarner, G.	44 50 N	14 10 E
63	Kvarneric	44 43 N	14 37 E
145	Kwakoegron	5 25 N	55 25W
168	Kwando, R.	16 48 S	22 45 E
95	Kwatisore	3 7 S	139 59 E
110	Kwinana	32 15 S	115 47 E
50	Kwisa, R.	51 35 N	15 25 E
77	Kyakhta	50 30 N	106 25 E
87	Kyaukpadaung	20 52 N	95 8 E
87	Kyaukpyu	19 28 N	93 30 E
87	Kyaukse	21 36 N	96 10 E
169	Kyle Dam	20 14 S	31 0 E
113	Kynuna	21 35 S	141 55 E
165	Kyoga, L.	1 35 N	33 0 E
87	Kyonpyaw	17 12 N	95 10 E
102	Kyōto	35 0 N	135 45 E
80	Kyrenia	35 20 N	33 19 E
77	Kystatyam	67 15 N	123 0 E
77	Kytal Ktakh	65 30 N	123 40 E
87	Kyunhla	23 25 N	95 15 E
102	Kyūshū, I.	32 30 N	131 0 E
77	Kyzyl	51 50 N	94 30 E
76	Kzyl Orda	44 50 N	65 10 E

L

55	La Alcarria	40 31 N	2 45W
55	La Almarcha	39 41 N	2 24W
55	La Almunia de Doña Godino	41 29 N	1 23W
53	La Bañeza	42 17 N	5 54W
137	La Barca	20 20 N	102 40W
29	La Bassée	50 31 N	2 49 E
30	La Bastide-Puylaurent	44 35 N	3 55 E
28	La Baule	47 18 N	2 23 E
55	La Bisbal	41 58 N	3 2 E
137	La Boca	9 0 N	79 30 E
29	La Bresse	48 0 N	6 53 E
53	La Bureba	42 36 N	3 24W
53	La Campiña	37 45 N	4 45W
29	La Capelle	49 59 N	3 50 E
53	La Carolina	38 17 N	3 38W
29	La Chapelle-d'Angillon	47 21 N	2 25 E
30	La Charité-sur-Loire	47 10 N	3 0 E
30	La Châtre	46 35 N	1 59 E
45	La Chaux-de-Fonds	47 7 N	6 50 E
31	La Ciotat	43 12 N	5 36 E
53	La Coruña □	43 10 N	8 30W
144	La Dorada	5 30 N	74 40W
53	La Estrada	42 43 N	8 27W
29	La Fere	49 40 N	3 20 E
29	La Ferté	48 57 N	3 6 E
28	La Ferté-Bernard	48 10 N	0 40 E
28	La Ferté-Mace	48 35 N	0 21W
28	La Flèche	47 42 N	0 5W
53	La Fregeneda	40 58 N	6 54W
53	La Fuente de S. Esteban	40 49 N	6 15W
55	La Gineta	39 8 N	2 1W
31	La Grand' Comb	44 13 N	4 2 E
31	La Grande-Motte	48 35 N	1 4 E
110	La Grange	33 4 N	85, 0W
144	La Guaira	10 36 N	66 56W
53	La Guardia	41 56 N	8 52W
139	La Mabana	23 8 N	82 22W
28	La Haye du Puits	49 17 N	1 33W
55	La Junquera	42 25 N	2 53 E
53	La Linea de la Concepción	36 15 N	5 23W
125	La Loche	56 29 N	109 27W
53	La Lora	42 45 N	4 0W
34	La Louvière	50 27 N	4 10 E
30	La Machine	46 54 N	3 27 E
123	La Malbaie	47 40 N	70 10W
55	La Mancha	39 10 N	2 54W
120	La Martre, L.	63 0 N	118 0W
131	La Mesa	32 48 N	117 5W
55	La Muela	41 36 N	1 7W
31	La Mure	44 55 N	5 48 E
31	La Napoule	43 31 N	6 56 E
144	La Oroya	11 32 S	75 54W
53	La Palma	37 21 N	6 38W
139	La Palma	8 15 N	78 0W
158	La Palma, I.	28 40 N	17 52W
144	La Paragua	6 50 N	63 20W
148	La Paz, Arg.	30 50 S	59 45W
144	La Paz, Bolivia	16 20 S	68 10W
137	La Paz, Mexico	24 10 N	110 20W
102	La Perouse, Str.	45 40 N	142 0 E
137	La Piedad	20 20 N	102 1W
131	La Pine	40 53 N	80 45W
148	La Plata	35 0 S	57 55W
53	La Pola de Gordón	42 51 N	5 41W
127	La Porte	41 40 N	86 40W
53	La Puebla de Cazalla	37 14 N	5 19W
53	La Puebla de Montalbán	39 52 N	4 22W
55	La Puerta	38 22 N	2 45W
144	La Quiaca	22 5 S	65 35W
122	La Reine	48 50 N	79 30W
30	La Réole	44 35 N	0 1W
148	La Rioja, Arg.	29 20 S	67 0W
55	La Rioja, Sp.	42 20 N	2 20W
28	La Roche Bernard	47 32 N	2 18W
30	La Roche-sur-Yon	46 40 N	1 25W
30	La Rochelle	46 10 N	1 9W
55	La Roda	39 13 N	2 15W
139	La Romana	18 27 N	68 57W
55	La Sagra, Mt.	38 0 N	2 35W
128	La Salle	41 20 N	89 5W
122	La Sarre	48 45 N	79 15W
55	La Selva	42 0 N	2 45 E
31	La Seyne-sur-Mer	43 7 N	5 52 E
65	La Sila, Mt.	39 15 N	16 35 E
53	La Solana	38 59 N	3 14W
62	La Spézia	44 8 N	9 50 E
28	La Suze	47 54 N	0 2 E
144	La Tagua	0 3 N	74 40W
30	La Teste	44 34 N	1 9W
31	La-Tour-du-Pin	45 34 N	5 27 E
30	La Tranche	46 20 N	1 26W
122	La Tuque	47 30 N	72 50W
148	La Unión, Chile	40 10 S	73 0W
55	La Unión, Sp.	37 38 N	0 53W
144	La Urbana	7 8 N	66 56W
144	La Victoria	10 14 N	67 20W
158	Labé	11 24 N	12 16W
91	Labis	2 22 N	103 2 E
30	Labouheyre	44 13 N	0 55W
148	Laboulaye	34 10 S	63 30W
118	Labrador, Reg.	53 20 N	61 0W
123	Labrador City	52 42 N	67 0W
95	Labuha	0 30 S	127 30 E
95	Labuhan	6 26 S	105 50 E
125	Lac Seul	50 28 N	92 0W
30	Lacanau, Étang de	44 58 N	1 7W
30	Lacanau-Médoc	44 59 N	1 5W
30	Lacaune, Mts. de	43 43 N	2 50 E
72	Laccadive Is.	10 0 N	72 30 E
122	Lachine	45 30 N	73 40W
113	Lachlan, R.	34 21 S	143 57 E
122	Lachute	45 39 N	74 21W
124	Lacombe	52 30 N	113 50W
64	Laconi	39 54 N	9 4 E
127	Laconia	43 32 N	71 30W
30	Lacq	43 25 N	0 35W
86	Ladakh Ra.	34 0 N	78 0 E
68	Ládhon, R.	37 40 N	21 50 E
81	Lādīz	28 55 N	61 15 E
75	Ladozhskoye, Oz.	61 15 N	30 30 E
124	Ladysmith, Canada	49 0 N	124 0W
169	Ladysmith, S. Africa	28 32 S	29 46 E
106	Lae	6 40 S	147 2 E
128	Lafayette	30 18 N	92 0W
158	Lafia	8 30 N	8 34 E
38	Lagan, R.	56 33 N	12 56 E
53	Lage, Sp.	43 13 N	9 0W
45	Lage, W. Germany	52 0 N	8 47 E
38	Lågen, R.	61 8 N	10 25 E
81	Laghmān □	34 20 N	70 0 E
158	Laghouat	33 50 N	2 59 E
53	Lagõa	37 8 N	8 27W
53	Lagoaça	41 11 N	6 44W
65	Lagónegro	40 8 N	15 45 E
158	Lagos, Nigeria	6 25 N	3 27 E
53	Lagos, Port.	37 5 N	8 41W
30	Laguépie	44 8 N	1 57 E
148	Laguna	28 30 S	48 50 E
94	Lahat	3 45 S	103 30 E
80	Lahijan	37 12 N	50 1 E
86	Lahore	31 32 N	74 22 E
86	Lahore □	31 55 N	74 5 E
45	Lahr	48 20 N	7 52 E
113	Laidley	27 39 S	152 20 E
28	L'Aigle	48 45 N	0 38 E
24	Lairg	58 1 N	4 24W
94	Lais	3 35 S	102 0 E
148	Lajes	27 48 S	50 20W
49	Lajosmizse	47 3 N	19 32 E
127	Lake City, Fla.	30 10 N	82 40W
127	Lake City, S.C.	33 51 N	79 44W
121	Lake Harbour	62 30 N	69 50W
131	Lake Havasu City	34 25 N	114 20W
131	Lake Mead Nat. Rec. Area	36 20 N	114 30W
113	Lake Nash	20 57 S	138 0 E
122	Lake Superior Prov. Park	47 45 N	85 0W
122	Lake Traverse	45 56 N	78 4W
127	Lake Worth	26 36 N	80 3W
127	Lakeland	28 0 N	82 0W
131	Lakeport	39 1 N	122 56W
131	Lakeview	34 12 N	109 59W
87	Lakhimpur	27 14 N	94 7 E
68	Lakonía □	36 55 N	22 30 E
37	Lakselv	70 2 N	24 56 E
87	Lakshmi Kantapur	22 5 N	88 20 E
30	Lalinde	44 50 N	0 44 E
86	Lalitpur	24 42 N	78 28 E
87	Lamaing	15 25 N	97 53 E
48	Lambach	48 6 N	13 51 E
28	Lamballe	48 29 N	2 31W
165	Lambaréné	0 20 S	10 12 E
68	Lámbia	37 52 N	21 53 E
158	Lame	10 27 N	9 12 E
53	Lamego	41 5 N	7 52W
128	Lamesa	32 45 N	101 57W
24	Lammermuir Hills	55 50 N	24 0W
95	Lamon B.	14 30 N	122 20 E
91	Lampang	18 18 N	99 31 E
28	Lampaul	48 28 N	5 7 E
159	Lampedusa, I.	35 36 N	12 40 E
21	Lampeter	52 6 N	4 6W
125	Lampman	49 25 N	102 50W
94	Lampung □	5 30 S	105 0 E
165	Lamu	2 10 S	40 55 E
24	Lanark	55 40 N	3 48W
21	Lancashire □	53 40 N	2 30W
123	Lancaster, Canada	45 17 N	66 10W
21	Lancaster, U.K.	54 3 N	2 48W
127	Lancaster, Ky.	37 40 N	84 40W
127	Lancaster, S.C.	34 45 N	80 47W
121	Lancaster Sd.	74 0 N	84 0W
45	Landau	49 12 N	8 7 E
48	Landeck	47 9 N	10 34 E
131	Lander	42 50 N	108 49W
28	Landerneau	48 28 N	4 17W
30	Landes □	43 57 N	0 48W
30	Landes, Reg.	44 0 N	1 5W
28	Landivisiau	48 31 N	4 6W
19	Land's End	50 4 N	5 42W
45	Landsberg	48 3 N	10 52 E
41	Landskrona	56 53 N	12 50 E
127	Lanett	33 0 N	85 15W
30	Langeac	45 7 N	3 29 E
28	Langeais	47 20 N	0 24 E
41	Langeland, I.	54 56 N	10 48 E
45	Langen	53 36 N	8 36 E
45	Langeoog, I.	53 44 N	7 33 E
24	Langholm	55 9 N	2 59W
30	Langogne	44 43 N	3 50 E
30	Langon	44 33 N	0 16W
29	Langres	47 52 N	5 20 E
29	Langres, Plat. de	47 45 N	5 20 E
94	Langsa	4 30 N	97 57 E
91	Langson	21 52 N	106 42 E
30	Languedoc, Reg.	43 58 N	3 22 E
30	Lannemezan	43 8 N	0 23 E
28	Lannion	48 46 N	3 29W
122	Lansdowne House	52 5 N	88 0W
123	L'Anse au Loup	51 32 N	56 50W
64	Lanusei	39 53 N	9 31 E
158	Lanzarote, I.	29 0 N	13 40W
99	Lanzhou	36 1 N	103 52 E
91	Lao Cai	22 30 N	103 57 E
95	Laoag	18 7 N	120 34 E
95	Laoang	12 32 N	125 8 E
27	Laois □	53 0 N	7 20W
29	Laon	49 33 N	3 35 E
91	Laos ■	17 45 N	105 0 E
148	Lapa	25 46 S	49 44W
30	Lapalisse	46 15 N	3 44 E
60	Lapovo	44 10 N	21 2 E
37	Lappi □	64 33 N	25 10 E
37	Lappland, Reg.	68 7 N	24 0 E
77	Laptev Sea	76 0 N	125 0 E
63	L'Aquila	42 21 N	13 24 E
81	Lār	27 40 N	54 14 E
158	Larache	35 10 N	6 5W
31	Laragne-Montéglin	44 18 N	5 49 E
128	Laramie	41 15 N	105 29W
53	Laredo, Sp.	43 26 N	3 28W
128	Laredo, U.S.A.	27 34 N	99 29W
31	L'Argens, R.	43 24 N	6 44 E
31	L'Argentière	44 40 N	6 30 E
24	Largs	55 48 N	4 51W
68	Lárisa	39 38 N	22 28 E
68	Lárisa □	39 39 N	22 24 E
86	Larkana	27 32 N	68 2 E
80	Lárnaca	35 0 N	33 35 E
27	Larne	54 52 N	5 50W
110	Larrimah	15 35 S	133 12 E
174	Larsen Ice Shelf	67 0 S	62 0W
38	Larvik	59 4 N	10 0 E
30	Larzac, Causse du	44 0 N	3 17 E
85	Las Anod	8 26 N	47 19 E
55	Las Blancos	37 38 N	0 49W
131	Las Cruces	32 25 N	106 50W
148	Las Flores	36 0 S	59 0W
85	Las Khoreh	11 4 N	48 20 E
53	Las Marismas	37 5 N	6 20W
158	Las Palmas	28 10 N	15 28W
131	Las Vegas, Nev.	36 10 N	115 5W
128	Las Vegas, N. Mex.	35 35 N	105 10W
125	Lashburn	53 10 N	109 40W
87	Lashio	22 56 N	97 45 E
28	Lassay	48 27 N	0 30W
131	Lassen Pk.	40 20 N	121 0W
60	Lastovo, I.	42 46 N	16 55 E
144	Latacunga	0 50 S	78 35W
122	Latchford	47 20 N	79 50W
64	Latina	41 26 N	12 53 E
49	Latorica, R.	48 28 N	21 50 E
120	Latouche	60 0 N	147 55W
113	Latrobe	41 14 S	146 30 E
75	Latvian S.S.R. □	57 0 N	25 0 E
114	Lau Is.	17 0 S	178 30W
45	Lauchhammer	51 35 N	13 40 E
45	Lauenburg	53 23 N	10 33 E
113	Launceston, Australia	41 24 S	147 8 E
21	Launceston, U.K.	50 38 N	4 21W
113	Laura	33 10 S	138 18 E
65	Laureana di Borrello	38 28 N	16 5 E
128	Laurel, Miss.	31 50 N	89 0W
131	Laurel, Mont.	45 46 N	108 49W
24	Laurencekirk	56 50 N	2 30W
127	Laurens	34 32 N	82 2W
118	Laurentian Plat.	51 30 N	65 0W
123	Laurentides Prov. Park	47 50 N	71 50W
65	Lauria	40 3 N	15 50 E
45	Lausanne	46 32 N	6 38 E
123	Lauzon	46 48 N	71 4W
28	Laval	48 4 N	0 48W
30	Lavaur	43 42 N	1 49 E
30	Lavelanet	42 57 N	1 51 E
65	Lavello	41 4 N	15 47 E
110	Laverton	28 44 S	122 29 E
145	Lavras	21 20 S	45 0W
95	Lawu, Mt.	7 40 S	111 13 E
41	Laxå	59 0 N	14 37 E
30	Laye, R.	43 54 N	5 48 E
80	Laylá	22 10 N	46 40 E
107	Laysan I.	25 30 N	167 0W
63	Lazio □	42 10 N	12 30 E
30	Le Bouscat	44 53 N	0 32 E
30	Le Cap d'Agde	43 18 N	3 29 E
31	Le Chambon-Feugerolles	45 24 N	4 18 E
31	Le Creusot	46 50 N	4 24 E
28	Le Croisic	47 18 N	2 30W
30	Le Dorat	46 14 N	1 5 E
28	Le Havre	49 30 N	0 5 E
45	Le Locle	47 3 N	6 44 E
64	Le Madonie, Mts.	37 50 N	13 50 E
28	Le Mans	48 0 N	0 10 E
165	Le Marinel	10 25 S	25 17 E
128	Le Mars	43 0 N	96 0W
28	Le Mont-St-Michel	48 40 N	1 30W
28	Le Palais	47 21 N	3 10W
28	Le Petit-Quevilly	49 26 N	1 0 E
30	Le Puy	45 3 N	3 52 E
29	Le Quesnoy	50 15 N	3 38 E
31	Le Teil	44 34 N	4 41 E
29	Le Thillot	47 52 N	6 55 E
29	Le Touquet-Paris-Plage	50 30 N	1 36 E
28	Le Tréport	50 3 N	1 20 E
21	Lea, R.	51 30 N	0 1 E
128	Lead	44 20 N	103 40W
125	Leader	50 50 N	109 30W
24	Leadhills	55 25 N	3 47W
122	Leamington, Canada	42 10 N	82 30W
21	Leamington, U.K.	52 18 N	1 32W
110	Learmonth	22 40 S	114 10 E
125	Leask	53 5 N	106 45W
50	Łeba	54 45 N	17 32 E
127	Lebanon, Ind.	40 3 N	86 55W
128	Lebanon, Mo.	37 40 N	92 40W
131	Lebanon, Ore.	44 31 N	122 57W
127	Lebanon, Pa.	40 20 N	76 28W
127	Lebanon, Tenn.	36 15 N	86 20W
80	Lebanon ■	34 0 N	36 0 E
50	Lębork	54 33 N	17 46 E
53	Lebrija	36 53 N	6 5W
148	Lebu	37 40 S	73 47W
65	Lecce	40 20 N	18 10 E
62	Lecco	45 50 N	9 27 E
62	Lecco, L. di	45 51 N	9 22 E
55	Lécera	41 13 N	0 43W
48	Lech	47 13 N	10 9 E
45	Lech, R.	47 19 N	10 27 E
30	Lectoure	43 56 N	0 38 E
50	Łęczyca	52 5 N	19 45 E
21	Ledbury	52 3 N	2 25W
53	Ledesma	41 6 N	5 59W
124	Leduc	53 20 N	113 30W
27	Lee, R.	51 51 N	9 2W
21	Leeds	53 48 N	1 34W
21	Leek	53 7 N	2 2W
45	Leer	53 13 N	7 29 E
34	Leeuwarden	53 15 N	5 48 E
139	Leeward Is.	16 30 N	63 30W
95	Legazpi	13 10 N	123 46 E
63	Legnago	45 10 N	11 19 E
62	Legnano	45 35 N	8 55 E
50	Legnica □	51 20 N	16 0 E
45	Lehrte	52 22 N	9 58 E
21	Leicester	52 39 N	1 9W
21	Leicester □	52 40 N	1 10W
34	Leiden	52 9 N	4 30 E
45	Leine, R.	48 54 N	10 1 E
27	Leinster □	53 0 N	7 10W
53	Leipzig	51 20 N	12 23 E
53	Leiria	39 46 N	8 53W
24	Leith	55 59 N	3 10W
21	Leith Hill	51 10 N	0 23W
49	Leitha, R.	47 54 N	17 17 E
27	Leitrim	54 0 N	8 5W
68	Lekhainá	37 57 N	21 16 E
128	Leland	33 25 N	90 52W
45	Léman, L.	46 26 N	6 30 E
95	Lemery	13 58 N	120 56 E
45	Lemgo	52 2 N	8 52 E
41	Lemvig	56 33 N	8 20 E
77	Lena	72 25 N	126 40 E
63	Lendinara	45 4 N	11 37 E
45	Lengerich	52 12 N	7 50 E
76	Leninabad	40 17 N	69 37 E
75	Leninakan	41 0 N	42 50 E
75	Leningrad	59 55 N	30 20 E
75	Leninsk	48 40 N	45 15 E
76	Leninsk Kuznetskiy	55 10 N	86 10 E
77	Leninskoye	47 56 N	132 38 E
45	Lenne, R.	51 25 N	7 30 E
62	Leno	45 24 N	10 14 E
29	Lens	50 26 N	2 50 E
77	Lensk	60 48 N	114 55 E
65	Lentini	37 18 N	15 0 E
48	Leoben	47 22 N	15 5 E
21	Leominster, U.K.	52 15 N	2 43W
127	Leominster, U.S.A.	42 30 N	71 44W
137	León, Mexico	21 7 N	101 30W
139	León, Nic.	12 20 N	86 51W
53	León, Sp.	42 38 N	5 34W
53	Léon, Mt. de	42 30 N	6 18W
165	Léopold II, L. = Mai-Ndombe, L.	2 0 S	18 0 E
165	Léopoldville = Kinshasa	4 20 S	15 15 E
53	Lepe	37 15 N	7 12W
75	Lepel	54 50 N	28 40 E
77	Lepikha	64 45 N	125 55 E
53	Lequeito	43 20 N	2 32W
62	Lérici	44 4 N	9 48 E
55	Lérida	41 37 N	0 39 E
53	Lerma	42 0 N	3 47W
68	Léros, I.	37 10 N	26 50 E
29	Lérouville	48 50 N	5 30 E
41	Lerum	57 46 N	12 16 E
24	Lerwick	60 10 N	1 10W
31	Les Ares	43 27 N	6 29 E
30	Les Herbiers	46 52 N	1 0W
28	Les Ponts-de-Cé	47 25 N	0 30W
30	Les Sables-d'Olonne	46 30 N	1 45W
137	Les Tres Marías, Is.	12 20 N	106 30W
65	Lésina, L. di	41 53 N	15 25 E
60	Leskovac	43 0 N	21 58 E
28	Lesneven	48 35 N	4 20W
60	Lešnica	44 39 N	19 20 E
77	Lesosibirsk	58 16 N	92 29 E
169	Lesotho ■	29 40 S	28 0 E
77	Lesozarodsk	45 30 N	133 20 E
30	Lesparre-Médoc	45 18 N	0 57W
28	Lessay	49 14 N	1 30W
139	Lesser Antilles, Is.	12 30 N	61 0W
95	Lesser Sunda Is.	7 30 S	117 0 E
68	Lésvos, I.	39 0 N	26 20 E
50	Leszno	51 50 N	16 30 E
21	Letchworth	51 58 N	0 13W
95	Leti, Kep.	8 10 S	128 0 E
144	Leticia	4 0 S	70 0W
87	Letpadan	17 45 N	96 0 E
87	Letpan	19 28 N	93 52 E
27	Letterkenny	54 57 N	7 42W
51	Leu	44 10 N	24 0 E
30	Leucate	42 56 N	3 3 E
94	Leuser, Mt.	4 0 N	96 51 E
34	Leuven	50 52	4 42 E
68	Levádhia	38 26 N	22 54 E
31	Levant, Î. du	43 3 N	6 28 E
62	Lévanto	44 10 N	9 37 E
128	Levelland	33 38 N	102 17W
24	Leven	56 12 N	3 0W
24	Leven, L.	56 12 N	3 22W
45	Leverkusen	51 2 N	6 59 E
30	Levet	46 56 N	2 22 E
49	Levice	48 13 N	18 35 E
114	Levin	40 37 S	175 18 E
123	Levis	46 48 N	71 9W
68	Levítha, I.	37 0 N	26 28 E
68	Lévka, Mt.	35 18 N	24 3 E
68	Levkás	38 48 N	20 43 E
61	Levski	43 21 N	25 10 E
21	Lewes	50 53 N	0 2 E
24	Lewis, I.	58 10 N	6 40W
131	Lewis Ra.	20 3 S	128 50 E
123	Lewisporte	49 15 N	55 3W
127	Lexington, Ky.	38 6 N	84 30W
128	Lexington, Mo.	39 7 N	93 55W
128	Lexington, Neb.	40 48 N	99 45W
127	Lexington, N.C.	35 50 N	80 13W
30	Leze, R.	43 40 N	5 28 E
68	Lezha	41 47 N	19 42 E
30	Lezoux	45 49 N	3 21 E
96	Lhasa	29 25 N	90 58 E
99	Lianyungang	34 43 N	119 28 E
99	Liaoning □	42 0 N	122 0 E
99	Liaoyang	41 15 N	122 58 E
99	Liaoyuan	42 58 N	125 2 E
120	Liard, R.	61 52 N	121 18W
128	Liberal	37 4 N	101 0W
48	Liberec	50 47 N	15 7 E
158	Liberia ■	6 30 N	9 30W
159	Lîbîya, Sahrâ', Des.	27 35 N	25 0 E

M

Maranhão Montevarchi

145	Maranhão = São Luís	2 39 S	44 15W
63	Marano, L. di	45 42 N	13 13 E
144	Marañón, R.	4 50 S	75 35W
80	Maraş	37 37 N	36 53 E
51	Mărăşeşti	45 52 N	27 5 E
68	Marathókambos	37 43 N	26 42 E
113	Marathon	20 51 S	143 32 E
53	Marbella	36 30 N	4 57W
110	Marble Bar	21 9 S	119 44 E
49	Marcal, R.	47 41 N	17 32 E
62	Marcaria	45 7 N	10 34 E
21	March	57 33 N	0 5 E
63	Marche □	43 22 N	13 10 E
30	Marche, Reg.	46 5 N	2 10 E
34	Marche-en-Famenne	50 14 N	5 19 E
65	Marcianise	41 3 N	14 16 E
29	Marck	50 57 N	1 57 E
106	Marcus I.	24 0 N	153 45 E
86	Mardan	34 12 N	72 2 E
24	Maree, L.	57 40 N	5 30W
113	Mareeba	16 59 S	145 28 E
63	Maremma, Reg.	42 45 N	11 15 E
124	Margaret Bay	51 20 N	127 20W
30	Margaride, Monts de la	44 43 N	3 38 E
144	Margarita, Is. de	11 0 N	64 0W
21	Margate	51 23 N	1 24 E
65	Margharita d'Savoia	41 25 N	16 5 E
75	Mari A.S.S.R. □	56 30 N	48 0 E
114	Maria van Diemen, C.	34 29 S	172 40 E
106	Mariana Is.	17 0 N	145 0 E
139	Marianao	23 8 N	82 24W
48	Mariánské Lázně	49 57 N	12 41 E
63	Maribor	46 36 N	15 40 E
121	Maricourt	61 36 N	71 57W
139	Marie-Galante, I.	15 56 N	61 16W
37	Mariehamn	60 5 N	19 57 E
168	Mariental	24 36 S	18 0 E
127	Marietta, Ga.	34 0 N	84 30W
127	Marietta, Ohio	39 27 N	81 27W
139	Marigot	15 32 N	61 18W
76	Marniisk	56 10 N	87 20 E
145	Marília	22 0 S	50 0W
148	Maringá	23 35 S	51 50W
128	Marion, Ill.	37 45 N	88 55W
127	Marion, Ind.	40 35 N	85 40W
128	Marion, Iowa	42 2 N	91 36W
127	Marion, Ohio	40 38 N	83 8W
127	Marion, S.C.	34 11 N	79 22W
127	Marion, Va.	36 51 N	81 29W
31	Maritimes, Alpes, Mts.	44 10 N	7 10 E
61	Maritsa	42 1 N	25 50 E
41	Markaryd	56 28 N	13 35 E
21	Market Drayton	52 55 N	2 30W
21	Market Harborough	52 29 N	0 55W
21	Market Rasen	53 24 N	0 20W
174	Markham, Mt.	83 0 S	164 0 E
50	Marki	52 20 N	21 2 E
60	Markovac	44 14 N	21 7 E
114	Marlborough □	41 45 S	173 33 E
113	Marlborough	22 46 S	149 52 E
21	Marlborough Downs	51 25 N	1 55W
128	Marlin	31 25 N	96 50W
86	Marmagao	15 25 N	73 56 E
80	Marmara Denizi, Sea	40 45 N	28 15 E
63	Marmolada, Mt.	46 25 N	11 55 E
122	Marmora	44 28 N	77 41W
29	Marne □	49 0 N	4 10 E
29	Marne, R.	48 49 N	2 24 E
49	Maros, R.	46 15 N	20 13 E
107	Marquesas Is.	9 0 S	139 30W
127	Marquette	46 30 N	87 21W
159	Marra, J.	7 20 N	27 35 E
158	Marrakech	31 40 N	8 0W
113	Marrawah	40 56 S	144 41 E
113	Marree	29 39 S	138 1 E
159	Marsá Susah	32 52 N	21 59 E
165	Marsabit	2 18 N	38 0 E
64	Marsala	37 48 N	12 25 E
113	Marsden	33 47 N	147 32 E
31	Marseille	43 18 N	5 23 E
128	Marshall, Minn.	44 25 N	95 45W
128	Marshall, Mo.	39 8 N	93•15W
128	Marshall, Tex.	32 29 N	94 20W
106	Marshall Is.	9 0 N	171 0 E
128	Marshfield	44 42 N	90 10W
87	Martaban	16 30 N	97 35 E
87	Martaban, G. of	15 40 N	96 30 E
30	Martagne-s.-Sèvre	49 59 N	0 57W
94	Martapura, Kalimantan	3 22 S	114 56 E
94	Martapura, Sumatera	4 19 S	104 22 E
159	Marte	12 23 N	13 46 E
113	Marthaguy Creek	30 16 S	147 35 E
127	Martha's Vineyard	41 25 N	70 35W
45	Martigny	46 6 N	7 3 E
31	Martigues	43 24 N	5 4 E
49	Martin	49 6 N	18 48 E
55	Martín, R.	41 18 N	0 19W
152	Martin Vaz, I.	20 30 S	28 15W
65	Martina Franca	40 42 N	17 20 E
139	Martinique, I.	14 40 N	61 0W
127	Martins Ferry	40 5 N	80 46W
48	Martinsberg	48 22 N	15 9 E
127	Martinsburg	39 30 N	77 57W
127	Martinsville, Ind.	39 29 N	86 23W
127	Martinsville, Va.	36 41 N	79 52W
114	Marton	40 4 S	175 23 E
53	Martos	37 44 N	3 58W
102	Marugame	34 15 N	133 55 E
113	Marulan	34 43 S	150 3 E
30	Marvejols	44 33 N	3 19 E
86	Marwar	25 43 N	73 45 E
76	Mary	37 40 N	61 50 E
113	Maryborough	25 31 S	152 37 E
127	Maryland □	39 10 N	76 40W
21	Maryport	54 43 N	3 30W
123	Marystown	47 10 N	55 10W
131	Marysville	39 14 N	121 40W
127	Maryville	35 50 N	84 0W
159	Marzūq	25 53 N	14 10 E
165	Masaka	0 21 S	31 45 E
95	Masamba	2 30 S	120 15 E
55	Masanasa	39 25 N	0 25W
81	Masandam, Ras.	26 30 N	56 30 E
165	Masasi	10 45 S	38 52 E
139	Masaya	12 0 N	86 7W
95	Masbate	12 20 N	123 30 E
158	Mascara	35 26 N	0 6 E
168	Maseru	29 18 S	27 30 E
81	Mashhad	36 20 N	59 35 E
122	Mashkode	47 2 N	84 7W
81	Mashūray	32 5 N	68 20 E
165	Masindi	1 40 N	41 43 E
80	Masjed Soleyman	31 55 N	49 25 E
81	Maskin	23 44 N	56 52 E
55	Masnou	41 28 N	2 20 E
81	Masqay	23 37 N	58 36 E
62	Massa	44 2 N	10 7 E
62	Massa Maríttima	43 3 N	10 52 E
127	Massachusetts □	42 25 N	72 0W
62	Massarossa	43 53 N	10 17 E
159	Massawa = Mitsiwa	15 35 N	39 25 E
127	Massena	44 52 N	74 55W
30	Massiac	45 15 N	3 11 E
30	Massif Central Reg.	45 30 N	2 21 E
127	Massillon	40 47 N	81 30W
114	Masterton	40 56 S	175 39 E
80	Mastūrah	23 7 N	38 52 E
102	Masuda	34 40 N	131 51 E
95	Mataboor	1 41 S	138 3 E
122	Matachewan	47 50 N	80 55W
165	Matadi	5 52 S	13 31 E
139	Matagalpa	13 10 N	85 40W
122	Matagami	49 45 N	77 34W
86	Matale	7 30 N	80 44 E
137	Matamoros	18 2 N	98 17W
139	Matanzas	23 0 N	81 40W
86	Matara	5 58 N	80 30 E
55	Mataró	41 32 N	2 29 E
55	Matarraña, R.	41 14 N	0 22 E
114	Mataura	46 11 S	168 51 E
137	Matehuala	23 40 N	100 50W
63	Matélica	43 15 N	13 0 E
65	Matera	40 40 N	16 37 E
49	Mátészalka	47 58 N	22 20 E
86	Mathura	27 30W	77 48 E
21	Matlock	53 8 N	1 32W
158	Matmata	33 30 N	9 59 E
145	Mato Grosso □	14 0 S	54 0W
156	Matopo	20 36 S	28 20 E
53	Matosinhos	41 11 N	8 42W
81	Matrah	23 37 N	58 30 E
159	Matrûh	31 19 N	27 9 E
102	Matsumoto	36 15 N	138 0 E
102	Matsusaka	34 34 N	136 32 E
102	Matsuyama	33 45 N	132 45 E
86	Mattancheri	9 50 N	76 15 E
122	Mattawa	46 20 N	78 45W
45	Matterhorn, Mt.	45 58 N	7 39 E
139	Matthew Town	20 57 N	73 40W
94	Matua	2 58 S	110 52 E
144	Maturín	9 45 N	63 11W
29	Maubeuge	50 17W	3 57 E
144	Maués	3 20 S	57 45W
133	Maui, I.	20 45 N	156 20 E
87	Maulamyaing	16 30 N	97 40 E
133	Mauna Loa, Mt.	19 50 N	155 28 E
87	Maungmagan Is.	41 0 S	97 48 E
31	Maures, Mts.	43 15 N	6 15 E
31	Maurienne	45 15 N	6 20 E
158	Mauritania ■	20 50 N	10 0W
153	Mauritius ■	20 0 S	57 0 E
113	Maxwelton	39 51 S	174 49 E
139	May Pen	17 58 N	77 15W
55	Maya	43 12 N	1 29W
137	Maya Mts.	16 30 N	89 0W
139	Mayagüez	18 12 N	67 9W
113	Maydena	42 45 S	146 39 E
45	Mayen	50 18 N	7 10 E
28	Mayenne	48 20 N	0 38W
28	Mayenne □	48 10 N	0 40W
127	Mayfield	36 45 N	88 40W
75	Maykop	44 35 N	40 25 E
122	Maynooth, Canada	45 14 N	77 56W
27	Maynooth, Eire	53 22 N	6 38W
27	Mayo □	53 47 N	9 7W
53	Mayorga	42 10 N	5 16W
127	Maysville	38 43 N	84 16W
165	Mayumba	3 25 S	10 39 E
77	Mayya	61 44 N	130 18 E
165	Mazabuka	15 52 S	27 44 E
145	Mazagão	0 20 S	51 50W
124	Mazama	49 43 N	120 8W
30	Mazamet	43 30 N	2 20 E
81	Mazan Darān □	36 30 N	53 30 E
64	Mazara del Vallo	37 40 N	12 34 E
81	Mazār-e-Sharīf	36 41 N	67 0 E
148	Mazarredo	47 10 S	66 50W
55	Mazarrón	37 38 N	1 19W
55	Mazarrón, G. de	37 27 N	1 19W
137	Mazatlán	23 10 N	106 30W
65	Mazzarino	37 19 N	14 12 E
169	Mbabane	26 18 S	31 6 E
165	M'Baiki	3 53 N	18 1 E
165	Mbala	8 46 S	31 17 E
165	Mbandaka	0 1 S	18 18 E
165	Mbanza Congo	6 18 S	14 16 E
165	Mbarara	0 35 S	30 25 E
165	Mbeya	8 54 S	33 29 E
165	Mbuji Maya	6 9 S	23 40 E
165	Mbulu	3 45 S	35 30 E
165	Mchinji	13 47 S	32 58 E
131	Mead, L.	36 10 N	114 10W
125	Meadow Lake	54 10 N	108 10W
127	Meadville	41 39 N	80 9W
27	Meath □	53 32 N	6 40W
30	Meaulne	46 36 N	2 28 E
29	Meaux	48 58 N	2 50 E
80	Mecca = Makkah	21 30 N	39 54 E
34	Mechelen	51 2 N	4 29 E
45	Mecklenburger, B.	54 20 N	11 40 E
94	Medan	3 40 N	98 38 E
148	Medanosa, Pta.	48 0 S	66 0W
158	Medéa	36 12 N	2 50 E
144	Medellín	6 15 N	75 35W
158	Mederdra	17 0 N	15 38W
131	Medford	42 20 N	122 52W
51	Mediaş	46 9 N	24 22 E
63	Medicina	44 29 N	11 38 E
131	Medicine Bow	41 56 N	106 11W
125	Medicine Hat	50 0 N	110 45W
127	Medina	43 15 N	78 27W
53	Medina del Campo	41 18 N	4 55W
53	Medina-Sidonia	36 28 N	5 57W
55	Medinaceli	41 12 N	2 30W
17	Mediterranean Sea	36 0 N	15 0 E
30	Médoc, Reg.	45 10 N	0 56W
75	Medveditsa, R.	49 0 N	43 58 E
77	Medvezhi Oshova	71 0 N	161 0 E
75	Medvezhyegorsk	63 0 N	34 25 E
21	Medway, R.	51 27 N	0 44 E
110	Meekatharra	26 32 S	118 29 E
45	Meerane	50 51 N	12 30 E
86	Meerut	29 1 N	77 50 E
68	Megalópolis	37 25 N	22 7 E
123	Mégantic	45 36 N	70 56W
31	Mégève	45 51 N	6 37 E
87	Meghalaya □	25 50 N	91 0 E
51	Mehadia	44 56 N	22 23 E
86	Mehsana	23 39 N	72 26 E
30	Mehun-sur-Yèvre	47 10 N	2 13 E
87	Meiktila	21 0 N	96 0 E
45	Meiningen	50 32 N	10 25 E
53	Meira, Sa. de	43 15 N	7 15W
30	Méjean, Causse	44 15 N	3 30 E
158	Meknès	33 57 N	5 33W
91	Mekong, R.	10 33 N	105 24 E
91	Melaka □	2 17 N	102 18 E
91	Melaka	2 15 N	102 15 E
94	Melalap	5 10 N	116 5 E
68	Mélambes	35 8 N	24 40 E
106	Melanesia, Arch.	4 0 S	155 0 E
113	Melbourne	37 40 S	145 0 E
137	Melchor Múzquiz	27 50 N	101 40W
45	Meldorf	54 5 N	9 5 E
62	Melegnano	45 21 N	9 20 E
75	Melekess = Dimitrovgrad	54 25 N	49 33 E
65	Melfi	41 0 N	15 40 E
125	Melfort	52 50 N	105 40W
53	Melgar de Fernamental	42 27 N	4 17W
158	Melilla	35 21 N	2 57W
125	Melita	49 15 N	101 5W
75	Melitopol	46 50 N	35 22 E
48	Melk	48 13 N	15 20 E
30	Melle	46 14 N	0 10W
48	Mělník	50 22 N	14 23 E
113	Melrose	55 35 N	2 44W
21	Melton Mowbray	52 46 N	0 52W
29	Melun	48 32 N	2 39 E
110	Melville, I	75 30 N	111 0W
123	Melville, L.	53 45 N	59 40W
121	Melville Pen.	68 0 N	84 0W
75	Memel = Klaipeda	55 43 N	21 10 E
45	Memmingen	47 59 N	10 12 E
128	Memphis	35 7 N	90 0W
21	Menai Str.	53 7 N	4 20W
30	Mende	44 31 N	3 30 E
21	Mendip Hills	51 17 N	2 40W
131	Mendocino	39 26 N	123 50W
148	Mendoza	32 50 S	68 52W
144	Mene Grande	9 49 N	70 56W
80	Menemen	38 36 N	27 4 E
34	Menen	50 47 N	3 7 E
64	Menfi	37 36 N	12 57 E
94	Menggala	4 20 S	105 15 E
53	Mengíbar	37 58 N	3 48W
113	Menindee	32 20 N	142 25 E
128	Menominee	45 9 N	87 39W
55	Menorca, I.	40 0 N	4 0 E
94	Mentawai, Kep.	2 0 S	99 0 E
31	Menton	43 50 N	7 29 E
159	Menzel-Temime	36 46 N	11 0 E
75	Menzelinsk	55 43 N	53 8 E
34	Meppel	52 42 N	6 12 E
55	Mequinenza	41 22 N	0 17 E
68	Merabéllou, Kól.	35 10 N	25 50 E
95	Merak	5 55 S	106 1 E
63	Merano	46 40 N	11 10 E
95	Merauke	8 29 S	120 24 E
63	Mercato Saraceno	43 57 N	12 11 E
131	Merced	37 25 N	120 30W
148	Mercedes, Buenos Aires	34 40 S	59 30W
148	Mercedes, Corrientes	29 10 S	58 5W
148	Mercedes, San Luis	33 40 S	65 30W
148	Mercedes, Uruguay	33 12 S	58 0W
114	Mercer	37 16 S	175 5 E
121	Mercy, C.	65 0 N	62 30W
148	Meredith, C.	52 15 S	60 40W
51	Merei	45 7 N	26 43 E
29	Méréville	48 20 N	2 5 E
91	Mergui	12 30 N	98 35 E
91	Mergui Arch. = Myeik Kyunzu	11 30 N	97 30 E
137	Mérida, Mexico	20 50 N	89 40W
53	Mérida, Sp.	38 55 N	6 25W
144	Mérida, Ven.	8 36 N	71 8W
127	Meriden	41 33 N	72 47W
131	Meridian, Id.	43 41 N	116 20W
128	Meridian, Miss.	32 20 N	88 42W
145	Meriruma	1 15 N	54 50W
34	Merksem	51 16 N	4 25 E
29	Merlebach	49 5 N	6 52 E
159	Merowe	18 29 N	31 46 E
128	Merrill	45 11 N	89 41W
21	Mersea I.	51 48 N	0 55 E
45	Merseburg	51 20 N	12 0 E
21	Mersey, R.	53 25 N	3 0W
21	Merseyside □	53 25W	2 55W
21	Merthyr Tydfil	51 45 N	3 23W
53	Mértola	37 40 N	7 40 E
29	Méru	49 13 N	2 8 E
165	Meru	0 3 N	37 40 E
29	Méry	48 30 N	3 52 E
45	Merzig	49 26 N	6 37 E
131	Mesa	33 20 N	111 56W
81	Meshed = Mashhad	36 20 N	59 35 E
131	Mesilla	32 20 N	107 0W
68	Mesolóngion	38 27 N	21 28 E
80	Mesopotamia, Reg. = Al Jazirah, Reg.	33 30 N	44 0 E
65	Messina, It.	38 10 N	15 32 E
169	Messina, S.Africa	22 20 S	30 12 E
65	Messina, Str. di	38 5 N	15 35 E
68	Messíni	37 4 N	22 1 E
68	Messinía □	37 10 N	22 0 E
68	Messiniakós Kól.	36 45 N	22 5 E
144	Meta, R.	6 12 N	67 28W
122	Metagama	47 0 N	81 55W
148	Metán	25 30 S	65 0W
114	Methven	43 38 S	171 40 E
61	Metkovets	43 37 N	23 10 E
60	Metković	43 6 N	17 39 E
63	Metlika	45 40 N	15 20 E
128	Metropolis	37 10 N	88 47W
68	Métsovon	39 48 N	21 12 E
29	Metz	49 8 N	6 10 E
94	Meulaboh	4 11 N	96 3 E
29	Meulan	49 0 N	1 52 E
29	Meurthe, R.	48 47 N	6 9 E
29	Meurthe-et-Moselle □	48 52 N	6 0 E
29	Meuse □	49 8 N	5 25 E
34	Meuse, R.	51 49 N	5 1 E
128	Mexia	31 38 N	96 32W
145	Mexiana, I.	0 0	49 30W
137	Mexicali	32 40 N	115 30W
137	Mexico, Mexico	19 20 N	99 10W
128	Mexico, U.S.A.	39 10 N	91 55W
137	Mexico ■	20 0 N	100 0W
139	Mexico, Gulf of	26 0 N	90 0W
45	Meyenburg	53 19 N	12 15 E
75	Mezen, R.	66 11 N	43 59 E
30	Mèze	43 27 N	3 36 E
75	Mezen	65 50 N	44 20 E
28	Mézidon	49 5 N	0 1W
30	Mézin	44 4 N	0 16 E
49	Mezóberény	46 49 N	21 3 E
49	Mezökövesd	47 49 N	20 35 E
49	Mezötur	47 0 N	20 41 E
86	Mhow	22 33 N	75 50 E
127	Miami	25 52 N	80 15W
127	Miami Beach	25 49 N	80 6W
80	Mīāndowāb āb Zanjān	37 0 N	46 5 E
80	Mīāneh	37 30 N	47 40 E
86	Mianwali	32 38 N	71 28 E
99	Miaoli	24 37 N	120 49 E
76	Miass	54 59 N	60 6 E
51	Micăsasa	46 7 N	24 7 E
49	Michalovce	48 44 N	21 54 E
127	Michigan □	44 40 N	85 40W
127	Michigan, L.	44 0 N	87 0W
127	Michigan City	41 42 N	86 56W
123	Michikamau L.	54 0 N	6 0W
122	Michipicoten I.	47 55 N	85 45W
122	Michipicoten River	47 50 N	84 58W
106	Micronesia, Arch.	17 0 N	160 0 E
21	Mid Glamorgan □	51 40 N	3 25W
34	Middelburg, Neth.	51 30 N	3 36 E
168	Middelburg, S. Africa	31 30 S	25 0 E
41	Middelfart	55 30 N	9 43 E
91	Middle Andaman, I.	12 30 N	92 30 E
21	Middlesbrough	54 35 N	1 14W
127	Middletown, Conn.	41 37 N	72 40W
127	Middletown, N.Y.	41 28 N	74 28W
127	Middletown, Ohio	39 29 N	84 25W
127	Middletown, Pa.	40 12 N	76 44W
123	Middleton	44 50 N	65 5W
113	Middleton P.O.	22 22 S	141 32 E
30	Midi, Canal du	43 45 N	1 21 E
122	Midland, Canada	44 45 N	79 50W
127	Midland, Mich.	43 37 N	84 17W
128	Midland, Tex.	32 0 N	102 3W
87	Midnapore	22 25 N	87 21 E
106	Midway Is.	28 13 N	177 22W
60	Midžor, Mt.	43 24 N	22 40 E
102	Mie □	34 20 N	136 20 E
50	Międzychod	52 35 N	15 53 E
50	Międzyrzec Podlaski	51 58 N	22 45 E
50	Międzyrzecz	52 26 N	15 35 E
51	Miercurea Ciuc	46 21 N	25 48 E
29	Migennes	47 58 N	3 31 E
63	Migliarino	44 54 N	11 56 E
102	Mihara	34 25 N	133 5 E
55	Mijares, R.	39 55 N	0 1W
53	Mijas	36 36 N	4 40W
68	Mikínai	37 43 N	22 46 E
165	Mikindani	10 15 S	40 2 E
37	Mikkeli □	61 56 N	28 0 E
68	Míkonos, I.	37 30 N	25 25 E
49	Mikołow	50 10 N	18 50 E
68	Mikrí Prespa, L.	40 46 N	21 4 E
75	Mikun	62 20 N	50 0 E
113	Milang	35 20 S	138 55 E
62	Milano	45 28 N	9 10 E
21	Mildenhall	52 20 N	0 30 E
113	Mildura	34 13 S	142 9 E
68	Miléai	39 20 N	23 9 E
125	Milestone	50 0 N	104 30W
118	Milford, Conn.	41 13 N	73 4W
127	Milford, Del.	38 52 N	75 26W
131	Milford, Utah	38 20 N	113 0W
21	Milford Haven	51 43 N	5 2W
50	Milicz	51 31 N	17 19 E
65	Militello in Val di Catania	37 16 N	14 46 E
30	Millau	44 8 N	3 4 E
30	Millevaches, Plat. de	45 45 N	2 0 E
21	Millom	54 13 N	3 16W
127	Millville	39 22 N	74 0W
121	Milne Inlet	72 30 N	80 0W
124	Milo	24 28 N	103 23 E
68	Mílos, I.	36 44 N	24 25 E
114	Milton, N.Z.	46 7 S	169 59 E
127	Milton, U.S.A..	41 0 N	76 53W
21	Milton Keynes	52 3 N	0 42W
27	Miltown Malbay	52 51 N	9 25W
127	Milwaukee	43 9 N	87 58W
131	Milwaukie	45 33 N	122 39W
48	Mimoň	50 38 N	14 45 E
80	Mīnā Su'ud	28 45 N	48 20 E
81	Mīnāb	27 10 N	57 1 E
148	Minas	34 20 S	55 15W
145	Minas Gerais □	18 50 S	46 0W
137	Minatitlán	17 58 N	94 35W
24	Minch, North, Chan.	58 0 N	6 0W
95	Mindanao, I.	8 0 N	125 0 E
95	Mindanao Sea	9 0	124 0 E
95	Mindanao Trench	8 0 N	128 0 E
45	Minden	52 18 N	8 54 E
95	Mindoro, I.	13 0 N	121 0 E
95	Mindoro Str.	12 30 N	120 30 E
21	Minehead	51 12 N	3 29W
123	Mingan	50 20 N	64 0W
113	Mingela	19 52 S	146 38 E
55	Minglanilla	39 34 N	1 38W
53	Mingorria	40 42 N	4 40 N
60	Minićevo	43 42 N	22 18 E
158	Minna	9 37 N	6 30 E
128	Minneapolis	44 58 N	93 20W
128	Minnesota □	46 40 N	94 0W
110	Minnipa	32 51 S	135 9 E
102	Mino	35 32 N	136 55 E
53	Miño, R.	41 52 N	8 51W
128	Minot	48 10 N	101 15W
75	Minsk	53 52 N	27 30 E
50	Mińsk Mazowiecki	52 10 N	21 33 E
123	Minto	34 1 S	150 51 E
121	Minto, L.	48 0 N	84 45W
131	Minturn	39 45 N	106 25W
64	Minturno	41 15 N	13 43 E
87	Minutang	28 15 N	96 30 E
123	Miquelon, I.	47 8 N	56 24W
63	Mira	45 26 N	12 9 E
53	Mira, R.	37 43 N	8 47W
65	Mirabella Eclano	41 3 N	14 59 E
86	Miraj	16 50 N	74 45 E
31	Miramas	43 33 N	4 59 E
30	Miramont	44 37 N	0 21 E
145	Miranda	20 10 S	50 15W
53	Miranda de Ebro	42 41 N	2 57W
53	Miranda do Corvo	40 6 N	8 20W
53	Miranda do Douro	41 30 N	6 16W
62	Mirandola	44 53 N	11 2 E
63	Mirano	45 29 N	12 6 E
85	Mirbāṭ	17 0 N	54 45 E
94	Miri	4 18 N	114 0 E
113	Miriam L.	32 45 S	52 50W
87	Mirzapur	25 10 N	82 45 E
102	Mishima	35 10 N	138 52 E
139	Miskitos, Cayos	14 26 N	82 50W
49	Miskolc	48 7 N	20 50 E
95	Misool, I.	2 0 S	130 0 E
159	Misrātah	32 18 N	15 3 E
128	Mississippi □	33 0 N	90 0W
128	Mississippi, R.	29 0 N	89 15W
131	Missoula	47 0 N	114 0W
128	Missouri □	38 25 N	92 30W
128	Missouri, R.	38 50 N	90 8W
122	Mistassini, L.	51 0 N	73 40W
65	Mistretta	37 56 N	14 20 E
113	Mitchell, Australia	26 29 S	147 58 E
128	Mitchell, U.S.A.	43 40 N	98 0W
27	Mitchelstown	52 16 N	8 18W
68	Míthimna	39 20 N	26 12 E
68	Mitilíni	39 6 N	26 35 E
137	Mitla	16 55 N	96 17W
159	Mitsiwa	15 35 N	39 25 E
113	Mittagong	34 28 S	150 29 E
45	Mittelland-kanal	52 23 N	7 45 E
45	Mittwelda	50 59 N	13 0 E
165	Mitumba, Chaîne des	10 0 S	26 20 E
102	Miyagi □	38 15 N	140 45 E
102	Miyako	39 40 N	141 75 E
102	Miyazaki	31 56 N	131 30 E
80	Miyet, Bahr el	31 30 N	35 30 E
102	Miyoshi	34 48 N	132 32 E
27	Mizen Hd., Cork	51 27 N	9 50W
27	Mizen Hd., Wicklow	52 52 N	6 4W
51	Mizil	44 59 N	26 29 E
87	Mizoram □	23 0 N	92 40 E
41	Mjölby	58 20 N	15 10 E
48	Mladá Boleslav	50 27 N	14 53 E
60	Mladenovac	44 28 N	20 44 E
50	Mława	53 9 N	20 25 E
156	Mlanje, Mt.	16 2 S	35 33 E
60	Mljet, I.	42 43 N	17 30 E
38	Mo	66 15 N	14 8 E
95	Moa, I.	8 0 S	128 0 E
131	Moab	38 40 N	109 35W
165	Moba	7 3 S	29 47 E
165	Mobaye	4 25 N	21 5 E
127	Mobile	30 41 N	88 3W
165	Mobutu Sese Seko, L.	1 30 N	31 0 E
165	Moçambique	15 3 S	40 42 E
165	Moçâmedes	16 35 S	12 30 E
168	Mochudi	24 27 S	26 7 E
137	Moctezuma, R.	21 59 N	98 34W
169	Mocubu	16 54 S	37 25 E
62	Módena	44 39 N	10 55 E
131	Modesto	37 43 N	121 0W
65	Módica	36 52 N	14 45 E
49	Mödling	48 5 N	16 17 E
113	Moe	38 12 S	146 19 E
165	Moero, L.	9 0 S	28 45 E
24	Moffat	55 20 N	3 27W
85	Mogadiscio	2 2 N	45 25 E
85	Mogadishu = Mogadiscio	2 2 N	45 25 E
158	Mogador = Essaouira	31 32 N	9 42W
87	Mogaung	25 20 N	97 0 E
55	Mogente	38 52 N	0 45W
148	Mogi das Cruzes	23 45 S	46 20W
145	Mogi Mirim	22 20 S	47 0W
75	Mogilev	53 55 N	30 18 E
75	Mogilvev Podolskiy	48 20 N	27 40 E
63	Mogliano Venteto	45 33 N	12 15 E
49	Mohács	45 58 N	18 41 E
45	Möhne, R.	51 27 N	7 57 E
29	Mohon	49 45 N	4 44 E
76	Mointy	47 40 N	73 45 E
30	Moissac	44 7 N	1 5 E
53	Moita	38 38 N	8 58W
55	Mojácar	37 6 N	1 55W
131	Mojave	35 8 N	118 8W
131	Mojave Des.	35 0 N	117 30W
95	Mojokerto	7 29 S	112 25 E
114	Mokau, R.	38 42 S	174 37 E
68	Mokhós	35 16 N	25 27 E
34	Mol	51 11 N	5 5 E
65	Mola di Bari	41 3 N	17 5 E
21	Mold	53 10 N	3 10W
75	Moldavian S.S.R. □	47 0 N	28 0 E
60	Moldova Nouă	44 45 N	21 41 E
61	Moldoveanu, Mt.	45 36 N	24 45 E
168	Molepolole	24 28 S	25 28 E
128	Moline	41 30 N	90 30W
63	Molinella	44 38 N	11 40 E
65	Molise □	41 45 N	14 30 E
53	Mollina	37 8 N	4 38W
45	Mölln	53 37 N	10 41 E
41	Mölndal	57 40 N	12 3 E
133	Molokai, I.	21 8 N	156 0W
113	Molong	33 5 S	148 54 E
168	Molopo, R.	28 30 S	20 13 E
68	Mólos	38 47 N	22 37 E
95	Molucca Sea	4 0 S	124 0 E
95	Moluccas, Is. = Maluku, Is.	1 0 S	127 0 E
165	Mombasa	4 2 S	39 43 E
53	Mombuey	42 3 N	6 20W
144	Mompos	9 14 N	74 26W
41	Møn, I.	54 57 N	12 15 E
139	Mona, Pta.	9 37 N	82 36W
139	Mona, I.	18 5 N	67 54W
24	Monach Is.	57 32 N	7 40W
31	Monaco ■	43 46 N	7 23 E
24	Monadhliath Mts.	57 10 N	4 4W
27	Monaghan □	54 10 N	7 0W
159	Monastir	35 50 N	10 49 E
55	Moncada	39 30 N	0 24W
53	Monção	42 4 N	8 27W
55	Moncayo, Sa. del	41 48 N	1 50W
45	Mönchengladbach	51 12 N	6 23 E
123	Moncton	46 7 N	64 51W
53	Mondego, R.	40 9 N	8 52W
53	Mondoñedo	43 25 N	7 23W
62	Mondovi	44 23 N	7 56 E
64	Mondragone	41 8 N	13 52 E
127	Monessen	40 9 N	79 50W
53	Monesterio	38 6 N	6 15W
122	Monet	48 10 N	75 40W
63	Monfalcone	45 49 N	13 32 E
53	Monforte de Lemos	42 31 N	7 33W
87	Mong Kung	21 35 N	97 35 E
87	Mong Pan	20 19 N	98 22 E
87	Mong Pawk	22 4 N	99 16 E
87	Mong Yai	22 28 N	98 3 E
110	Monger, L.	29 25 S	117 5 E
87	Mongolia ■	46 30 N	105 0 E
87	Monghyr	25 23 N	86 30 E
159	Mongo	12 14 N	18 43 E
165	Mongu	15 16 S	23 12 E
30	Monistrol-sur-Loire	45 17 N	14 11 E
125	Monk	47 7 N	69 59W
21	Monmouth, U.K.	51 48 N	2 43W
128	Monmouth, U.S.A.	40 50 N	90 40W
139	Mono, Pta. del	12 0 N	83 30W
65	Monópoli	40 57 N	17 18 E
49	Monor	47 21 N	19 27 E
55	Monóvar	38 28 N	0 53W
128	Monroe, La.	32 32 N	92 4W
127	Monroe, Mich.	41 55 N	83 26W
127	Monroe, N.C.	35 2 N	80 37W
128	Monroe, Wis.	42 38 N	89 40W
158	Monrovia, Liberia	6 18 N	10 47W
131	Monrovia, U.S.A.	34 7 N	118 1W
34	Mons	50 27 N	3 58 E
63	Monsélice	43 13 N	11 45 E
41	Monsterås	57 3 N	16 33 E
31	Mont Cenis, Col du	45 15 N	6 54 E
124	Mont Joli	48 37 N	68 10W
122	Mont Laurier	46 35 N	75 30W
122	Mont Tremblant Prov. Park	46 30 N	74 30W
137	Montague, I.	31 40 N	144 46W
30	Montaigu	46 59 N	1 18W
55	Montalbán	40 50 N	0 45W
65	Montalbano Iónica	40 17 N	16 33 E
55	Montalbo	39 53 N	2 42W
65	Montalto Uffugo	39 25 N	16 9 E
131	Montana □	6 0 S	73 0W
29	Montargis	48 0 N	2 43 E
30	Montauban	44 0 N	1 21 E
127	Montauk Pt.	41 4 N	71 52W
29	Montbard	47 38 N	4 20 E
29	Montbéliard	47 31 N	6 48 E
55	Montblanch	41 23 N	1 4 E
31	Montbrison	45 36 N	4 3 E
30	Montcalm, Pic de	42 40 N	1 25 E
31	Montceau-les-Mines	46 40 N	4 23 E
30	Mont-de-Marsan	43 54 N	0 31W
29	Montdidier	49 38 N	2 35 E
145	Monte Alegre	2 0 S	54 0W
145	Monte Azul	15 9 S	42 53W
31	Monte Carlo	43 46 N	7 23 E
53	Monte Redondo	39 53 N	8 50W
62	Monte Rosa	45 55 N	7 50 E
64	Monte San Giovanni	41 38 N	13 31 E
64	Monte Santu, C. di	40 5 N	9 42 E
28	Montebourg	49 30 N	1 20W
62	Montecatini	43 55 N	10 48 E
144	Montecristi	1 0 S	80 40W
62	Montecristo, I.	42 20 N	10 20 E
63	Montefiascone	42 31 N	12 2 E
139	Montego Bay	18 30 N	78 0W
31	Montélimar	44 33 N	4 45 E
53	Montellano	36 59 N	5 36W
137	Montemorelos	25 11 N	99 42W
53	Montemor-o-Nova	38 40 N	8 12W
131	Monterey	36 35 N	121 57W
144	Montería	8 46 N	75 53W
137	Monterrey	25 40 N	100 30W
145	Montes Claros	16 30 S	43 50W
55	Montes de Toledo	39 35 N	4 30W
131	Montesano	47 0 N	123 39W
63	Montevarchi	43 30 N	11 32 E

Montevideo

Nîl, Nahr en

148 Montevideo 34 50 S 56 11W
28 Montfort-sur Meuse 48 8 N 1 58W
21 Montgomery, U.K. 52 34 N 3 9W
127 Montgomery, U.S.A. 32 20 N 86 20W
65 Monti Nébrodi, Mts. 37 48 N 14 20 E
62 Montichiari 45 28 N 10 29 E
29 Montigny-les-Metz 49 7 N 6 10 E
53 Montijo 38 52 N 6 39W
53 Montilla 37 36 N 4 40W
128 Montivideo 44 55 N 95 40W
30 Montluçon 46 22 N 2 36 E
123 Montmagny 46 58 N 70 43 E
29 Montmédy 49 30 N 5 20 E
31 Montmélian 45 30 N 6 4 E
29 Montmirail 48 51 N 3 30 E
30 Montmoreau 45 23 N 0 7 E
123 Montmorency 46 53 N 71 11W
30 Montmorillon 46 26 N 0 50 E
131 Montpelier, Id. 42 15 N 11 29W
127 Montpelier, Vt. 44 15 N 72 38W
30 Montpellier 43 37 N 3 52 E
122 Montreal 45 31 N 73 34W
30 Montrejeau 43 6 N 0 35 E
29 Montreuil 50 27 N 1 45 E
28 Montreuil-Bellay 47 8 N 0 9W
45 Montreux 46 26 N 6 55 E
28 Montrichard 47 20 N 1 10 E
24 Montrose, U.K. 56 43 N 2 28W
131 Montrose, U.S.A. 38 30 N 107 52W
139 Montserrat, I. 16 40 N 62 10W
55 Montuiri 39 34 N 2 59 E
87 Monywa 22 7 N 95 11 E
62 Monza 45 35 N 9 15 E
34 Monze 16 17 S 27 29 E
86 Monze, C. 24 47 N 66 37 E
55 Monzón 41 52 N 0 10 E
122 Moonbeam 49 20 N 82 10W
113 Moonie 27 46 S 150 20 E
113 Moonta 34 6 S 137 32 E
113 Mooraberree 25 13 S 140 54 E
110 Moore, L. 29 50 S 117 35 E
24 Moorfoot Hills 55 44 N 3 8W
122 Moose, R. 43 37 N 75 22W
122 Moose Factory 52 20 N 80 40W
125 Moose Jaw 50 30 N 105 30W
128 Moose Lake 46 27 N 92 48W
125 Moosomin 50 9 N 101 40W
122 Moosonee 51 25 N 80 51W
169 Mopeia Velha 17 30 S 35 40 E
49 Mór 47 25 N 18 12 E
53 Móra, Sp. 40 15 N 0 45W
41 Mora, Sweden 61 2 N 14 38 E
55 Mora de Ebro 41 6 N 0 38 E
55 Mora la Nueva 41 7 N 0 39 E
86 Moradabad 28 50 N 78 50 E
50 Morag 53 55 N 19 56 E
53 Moral de Calatrava 38 51 N 3 33W
53 Moraleja 40 6 N 6 43W
139 Morant Pt. 17 55 N 76 12W
24 Morar, L. 56 57 N 5 40W
55 Moratalla 38 14 N 1 49W
86 Moratuwa 6 45 N 79 55 E
49 Morava, R. 48 10 N 16 59 E
60 Moravița 45 17 N 21 14 E
144 Morawhanna 8 30 N 59 40W
24 Moray Firth 57 50 N 3 30W
62 Morbegno 46 8 N 9 34 E
28 Morbihan □ 47 55 N 2 50W
75 Mordovian A.S.S.R. □ 54 20 N 44 30 E
41 Møre og Romsdal □ 63 0 N 9 0 E
21 Morecambe 54 5 N 2 52W
21 Morecambe B. 54 7 N 3 0W
113 Moree 29 28 S 149 54 E
53 Morena, Sa. 38 20 N 4 0W
131 Morenci 33 7 N 109 20W
29 Moret 48 22 N 2 48 E
113 Moreton, I. 27 10 S 153 25 E
29 Moreuil 49 46 N 2 30 E
31 Morez 46 31 N 6 2 E
128 Morgan City 29 40 N 91 15W
127 Morgantown 39 39 N 75 58W
28 Morgat 48 15 N 4 32 E
76 Morghāb 38 10 N 73 59 E
29 Morhange 48 55 N 6 38 E
28 Morlaix 48 36 N 3 52W
29 Mormant 48 37 N 2 52 E
113 Mornington, I., Australia 16 30 S 139 30 E
148 Mornington, I., Chile 49 50 S 75 30W
95 Moro G. 6 30 N 123 0 E
158 Morocco ■ 31 0 N 6 0W
137 Moroleón 20 8 N 101 32W
139 Morón 22 0 N 78 30W
55 Morón de Almazán 41 29 N 2 27W
53 Morón de la Frontera 37 6 N 5 28W
169 Morondavo 20 17 S 44 27 E
95 Morotai, I. 2 10 N 128 30 E
165 Moroto 2 28 N 34 42 E
21 Morpeth 55 11 N 1 41W
128 Morrilton 35 10 N 92 45W
145 Morrinhos 17 45 S 49 10W
114 Morrinsville 37 40 S 175 32 E
125 Morris 49 25 N 97 30W
122 Morrisburg 44 55 N 75 7W
127 Morristown 36 18 N 83 20W
131 Morro Bay 35 27 N 120 54W
144 Morrosquillo, G. de 9 35 N 75 40W
75 Morshansk 53 28 N 41 50 E
41 Mörsil 63 19 N 13 40 E
28 Mortagne-au-Perche 48 30 N 0 32 E
29 Mortagne, R. 48 33 N 6 27 E
148 Morteros 30 50 S 62 0W
145 Mortes, R. 11 45 S 50 44W
113 Morundah 34 57 S 146 19 E
31 Morvan, Mts. du 47 5 N 4 0 E
113 Morven 26 22 S 147 5 E
24 Morvern, Reg. 56 38 N 5 44W
87 Moscos Is. 14 0 N 97 45 E
131 Moscow 46 45 N 116 59W
75 Moscow = Moskva 55 45 N 37 35 E
45 Mosel, R. 50 22 N 7 36 E
29 Moselle □ 48 59 N 6 33 E
114 Mosgiel 45 53 S 170 21 E
165 Moshi 3 22 S 37 18 E
37 Mosjøen 65 51 N 13 12 E
75 Moskva 55 45 N 27 35 E
75 Moskva, R. 55 5 N 38 50 E
144 Mosquera 2 35 N 78 30W
139 Mosquitos, G. de los 9 15 N 81 0W
38 Moss 59 27 N 10 40 E
113 Moss Vale 34 32 S 150 25 E
168 Mosselbaai 34 11 S 22 8 E
165 Mossendjo 2 55 S 12 42 E
113 Mossgiel 33 15 S 144 30 E
113 Mossman 16 28 S 145 23 E
145 Mossoró 5 10 S 37 15W
165 Mossuril 14 58 S 40 42 E
48 Most 50 31 N 13 38 E
158 Mostaganem 35 54 N 0 5 E
60 Mostar 43 22 N 17 50 E
80 Mosul = Al Mawsil 36 20 N 43 5 E
24 Motherwell 55 48 N 4 0W
87 Motihari 26 37 N 85 1 E
55 Motilla del Palancar 39 34 N 1 55W
65 Mótlola 40 38 N 17 0 E
165 Mouila 1 50 S 11 0 E
30 Moulins 46 35 N 3 19¼
87 Moulmein = Maulamyaing 16 30 N 97 40 E
127 Moultrie 31 11 N 83 47W
159 Moundou 8 40 N 16 10 E
127 Moundsville 39 53 N 80 43W
110 Mount Barker 34 38 S 117 40 E
127 Mount Clemens 42 35 N 82 50W
113 Mount Coolon 21 25 S 147 25 E
169 Mount Darwin 16 47 S 31 38 E
113 Mount Douglas 21 35 S 146 50 E
122 Mount Forest 43 59 N 80 43W
113 Mount Gambier 37 50 S 140 46 E
113 Mount Garnet 17 41 S 145 7 E
113 Mount Hope 34 7 S 135 23 E
113 Mount Isa 20 42 S 139 26 E
113 Mount Larcom 23 48 S 150 59 E
113 Mount Molloy 16 42 S 145 20 E
113 Mount Morgan 23 40 S 150 25 E
128 Mount Pleasant, Iowa 41 0 N 91 35W
127 Mount Pleasant, Mich. 43 38 N 84 46W
128 Mount Pleasant, Texas 33 5 N 95 0W
131 Mount Pleasant, Utah 39 40 N 111 29W
131 Mount Rainier Nat. Park 46 50 N 121 20W
124 Mt. Revelstoke Nat. Park 51 6 N 118 0W
124 Mount Robson 52 56 N 119 15W
127 Mount Sterling 38 0 N 84 0W
113 Mount Surprise 18 10 S 144 17 E
127 Mount Vernon, Ill. 38 19 N 88 55W
127 Mount Vernon, N.Y. 40 57 N 73 49W
131 Mount Vernon, Wash. 48 27 N 122 18W
110 Mount Willoughby 27 58 S 134 8 E
131 Mountain View 37 26 N 122 5W
113 Moura, Australia 24 35 S 149 58 E
144 Moura, Brazil 1 25 S 61 45W
53 Moura, Port. 38 7 N 7 30W
159 Mourdi, Depression du 18 10 N 23 0 E
30 Mourenx 43 23 N 0 36W
29 Mourmelon-le Grand 49 8 N 4 22 E
27 Mourne, Mts. 54 10 N 6 0W
27 Mourne, R. 54 45 N 7 25W
34 Mouscron 50 45 N 3 12 E
45 Moutier 47 16 N 7 21 E
31 Moutiers 45 29 N 6 31 E
165 Moyale 3 30 N 39 0 E
75 Moy, R. 54 5 N 9 6W
27 Moyle □ 55 10 N 6 15W
169 Mozambique ■ 19 0 S 35 0 E
169 Mozambique Chan. 20 0 S 39 0 E
165 Mpanda 6 23 S 31 40 E
165 Mpika 11 51 S 31 25 E
165 Msoro 13 35 S 31 50 E
145 Muaná 1 25 S 49 15W
91 Muang Chiang Rai 19 52 N 99 50 E
91 Muang Lamphun 18 40 N 98 53 E
91 Muang Phichit 16 29 N 100 21 E
91 Muar = Bandar Maharani 2 3 N 102 34 E
94 Muarabungo 1 40 S 101 10 E
94 Muaratewe 0 50 S 115 0 E
165 Mubende 0 33 N 31 22 E
159 Mubi 10 18 N 13 16 E
45 Mücheln 51 18 N 11 49 E
24 Muck, I. 56 50 N 6 15W
145 Mucuri 18 0 S 40 0W
99 Mudanjiang 44 38 N 129 30 E
165 Mufulira 12 32 S 28 15W
53 Mugia 43 3 N 9 17W
159 Muhammad Qol 20 53 N 37 9 E
45 Mühldorf 48 14 N 12 23 E
45 Mühlhausen 51 12 N 10 29 E
94 Mukomuko 2 20 S 101 10 E
86 Muktsar 30 30 N 74 30 E
55 Mula 38 3 N 1 33W
139 Mulatas, Arch. de las 6 51 N 78 31W
148 Mulchén 37 45 S 72 20W
45 Mulde, R., 51 10 N 12 48 E
123 Mulgrave 45 38 N 61 31W
53 Mulhacén, Mt. 37 4 N 3 20W
45 Mülheim 51 26 N 6 53W
29 Mulhouse 47 40 N 7 20 E
24 Mull of Galloway, Pt. 54 40 N 4 55W
24 Mull of Kintyre, Pt. 55 20 N 5 45W
24 Mull, I. 56 27 N 6 0W
113 Mullengudgery 31 43 S 147 29 E
27 Mullet, Pen. 54 10 N 10 2W
110 Mullewa 28 29 S 115 30 E
27 Mullingar 53 31 N 7 20W
113 Mullumbimby 28 30 S 153 30 E
86 Multan 30 15 N 71 30 E
91 Mun, R. 15 19 N 105 31 E
95 Muna, I. 5 0 S 122 30 E
45 München 48 8 N 11 33 E
127 Muncie 40 10 N 85 20W
45 Münden 51 25 N 9 42 E
55 Munera 39 2 N 2 29W
113 Mungallala 26 25 S 147 34 E
113 Mungana 17 8 S 144 27 E
113 Mungindi 28 58 S 149 1 E
165 Munhango 12 9 S 18 36 E
45 Munich = München 48 8 N 11 33 E
41 Munkedal 58 28 N 11 40 E
148 Muñoz Gamero, Pen. 52 30 S 73 5 E
29 Munster 48 2 N 7 8 E
27 Munster □ 52 20 N 8 40W
45 Münster, Niedersachsen 52 59 N 10 5 E
45 Münster, Nordrhein-Westfalen 51 58 N 7 37 E
94 Muntok 2 5 S 105 10 E
37 Muonio, R. 67 48 N 23 25 E
48 Mur, R. 46 18 N 16 53 E
63 Mura, R. 46 18 N 16 53 E
75 Murashi 59 30 N 49 0 E
30 Murat 45 7 N 2 53 E
48 Murau 47 6 N 14 10 E
64 Muravera 39 25 N 9 35 E
53 Murça 41 24 N 7 28W
110 Murchison, R. 26 1 S 117 6 E
55 Murcia 38 2 N 1 10W
55 Murcia □ 37 50 N 1 30W
51 Mureș 46 45 N 24 40 E
51 Mureșul, R. 46 15 N 20 13 E
30 Muret 43 30 N 1 20 E
113 Murgon 26 15 S 151 54 E
45 Müritzsee 53 25 N 12 40 E
75 Murmansk 68 57 N 33 10 E
55 Muro 39 45 N 3 3 E
53 Muros 42 45 N 9 5W
127 Murray, Ky. 36 40 N 88 20W
131 Murray, Utah 40 41 N 111 58W
113 Murray, R. 35 22 S 139 22 E
113 Murray Bridge 35 6 S 139 14 E
86 Murree 33 56 N 73 28 E
113 Murrumbidgee, R. 34 43 S 143 12 E
113 Murrurundi 31 42 S 150 51 E
113 Murtoa 36 35 S 142 28 E
53 Murtosa 40 44 N 8 40W
114 Murupara 38 30 S 178 40 E
87 Murwara 23 46 N 80 28 E
113 Murwillumbah 28 18 S 153 27 E
48 Mürzzuschlag 47 36 N 15 41 E
61 Musala, Mt. 41 13 N 23 27 E
81 Muscat = Masqat 23 37 N 58 36 E
128 Muscatine 41 25 N 91 5W
165 Mushie 2 56 S 17 4 E
127 Muskegon 43 15 N 86 17W
127 Muskegon Heights 43 12 N 86 17W
128 Muskogee 35 50 N 95 25W
159 Musmar 18 6 N 35 40 E
165 Musoma 1 30 S 33 48 E
24 Musselburgh 55 57 N 3 3W
30 Mussidan 45 2 N 0 22 E
64 Mussomeli 37 35 N 13 43 E
148 Musters, L. 45 20 S 69 25W
113 Muswellbrook 32 16 S 150 56 E
159 Mût 25 28 N 28 58 E
113 Muttaburra 22 38 S 144 29 E
123 Mutton Bay 50 50 N 59 2W
77 Muya 56 27 N 115 39 E
86 Muzaffarabad 34 25 N 73 30 E
86 Muzaffarnagar 29 26 N 77 40 E
87 Muzaffarpur 26 7 N 85 32 E
76 Muzhi 65 25 N 64 40 E
28 Muzillac 47 35 N 2 30W
165 Mvadhi Ousye 1 13 N 13 12 E
165 Mwanza, Tanzania 2 30 S 32 58 E
165 Mwanza, Zaïre 7 55 S 26 43 E
165 Mweka 4 50 S 21 40 E
165 Mweru, L. 9 0 S 28 45 E
91 My Tho 10 29 N 106 23 E
87 Myanaung 18 25 N 95 10 E
87 Myaungmya 16 30 N 95 0 E
87 Myingyan 21 30 N 95 30 E
87 Myitkyina 25 30 N 97 26 E
49 Myiava 48 41 N 17 37 E
131 Myrtle Creek 43 0 N 123 19W
131 Myrtle Point 43 0 N 124 4W
50 Myślibórz 52 55 N 14 50 E
49 Mystowice 50 15 N 19 12 E
86 Mysore 12 17 N 76 41 E
49 Myszkow 50 45 N 19 22 E
37 Mývatn, L. 65 36 N 17 0W
48 Mźe, R. 49 46 N 13 24 E

N

37 Naantali 60 27 N 21 57 E
27 Naas 53 12 N 6 40W
87 Nabadwip 23 34 N 88 20 E
159 Nabenl 36 30 N 10 51 E
80 Nābulus 32 14 N 35 15 E
165 Nachingwea 10 49 S 38 49 E
49 Náchod 50 25 N 16 8 E
128 Nacogdoches 31 33 N 95 30W
137 Nacozari 30 30 N 109 50W
86 Nadiad 22 41 N 72 56 E
76 Nadym 63 35 N 72 42 E
41 Næstved 55 13 N 11 44 E
158 Nafada 11 8 N 11 20 E
95 Naga 13 38 N 123 15 E
95 Naga Hills 27 0 N 96 0 E
87 Nagaland □ 26 0 N 95 0 E
102 Nagano 36 40 N 138 10 E
86 Nagappattinam 10 46 N 79 51 E
102 Nagasaki 32 47 N 129 50 E
86 Nagaur 27 15 N 73 45 E
86 Nagercoil 8 12 N 77 33 E
77 Nagornyy 55 58 N 124 57 E
102 Nagoya 35 10 N 136 50 E
86 Nagpur 21 8 N 79 10 E
99 Naha 26 13 N 127 42 E
120 Nahannai Butte 61 5 N 123 30W
80 Nahavand 34 10 N 48 30 E
148 Nahuel Huapi, L. 41 0 S 71 32W
125 Naicam 52 30 N 104 30W
45 Naila 50 19 N 11 43 E
123 Nain 56 34 N 61 40W
28 Naintré 46 46 N 0 29 E
24 Nairn 57 35 N 3 54W
165 Nairobi 1 17 S 36 48 E
165 Naivasha 0 40 S 36 30 E
81 Najafābād 32 40 N 51 15 E
80 Najd, Reg. 26 30 N 42 0 E
102 Nakamura 33 0 N 133 0 E
75 Nakhichevan 39 14 N 45 30 E
77 Nakhodka 43 10 N 132 45 E
91 Nakhon Phanom 17 23 N 104 43 E
91 Nakhon Ratchasima 14 59 N 102 12 E
91 Nakhon Sawan 15 35 N 100 12 E
41 Nakskov 54 50 N 11 8 E
165 Nakuru 0 15 S 35 5 E
124 Nakusp 50 20 N 117 45W
86 Nal, R. 26 2 N 65 19 E
86 Nalgonda 17 6 N 79 15 E
86 Nallamalai Hills 15 30 N 78 50 E
53 Nalon, R. 43 32 N 6 4W
159 Nālūt 31 54 N 11 0 E
91 Nam Dinh 20 25 N 106 5 E
91 Nam-Phan, Reg. 10 30 N 106 0 E
91 Nam Tha 20 58 N 101 30 E
91 Nam Tok 14 21 N 99 0 E
168 Namaland, Reg. 29 43 S 19 5 E
95 Namber 1 2 S 134 57 E
113 Nambour 26 38 S 152 49 E
113 Nambucca Heads 30 40 S 152 48 E
168 Namib Des. = Namibwoestyn 22 30 S 15 0W
168 Namibia ■ 22 0 S 18 9 E
168 Namibwoestyn 22 30 S 15 0W
95 Namlea 3 10 S 127 5 E
131 Nampa 43 40 N 116 40W
165 Nampula 15 6 S 39 7 E
37 Namsos 64 29 N 11 30 E
87 Namtu 23 5 N 97 28 E
34 Namur 50 27 N 4 52 E
34 Namur □ 50 17 N 5 0 E
168 Namutoni 18 49 S 16 55 E
165 Namwala 15 44 S 26 30 E
50 Namysłów 51 6 N 17 42 E
124 Nanaimo 49 10 N 124 0W
102 Nanao 37 0 N 137 0 E
99 Nanchang 28 42 N 115 55 E
99 Nanchong 30 43 N 106 2 E
29 Nancy 48 42 N 6 12 E
86 Nanda Devi, Mt. 30 30 N 80 30 E
86 Nandurbar 21 20 N 74 15 E
86 Nandyal 15 30 N 78 30 E
99 Nanjing 32 2 N 118 44 E
99 Nanking = Nanjing 32 2 N 118 44 E
102 Nankoku 33 39 N 133 44 E
110 Nannine 26 51 S 118 18 E
99 Nanning 22 48 N 108 20 E
99 Nanping 26 38 N 118 10 E
102 Nansei-Shotō, Is. 29 0 N 129 0 E
28 Nantes 47 12 N 1 33W
30 Nantiat 46 1 N 1 11 E
127 Nanticoke 41 12 N 76 1W
99 Nantong 32 1 N 120 52 E
31 Nantua 46 10 N 5 35 E
118 Nantucket I. 41 16 N 70 3W
145 Nanuque 17 50 S 40 21W
165 Nanyuki 0 2 N 37 4 E
68 Náousa 40 42 N 22 9 E
131 Napa 38 18 N 122 17W
122 Napanee 44 15 N 77 0W
114 Napier 39 30 S 176 56 E
65 Nápoli 40 50 N 14 5 E
102 Nara 34 40 N 135 49 E
102 Nara □ 34 30 N 136 0 E
86 Nara, R. 24 7 N 69 7 E
113 Naracoorte 36 50 S 140 44 E
91 Narathiwat 6 40 N 101 55 E
30 Narbonne 43 11 N 3 0 E
53 Narcea, R. 43 28 N 6 6W
65 Nardo 40 10 N 18 0 E
50 Narew 52 55 N 23 30 E
50 Narew, R. 52 26 N 20 42 E
86 Narmada, R. 21 35 N 72 35 E
63 Narni 42 30 N 12 30 E
64 Naro 37 18 N 13 48 E
113 Narrandera 34 42 S 146 31 E
110 Narrogin 32 58 S 117 14 E
113 Narromine 32 12 S 148 12 E
102 Naruto 35 36 N 140 25 E
37 Narvik 68 28 N 17 26 E
53 Naryilco 28 37 S 141 53 E
76 Narym 59 0 N 81 58 E
76 Narymskoye 49 10 N 84 15 E
76 Naryn 41 30 N 76 10 E
158 Nasarawa 8 32 N 7 41 E
159 Naser, Buheiret en 23 0 N 32 30 E
127 Nashville 36 12 N 86 46W
60 Nasice 45 32 N 18 4W
86 Nasik 20 2 N 73 50 E
86 Nasirabad, India 26 15 N 74 45 E
86 Nasirabad, Pak. 28 25 N 68 25 E
139 Nassau 25 0 N 77 30W
148 Nassau, B. 55 20 S 68 0W
159 Nasser, L. = Naser, Buheiret en 23 0 N 32 30 E
41 Nässjö 57 38 N 14 45 E
122 Nastapoka Is. 57 0 N 77 0W
144 Natagaima 3 37 N 75 6W
145 Natal, Brazil 5 47 S 35 13W
94 Natal, Indonesia 0 35 N 99 0 E
169 Natal □ 28 30 S 30 30 E
123 Natashquan 50 14 N 61 46W
123 Natashquan, R. 50 6 N 61 49W
128 Natchez 31 35 N 91 25W
128 Natchitoches 31 47 N 93 4W
86 Nathdwara 24 55 N 73 50 E
145 Natividade 11 43 S 47 47W
165 Natron, L. 2 20 S 36 0 E
94 Natuna Besar, Kep. 4 0 N 108 0 E
94 Natuna Selatan, Kep. 3 0 N 109 55 E
86 Naushahra 33 9 N 74 15 E
53 Nava del Rey 41 22 N 5 6W
53 Navahermosa 39 41 N 4 28W
131 Navajo Res. 36 55 N 107 30W
53 Navalcarnero 40 17 N 4 5W
53 Navalmoral de la Mata 39 52 N 5 16W
27 Navan = An Uaimh 53 39 N 6 40W
148 Navarino, I. 55 0 S 67 30W
55 Navarra □ 42 40 N 1 40W
30 Navarre, Reg. 43 15 N 1 20 E
139 Navassa, I. 18 30 N 75 0W
53 Navia 43 24 N 6 42W
137 Navojoa 27 0 N 109 30W
75 Navolok 62 33 N 39 57 E
68 Návpaktos 38 23 N 21 42 E
68 Navplion 37 33 N 22 50 E
86 Nawabshah 26 15 N 68 25 E
86 Nawalgarh 27 50 N 75 15 E
68 Náxos, I. 37 5 N 25 30 E
81 Nāy Band 27 20 N 52 40 E
77 Nayakhan 62 10 N 159 0 E
137 Nayarit □ 22 0 N 105 0W
145 Nazaré, Brazil 13 0 S 39 0W
53 Nazaré, Port. 39 36 N 9 4W
87 Nazir Hat 22 35 N 91 55 E
165 Ndalatando 9 18 S 14 54 E
165 Ndélé 8 25 N 20 36 E
165 Ndendé 2 29 S 10 46 E
159 Ndjamena 12 4 N 15 8 E
165 Ndola 13 0 S 28 34 E
27 Neagh, L. 54 35 N 6 25W
120 Near Is. 53 0 N 172 0W
21 Neath 51 39 N 3 49W
113 Nebo 39 27 N 90 47W
128 Nebraska □ 41 30 N 100 0W
128 Nebraska City 40 40 N 95 52W
45 Neckar, R. 49 31 N 8 26 E
148 Necochea 38 30 S 58 50W
131 Needles 34 50 N 114 35W
86 Neemuch 24 30 N 74 50 E
128 Neenah 44 10 N 88 30W
21 Nefyn 52 57 N 4 31W
86 Negombo 7 12 N 79 50 E
60 Negotin 44 16 N 22 37 E
95 Negra Pt. 18 40 N 120 50 E
144 Negra, Pta. 6 6 S 81 10W
53 Negreira 42 54 N 8 45W
148 Negro, R., Arg. 41 2 S 62 47W
144 Negro, R., Brazil 3 10 S 59 58W
95 Negros, I. 10 0 N 123 0 E
61 Negru Vodă 43 47 N 28 21 E
81 Nehbandān 31 35 N 60 5 E
45 Neheim 51 27 N 7 58 E
51 Nehoiașu 45 24 N 26 20 E
99 Nei Monggol Zizhiqu □ 42 0 N 112 0 E
99 Neijiang 29 35 N 104 55 E
53 Neira de Jusá 42 53 N 7 14W
50 Neisse, R. 52 4 N 14 47 E
53 Nelas 40 32 N 7 52W
77 Nelkan 57 50 N 136 15 E
86 Nellore 14 27 N 79 59 E
77 Nelma 47 30 N 139 0 E
124 Nelson, Canada 49 30 N 117 20W
114 Nelson, N.Z. 41 18 S 173 16 E
21 Nelson, U.K. 53 50 N 2 14W
125 Nelson, R. 55 30 N 96 50W
124 Nelson Forks 59 30 N 124 0W
169 Nelspruit 25 29⅜ 30 59 E
158 Néma 16 40 N 7 15W
29 Nemours 48 16 N 2 40 E
102 Nemuro 43 20 N 145 35 E
102 Nemuro-Kaikyō, Str. 43 30 N 145 30 E
77 Nemuy 55 40 N 135 55 E
21 Nene, R. 52 48 N 0 13 E
68 Néon Petritsi 41 16 N 23 15 E
128 Neosho 35 59 N 95 10W
87 Nepal ■ 28 0 N 84 30 E
131 Nephi 39 43 N 111 52W
51 Néra, R. 42 26 N 12 24 E
30 Nérac 44 19 N 0 20 E
77 Nerchinsk 52 0 N 116 39 E
77 Nerchinskiyzavod 51 10 N 119 30 E
60 Neretva, R. 43 1 N 17 27 E
38 Neslandvatn 58 57 N 9 10 E
29 Nesle 49 45 N 2 53 E
24 Ness, L. 57 15 N 4 30W
68 Néstos, R. 41 20 N 24 35 E
37 Nesttun 60 19 N 5 21 E
80 Netanya 32 20 N 34 51 E
34 Netherlands ■ 52 0 N 5 30 E
29 Nettancourt 48 51 N 4 57 E
121 Nettilling L. 66 30 N 71 0W
45 Neu-Isenburg 50 3 N 8 42 E
45 Neu-Ulm 48 23 N 10 2 E
45 Neubrandenburg 53 33 N 13 17 E
45 Neubrandenburg □ 53 30 N 13 20 E
45 Neuchâtel 47 0 N 6 55 E
29 Neufchâteau 48 21 N 5 40 E
28 Neufchâtel 49 43 N 1 30 E
29 Neufchâtel-sur-Aisne 49 26 N 4 0 E
28 Neuillé-Pont-Pierre 47 33 N 0 33 E
45 Neumarkt 49 16 N 11 28 E
45 Neumünster 54 4 N 9 58 E
48 Neunkirchen, Austria 47 43 N 16 4 E
45 Neunkirchen, Germany 49 23 N 7 6 E
148 Neuquén 38 0 S 68 0 E
49 Neusiedler See, L. 47 50 N 16 47 E
45 Neuss 51 12 N 6 39 E
45 Neustadt, Bayern 49 42 N 12 10 E
45 Neustadt, Bayern 50 23 N 11 0 E
45 Neustadt, Potsdam 52 50 N 12 27 E
45 Neustadt, Rheinland-Pfalz 49 21 N 8 10 E
45 Neustrelitz 53 22 N 13 4 E
30 Neuvic 45 23 N 2 16 E
30 Neuville 45 52 N 4 51 E
45 Neuwied 50 26 N 7 29 E
128 Nevada 37 20 N 94 40W
131 Nevada □ 39 20 N 117 0W
53 Nevada, Sa. 37 3 N 3 15W
144 Nevada de Sta. Marta, Sa. 10 55 N 73 50W
77 Nevanka 56 45 N 98 55 E
30 Nevers 47 0 N 3 9 E
113 Nevertire 31 50 S 147 44 E
139 Nevis, I. 17 0 N 62 30W
127 New Albany 38 20 N 85 50W
144 New Amsterdam 6 15 N 57 30W
127 New Bedford 41 40 N 70 52W
106 New Britain, I. 6 0 S 151 0 E
127 New Brunswick 40 30 N 74 28W
123 New Brunswick □ 46 50 N 66 30W
106 New Caledonia, I. 21 0 S 165 0 E
127 New Castle, Ind. 39 55 N 85 23W
127 New Castle, Pa. 41 0 N 80 20W
86 New Delhi 28 37 N 77 13 E
21 New Forest, Reg. 50 53 N 1 40W
123 New Glasgow 45 35 N 62 36W
106 New Guinea, I. 4 0 S 146 0 E
127 New Hampshire □ 43 40 N 71 40W
127 New Haven 41 20 N 72 54W
106 New Hebrides 15 0 S 168 0 E
128 New Iberia 30 2 N 91 54W
106 New Ireland, I. 3 0 S 151 30 E
127 New Jersey □ 39 50 N 74 10W
127 New London 41 23 N 72 8W
131 New Mexico □ 34 30 N 106 0W
113 New Norfolk 42 46 S 147 2 E
128 New Orleans 30 0 N 90 5W
139 New Providence I. 25 0 N 77 30W
21 New Radnor 52 15 N 3 10W
21 New Romney 50 59 N 0 57 E
113 New South Wales □ 33 0 S 146 0 E
124 New Westminster 49 10 N 122 52W
127 New York 40 45 N 74 0W
127 New York □ 42 40 N 76 0W
114 New Zealand ■ 40 0 S 173 0 E
21 Newark, U.K. 53 6 N 0 48W
127 Newark, N.J. 40 41 N 74 12W
127 Newark, N.Y. 43 2 N 77 10W
127 Newark, Ohio 40 5 N 82 30W
21 Newbury 51 24 N 1 19W
127 Newburyport 42 48 N 70 50W
113 Newcastle, Australia 32 52 S 151 49 E
123 Newcastle, Canada 47 1 N 65 38W
27 Newcastle, Eire 52 27 N 9 3W
169 Newcastle, S.Africa 27 45 S 29 58 E
27 Newcastle, N. Ireland 54 13 N 5 54W
21 Newcastle, Tyne and Tees 54 59 N 1 37W
21 Newcastle Emlyn 52 2 N 4 29W
110 Newcastle Waters 17 30 S 133 28 E
21 Newcastle-under-Lyme 53 2 N 2 15W
110 Newdegate 33 17 N 118 58 E
123 Newfoundland □ 48 28 N 56 0W
21 Newhaven 50 47 N 0 4 E
27 Newmarket, Eire 52 13 N 9 0W
21 Newmarket, U.K. 52 15 N 0 23 E
21 Newport, Gwent 51 35 N 3 0W
21 Newport, I. of Wight 50 42 N 1 18W
128 Newport, Ark. 35 38 N 91 15W
127 Newport, Ky. 39 5 N 84 23W
127 Newport, N.H. 43 23 N 72 8W
131 Newport, Oreg. 44 41 N 124 2W
127 Newport News 37 2 N 76 54W
21 Newquay 50 24 N 5 6W
27 Newry 54 10 N 6 20W
27 Newry & Mourne □ 54 10W 6 20W
128 Newton, Iowa 41 40 N 93 3W
128 Newton, Kans. 38 2 N 97 30W
127 Newton, N.J. 41 3 N 74 46W
21 Newton Abbot 50 32 N 3 37W
24 Newton Stewart 54 57 N 4 30W
24 Newtonmore 57 4 N 4 7W
21 Newtown 52 31 N 3 19W
27 Newtownabbey □ 54 40 N 5 55W
27 Newtownards 54 37 N 5 40W
75 Nezhin 51 5 N 31 55 E
168 Ngami Depression 20 30 S 22 46 E
95 Nganjuk 7 32 S 111 55 E
159 Ngaoundéré 7 15 N 13 35 E
165 Ngunzu 11 10 S 13 18 E
158 Nguru 12 56 N 10 29 E
91 Nha Trang 12 16 N 109 10 E
122 Niagara Falls, Canada 43 7 N 79 5W
127 Niagara Falls, U.S.A. 43 5 N 79 0W
158 Niamey 13 27 N 2 6 E
165 Niangara 3 50 N 27 50 E
94 Nias, I. 1 0 N 97 40 E
62 Nibbiano 44 54 N 9 20 E
139 Nicaragua ■ 11 40 N 85 30W
65 Nicastro 39 0 N 16 18 E
31 Nice 43 42 N 7 14 E
102 Nichinan 31 28 N 131 26 E
72 Nicobar Is. 9 0 N 93 0 E
124 Nicola 50 8 N 120 40W
122 Nicolet 46 17 N 72 35W
80 Nicosia 35 10 N 33 25 E
139 Nicoya, Pen. de 9 45 N 85 40W
49 Nida, R. 50 18 N 20 52 E
21 Nidd, R. 54 1 N 1 12W
50 Nidzica 53 25 N 20 28 E
45 Niebüll 54 45 N 8 49 E
29 Niéderbronn-les-Bains 48 57 N 7 39 E
48 Niederösterreich □ 48 25 N 15 40 E
45 Niedersachsen □ 52 45 N 9 0 E
48 Niedere Tauern, Mts 47 18 N 14 E
145 Nieuw Amsterdam 5 53 N 55 5W
145 Nieuw Nickerie 6 0 N 57 10W
53 Nieves 42 7 N 7 26W
29 Nièvre □ 47 10 N 5 40 E
80 Niğde 37 59 N 34 42 E
158 Niger ■ 13 30 N 10 0 E
158 Niger, R. 5 33 N 6 33 E
158 Nigeria ■ 8 30 N 8 0 E
102 Niigata 37 58 N 139 0 E
102 Niihama 33 55 N 133 10 E
133 Niihau, I. 21 55 N 160 10W
34 Nijmegen 51 50 N 5 52 E
95 Nikiniki 9 40 S 124 30 E
75 Nikolayev 46 58 N 32 7 E
75 Nikolayevsk 50 10 N 45 35 E
61 Nikopol, Bulgaria 43 43 N 24 54 E
75 Nikopol, U.S.S.R. 47 35 N 34 25 E
60 Nikšić 42 50 N 18 57 E
159 Nîl, Nahr en, R. 30 10 N 31 6 E

Nîl el Abyad

Padstow

159 Nîl el Abyad, R. 15 40 N 32 30 E
131 Niland 33 16 N 115 30W
159 Nile, R. = Nîl, Nahren, R. 30 10 N 31 6 E
127 Niles 41 8 N 80 40W
31 Nîmes 43 50 N 4 23 E
81 Nīmrūz 31 10 N 62 0 E
165 Nimule 3 32 N 32 3 E
80 Nīnawá 36 25 N 43 10 E
53 Nindigully 28 21 S 148 49 E
99 Ningbo 29 51 N 121 28 E
99 Ningxia Huizu Zizhiqu □ 38 0 N 106 0 E
91 Ninh Binh 20 15 N 105 55 E
34 Ninove 50 51 N 4 2 E
30 Niort 46 19 N 0 29W
125 Nipawin 53 20 N 104 0W
125 Nipawin Prov. Park 54 0 N 104 40W
122 Nipigon 49 0 N 88 17W
122 Nipigon, L. 49 40 N 88 30W
145 Niquelandia 14 27 S 48 27W
60 Niš 43 19 N 21 58 E
53 Nisa 39 30 N 2 41W
85 Niṣāb 14 25 N 46 29 E
60 Nišava, R. 43 22 N 21 46 E
68 Nísiros, I. 36 35 N 27 12 E
41 Nissan, R. 43 22 N 21 46 E
41 Nissum, Fd. 56 20 N 8 11 E
145 Niterói 22 52 S 43 0W
24 Nith, R. 55 0 N 3 35W
49 Nitra 48 19 N 18 4 E
49 Nitra, R. 47 46 N 18 10 E
34 Nivelles 50 35 N 4 20 E
29 Nivernais, Reg. 47 0 N 3 40 E
86 Nizamabad 18 45 N 78 7 E
87 Nizamghat 28 20 N 95 45 E
77 Nizhneudinsk 55 0 N 99 20 E
76 Nizhniy Tagil 57 45 N 60 0 E
80 Nizip 37 1 N 37 46 E
49 Nizké Tatry, Mts. 48 55 N 20 0 E
165 Njombe 9 0 S 34 35 E
158 Nkambe 6 35 N 10 40 E
158 Nkawkaw 6 36 N 0 49W
165 Nkhata Bay 11 33 S 34 16 E
165 Nkhota Kota 12 55 S 34 15 E
158 Nkongsamba 4 55 N 9 55 E
120 Noatak 67 34 N 162 59W
102 Nobeoka 32 36 N 131 41 E
65 Noci 40 47 N 17 7 E
102 Noda 47 30 N 142 5 E
137 Nogales, Mexico 31 36 N 94 29W
131 Nogales, U.S.A. 31 33 N 110 59W
102 Nōgata 33 48 N 130 54 E
28 Nogent-le-Rotrou 48 20 N 0 50 E
29 Nogent-sur-Seine 48 30 N 3 30 E
49 Nograd □ 48 0 N 19 30 E
53 Nogueira de Ramuin 42 21 N 7 43W
55 Noguera Pallaresa, R. 42 15 N 0 54 E
55 Noguera Ribagorzana, R. 41 40 N 0 43 E
91 Noi, R. 17 5 N 105 2 E
28 Noire, Mts., Finistère 48 11 N 3 40W
30 Noire, Mts., Tarn 43 26 N 2 12W
30 Noirmoutier 47 0 N 2 15W
30 Noirmoutier, Î. de 46 58 N 2 10W
65 Nola 40 54 N 14 29 E
31 Nolay 46 58 N 4 35 E
62 Noli, C. di 44 12 N 8 26 E
120 Nome 64 30 N 165 30W
28 Nonancourt 48 47 N 1 11 E
28 Nonant-le-Pin 48 42 N 0 12 E
113 Nonda 20 40 S 142 28 E
30 Nontron 45 31 N 0 40 E
113 Noondoo 28 35 S 148 30 E
34 Noord Beveland, I. 51 45 N 3 50 E
34 Noord Brabant □ 51 40 N 5 0 E
34 Noord Holland □ 52 30 N 4 45 E
34 Noordoost-Polder 52 45 N 5 45 E
34 Noordwijk 52 14 N 4 26 E
124 Nootka I. 49 40 N 126 50W
41 Nora 59 32 N 15 2 E
122 Noranda 48 20 N 79 0 E
41 Norberg 60 4 N 15 56 E
29 Nord □ 50 15 N 3 30 E
45 Nord-Friesische, Is. 54 50 N 8 20 E
45 Nord-Ostsee Kanal 54 5 N 9 15 E
173 Nordaustlandet 79 55 N 23 0 E
41 Nordborg 55 5 N 9 50 E
45 Norddeich 53 37 N 7 10 E
124 Nordegg 52 29 N 116 5W
45 Norden 53 35 N 7 12 E
45 Nordenham 53 29 N 8 28 E
45 Norderney, I. 53 42 N 7 15 E
37 Nordkapp, Norway 71 11 N 25 48 E
173 Nordkapp, Svalbard 80 31 N 20 0 E
37 Nordland □ 65 40 N 13 0 E
45 Nördlingen 48 50 N 10 30 E
45 Nordrhein Westfalen □ 51 45 N 7 30 E
45 Nordstrand, I. 54 27 N 8 50 E
77 Nordvik 73 40 N 110 57 E
41 Nordyllands □ 57 0 N 10 0 E
27 Nore, R. 52 25 N 6 58W
128 Norfolk, Nebr. 42 3 N 97 25W
127 Norfolk, Va. 36 52 N 76 15W
21 Norfolk □ 52 39 N 1 0 E
106 Norfolk I. 28 58 S 168 3 E
77 Norilsk 69 20 N 88 0 E
28 Normandie, Reg. 48 45 N 0 10 E
28 Normandie, Collines de 48 55 N 0 45W
122 Normandin 48 49 N 72 31W
113 Normanton 17 40 S 141 10 E
37 Norrbotten □ 66 45 N 23 0 E
41 Nørresundby 57 5 N 9 52 E
127 Norristown 40 9 N 75 15W
41 Norrköping 58 37 N 16 11 E
41 Norrtälje 59 46 N 18 42 E
110 Norseman 32 8 S 121 43 E
41 Norsholm 58 31 N 15 59 E
77 Norsk 52 30 N 130 0 E
145 Norte, C. do 1 40 N 49 55W
114 North, C. 34 23 S 173 4 E
114 North I. 38 0 S 176 0 E
91 North Andaman, I. 13 15 N 92 40 E
152 North Atlantic Ocean 30 0 N 50 0W
122 North Bay 46 20 N 79 30W
122 North Belcher Is. 56 30 N 79 0W
124 North Bend, Canada 49 50 N 121 35W
131 North Bend, Oreg. 43 28 N 124 7W
24 North Berwick 56 4 N 2 44W
127 North Carolina □ 35 30 N 80 0W
24 North Channel 55 0 N 5 30W
128 North Dakota □ 47 30 N 100 0W
27 North Down □ 54 40 N 5 45W
21 North Downs 51 17 N 0 30W
17 North European Plain 55 0 N 25 0 E
21 North Foreland, Pt. 51 22 N 1 28 E
114 North Island 38 0 S 176 0 E
124 North Kamloops 50 40 N 120 25W
87 North Lakhimpur 27 15 N 94 10 E
128 North Platte 41 10 N 100 50W
173 North Pole 90 0 N 0 0 E
24 North Ronaldsay, I. 59 20 N 2 30W
125 North Saskatchewan, R. 53 15 N 105 6W
16 North Sea 56 0 N 4 0 E
128 North Truchas Pk. 36 0 N 105 30W
21 North Tyne, R. 54 59 N 2 8W
24 North Uist, I. 57 40 N 7 15W
124 North Vancouver 49 25 N 123 20W
21 North Walsham 52 49 N 1 22 E
110 North West, C. 21 45 S 114 9 E
24 North West Highlands, Mts. 57 35 N 5 2W
120 North West Territories □ 65 0 N 100 0W
21 North York Moors 54 25 N 0 50W
21 North Yorkshire □ 54 10 N 1 25W
21 Northallerton 54 20 N 1 26W
110 Northam 31 35 S 116 42 E
110 Northampton, Australia 28 21 S 114 33 E
21 Northampton, U.K. 52 14 N 0 54W
127 Northampton, Mass. 42 22 N 72 39W
127 Northampton, Pa. 40 38 N 75 24W
21 Northampton □ 52 16 N 0 55W
27 Northern Ireland ■ 54 45 N 7 0W
110 Northern Territory □ 16 0 S 133 0 E
21 Northumberland □ 55 12 N 2 0W
113 Northumberland, Is. 21 45 S 150 20 E
123 Northumberland Str. 46 20 N 64 0W
120 Northwest Territories 67 0 N 90 0W
21 Northwich 53 16 N 2 30W
127 Norwalk, Conn. 41 7 N 73 27W
127 Norwalk, Ohio 41 15 N 82 37W
37 Norway ■ 67 0 N 11 0 E
174 Norwegian Dependency 75 0 S 15 0 E
173 Norwegian Sea 66 0 N 1 0 E
21 Norwich, U.K. 52 38 N 1 17 E
127 Norwich, N.Y. 42 32 N 75 30W
76 Nosok 70 10 N 82 20 E
168 Nossob, R. 26 55 S 20 37 E
50 Noteć R. 52 44 N 15 26 E
68 Notios Evvoïkos, Kól. 38 20 N 24 0 E
124 Notikewin 57 15 N 117 5W
65 Noto 36 52 N 15 4 E
38 Notodden, Reg. 59 35 N 9 17 E
123 Notre Dame B. 49 45 N 55 30W
121 Notre Dame de Koartac = Koartac 60 55 N 69 40W
121 Notre Dame d'Ivugivik = Ivugivik 62 20 N 78 0W
21 Nottingham 52 57 N 1 10W
21 Nottinghamshire □ 53 10 N 1 0W
158 Nouâdhibou 21 0 N 17 0W
158 Nouakchott 18 20 N 15 50W
106 Noumea 22 17 S 166 30 E
29 Nouzonville 49 48 N 4 44 E
49 Nová Bana 48 28 N 18 39 E
48 Nová Bystrice 49 2 N 15 8 E
145 Nova Cruz 6 28 S 35 25W
145 Nova Friburgo 22 10 S 42 30W
145 Nova Granada 20 29 S 49 19W
60 Nova Gradiška 45 17 N 17 28 E
165 Nova Lisboa = Huambo 12 42 S 15 54 E
48 Nova Paka 50 29 N 15 30 E
123 Nova Scotia □ 45 10 N 63 0W
61 Nova Zagora 42 32 N 25 59 E
51 Novaci 45 10 N 23 42 E
62 Novara 45 27 N 8 36 E
75 Novaya Ladoga 60 7 N 32 16 E
76 Novaya Lyalya 58 50 N 60 35 E
77 Novaya Sibir, Os. 75 10 N 150 0 E
76 Novaya Zemlya, I. 75 0 N 56 0 E
49 Nové Mesto 49 33 N 16 7 E
49 Nové Zámky 47 59 N 18 11 E
62 Novellara 44 50 N 10 43 E
75 Novgorod 58 30 N 31 25 E
60 Novi Bečej 45 36 N 20 10 E
60 Novi Kneževac 46 4 N 20 8 E
61 Novi Krichim 42 22 N 24 31 E
62 Novi Lígure 44 45 N 8 47 E
61 Novi Pazar, Bulgaria 43 25 N 27 15 E
60 Novi Pazar, Yug. 43 12 N 20 28 E
60 Novi-Sad 45 18 N 19 52 E
63 Novi Vinodolski 45 10 N 14 48 E
75 Novocherkassk 47 27 N 40 5 E
76 Novokazalinsk 45 40 N 61 40 E
75 Novokiybyshevsk 53 7 N 49 58 E
76 Novo-kuznetsk 54 0 N 87 10 E
75 Novomoskovsk 54 5 N 38 15 E
76 Novosibirsk 55 0 N 83 5 E
77 Novosibirskiye Os. 75 0 N 140 0 E
60 Novska 45 19 N 17 0 E
48 Novy Bydžov 50 14 N 15 29 E
50 Nŏvy Dwór 52 26 N 20 44 E
49 Nový Jičín 49 15 N 18 0 E
81 Now Shahr 36 40 N 51 40 E
50 Nowa Sól 51 48 N 15 44 E
50 Nowogrod 53 14 N 21 53 E
113 Nowra 34 53 S 150 35 E
49 Nowy Sącz 49 40 N 20 41 E
53 Noya 42 48 N 8 53W
28 Noyant 47 30 N 0 6 E
29 Noyers 47 40 N 4 0 E
29 Noyon 49 34 N 3 0 E
28 Nozay 47 34 N 1 38W
169 Nsanje 16 55 S 35 12 E
158 Nsawam 5 50 N 0 24W
169 Nuanetsi 21 22 S 30 45 E
156 Nubian Des. 21 30 N 33 30 E
159 Nûbîya, Es Sahrâ en 21 30 N 33 30 E
139 Nuevitas 21 30 N 77 20W
148 Nuevo, G. 43 0 S 64 30W
137 Nuevo Laredo 27 30 N 99 40W
137 Nuevo León □ 25 0 N 100 0W
114 Nuhaka 39 3 S 177 45 E
31 Nuits St. Georges 47 10 N 4 56 E
120 Nulato 64 43 N 158 6W
55 Nules 39 51 N 0 9W
110 Nullagine 21 53 S 120 6 E
110 Nullarbor Plain 31 20 S 128 0 E
38 Numedal 60 6 N 9 6 E
113 Numurkah 36 0 S 145 26 E
21 Nuneaton 52 32 N 1 29W
120 Nunivak I. 60 0 N 166 0W
34 Nunspeet 52 21 N 5 45 E
64 Núoro 40 20 N 9 20 E
45 Nürnberg 49 26 N 11 5 E
94 Nusa Tenggara Barat 8 50 S 117 30 E
95 Nusa Tenggara Timur □ 9 30 S 122 0 E
168 Nuweveldberge 32 10 S 21 45 E
110 Nyabing 33 30 S 118 7 E
165 Nyahanga 2 20 S 33 37 E
159 Nyâlâ 12 2 N 24 58 E
165 Nyasa, L. 12 0 S 34 30 E
41 Nyborg 55 18 N 10 47 E
41 Nybro 56 44 N 15 55 E
76 Nyda 66 40 N 73 10 E
49 Nyirbátor 47 49 N 22 9 E
37 Nykarleby 63 32 N 22 31 E
41 Nykøbing 54 56 N 11 52 E
41 Nykøbing Mors 56 49 N 8 51 E
41 Nyköping 58 45 N 17 0 E
169 Nylstroom 24 42 S 28 22 E
113 Nyngan 31 30 S 147 8 E
45 Nyon 46 23 N 6 14 E
31 Nyons 44 22 N 5 10 E
49 Nysa 50 40 N 17 22 E
50 Nysa, R. 52 4 N 14 46 E
158 Nzerekore 7 49 N 8 48W

O

128 Oahe Dam 44 28 N 100 25W
128 Oahe Res. 45 30 N 100 15W
133 Oahu, I. 21 30 N 158 0W
127 Oak Park 41 55 N 87 45W
127 Oak Ridge 36 1 N 84 5W
21 Oakengates 52 42 N 2 29W
131 Oakesdale 47 11 N 117 9W
113 Oakey 27 25 S 151 43 E
21 Oakham 52 40 N 0 43W
131 Oakland 37 50 N 122 18W
125 Oakville 49 56 N 97 58W
137 Oaxaca □ 17 0 N 97 0W
76 Ob, R. 62 40 N 66 0 E
24 Oban 56 25 N 5 30W
124 Obed 53 30 N 117 10W
45 Oberammergau 47 35 N 11 3 E
45 Oberhausen 51 28 N 6 50 E
48 Oberösterreich □ 48 10 N 14 0 E
45 Oberpfälzer Wald 49 30 N 12 25 E
76 Obskaya Guba 70 0 N 73 0 E
158 Obuasi 6 17 N 1 40W
61 Obzor 42 50 N 27 52 E
144 Ocaña, Col. 8 15 N 73 20W
144 Ocaña, Sp. 39 55 N 3 30W
144 Occidental, Cord. 5 0 N 76 0W
127 Ocean City 39 18 N 74 34W
131 Oceanlake 45 0 N 124 0W
131 Oceanside 33 13 N 117 26W
24 Ochil Hills 56 14 N 3 40W
128 Oconto 44 52 N 87 53W
137 Ocatlán 20 21 N 102 42W
28 Octeville 49 38 N 1 40W
144 Ocumare del Tuy 10 7 N 66 46W
95 Ocussi 9 20 S 124 30 E
102 Ōda 5 50 N 1 5W
37 Odáðahraun 65 5 N 17 0W
41 Ödåkra 56 9 N 12 45 E
38 Odda 60 3 N 6 35 E
41 Odder 55 58 N 10 10 E
85 Oddur 4 0 N 43 35 E
41 Odense 55 22 N 10 23 E
45 Odenwald, Mts. 49 18 N 9 0 E
50 Oder = Odra R. 53 0 N 14 12 E
75 Odessa 46 30 N 30 45 E
53 Odiel, R. 37 30 N 6 55W
61 Odorheiul Secuiesc 46 21 N 25 21 E
50 Odra, R., Poland 53 33 N 14 38 E
53 Odra, R., Sp. 42 30 N 4 15W
60 Odžaci 45 30 N 19 17 E
145 Oeiras 7 0 S 42 8W
45 Oelsnitz 50 24 N 12 11 E
128 Oelwein 42 39 N 91 55W
158 Offa 8 13 N 4 42 E
27 Offaly □ 53 20 N 7 30W
45 Offenbach 50 6 N 8 46 E
122 Ogahalla 50 6 N 85 51W
102 Ōgaki 35 25 N 136 35 E
158 Ogbomosho 8 1 N 3 29 E
131 Ogden 41 13 N 112 1W
127 Ogdensburg 44 40 N 75 27W
62 Oglio, R. 45 15 N 10 15 E
113 Ogmore 22 37 S 149 35 E
165 Ogooué, R. 1 0 S 10 0 E
148 O'Higgins, L. 49 0 S 72 40W
114 Ohakune 39 24 S 175 24 E
127 Ohio, R. 38 0 N 86 0W
127 Ohio □ 40 20 N 83 0W
45 Ohre, R. 50 10 N 12 30 E
60 Ohrid 41 8 N 20 52 E
60 Ohrid, L. = Ohridsko, J. 41 8 N 20 52 E
60 Ohridsko, J. 41 8 N 20 52 E
127 Oil City 41 26 N 79 40W
29 Oise, R. 49 53 N 3 50 E
29 Oise □ 49 28 N 2 30 E
102 Ōita 33 15 N 131 36 E
148 Ojos del Salado, Cerro, Mt. 27 0 S 68 40W
131 Okanagan 48 24 N 119 24W
168 Okavango, R. 17 40 S 19 30 E
168 Okavango Swamps 19 30 S 23 0 E
102 Okaya 36 0 N 138 10 E
102 Okayama 34 40 N 133 54 E
102 Okazaki 34 36 N 137 0 E
127 Okeechobee, L. 21 0 N 80 50W
127 Okefenokee Swamp 30 50 N 82 15W
21 Okehampton 50 44 N 4 1W
45 Oker, R. 52 7 N 10 34 E
86 Okha 53 40 N 143 0 E
77 Okhotsk 59 20 N 143 10 E
77 Okhotsk, Sea of 55 0 N 145 0 E
77 Okhotskiy Perevoz 61 52 N 135 35 E
102 Oki-Shotō 36 15 N 133 15 E
128 Oklahoma □ 35 20 N 97 30W
128 Oklahoma City 35 25 N 97 30W
158 Okrika 4 47 N 7 4 E
77 Oktyabriskoy Revolyutsii Os. 79 30 N 97 0 E
75 Oktyabrski 53 11 N 48 40 E
114 Okura 43 55 S 168 55 E
102 Okushiri-Tō, I. 42 15 N 139 30 E
41 Öland, I. 56 45 N 16 50 E
128 Olathe 38 50 N 94 50W
148 Olavarría 36 55 S 60 20W
64 Ólbia 40 55 N 9 30 E
64 Ólbia, G. di 40 55 N 9 35 E
122 Old Factory 52 36 N 78 43W
127 Old Town 45 0 N 68 50W
27 Oldcastle 53 46 N 7 10W
45 Oldenburg 53 10 N 8 10 E
21 Oldham 53 32 N 2 8W
34 Oldenzaal 52 19 N 6 53 E
124 Olds 51 50 N 114 10W
50 Olecko 54 3 N 22 30 E
77 Olekminsk 60 40 N 120 30 E
75 Olenegorsk 68 9 N 33 15 E
30 Oléron, Î. d' 45 55 N 1 15W
50 Oleśnica 51 13 N 17 22 E
77 Olga 43 50 N 135 0 E
110 Olga, Mt. 25 20 S 130 40 E
169 Olifants, R. 24 10 S 32 40 S
53 Oliva, Pta. del 43 37 N 5 28W
53 Oliva de la Frontera 38 17 N 6 54W
145 Oliveira 20 50 S 44 50W
53 Oliveira de Azemeis 40 49 N 8 29W
124 Oliver 49 20 N 119 30W
53 Olmedo 41 20 N 4 43W
127 Olney 38 40 N 88 0W
41 Olofström 56 17 N 14 32 E
49 Olomouc 49 38 N 17 12 E
55 Olot 42 11 N 2 30 E
60 Olovo 44 8 N 18 35 E
77 Olovyannaya 50 50 N 115 10 E
50 Olsztyn 53 48 N 20 29 E
50 Olsztyn □ 54 0 N 21 0 E
51 Olt, R. 43 50 N 24 40 E
45 Olten 47 21 N 7 53 E
53 Olvera 36 55 N 5 18W
131 Olympia 47 0 N 122 58W
131 Olympic Mts. 48 0 N 124 0W
131 Olympic Nat. Park 47 35 N 123 30W
131 Olympus Mt. 47 52 N 123 40W
68 Olympus, Mt. = Óros Ólimbos 40 6 N 22 23 E
80 Olympus = Tróodus, Mt. 34 58 N 32 55 E
27 Omagh 54 36 N 7 20W
128 Omaha 41 15 N 96 0W
85 Oman ■ 23 0 N 58 0 E
81 Oman, G. of 24 30 N 58 30 E
168 Omaruru 21 26 S 16 0 E
144 Omate 16 45 S 71 0W
95 Ombai, Selat, Str. 8 30 S 124 50 E
159 Omdurmân 15 40 N 32 28 E
62 Omegna 45 52 N 8 23 E
102 Ōmiya 35 54 N 139 38 E
76 Omsk 55 0 N 73 38 E
61 Omul, Mt. 45 27 N 25 29 E
102 Ōmura 33 8 N 130 0 E
102 Ōmuta 33 0 N 130 26 E
55 Onda 39 55 N 0 17W
168 Ondangua 17 57 S 16 4 E
53 Ondárroa 43 19 N 2 25W
158 Ondo 7 4 N 4 47 E
75 Onega 64 0 N 38 10 E
75 Onega, R. 63 0 N 39 0 E
114 Onehunga 36 55 N 174 30 E
128 O'Neill 42 30 N 98 38W
127 Oneonta 42 26 N 75 5W
75 Onezhskaya Guba 64 30 N 37 0 E
75 Onezhskoye, Oz 62 0 N 35 30 E
158 Onitsha 6 6 N 6 42 E
53 Ons, Is. 42 23 N 8 55W
110 Onslow 21 40 S 115 0 E
131 Ontario 34 2 N 117 40W
127 Ontario, L. 43 40 N 78 0W
122 Ontario □ 52 0 N 88 10W
110 Oodnadatta 27 33 S 135 30 E
110 Ooldea 30 27 S 131 50 E
34 Oostende 51 15 N 2 50 E
34 Oosterhout 51 38 N 4 51 E
34 Oosterschelde, R. 51 30 N 4 0 E
86 Ootacamund 11 30 N 76 44 E
77 Opala, U.S.S.R. 52 15 N 156 15 E
165 Opala, Zaïre 0 37 S 24 21 E
63 Opatija 45 21 N 14 17 E
49 Opava 49 57 N 17 58 E
120 Ophir 63 10 N 156 31W
50 Opoczno 51 22 N 20 18 E
49 Opole 50 42 N 17 58 E
114 Opotiki 38 1 S 177 19 E
127 Opp 31 19 E 86 13W
41 Oppland □ 61 15 N 9 30 E
125 Optic Lake 54 46 N 101 13W
114 Opua 35 19 S 174 9 E
114 Opunake 39 26 S 173 52 E
29 Or, Côtes d' 47 10 N 4 50 E
63 Ora 46 20 N 11 19 E
51 Oradea 47 2 N 21 58 E
37 Öraefajökull, Mt. 64 2 N 16 15W
148 Oran 35 37 N 0 39W
31 Orange, Fr. 44 8 N 4 47 E
128 Orange, U.S.A. 30 0 N 93 40W
165 Orange = Oranje, R. 28 30 S 18 0 E
145 Orange, C. 4 20 N 51 30W
165 Orange Free State □ 28 30 S 27 0 E
137 Orange Walk 17 15 N 88 47W
127 Orangeburg 33 27 N 80 53W
122 Orangeville 43 55 N 80 5W
45 Oranienburg 52 45 N 13 15 E
168 Oranje, R. 28 41 S 16 28 E
168 Oranje-Vrystaat □ 28 30 S 27 0 E
168 Oranjemund 28 32 S 16 29 E
165 Orapa 24 13 S 25 25 E
60 Orašje 45 1 N 18 42 E
51 Orăştie 45 50 N 23 10 E
30 Orb, R. 43 15 N 3 18 E
113 Orbost 37 40 S 148 29 E
41 Örbynus 60 15 N 17 43 E
55 Orce 37 44 N 2 28W
29 Orchies 50 28 N 3 14 E
24 Orchy, Bridge of 56 30 N 4 46W
110 Ord, Mt. 17 20 S 125 34 E
110 Ord, R. 15 30 S 128 21 E
24 Ord of Caithness 58 35 N 3 37W
80 Ordu 40 55 N 37 53 E
53 Orduña 42 58 N 2 58W
53 Orduña, Mt. 37 20 N 3 30W
75 Ordzhonlkidze 43 0 N 44 35 E
41 Örebro 59 20 N 15 18 E
41 Örebro □ 59 27 N 15 0 E
131 Oregon □ 44 0 N 120 0W
131 Oregon City 45 28 N 122 35W
75 Orekhovo-Zuyevo 55 50 N 38 55 E
75 Orel 52 59 N 36 5 E
53 Orellana La Vieja 39 1 N 5 32W
131 Orem 40 27 N 111 45W
75 Orenburg 51 45 N 55 6 E
114 Orepuki 46 19 S 167 46 E
68 Orestiás 41 30 N 26 33 E
41 Øresund 55 45 N 12 45 E
21 Orford Ness, C. 52 6 N 1 31 E
65 Ória 40 30 E 17 38 E
122 Orient Bay 49 20 N 88 10W
144 Oriental, Cord. 5 0 N 74 0W
29 Origny 49 50 N 3 30 E
122 Orillia 44 40 N 79 24W
144 Orinoco, R. 8 37 N 62 15W
125 Orion 49 28 N 110 49W
87 Orissa □ 21 0 N 85 0 E
64 Oristano 39 54 N 8 35 E
64 Oristano, G. di 39 50 N 8 22 E
38 Orkanger 63 18 N 9 52 E
41 Örken 51 6 N 6 34 E
24 Orkney □ 59 0 N 3 0W
131 Orland 39 46 N 120 10W
127 Orlando 28 30 N 81 25W
29 Orléanais, Reg. 48 0 N 2 0 E
29 Orléans 47 54 N 1 52 E
123 Orleans, I. d' 46 54 N 70 58W
158 Orléansville = El Asnam 36 10 N 1 20 E
49 Orlické hory 50 15 N 16 30 E
77 Orlik 52 30 N 99 55 E
49 Orlov 49 17 N 20 51 E
86 Ormara 25 16 N 64 33 E
95 Ormoc 11 0 N 124 37 E
114 Ormond 38 33 S 177 56 E
63 Ormož 46 25 N 16 10 E
21 Ormskirk 53 35 N 2 54W
28 Orne, R. 49 18 N 0 14 E
28 Orne □ 48 40 N 0 0 E
41 Örnsköldsvik 63 17 N 18 40 E
144 Orocué 4 48 N 71 20W
123 Oromocto 45 54 N 66 37W
145 Orós 6 15 S 38 55W
68 Óros Ólimbos, Mt. 40 6 N 22 23 E
68 Óros Óthris, Mt. 39 4 N 22 42 E
64 Orosei, G. di 40 15 N 9 40 E
49 Orosháza 46 32 N 20 42 E
131 Oroville 39 40 N 121 30W
41 Orsa 61 7 N 14 37 E
75 Orsha 54 30 N 30 25 E
75 Orsk 51 20 N 58 34 E
51 Orşova 44 41 N 22 25 E
62 Orta, L. d' 45 48 N 8 21 E
65 Orta Nova 41 20 N 15 40 E
30 Orthez 43 29 N 0 48W
53 Ortigueira 43 40 N 7 50W
62 Ortles, Mt. 46 31 N 10 33 E
63 Ortona 42 21 N 14 24 E
144 Oruro 18 0 S 67 19W
28 Orvault 47 17 N 1 38 E
63 Orvieto 42 43 N 12 8 E
21 Orwell, R. 51 57 N 1 17 E
61 Oryakhovo 43 40 N 23 57 E
62 Orzinuovi 45 24 N 9 55 E
50 Orzyc, R. 52 47 N 21 13 E
139 Osa, Pen. de 8 0 N 84 0W
128 Osage, R. 38 35 N 91 57W
102 Ōsaka 34 40 N 135 30 E
102 Ōsaka □ 34 40 N 135 30 E
128 Osborne 39 30 N 98 45W
41 Osby 56 23 N 13 59 E
128 Osceola 35 40 N 90 0W
45 Oschatz 51 17 N 13 8 E
64 Oschiri 40 43 N 9 7 E
122 Oshawa 43 50 N 78 45W
128 Oshkosh 44 3 N 88 35W
158 Oshogbo 7 48 N 4 37 E
50 Osieczna 51 55 N 16 40 E
63 Osimo 43 40 N 13 30 E
75 Osipenko = Berdyansk 46 45 N 36 49 E
41 Oskarshamn 57 15 N 16 27 E
38 Oslo 59 55 N 10 45 E
41 Oslofjorden 58 30 N 10 0 E
80 Osmaniye 37 5 N 36 10 E
45 Osnabrück 52 16 N 8 2 E
148 Osorno 40 25 S 73 0W
34 Oss 51 46 N 5 32 E
113 Ossa, Mt. 41 80 S 146 0 E
55 Ossa de Montiel 38 58 N 2 45W
45 Oste, R. 53 33 N 9 10 E
34 Ostend = Oostende 51 15 N 2 50 E
45 Osterburg 52 47 N 11 44 E
41 Østerdalen 62 0 N 10 40 E
41 Östergötlands □ 58 24 N 15 34 E
41 Östersund 63 10 N 14 38 E
38 Østfold □ 59 25 N 11 25 E
45 Ostfriesische Is. 53 45 N 7 15 E
45 Ostfriesland, Reg. 53 20 N 7 40 E
41 Östhammar 60 16 N 18 22 E
49 Ostrava 49 51 N 18 18 E
50 Ostróda 53 42 N 19 58 E
50 Ostrołeka 53 4 N 21 38 E
51 Ostrov 43 40 N 24 9 E
50 Ostrów Mazowiecka 52 50 N 21 51 E
50 Ostrów Wielkopolski 51 39 N 17 49 E
49 Ostrowiec-Swietokrzyski 50 57 N 21 23 E
50 Ostrzeszów 51 25 N 17 52 E
68 Osumi, R. 40 48 N 19 52 E
102 Ōsumi-Kaikyō, Str. 30 55 N 131 0 E
102 Ōsumi-Shotō, Is. 30 30 N 130 45 E
127 Oswego 43 29 N 76 30W
21 Oswestry 52 52 N 3 3W
49 Oświęcim 50 2 N 19 11 E
114 Otago □ 44 45 S 169 10 E
102 Ōtake 34 27 N 132 25 E
114 Otaki 40 45 S 175 10 E
102 Otaru 43 13 N 141 0 E
48 Otava 61 39 N 27 4 E
68 Otelec 45 36 N 20 50 E
53 Otero de Rey 43 6 N 7 36W
131 Othello 46 53 N 119 8W
114 Otira Gorge 42 53 S 171 33 E
114 Otorohanga 38 11 S 175 12 E
65 Otranto 40 9 N 18 28 E
102 Otsu 42 35 N 143 40 E
38 Otta 61 46 N 9 32 E
122 Ottawa, Canada 45 27 N 75 42W
128 Ottawa, Ill. 41 20 N 88 55W
128 Ottawa, Kans 38 40 N 95 10W
121 Ottawa Is. 59 50 N 80 0W
122 Ottawa, R. 45 20 N 73 58W
125 Otter Rapids 55 42 N 104 46W
41 Otterup 55 30 N 10 22 E
148 Otway, B. 53 30 S 74 0W
113 Otway, C. 38 52 S 143 31 E
148 Otway, Seno de 53 5 S 71 30W
50 Otwock 52 5 N 21 20 E
48 Ötz 47 13 N 10 53 E
48 Ötztaler Alpen, Mts. 46 58 N 11 0 E
158 Ouagadougou 12 25 N 1 30W
158 Ouargla 31 59 N 5 25 E
158 Ouarzazate 30 55 N 6 55W
165 Oubangi, R. 0 30 S 17 42 E
29 Ouche, R. 47 6 N 5 16 E
34 Oudenaarde 50 50 N 3 37 E
168 Oudtshoorn 33 35 S 22 14 E
28 Ouessant, I. d' 48 28 N 5 6W
158 Ouezzane 34 51 N 5 42W
158 Ouidah 6 25 N 2 0 E
158 Oujda 34 41 N 1 45W
158 Ouled Djellal 34 28 N 5 2 E
37 Oulu 65 1 N 25 29 E
37 Oulujärvi, L. 64 25 N 27 0 E
34 Our, R. 49 53 N 6 18 E
113 Ouse 42 25 S 146 42 E
21 Ouse, R., Gt. 52 35 N 0 18 E
21 Ouse, R., Little 52 31 N 0 30 E
21 Ouse, R., E. Sussex 50 47 N 0 3 E
21 Ouse, R., N. Yorks 53 42 N 0 41W
28 Oust, R. 47 39 N 2 6W
19 Outer Hebrides 57 30 N 7 40W
125 Outlook 51 30 N 107 0W
29 Outreau 50 40 N 1 36 E
113 Ouyen 35 1 S 142 22 E
114 Ovalau, I. 17 40 S 178 48 E
148 Ovalle 30 33 S 71 18W
165 Ovamboland, Reg. 17 20 S 16 30 E
34 Over Flakkee, I. 51 45 N 4 5 E
34 Overijssel □ 52 25 N 6 35 E
34 Overpelt 51 12 N 5 20 E
53 Oviedo 43 25 N 5 50W
41 Oviksfjällen, Mts. 63 0 N 13 49 E
114 Owaka 46 27 S 169 40 E
165 Owando 0 29 S 15 55 E
127 Owego 42 6 N 76 17W
122 Owen Sound 44 35 N 80 55W
165 Owendo 0 17 N 9 30 E
127 Owensboro 37 40 N 87 5W
158 Owo 7 18 N 5 30 E
41 Oxelösund 58 43 N 17 15 E
21 Oxford, U.K. 51 45 N 1 15W
127 Oxford, N.C. 36 19 N 78 36W
21 Oxford □ 51 45 N 1 15W
125 Oxford House 54 46 N 95 16W
131 Oxnard 34 10 N 119 14W
102 Oyama 36 18 N 139 48 E
165 Oyem 1 37 N 11 35 E
158 Oyo 7 46 N 3 56 E
95 Ozamiz 8 15 N 123 50 E
127 Ozark 31 29 N 85 39W
118 Ozark Plat. 37 20 N 91 40W
128 Ozarks, L. of the 38 10 N 93 0W
64 Ozieri 40 35 N 9 0 E

P

87 Pa-an 16 45 N 97 40 E
168 Paarl 13 45 S 18 46 E
87 Pabna 24 1 N 89 18 E
144 Pacaraima, Sa. 5 0 N 63 0W
144 Pacasmayo 7 20 S 79 35W
65 Pachino 36 43 N 15 4 E
131 Pacific Groves 37 36 N 121 58W
107 Pacific Ocean 10 0 N 140 0W
28 Pacy 49 2 N 1 22 E
94 Padang 1 0 S 100 20 E
125 Paddockwood 53 30 N 105 30W
45 Paderborn 51 42 N 8 44 E
121 Padloping Island 67 0 N 63 0W
63 Pádova 45 24 N 11 52 E
21 Padstow 50 33 N 4 57W

Portomaggiore

Rødby

63 Portomaggiore 44 41 N 11 47 E
62 Portovénere 44 2 N 9 50 E
24 Portpatrick 54 50 N 5 7W
24 Portree 57 25 N 6 11W
27 Portrush 55 13 N 6 40W
21 Portsmouth, U.K. 50 48 N 1 6W
127 Portsmouth, N.H. 43 5 N 70 45W
127 Portsmouth, Ohio 38 45 N 83 0W
127 Portsmouth, R.I. 41 35 N 71 44W
127 Portsmouth, Va. 36 50 N 76 50W
24 Portsoy 57 41 N 2 41W
53 Portugal ■ 40 19 N 8 4W
158 Portuguese Guinea
= Guinea Bissau ■ 12 0 N 15 0W
27 Portumna 53 5 N 8 12W
148 Porvenir 53 10 S 70 30W
148 Posadas, Arg. 27 30 S 56 0W
53 Posadas, Sp. 37 47 N 5 11W
145 Posse 14 4 S 46 18W
45 Pössneck 50 42 N 11 34 E
122 Poste de la Baleine 55 20 N 77 40W
158 Poste Maurice
Cortier 22 14 N 1 2 E
63 Postojna 45 46 N 14 12 E
168 Potchefstroom 26 41 S 27 7 E
65 Potenza 40 40 N 15 50 E
63 Potenza, R. 43 25 N 13 40 E
63 Potenza Picena 43 22 N 13 37 E
169 Potgietersrus 24 10 S 29 3 E
127 Potomac, R. 38 0 N 76 20W
144 Potosí 19 38 S 65 50W
45 Potsdam,
E. Germany 52 23 N 13 4 E
127 Potsdam, U.S.A. 44 40 N 74 59W
45 Potsdam □ 52 40 N 13 30 E
127 Pottsville 40 39 N 76 12W
127 Poughkeepsie 41 40 N 73 57W
29 Pouilly 47 18 N 2 57 E
114 Poverty B. 38 43 S 178 0 E
53 Póvoa de Varzim 41 25 N 8 46W
75 Povenets 62 48 N 35 0 E
128 Powder, R. 46 44 N 105 26W
131 Powder River 43 5 N 107 0W
131 Powell 44 45 N 108 45W
131 Powell, L. 37 25 N 110 45W
124 Powell River 49 48 N 125 20W
21 Powys □ 52 20 N 3 30W
99 Poyang Hu, L. 29 5 N 116 20 E
53 Poza de la Sal 42 35 N 3 31W
50 Poznań 52 25 N 17 0 E
55 Pozo Alcón 37 42 N 2 56W
53 Pozoblanco 38 23 N 4 51W
65 Pozzallo 36 44 N 15 40 E
65 Pozzuoli 40 49 N 14 7 E
60 Praca 43 47 N 18 43 E
145 Prado 17 20 S 39 20W
48 Prague = Praha 50 5 N 14 22 E
48 Praha 50 5 N 14 22 E
51 Prahova, R. 44 43 N 26 27 E
51 Prahovo 44 18 N 22 39 E
145 Prainha 1 45 S 53 30W
113 Prairie 20 50 S 144 35 E
131 Prairie City 45 27 N 118 44W
128 Prairie du Chien 43 1 N 91 9W
128 Prairies,
Coteau des 44 0 N 97 0W
94 Praja 8 39 S 116 37 E
145 Prata 19 25 S 49 0W
63 Prato 43 53 N 11 5 E
128 Pratt 37 40 N 98 45W
53 Pravia 43 30 N 6 12W
63 Predáppio 44 7 N 11 58 E
60 Predejane 42 51 N 22 9 E
125 Preeceville 52 0 N 102 50W
124 Premier 56 4 N 130 1W
45 Prenzlau 53 19 N 13 51 E
60 Prepansko, J. 40 45 N 21 0 E
91 Preparis North
Chan. 15 12 N 93 40 E
91 Preparis South
Chan. 14 36 N 93 40 E
122 Prescott, Canada 44 45 N 75 30W
131 Prescott, U.S.A. 34 35 N 112 30W
60 Preševo 42 19 N 21 39 E
145 Presidente Epitácio 21 46 S 52 6W
145 Presidente Prudente 15 45 S 54 0W
61 Preslav 43 10 N 26 52 E
49 Prešov 49 0 N 21 15 E
127 Presque Isle 46 40 N 68 0W
158 Prestea 5 22 N 2 7W
21 Presteign 52 17 N 3 0W
21 Preston, 53 46 N 2 42W
24 Prestonpans 55 58 N 3 0W
24 Prestwick 55 30 N 4 38W
169 Pretoria 25 44 S 28 12 E
68 Préveza 38 57 N 20 47 E
120 Pribilov Is. 56 0 N 170 0W
55 Priego 40 38 N 2 21W
53 Priego de
Córdoba 37 27 N 4 12W
168 Prieska 29 40 S 22 42 E
49 Prievidza 48 46 N 18 36 E
75 Prikaspiyskaya
Nizmennost 47 30 N 50 0 E
60 Prilep 41 21 N 21 37 E
125 Prince Albert 53 15 N 105 50W
120 Prince Albert Pen. 72 0 N 116 0W
120 Prince Albert Sd. 70 25 N 115 0W
121 Prince Charles I. 68 0 N 76 0W
123 Prince Edward I. □ 44 2 N 77 20W
124 Prince George 53 50 N 122 50W
118 Prince of Wales, C. 53 50 N 131 30W
113 Prince of Wales, I.,
Australia 10 35 S 142 0 E
120 Prince of Wales I.,
Canada 73 0 N 99 0W
124 Prince of Wales I.,
U.S.A. 53 30 N 131 30W
124 Prince Rupert 54 20 N 130 20W
113 Princess Charlotte,
B. 14 15 S 144 0 E
174 Princesse Astrid
Kyst 71 0 S 10 0 E
174 Princesse Ragnhild
Kyst 71 0 S 30 0 E
124 Princeton, Canada 49 27 N 120 30W
127 Princeton, Ind. 38 20 N 87 35W
127 Princeton, Ky. 37 6 N 87 55W
127 Princeton, N.J. 40 18 N 74 40W
127 Princeton, W.Va. 37 21 N 81 8W
75 Priozersk 61 2 N 30 4 E
75 Pripyat, R. 51 20 N 30 20 E
60 Priština 42 40 N 21 13 E
127 Pritchard 30 47 N 88 5W
64 Priverno 41 29 N 13 10 E
60 Prizren 42 13 N 20 45 E
64 Prizzi 37 44 N 13 24 E
95 Probolinggo 7 46 S 113 13 E
137 Progreso 21 20 N 89 40W
68 Prokletije, Mt. 42 30 N 19 45 E
76 Prokopyevsk 54 0 N 87 3 E
87 Prome 18 45 N 95 30 E
145 Propriá 10 13 S 36 51W
31 Propriano 41 41 N 8 52 E
113 Proserpine 20 21 S 148 36 E
61 Provadiya 43 12 N 27 30 E
31 Provence, Reg. 43 40 N 5 45 E
127 Providence 41 41 N 71 15W
122 Providence Bay 45 41 N 82 15W
124 Provincial Cannery 51 33 N 127 36W
29 Provins 48 33 N 3 15 E
131 Provo 40 16 N 111 37W
125 Provost 52 25 N 110 20W
113 Prudhoe, I. 21 23 S 149 45 E
120 Prudhoe Bay 70 10 N 148 0W
125 Prudhomme 52 22 N 105 47W
49 Prudnik 50 20 N 17 38 E
50 Pruszez Gdańska 54 17 N 19 40 E
50 Pruszków 52 9 N 20 49 E
75 Prut, R. 45 28 N 28 12 E
174 Prydz B. 69 0 S 74 0 E
50 Przasnysz 53 2 N 20 45 E
49 Przemysl 49 50 N 22 45 E
49 Przemysl □ 50 0 N 22 0 E
76 Przhevalsk 42 30 N 78 20 E
68 Psará, I. 38 37 N 25 38 E
75 Pskov 57 50 N 28 25 E
49 Pszczyna 49 59 N 18 58 E
68 Ptolemaís 40 30 N 21 43 E
144 Pucallpa 8 25 S 74 30W
51 Pucioasia 45 4 N 25 26 E
86 Pudukkottai 10 28 N 78 47 E
137 Puebla 19 0 N 98 10W
137 Puebla □ 18 30 N 98 0W
53 Puebla de Guzman 37 33 N 7 15W
53 Puebla de Sanabria 42 4 N 6 38W
128 Pueblo 38 20 N 104 40W
148 Puente Alto 33 32 S 70 35W
53 Puente Genil 37 22 N 4 47W
55 Puente la Reina 42 40 N 1 49W
53 Puenteareas 42 10 N 8 28W
53 Puentedeume 43 24 N 8 10W
139 Puerto Armuelles 8 20 N 83 10W
144 Puerto Asís 0 30 N 76 30W
144 Puerto Ayacucho 5 40 N 67 35W
137 Puerto Barrios 15 40 N 88 40W
144 Puerto Berrío 6 30 N 74 30W
144 Puerto Bolívar 3 10 S 79 55W
144 Puerto Cabello 10 28 N 68 1W
139 Puerto Cabezas 14 0 N 83 30W
144 Puerto Carreño 6 12 N 67 22W
139 Puerto Cortes 15 51 N 88 0W
137 Puerto Cortés 8 20 N 82 20W
148 Puerto Coyle 50 54 S 69 15W
144 Puerto Cumarebo 11 29 N 69 21W
53 Puerto de Santa
María 36 35 N 6 15W
158 Puerto del Rosario 28 30 N 13 52W
148 Puerto Deseado 47 45 S 66 0W
144 Puerto Páez 6 13 N 67 28W
144 Puerto Leguizamo 0 12 S 74 46W
148 Puerto Lobos 42 0 S 65 3W
55 Puerto Lumbreras 37 34 N 1 48W
148 Puerto Madryn 42 48 S 65 4W
55 Puerto Mazarrón 37 34 N 1 15W
148 Puerto Montt 41 28 S 72 57W
148 Puerto Natales 51 45 S 72 25W
139 Puerto Padre 21 13 N 76 35W
144 Puerto Pinasco 22 30 S 57 50W
148 Puerto Pirámides 42 35 S 64 20W
144 Puerto Piritu 10 5 N 65 0W
139 Puerto Plata 19 40 N 70 45W
95 Puerto Princesa 9 55 N 118 50 E
148 Puerto Quellón 43 7 S 73 37W
53 Puerto Real 36 33 N 6 12W
139 Puerto Rico, I. 18 15 N 66 45W
148 Puerto Saavedra 38 47 S 73 24W
144 Puerto Suárez 18 58 S 57 52W
148 Puerto Varas 41 19 S 72 59W
53 Puertollano 38 43 N 4 7W
148 Pueyrredón, L. 47 20 S 72 0W
75 Pugachev 52 0 N 48 55 E
131 Puget Sd. 47 15 N 123 30W
65 Puglia □ 41 0 N 16 30 E
51 Pui 45 30 N 23 4 E
55 Puig Mayor, Mt. 39 49 N 2 47 E
55 Puigcerda 42 24 N 1 50 E
29 Puisaye, Collines
de la 47 35 N 3 30 E
114 Pukaki, L. 44 5 S 170 1 E
125 Pukatawagan 55 45 N 101 20W
114 Pukekohe 37 12 S 174 55 E
63 Pula 39 0 N 9 0 E
144 Pulacayo 20 25 S 66 41W
127 Pulaski, N.Y. 43 32 N 76 9W
127 Pulaski, Tenn. 35 10 N 87 0W
127 Pulaski, Va. 37 4 N 80 49W
50 Puławy 51 23 N 21 59 E
86 Pulicat L. 13 40 N 80 15 E
131 Pullman 46 49 N 117 10W
94 Puloraja 4 55 N 95 24 E
50 Pułtusk 52 43 N 21 6 E
86 Punch 33 48 N 74 4 E
86 Pune 18 29 N 73 57 E
86 Punjab □ 31 0 N 76 0 E
144 Puno 15 55 S 70 3W
148 Punta Alta 38 53 S 62 4W
148 Punta Arenas 53 0 S 71 0W
148 Punta Delgada 42 43 S 63 38W
137 Punta Gorda 16 10 N 88 45W
113 Puntabie 32 12 S 134 5 E
139 Puntarenas 10 0 N 84 50W
144 Punto Fijo 11 42 N 70 13W
144 Purace, Mt. 2 21 N 76 23W
21 Purbeck, I. of 50 40 N 2 5W
55 Purchena Tetica 37 21 N 2 21W
87 Puri 19 50 N 85 58 E
87 Purnea 25 45 N 87 31 E
91 Pursat 12 34 N 103 50 E
87 Purulia 23 17 N 86 33 E
144 Purus, R. 3 42 S 61 28W
61 Pŭrvomay 42 8 N 25 17 E
95 Purwakarta 6 35 S 107 29 E
95 Purwodadi, Jawa 7 7 S 110 55 E
95 Purwodadi, Jawa 7 51 S 110 0 E
95 Purwokerto 7 25 S 109 14 E
95 Purworedjo 7 43 S 110 2 E
99 Pusan 35 5 N 129 0 E
77 Pushchino 54 20 N 158 10 E
75 Pushkino 51 16 N 47 9 E
49 Püspökladány 47 19 N 21 6 E
87 Putao 27 28 N 97 30 E
114 Putaruru 38 3 S 175 47 E
65 Putignano 40 50 N 17 5 E
51 Putna, R. 45 35 N 27 30 E
45 Puttgarden 54 28 N 11 15 E
144 Putumayo, R. 3 7 S 67 58 E
30 Puy de Dôme, Mt. 45 46 N 2 57 E
30 Puy de Sancy, Mt. 45 32 N 2 41 E
30 Puy l'Evêque 44 31 N 1 9 E
131 Puyallup 47 10 N 122 22W
30 Puy-de-Dôme □ 45 47 N 3 0 E
30 Puyoô 43 33 N 0 56W
21 Pwllheli 52 54 N 4 24W
75 Pyatigorsk 44 2 N 43 0 E
87 Pyinmana 19 45 N 96 20 E
99 Pyŏngyang 39 0 N 125 45 E
30 Pyrénées-
Atlantiques □ 43 15 N 0 45W
30 Pyrénées-
Orientales □ 42 35 N 2 25 E
50 Pyrzyce 53 10 N 14 55 E
87 Pyu 18 30 N 96 35 E

Q

102 Qalāt 32 15 N 66 58 E
80 Qal'at Şalih 31 31 N 47 16 E
81 Qandahār 31 32 N 65 30 E
159 Qâra 29 38 N 26 30 E
81 Qarāvol 37 15 N 68 50 E
159 Qasr Farâfra 27 0 N 28 1 E
85 Qaşr Hamām 21 5 N 46 5 E
81 Qatar ■ 25 30 N 51 15 E
159 Qattara,
Munkhafed el 29 30 N 27 30 E
159 Qena 26 10 N 32 43 E
81 Qeshm 26 55 N 56 10 E
81 Qeys, Jazireh-ye 26 32 N 53 56 E
86 Qila Safed 29 0 N 61 30 E
85 Qîzân 16 57 N 42 3 E
81 Qom 34 40 N 51 4 E
81 Qondūz 36 50 N 68 50 E
81 Qondūz □ 36 50 N 68 50 E
91 Quang Ngai 15 13 N 108 58 E
91 Quang Yen 21 3 N 106 52 E
21 Quantock Hills 51 8 N 3 10W
148 Quaraí 30 15 S 56 20W
99 Quanzhou 24 55 N 118 34 E
81 Qūchān 37 10 N 58 27 E
169 Que Que 18 58 S 29 48 E
113 Queanbeyan 35 17 S 149 14 E
123 Québec 46 52 N 71 13W
45 Quedlinburg 51 47 N 11 9 E
174 Queen Alexandra
Ra. 85 0 S 170 0 E
124 Queen Charlotte
Is. 53 10 N 132 0W
124 Queen Charlotte
Str. 51 0 N 128 0W
118 Queen Elizabeth Is. 75 0 N 95 0W
174 Queen Mary Coast 70 0 S 95 0 E
174 Queen Maud Ra. 86 0 S 160 0W
111 Queensland □ 15 0 S 142 0 E
113 Queenstown, Australia 42 4 S 145 35 E
114 Queenstown, N.Z. 45 1 S 168 40 E
168 Queenstown, S.Africa 31 52 S 26 52 E
165 Quela 9 10 S 16 56 E
169 Quelimane 17 53 S 36 58 E
99 Quemoy = Jinmen, I. 24 25 N 118 25 E
137 Querêtaro 20 40 N 100 23W
55 Quesada 37 51 N 3 4W
124 Quesnel 53 5 N 122 30W
28 Questembert 47 40 N 2 28W
122 Quetico 48 45 N 90 55W
86 Quetta 30 15 N 66 55 E
137 Quezaltenango 14 40 N 91 30W
95 Quezon City 14 38 N 121 0 E
91 Qui Nhon 13 40 N 109 13 E
144 Quibdo 5 42 N 76 40W
148 Quilân, C. 43 15 S 74 30W
165 Quilengues 14 12 S 15 12 E
96 Qilian Shan, mts. 39 0 N 98 0 E
148 Quillota 32 54 S 71 16W
86 Quilon 8 50 N 76 38 E
28 Quimper 48 0 N 4 9W
28 Quimperlé 47 53 N 3 33W
127 Quincy,Fla. 30 34 N 84 34W
128 Quincy, Ill. 39 55 N 91 20W
99 Qingdao 36 5 N 120 20 E
99 Qinghai □ 36 0 N 98 0 E
99 Qinhuangdao 39 56 N 119 30 E
137 Quintana Roo □ 19 0 E 88 0W
148 Quintero 32 45 S 71 30W
55 Quinto 41 25 N 0 32W
99 Qiqihar 47 26 N 124 0 E
53 Quiroga 42 28 N 7 18W
144 Quito 0 15 S 78 35W
145 Quixadâ 4 55 S 39 0W
113 Quorn 32 25 S 138 0 E
159 Quseir 26 7 N 34 16 E
68 Qytet Stalin 40 47 N 19 57 E

R

48 Raab 47 42 N 17 38 E
37 Raane 64 40 N 24 28 E
24 Raasay, I. 57 25 N 6 4W
49 Raba, R. 50 9 N 20 30 E
95 Raba 8 36 S 118 55 E
53 Rabaçal, R. 41 30 N 7 12W
158 Rabat 34 2 N 6 48W
106 Rabaul 4 24 S 152 18 E
80 Rābigh 22 50 N 39 5 E
49 Rabka 49 37 N 19 59 E
64 Racalmuto 37 25 N 13 41 E
123 Race, C. 46 40 N 53 18W
49 Racibórz 50 7 N 18 18 E
127 Racine 42 41 N 87 51W
48 Radbuza, R. 49 46 N 13 24 E
127 Radford 37 8 N 80 32W
50 Radom □ 51 20 N 21 0 E
50 Radomka R. 51 43 N 21 26 E
50 Radomsko 51 5 N 19 28 E
63 Radovljica 46 22 N 14 12 E
48 Radstadt 47 24 N 13 28 E
21 Radstock 51 17 N 2 25W
60 Raduša 42 7 N 21 15 E
125 Radville 49 30 N 104 15W
124 Rae 62 45 N 115 50W
87 Rae Bareli 26 18 N 81 20 E
121 Rae Isthmus 66 40 N 87 30W
114 Raetihi 39 25 S 175 17 E
148 Rafaela 31 10 S 61 30W
64 Raffadali 37 23 N 13 29 E
80 Rafhā 29 35 N 43 35 E
159 Râgâ 8 28 N 25 41 E
113 Raglan, Australia 23 42 S 150 49 E
114 Raglan, N.Z. 37 55 S 174 55 E
65 Rāgusa 36 56 N 14 42 E
86 Raichur 16 10 N 77 20 E
87 Raigarh 21 56 N 83 25 E
131 Rainier, Mt. 46 50 N 121 50W
125 Rainy River 48 50 N 94 30W
87 Raipur 21 17 N 81 45 E
122 Raith 48 50 N 90 0W
27 Raith Luirc 52 22 N 8 43W
87 Rajahmundry 17 1 N 81 48 E
86 Rajasthan □ 26 45 N 73 30 E
86 Rajgarh, Mad. P. 24 2 N 76 45 E
86 Rajgarh, Rajasthan 28 40 N 75 25 E
86 Rajkot 22 15 N 70 56 E
87 Rajshahi 24 22 N 88 39 E
114 Rakaia 43 45 S 172 1 E
49 Rákospalota 47 30 N 19 5 E
48 Rakovník 50 6 N 13 42 E
61 Rakovski 42 21 N 24 57 E
125 Raleigh, Australia 30 27 S 153 2 E
127 Raleigh, Canada 49 30 N 92 5W
113 Ram Head 37 47 S 149 30 E
65 Ramacca 37 24 N 14 40 E
29 Rambouillet 48 40 N 1 48 E
95 Ramelau, Mt. 8 55 S 126 22 E
131 Ramona 33 1 N 116 56W
86 Rampur 23 25 N 73 53 E
122 Ramsey, Canada 47 25 N 82 20W
21 Ramsey, U.K. 54 20 N 4 21W
21 Ramsgate 51 20 N 1 25 E
87 Ranaghat 23 15 N 88 35 E
148 Rancagua 34 10 S 70 50W
28 Rance, R. 48 31 N 1 59W
131 Ranchester 44 57 N 107 12W
87 Ranchi 23 19 N 85 27 E
51 Rancu 44 32 N 24 15 E
65 Rándazzo 37 53 N 14 56 E
41 Randers 56 29 N 10 1 E
41 Randers, Fd. 56 37 N 10 20 E
127 Randolph 43 55 N 72 39W
37 Râneå 65 53 N 22 18 E
114 Rangaunu, B. 34 51 S 173 15 E
114 Rangitaiki, R. 37 54 S 176 53 E
114 Rangitata, R. 44 11 S 171 30 E
87 Rangoon 16 45 N 96 20 E
87 Rangpur 25 42 N 89 22 E
86 Ranibennur 14 35 N 75 30 E
113 Rankins Springs 33 49 S 146 14 E
24 Rannoch 56 41 N 4 20W
24 Rannoch, L. 56 41 N 4 20W
91 Ranong 9 56 N 98 40 E
95 Rantemario, Mt. 3 15 S 119 57 E
127 Rantoul 40 18 N 88 10W
62 Rapallo 44 21 N 9 12 E
95 Rapang 3 45 S 119 55 E
128 Rapid City 44 0 N 103 0W
107 Rarotonga, I. 21 30 S 160 0W
81 Ra's al Khaymah 25 50 N 56 5 E
80 Ra's al Mishā'b 29 5 N 48 10 E
159 Ra's Al-Unuf 30 25 N 18 15 E
80 Ra's al Tannūrah 26 40 N 50 10 E
159 Rashad 11 55 N 31 0 E
159 Rashîd 31 21 N 30 22 E
80 Rasht 37 20 N 49 40 E
45 Rastatt 48 50 N 8 12 E
91 Rat Buri 13 30 N 99 54 E
120 Rat Is. 51 50 N 178 15 E
86 Ratangarh 28 5 N 74 35 E
27 Rath Luirc 52 21 N 8 40W
27 Rathdrum, Eire 52 57 N 6 13W
131 Rathdrum, U.S.A 47 50 N 116 58W
45 Rathenow 52 38 N 12 23 E
27 Rathkeale 52 32 N 8 57W
27 Rathlin, I. 55 18 N 6 14W
48 Ratikon, Ra. 47 3 N 9 50 E
86 Ratnagiri 16 57 N 73 18 E
128 Raton 37 0 N 104 30W
48 Ratten 47 28 N 15 44 E
24 Rattray Hd. 57 38 N 1 50W
91 Raub 3 47 N 101 52 E
114 Raukumara, Ra. 38 5 S 177 55 E
64 Ravanusa 37 16 N 13 58 E
81 Rāvar 31 20 N 56 51 E
63 Ravenna 44 28 N 12 15 E
113 Ravenshoe 17 37 S 145 29 E
110 Ravensthorpe 33 35 S 120 2 E
86 Rawalpindi 33 38 N 73 8 E
86 Rawalpindi □ 33 38 N 73 8 E
91 Rawang 3 19 N 101 35 E
122 Rawdon 46 3 N 73 40W
50 Rawicz 51 36 N 16 52 E
50 Rawka R. 52 9 N 20 8 E
110 Rawlinna 30 58 S 125 28 E
131 Rawlins 41 50 N 107 20W
148 Rawson 43 15 S 65 0W
123 Ray, C. 47 33 N 59 15W
77 Raychikhinsk 49 46 N 129 25 E
124 Raymond, Canada 49 30 N 112 35W
131 Raymond, U.S.A. 46 45 N 123 48W
128 Raymondville 26 30 N 97 50W
125 Raymore 50 25 N 104 31W
28 Raz, Pte. du 48 2 N 4 47W
60 Ražana 44 6 N 19 55 E
60 Ražanj 43 40 N 21 31 E
61 Razdelna 43 13 N 27 41 E
61 Razgrad 43 33 N 26 34 E
61 Razlog 41 53 N 23 28 E
30 Ré, Ï. de 46 12 N 1 30W
21 Reading, U.K. 51 27 N 0 57W
127 Reading, U.S.A. 40 20 N 75 53W
148 Realicó 35 0 S 64 15W
30 Réalmont 43 48 N 2 10 E
63 Recanati 43 24 N 13 32 E
60 Recas 45 46 N 21 30 E
145 Recife 8 0 S 35 0W
45 Recklinghausen 51 36 N 7 10 E
148 Reconquista 29 10 S 59 45W
128 Red, R. 48 10 N 97 0W
124 Red Deer 52 20 N 113 50W
125 Red Lake 51 1 N 94 1W
73 Red Sea 20 0 N 40 0 E
128 Red Wing 44 32 N 92 35W
21 Redbridge 51 35 N 0 7 E
21 Redcar 54 37 N 1 4W
125 Redcliff 50 10 N 110 50W
113 Redcliffe 27 12 S 153 0 E
21 Redditch 52 18 N 1 57W
131 Redlands 34 0 N 117 0W
131 Redmond 44 19 N 121 11W
139 Redonda, I. 16 58 N 62 19W
53 Redondela 42 15 N 8 38W
53 Redondo 38 39 N 7 37W
131 Redondo Beach 33 52 N 118 26W
21 Redruth 50 14 N 5 14W
124 Redstone 52 8 N 123 42W
124 Redwater 53 55 N 113 0W
131 Redwood City 37 30 N 122 15W
27 Ree, L. 53 35 N 8 0W
114 Reefton 42 6 S 171 51 E
50 Rega, R. 53 52 N 15 16 E
45 Regen 48 58 N 13 9 E
45 Regensburg 49 1 N 12 7 E
62 Reggio nell'Emilia 44 42 N 10 38 E
65 Réggio di Calábria 38 7 N 15 38 E
125 Regina 50 30 N 104 35W
80 Rehovot 31 54 N 34 48 E
45 Reichenbach 50 36 N 12 19 E
127 Reidsville 36 21 N 79 40W
21 Reigate 51 14 N 0 11W
55 Reillo 39 54 N 1 53W
29 Reims 49 15 N 4 0 E
125 Reindeer L. 57 20 N 102 20W
114 Reinga, C. 34 25 S 172 43 E
53 Reinosa 43 2 N 4 15W
53 Reinosa, P. 42 56 N 4 10W
145 Remanso 9 41 S 42 4W
95 Rembang 6 42 S 111 21 E
81 Remeshk 26 55 N 58 50 E
29 Remiremont 48 0 N 6 36 E
45 Remscheid 51 11 N 7 12 E
77 Rene 66 2 N 179 25W
122 Renfrew, Canada 45 30 N 76 40W
24 Renfrew, U.K. 55 52 N 4 24W
94 Rengat 0 30 S 102 45 E
113 Renmark 34 11 S 140 43 E
28 Rennes 48 7 N 1 41W
28 Rennes, Bassin de 48 0 N 2 0W
131 Reno 39 30 N 119 0W
131 Renton 47 30 N 122 9W
128 Republican, R. 39 3 N 96 48W
121 Repulse Bay 66 30 N 86 30W
60 Resen 41 5 N 21 0 E
125 Reserve 33 50 N 108 54W
148 Resistencia 27 30 S 59 0W
51 Reşita 45 18 N 21 53 E
121 Resolution I.,Canada 61 30 N 65 0W
114 Resolution, I., N.Z. 45 40 S 166 40 E
29 Rethel 49 30 N 4 20 E
68 Réthímnon 35 15 N 24 40 E
68 Réthímnon □ 35 23 N 24 28 E
28 Rétiers 47 55 N 1 25W
55 Reus 41 10 N 1 5 E
45 Reutlingen 48 28 N 9 13 E
48 Reutte 47 29 N 10 42 E
30 Revel 43 28 N 2 0 E
29 Revigny 48 50 N 5 0 E
107 Revillagigedo, Is.de 18 40 N 112 0W
29 Revin 49 55 N 4 39 E
87 Rewa 24 33 N 81 25 E
131 Rexburg 43 45 N 111 50W
158 Rey Malabo 3 45 N 8 50 E
37 Reykanes, Pen. 63 48 N 22 40W
37 Reykjavik 64 10 N 21 57 E
137 Reynosa 26 5 N 98 18W
80 Rezā'īyeh 37 40 N 45 0 E
21 Rhayader 52 19 N 3 30W
42 Rhein, R. 51 42 N 6 20 E
45 Rheine 52 17 N 7 25 E
45 Rheinland-Pfalz □ 50 50 N 7 0 E
45 Rheydt 51 10 N 6 24 E
42 Rhine, R. =
Rhein, R. 51 42 N 6 20 E
128 Rhinelander 45 38 N 89 29W
62 Rho 45 31 N 9 2 E
127 Rhode Island □ 41 38 N 71 37W
61 Rhodope, Mts. =
Rhodopi Planina 41 40 N 24 20 E
61 Rhodopi Planina 41 40 N 24 20 E
21 Rhondda 51 39 N 3 30W
31 Rhône □ 45 54 N 4 35 E
31 Rhône, R. 43 28 N 4 42 E
24 Rhum, I. 57 0 N 6 20W
21 Rhyl 53 19 N 3 29W
53 Riansares, R. 39 32 N 3 18W
94 Riau □ 1 0 N 102 35 E
53 Riaza, R. 41 16 N 3 29W
53 Ribadavia 42 17 N 8 8W
53 Ribadesella 43 30 N 5 7W
55 Ribas 42 19 N 2 15 E
145 Ribas do Rio Pardo 20 27 S 53 46W
21 Ribble, R. 54 13 N 2 20W
41 Ribe 55 19 N 8 44 E
29 Ribeauville 48 10 N 7 20 E
29 Ribécourt 49 30 N 2 55 E
53 Ribeira 42 36 N 8 58W
145 Ribeirão Prêto 21 10 S 47 50W
64 Ribera 37 30 N 13 13 E
48 Říčany 50 0 N 14 40 E
114 Riccarton 43 32 S 172 37 E
63 Riccione 44 0 N 12 39 E
128 Rice Lake 44 10 N 78 10W
165 Richards B. 28 48 S 32 6 E
131 Richland 44 49 N 117 9W
113 Richmond, Australia 20 43 S 143 8 E
114 Richmond, N.Z. 41 4 S 173 12 E
169 Richmond, S. Africa 29 54 S 30 8 E
21 Richmond, Surrey 51 28 N 0 18W
21 Richmond, Yorks. 54 24 N 1 43W
131 Richmond, Calif. 38 0 N 122 30W
127 Richmond, Ind. 39 50 N 84 50W
127 Richmond, Ky. 37 40 N 84 20W
127 Richmond, Va. 37 33 N 77 27W
122 Richmond Gulf, L. 56 20 N 75 50W
127 Richwood 38 17 N 80 32W
122 Ridgetown 42 26 N 81 52W
127 Ridgway 41 25 N 78 43W
48 Ried 48 14 N 13 30 E
45 Riesa 51 19 N 13 19 E
65 Riesi 37 16 N 14 4 E
63 Rieti 42 23 N 12 50 E
75 Riga 56 53 N 24 8 E
81 Rīgestān, Reg 30 15 N 65 0 E
123 Rigolet 54 10 N 58 23W
63 Rijeka 45 20 N 14 21 E
60 Rijeka Crnojevica 42 24 N 19 1 E
34 Rijssen 52 19 N 6 30 E
131 Riley 39 18 N 96 50W
41 Rimbo 59 44 N 18 21 E
63 Rímini 44 3 N 12 33 E
51 Rîmnicu Sărat 45 26 N 27 3 E
51 Rîmnicu Vîlcea 45 9 N 24 21 E
123 Rimouski 48 27 N 68 30W
41 Ringe 55 13 N 10 28 E
38 Ringerike 60 7 N 10 16 E
41 Ringsjön, L. 55 55 N 13 30 E
41 Ringsted 55 25 N 11 46 E
45 Rinteln 52 11 N 9 3 E
55 Rio, Pta. del 36 49 N 2 24W
144 Rio Branco, Brazil 9 58 S 67 49W
148 Rio Branco,
Uruguay 32 34 S 53 25W
148 Rio Cuarto 33 10 S 64 25W
148 Rio de la Plata 35 0 S 57 0W
145 Rio de Janeiro 23 0 S 43 12W
145 Rio de Janeiro □ 22 50 S 43 0W
148 Rio do Sul 27 95 S 49 37W
148 Rio Grande 32 0 S 52 20W
145 Rio Grande do
Norte □ 5 45 S 36 0W
148 Rio Grande do
Sul □ 30 0 S 54 0W
145 Rio Largo 9 28 S 35 50W
165 Rio Muni □ 1 30 N 10 0 E
148 Rio Negro 26 0 S 50 0W
53 Rio Tinto 41 11 N 8 34W
145 Rio Verde, Brazil 17 43 S 50 56W
137 Río Verde,
Mexico 21 56 N 99 59W
131 Rio Vista 38 11 N 121 44W
30 Riom 45 54 N 3 7 E
144 Ríohacha 11 33 N 72 55W
65 Rionero in
Vulture 40 55 N 15 40 E
144 Ríosucio 5 30 N 75 40W
144 Rioscio 7 27 N 77 7W
21 Ripon, U.K. 54 8 N 1 31W
128 Ripon, U.S.A. 43 51 N 88 50W
65 Riposto 37 44 N 15 12 E
60 Risan 42 32 N 18 42 E
28 Risle, R. 49 26 N 0 23 E
51 Rîsnov 45 35 N 25 27 E
38 Risør 58 43 N 9 13 E
131 Ritzville 47 10 N 118 21W
62 Riva 45 53 N 10 50 E
148 Rivadavia 29 50 S 70 35W
139 Rivas 11 30 N 85 50W
31 Rive-de-Gier 45 32 N 4 37 E
148 Rivera 31 0 S 55 50W
127 Riverhead 40 53 N 72 40W
125 Riverhurst 50 55 N 106 50W
168 Riversdale 34 7 S 21 15 E
131 Riverside, Calif. 34 0 N 117 15W
131 Riverside, Wyo. 41 12 N 106 57W
113 Riverton, Australia 34 10 S 138 46 E
125 Riverton, Canada 51 5 N 97 0W
131 Riverton, U.S.A. 43 1 N 108 27W
62 Riviera 44 0 N 8 30 E
123 Rivière Bleue 47 26 N 69 2W
123 Rivière du Loup 47 50 N 69 30W
62 Rivoli 45 3 N 7 31 E
80 Riyadh = Ar Riyād 24 41 N 46 42 E
80 Rize 41 0 N 40 30 E
38 Rjukan 59 54 N 8 33 E
31 Roanne 46 3 N 4 4 E
127 Roanoke, Ala. 33 9 N 85 23W
127 Roanoke, Va 37 19 N 79 55W
127 Roanoke Rapids 36 36 N 77 42W
168 Robertson 33 46 S 19 50 E
122 Roberval 48 32 N 72 15W
107 Robinson Crusoe, I. 33 50 S 78 30W
125 Roblin 51 21 N 101 25W
124 Robson, Mt. 53 10 N 119 10W
53 Roca, C. da 38 40 N 9 31W
145 Rocas, Is. 4 0 S 34 1W
63 Roccastrada 43 0 N 11 10 E
148 Rocha 34 30 S 54 25W
21 Rochdale 53 36 N 2 10W
30 Rochefort 45 56 N 0 57W
128 Rochelle 41 55 N 89 5W
21 Rochester, U.K. 51 22 N 0 30 E
128 Rochester, Minn. 44 1 N 92 28W
127 Rochester, N.H. 43 19 N 70 57W
127 Rochester, N.Y. 43 10 N 77 40W
127 Rock Hill 34 55 N 81 2W
128 Rock Island 41 30 N 90 35W
131 Rock Springs 46 55 N 106 11W
16 Rockall, I. 57 37 N 13 42W
174 Rockefeller Plat. 84 0 S 130 0W
128 Rockford, Ill. 42 20 N 89 0W
128 Rockford, Mich. 43 7 N 85 33W
113 Rockhampton 23 22 S 150 32 E
127 Rockville, Md. 39 7 N 77 10W
127 Rocky Mount 35 55 N 77 48W
118 Rocky Mts. 48 0 N 113 0W
124 Rockyford 51 13 N 113 8W
38 Rødberg 60 17 N 8 56 E
41 Rødby 54 41 N 11 23 E

Rødbyhavn Santa Clara

41 Rødbyhavn 54 39 N 11 22 E
30 Rodez 44 21 N 2 33 E
68 Rodhópi □ 41 10 N 25 30 E
68 Ródhos 36 15 N 28 10 E
110 Roebourne 20 44 S 117 9 E
110 Roebuck, B. 18 5 S 122 20 E
121 Roes Welcome Sd. 65 0 N 87 0W
34 Roeselare 50 57 N 3 7 E
37 Rogaland □ 59 12 N 6 20 E
128 Rogers 36 20 N 94 0W
122 Roggan River 54 24 N 78 5W
31 Rogliano 42 57 N 9 30 E
29 Roisel 49 58 N 3 6 E
148 Rolândia 23 5 S 52 0W
113 Rollingstone 19 2 S 146 24 E
113 Rolleston 43 35 S 172 24 E
113 Roma, Australia 26 32 S 148 49 E
63 Roma, Italy 41 54 N 12 30 E
51 Romania ■ 46 0 N 25 0 E
31 Romans 45 3 N 5 3 E
120 Romanzof, C. 61 49 N 165 56W
63 Rome, Italy = Roma 41 54 N 12 30 E
127 Rome, Ga. 34 20 N 85 0W
127 Rome, N.Y. 43 14 N 75 29W
29 Romilly 48 31 N 3 44 E
21 Romney Marsh 51 0 N 1 0 E
41 Rømø, I. 55 10 N 8 30 E
41 Romsdalen 62 25 N 7 50 E
24 Ronaldsay, North I. 59 23 N 2 26W
24 Ronaldsay, South I. 58 47 N 2 56W
145 Roncador, S. do 12 30 S 52 30W
53 Ronda, Sa. de 36 44 N 5 3W
41 Rondane, Reg. 61 57 N 9 50 E
144 Rondônia □ 11 0 S 63 0W
41 Rønne 55 6 N 14 44 E
174 Ronne Ld. 83 0 S 70 0W
41 Ronneby 56 12 N 15 17 E
165 Roodepoort-Maraisburg 26 11 S 27 54 E
34 Roosendaal 51 32 N 4 29 E
131 Roosevelt Res. 33 46 N 111 0W
110 Roper, R. 14 43 S 135 27 E
30 Roquefort 44 2 N 0 20W
144 Roraima □ 2 0 N 61 30W
144 Roraima, Mt. 5 10 N 60 40W
53 Rosal de la Frontera 37 59 N 7 13W
145 Rosário, Brazil 3 0 S 44 15W
137 Rosario, Mexico 23 0 S 105 52W
148 Rosario, Urug. 34 20 S 57 20W
148 Rosario de la Frontera 25 50 S 65 0W
148 Rosário do Sul 30 15 S 54 55W
28 Roscoff 48 44 N 4 0W
27 Roscommon 53 38 N 8 11W
27 Roscrea 52 57 N 7 47W
123 Rose Blanche 47 38 N 58 45W
124 Rose Harbour 52 15 N 131 10W
125 Rose Valley 52 19 N 103 49W
139 Roseau 48 56 N 96 0W
128 Rosenberg 29 30 N 95 48W
131 Roseburg 43 10 N 123 10W
29 Rosendaël 51 3 N 2 24 E
45 Rosenheim 47 51 N 12 9 E
125 Rosetown 57 33 N 108 0 E
159 Rosetta = Rashîd 31 21 N 30 22 E
131 Roseville 38 46 N 121 41W
41 Roshage, C. 57 7 N 8 35 E
29 Rosières 48 36 N 6 20 E
62 Rosignano 43 23 N 10 28 E
144 Rosignol 6 15 N 57 30W
41 Roskilde 55 38 N 12 3 E
41 Roskilde, Fd. 55 50 N 12 2 E
75 Roslavl 53 57 N 32 55 E
114 Ross, N.Z. 42 53 S 170 49 E
21 Ross, U.K. 51 55 N 2 34W
27 Ross □ 70 0 S 170 5W
174 Ross Ice Shelf 80 0 S 180 0W
174 Ross Sea 74 0 S 178 0 E
124 Rossland 49 6 N 117 50W
27 Rosslare 52 17 N 6 23W
45 Rosslau 57 52 N 12 15 E
158 Rosso 16 30 N 15 49W
125 Rosthern 52 40 N 106 20W
45 Rostock 54 4 N 12 9 E
75 Rostov 47 15 N 39 45 E
24 Rosyth 56 2 N 3 26W
53 Rota 36 37 N 6 20W
45 Rotenburg 53 6 N 9 24 E
45 Rothenburg ob der Tauber 49 21 N 10 11 E
21 Rother, R. 50 59 N 0 40W
21 Rotherham 53 26 N 1 21W
24 Rothes 57 31 N 3 12W
24 Rothesay 55 50 N 5 3W
113 Roto 33 0 S 145 30 E
114 Rotorua 38 9 S 176 16 E
114 Rotorua, L. 38 5 S 176 18 E
48 Rottenmann 47 31 N 14 22 E
34 Rotterdam 51 55 N 4 30 E
106 Rotuma, I. 12 25 S 177 5 E
29 Roubaix 50 40 N 3 10 E
48 Roudnice 50 25 N 14 15 E
28 Rouen 49 27 N 1 4 E
113 Round, Mt. 30 26 S 152 16 E
131 Roundup 46 25 N 108 35W
24 Rousay, I. 59 10 N 3 2W
30 Roussillon, Reg. 45 24 N 4 49 E
62 Rovereto 45 53 N 11 3 E
63 Rovigo 45 4 N 11 48 E
51 Rovinari 44 55 N 23 11 E
63 Rovinj 45 18 N 13 40 E
95 Roxas 11 36 N 122 49 E
114 Roxburgh 45 33 S 169 19 E
41 Roxen, L. 58 30 N 15 41 E
127 Royal Oak 42 30 N 83 5W
128 Royale, I. 48 0 N 89 0W
30 Royan 45 37 N 1 2W
29 Roye 47 40 N 6 31 E
49 Rožnava 48 37 N 20 35 E
53 Rúa 42 24 N 7 6W
114 Ruapehu, Mt. 39 18 S 175 35 E
85 Rub'al Khali 21 0 N 51 0 E
144 Rubio 7 43 N 72 22W
120 Ruby 38 27 S 145 55 E
49 Ruda Slaska 50 16 N 18 50 E
110 Rudall 33 43 S 136 17 E
45 Rüdersdorf 52 28 N 13 48 E
41 Rudkøbing 54 56 N 10 41 E
77 Rudnogorsk 57 15 N 103 42 E
76 Rudnyy 52 57 N 63 7 E
165 Rudolf, L. = Turkana, L. 4 10 N 36 10 E
29 Rue 50 15 N 1 40 E
159 Rufa'a 14 44 N 33 32 E
30 Ruffec 46 2 N 0 42 E
165 Rufiji, R. 8 0 S 39 20 E
158 Rufisque 14 43 N 17 17W
21 Rugby, U.K. 52 23 N 1 16W
128 Rugby, U.S.A. 48 21 N 100 0W
45 Rügen, I. 54 22 N 13 25 E
45 Ruhr, R. 51 27 N 6 44 E
165 Rukwa, L. 7 50 S 32 10 E
60 Ruma 45 8 N 19 50 E
110 Rumbalara 25 20 S 134 29 E
127 Rumford 44 30 N 70 30W
31 Rumilly 45 53 N 5 56 E
114 Runanga 42 25 S 171 15 E
21 Runcorn 53 20 N 2 44W
165 Rungwa 6 55 S 33 32 E
169 Rusape 18 35 S 32 8 E
61 Ruse 43 48 N 25 59 E
21 Rushden 52 17 N 0 37W
145 Russas 4 56 S 37 58W
125 Russell, Canada 50 50 N 101 20W
128 Russell, Kans. 38 56 N 98 55W
76 Russkaya Polyana 53 47 N 73 53 E
168 Rustenburg 25 41 S 27 14 E
128 Ruston 32 30 N 92 40W
53 Rute 37 19 N 4 29W
95 Ruteng 8 26 S 120 30 E
131 Ruth 39 15 N 115 1W
24 Rutherglen 55 50 N 4 11W
127 Rutland 43 38 N 73 0W
165 Rutshuru 1 13 S 29 25 E
65 Ruvo di Púglia 41 7 N 16 27 E
165 Ruvuma, R. 10 29 S 40 28 E
165 Ruwenzori, Mts. 0 30 N 29 55 E
49 Ruzomberok 49 3 N 19 17 E
165 Rwanda ■ 2 0 S 30 0 E
24 Ryan, L. 55 0 N 5 2W
75 Ryazan 54 38 N 39 44 E
76 Rybache 46 40 N 81 20 E
75 Rybachiy Pol. 69 43 N 32 0 E
75 Rybinsk 58 3 N 38 52 E
75 Rybinsk Res. 58 30 N 38 0 E
49 Rybnik 50 6 N 18 32 E
21 Ryde 50 44 N 1 9W
21 Rye 50 57 N 0 46 E
21 Rye, R. 54 12 N 0 53W
50 Rzepin 52 20 N 14 49 E
49 Rzeszów 50 5 N 21 58 E

S

45 Saale, R. 51 57 N 11 55 E
45 Saalfeld 50 39 N 11 21 E
48 Saalfelden 47 26 N 12 51 E
45 Saarbrücken 49 15 N 6 58 E
45 Saarburg 49 36 N 6 32 E
75 Saaremaa, I. 58 30 N 22 30 E
45 Saarland □ 49 20 N 0 75 E
139 Saba, I. 17 30 N 63 10W
60 Šabac 44 48 N 19 42 E
55 Sabadell 41 28 N 2 7 E
94 Sabah □ 6 0 N 117 0 E
80 Sabalan, Kuhha-ye 38 15 N 47 49 E
94 Sabang 5 50 N 95 15 E
145 Sabará 19 55 S 43 55W
159 Sabhah 27 9 N 14 29 E
55 Sabinal, Pta. del 36 43 N 2 44W
137 Sabinas 27 50 N 101 10W
128 Sabine, R. 30 0 N 93 45W
118 Sable, C., Canada 43 29 N 65 38W
123 Sable, C., U.S.A. 25 5 N 81 0W
123 Sable I. 44 0 N 60 0W
30 Sables-d'Olonne, Les 46 30 N 1 45W
28 Sablé-sur-Sarthe 47 50 N 0 21W
53 Sabôr, R. 41 10 N 7 7W
81 Sabzvārān 28 45 N 57 50 E
55 Sacedón 40 29 N 2 41W
45 Säckingen 47 34 N 7 56 E
131 Sacramento 38 39 N 121 30 E
131 Sacramento, R. 38 3 N 121 56W
131 Sacramento Mts. 32 30 N 105 30W
53 Sacratif, C. 36 42 N 3 28W
55 Sádaba 2 19 N 1 12W
159 Sadd el Aali 24 5 N 32 54 E
102 Sado, I. 38 15 N 138 30 E
53 Sado, R. 38 29 N 8 55W
55 Saelices 39 55 N 2 49W
41 Säffle 59 8 N 12 55 E
131 Safford 32 54 N 109 52W
21 Saffron Walden 52 5 N 0 15 E
158 Safi 32 20 N 9 17W
95 Saga, Indonesia 2 40 S 132 55 E
102 Saga, Japan 33 15 N 130 18 E
87 Sagaing 22 0 N 96 0 E
86 Sagar 23 50 N 78 50 E
127 Saginaw 43 26 N 83 55W
127 Saginaw B. 43 50 N 83 40W
121 Saglouc 62 30 N 74 15W
31 Sagone, G. de 42 4 N 8 40 E
53 Sagres 37 0 N 8 58W
139 Sagua la Grande 22 50 N 80 10W
131 Saguache 38 10 N 106 4W
123 Saguenay, R. 48 10 N 69 45W
53 Sahagun 42 18 N 5 2W
158 Sahara 23 0 N 5 0 E
86 Saharanpur 29 58 N 77 33 E
86 Sahiwal 30 45 N 73 8 E
49 Sahy 48 4 N 18 55 E
49 Saida 34 50 N 0 11 E
81 Sa'īdābād 29 30 N 55 45 E
86 Saidu 34 50 N 72 15 E
30 Saignes 45 20 N 2 31 E
91 Saigon = Phan Bho Ho Chi Minh 10 58 N 106 40 E
102 Saiki 32 35 N 131 50 E
24 St. Abbs Hd. 55 55 N 2 10W
48 St. Aegyd 47 52 N 15 33 E
30 St-Affrique 43 57 N 2 53 E
21 St. Albans, U.K. 51 46 N 0 21W
127 St. Albans, U.S.A. 44 49 N 73 5W
21 St. Albans Hd. 50 34 N 2 3W
29 St-Amand 50 25 N 3 6 E
29 St-Amarin 47 54 N 7 0 E
31 St-Amour 46 26 N 5 21 E
30 St-André-de-Cubzac 44 59 N 0 26W
31 St-André-les-Alpes 43 58 N 6 30 E
24 St. Andrews 56 20 N 2 48W
113 St. Arnaud 36 32 S 143 16 E
21 St. Asaph 53 15 N 3 27W
28 St-Aubin de Cormier 48 15 N 1 26W
123 St. Augustin 51 19 N 58 48W
127 St. Augustine 29 52 N 81 20W
21 St. Austell 50 20 N 4 48W
139 St. Barthélemy, I. 17 50 N 62 50W
21 St. Bees Hd. 54 30 N 3 38 E
30 St-Benoit-du-Sault 46 26 N 1 24 E
125 St. Boniface 49 50 N 97 10W
30 St-Bonnet 44 40 N 6 5 E
21 St. Bride's B. 51 48 N 5 15W
28 St-Brieuc 48 30 N 2 46W
21 St. Catherine's Pt. 50 34 N 1 18W
31 St-Chamond 45 28 N 4 31 E
128 St. Charles 38 46 N 90 30W
30 St-Chinian 43 25 N 2 56 E
139 St. Christopher, I. 17 20 N 62 40W
127 St. Clair 40 42 N 76 12W
127 St. Clair, L. 42 30 N 82 45W
125 St. Claude, Canada 49 40 N 98 22W
31 St-Claude, Fr. 46 22 N 5 52 E
128 St. Cloud 45 30 N 94 11W
123 St. Cur de Marie 48 39 N 71 43W
31 St-Cyr 43 11 N 5 43 E
21 St. Davids 51 54 N 5 16W
21 St. David's Hd. 51 54 N 5 16W
139 St. David's I. 32 22 N 64 39W
153 St-Denis 48 56 N 2 22 E
29 St-Dié 48 17 N 6 56 E
29 St-Dizier 48 40 N 5 0 E
120 St. Elias, Mt. 60 20 N 141 59W
30 St-Eloy-les Mines 46 10 N 2 51 E
30 St-Émilion 44 53 N 0 9W
30 St-Étienne 45 27 N 4 22 E
31 St-Étienne de Tinée 44 16 N 6 56 E
123 St. Fintan's 48 10 N 58 50W
31 St-Florent 42 41 N 9 18 E
30 St-Florent-sur-Cher 46 59 N 2 15 E
29 St-Florentin 48 0 N 3 45 E
31 St-Fons 45 42 N 4 52 E
30 St-Foy-la Grande 44 50 N 0 13 E
168 St. Francis, C. 34 14 S 24 49 E
45 St. Gallen 47 25 N 9 23 E
45 St. Gallen □ 47 10 N 9 8 E
30 St-Gaultier 46 39 N 1 26 E
139 St. George, Bermuda 32 24 N 64 42W
123 St. George, Canada 45 11 N 66 57W
131 St. George, U.S.A. 37 10 N 113 35W
127 St. George, C. 29 36 N 85 2W
113 St. George Hd. 35 11 S 150 45 E
34 St. Georges, Belgium 50 37 N 4 20 E
122 St. Georges, Canada 46 42 N 72 35W
145 St. George's, Fr. Guiana 4 0 N 52 0W
123 St. George's B. 48 20 N 59 0W
19 St. George's Chan. 52 0 N 6 0W
139 St. George's I. 32 22 N 64 40W
29 St-Germain 48 53 N 2 5 E
30 St-Germain-des-Fossés 46 12 N 3 26 E
31 St-Gervais, Haute Savoie 45 53 N 6 42 E
30 St-Gervais, Puy de Dôme 46 4 N 2 50 E
30 St-Gilles-Croix-de-Vie 46 41 N 1 55W
30 St-Girons 42 59 N 1 8 E
45 St. Goar 50 31 N 7 43 E
152 St. Helena, I. 15 55 S 5 44W
113 St. Helens, Australia 41 20 S 148 15 E
21 St. Helens, U.K. 53 28 N 2 44W
131 St. Helens, U.S.A. 45 55 N 122 50W
28 St-Helier 49 11 N 2 6W
21 St. Ives, Cambridge 52 20 N 0 5W
21 St. Ives, Cornwall 50 13 N 5 29W
122 St. Jean 45 20 N 73 50W
30 St-Jean-d'Angély 45 57 N 0 31W
31 St-Jean-de-Maurienne 45 16 N 6 28 E
30 St-Jean-de-Monts 46 47 N 2 4W
122 St. Jérôme 45 55 N 74 0W
48 St. Johann 47 22 N 13 12 E
123 St. John 45 20 N 66 8W
123 St. John, L. 48 40 N 72 0W
139 St. John's, Antigua 17 6 N 61 51W
123 St. John's, Canada 47 45 N 52 40W
127 St. Joseph, Mich. 42 6 N 86 29W
128 St. Joseph, Mo. 39 46 N 94 51W
31 St-Julien La Roche 46 4 N 6 19 E
114 St. Kilda 45 53 S 170 31 E
139 St. Kitts, I. 17 20 N 62 40W
125 St. Laurent 50 25 N 97 58W
123 St. Lawrence 46 54 N 55 23W
123 St. Lawrence, G. of 48 25 N 62 0W
120 St. Lawrence, I. 63 0 N 170 0W
123 St. Lawrence, R. 49 15 N 67 0W
123 St. Leonard 47 12 N 67 58W
123 St. Lin 45 44 N 73 46W
158 St. Louis, Senegal 16 8 N 16 27W
128 St. Louis, U.S.A. 38 40 N 90 20W
139 St. Lucia, I. 14 0 N 60 50W
169 St. Lucia, L. 28 5 S 32 30 E
139 St. Lucia Chan. 14 15 N 61 0W
139 St. Maarten, I. 18 0 N 63 5W
30 St-Maixent-L'École 46 24 N 0 12W
28 St-Malo 48 39 N 2 1W
28 St-Malo, G. de 48 50 N 2 30W
31 St-Mandrier 43 4 N 5 56 E
139 St. Marc 19 10 N 72 5W
131 St. Maries 47 17 N 116 34W
29 St-Martin 50 42 N 1 38 E
139 St. Martin, I. 18 0 N 63 0W
123 St. Martins 45 22 N 65 38W
113 St. Marys 41 32 S 148 11 E
21 St. Marys, I. 49 55 N 6 17W
28 St-Mathieu, Pte. de. 48 20 N 4 45W
120 St. Matthew I. 60 30 N 172 45W
21 St. Michael's Mt. 50 7 N 5 29W
45 St. Moritz 46 30 N 9 50 E
28 St-Nazaire 47 17 N 2 12W
21 St. Neots 52 14 N 0 16W
29 St-Nicolas-de-Port 48 38 N 6 18 E
29 St-Omer 50 45 N 2 15 E
23 St. Pacôme 47 24 N 69 58W
30 St-Palais 43 20 N 1 8W
23 St. Pascal 47 32 N 69 48W
124 St. Paul, Canada 51 34 N 57 47W
128 St. Paul, U.S.A. 44 54 N 93 5W
30 St-Paul-les-Dax 43 44 N 1 3W
128 St. Peter 44 15 N 93 57W
21 St. Peter Port 49 27 N 2 31W
127 St. Petersburg 27 45 N 82 40W
123 St. Pierre, Canada 46 40 N 56 0W
30 St-Pierre, Fr. 45 57 N 1 19W
122 St. Pierre, L. 46 10 N 72 50W
28 St-Pierre-en-Port 49 48 N 0 30 E
123 St. Pierre et Miquelon □ 46 49 N 56 15W
30 St-Pierre-le-Moutier 46 48 N 3 7 E
28 St-Pierre-sur-Dives 49 2 N 0 1W
29 St-Pol 50 21 N 2 20 E
29 St-Pol-sur-Mer 51 1 N 2 20 E
30 St-Pons 43 30 N 2 45 E
29 St-Quentin 49 50 N 3 16 E
31 St-Rambert d'Albon 45 17 N 1 35 E
31 St-Raphaël 43 25 N 6 46 E
28 St-Servan 48 38 N 2 0 E
28 St-Sever Calvados 48 50 N 1 3W
123 St. Stephen 45 16 N 67 17W
30 St-Sulpice-Laurière 46 3 N 1 29 E
122 St. Thomas, Canada 42 47 N 81 12W
139 St. Thomas, Virgin Is. 18 21 N 64 56W
31 St-Tropez 43 17 N 6 38 E
34 St. Troud 50 48 N 5 10 E
28 St-Vaast-la-Hougue 49 35 N 1 17W
48 St. Valentin 48 10 N 14 32 E
29 St-Valéry 50 10 N 1 38 E
31 St-Vallier-de-Thiey 43 42 N 6 51 E
31 St-Varent 46 53 N 0 13W
48 St. Veit 46 46 N 14 21 E
139 St. Vincent, I. 13 10 N 61 10W
139 St. Vincent Pass. 13 30 N 61 0W
125 St. Walburg 53 39 N 109 12W
45 St. Wendel 49 28 N 7 10 E
48 St. Wolfgang 47 44 N 13 27 E
28 Ste. Adresse 49 31 N 0 5 E
123 Ste. Anne de Beaupré 47 2 N 70 58W
29 Ste. Benoite 49 47 N 3 30 E
125 Ste. Cecile 47 56 N 64 34W
139 Ste. Marie 14 48 N 61 1W
29 Ste. Marie-aux-Mines 48 10 N 7 12 E
123 Ste. Marie de la Madeleine 46 26 N 71 0W
31 Ste. Maries-de-la-Mer 43 27 N 4 25 E
28 Ste. Maur 47 7 N 0 37 E
29 Ste. Menehould 49 5 N 4 54 E
28 Ste. Mère Église 49 24 N 1 19W
139 Ste. Rose 16 20 N 61 45W
125 Ste. Rose du lac 51 10 N 99 30W
30 Saintes 45 45 N 0 37W
87 Sairang 23 50 N 92 45 E
102 Saitama □ 36 25 N 137 0 E
144 Sajama, Mt. 18 6 S 68 54W
102 Sakai 34 30 N 135 30 E
102 Sakaiminato 35 33 N 133 15 E
102 Sakata 38 55 N 139 56 E
77 Sakhalin 51 0 N 143 0 E
168 Sakrivier 30 54 S 20 28 E
41 Sala 59 58 N 16 35 E
65 Sala Consilina 40 23 N 15 35 E
158 Salaga 8 31 N 0 31W
53 Salamanca, Sp. 40 58 N 5 39W
127 Salamanca, U.S.A. 42 10 N 78 42W
68 Salamis 37 56 N 23 30 E
53 Salas 43 25 N 6 15W
75 Salavat 53 21 N 55 55 E
95 Salawati, I. 1 7 S 130 54 E
29 Salbris 47 25 N 2 3 E
168 Saldanha 33 0 S 17 58 E
113 Sale, Australia 38 7 S 147 0 E
21 Sale, U.K. 53 26 N 2 19W
158 Salé 34 3 N 6 48W
76 Salekhard 66 30 N 66 25 E
127 Salem, Mass. 42 29 N 70 53W
127 Salem, Ohio 40 52 N 80 50W
127 Salem, Va. 37 19 N 80 8W
31 Salernes 43 34 N 6 15 E
65 Salerno 40 40 N 14 44 E
65 Salerno, G. di 40 35 N 14 45 E
21 Salford 53 30 N 2 17W
165 Salima 13 47 S 34 26 E
128 Salina 38 50 N 97 40W
137 Salina Cruz 16 10 N 95 10W
145 Salinas, Brazil 16 20 S 42 10W
131 Salinas, U.S.A. 36 40 N 121 38W
139 Salinas, B. de 11 4 N 85 45W
131 Salinópolis 0 40 S 47 20W
113 Salisbury, Australia 34 46 S 138 38 E
169 Salisbury, Zimbabwe 17 50 S 31 2 E
21 Salisbury, U.K. 51 4 N 1 48W
127 Salisbury, Md. 38 20 N 75 38W
127 Salisbury, N.C. 35 42 N 80 29W
121 Salisbury Plain 51 13 N 2 0W
131 Salmon 45 12 N 113 56W
131 Salmon, R. 45 51 N 116 46W
124 Salmon Arm 50 40 N 119 15W
37 Salo-de-P. 60 22 N 23 3 E
31 Salon 43 39 N 5 6 E
21 Salop □ 52 36 N 2 45W
75 Salou, C. 41 3 N 1 10 E
75 Salsk 46 28 N 41 30 E
62 Salsomaggiore 44 48 N 9 59 E
131 Salt Lake City 40 45 N 111 58W
148 Salta 24 47 S 65 25W
21 Saltcoats 55 38 N 4 47W
41 Saltholm, I. 55 38 N 12 43 E
137 Saltillo 25 30 N 100 57W
148 Salto, Uruguay 31 20 S 58 10W
131 Salton Sea 33 20 N 116 0W
41 Saltsjöbaden 59 15 N 18 20 E
124 Saltspring 48 54 N 123 37W
159 Salûm 31 31 N 25 7 E
62 Saluzzo 44 39 N 7 29 E
145 Salvador, Brazil 13 0 S 38 30W
125 Salvador, Canada 52 20 N 109 25W
137 Salvador ■ 13 50 N 89 0W
53 Salvora, I. 42 30 N 8 58W
87 Salween, R. 16 31 N 97 37 E
48 Salza, R. 47 40 N 14 43 E
48 Salzach, R. 48 12 N 12 56 E
48 Salzburg 47 48 N 13 2 E
48 Salzburg □ 47 25 N 13 15 E
45 Salzgitter 52 2 N 10 22 E
91 Sam Neua 20 29 N 104 0 E
91 Sam Ngao 17 18 N 99 0 E
128 Sam Rayburn Res. 31 15 N 94 20W
76 Sama 60 10 N 60 15 E
77 Samagaltai 50 36 N 95 3 E
81 Samangān □ 36 15 N 67 40 E
95 Samar, I. 12 0 N 125 0 E
76 Samarkand 39 40 N 67 0 E
87 Sambalpur 21 28 N 83 58 E
34 Sambre, R. 50 28 N 4 52 E
29 Samer 50 38 N 1 44 E
114 Samoa Is. 14 0 S 171 0W
61 Samokov 42 20 N 23 33 E
53 Samos 42 44 N 7 20W
95 Sampang 7 11 S 113 13 E
55 Sampeer de Calanda 41 11 N 2 4W
41 Samsø, I. 55 52 N 10 37 E
80 Samsun 41 15 N 36 15 E
91 Samut Sakhon 13 31 N 100 20 E
91 Samut Songkhram 13 24 N 100 1 E
158 San 13 15 N 4 45W
107 San Ambrosio, I. 26 21 S 79 52W
139 San Andrés, I. de 12 42 N 81 46W
137 San Andrés Tuxtla 18 30 N 95 20W
148 San Antonio, Chile 33 40 S 71 40W
128 San Antonio, U.S.A. 29 30 N 98 30W
139 San Antonio, C. 21 50 N 84 57W
55 San Antonio, C. de 38 48 N 0 12 E
148 San Antonio Oeste 40 40 S 65 0W
65 San Bartolomeo 41 24 N 15 1 E
62 San Benedetto 45 2 N 10 57 E
131 San Bernardino 34 7 N 117 18W
95 San Bernardino Str. 12 37 N 124 12 E
144 San Bernardo, I. de 9 45 N 75 50W
139 San Blas, Cord. de 9 15 N 78 30W
95 San Carlos, Philippines 10 29 N 123 25 E
144 San Carlos, Ven. 1 55 N 67 4W
144 San Carlos, Ven. 9 40 N 68 36W
55 San Carlos de la Rápita 40 37 N 0 35 E
144 San Carlos del Zulia 9 1 N 71 55W
131 San Carlos L. 33 13 N 110 24W
64 San Cataldo 37 30 N 13 58 E
55 San Clemente, Sp. 39 24 N 2 25W
131 San Clemente, U.S.A. 33 29 N 117 45W
131 San Clemente I. 33 0 N 118 30W
137 San Cristóbal de las Casas 16 50 N 92 33W
131 San Diego 32 50 N 117 10W
148 San Diego, C. 54 40 S 65 10W
63 San Dona di
53 San Esteban de Gormaz 41 34 N 3 13W
62 San Felice sul Panaro 44 51 N 11 9 E
55 San Feliu de Guixals 41 45 N 3 1 E
95 San Fernando, Philippines 15 5 N 120 37 E
95 San Fernando, Philippines 16 40 N 120 23 E
53 San Fernando, Sp. 36 22 N 6 17W
139 San Fernando, Trinidad 10 20 N 61 30W
131 San Fernando, U.S.A. 34 15 N 118 29W
144 San Fernando de Apure 7 54 N 67 28W
65 San Fernando di Puglia 41 18 N 16 5 E
131 San Francisco, U.S.A. 37 35 N 122 30W
131 San Francisco, R. 32 59 N 109 22W
139 San Francisco de Macoris 19 19 N 70 15W
55 San Francisco Javier 38 40 N 1 25 E
65 San Fratello 38 1 N 14 33 E
62 San Gimignano 43 28 N 11 3 E
65 San Giovanni Rotondo 41 44 N 15 42 E
62 San Giuliano Terme 43 45 N 10 26 E
45 San Gottardo, P. del 46 33 N 8 33 E
131 San Joaquin, R. 36 43 N 121 50W
148 San Jorge, G. de, Arg. 46 0 S 66 0W
55 San Jorge, G. de, Sp. 40 50 N 0 55W
137 San José, Guatemala 14 0 N 90 50W
95 San Jose, Philippines 15 45 N 120 55 E
55 San Jose, Sp. 38 55 N 1 18 E
131 San Jose, U.S.A. 37 20 N 122 0W
148 San José, G. 42 20 S 64 20W
144 San José de Ocune 4 15 N 70 20W
137 San José del Cabo 23 0 N 109 50W
144 San José del Guaviare 2 35 N 72 38W
139 San Juan, Dom. Rep. 18 49 N 71 12W
137 San Juan, Mexico 21 20 N 102 50W
131 San Juan, R. 37 18 N 110 28W
144 San Juan de los Morros 9 55 N 67 21W
139 San Juan del Norte, B. de 11 30 N 83 40W
53 San Juan del Puerto 37 20 N 6 50W
131 San Juan Mts. 38 30 N 108 30W
55 San Just, Sa. de 40 45 N 0 41W
131 San Leandro 37 40 N 122 6W
53 San Leonardo 41 51 N 3 5W
144 San Lorenzo, Ecuador 1 15 N 78 50W
148 San Lorenzo, Mt. 47 40 S 72 20W
137 San Lucas, C. de 22 50 N 110 0W
137 San Luis de la Paz 21 18 N 100 31W
137 San Luis Potosí 22 9 N 100 59W
65 San Marco Argentano 39 34 N 16 8 E
65 San Marco in Lamis 41 43 N 15 38 E
63 San Marino ■ 43 56 N 12 25 E
62 San Martino de Calvi 45 57 N 9 41 E
131 San Mateo 37 32 N 122 25W
148 San Matías, G. 41 30 S 64 0W
137 San Miguel, Salvador 13 30 N 88 12W
55 San Miguel, Sp. 39 3 N 1 26 E
53 San Pedro, Sa. de 39 18 N 6 40W
137 San Pedro de las Colonias 25 50 N 102 59W
55 San Pedro del Pinatar 37 50 N 0 50W
137 San Pedro Sula 15 30 N 88 0W
64 San Pietro, I. 39 9 N 8 17 E
62 San Remo 43 48 N 7 47 E
137 San Salvador 13 40 N 89 20W
147 San Salvador, I. 24 0 N 74 40W
148 San Sebastián, Arg. 53 10 S 68 30W
55 San Sebastián, Spain 43 17 N 1 58W
63 San Severino Marche 43 13 N 13 10 E
65 San Severo 41 41 N 15 23 E
131 San Simon 32 14 N 109 16W
63 San Stéfano di Cadore 46 34 N 12 33 E
53 San Vicente de Alcantara 39 22 N 7 8W
53 San Vicente de la Barquera 43 30 N 4 29W
62 San Vincenzo 43 9 N 10 32 E
65 San Vito dei Normanni 40 39 N 17 42 E
63 San Vito di Tagliamento 45 55 N 12 50 E
85 Sana 15 27 N 44 12 E
63 Sana, R. 45 3 N 16 23 E
95 Sanana 2 5 S 125 50 E
31 Sanary 43 7 N 5 48 E
29 Sancerre 47 20 N 2 50 E
30 Sancoins 46 47 N 2 55 E
122 Sand Lake 47 46 N 84 31W
128 Sand Springs 36 12 N 96 5W
94 Sandakan 5 53 N 118 10 E
91 Sandan 12 46 N 106 0 E
24 Sanday, I. 59 14 N 2 30W
41 Sandefjord 59 10 N 10 15 E
131 Sanders 35 12 N 109 25W
113 Sandgate 27 20 S 153 5 E
80 Sandikli 38 30 N 30 20 E
37 Sandnes 58 50 N 5 45 E
131 Sandpoint 48 20 N 116 40W
21 Sandringham 52 50 N 0 30 E
41 Sandvig 55 18 N 14 48 E
41 Sandviken 60 38 N 16 46 E
113 Sandy, C. 24 41 S 153 8 E
45 Sangerhausen 51 28 N 11 18 E
94 Sanggau 0 5 N 110 30 E
95 Sangihe, Pulau 3 45 N 125 30 E
55 Sangonera, R. 37 59 N 1 4W
128 Sangre de Cristo Mts. 37 0 N 105 0W
65 Sangro, R. 42 14 N 14 32 E
55 Sanguesa 42 37 N 1 17W
53 Sanlucar de Barrameda 36 47 N 6 21W
53 Sanlúcar-la-Mayor 37 26 N 6 18W
64 Sanluri 39 55 N 8 55 E
65 Sannicandro Gargánico 41 50 N 15 34 E
49 Sanok 49 35 N 22 10 E
24 Sanquhar 55 21 N 3 56W
63 Sanski Most 44 46 N 16 40 E
65 Sant' Ágata di Militello 38 2 N 14 40 E
144 Santa Ana, Ecuador 1 10 S 80 20W
137 Santa Ana, Mexico 30 31 N 111 8W
137 Santa Ana, Salvador 14 0 N 89 40W
131 Santa Ana, U.S.A. 33 48 N 117 55W
62 Sant' Angelo 45 14 N 9 25 E
64 Sant' Antioco, I. 39 2 N 8 30 E
63 Sant' Arcángelo di Romagna 44 4 N 12 26 E
131 Santa Barbara, U.S.A. 34 25 N 119 40W
55 Santa Barbara, Mt. 37 23 N 2 50W
131 Santa Catalina, G. of 33 0 N 118 0W
139 Santa Clara, Cuba 22 20 N 80 0W

Santa Clara Sonepat

131	Santa Clara, U.S.A.	37 21 N	122 0W
148	Santa Cruz, Arg.	50 0 S	68 50W
158	Santa Cruz, Canary Is.	28 29 N	16 26W
139	Santa Cruz, Costa Rica	10 15 N	85 41W
95	Santa Cruz, Philippines	14 20 N	121 30 E
131	Santa Cruz, Calif.	36 55 N	122 10W
131	Santa Cruz, N. Mex.	35 59 N	106 1W
106	Santa Cruz, I.	0 38 S	90 23W
148	Santa Cruz, R.	50 10 S	68 20W
65	Sant' Eufémia, G. di	38 50 N	16 10 E
55	Santa Eulalia	40 34 N	1 20W
53	Santa Fé, Sp.	37 11 N	3 43W
131	Sante Fe, U.S.A.	35 40 N	106 0W
145	Santa Filomena	9 0 S	45 50W
55	Santa Lucia, Sp.	37 35 N	0 58W
131	Santa Lucia Ra.	36 0 N	121 30W
137	Santa Margarita, I.	24 30 N	112 0W
65	Santa Maria, Italy	41 3 N	14 29 E
55	Santa Maria, Sp.	39 39 N	2 45 E
131	Santa Maria, U.S.A.	34 58 N	120 29W
53	Santa Maria, C. de	36 39 N	7 53W
145	Santa Maria de Vitória	13 24 S	44 12W
65	Santa Maria di Leuca, C.	39 48 N	18 20 E
131	Santa Monica	34 0 N	118 30W
131	Santa Paula	34 20 N	119 2W
55	Santa Pola	38 13 N	0 35W
137	Santa Rosa, Honduras	14 40 N	89 0W
131	Santa Rosa, Calif.	38 20 N	122 50W
128	Santa Rosa, N. Mex.	34 58 N	104 40W
137	Santa Rosalía	27 20 N	112 30W
55	Santanyi	39 20 N	3 5 E
145	Santarem, Brazil	2 25 S	54 42W
53	Santarém, Port.	39 12 N	8 42W
65	Santéramo in Colie	40 48 N	16 45 E
148	Santiago, Chile	33 24 S	70 50W
139	Santiago, Dom. Rep.	19 30 N	70 40W
139	Santiago, Panama	8 0 N	81 0W
139	Santiago de Cuba	20 0 N	75 49W
137	Santiago Ixcuintla	21 50 N	105 11W
53	Santillana del Mar	43 24 N	4 6W
145	Santo Amaro	12 30 S	38 50W
148	Santo Angelo	28 15 S	54 15W
139	Santo Domingo	18 30 N	70 0W
53	Santo Domingo de la Calzada	42 26 N	2 27W
53	Santo Tirso	41 29 N	8 18W
148	Santo Tomé	28 40 S	56 5W
148	Santos	24 0 S	46 20W
53	Santos, Sa. de los	38 7 N	5 12W
53	São Bartholomeu de Messines	37 15 N	8 17W
148	São Borja	28 45 S	56 0W
145	São Carlos	22 0 S	47 50W
145	São Cristóvão	11 15 S	37 15W
145	São Domingos	13 25 S	46 10W
145	São Francisco	16 0 S	44 50W
145	São Francisco, R.	10 30 S	36 24W
148	São Francisco do Sul	26 15 S	48 36W
53	São João da Pesqueira	41 8 N	7 24W
145	São João del Rei	21 8 S	44 15W
145	São João do Araguaia	5 23 S	48 46W
145	São João do Piaui	8 10 S	42 15W
145	São Marcos, B. de	2 0 S	44 0W
145	São Mateus	18 44 S	39 50W
16	São Miguel, I.	37 33 N	25 27W
145	São Paulo	23 40 S	56 50W
145	São Paulo □	22 0 S	49 0W
53	São Pedro do Sul	40 46 N	8 4W
145	São Roque, C. de	5 30 S	35 10W
148	São Sebastião, I. de	23 50 S	45 18W
152	São Vicente	23 57 S	46 23W
53	São Vicente, C. de	37 0 N	9 0W
31	Saône, R.	45 44 N	4 50 E
31	Saône-et-Loire □	46 25 N	4 50 E
158	Sapele	5 50 N	5 40 E
102	Sapporo	43 0 N	141 15 E
65	Sapri	40 5 N	15 37 E
80	Saqqez	36 15 N	46 20 E
55	Saragossa	41 39 N	0 53W
60	Sarajevo	43 52 N	18 26 E
68	Saranda	39 59 N	19 55 E
148	Sarandí del Yi	33 21 S	55 58W
95	Sarangani B.	6 0 N	125 13 E
127	Sarasota	27 10 N	82 30W
127	Saratoga Springs	43 5 N	73 47W
75	Saratov	51 30 N	46 2 E
94	Sarawak □	2 0 S	113 0 E
81	Sarbāz	26 38 N	61 19 E
81	Sarbīsheh	32 30 N	59 40 E
49	Sârbogârd	46 55 N	18 40 E
64	Sardegna, I.	39 57 N	9 0 E
64	Sardinia, I. = Sardegna, I.	39 57 N	9 0 E
152	Sargasso Sea	27 0 N	67 0W
159	Sarh	9 5 N	18 23 E
81	Sarī	36 30 N	53 11 E
80	Sarikamiş	40 22 N	42 35 E
94	Sarikei	2 8 N	111 30 E
113	Sarina	21 22 S	149 13 E
55	Sariñena	41 47 N	0 10W
21	Sark, I.	49 25 N	2 20W
49	Sarked	46 47 N	21 17 E
30	Sarlat-la-Canéda	44 54 N	1 13 E
148	Sarmiento	45 35 S	69 5W
63	Sarnano	43 2 N	13 17 E
122	Sarnia	43 0 N	82 30W
65	Sarno	40 48 N	14 35 E
75	Sarny	51 17 N	26 40 E
68	Saronikós Kól.	37 45 N	23 45 E
62	Saronno	45 38 N	9 2 E
49	Sárospatak	58 18 N	21 33 E
53	Sarracín	42 15 N	3 45W
29	Sarralbe	48 55 N	7 1 E
29	Sarrebourg	48 43 N	7 3 E
29	Sarreguemines	49 1 N	7 4 E
53	Sarriá	42 41 N	7 49W
55	Sarrión	40 9 N	0 49W
28	Sarthe □	47 58 N	0 10 E
28	Sarthe, R.	47 30 N	0 32W
28	Sarzeau	47 31 N	2 48W
62	Sarzana	44 7 N	9 57 E
87	Sasaram	24 57 N	84 5 E
102	Sasebo	33 15 N	129 50 E
125	Saskatchewan □	53 40 N	103 30W
125	Saskatchewan, R.	53 12 N	99 16W
125	Saskatoon	52 10 N	106 45W
75	Sasovo	54 25 N	41 55 E
158	Sassandra	5 0 N	6 8W
64	Sássari	40 44 N	8 33 E
45	Sassnitz	54 29 N	13 39 E
62	Sassuolo	44 31 N	10 47 E
75	Satka	55 3 N	59 1 E
49	Sátoraljaújhely	48 25 N	21 41 E
91	Sattahip	12 41 N	100 54 E
49	Satu Mare	47 48 N	22 53 E
37	Sauđarkrókur	65 45 N	19 40W
85	Saudi Arabia ■	26 0 N	44 0 E
30	Saujon	45 41 N	0 55W
29	Sauldre, R.	47 16 N	1 30 E
29	Saulieu	47 17 N	4 14 E
122	Sault Ste. Marie, Canada	46 30 N	84 20W
127	Saulte Ste. Marie, U.S.A.	46 27 N	84 22W
28	Saumur	47 15 N	0 5W
37	Saurbaer	64 24 N	21 35W
165	Saurimo	9 39 S	20 24 E
60	Sava, R.	44 50 N	20 26 E
114	Savaii, I.	13 35 S	172 25W
158	Savalou	7 57 N	2 4 E
128	Savanna	42 5 N	90 10W
127	Savannah	32 4 N	81 4W
127	Savannah, R.	32 2 N	80 53W
91	Savannakhet	16 30 N	104 49 E
122	Savant Lake	50 20 N	90 40W
158	Savé	8 2 N	2 17 E
30	Save, R.	43 47 N	1 17 E
80	Sáveh	35 2 N	50 20 E
158	Savelugu	9 38 N	0 54W
28	Savenay	47 20 N	1 55W
29	Saverne	48 39 N	7 20 E
62	Savigliano	44 39 N	7 40 E
53	Saviñao	42 35 N	7 38W
31	Savoie □	45 26 N	6 35 E
62	Savona	44 19 N	8 29 E
95	Sawai	3 0 S	129 5 E
91	Sawankhalok	17 19 N	99 54 E
131	Sawatch Mts.	38 30 N	106 30W
169	Sawmills	19 30 S	28 2 E
95	Sawu Sea	9 30 S	121 50 E
123	Sayabec	38 35 N	67 41W
80	Saydā	33 35 N	35 25 E
81	Şayghān	35 10 N	67 55 E
85	Sayhūt	15 12 N	51 10 E
127	Sayre	42 0 N	76 30W
48	Sazava	49 50 N	15 0 E
21	Sca Fell, Mt	54 27 N	3 14W
28	Scaër	48 2 N	3 42 E
37	Scandinavia	65 0 N	15 0 E
24	Scapa Flow	58 52 N	3 0W
21	Scarborough	54 17 N	0 24W
45	Schaal See	53 40 N	10 57 E
45	Schaffhausen	47 42 N	8 36 E
48	Schärding	48 27 N	13 27 E
123	Schefferville	54 50 N	66 40W
48	Scheibbs	48 1 N	15 9 E
34	Schelde, R.	51 22 N	4 15 E
127	Schenectady	42 50 N	73 58W
34	Scheveningen	52 6 N	4 18 E
34	Schiedam	51 55 N	4 25 E
29	Schiltigheim	48 35 N	7 45 E
63	Schio	45 42 N	11 21 E
45	Schleswig	54 32 N	9 34 E
45	Schleswig-Holstein □	54 10 N	9 40 E
45	Schmalkalden	50 43 N	10 28 E
45	Schmölin	50 54 N	12 22 E
45	Schönebeck	52 2 N	11 42 E
45	Schramberg	48 12 N	8 24 E
122	Schreiber	48 45 N	87 20W
122	Schumacher	48 30 N	81 16W
131	Schurz	38 59 N	118 57W
45	Schwabach	49 19 N	11 3 E
45	Schwäbische Alb, Mts.	48 30 N	9 30 E
48	Schwarzach R.	50 30 N	11 30 E
45	Schwarzwald	48 0 N	8 0 E
48	Schwaz	47 20 N	11 44 E
45	Schweinfurt	50 3 N	10 12 E
45	Schwenningen	48 3 N	8 32 E
45	Schwerin	53 37 N	11 22 E
45	Schweriner See, L.	53 45 N	11 26 E
45	Schwetzingen	49 22 N	8 35 E
64	Sciacca	37 30 N	13 3 E
65	Scicli	36 48 N	14 41 E
21	Scilly Is.	49 55 N	6 15W
128	Scobey	48 47 N	105 30W
113	Scone, Australia	32 0 S	150 52 E
24	Scone, U.K.	56 25 N	3 26W
173	Scoresbysund	70 20 N	23 0W
174	Scotia Sea	56 5 S	56 0W
24	Scotland ■	57 0 N	4 0W
174	Scott, C.	71 30 S	168 0 E
128	Scott City	38 30 N	100 52W
128	Scottsbluff	41 55 N	103 35W
127	Scranton	41 22 N	75 41W
21	Scunthorpe	53 35 N	0 38W
122	Seaforth	43 35 N	81 25W
125	Seal, R.	59 4 N	94 48W
131	Searchlight	35 31 N	111 57W
128	Searcy	35 15 N	91 45W
131	Seattle	47 41 N	122 15W
137	Sebastián Vizcaíno, B.	28 0 N	114 0W
131	Sebastopol	38 16 N	122 56W
60	Sečanj	45 25 N	20 47 E
29	Seclin	50 33 N	3 2 E
114	Secretary, I.	45 15 S	166 56 E
86	Secunderabad	17 28 N	78 30 E
128	Sedalia	38 40 N	93 18W
29	Sedan	49 43 N	4 57 E
114	Seddon	41 40 S	174 7 E
114	Seddonville	41 33 E	172 1 E
131	Sedro Woolley	48 30 N	122 15W
48	Seefeld	51 53 N	13 17 E
168	Seeheim	26 32 S	17 52 E
28	Sées	48 38 N	0 10 E
45	Seesen	51 35 N	10 10 E
91	Segamat	2 30 N	102 50 E
55	Segorbe	39 50 N	0 30W
158	Ségou	13 30 N	6 10W
28	Segré	47 40 N	0 52W
158	Séguéla	7 57 N	6 40W
55	Segura, R.	38 6 N	0 54W
55	Segura, Sa. de	38 5 N	2 45W
81	Sehkonj, Kuh-e	30 0 N	57 30 E
51	Şeica Mare	46 1 N	24 7 E
31	Seille, R.	49 7 N	6 11 E
37	Seinäjoki	62 47 N	22 50 E
28	Seine, B. de la	49 30 N	0 30W
28	Seine, R.	49 26 N	0 26 E
29	Seine-et-Marne □	48 45 N	3 0 E
28	Seine-Maritime □	49 40 N	1 0 E
81	Seistan	27 0 N	62 0 E
158	Sekondi-Takoradi	5 2 N	1 48W
91	Selangor □	3 20 N	101 30 E
94	Selatan N, Kalimantan	3 0 S	115 0 E
95	Selatan N, Sulawesi	3 0 S	120 0 E
94	Selatan N, Sumatera	3 0 S	105 0 E
45	Selb	50 9 N	12 9 E
21	Selby	53 47 N	1 5W
169	Selebi-Pikwe	22 0 S	27 45 E
29	Sélestat	48 10 N	7 26 E
158	Sélibabi	15 20 N	12 15W
125	Selkirk, Canada	50 10 N	97 20W
24	Selkirk, U.K.	55 33 N	2 50W
124	Selkirk Mts.	51 0 N	117 10W
127	Selma, Ala.	32 30 N	87 0W
131	Selma, Calif.	36 39 N	119 30W
21	Selsey Bill	50 43 N	0 48W
29	Seltz	48 48 N	8 4W
169	Selukwe	19 40 S	30 0 E
95	Semarang	7 0 S	110 26 E
95	Semeru, Mt.	8 4 S	113 3 E
131	Seminoe Res.	42 0 N	107 0W
76	Semipalatinsk	50 30 N	80 10 E
48	Semmering P.	47 41 N	15 45 E
95	Semporna	4 30 N	118 33 E
144	Sena Madureira	9 5 S	68 45W
91	Senai	1 38 S	103 38 E
168	Senanga	16 2 S	23 14 E
102	Sendai, Kagoshima	31 50 N	130 20 E
102	Sendai, Miyagi	38 15 N	141 0 E
158	Senegal ■	14 30 N	14 30W
158	Senegal, R.	16 30 N	15 30W
156	Senegambia, Reg.	14 0 N	14 0W
45	Senftenberg	51 30 N	13 51 E
63	Senigállia	43 42 N	13 12 E
63	Senj	45 0 N	14 58 E
159	Sennâr	13 30 N	33 35 E
29	Sens	48 11 N	3 15 E
60	Senta	45 55 N	20 3 E
95	Sentolo	7 55 S	110 13 E
55	Seo de Urgel	42 22 N	1 23 E
123	Separation Pt.	53 40 N	57 16W
91	Sepone	16 45 N	106 13 E
61	Septemvri	42 13 N	24 6 E
131	Sequim	48 3 N	123 9W
34	Seraing	50 35 N	5 32 E
95	Seram, I.	3 10 S	129 0 E
95	Seram Sea	3 0 S	130 0 E
95	Serang	6 8 S	106 10 E
75	Serdobsk	52 28 N	44 10 E
62	Seregno	45 40 N	9 12 E
91	Seremban	2 43 N	101 53 E
165	Serenje	13 11 S	30 52 E
145	Sergipe □	10 30 S	37 30W
94	Seria	4 37 N	114 30 E
29	Sérifontaine	49 20 N	1 45 E
68	Sérifos, I.	37 9 N	24 30 E
63	Sérmide	45 0 N	11 17 E
76	Serov	59 40 N	60 20 E
165	Serpa Pinto	14 48 S	17 52 E
64	Serpeddi, Pta.	39 19 N	9 28 E
55	Serpis, R.	38 45 N	0 21W
68	Sérrai	41 5 N	23 32 E
68	Sérrai □	41 5 N	23 37 E
64	Serramanna	39 26 N	8 56 E
145	Sertania	8 5 S	37 20W
68	Sérvia	40 9 N	21 58 E
53	Sesimbra	38 28 N	9 20W
53	Sestao	43 18 N	3 0W
62	Sesto S. Giovanni	45 32 N	9 14 E
62	Sestri Levante	44 17 N	9 22 E
30	Sète	43 25 N	3 42 E
158	Sétif	36 9 N	5 26 E
102	Seto	35 14 N	137 6 E
158	Settat	33 0 N	7 40W
165	Setté Cama	2 32 S	9 57 E
21	Settle	54 5 N	2 18W
53	Setúbal	38 30 N	8 58W
53	Setúbal, B. de	38 40 N	8 56W
75	Sevan L.		
75	Sevastopol	44 35 N	33 30 E
122	Severn, R., Canada	56 2 N	87 36W
21	Severn, R., U.K.	51 25 N	3 0W
77	Severnaya Zemlya, I.	79 0 N	100 0 E
75	Severnyye Uvaly, Reg.	58 0 N	48 0 E
75	Severodvinsk	64 27 N	39 58 E
49	Severomoravsky □	49 38 N	17 40 E
53	Sevilla	37 23 N	6 0W
61	Sevlievo	43 1 N	25 6 E
120	Seward	60 0 N	149 40W
120	Seward Pen.	65 0 N	164 0W
153	Seychelles, Is.	5 0 S	56 0 E
31	Seyssel	45 57 N	5 49 E
29	Sézanne	48 40 N	3 40 E
64	Sezze	41 30 N	13 3 E
159	Sfax	34 49 N	10 48 E
34	's-Gravenhage	52 7 N	4 17 E
99	Shaanxi □	35 0 N	109 0 E
169	Shabani	20 17 S	30 2 E
61	Shabla	43 31 N	28 32 E
96	Shache	38 20 N	77 10 E
21	Shaftesbury	51 0 N	2 12W
81	Shāhābād, Iran	37 40 N	56 50 E
80	Shāhābād, Iran	34 10 N	46 30 E
81	Shahdād	30 30 N	57 40 E
81	Shāhī	36 30 N	52 55 E
80	Shāhpūr	38 12 N	44 45 E
81	Shahrezā	32 0 N	51 55 E
81	Shāhrūd	36 30 N	55 0 E
81	Shahsavār	36 45 N	51 12 E
75	Shakhty	47 40 N	40 10 E
75	Shakhunya	57 40 N	47 0 E
158	Shaki	8 41 N	3 21 E
81	Shām, Jabal ash	23 10 N	57 5 E
81	Shamīl	29 32 N	77 18 E
165	Shamo, L.	5 45 N	37 30 E
87	Shan □	21 30 N	98 30 E
99	Shandong □	36 0 N	118 0 E
158	Shanga	9 1 N	5 2 E
169	Shangani, R.	18 41 S	27 10 E
99	Shanghai	31 15 N	121 26 E
99	Shangqiu	34 26 N	115 36 E
114	Shannon	40 33 S	17 25 E
27	Shannon, R.	52 30 N	9 53W
99	Shantou	23 18 N	116 40 E
99	Shaoxing	30 0 N	120 35 E
99	Shaoyang	27 14 N	111 25 E
24	Shapinsay, I.	59 2 N	2 50W
80	Shaqrā	25 15 N	45 16 E
110	Shark, B.	25 15 S	133 20 E
75	Sharya	58 12 N	45 40 E
169	Shashi	21 40 S	28 40 E
125	Shaunavon	49 35 N	108 40W
128	Shawano	44 45 N	88 38W
122	Shawinigan	46 35 N	72 50W
128	Shawnee	35 15 N	97 0W
127	Sheboygan	43 46 N	87 45W
123	Shediac	46 14 N	64 32W
21	Sheerness	51 26 N	0 47 E
21	Sheffield	53 23 N	1 28W
81	Shēkhābād	34 0 N	68 45 E
123	Shelburne, Nova Scotia	43 47 N	65 20W
127	Shelbyville, Ind.	39 30 N	85 42W
127	Shelbyville, Tenn.	35 30 N	86 25W
77	Shelikhova Zaliv	59 30 N	157 0 E
125	Shell Lake	53 19 N	107 6W
125	Shellbrook	53 13 N	106 24W
123	Shelter Bay	50 30 N	67 20W
75	Shemakha	40 50 N	48 28 E
128	Shenandoah, Iowa	40 50 N	95 25W
127	Shenandoah, Pa.	40 49 N	76 13W
127	Shenandoah, R.	39 19 N	77 44W
159	Shendî	16 46 N	33 33 E
68	Shëngjeni	41 50 N	19 35 E
99	Shenyang	41 48 N	123 27 E
113	Shepparton	36 18 S	145 25 E
81	Sherberghān	36 40 N	65 48 E
21	Sherborne	50 56 N	2 31W
158	Sherbro I.	7 30 N	12 40W
131	Sheridan	44 50 N	107 0W
128	Sherman	33 40 N	96 35W
34	s'Hertogenbosch	51 41 N	5 19 E
21	Sherwood Forest	53 5 N	1 5W
24	Shetland □	60 30 N	1 30W
76	Shevchenko	44 25 N	51 20 E
102	Shibushi	31 25 N	131 0 E
24	Shiel, L.	56 48 N	5 32W
102	Shiga □	35 20 N	136 0 E
68	Shijaku	41 21 N	19 33 E
99	Shijiazhuang	38 2 N	114 28 E
102	Shikoku, I.	33 45 N	133 30 E
27	Shillelagh	52 46 N	6 32 E
77	Shilka	52 0 N	115 55 E
87	Shillong	25 30 N	92 0 E
102	Shimada	34 49 N	138 19 E
102	Shimane □	35 0 N	132 30 E
102	Shimizu	35 0 N	138 30 E
102	Shimodate	36 20 N	139 55 E
86	Shimoga	13 57 N	75 32 E
24	Shin, L.	58 7 N	4 30W
81	Shīndand	33 12 N	62 8 E
102	Shingú	33 40 N	135 33 E
123	Shippegan	47 45 N	64 45W
102	Shirane-San, Mt.	35 40 N	138 15 E
81	Shíráz	29 42 N	52 30 E
86	Shivpuri	25 18 N	77 42 E
102	Shizuoka	35 0 N	138 30 E
68	Shkodra	42 6 N	19 20 E
68	Shkumbini, R.	41 1 N	19 26 E
21	Shoeburyness	51 13 N	0 49 E
77	Shologontsy	66 13 N	114 14 E
131	Shoshone	43 0 N	114 27W
131	Show Low	34 16 N	110 0W
128	Shreveport	32 30 N	93 50W
21	Shrewsbury	52 42 N	2 45W
99	Shuangliao	43 29 N	123 30 E
76	Shumikha	55 15 N	63 30 E
81	Shúsf	31 50 N	60 5 E
80	Shushtar	32 0 N	48 50 E
91	Si Racha	13 20 N	101 10 E
86	Siahan Ra.	27 30 N	64 40 E
86	Sialkot	32 32 N	74 30 E
91	Siam = Thailand ■	15 0 N	100 0 E
91	Siam, G. of	11 30 N	101 E
95	Siargao, I.	9 52 N	126 3 E
68	Siátista	40 15 N	21 33 E
125	Sibbald	51 24 N	110 10W
63	Sibenik	43 48 N	15 54 E
94	Siberut, I.	1 30 S	99 0 E
165	Sibiti	3 38 S	13 19 E
51	Sibiu	45 45 N	24 9 E
94	Sibolga	1 50 N	98 45 E
87	Sibsagar	27 0 N	94 36 E
94	Sibu	2 19 N	111 51 E
95	Sibutu Pass.	4 50 N	120 0 E
95	Sibuyan, I.	12 25 N	122 40 E
95	Sibuyan Sea	12 50 N	122 20 E
99	Sichuan □	31 0 N	104 0 E
64	Sicilian Chan.	37 20 N	12 20 E
65	Sicily, I.	37 30 N	14 30 E
60	Šid	45 6 N	19 16 E
86	Siddipet	18 0 N	79 0 E
68	Sidhirókastron	37 20 N	21 46 E
159	Sîdi Barrâni	31 32 N	25 58 E
158	Sidi-Bel-Abbès	35 13 N	0 10W
24	Sidlaw Hills	56 32 N	3 10W
21	Sidmouth	50 40 N	3 13W
124	Sidney, Canada	48 39 N	123 24W
127	Sidney, U.S.A.	40 18 N	84 6W
95	Sidoardjo	7 30 S	112 46 E
45	Sieburg	50 48 N	7 12 E
50	Siedice	52 10 N	22 20 E
45	Sieg, R	50 45 N	7 5 E
45	Siegen	50 52 N	8 2 E
63	Siena	43 20 N	11 20 E
50	Sieradź	51 37 N	18 41 E
50	Sierpc	52 55 N	19 43 E
158	Sierra Leone ■	9 0 N	12 0W
45	Sierre	46 17 N	7 31 E
68	Sifnos, I.	37 0 N	24 45 E
30	Sigean	43 2 N	2 58 E
51	Sighisoara	46 12 N	24 50 E
94	Sigli	5 25 N	96 0 E
37	Siglufjörđur	66 12 N	18 55W
53	Sigüenza	41 3 N	2 40W
158	Siguiri	11 31 N	9 10W
131	Sigurd	38 57 N	112 0W
91	Sihanoukville = Kompong Som	10 40 N	103 30 E
80	Siirt	37 57 N	41 55 E
158	Sikasso	11 7 N	5 35W
77	Sikhote Alin Khrebet	46 0 N	136 0 E
68	Sikinos, I.	36 40 N	25 8 E
87	Sikkim □	27 50 N	88 50 E
53	Sil, R.	42 27 N	7 43W
63	Silba	44 24 N	14 41 E
87	Silghat	26 35 N	93 0 E
61	Silistra	44 6 N	27 19 E
41	Silkeborg	56 10 N	9 32 E
165	Silva Porto = Bié	12 22 S	16 55 E
53	Silves	37 11 N	8 26W
48	Silz	47 16 N	10 56 E
94	Simanggang	1 15 N	111 25 E
77	Simenga	62 50 N	107 55 E
51	Simeria	45 51 N	23 1 E
94	Simeulue, I.	2 45 N	95 45 E
75	Simferopol	44 55 N	34 3 E
68	Sími, I.	36 35 N	27 50 E
86	Simla	31 2 N	77 15
125	Simmie	49 56 N	108 6W
91	Simpang	4 50 N	100 40 E
45	Simplonpass	46 15 N	8 0 E
110	Simpson, Des.	25 0 S	137 0 E
159	Sinâ', Gebel el Tih Es	29 0 N	33 30 E
159	Sinai = Es Sinâ'	29 0 N	34 0 E
51	Sinaia	45 21 N	25 38 E
137	Sinaloa □	25 50 N	108 20W
60	Sînandrei	45 52 N	21 13 E
144	Sincelejo	9 18 N	75 24W
53	Sines	37 56 N	8 51 E
53	Sines, C. de	37 58 N	8 53W
95	Singaparna	7 23 S	108 4 E
91	Singapore ■	1 17 N	103 51 E
91	Singapore, Str. of	1 10 N	103 40 E
45	Singen	47 45 N	8 50 E
87	Singkling Hkamti	26 0 N	95 45 E
159	Sinkat	18 55 N	36 49 E
64	Sínnai	39 18 N	9 13 E
145	Sinnamary	5 23 N	52 57W
159	Sinnuris	29 26 N	30 31 E
61	Sinoe, L.	44 35 N	28 50 E
80	Sinop	42 1 N	35 11 E
94	Sintang	0 5 N	111 35 E
53	Sintra	38 47 N	9 25W
45	Sion	46 14 N	7 20 E
128	Sioux City	42 32 N	96 25W
139	Siparia	10 15 N	61 30W
99	Siping	43 8 N	124 21 E
139	Siquia, R.	12 30 N	84 30W
81	Şīr Banī Yās, I.	24 20 N	54 0 E
120	Sir James McBrien, Mt.	62 7 N	127 41W
38	Sira	13 41 N	76 49 E
65	Siracusa	37 4 N	15 17 E
87	Sirajganj	24 25 N	89 47 E
51	Siret, R.	47 55 N	26 5 E
86	Sironj	24 5 N	77 45 E
68	Síros, I.	37 28 N	24 57 E
63	Sisak	45 30 N	16 21 E
55	Sisante	39 25 N	2 12W
91	Sisophon	13 31 N	102 59 E
87	Sitapur	27 38 N	80 45 E
55	Sitges	41 17 N	1 47 E
68	Sithonia, Pen.	40 0 N	23 45 E
87	Sittang Myit, R.	18 20 N	96 45 E
34	Sittard	51 0 N	5 52 E
159	Sîwa	29 11 N	25 31 E
87	Siwalik Ra.	28 0 N	83 0 E
87	Siwan	26 13 N	84 27 E
21	Sizewell	52 13 N	1 38 E
41	Sjaelland, I.	55 30 N	11 30 E
	Jezero, L.	42 10 N	19 15 E
41	Skaerbaek	55 31 N	9 38 E
41	Skagen	57 43 N	10 35 E
38	Skagerrak, Str.	57 30 N	9 0 E
124	Skagway	59 30 N	135 20W
41	Skanderborg	56 2 N	9 55 E
41	Skanör	55 24 N	12 50 E
41	Skara	58 25 N	13 30 E
41	Skaraborg □	58 20 N	13 30 E
86	Skardu	35 20 N	73 35 E
50	Skarzysko Kamienna	51 7 N	20 52 E
124	Skenna Mts.	56 40 N	128 0W
21	Skegness	53 9 N	0 20 E
144	Skeldon	6 0 N	57 20W
37	Skellefteå	64 45 N	20 59 E
37	Skelleftehamn	64 41 N	21 14 E
68	Skíathos, I.	39 12 N	23 30 E
27	Skibbereen	51 33 N	9 16W
21	Skiddaw, Mt.	54 39 N	3 9W
38	Skien	59 12 N	9 35 E
50	Skierniewice	51 58 N	20 19 E
158	Skikda	36 50 N	6 58 E
21	Skipton	53 57 N	2 1W
68	Skíros, I.	38 55 N	24 34 E
41	Skive	56 33 N	9 2 E
41	Skoghall	59 20 N	13 30 E
41	Skönsberg	62 25 N	17 21 E
68	Skópelos, I.	39 9 N	23 47 E
60	Skopje	42 1 N	21 32 E
50	Skórcz	43 47 N	18 30 E
41	Skövde	58 24 N	13 50 E
127	Skowhegan	44 49 N	69 40W
38	Skudeneshavn	59 10 N	5 10 E
27	Skull	51 32 N	9 40W
41	Skurup	55 28 N	13 30 E
41	Skutskär	60 37 N	17 25 E
24	Skye, I.	57 15 N	6 10W
41	Slagelse	55 23 N	11 19 E
27	Slaney, R.	52 52 N	6 45W
60	Slano	42 48 N	17 53 E
48	Slaný	50 13 N	14 6 E
51	Slatina	44 28 N	24 22 E
128	Slaton	33 27 N	101 38W
124	Slave Lake	55 25 N	114 50W
76	Slavgorod	53 10 N	78 50 E
60	Slavonska Požega	45 20 N	17 41 E
60	Slavonski Brod	45 11 N	18 0 E
21	Sleaford	53 0 N	0 22W
24	Sleat, Sd. of	57 5 N	5 47W
27	Sligo	54 17 N	8 28W
91	Slim River	3 48 N	101 25 E
61	Sliven	42 42 N	26 19 N
60	Slivnitsa	42 50 N	23 0 E
63	Sljeme, Mt.	45 57 N	15 58 E
21	Slough	51 30 N	0 35W
63	Slovenska Bistrica	46 24 N	15 35 E
49	Slovenská Socialistická Rep. □	48 40 N	19 0 E
49	Slovenské Rudohorie, Mts.	50 25 N	13 0 E
49	Slovensko, Reg.	48 50 N	20 0 E
50	Słubice	52 50 N	14 35 E
50	Słubia, R.	54 35 N	16 50 E
50	Słupsk	54 28 N	17 1 E
77	Slyudyanka	51 40 N	103 30 E
125	Smeaton	53 30 N	105 49W
60	Smederevo	44 40 N	20 57 E
124	Smith	55 10 N	114 0W
120	Smith Arm, B.	66 30 N	123 0W
124	Smithers	54 45 N	127 10W
127	Smithfield	35 31 N	78 16W
110	Smoky Bay	32 22 S	133 56 E
122	Smoky Falls	50 10 N	82 10W
128	Smoky Hill, R.	39 3 N	96 48W
75	Smolensk	54 50 N	32 1 E
61	Smolyan	41 36 N	24 38 E
122	Smooth Rock Falls	49 17 N	81 37W
21	Snaefell, Mt.	54 18 N	4 26W
37	Snaefellsjökull,Mt.	64 50 N	23 49W
131	Snake, R.	46 12 N	119 2W
34	Sneek	53 2 N	5 40 E
50	Sniardwy, Sezero, L.	53 46 N	21 44 E
125	Snow Lake	54 53 N	101 2W
21	Snowdon, Mt.	53 4 N	4 8W
53	Snowtown	33 47 S	138 13 E
113	Snowy, Mts.	36 15 S	148 20 E
131	Soap Lake	47 29 N	119 31W
145	Sobral	3 50 S	40 30W
50	Sochaczew	52 15 N	20 13 E
75	Sochi	43 35 N	39 40 E
144	Socorro, Col.	6 29 N	73 16W
131	Socorro, U.S.A.	34 3 N	106 58W
85	Socotra, I.	12 30 N	54 0 E
55	Socúellamas	39 16 N	2 47W
124	Soda Creek	52 25 N	122 10W
131	Soda Springs	42 4 N	111 40W
165	Sodo	7 0 N	37 57 E
34	Soest, Neth.	52 9 N	5 19 E
45	Soest, W. Germany	51 34 N	8 7 E
68	Sofádhes	39 28 N	22 4 E
165	Sofala = Beira	19 50 S	34 52 E
61	Sofiya	42 45 N	23 20 E
144	Sogamoso	5 43 N	72 56W
38	Sogn og Fjordane □	61 40 N	6 0 E
37	Sognefjorden	61 10 N	5 30 E
159	Sohâg	26 27 N	31 43 E
34	Soignes	50 35 N	4 5 E
29	Soissons	49 25 N	3 19 E
80	Soke	37 48 N	27 28 E
158	Sokodé	9 0 N	1 11 E
75	Sokol	59 30 N	40 5 E
48	Sokolov	50 12 N	22 7 E
158	Sokoto	13 2 N	5 16 E
95	Solano	16 25 N	121 15 E
50	Solec Kujawski	53 6 N	18 14 E
31	Solenzara	41 53 N	9 23 E
29	Solesmes	50 10 N	3 30 E
75	Soligalich	59 5 N	42 10 E
75	Solikamsk	59 38 N	56 50 E
45	Solingen	51 10 N	7 4 E
41	Sollefteå	63 10 N	17 20 E
55	Sóller	39 43 N	2 45 E
41	Solna	59 22 N	18 1 E
29	Sologne, Reg.	47 40 N	2 0 E
94	Solok	0 55 S	100 40 E
137	Sololá	14 49 N	91 10 E
106	Solomon Is.	8 0 S	159 0 E
45	Solothurn	47 13 N	7 32 E
63	Solta, I.	43 24 N	16 15 E
81	Solţānābād	36 29 N	58 5 E
80	Solţānīyeh	36 20 N	48 55 E
45	Soltau	52 59 N	9 50 E
127	Solvay	43 5 N	76 17W
41	Sölvesborg	56 5 N	14 35 E
165	Solwezi	12 20 S	26 26 E
24	Solway Firth	54 45 N	3 38W
85	Somali Rep. ■	7 0 N	47 0 E
60	Sombor	45 46 N	19 17 E
127	Somerset	37 5 N	84 40W
21	Somerset □	51 9 N	3 0W
168	Somerset East	32 42 S	25 35 E
139	Somerset I., Bermuda	32 20 N	64 55W
120	Somerset I., Canada	73 30 N	93 0W
29	Somme □	40 0 N	2 15 E
28	Somme, B. de la	5 22 N	1 30 E
29	Somme, R.	50 11 N	1 39 E
41	Sommen, L.	58 0 N	15 15 E
29	Sommesous	48 44 N	4 12 E
49	Somogy □	46 19 N	17 30 E
53	Somosierra, P. de	41 9 N	3 35W
30	Somport, Col du	42 48 N	0 31W
41	Sønderborg	54 55 N	9 49 E
45	Sondershausen	51 22 N	10 50 E
41	Sonderyllands □	55 10 N	9 10 E
62	Sóndrio	46 10 N	9 53 E
86	Sonepat	29 0 N	77 5 E

Uaupés

Wakre

U

144	Uaupés	0 8 S	67 5W
145	Ubaitaba	14 18 S	39 20W
31	Ubaye, R.	44 28 N	6 18 E
102	Ube	34 6 N	131 20 E
53	Ubeda	38 3 N	3 23W
145	Uberaba	19 50 S	48 0W
145	Uberlândia	19 0 S	48 20W
91	Ubon Ratchathani	15 15 N	104 50 E
165	Ubundu	0 22 S	25 30 E
144	Ucayali, R.	4 30 S	73 30W
125	Uchi Lake	51 10 N	92 40W
102	Uchiura-Wan, G.	42 25 N	140 40 E
124	Ucluelet	48 57 N	125 32W
63	Udbina	44 31 N	15 47 E
41	Uddevalla	58 21 N	11 55 E
37	Uddjaur, L.	65 55 N	17 50 E
86	Udgir	18 25 N	77 5 E
86	Udhampur	33 0 N	75 5 E
158	Udi	6 23 N	7 21 E
63	Údine	46 5 N	13 10 E
75	Udmurt A.S.S.R. □	57 30 N	52 30 E
91	Udon Thani	17 29 N	102 46 E
61	Udvoy, Mts.	42 50 N	26 50 E
45	Ueckermünde	53 45 N	14 1 E
102	Ueda	36 30 N	138 10 E
77	Uelen	66 10 N	170 0W
45	Uelzen	53 0 N	10 33 E
75	Ufa	54 45 N	55 55 E
165	Uganda ■	2 0 N	32 0 E
120	Ugashik Lakes	57 0 N	157 0W
31	Ugine	45 45 N	6 25 E
77	Uglegorsk	49 10 N	142 5 E
49	Uherské Hradiště	49 4 N	17 30 E
49	Uhersky Brod	49 1 N	17 40 E
48	Uhlava, R.	49 45 N	13 20 E
127	Uhrichsville	40 23 N	81 22W
168	Uitenhage	33 40 S	25 28 E
49	Ujpest	47 33 N	19 6 E
95	Ujung Pandang	5 10 S	119 0 E
165	Ukerewe I.	2 0 S	33 0 E
87	Ukhrul	25 10 N	94 25 E
75	Ukhta	63 55 N	54 0 E
75	Ukrainian S.S.R. □	48 0 N	35 0 E
77	Ulan-Bator	47 50 N	106 40 E
77	Ulan Ude	52 0 N	107 30 E
60	Ulcinj	41 58 N	19 10 E
86	Ulhasnagar	19 15 N	73 10 E
60	Uljma	45 2 N	21 10 E
53	Ulla, R.	42 39 N	8 44W
24	Ullapool	57 54 N	5 10W
55	Ulldecona	40 36 N	0 20 E
21	Ullswater, L.	54 35 N	2 52W
45	Ulm	48 23 N	10 0 E
51	Ulmeni	45 4 N	46 40 E
38	Ulsberg	62 45 N	10 3 E
27	Ulster □	54 45 N	6 30W
21	Ulverston	54 13 N	3 7W
113	Ulverstone	41 11 S	146 11 E
75	Ulyanovsk	54 25 N	48 25 E
75	Uman	48 40 N	30 12 E
63	Umbertide	43 18 N	12 20 E
63	Umbria □	42 53 N	12 30 E
159	Umm Keddada	13 36 N	26 42 E
80	Umm Lajj	25 0 N	37 23 E
120	Umnak I.	53 0 N	168 0W
169	Umtali	18 58 S	32 38 E
169	Umvuma	19 16 S	30 30 E
169	Umzimvubu	31 38 S	29 33 E
63	Unac, R.	44 30 N	16 9 E
120	Unalaska I.	54 0 N	164 30W
131	Uncompahgre Pk.	38 5 N	107 32W
113	Underbool	35 10 S	141 51 E
113	Ungarie	33 38 S	146 56 E
121	Ungava B.	59 30 N	67 0W
121	Ungava Pen.	60 0 N	75 0W
148	União da Vitoría	26 5 S	51 0W
120	Unimak I.	54 30 N	164 30W
127	Union City	40 47 N	74 5W
72	Union of Soviet Socialist Republics ■	60 0 N	60 0 E
127	Uniontown	39 54 N	79 45W
81	United Arab Emirates ■	24 0 N	54 30 E
19	United Kingdom ■	55 0 N	3 0W
119	United States ■	40 0N	100 0W
24	Unst, I.	60 50 N	0 55W
45	Unterwalden □	46 50 N	8 15 E
102	Uozu	36 48 N	137 24 E
144	Upata	8 1 N	62 24W
173	Upernavik	72 45 N	56 0W
168	Upington	28 25 S	21 15 E
114	Upolu, I.	13 58 S	172 0W
114	Upper Hutt	41 8 S	175 5 E
158	Upper Volta ■	12 0 N	0 30W
41	Uppsala	59 53 N	17 42 E
41	Uppsala □	60 0 N	17 30 E
80	Ur	30 55 N	46 25 E
75	Ural Mts. = Uralskie Gory	60 0 N	59 0 E
76	Ural, R.	47 0 N	51 48 E
113	Uralla	30 37 S	151 29 E
75	Uralskie Gory	60 0 N	59 0 E
113	Urandangi	21 32 S	138 14 E
125	Uranium City	59 28 N	108 40W
102	Urawa	35 50 N	139 40 E
128	Urbana, Ill.	40 7 N	88 12W
127	Urbana, Ohio	40 9 N	83 44W
63	Urbino	43 43 N	12 38 E
30	Urdos	42 51 N	0 35W
21	Ure, R.	54 1 N	1 12W
76	Urengoy	66 0 N	78 0 E
80	Urfa	37 12 N	38 50 E
48	Urfahr	48 19 N	14 17 E
45	Uri □	46 43 N	8 35 E
144	Uribia	11 43 N	72 16W
51	Urlati	44 59 N	26 15 E
80	Urmia, L. = Daryâcheh-ye Reza'iyeh	37 30 N	45 30 E
60	Uroševac	42 23 N	21 10 E
145	Uruaca	14 35 S	49 16W
137	Uruapán	19 30 N	102 0W
148	Uruguaiana	29 50 S	57 0W
148	Uruguay ■	32 30 S	55 30W
148	Uruguay, R.	34 12 S	58 18W
96	Ürümqi	43 45 N	87 45 E
51	Urziceni	44 46 N	26 42 E
75	Usa, R.	65 57 N	56 55 E
80	Uşak	38 43 N	29 28 E
45	Usedom, I.	53 50 N	13 55 E
76	Ush-Tobe	45 16 N	78 0 E
148	Ushuaia	54 50 S	68 23W
77	Ushuman	52 47 N	126 32 E
21	Usk, R.	51 36 N	2 58W
80	Üsküdar	41 0 N	29 5 E
75	Usman	52 5 N	39 48 E
77	Usolye Sibirskoye	52 40 N	103 40 E
76	Uspenskiy	48 50 N	72 55 E
30	Ussel	45 32 N	2 18 E
77	Ussuriysk	43 40 N	131 50 E
77	Ust-Ilimsk	58 3 N	102 39 E
76	Ust Ishim	57 45 N	71 10 E
77	Ust-Kamchatsk	56 10 N	162 0 E
76	Ust Kamenogorsk	50 0 N	82 20 E
77	Ust Kuyga	70 1 N	135 36 E
77	Ust Olenck	73 0 N	120 10 E
76	Ust Post	70 0 N	84 10 E
75	Ust Tsilma	65 25 N	52 0 E
75	Ust Usa	66 0 N	56 30 E
77	Ustchaun	68 47 N	170 30 E
49	Ustí na Orlici	49 58 N	16 38 E
48	Ustí nad Labem	50 41 N	14 3 E
77	Ustye	55 30 N	97 30 E
131	Utah □	39 30 N	111 30W
94	Utara □	2 0 N	99 0 E
45	Ütersen	53 40 N	9 40 E
91	Uthai Thani	15 22 N	100 3 E
127	Utica	43 5 N	75 18W
55	Utiel	39 37 N	1 11W
34	Utrecht, Neth.	52 3 N	5 8 E
34	Utrecht, Netherlands □	52 6 N	5 7 E
102	Utsunomiya	36 30 N	139 50 E
86	Uttar Pradesh □	27 0 N	80 0 E
91	Uttaradit	17 36 N	100 5 E
21	Uttoxeter	52 53 N	1 50W
37	Uudenmaa □	60 25 N	23 0 E
37	Uusikaupunki	60 47 N	21 28 E
128	Uvalde	29 15 N	99 48W
76	Uvat	59 5 N	68 50 E
165	Uvira	3 22 S	29 3 E
102	Uwajima	33 10 N	132 35 E
137	Uxmal	20 22 N	89 46W
144	Uyuni	20 35 S	66 55W
76	Uzbek S.S.R.	40 5 N	65 0 E
31	Uzès	44 1 N	4 26 E

V

168	Vaal, R.	29 4 S	23 38 E
37	Vaasa	63 10 N	21 35 E
31	Vaccares, Étang de	43 32 N	4 34 E
37	Vadsø	70 3 N	29 50 E
48	Vaduz	47 8 N	9 31 E
53	Vagos	40 33 N	8 42W
49	Váh, R.	47 55 N	18 0 E
76	Vaigach	70 10 N	59 0 E
28	Vaiges	48 2 N	0 30W
122	Val d'Or	48 7 N	77 47W
125	Val Marie	49 15 N	107 45W
53	Valadares	41 5 N	8 38W
45	Valais □	46 12 N	7 45 E
49	Valasské Meziřičí	49 29 N	17 59 E
41	Valbo	60 40 N	17 4 E
29	Val-d'Oise □	49 5 N	2 0 E
63	Valdagno	45 38 N	11 18 E
75	Valdayskaya Vozvyshennost	57 0 N	33 40 E
53	Valdeazogues, R.	38 45 N	4 55W
41	Valdemarsvik	58 14 N	16 40 E
53	Valderaduey, R.	41 31 N	5 42W
55	Valderrobres	40 53 N	0 9 E
148	Valdés, Pen.	42 30 S	63 45W
120	Valdez	61 14 N	146 10W
63	Valdobbiádene	45 53 N	12 0 E
127	Valdosta	30 50 N	83 48W
145	Valença, Brazil	13 20 S	39 5W
53	Valença, Port.	42 1 N	8 34W
145	Valença da Piaui	6 20 S	41 45W
31	Valence	44 57 N	4 54 E
30	Valence-d'Agen	44 8 N	0 54 E
55	Valencia, Sp.	39 27 N	0 23W
144	Valencia, Ven.	10 11 N	68 0W
55	Valencia, Reg.	39 25 N	0 45W
53	Valencia de Alcantara	39 25 N	7 14W
53	Valencia de Don Juan	42 17 N	5 31W
53	Valencia del Ventoso	38 15 N	6 29W
29	Valenciennes	50 20 N	3 34 E
51	Vălenii-de-Munte	45 12 N	26 3 E
128	Valentine	42 50 N	100 35W
62	Valenza	45 2 N	8 39 E
144	Valera	9 19 N	70 37W
65	Valguarnera Caropepe	37 30 N	14 22 E
31	Valinco, G. de	41 40 N	8 52 E
34	Valkenswaard	51 21 N	5 29 E
55	Vall de Uxó	40 49 N	0 15W
137	Valladolid, Mexico	20 30 N	88 20W
53	Valladolid, Sp.	41 38 N	4 43W
62	Valle d'Aosta □	45 45 N	7 22 E
137	Valle de Santiago	20 25 N	101 15W
53	Vallecas	40 23 N	3 41W
131	Vallejo	38 12 N	122 15W
128	Valley City	46 57 N	98 0W
122	Valleyfield	45 15 N	74 8W
124	Valleyview	55 5 N	117 25W
55	Valls	41 18 N	1 15 E
29	Valmy	49 5 N	4 45 E
28	Valognes	49 30 N	1 28W
148	Valparaíso	33 2 S	71 40W
62	Valtellino	46 9 N	10 2 E
53	Valverde del Camino	37 35 N	6 47W
53	Valverde del Fresno	40 15 N	6 51W
128	Van Buren, Ark.	35 28 N	94 18W
123	Van Buren, Me.	47 10 N	68 1W
110	Van Diemen, G.	12 0 S	132 0 E
127	Van Wert	40 52 N	84 31W
124	Vancouver, Canada	49 20 N	123 10W
131	Vancouver, U.S.A.	45 44 N	122 41W
124	Vancouver I.	49 50 N	126 30W
128	Vandalia	38 57 N	89 4W
124	Vanderhoof	54 0 N	124 0W
113	Vandyke	24 8 S	142 45 E
41	Vänern, L.	58 47 N	13 50 E
41	Vänersborg	58 26 N	12 27 E
91	Vang Vieng	18 58 N	102 32 E
77	Vankarem	67 51 N	175 50W
122	Vankleek Hill	45 32 N	74 40W
28	Vannes	47 40 N	2 47W
114	Vanua Levu, I.	15 45 S	179 10 E
31	Var, R.	43 39 N	7 12 E
31	Var □	43 27 N	6 18 E
87	Varanasi	25 22 N	83 8 E
63	Varaždin	46 20 N	16 20 E
62	Varazze	44 21 N	8 36 E
41	Varberg	57 17 N	12 20 E
81	Vardak □	34 15 N	68 0 E
41	Varde	55 38 N	8 29 E
45	Varel	53 23 N	8 9 E
30	Varennes-sur-Allier	49 12 N	5 0 E
60	Vareš	44 12 N	18 23 E
41	Värmdö, I.	59 18 N	18 45 E
41	Värmlands □	59 45 N	13 0 E
41	Värnamo	57 10 N	14 3 E
48	Varnsdorf	49 56 N	14 38 E
60	Varvarin	43 43 N	21 20 E
29	Varzy	47 22 N	3 20 E
49	Vas □	47 10 N	16 55 E
53	Vascâo, R.	37 31 N	7 31W
55	Vascongadas, Reg.	42 50 N	2 45W
41	Västerås	59 37 N	16 38 E
37	Västerbotten □	64 58 N	18 0 E
41	Västerdalälven, R.	60 33 N	15 8 E
41	Västernorrlands □	63 30 N	17 40 E
41	Västervik	57 43 N	16 43 E
41	Västmanlands □	89 5 N	16 20 E
63	Vasto	42 8 N	14 40 E
63	Vatican City	41 54 N	12 27 E
65	Vaticano, C.	38 38 N	15 50 E
37	Vatnajökull	64 30 N	16 30W
41	Vättern, L.	58 25 N	14 30 E
31	Vaucluse □	44 3 N	5 10 E
29	Vaucouleurs	48 37 N	5 40 E
45	Vaud □	46 35 N	6 30 E
31	Vauvert	43 42 N	4 17 E
124	Vauxhall	50 5 N	112 9W
41	Växjö	56 52 N	14 50 E
76	Vaygach, Os.	70 0 N	60 0 E
45	Vechta	52 47 N	8 18 E
34	Vechte, R.	52 35 N	6 5 E
49	Vecsés	47 26 N	19 19 E
34	Veendam	53 5 N	6 25 E
34	Veenendaal	52 2 N	5 34 E
37	Vefsna, R.	65 50 N	13 12 E
37	Vegafjord	65 37 N	12 0 E
124	Vegreville	53 30 N	112 5W
53	Vejer de la Frontera	36 15 N	5 59W
41	Vejle □	55 2 N	11 22 E
63	Vela Luka	42 59 N	16 44 E
30	Velay, Mts. du	45 0 N	3 40 E
63	Velebit Planina, Mts.	44 50 N	15 20 E
68	Velestínon	39 23 N	22 45 E
144	Vélez	6 2 N	73 43W
55	Velez Blanco	37 41 N	2 5W
53	Vélez Málaga	36 48 N	4 5W
55	Vélez Rubio	37 41 N	2 5W
63	Velika Kapela, Mts.	45 10 N	15 5 E
60	Velika Plana	44 20 N	21 1 E
60	Veliki Backu, Kanal	45 45 N	19 15 E
75	Velikiy Ustyug	60 47 N	46 20 E
86	Velikonda Ra.	14 45 N	79 10 E
61	Velingrad	42 4 N	23 58 E
63	Velino, Mt.	42 10 N	13 20 E
48	Velke Meziřici	49 21 N	16 1 E
64	Velletri	41 43 N	12 43 E
86	Vellore	12 57 N	79 10 E
34	Velsen	52 27 N	4 40 E
75	Velsk	61 10 N	42 5 E
31	Venaco	42 14 N	9 10 E
148	Venado Tuerto	33 50 S	62 0W
53	Vendas Novas	38 39 N	8 27W
30	Vendée □	46 40 N	1 20W
29	Vendeuvre	48 14 N	4 27 E
28	Vendôme	47 47 N	1 3 E
55	Vendrell	41 10 N	1 30 E
41	Vendsyssel, Reg.	57 22 N	10 15 E
63	Veneto □	45 30 N	12 0 E
63	Venézia	45 27 N	12 20 E
144	Venezuela ■	8 0 N	65 0W
144	Venezuela, G. de	11 30 N	71 0W
63	Venice = Venézia	45 27 N	12 20 E
31	Vénissieux	45 43 N	4 53 E
87	Venkatapuram	18 20 N	80 30 E
34	Venlo	51 22 N	6 11 E
53	Venta de S. Rafael	40 42 N	4 12W
62	Ventimiglia	43 50 N	7 39 E
21	Ventnor	50 35 N	1 12W
75	Ventspils	57 25 N	21 32 E
131	Ventura	34 16 N	119 25W
148	Vera, Arg.	29 30 S	60 20W
55	Vera, Sp.	37 15 N	1 15W
137	Veracruz	19 10 N	96 10W
137	Veracruz □	19 0 N	96 15W
86	Veraval	20 53 N	70 27 E
148	Verde, R.	41 56 S	65 5W
45	Verden	52 56 N	9 15 E
29	Verdun	49 12 N	5 24 E
31	Verdun-sur-le-Doubs	46 54 N	5 0 E
169	Vereeniging	26 38 S	27 57 E
55	Vergara	43 9 N	2 28W
53	Verín	41 57 N	7 27W
75	Verkhniy Baskunchak	48 5 N	46 50 E
77	Verkhoyansk	67 50 N	133 50 E
77	Verkhoyanskiy Khrebet	66 0 N	129 0 E
125	Vermilion	53 20 N	110 50W
125	Vermilion Bay	49 50 N	93 20W
128	Vermillion	42 50 N	96 56W
127	Vermont □	43 40 N	72 50W
29	Vermenton	47 40 N	3 42 E
131	Vernal	40 28 N	109 35W
28	Verneuil	48 45 N	0 56 E
124	Vernon, Canada	50 20 N	119 15W
28	Vernon, Fr.	49 5 N	1 30 E
68	Véroia	40 34 N	22 18 E
64	Véroli	41 43 N	13 24 E
62	Verona	45 27 N	11 0 E
29	Versailles	48 48 N	2 8 E
158	Verte, C.	14 45 N	17 30W
28	Vertou	47 10 N	1 28W
34	Verviers	50 37 N	5 52 E
29	Vervins	49 50 N	3 53 E
31	Vescovato	42 30 N	9 26 E
75	Veselovskoye, Vdkhr.	47 0 N	41 0 E
29	Vesle, R.	49 23 N	3 38 E
29	Vesoul	60 40 N	6 11 E
38	Vestfold □	59 15 N	10 0 E
41	Vestjællands □	55 30 N	11 20 E
37	Vestmannaejar, Is.	63 27 N	20 15W
65	Vesuvio, Mt.	40 50 N	14 22 E
49	Veszprém	47 8 N	17 57 E
41	Vetlanda	57 24 N	15 3 E
61	Vetovo	43 42 N	26 16 E
63	Vettore, Mt.	44 38 N	7 5 E
45	Vevey	46 28 N	6 51 E
30	Vézère, R.	44 53 N	0 53 E
144	Viacha	16 30 S	68 5W
62	Viadana	44 55 N	10 30 E
145	Viana	3 0 S	44 40W
53	Viana do Alentejo	38 20 N	8 0W
53	Viana do Castelo	41 42 N	8 50W
53	Vianna do Castelo □	41 50 N	8 30W
53	Viar, R.	37 36 N	5 50W
62	Viaréggio	43 52 N	10 13 E
65	Vibo Valéntia	38 40 N	16 5 E
41	Viborg	56 27 N	9 23 E
30	Vic-Fézensac	43 47 N	0 19 E
63	Vicenza	45 32 N	11 31 E
55	Vich	41 58 N	2 19 E
30	Vichy	46 9 N	3 26 E
128	Vicksburg	32 22 N	90 56W
65	Vico del Gargano	41 54 N	15 57 E
30	Vic-sur-Cère	44 59 N	2 38 E
113	Victor Harbour	35 30 S	138 37 E
111	Victoria, Australia	21 16 S	149 3 E
124	Victoria, Canada	48 30 N	123 25W
148	Victoria, Chile	38 22 S	72 29W
101	Victoria, Hong Kong	22 25 N	114 15 E
94	Victoria, Malaysia	5 20 N	115 20 E
128	Victoria, U.S.A.	28 50 N	97 0W
165	Victoria, L.	1 0 S	33 0 E
110	Victoria, R.	15 12 S	129 43 E
139	Victoria de las Tunas	20 58 N	76 59W
49	Victoria Falls	17 58 S	25 45 E
153	Victoria I.	71 0 N	11 0W
27	Victoria Ld.	75 0 S	160 0 E
168	Victoria West	31 25 S	23 4 E
123	Victoriaville	46 4 N	71 56W
131	Victorville	34 32 N	117 18W
127	Vidalia	32 13 N	82 25W
31	Vidauban	43 25 N	6 27 E
53	Vidio, C.	43 35 N	6 14W
148	Viedma	40 50 S	63 0W
148	Viedma, L.	49 30 S	72 30W
53	Vieira	41 38 N	8 8W
45	Vienenburg	51 57 N	10 35 E
49	Vienna = Wien	48 12 N	16 22 E
31	Vienne	45 31 N	4 53 E
91	Vientiane	18 7 N	102 35 E
45	Viersen	51 15 N	6 23 E
45	Vierwald-stättersee, L.	47 0 N	8 30 E
65	Vieste	41 53 N	16 10 E
91	Vietnam ■	16 0 N	108 0 E
31	Vif	45 5 N	5 41 E
95	Vigan	17 35 N	120 28 E
62	Vigévano	45 18 N	8 50 E
145	Vigia	0 50 S	48 5W
30	Vignemale, Pic de	42 47 N	0 10W
62	Vignola	44 29 N	11 0 E
53	Vigo	42 12 N	8 41W
87	Vijayawada	16 31 N	80 39 E
165	Vila Cabral = Lichinga	13 13 S	35 11 E
53	Vila de Rei	39 41 N	8 9W
53	Vila do Conde	41 21 N	8 45W
53	Vila Franca de Xira	38 57 N	8 59W
53	Vila Nova de Foscôa	41 5 N	7 9W
53	Vila Nova de Gaia	41 4 N	8 40W
53	Vila Nova de Ourém	39 40 N	8 35W
53	Vila Real	41 17 N	7 48W
53	Vila Real de Sto. António	37 10 N	7 28W
53	Vilaboa	42 21 N	8 39W
28	Vilaine, R.	47 30 N	2 27W
53	Vilar Formosa	40 38 N	6 45W
53	Vilareal □	41 36 N	7 35W
148	Villa Ángela	27 34 S	60 45W
158	Villa Cisneros = Dakhla	23 50 N	15 53W
148	Villa Colón	31 38 S	68 20W
148	Villa Hayes	25 0 S	57 20W
139	Villa Julia Molina	19 5 N	69 45W
148	Villa María	32 20 S	63 10W
62	Villa Minozzo	44 21 N	10 30 E
53	Villablino	42 57 N	6 19W
53	Villacañas	39 38 N	3 20W
55	Villacarlos	39 53 N	4 17 E
55	Villacarrillo	38 7 N	3 3W
53	Villacastín	40 46 N	4 25W
48	Villach	46 37 N	13 51 E
53	Villada	42 15 N	4 59W
55	Villafeliche	41 10 N	1 30W
55	Villafranca	42 17 N	1 46W
53	Villafranca de los Barros	38 35 N	6 18W
53	Villafranca del Bierzo	42 38 N	6 50W
55	Villafranca del Panadés	41 21 N	1 40 E
62	Villafranca di Verona	45 20 N	10 51 E
148	Villaguay	32 0 S	58 45W
137	Villahermosa	17 45 N	92 50W
55	Villajoyosa	38 30 N	0 12W
53	Villalba	40 36 N	3 59W
53	Villalba de Guardo	42 42 N	4 49W
53	Villalón de Campos	42 5 N	5 4W
53	Villalpando	41 51 N	5 25W
53	Villaluenga	40 2 N	3 54W
53	Villamartín	36 52 N	5 38W
55	Villamayor	41 42 N	0 43W
131	Villanueva	35 16 N	105 31W
55	Villanueva de Castellón	39 5 N	0 31W
53	Villanueva de la Serena	38 59 N	5 50W
55	Villanueva del Arzobispo	38 10 N	3 0W
53	Villanueva del Fresno	38 23 N	7 10W
55	Villanueva y Geltrú	41 13 N	1 40 E
65	Villaroso	37 36 N	14 9 E
148	Villarrica	39 15 S	72 30W
55	Villarrobledo	39 18 N	2 36W
55	Villarroya de la Sierra	41 27 N	1 46W
53	Villarta de San Juan	39 15 N	3 25W
53	Villatobas	39 54 N	3 20W
144	Villavicencio	4 9 N	73 37W
144	Villazón	22 0 S	65 35W
122	Ville Marie	47 20 N	79 30W
28	Villedieu	48 50 N	1 12W
30	Villefort	44 28 N	3 56 E
29	Villefranche	47 19 N	1 46 E
30	Villefranche-de-Lauragais	43 25 N	1 44 E
30	Villefranche-de-Rouergue	44 21 N	2 2 E
31	Villefranche-sur- Saône	45 59 N	4 43 E
29	Villemaur	48 14 N	3 40 E
55	Villena	38 39 N	0 52W
29	Villeneuve	48 42 N	2 25 E
31	Villeneuve-les-Avignon	43 57 N	4 49 E
30	Villeneuve-sur-Lot	44 24 N	0 42 E
28	Villers-Bocage	49 3 N	0 40 E
29	Villers-Cotterets	49 15 N	3 4 E
29	Villerupt	49 28 N	5 55 E
45	Villingen-Schwenningen	48 3 N	8 29 E
75	Vilnius	54 38 N	25 25 E
48	Vils	47 33 N	10 37 E
34	Vilvoorde	50 56 N	4 26 E
77	Vilyuysk	63 40 N	121 20 E
62	Vimercate	45 38 N	9 25 E
41	Vimmerby	57 40 N	15 55 E
148	Viña del Mar	33 0 S	71 30W
127	Vincennes	38 42 N	87 29W
86	Vindhya Ra.	22 50 N	77 0 E
91	Vinh	18 45 N	105 38 E
63	Vinica	45 28 N	15 16 E
128	Vinita	36 40 N	95 12W
75	Vinnitsa	49 15 N	28 30 E
38	Vinstra	61 37 N	9 44 E
51	Vinţu de Jos	46 0 N	23 30 E
63	Vipava	45 51 N	13 38 E
95	Viqueque	8 42 S	126 30 E
125	Virden	49 50 N	101 0W
148	Vírgenes, C.	52 19 S	68 21W
139	Virgin Gorda, I.	18 45 N	64 26W
139	Virgin Is., Br.	18 40 N	64 30W
139	Virgin Is., U.S.	18 20 N	64 50W
128	Virginia	47 30 N	92 32W
127	Virginia □	37 45 N	78 0W
127	Virginia Beach	36 54 N	75 58W
131	Virginia City	45 25 N	111 58W
60	Virovitica	45 51 N	17 21 E
60	Virpazar	42 15 N	19 5 E
34	Virton	49 35 N	5 32 E
86	Virudunagar	9 30 N	78 0 E
131	Visalia	36 25 N	119 18W
95	Visayan Sea	11 30 N	123 30 E
41	Visby	57 37 N	18 18 E
34	Visé	50 44 N	5 41 E
60	Višegrad	43 47 N	19 17 E
53	Viseu	40 40 N	7 55W
87	Vishakhapatnam	17 45 N	83 20 E
63	Višnja Gora	45 58 N	14 45 E
63	Viterbo	42 25 N	12 8 E
114	Viti Levu, I.	17 30 S	177 30 E
77	Vitim	59 45 N	112 25 E
55	Vitória	42 50 N	2 41W
145	Vitória da Conquista	14 51 S	40 51W
145	Vitoria de Santo Antão	8 10 S	37 20W
29	Vitry-le-François	48 43 N	4 33 E
68	Vitsi, Mt	40 40 N	21 25 E
29	Vitteaux	47 24 N	4 30 E
65	Vittória	36 58 N	14 30 E
63	Vittório Véneto	45 59 N	12 18 E
55	Viver	39 55 N	0 36W
30	Vivonne	46 36 N	0 15 E
53	Vizcaya □	43 15 N	2 45W
87	Vizianagaram	18 6 N	83 10 E
51	Viziru	45 0 N	27 43 E
49	Vizovice	49 12 N	17 56 E
34	Vlaardingen	51 55 N	4 21 E
60	Vladicin Han	42 42 N	22 1 E
75	Vladimir	56 0 N	40 30 E
60	Vladimirovac	45 1 N	20 53 E
77	Vladivostok	43 10 N	131 53 E
60	Vlasenica	44 11 N	18 59 E
34	Vlissingen	51 26 N	3 34 E
68	Vlóra	40 32 N	19 28 E
68	Vlora □	40 12 N	20 0 E
48	Vltava, R.	49 35 N	14 10 E
62	Vobarno	45 38 N	10 30 E
48	Vöcklabruck	48 1 N	13 39 E
63	Vodnjan	44 59 N	13 52 E
45	Vogelsberg, Mts.	50 30 N	9 15 E
169	Vohimarina	13 25 S	50 0 E
165	Voi	3 25 S	38 32 E
68	Voíotía □	38 20 N	23 0 E
31	Voiron	45 22 N	5 35 E
48	Voitsberg	47 3 N	15 9 E
68	Voiviis, L.	39 30 N	22 45 E
106	Volcano Is.	25 0 N	141 0 E
75	Volga, R.	45 55 N	47 52 E
75	Volga Heights, Mts.	51 0 N	46 0 E
75	Volgograd	48 40 N	44 25 E
75	Volgogradskoye, Vdkhr.	50 0 N	45 20 E
48	Völkermarkt	46 34 N	14 39 E
45	Völkingen	49 15 N	6 50 E
77	Volochanka	71 0 N	94 28 E
75	Vologda	59 25 N	40 0 E
68	Vólos	39 24 N	22 59 E
158	Volta, L.	7 30 N	0 15 E
158	Volta Noire, R.	8 41 N	1 33W
145	Volta Redonda	22 31 S	44 5W
62	Volterra	43 24 N	10 50 E
62	Voltri	44 25 N	8 43 E
64	Volturno, R.	41 1 N	13 55 E
75	Volzhskiy	48 56 N	44 46 E
34	Voorburg	52 5 N	4 24 E
48	Voralberg □	47 20 N	10 0 E
68	Vóras Oros, Mt.	40 57 N	21 45 E
41	Vordingborg	55 0 N	11 54 E
68	Voríai Sporádhes, Is.	39 15 N	23 30 E
68	Vóras Evvoïkos Kól.	38 45 N	23 15 E
75	Vorkuta	67 48 N	64 20 E
75	Voronezh	51 40 N	39 10 E
75	Voroshilovgrad	48 38 N	39 15 E
41	Vorså	57 15 N	10 30W
29	Vosges, Mts.	48 20 N	7 10 E
29	Vosges □	48 12 N	6 20 E
77	Vostochnyy Sayan	54 0 N	96 0 E
107	Vostok, I.	10 5 S	152 23W
75	Votkinsk	57 0 N	53 55 E
75	Votkinskoye, Vdkhr.	57 30 N	55 0 E
53	Vouga, R.	40 41 N	8 40W
29	Vouziers	49 22 N	4 40 E
75	Vozhe, Oz.	60 45 N	39 0 E
75	Voznesensk	47 35 N	31 15 E
75	Voznesenye	61 0 N	35 45 E
77	Vrangelya, Os.	71 0 N	180 0 E
60	Vranica, Mt.	43 59 N	18 0 E
60	Vranje	42 34 N	21 54 E
63	Vransko	46 17 N	14 58 E
61	Vratsa	43 13 N	23 30 E
60	Vrbas	45 0 N	17 27 E
60	Vrbas, R.	45 6 N	17 31 E
63	Vrbnik	45 4 N	14 32 E
48	Vřchlabí	49 38 N	15 37 E
168	Vredenburg	32 51 S	18 0 E
68	Vrondádhes	38 25 N	26 7 E
60	Vršac	45 8 N	21 18 E
60	Vrsacki, Kanal	45 15 N	21 0 E
168	Vryburg	26 55 S	24 45 E
169	Vryheid	27 54 S	30 47 E
34	Vught	51 38 N	5 20 E
60	Vukovar	45 21 N	18 59 E
124	Vulcan, Canada	50 25 N	113 15W
51	Vulcan, Romania	45 23 N	23 17 E
63	Vulci	42 23 N	11 37 E
75	Vyatskiye	56 5 N	51 0 E
75	Vyborg	60 42 N	28 45 E
49	Vyehodné Beskydy, Mts.	49 30 N	22 0 E
48	Vychodoceský □	50 20 N	15 45 E
49	Východoslovenský □	48 50 N	21 0 E
75	Vyg, Oz.	63 30 N	34 0 E
21	Vyrnwy, L.	52 48 N	3 30W
48	Vyšší Brod	48 36 N	14 20 E
75	Vytegra	61 15 N	36 40 E

W

158	Wa	10 7 N	2 25W
34	Waal, R.	51 55 N	4 30 E
123	Wabana	47 40 N	53 0W
127	Wabash	40 48 N	85 46W
127	Wabash, R.	37 46 N	88 2W
50	Wabrzeźno	53 16 N	18 57 E
123	Wabush City	52 40 N	67 0W
128	Waco	31 33 N	97 5W
159	Wad Banda	13 10 N	27 50 E
159	Wad Hamid	16 20 N	32 45 E
159	Wâd Medanî	14 28 N	33 30 E
34	Waddeniladen, Is.	53 30 N	5 30 E
34	Waddenzee	53 15 N	5 15 E
124	Waddington, Mt.	51 10 N	125 20W
53	Waddy, Pt.	24 58 S	153 21 E
159	Wadi Halfa	21 53 N	31 19 E
49	Wadowice	49 52 N	19 30 E
34	Wageningen	51 58 N	5 40 E
113	Wagga Wagga	35 7 S	147 24 E
110	Wagin	33 17 S	117 25 E
50	Wagrowiec	52 48 N	17 19 E
95	Wahai	2 48 S	129 35 E
128	Wahpeton	46 20 N	96 35W
114	Waiau	42 39 S	173 5 E
114	Waiau, R.	42 46 S	173 23 E
95	Waigeo, I.	0 20 S	130 40 E
114	Waihi	37 23 S	175 52 E
114	Waihou, R.	37 10 S	175 32 E
114	Waikaremoana, L.	38 49 S	177 9 E
114	Waikari	42 58 S	72 41 E
114	Waikato, R.	37 23 S	174 43 E
114	Waikerie	34 9 S	140 0 E
114	Waikokopu	39 3 S	177 52 E
114	Waikouaiti	45 36 S	170 41 E
114	Waimakariri, R.	43 24 S	172 42 E
114	Waimarino	40 40 S	175 20 E
114	Waimate	44 53 S	171 3 E
114	Waiouru	39 29 S	175 40 E
114	Waipara	43 3 N	172 46 E
114	Waipawa	39 56 S	176 38 E
114	Waipiro	38 2 S	176 22 E
114	Waipu	35 59 S	174 29 E
114	Waipukurau	40 1 S	176 33 E
114	Wairoa	39 3 S	177 25 E
114	Waitaki, R.	44 56 S	171 7 E
114	Waitara	38 59 S	174 15 E
114	Waiuku	37 15 S	174 45 E
165	Wajir	1 42 N	40 20 E
102	Wakasa	35 20 N	134 24 E
114	Wakatipu, L.	45 6 S	168 30 E
125	Wakaw	52 39 N	105 44W
102	Wakayama	34 15 N	135 15 E
106	Wake, I.	19 18 N	166 36 E
21	Wakefield, U.K.	53 41 N	1 31W
114	Wakefield, N.Z.	41 24 S	173 5 E
121	Wakeham Bay = Maricourt	61 36 N	71 57W
102	Wakkanai	45 28 N	141 35 E
95	Wakre	0 30 S	131 5 E

Map	Name	Lat	Long
61	Walachia = Valahia □	44 40 N	25 0 E
49	Walbrzych	50 45 N	16 18 E
21	Walbury Hill	51 22 N	1 28W
113	Walcha	30 55 S	151 31 E
34	Walcheren, I.	51 30 N	3 35 E
50	Walcz	53 17 N	16 28 E
45	Waldbröl	50 52 N	7 36 E
125	Waldron	50 53 N	102 35W
19	Wales ■	52 30 N	3 30W
113	Walgett	30 0 S	148 5 E
122	Walkerton	44 10 N	81 10W
131	Walla Walla	46 3 N	118 25W
131	Wallace	47 30 N	116 0W
113	Wallaroo	33 56 S	137 39 E
21	Wallasey	53 26 N	3 2W
113	Wallerawang	33 25 S	150 4 E
106	Wallis Arch.	13 20 S	176 20 E
131	Wallowa	45 40 N	117 35W
21	Wallsend	54 59 N	1 30W
113	Wallumbilla	26 33 S	149 9 E
21	Walney, I.	54 5 N	3 15W
21	Walsall	52 36 N	1 59W
128	Walsenburg	37 42 N	104 45W
45	Walsrode	52 51 N	9 37 E
45	Waltershausen	50 53 N	10 33 E
122	Waltham	45 57 N	76 57W
168	Walvisbaai	23 0 S	14 28 E
168	Walvis Bay = Walvisbaai	23 0 S	14 28 E
114	Wanaka, L.	44 33 S	169 7 E
95	Wanapiri	4 30 S	135 50 E
113	Wandoan	26 5 S	149 55 E
114	Wanganui	39 35 S	175 3 E
113	Wangaratta	36 21 S	146 19 E
168	Wankie	18 18 S	26 30 E
125	Wanless	54 11 N	101 21W
99	Wanxian	30 42 N	108 20 E
131	Wapato	46 30 N	120 25W
85	Warandab	7 20 N	44 2 E
86	Warangal	17 58 N	79 45 E
45	Waren	53 30 N	12 41 E
45	Warendorf	51 57 N	8 0 E
113	Warialda	29 29 S	150 33 E
95	Warkopi	1 12 S	134 9 E
114	Warkworth	36 24 S	174 41 E
21	Warley	52 30 N	2 0W
125	Warman	52 25 N	106 30W
168	Warmbad, S.W. Africa	28 25 S	18 42 E
169	Warmbad, S.W. Africa	19 14 S	13 51 E
131	Warner Ra.	41 30 S	120 20W
45	Warnemünde	54 9 N	12 5 E
113	Warrego, R.	30 24 S	145 21 E
127	Warren, Ohio	41 18 N	80 52W
127	Warren, Pa.	41 52 N	79 10W
27	Warrenpoint	54 7 N	6 15W
128	Warrensburg	38 45 N	93 45W
168	Warrenton, S. Africa	28 9 S	24 47 E
131	Warrenton, U.S.A.	46 11 N	123 59W
158	Warri	5 30 N	5 41 E
21	Warrington, U.K.	53 25 N	2 38W
127	Warrington, U.S.A.	30 22 N	87 16W
113	Warrnambool	38 25 S	142 30 E
50	Warszawa	52 13 N	21 0 E
50	Warszawa □	52 35 N	21 0 E
50	Warta, R.	52 35 N	14 39 E
113	Warwick, Australia	28 10 S	152 1 E
21	Warwick, U.K.	52 17 N	1 36W
127	Warwick, U.S.A.	41 43 N	71 25W
124	Wasa	49 45 N	115 50W
118	Wasatch Mts.	40 30 N	111 15W
131	Wasco, Calif.	35 37 N	119 16W
131	Wasco, Oreg.	45 45 N	120 46W
128	Waseca	44 3 N	93 31W
21	Wash, The	52 58 N	0 20W
131	Washington	47 45 N	120 30W
127	Washington, D.C.	38 52 N	77 0W
127	Washington, Ind.	38 40 N	87 8W
127	Washington, N.C.	35 35 N	77 1W
127	Washington, Ohio	39 34 N	83 26W
127	Washington, Pa.	40 10 N	80 20W
107	Washington I.	4 43 N	160 24W
127	Washington, Mt.	44 15 N	71 18W
122	Waswanipi	49 30 N	77 0W
95	Watampone	4 29 S	120 25 E
127	Waterbury	41 32 N	73 0W
27	Waterford	52 16 N	7 8W
34	Waterloo, Belgium	50 43 N	4 25 E
128	Waterloo, Iowa	42 27 N	92 20W
127	Waterloo, N.Y.	42 54 N	76 53W
128	Watertown, S.D.	44 57 N	97 5W
128	Watertown, Wis.	43 15 N	88 45W
95	Wates	7 53 S	110 6 E
21	Watford	51 38 N	0 23W
139	Watling, I.	24 0 N	74 30W
125	Watrous	51 40 N	105 25W
165	Watsa	3 4 N	29 30 E
124	Watson Lake	60 12 N	129 0W
131	Watsonville	37 58 N	121 49W
113	Wauchope	31 28 S	152 45 E
125	Waugh	49 40 N	95 20W
127	Waukegan	42 22 N	87 54W
128	Waukesha	43 0 N	88 15W
128	Waupun	43 38 N	88 44W
128	Wausau	44 57 N	89 40W
21	Waveney, R.	52 28 N	1 45 E
114	Waverley	39 46 S	174 37 E
127	Waverly	42 40 N	92 30W
34	Wavre	50 43 N	4 38 E
159	Waw	7 45 N	28 1 E
128	Waxahachie	32 22 N	96 53W
113	Wayatinah	42 19 S	146 27 E
127	Waycross	31 12 N	82 25W
127	Waynesboro, Pa.	39 46 N	77 32W
127	Waynesboro, Va.	38 4 N	78 57W
127	Waynesville	35 31 N	83 0W
86	Wazirabad	32 30 N	74 8 E
21	Weald, The	51 7 N	0 9 E
21	Wear, R.	54 55 N	1 22W
128	Webster City	42 30 N	93 50W
95	Weda	0 30 N	127 50 E
148	Weddell I.	51 50 S	61 0W
174	Weddell Sea	72 30 S	40 0W
113	Wedderburn	36 20 S	143 33 E
123	Wedgeport	43 44 N	65 59W
113	Wee Waa	30 11 S	149 26 E
50	Wegliniec	51 18 N	15 10 E
99	Wei He, R.	34 38 N	110 15 E
45	Weida	50 47 N	12 3 E
99	Weifang	36 44 N	119 7 E
45	Weimar	51 0 N	11 20 E
45	Weingarten	47 49 N	9 39 E
45	Weinheim	47 50 N	11 9 E
113	Weipa	12 24 S	141 50 E
125	Weir River	57 0 N	94 10W
131	Weiser	44 10 N	117 0W
45	Weissenburg	49 2 N	10 58 E
45	Weissenfels	51 11 N	11 58 E
45	Weisswasser	51 30 N	14 36 E
48	Weitra	48 41 N	14 54 E
48	Weiz	47 13 N	15 39 E
50	Wejherowo	54 35 N	18 12 E
168	Welkom	28 0 S	26 50 E
122	Welland	43 0 N	79 10W
21	Welland, R.	52 53 N	0 2W
113	Wellesley, Is.	17 20 S	139 30 E
21	Wellingborough	52 18 N	0 41W
113	Wellington, Australia	32 30 S	149 0 E
122	Wellington, Canada	43 57 N	77 20W
114	Wellington, N.Z.	41 19 S	174 46 E
21	Wellington, U.K.	52 42 N	2 31W
128	Wellington, U.S.A.	37 15 N	97 25W
148	Wellington, I.	49 30 S	75 0W
21	Wells, Norfolk	52 57 N	0 51 E
21	Wells, Somerset	51 12 N	2 39W
131	Wells, U.S.A.	41 8 N	115 0W
110	Wells, L.	26 44 S	123 15W
50	Welna, R.	52 9 N	17 53 E
21	Welshpool	52 40 N	3 9W
21	Wem	52 52 N	2 45W
158	Wenchi	7 46 N	2 8W
99	Wenchow = Wenzhou	28 0 N	120 38 E
131	Wendell	42 50 N	114 51W
21	Wensleydale	54 20 N	2 0W
113	Wentworth	34 2 S	141 54 E
99	Wenzhou	28 0 N	120 38 E
168	Werda	25 15 S	23 16 E
45	Werdau	50 45 N	12 20 E
45	Werder	52 23 N	12 56 E
45	Werdohl	51 15 N	7 47 E
45	Werne	51 38 N	7 38 E
113	Werribee	37 54 S	144 40 E
45	Wesel	51 39 N	6 34 E
45	Weser, R.	53 32 N	8 34 E
123	Wesleyville	49 8 N	53 36W
111	Wessel, Is.	11 10 S	136 45 E
87	West Bengal □	25 0 N	90 0 E
21	West Bromwich	52 32 N	2 1W
148	West Falkland, I.	51 30 S	60 0W
128	West Frankfort	37 56 N	89 0W
45	West Frankfort	51 0 N	9 0 E
21	West Glamorgan □	51 40 N	3 55W
139	West Indies	22 30 N	65 0W
21	West Midlands □	52 30 N	2 0W
128	West Monroe	32 32 N	92 7W
128	West Point, Miss.	33 36 N	88 38W
127	West Point, Va.	37 35 N	76 47W
21	West Sussex □	50 55 N	0 30W
127	West Virginia □	39 0 N	18 0W
113	West Wyalong	33 56 S	147 10 E
21	West Yorkshire □	53 45 N	1 40W
127	Westbrook	43 41 N	70 21W
113	Westbury	41 30 S	146 51 E
45	Westerland	54 51 N	8 20 E
110	Western Australia □	25 0 S	118 0 E
86	Western Ghats, Mts.	15 30 N	74 30 E
21	Western Isles □	57 30 N	7 10W
114	Western Samoa ■	14 0 S	172 0W
34	Westerschelde, R.	51 25 N	4 0 E
45	Westerwald, Mts.	50 39 N	8 0 E
114	Westland □	43 33 S	169 59 E
124	Westlock	54 20 N	113 55W
27	Westmeath □	53 30 N	7 30W
127	Westminster	39 34 S	77 1W
131	Westmorland	33 2 N	115 42W
21	Weston-super-Mare	51 20 N	2 59W
27	Westport, Eire	53 44 N	9 31W
114	Westport, N.Z.	41 46 S	171 37 E
24	Westray, I.	59 18 N	3 0W
124	Westview	49 50 N	124 31W
131	Westwood	40 26 N	121 0W
95	Wetar, I.	7 30 S	126 30 E
34	Wetteren	51 0 N	3 53 E
45	Wetzlar	50 33 N	8 30 E
114	Wewaka	35 10 N	96 35W
87	Wexford	52 20 N	6 28W
21	Weymouth	50 36 N	2 28W
114	Whakatane	37 57 S	177 1 E
121	Whale, R.	57 40 N	67 0W
24	Whalsay, I.	60 22 N	1 0W
114	Whangamomona	39 8 S	174 44 E
114	Whangarei	35 43 S	174 21 E
114	Whangaroa, Harbour	35 4 S	173 46 E
21	Wharfe, R.	53 51 N	1 7W
131	Wheeier Pk.	38 57 N	114 15W
127	Wheeling	40 2 N	80 41W
21	Whernside, Mt.	54 14 N	2 24W
21	Whitby	54 29 N	0 37W
127	White, R., Ind.	38 25 N	87 44W
128	White, R., Ark.	33 53 N	91 3W
113	White Cliffs	30 50 S	143 10 E
21	White Horse, Vale of	51 37 N	1 30W
159	White Nile, R. = Nil el Abyad	9 30 N	31 40 E
75	White Sea = Beloye More	66 30 N	38 0 E
131	White Sulphur Springs	46 35 N	110 0W
114	Whitecliffs	43 26 S	171 55 E
127	Whitehall, N.Y.	43 32 N	73 28W
131	Whitehall, Wis.	44 20 N	91 19W
21	Whitehaven	54 33 N	3 35W
124	Whitehorse	60 45 N	135 10W
125	Whiteshell Prov. Park	50 0 N	95 25W
24	Whithorn	54 55 N	4 25W
114	Whitianga	36 47 S	175 41 E
131	Whitney, Mt.	36 35 N	118 14W
21	Whitstable	51 21 N	1 2 E
113	Whitsunday, I.	20 15 S	149 4 E
113	Whyalla	33 2 S	137 30 E
122	Wiarton	44 50 N	81 10W
128	Wichita	37 40 N	97 29W
128	Wichita Falls	33 57 N	98 30W
24	Wick	58 26 N	3 5W
131	Wickenburg	33 58 N	112 45W
27	Wicklow	53 0 N	6 2W
27	Wicklow Mts.	53 0 N	6 30W
21	Widnes	53 22 N	2 44W
50	Wiecbork	53 22 N	17 30 E
45	Wiedenbrück	51 50 N	8 18 E
50	Wielbark	53 24 N	20 55 E
50	Wielun	51 15 N	18 40 E
48	Wien	48 12 N	16 22 E
49	Wiener Neustadt	47 49 N	16 16 E
50	Wieprz, R.	51 34 N	21 49 E
34	Wierden	52 22 N	6 35 E
45	Wiesbaden	50 7 N	8 17 E
21	Wigan	53 33 N	2 38W
24	Wigtown	54 52 N	4 27W
45	Wildeshausen	52 54 N	8 25 E
48	Wildon	46 52 N	15 31 E
127	Wildwood	39 0 N	74 46W
48	Wilhelmsburg, Austria	48 6 N	15 36 E
45	Wilhelmsburg, W. Germany	53 28 N	10 1 E
45	Wilhelshaven	53 30 N	8 9 E
45	Wilkes-Barre	41 15 N	75 52W
131	Wilkie	52 27 N	108 42W
131	Wilcox	32 13 N	109 53W
139	Willemstad	12 5 N	69 0W
110	William Creek	28 58 S	136 22 E
131	Williams	35 16 N	112 11W
124	Williams Lake	52 20 N	122 10W
127	Williamsburg	37 17 N	76 44W
127	Williamston	37 46 N	82 17W
128	Williston	48 10 N	103 35W
168	Willowmore	33 15 S	23 30 E
113	Willows, Australia	23 45 S	147 25 E
131	Willows, U.S.A.	39 30 N	122 10W
127	Wilmington, Del.	39 45 N	75 0W
127	Wilmington, N.C.	34 14 N	77 54W
127	Wilmington, Ohio	39 29 N	83 46W
127	Wilson	35 44 N	77 54W
131	Wilson, Mt.	37 55 N	105 3W
113	Wilson's Promontory	39 5 S	146 28 E
21	Wilton	51 5 N	1 52W
21	Wiltshire □	51 20 N	2 0W
110	Wiluna	26 40 S	120 40 E
29	Wimereux	50 45 N	1 37 E
21	Winchester, U.K.	51 4 N	1 19W
127	Winchester, Ind.	40 10 N	84 56W
127	Winchester, Ky.	38 0 N	84 8W
127	Winchester, Va.	39 14 N	78 8W
21	Windermere, L.	54 20 N	2 57W
168	Windhoek	22 35 S	17 4 E
113	Windorah	25 24 S	142 36 E
21	Windrush, R.	51 42 N	1 25W
113	Windsor, Australia	33 34 S	150 44 E
123	Windsor, Nova Scotia	44 59 N	64 5W
122	Windsor, Ont.	42 25 N	83 0W
21	Windsor, U.K.	51 28 N	0 36W
139	Windward Is.	13 0 N	63 0W
113	Wingen	31 50 S	150 58 E
113	Wingham	43 55 N	81 25W
48	Winklern	46 52 N	12 53 E
158	Winneba	5 25 N	0 36W
131	Winnemucca	40 58 N	117 45W
125	Winnipeg	49 50 N	97 15W
125	Winnipeg, L.	52 30 N	98 0W
125	Winnipegosis	52 40 N	100 0W
128	Winona	44 2 N	91 45W
127	Winooski	44 31 N	73 11W
34	Winschoten	53 9 N	7 3 E
131	Winslow	35 2 N	110 41W
127	Winston-Salem	36 7 N	80 15W
127	Winter Park	28 34 N	81 19W
45	Winterthur	47 30 N	8 44 E
113	Winton	22 21 S	143 0 E
21	Wirral	53 25 N	3 0W
110	Wirrulla	32 24 S	134 31 E
21	Wisbech	52 39 N	0 10 E
128	Wisconsin □	44 30 N	90 0W
24	Wishaw	55 46 N	3 55W
50	Wisla, R.	54 22 N	18 55 E
49	Wisloka, R.	50 27 N	21 23 E
45	Wismar	53 53 N	11 23 E
29	Wissant	50 52 N	1 40 E
29	Wissembourg	49 2 N	7 57 E
169	Witbank	25 51 S	29 14 E
21	Witham, R.	52 56 N	0 4 E
21	Withernsea	53 43 N	0 2W
21	Witney	51 47 N	1 29W
45	Witten	51 26 N	7 19 E
45	Wittenberg	51 51 N	12 39 E
45	Wittenberge	53 0 N	11 44 E
110	Wittenoom	22 15 S	118 20 E
45	Wittingen	52 43 N	10 43 E
45	Wittow, I.	54 37 N	13 21 E
45	Wittstock	53 10 N	12 30 E
95	Wlingi	8 5 S	112 25 E
50	Wloclawek	52 39 N	19 2 E
113	Wodonga	36 5 S	146 50 E
49	Wodzislaw Sl.	50 1 N	18 26 E
95	Wokam, I.	5 45 S	134 28 E
122	Wolfe I.	44 7 N	76 27 E
45	Wolfenbüttel	52 10 N	10 33 E
45	Wolfsberg	46 50 N	14 52 E
45	Wolfsburg	52 27 N	10 49 E
148	Wollaston, Is.	55 40 S	67 30W
125	Wollaston L.	58 20 N	103 30W
120	Wollaston Pen.	69 30 N	115 0W
113	Wollongong	34 25 S	150 54 E
50	Wolomin	52 19 N	21 15 E
50	Wolseley	50 25 N	103 15W
118	Wolstenholme, C.	62 50 N	78 0W
21	Wolverhampton	52 35 N	2 6W
111	Wonarah P.O.	19 55 S	136 20 E
113	Wonan	26 20 S	151 49 E
99	Wönsan	39 11 N	127 27 E
113	Wonthaggi	38 29 S	145 31 E
131	Woodland	38 40 N	121 50W
122	Woodridge	49 20 N	96 20W
110	Woodroffe, Mt.	26 20 S	131 45 E
24	Woods, L. of the	49 30 N	94 30W
113	Woodstock, Australia	19 22 S	142 45 E
122	Woodstock, Ont.	43 10 N	80 45W
123	Woodstock, N.B.	46 11 N	67 37W
21	Woodstock, U.K.	51 51 N	1 20W
114	Woodville	40 20 S	175 53 E
128	Woodward	36 24 N	99 28W
113	Woomera	31 9 S	136 56 E
127	Woonsocket	42 0 N	71 30W
110	Woornarel, R.	25 47 S	114 10 E
127	Wooster	40 38 N	81 55W
165	Worcester, S. Africa	33 39 S	19 27 E
21	Worcester, U.K.	52 12 N	2 12W
127	Worcester, U.S.A.	42 14 N	71 49W
48	Wörgl	47 29 N	12 3 E
21	Workington	54 39 N	3 34W
21	Worksop	53 19 N	1 9W
131	Worland	44 0 N	107 59W
45	Worms	49 37 N	8 21 E
48	Wörther See, L.	46 37 N	14 19 E
21	Worthing	50 49 N	0 21W
128	Worthington	43 35 N	95 30W
124	Wrangell	56 30 N	132 25W
124	Wrangell Mts.	61 40 N	143 30W
24	Wrath, C.	58 38 N	5 0W
21	Wrekin, The	52 41 N	2 35W
21	Wrexham	53 5 N	3 0W
120	Wrigley	63 0 N	123 30W
49	Wroclaw	51 5 N	17 5 E
50	Wroclaw □	51 0 N	17 0 E
50	Wrzesnia	52 21 N	17 36 E
99	Wuhan	30 31 N	114 18 E
99	Wuhu	31 22 N	118 21 E
158	Wukari	7 57 N	9 42 E
96	Wulumuchi = Urumqi	43 45 N	87 38 E
87	Wuntho	23 55 N	95 45 E
45	Wuppertal	51 15 N	7 8 E
45	Würzburg	49 46 N	9 55 E
45	Wurzen	51 21 N	12 45 E
99	Wutongqiao	29 22 N	103 50 E
99	Wuxi	31 33 N	120 18 E
99	Wuzhou	23 30 N	111 18 E
21	Wye, R.	51 37 N	2 39W
21	Wymondham	52 45 N	1 7 E
110	Wyndham	15 33 S	128 3 E
113	Wynnum	27 29 S	152 58 E
131	Wyoming □	42 48 N	109 0W
50	Wyrzysk	53 10 N	17 17 E
50	Wyszków	52 36 N	21 25 E
127	Wytheville	37 0 N	81 3W

X

Map	Name	Lat	Long
68	Xánthi	41 10 N	24 58 E
99	Xi Jiang, R.	22 5 N	113 20 E
96	Xiaguan	25 32 N	100 16 E
99	Xiamen	24 25 N	118 4 E
99	Xi'an	34 15 N	109 0 E
99	Xiangfan	29 40 N	109 8 E
99	Xiangtan	27 51 N	112 54 E
99	Xiao Hinggan Ling, mts.	49 0 N	127 0 E
68	Xilókastron	38 4 N	22 43 E
169	Xinavane	25 2 S	32 47 E
145	Xingu, R.	1 30 S	51 53W
68	Xiniás, L.	39 2 N	22 12 E
99	Xining	36 34 N	101 40 E
96	Xinjiang Uygur □	42 0 N	86 0 E
99	Xinxiang	35 18 N	113 50 E
99	Xinyang	32 6 N	114 3 E
145	Xique-Xique	10 40 S	42 40W
96	Xizang □	32 0 N	88 0 E

Map	Name	Lat	Long
99	Xuan hua	40 40 N	115 2 E
99	Xuzhou	34 18 N	117 10 E

Y

Map	Name	Lat	Long
113	Yaamba	23 8 S	150 22 E
77	Yablonovy Khrebet	53 0 N	114 0 E
144	Yacuiba	22 0 S	63 25W
131	Yakima	46 42 N	120 30W
102	Yaku-Shima, I.	30 20 N	130 30 E
77	Yakut A.S.S.R. □	66 0 N	125 0 E
77	Yakutsk	62 5 N	129 40 E
113	Yalboroo	20 50 S	148 30 E
137	Yalkubul, Pta.	21 32 N	88 37W
113	Yallourn	38 10 S	146 18 E
75	Yalta	44 30 N	34 10 E
102	Yamagata	37 55 N	140 20 E
102	Yamaguchi	34 10 N	131 32 E
76	Yamal Pol.	71 0 N	70 0 E
80	Yamma	24 5 N	47 30 E
102	Yamanashi □	35 40 N	138 40 E
61	Yambol	42 30 N	26 36 E
95	Yamdena, I.	7 45 S	131 20 E
87	Yamethin	20 26 N	96 9 E
110	Yampi, Sd.	15 15 S	123 30 E
87	Yamuna, R.	27 0 N	78 30 E
113	Yanac	33 58 N	132 7 E
75	Yanaul	56 25 N	55 0 E
87	Yandoon	17 2 N	95 39 E
76	Yangi-Yer	40 17 N	68 48 E
99	Yangquan	37 58 N	113 31 E
99	Yangtze Kiang = Chang Jiang, R.	31 20 N	121 52 E
99	Yangzhou	32 21 N	119 26 E
99	Yanji	42 59 N	129 30 E
131	Yanna	26 58 S	146 0 E
99	Yantai	37 34 N	121 22 E
165	Yaoundé	3 50 N	1 35 E
95	Yap Is.	9 30 N	138 10 E
95	Yapen, I.	1 50 S	136 0 E
95	Yapen, Teluk, G.	1 30 S	136 0 E
76	Yaransk	57 13 N	47 56 E
21	Yare, R.	52 40 N	1 45 E
96	Yarkand = Shache	38 20 N	77 10 E
75	Yaroslavl	57 35 N	39 55 E
113	Yarraman	26 46 S	152 1 E
76	Yar-Sale	66 50 N	70 50 E
144	Yarumal	6 58 N	75 24W
114	Yasawa Is.	17 0 S	177 23 E
91	Yasothon	15 50 N	104 10 E
102	Yatsushiro	32 30 N	130 40 E
102	Yawatahama	33 27 N	132 24 E
81	Yazd	31 55 N	54 27 E
128	Yazoo City	32 48 N	90 28W
87	Ye	15 15 N	97 51 E
77	Yebyu	14 15 N	98 13 E
77	Yeniseysk	58 39 N	92 4 E
76	Yenisey, R.	68 0 N	86 30 E
76	Yeniseyskiy Zaliv	72 20 N	81 0 E
21	Yeo, R.	51 1 N	2 46W
86	Yeola	20 2 N	74 30 E
86	Yeotmal	20 20 N	78 15 E
21	Yeovil	50 57 N	2 38W
113	Yeppoon	23 5 S	150 47 E
75	Yerevan	40 10 N	44 20 E
77	Yermakovo	52 35 N	126 20 E
77	Yerofey Pavlovich	54 0 N	122 0 E
21	Yes Tor	50 41 N	3 59 E
99	Yeu, Î.d'	46 42 N	2 20W
96	Yibin	28 45 N	104 32 E
99	Yichang	30 40 N	111 20 E
99	Yilan	24 51 N	121 44 E
99	Yinchuan	38 30 N	106 15 E
99	Yingkou	40 37 N	122 18 E
96	Yining	43 58 N	81 10 E
99	Yirga Alem	6 48 N	38 22 E
99	Yithion	36 46 N	22 34 E
99	Yixing	31 21 N	119 48 E
95	Yogyakarta	7 49 S	110 22 E
102	Yokkaichi	35 0 N	136 38 E
102	Yokohama	35 27 N	139 28 E
102	Yokosuka	35 20 N	139 40 E
102	Yonago	35 25 N	133 19 E
127	Yonkers	40 57 N	73 51W
29	Yonne □	47 50 N	3 40 E
21	York, U.K.	53 58 N	1 7W
127	York, Pa.	39 57 N	76 43W
113	York, C.	10 42 S	142 31 E
21	York Wolds	54 0 N	0 30W
113	Yorke, Pen.	34 50 S	137 40 E
125	Yorkton	51 11 N	102 28W
131	Yosemite Nat. Park	38 0 N	119 30W
75	Yoshkar Ola	56 49 N	47 10 E
27	Youghal	51 58 N	7 51W
113	Young	34 19 S	148 18 E
113	Younghusband, Pen.	34 45 S	139 15 E
127	Youngstown	43 16 N	79 2W
31	Yssingeaux	45 9 N	4 8 E
41	Ystad	55 26 N	13 50 E
24	Ythan, R.	57 26 N	1 12W
131	Yuba City	39 12 N	121 45W
137	Yucatán □	21 30 N	86 30W
131	Yucca	34 56 N	114 9W
60	Yugoslavia ■	44 0 N	20 0 E
120	Yukon Territory ■	63 0 N	135 0W
120	Yukon, R.	65 30 N	150 0W
99	Yulin	22 45 N	110 45 E
99	Yunlin	23 42 N	120 30 E
99	Yunnan □	25 0 N	102 0 E
113	Yunta	32 35 S	139 33 E
99	Yushu	33 5 N	96 55 E
76	Yuribei	71 20 N	76 30 E
77	Yuzhno-Sakhalinsk	47 5 N	142 5 E
29	Yvelines □	48 40 N	1 45 E
28	Yvetot	49 37 N	0 44 E

Z

Map	Name	Lat	Long
34	Zaandam	52 26 N	4 49 E
60	Žabalj	45 21 N	20 5 E
77	Zabaykalskiy	49 40 N	117 10 E
49	Zabkowice Slaskie	50 22 N	19 17 E
81	Zabol	31 0 N	61 25 E
81	Zaboli	27 10 N	61 35 E
49	Zabrze	50 24 N	18 50 E
137	Zacatecas	22 49 N	102 34W
137	Zacatecoluca	13 29 N	88 51W
63	Zadar	44 8 N	15 8 E
53	Zafra	38 26 N	6 30W
50	Zagan	51 39 N	15 22 E
159	Zagazig	30 40 N	31 12 E
68	Zagorá	39 27 N	23 6 E
63	Zagreb	45 50 N	16 0 E
80	Zagros, Kudha-ye	33 45 N	47 0 E
81	Zahedan	29 30 N	60 50 E
80	Zahlah	33 52 N	35 50 E
165	Zaïre ■	3 0 S	23 0 E
165	Zaïre, R.	6 4 S	12 24 E
77	Zakamensk	50 23 N	103 17 E
75	Zakavkazye	42 0 N	44 0 E
80	Zakho	37 10 N	42 50 E
68	Zákinthos, I.	37 45 N	27 45 E
49	Zakopane	49 18 N	19 57 E
49	Zalaegerszeg	46 53 N	16 47 E
53	Zalamea de la Serena	38 40 N	5 38W
63	Zalec	46 16 N	15 10 E
169	Zambeze, R.	18 46 S	36 16 E
165	Zambezi	13 30 S	23 15 E
169	Zambia ■	15 0 S	28 0 E
95	Zamboanga	6 59 N	122 3 E
137	Zamora, Mexico	20 0 N	102 21W
53	Zamora, Sp.	41 30 N	5 45W
50	Zamosc	50 50 N	23 22 E
55	Záncara, R.	39 18 N	3 18W
34	Zandvoort	52 22 N	4 32 E
110	Zanthus	30 55 S	123 29 E
165	Zanzibar	6 12 S	39 12 E
165	Zanzibar, I.	6 12 S	39 12 E
158	Zaouiet Reggane	26 32 N	0 3 E
60	Zapadna Morava, R.	43 50 N	20 15 E
49	Západné Beskydy, Mts.	49 30 N	19 0 E
48	Západočeský □	49 35 N	13 0 E
75	Zapolyarnyy	69 26 N	30 48 E
75	Zaporozhye	47 50 N	35 10 E
53	Zaragoza	41 39 N	0 53W
81	Zarand	30 46 N	56 34 E
144	Zaraza	9 21 N	65 19W
158	Zaria	11 0 N	7 40W
50	Zary	51 37 N	15 10 E
53	Zarza de Alange	38 49 N	6 13W
53	Zarza de Granadilla	40 14 N	6 3W
159	Zarzis	33 31 N	11 2 E
77	Zashiversk	67 25 N	142 40 E
86	Zaskar Mts.	33 15 N	77 30 E
54	Zavala	42 50 N	17 59 E
77	Zavidočići	44 27 N	18 13 E
77	Zavitinsk	50 10 N	129 20 E
49	Zawiercie	50 30 N	19 13 E
76	Zaysan	47 28 N	84 52 E
76	Zaysan, Oz.	48 0 N	83 0 E
124	Zeballos	49 49 N	126 50W
113	Zeehan	41 52 S	145 25 E
34	Zeeland □	51 30 N	3 50 E
85	Zeila	11 15 N	43 30 E
34	Zeist	52 5 N	5 15 E
45	Zeitz	51 3 N	12 9 E
50	Zelenik	44 43 N	20 23 E
48	Zell am See	47 19 N	12 47 E
45	Zella-Mehlis	50 40 N	10 41 E
60	Zemun	44 51 N	20 23 E
21	Zennor	50 11 N	5 34W
45	Zerbst	51 59 N	12 8 E
48	Zermatt	46 2 N	7 46 E
77	Zêzere, R.	40 0 N	7 55W
50	Zgierz	51 45 N	19 27 E
45	Zgorzelec	51 10 N	15 0 E
76	Zhanatas	43 11 N	81 18 E
99	Zhangjiakou	24 30 N	117 35 E
99	Zhanjiang	21 15 N	110 0 E
99	Zhdanov	47 5 N	37 31 E
99	Zhejiang □	29 0 N	120 0 E
99	Zhengzhou	34 45 N	113 34 E
99	Zhenjiang	32 11 N	119 26 E
99	Zhigansk	66 35 N	124 10 E
75	Zhitomir	50 20 N	28 40 E
77	Zhupanovo	51 59 N	15 9 E
99	Zhuzhou	27 49 N	113 12 E
49	Zielona Góra	51 57 N	15 31 E
50	Zielona Góra □	51 57 N	15 30 E
99	Zigong	29 15 N	104 48 E
158	Ziguinchor	12 25 N	16 20W
49	Zilina	49 12 N	18 42 E
48	Zillertaler Alpen, Mts.	47 6 N	11 45 E
76	Zima	54 0 N	102 5 E
169	Zimbabwe ■	20 0 S	28 30 E
158	Zinder	13 48 N	9 0 E
85	Zinjibar	13 5 N	46 0 E
131	Zion Nat. Park	37 25 N	112 50W
144	Zipaquira	5 0 N	74 0W
48	Zistersdorf	48 33 N	16 45 E
48	Zitava, R.	48 14 N	18 21 E
45	Zittau	50 54 N	14 47 E
49	Zivinice	44 27 N	18 36 E
61	Zlatitsa	42 41 N	24 7 E
49	Zlín = Gottwaldov	49 13 N	17 41 E
48	Zliten	32 25 N	14 35 E
63	Zlotoryja	51 8 N	15 55 E
49	Zmigród	51 28 N	16 53 E
49	Znin	52 51 N	17 15 E
48	Znojmo	48 50 N	16 2 E
158	Zóuerate	22 35 N	12 30W
53	Zuera	41 51 N	0 49W
45	Zossen	52 13 N	13 28 E
131	Zuni	35 7 N	108 48W
80	Zonguldak	41 28 N	31 50 E
60	Zorritos	3 50 S	80 40W
45	Zuger-see, Mt.	47 7 N	8 35 E
45	Zürich	47 22 N	8 32 E
45	Zürich-see	47 18 N	8 40 E
34	Zutphen	52 9 N	6 12 E
76	Zverinogolovskoye	54 30 N	62 30 E
49	Zvolen	48 33 N	19 10 E
60	Zvornik	44 26 N	19 7 E
45	Zweibrücken	49 15 N	7 20 E
45	Zwenkau	51 13 N	12 19 E
45	Zwickau	50 43 N	12 30 E
45	Zwischenahn	53 12 N	8 1 E
34	Zwolle	52 31 N	6 6 E
77	Zyryanka	65 45 N	150 51 E
77	Zyryanovsk	49 43 N	84 20 E
49	Zywiec	49 41 N	19 12 E